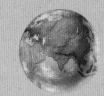

# OXFORD
# School
# Atlas

*Editorial Adviser*
Dr Patrick Wiegand

D0525835

# OXFORD
## UNIVERSITY PRESS

Great Clarendon Street, Oxford OX2 6DP

Oxford University Press is a department of the University of Oxford.
It furthers the University's objective of excellence in research, scholarship,
and education by publishing worldwide in

Oxford   New York

Auckland   Cape Town   Dar es Salaam   Hong Kong   Karachi
Kuala Lumpur   Madrid   Melbourne   Mexico City   Nairobi
New Delhi   Shanghai   Taipei   Toronto

With offices in

Argentina   Austria   Brazil   Chile   Czech Republic   France   Greece
Guatemala   Hungary   Italy   Japan   Poland   Portugal   Singapore
South Korea   Switzerland   Thailand   Turkey   Ukraine   Vietnam

Oxford is a registered trade mark of Oxford University Press
in the UK and in certain other countries

ISBN 978 0 19 832923 7

1 3 5 7 9 10 8 6 4 2

Printed in Singapore

Paper used in the production of this book is a natural, recyclable product
made from wood grown in sustainable forests. The manufacturing process
conforms to the environmental regulations of the country of origin.

## Acknowledgements

The publishers would like to thank the following for permission to reproduce photographs:

NASA images courtesy the MODIS Rapid Response Team at Goddard Space Flight Center p.97; Courtesy of NASA Visible Earth p.87;
Science Photo Library pp.67, 76 (t/Planetary Visions Ltd) & (bl/M-Sat Ltd), 84 (NASA), 106 (NASA), 113 (NOAA), 114; Corbis p.115;
Oxford Scientific Films pp.114, 115.

The page design is by Adrian Smith.

The publishers are grateful to the following colleagues in geography education for their helpful comments and advice during
the development stages of this atlas: Pam Boardman, Graham Butt, Kathryn Clayton, Alan Cottle, Ruth Crossley, Rachel Dean,
Bob Digby, Ian Douglass, Tony Field, Martyn Gill, Joel Griffiths, Matthew Gunn, Gareth Huws, Kathryn Jones, Irfon Morris Jones,
David Langham, Patrick Lewis, Bob Newman,  Andrew Parkinson, Liz Roodhouse, John Sadler, Toni Schiavone, Natasha Sirin,
Andrea Wade, Patrick Wherity, Steve Wilkes, and Malcolm Yates.

The publishers would also like to thank the many individuals, companies societies, and institutions
who gave assistance in the gathering of data.

# 2 Contents

*page*

**Maps and satellite images** ___ 4
**Map projections and graphics** ___ 5

## British Isles   Topographic maps

British Isles ___ 6
Orkney and Shetland Islands ___ 7
Scottish Highlands and Islands ___ 8–9
Northern Ireland   Southern Scotland ___ 10–11
Northern England ___ 12–13
Wales   West and East Midlands ___ 14–15
South East England ___ 16–17
South West England ___ 18–19
Ireland ___ 20–21

topographic maps of the British Isles

## British Isles   Thematic maps

| | | | |
|---|---|---|---|
| Political | 22–23 | Employment | 33 |
| Physical | 24 | Population | 34–35 |
| Geology | 25 | Sport   Tourism | 36 |
| Climate | 26–27 | Quality of life | 37 |
| Land use | 28 | Conservation | 38 |
| Farming | 29 | Pollution | 39 |
| Water   Minerals | 30 | Transport | 40 |
| Energy | 31 | Trade | 41 |
| Manufacturing industry | 32 | | |

## Europe   Thematic maps

Physical ___ 42
Climate   Ecosystems ___ 43
Political ___ 44
Population   Wealth ___ 45
Economy ___ 46
Tourism ___ 47

## Europe   Topographic maps

Benelux and the Ruhr ___ 48
Scandinavia and Iceland ___ 49
France ___ 50
Spain and Portugal ___ 51
Middle Europe ___ 52–53
Italy and the Balkans ___ 54–55
East Europe and Turkey ___ 56–57

topographic maps of Europe

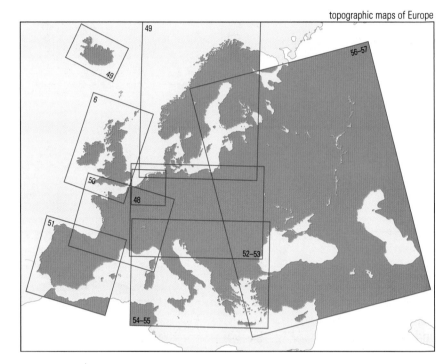

## Asia   Thematic maps

Physical ___ 58
Political ___ 59
Climate   Ecosystems ___ 60
Economy   Population ___ 61

## Asia   Topographic maps

Northern Eurasia ___ 62–63
Middle East ___ 64–65
South Asia ___ 66–67
China ___ 68–69
Japan ___ 70
South East Asia ___ 71

topographic maps of Asia

## Oceania   Topographic map

Australia and New Zealand ___ 72–73

## Oceania   Thematic maps

Climate   Ecosystems
Population   Economy ___ 74

topographic map of Oceania

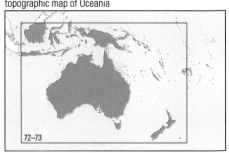

© Oxford University Press

# Contents 3

## Africa   Thematic maps

| | |
|---|---|
| Physical   Political | 75 |
| Satellite images | 76 |
| Climate   Ecosystems | 77 |
| Economy   Population | 78 |
| Tourism | 79 |

## Africa   Topographic maps

| | |
|---|---|
| Northern Africa | 80–81 |
| Southern Africa | 82 |
| East Africa | 83 |

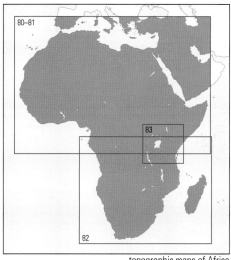

topographic maps of Africa

## North America   Thematic maps

| | |
|---|---|
| Physical   Political | 84 |
| Climate   Ecosystems | 85 |
| Economy   Population | 86 |
| Tourism | 87 |

## North America   Topographic maps

| | |
|---|---|
| Canada | 88–89 |
| United States of America | 90–91 |
| Great Lakes | 92–93 |
| Mexico, Central America and the Caribbean | 94–95 |

topographic maps of North America

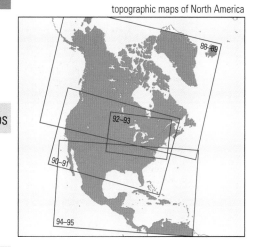

## South America   Topographic map

| | |
|---|---|
| South America | 96–97 |

## South America   Thematic maps

| | |
|---|---|
| Political | 97 |
| Climate   Ecosystems | 98 |
| Economy   Population | 99 |

topographic map of South America

## World   Thematic maps   *page*

| | |
|---|---|
| Political | 102–103 |
| Physical | 104–105 |
| Earthquakes and volcanoes | 106–107 |
| Temperature and ocean currents | 108 |
| Pressure, winds and precipitation | 109 |
| Climate regions | 110–111 |
| Climate data | 112 |
| Climate hazards | 113 |
| Ecosystems | 114–115 |
| Population | 116–117 |
| Population trends | 118–119 |
| Quality of life | 120–121 |
| Economic development | 122–123 |
| Energy | 124 |
| Trade   Transport | 125 |
| Environmental issues | 126 |
| Climate change | 127 |
| Tourism | 128–129 |
| Time, distance and cyberspace | 130 |
| Globalisation | 131 |
| Flags | 132–133 |
| Datasets | 134–141 |

## Index   142–160

## Oceans and Poles   Topographic maps

| | |
|---|---|
| Pacific Ocean | 100 |
| Arctic Ocean   Antarctica | 101 |

topographic maps of the Poles

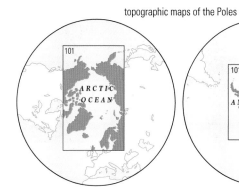

topographic map of the Pacific Ocean

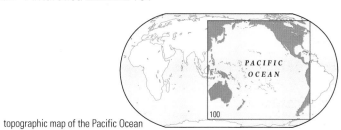

# 4  Maps and satellite images

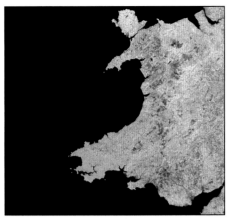

Satellite scanners 'read' the Earth's radiation. The data can be organised by computer to form a visual image. In this image the colours are not real but have been arranged to show how the land is used.

Orange: rough pasture
Red: forest and woodland
Green: improved pasture
Dark blue: urban areas

Topographic maps show the main features of the physical landscape as well as settlements, communications, and boundaries. Background colours show the height of the land.

Greens: low land
Browns: high land

Thematic maps show information about special topics such as agriculture, industry, population, the environment, and quality of life. This map shows land use.

Dark green: forest and woodland
Purple: built-up area

## Symbols on thematic maps

### Point symbols

**Dot map**
Each black dot represents 100 000 sheep.
*From p29*

**Economic map**
Blue squares represent a main centre of the motor vehicle industry.
*From p32*

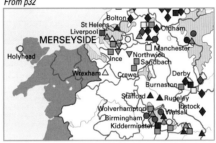

**Proportional symbols**
The size of the blue circles is proportional to the amount of cargo handled at each port.
*From p40*

### Line symbols

**Isopleth map**
Lines join places with equal amounts of sunshine.
*From p27*

**Isotherm map**
Some isopleths have special names. Isotherms join places with equal temperature.
*From p26*

**Line map**
The lines represent major transport routes.
*From p125*

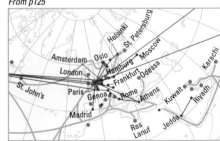

### Area symbols

**Choropleth map**
Darker colours show areas with a higher percentage of land used for growing potatoes.
*From p29*

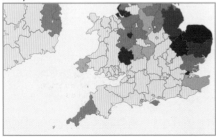

**Environmental map**
Each colour represents an ecosystem.
Purple stands for mountains.
*From p115*

**Political map**
Colours have no meaning but are simply used to show where one country ends and another begins.
*From p102*

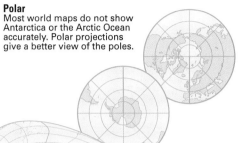

This map has been made by unpeeling strips from the Earth's surface. It would be difficult to use because gaps are left in the land and sea.

Parallels of latitude and meridians of longitude form a grid. Different grid patterns, called projections, can be used to turn the spherical surface of the Earth into a flat world map. It is impossible to make a world map in which both the sizes and shapes of the Earth's land masses are shown accurately. All world maps are distorted in some way.

There are many map projections. It is important that the projection used for a world map is suitable for the information shown on it.

Compare the shape and relative areas of Greenland and Africa on the Eckert IV and Mercator projections.

**Polar**
Most world maps do not show Antarctica or the Arctic Ocean accurately. Polar projections give a better view of the poles.

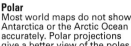

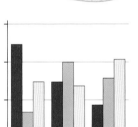

**Eckert IV**
Equal area. The land masses are the correct size in relation to each other but there is some distortion in shape.

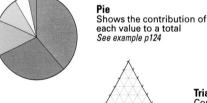

**Mercator**
Conformal. The shape of the land masses is correct but their size becomes larger further away from the equator.

**Oblique Aitoff**
Equal area. The arrangement of the land masses allows a good view of the northern hemisphere.

---

# Graphical representation of data

**Clustered column**
Compares values across categories
*See example p35*

**Line**
Shows trend over time across categories
*See example p33*

**Pie**
Shows the contribution of each value to a total
*See example p124*

**Stacked column**
Compares the contribution of each value to a total across categories
*See example p32*

**Triangular**
Compares trios of values
*See example p123*

**Simple bar**
Length of bar is proportional to each value
*See example p128*

**Scatter**
Compares pairs of values
*See example p61*

**100% stacked bar**
Compares the percentage each value contributes to a total across categories
*See example p116*

**Line and whisker**
Shows highest, average, and lowest values
*See example p30*

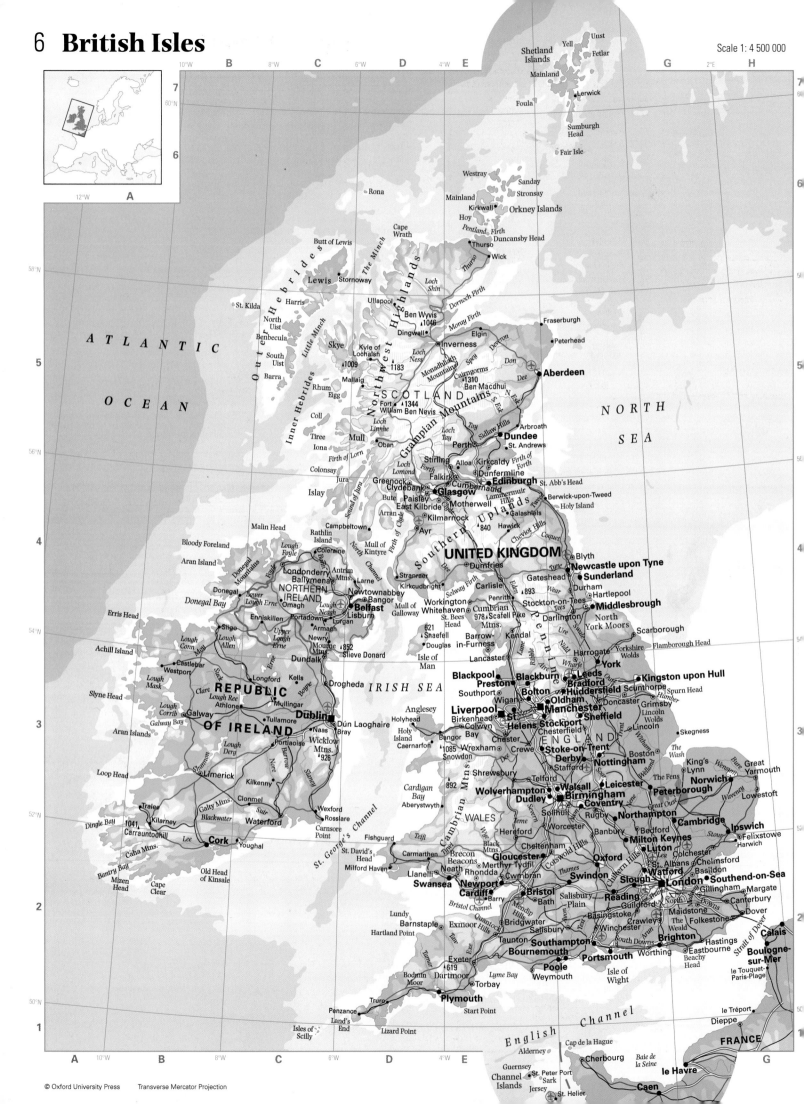

Scale 1: 4 500 000

© Oxford University Press    Transverse Mercator Projection

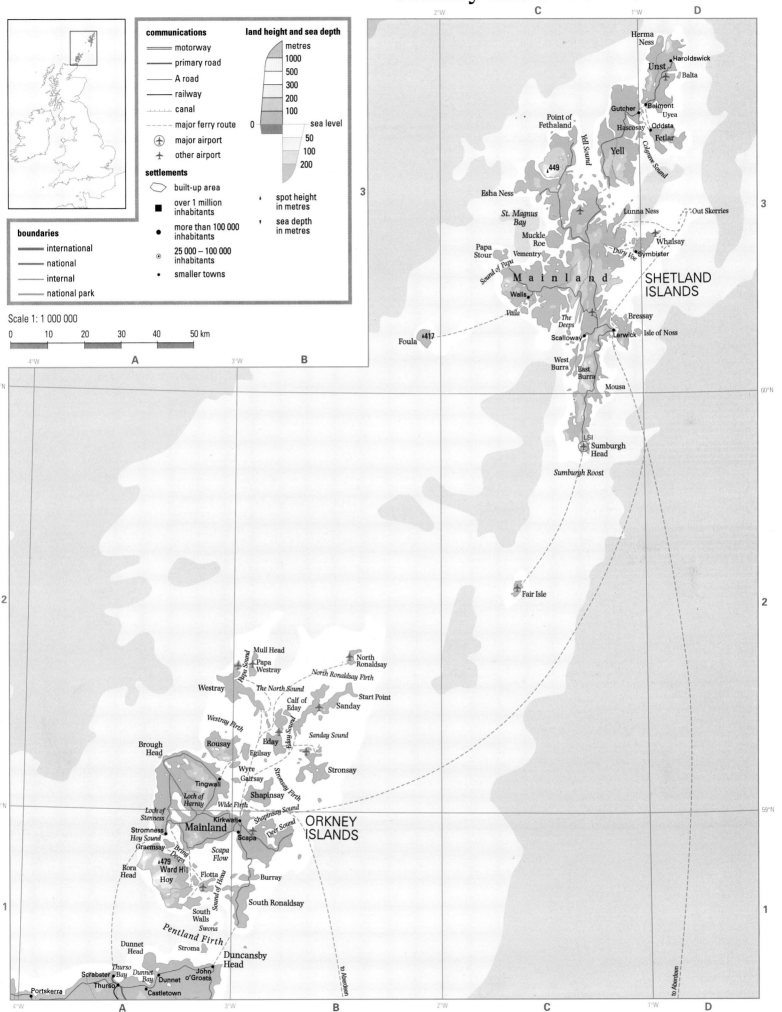

**communications**

motorway
primary road
A road
railway
canal
major ferry route
✈ major airport
✈ other airport

**settlements**

built-up area
■ over 1 million inhabitants
● more than 100 000 inhabitants
◉ 25 000 – 100 000 inhabitants
• smaller towns

**land height and sea depth**

metres
1000
500
300
200
100
0 — sea level
50
100
200

▲ spot height in metres
▼ sea depth in metres

**boundaries**

international
national
internal
national park

Scale 1: 1 000 000

0   10   20   30   40   50 km

SHETLAND ISLANDS

Herma Ness
Haroldswick
Unst
Balta
Point of Fethaland
Gutcher
Belmont
Uyea
Hascosay
Oddsta
Fetlar
Yell Sound
Yell
Colgrave Sound
▲449
Esha Ness
Lunna Ness
Out Skerries
St. Magnus Bay
Muckle Roe
Whalsay
Papa Stour
Vementry
Dury Voe
Symbister
Mainland
Sound of Papa
Walls
Bressay
Vaila
The Deeps
Lerwick
Isle of Noss
Foula  ▲417
Scalloway
West Burra
East Burra
Mousa

LSI ✈ Sumburgh Head
Sumburgh Roost

Fair Isle

Mull Head
Papa Westray
North Ronaldsay
Papa Sound
North Ronaldsay Firth
Westray
The North Sound
Calf of Eday
Start Point
Sanday
Westray Firth
Eday
Sanday Sound
Rousay
Eday Sound
Egilsay
Brough Head
Wyre
Gairsay
Stronsay
Tingwall
Stronsay Firth
Shapinsay
Loch of Harray
Wide Firth
Loch of Stenness
Kirkwall
Shapinsay Sound
Stromness
Scapa
Deer Sound
ORKNEY ISLANDS
Hoy Sound
Graemsay
Bring Deeps
Scapa Flow
Rora Head
▲479 Ward Hill
Flotta
Hoy
Burray
Sound of Hoxa
South Walls
South Ronaldsay
Swona
Pentland Firth
Stroma
Dunnet Head
Duncansby Head
Portskerra
Scrabster
Thurso Bay
Dunnet Bay
Dunnet
John o'Groats
Thurso
Castletown
to Aberdeen
to Aberdeen

Transverse Mercator Projection    © Oxford University Press

boundaries
| | international
| | national
| | internal
| | national park

communications
| | motorway
| | primary road
| | A road
| | railway
| | canal
| | major ferry route
✈ major airport
✈ other airport

settlements
built-up area
■ over 1 million inhabitants
● more than 100 000 inhabitants
◉ 25 000 – 100 000 inhabitants
• smaller towns

land height and sea depth

metres
1000
500
300
200
100
0 — sea level
50
100
200

▲ spot height in metres
▼ sea depth in metres

Scale 1: 1 000 000

0  10  20  30  40  50 km

© Oxford University Press

Butt of Lewis
Port of Ness
Cellar Head
Barvas
Tolsta Head
Carloway
Lewis
Broad Bay
Tiumpan Head
Portnaguran
Gallan Head
Great Bernera
Eye Peninsula
Loch Roag
Stornoway
Flannan Isles
574
Scarp
Loch Langavat
Loch Seaforth
Kebock Head
Loch Shell
The Minch
799
Clisham
West Loch Tarbert
Loch Erisort
Taransay
Tarbert
Scalpay
Shiant
Sound of Shiant
Sound of Taransay
Toe Head
Harris
East Loch Tarbert
Little Minch
Pabbay
Leverburgh
Berneray
Rodel
Sound of Harris
North Uist
230
Lochmaddy
Waternish Point
Rubha Hunish
Kilmaluag
Heisker
Baleshare
Loch Snizort
Uig
Ronay
Dunvegan Head
Trotternish
Rona
Benbecula
Wiay
Idrigill Point
719
The Storr
Dunvegan
Skye
Loch Bracadale
Raasay
East Suisnish
Sound of Raasay
Inner Sound
606
620
Rubha Ardvule
South Uist
Loch Eynort
Cuillin Hills
Sconser
Scalpay
993
Sgurr Alasdair
Loch Slapin
Soay
Elgol
Loch Eishort
Lochboisdale
Loch Boisdale
Armadale
Ardvasar
Calligarry
Eriskay
Point of Sleat
Fuday
Canna
Sound of Barra
Sanday
Sound of Canna
Barra
Rhum
Kinloch
Castlebay
Vatersay
Askival
812
Sandray
Eigg
393
Pabbay
Mingulay
Muck
Berneray
Sound of Rhum
Barra Head
Point of Ardnamurchan
Kilchoan
Salen
Coll
Arinagour
Tobermory
Scarinish
Tiree
Treshnish Isles
Ulva
Staffa
Ben More
967
Mull
Iona
Fionnphort
Loch Scridain
Ross of Mull

Scourie
Point of Stoer
Eddrachillis Bay
Lochinver
Rubha Coigeach
Enard Bay
Loch Broom
Greenstone Point
Ullapool
Grunard Bay
Little Loch Broom
Rubha Reidh
Loch Ewe
Loch Maree
Poolewe
Fionn Loch
Loch Gairloch
Gairloch
1053
Torridon
Loch a' Chroisg
Kinlochewe
Upper Loch Torridon
Shieldaig
HIGH
Loch Torridon
Lochcarron
Strathcarron
Loch Carron
Plockton
Stromeferry
Kyle of Lochalsh
Dornie
Kyleakin
Loch Alsh
Loch Duich
Glenaffric
Broadford
Loch Hourn
Loch Quoich
Sound of Sleat
Loch Cluanie
Mallaig
Loch Nevis
Loch Morar
Arisaig
Lochailort
Glenfinnan
Sound of Arisaig
Loch Eil
Kinlocheil
Loch Shiel
Loch Arkaig
Strontian
North Ballachulish
Loch Sunart
South Ballachulish
Ballachulish
Lochaline
Sound of Mull
Salen
Loch Linnhe
Loch Creran
Craignure
Lochdon
Lismore
Achnacroish
Loch Etive
Oban
Taynuilt
1124
Ben Cruachan
Kerrera
Firth of Lorn
to Colonsay

Outer Hebrides
Inner Hebrides
WESTERN ISLES
NORTHWE
St. Kilda

Pentland Firth
Dunnet Head
Stroma
Duncansby Head
to Kirkwall

Cape Wrath
Durness
Whiten Head
Strathy Point
Dunnet Head
Dunnet Bay
Scrabster
Thurso Bay
John o'Groats
Portskerra
Strathy
Dunnet
Melvich
Castletown

Oxford Bridge
Loch Eriboll
Kyle of Durness
Loch Hope
Ben Hope 927
Kyle of Tongue
Tongue
Loch Loyal
Ben Loyal 764
Bettyhill
Naver
Dyke
Halladale
Strathy
Thurso
Halkirk
Loch Watten
Mybster
Wick
Sinclair's Bay
Noss Head
Wick

HIGHLANDS
Reay Forest
Loch More
Loch Meadie
Altnaharra
Loch Naver
Ben Klibreck 961
Loch nan Clàr
Kinbrace
Morven 705
Berriedale Water
Dunbeath Water
Lybster
Latheron
Dunbeath

Ullapool
Unapool
Loch Assynt
Ben More Assynt 998
Loch Shin
Shin
Helmsdale
Berriedale

Canisp 847
Ledmore

Beinn Dearg 1081
Sgurr Mór 1109
Loch Fannich
Loch Luichart
Garve
Achnasheen
Bran
Meig

Helmsdale
Lairg
Brora
Brora
Golspie
Shin
Evelix
Bonar Bridge
Dornoch
Dornoch Firth
Tain
Tarbat Ness
Portmahomack

Loch Glass
Ben Wyvis 1046
Alness
Evanton
Nigg Bay
Invergordon
Cromarty Firth
Cromarty
Black Isle
Fortrose
Fort George
Moray Firth

Lossiemouth
Findochty
Portknockie
Portsoy
Whitehills
Troup Head
Rosehearty
Kinnaird Head
Burghead Bay
Burghead
Elgin
Cullen
Banff
Macduff
Gardenstown
Fraserburgh
Findhorn Bay
Findhorn
Kinloss
Fochabers
Loch of Strathbeg
Rattray Head

ROSS AND
Loch Monar
Carn Eige 1183
Loch Mullardoch
Loch Affric
Affric
Cannich
Beauly
Glass
Loch Meig
Orrin Reservoir
Muir of Ord
Beauly
Strathpeffer
Dingwall
Conon Bridge
Tore
North Kessock
Beauly Firth
Inverness
INV
Nairn
Forres
Nairn

MORAY
Rothes
Charlestown of Aberlour
Craigellachie
Dufftown
Spey
Keith
Huntly
Deveron
Aberchirder
Turriff
New Deer
Mintlaw
Ugie
Peterhead
Buchan Ness
Boddam
Hatton
Ellen

Loch Mhór
Invermoriston
Fort Augustus
Glen Mor
Drumnadrochit
Loch Ness
Tomatin
Findhorn
Strathspey
Grantown-on-Spey
Carrbridge
Aviemore
Tomintoul
Avon
Don
Rhynie
518
Oldmeldrum
Inverurie
Newmachar
Pitmedden
Ythan

Loch Garry
Invergarry
Loch Oich
935
Monadhliath Mountains
Kingussie
Newtonmore
Spey
Dulnain
CAIRNGORMS
Cairn Gorm 1244
Ben Macdui 1310
CAIRNGORMS NATIONAL PARK
Don
Alford
Kemnay
Kintore
ABZ
Dyce
Don
Bridge of Don
ABERDEENSHIRE
Westhill
Aberdeen
ABERDEEN CITY
Peterculter
Nigg
Nigg Bay
Cove Bay
Portlethen
Dee

Spean Bridge
Loch Lochy
1130
Roy
Loch Laggan
Dalwhinnie
Braemar
Balmoral
Crathie
Ballater
Aboyne
Banchory
Water of Feugh
Cowie Water
Stonehaven

Fort William
Ben Nevis 1344
Ben Alder 1148
Loch Ericht
Bridge of Dee
Lochnagar 1155
MOUNTAINS
North Esk
Fettercairn
Inverbervie

Blackwater Reservoir
Loch Treig
Glas Maol 1068
South Esk
Laurencekirk
Milton Ness

Kinlochleven
Loch Leven
Glencoe
1150
Glen Etive 1108
Loch Tulla
Bridge of Orchy
Rannoch Moor
Loch Ba
Ben Alder
Rannoch Station
Bridge of Ericht
Kinloch Rannoch
Loch Rannoch
Dunalastair Reservoir
Loch Tummel
Tummel
Tilt
Blair Atholl
Glen Garry
Glen Shee
Ardle
Prosen Water
ANGUS
Inverquharity
Brechin
Montrose Basin
Montrose
South Esk

GRAMPIAN
Loch Lyon
Loch an Daimh
Ben Lawers 1214
Lochay
Killin
Loch Tay
Aberfeldy
Tummel Bridge
Pitlochry
Isla
Glen Shee
Kirriemuir
Forfar
Lunan Water
Lunan Bay

Dalmally
Lochan Shira
Orchy
Tyndrum
Crianlarich
Ben More 1174
Ben Lui
Dochart
Loch Earn
Lochearnhead
Loch Lyon
Lyon
Almond
PERTH AND KINROSS
New Scone
Perth
Comrie
Crieff
Earn
Dunkeld
Isla
Blairgowrie
Rattray
Alyth
Coupar Angus
Sidlaw Hills
DUNDEE CITY
Dundee
Monifieth
Broughty Ferry
Tayport
Buddon Ness
Carnoustie
Arbroath
Newport-on-Tay
Newburgh
Leuchars
Eden Mouth
St. Andrews Bay
Cupar
St. Andrews
Firth of Tay

to Lerwick

**communications**
— motorway
— primary road
— A road
— railway
—|—|— canal
----- major ferry route
✈ major airport
✈ other airport

**settlements**
⬡ built-up area
■ over 1 million inhabitants
● more than 100 000 inhabitants
◉ 25 000 – 100 000 inhabitants
• smaller towns

**land height and sea depth**
metres
1000
500
300
200
100
0 sea level
50
100
200
▲ spot height in metres
▼ sea depth in metres

**boundaries**
— international
— national
— internal
— national park

Scale 1: 1 000 000

0 10 20 30 40 50 km
A B

© Oxford University Press

Scale 1 : 1 000 000

0   10   20   30   40   50 km

© Oxford University Press

Transverse Mercator Projection © Oxford University Press

Scale 1: 1 000 000

0   10   20   30   40   50 km

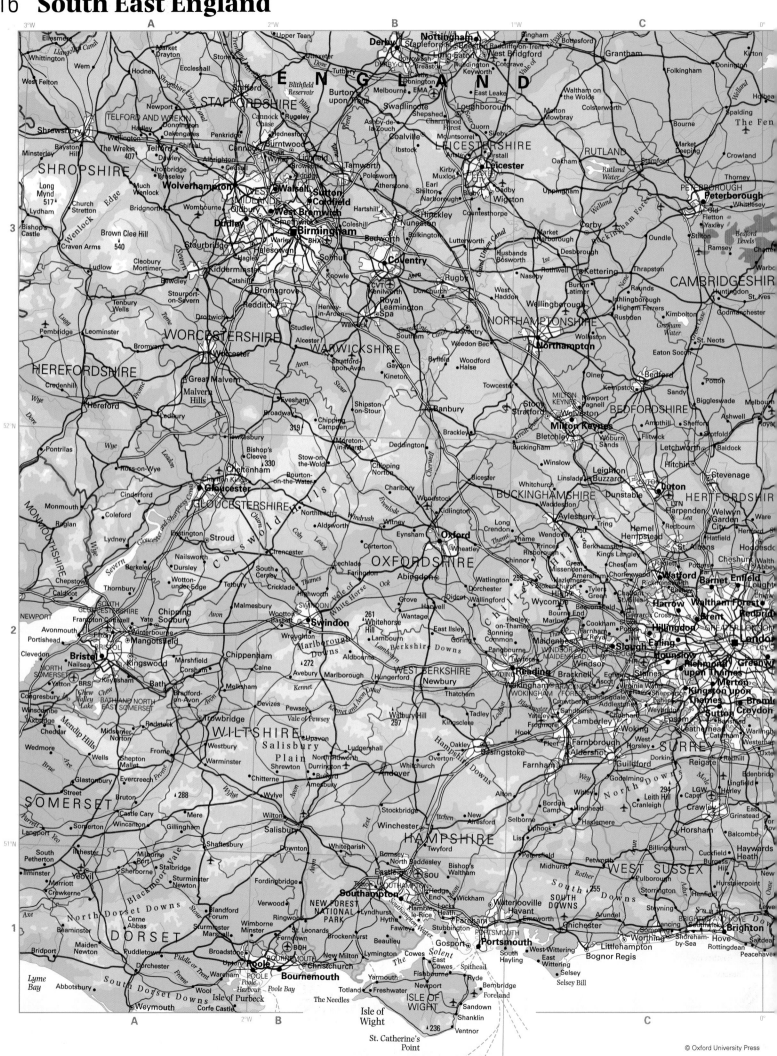

## Map Labels

**Sea / water features:**
The Wash, Blakeney Point, Great Ouse, Nar, Wensum, Bure, Yare, Waveney, Blyth, Alde, Deben, Orwell, Stour, Colne, Chelmer, Blackwater, Crouch, Thames, The Swale, Great Stour, Rother, Bewl Water, Romney Marsh, Strait of Dover (Pas de Calais), Canal de Calais, Aa, Liane

**Counties / regions:**
NORFOLK, Breckland, SUFFOLK, ESSEX, KENT, North Downs, EAST SUSSEX, THURROCK, MEDWAY, NORD-PAS-DE-CALAIS, FRANCE

**Settlements (Norfolk / Suffolk area):**
Burnham Market, Wells-next-the-Sea, Sheringham, Cromer, Mundesley, Hunstanton, Heacham, Holt, North Walsham, Docking, Saxthorpe, Dersingham, Fakenham, Aylsham, Winterton-on-Sea, Sandringham, Reepham, Coltishall, King's Lynn, East Dereham, Taverham, NWI, Wroxham, Acle, Caister-on-Sea, Great Yarmouth, Swaffham, Norwich, THE BROADS, Belton, Watton, Wymondham, Hopton on Sea, Downham Market, Wissey, Attleborough, Loddon, Feltwell, Bungay, Beccles, Lowestoft, Littleport, Little Ouse, Thetford, Harleston, Kessingland, Ely, Lakenheath, Brandon, Diss, Eye, Halesworth, Southwold, Isleham, Mildenhall, Ixworth, Yoxford, Soham, Fordham, Kentford, Debenham, Leiston, Saxmundham, Cambridge, Newmarket, Bury St. Edmunds, Stowmarket, Framlingham, Wickham Market, Aldeburgh, Great Shelford, Needham Market, Claydon, Orford, Sawston, Lavenham, Woodbridge, Orford Ness, Linton, Haverhill, Long Melford, Sudbury, Hadleigh, Ipswich, Bawdsey, Great Chesterford, Sible Hedingham, Saffron Walden, Felixstowe, Newport, Thaxted, Great Bardfield, Halstead, Earls Colne, Manningtree, Harwich, Stansted Mountfitchet, STN, Braintree, Coggeshall, Colchester, Wivenhoe, The Naze, Walton-on-the-Naze, Bishop's Stortford, Great Dunmow, Kelvedon, Abberton Reservoir, Tiptree, Thorpe-le-Soken, Frinton-on-Sea, Sawbridgeworth, Witham, West Mersea, Mersea Island, Brightlingsea, Chipping Ongar, Writtle, Chelmsford, Danbury, Clacton-on-Sea, Ingatestone, Hanningfield Reservoir, Maldon, Bradwell-on-Sea, Brentwood, Billericay, South Woodham Ferrers, Southminster, Havering, Hullbridge, Hockley, Burnham-on-Crouch, Foulness Point, Barking, Wickford, Rochford, Foulness Island, Aveley, South Ockendon, Basildon, Rayleigh, SOUTHEND, Southend-on-Sea, THURROCK, West Thurrock, South Benfleet, Canvey Island, Shoeburyness, Grays, Tilbury, Grain, Sheerness, Bexley, Swanscombe, MEDWAY, Hoo, Minster, Margate, Foreness Point, Dartford, Gravesend, Queenborough, Isle of Sheppey, Leysdown on Sea, Herne Bay, North Foreland, Swanley, Rochester, Broadstairs, New Ash Green, Stroud, Chatham, Whitstable, Minster, Ramsgate, Otford, Gillingham, Faversham, Sandwich, Sevenoaks, Wrotham, Aylesford, Sittingbourne, Canterbury, Ash, Tonbridge, Maidstone, Bearsted, Charing, Deal, Paddock Wood, Marden, Wye, Aylesham, Royal Tunbridge Wells, Pembury, Staplehurst, Bethersden, Ashford, Kennington, Brabourne Lees, Lyminge, Whitfield, St. Margaret's at Cliffe, Cranbrook, Tenterden, Hamstreet, Romney Marsh, Hythe, Dover, South Foreland, Wadhurst, Hawkhurst, Folkestone, Dymchurch, Northiam, New Romney, Heathfield, Rye, Lydd, Winchelsea, Dungeness, Hailsham, Battle, Fairlight, Polegate, Hastings, Pevensey, Bexhill, Eastbourne, Beachy Head, East Dean

**France:**
Bray-Dunes, Malo-les-Bains, Dunkerque, Grand Fort-Philippe, Gravelines, Bergues, Calais, Marck, Bourbourg, Esquelbecq, Wormhout, Guînes, Audruicq, Watten, Cassel, Ardres, Cap Gris-Nez, Slack, Marquise, St-Omer, Wimereux, Lumbres, Hazebrouck, Boulogne-sur-Mer, Desvres, Samer, Thérouanne, Aire-sur-la-Lys, Hardelot-Plage

**Ferry routes:**
to Esbjerg, to Amsterdam, to Hook of Holland, to Oostende, to Dieppe and le Havre

## Legend

**boundaries**
- international
- national
- internal
- national park

**communications**
- motorway
- primary road
- A road
- railway
- canal
- major ferry route
- ⊕ major airport
- ✈ other airport

**settlements**
- ⬡ built-up area
- ■ over 1 million inhabitants
- ● more than 100 000 inhabitants
- ⊙ 25 000 – 100 000 inhabitants
- • smaller towns

**land height and sea depth**

metres
1000
500
300
200
100
0 sea level
50
100
200

- ▲ spot height in metres
- ▾ sea depth in metres

Scale 1: 1 000 000

0  10  20  30  40  50 km

© Oxford University Press    Transverse Mercator Projection

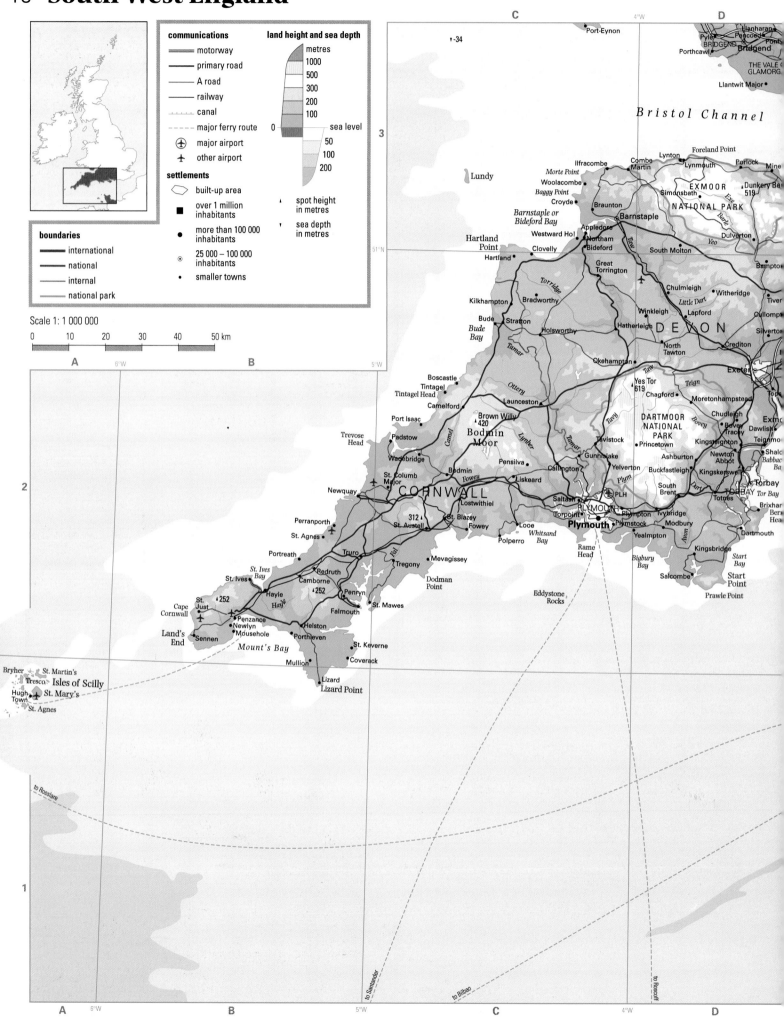

**communications**

| | |
|---|---|
| motorway | |
| primary road | |
| A road | |
| railway | |
| canal | |
| major ferry route | |

⊕ major airport
✈ other airport

**settlements**

⬡ built-up area

■ over 1 million inhabitants

● more than 100 000 inhabitants

⊙ 25 000 – 100 000 inhabitants

• smaller towns

**land height and sea depth**

metres
1000
500
300
200
100
0 — sea level
50
100
200

▲ spot height in metres
▼ sea depth in metres

**boundaries**

international
national
internal
national park

Scale 1: 1 000 000

0  10  20  30  40  50 km

*Bristol Channel*

Port-Eynon

Lundy

Ilfracombe
Combe Martin
Lynton
Foreland Point
Porlock
Mine
*Morte Point*
Woolacombe
Lynmouth
*Baggy Point*
Croyde
Braunton
**Barnstaple**
Simonsbath
EXMOOR
NATIONAL PARK
Dunkery Be
519
*Barnstaple or Bideford Bay*
Westward Ho!
Appledore
Northam
Bideford
Dulverton

Hartland Point
Clovelly
Great Torrington
South Molton
Bampton

Hartland
Kilkhampton
Bradworthy
Chulmleigh
Witheridge
Tiver
*Little Dart*
Bude
Stratton
Holsworthy
Winkleigh
Lapford
Cullomp
*Bude Bay*
Hatherleigh
D E V O N
Silverto
Boscastle
Tintagel
Tintagel Head
Camelford
*Torridge*
Okehampton
North Tawton
Crediton
*Tamar*
Yes Tor
619
Chagford
Exeter
Brown Willy
▲420
Launceston
*Ottery*
*Teign*
Moretonhampstead
Top
Port Isaac
Bodmin Moor
Chudleigh
Exm
Trevose Head
Padstow
*Camel*
Pensilva
DARTMOOR
NATIONAL PARK
*Bovey*
Bovey Tracey
Dawlish
Wadebridge
Bodmin
*Lynher*
Tavistock
Ashburton
Newton Abbot
Teignmo
St. Columb Major
*Fowey*
Liskeard
Princetown
Yelverton
Buckfastleigh
Kingsteignton
Shalc
Babbac
Ba
Newquay
CORNWALL
Callington
Gunnislake
*Plym*
South Brent
Kingskerswe
Torbay
Perranporth
312
▲
St. Austell
St. Blazey
Fowey
Saltash
PLH
Plympton
TORBAY
Totnes
*Tor Bay*
Brixhar
Ber
Hea
St. Agnes
Looe
*Whitsand Bay*
Torpoint
**Plymouth**
Plymstock
Ivybridge
Modbury
Dartmouth
Portreath
Truro
*Fal*
Tregony
Polperro
Rame Head
Yealmpton
*Avon*
Kingsbridge
*Start Bay*
*St. Ives Bay*
Redruth
Mevagissey
Eddystone Rocks
*Bigbury Bay*
Salcombe
Start Point
St. Ives
Camborne
252
▲
Penryn
Dodman Point
Prawle Point
St. ▲252
Just
Hayle
*Hayle*
Penzance
Helston
St. Mawes
Cape Cornwall
Newlyn
Mousehole
Porthleven
Land's End
Sennen
St. Keverne
*Mount's Bay*
Mullion
Coverack
Bryher
St. Martin's
Tresco
*Isles of Scilly*
Lizard
Hugh Town
St. Mary's
Lizard Point
St. Agnes

to Rosslare

to Santander

to Bilbao

to Roscoff

Llanharan
Pyle
Pencoed
Pont
BRIDGEND
**Bridgend**
Porthcawl
THE VALE
GLAMORG
Llantwit Major

-34

NORTHERN IRELAND

REPUBLIC OF IRELAND

North Channel

Counties and regions: MOYLE, BALLYMONEY, ANTRIM, BALLYMENA, COLERAINE, LIMAVADY, LONDONDERRY, MAGHERAFELT, STRABANE, COOKSTOWN, OMAGH, DUNGANNON, FERMANAGH, ARMAGH, CRAIGAVON, BANBRIDGE, DOWN, ARDS, NEWRY AND MOURNE, LISBURN, DONEGAL, SLIGO, LEITRIM, FERMANAGH, CAVAN, MONAGHAN, LOUTH, MEATH, WESTMEATH, LONGFORD, ROSCOMMON, MAYO, GALWAY, OFFALY

Dublin / Baile Átha Cliath, Belfast

Kintyre 446, Mull of Kintyre, Sanda Island, Machrihanish, Campbeltown, Southend, Lussa Loch

Rathlin Island, Fair Head, Benbane Head, Giants Causeway, Bushmills, Portrush, Portstewart, Coleraine, Ballycastle, Cushendun, Cushendall, Carnlough, Larne, Whitehead, Carrickfergus, Belfast, Bangor, Newtownards, Donaghadee, Ballyquintin Point, Strangford Lough, Downpatrick, Ardglass, Newcastle, Slieve Donard 852, Annalong, Kilkeel, Greencastle, Carlingford Lough, Greenore, Dundalk, Dundalk Bay, Drogheda, Balbriggan, Skerries, Rush, Lambay Island, Malahide, Howth, Dún Laoghaire, Dublin Bay, Bray

Malin Head, Inishowen Peninsula, Lough Swilly, Lough Foyle, Letterkenny, Donegal, Donegal Bay, Killybegs, Ballyshannon, Bundoran, Sligo, Sligo Bay, Ballina, Killala Bay, Westport, Clew Bay, Achill Island, Achill Head, Clare Island, Inishturk, Inishbofin, Inishshark, Clifden, Slyne Head, Galway Bay, Aran Islands

Lough Neagh, Lough Erne (Upper Lough Erne, Lower Lough Erne), Enniskillen, Lough Allen, Lough Gill, Lough Arrow, Lough Key, Lough Ree, Lough Corrib, Lough Mask, Lough Conn, Lough Cullin, Lough Derg, Shannon, Royal Canal, Grand Canal

Mountains: Antrim Mountains, Sperrin Mountains, Sawel 683, Slieve Snaght 615, Errigal 752, Blue Stack Mountains, Nephin Beg Range, Nephin 807, Ox Mountains, Slieve Gamph, Partry Mts., Sheeffry Hills, Mweelrea 814, Croagh Patrick 764, Joyce Country

to Douglas, to Liverpool, to Fleetwood, to Stranraer, to Holyhead

© Oxford University Press

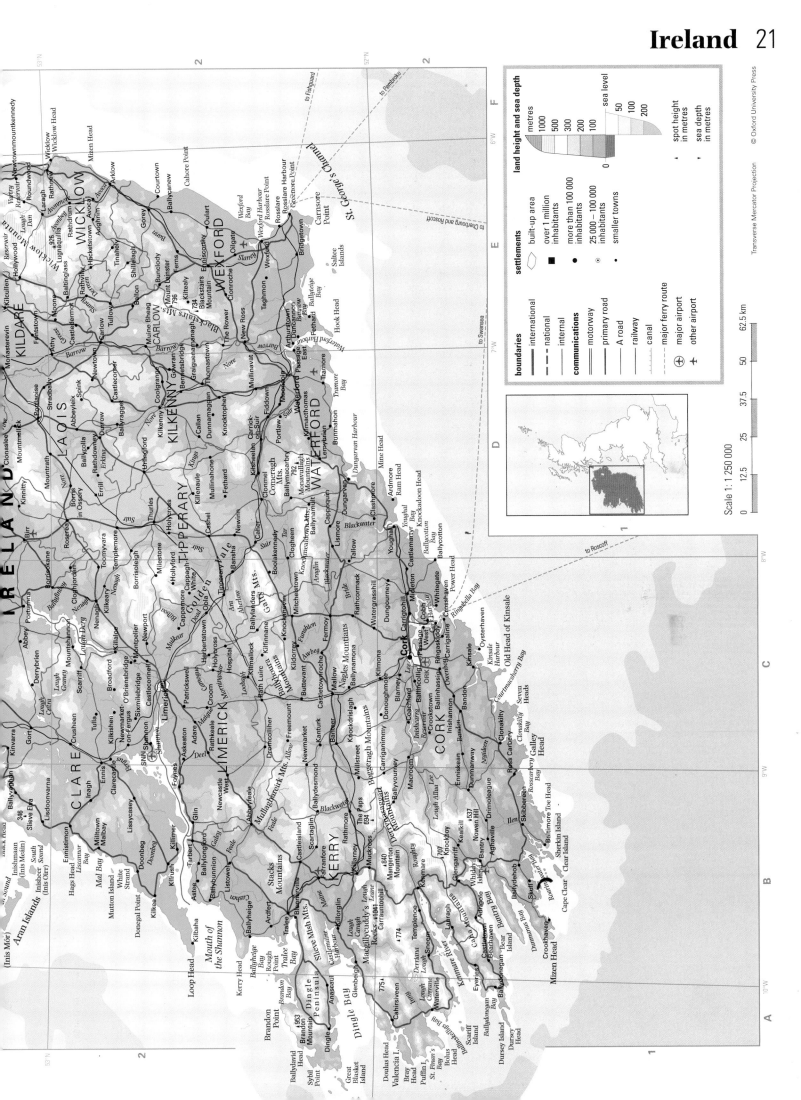

**Scale 1:1 250 000**

| settlements | |
| --- | --- |
| built-up area | |
| over 1 million inhabitants | |
| more than 100 000 inhabitants | |
| 25 000 – 100 000 inhabitants | |
| smaller towns | |

| boundaries | |
| --- | --- |
| international | |
| national | |
| internal | |

| communications | |
| --- | --- |
| motorway | |
| primary road | |
| A road | |
| railway | |
| canal | |
| major ferry route | |
| major airport | |
| other airport | |

**land height and sea depth**
metres
1000 500 300 200 100 sea level
50 100 200

spot height in metres
sea depth in metres

Transverse Mercator Projection

© Oxford University Press

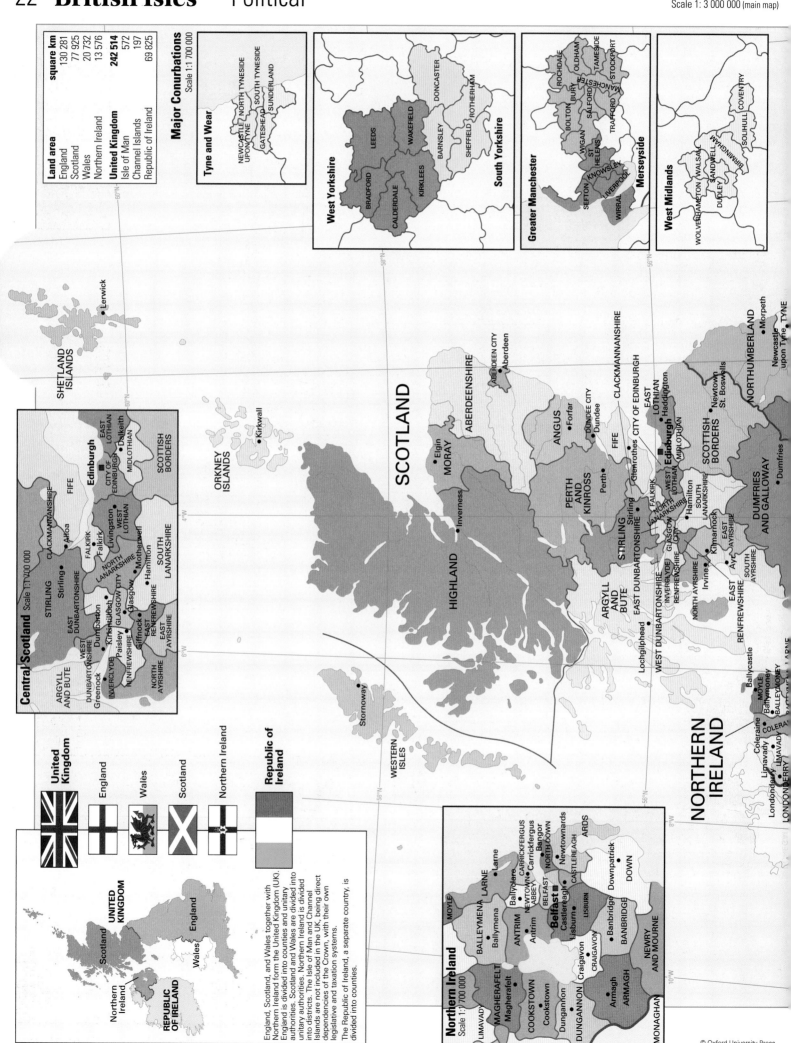

© Oxford University Press

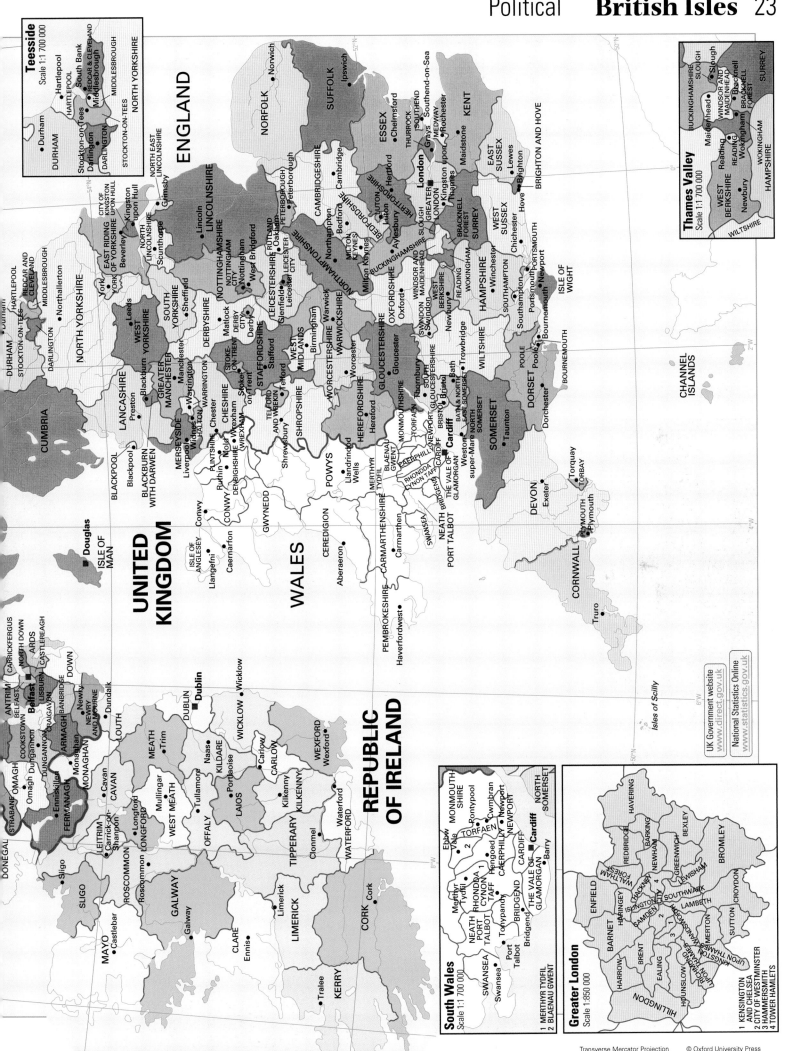

**Teesside** Scale 1:1 700 000

Durham • DURHAM
HARTLEPOOL • Hartlepool
STOCKTON-ON-TEES
Northallerton •
DARLINGTON
Darlington •
REDCAR & CLEVELAND
South Bank • Middlesbrough
Stockton on Tees
MIDDLESBROUGH
STOCKTON-ON-TEES
NORTH YORKSHIRE

**Thames Valley** Scale 1:1 700 000

BUCKINGHAMSHIRE
SLOUGH
Maidenhead • Slough
WINDSOR AND MAIDENHEAD
BRACKNELL FOREST
Reading • Bracknell
READING
WEST BERKSHIRE
Newbury • Wokingham
WOKINGHAM
SURREY
HAMPSHIRE
WILTSHIRE

ENGLAND

NORFOLK
Norwich •
Ipswich •
SUFFOLK
CAMBRIDGESHIRE
Cambridge •
Peterborough •
PETERBOROUGH
ESSEX
Chelmsford •
THURROCK
Grays • Southend-on-Sea
SOUTHEND
MEDWAY
Rochester •
London ■ GREATER LONDON
Kingston upon Thames
Maidstone •
KENT
EAST SUSSEX
Lewes •
Brighton •
BRIGHTON AND HOVE
Hove •
WEST SUSSEX
Chichester •

CITY OF KINGSTON UPON HULL
Kingston upon Hull
Grimsby •
NORTH LINCOLNSHIRE
NORTH EAST LINCOLNSHIRE
LINCOLNSHIRE
Lincoln •
Scunthorpe •
EAST RIDING OF YORKSHIRE
Beverley •
York •
NORTH YORKSHIRE
Sheffield •
SOUTH YORKSHIRE
NOTTINGHAMSHIRE
NOTTINGHAM CITY
Nottingham •
West Bridgford •
RUTLAND
Oakham •
LEICESTERSHIRE
LEICESTER CITY
Leicester •
Glenfield •
DERBYSHIRE
Matlock •
DERBY CITY
Derby •
NORTHAMPTONSHIRE
Northampton •
BEDFORDSHIRE
Bedford •
MILTON KEYNES
Milton Keynes •
BUCKINGHAMSHIRE
Aylesbury •
HERTFORDSHIRE
Hertford •
LUTON
Luton •
OXFORDSHIRE
Oxford •

DURHAM
HARTLEPOOL
STOCKTON-ON-TEES
REDCAR AND CLEVELAND
MIDDLESBROUGH
DARLINGTON
Darlington •
Northallerton •

NORTH YORKSHIRE
Leeds •
WEST YORKSHIRE
GREATER MANCHESTER
Manchester •
LANCASHIRE
Preston •
Blackburn •
BLACKBURN WITH DARWEN
BLACKPOOL
Blackpool •
CUMBRIA

MERSEYSIDE
Liverpool •
Widnes • HALTON
CHESHIRE
Chester •
Warrington •
WARRINGTON
STOKE-ON-TRENT
Stoke-on-Trent •
STAFFORDSHIRE
Stafford •
TELFORD AND WREKIN
Telford •
SHROPSHIRE
Shrewsbury •
WEST MIDLANDS
Birmingham •
WARWICKSHIRE
Warwick •
WORCESTERSHIRE
Worcester •
HEREFORDSHIRE
Hereford •
GLOUCESTERSHIRE
Gloucester •
Thornbury •
SOUTH GLOUCESTERSHIRE
MONMOUTHSHIRE
NEWPORT
Newport •
BRISTOL
Bristol •
BATH & NORTH EAST SOMERSET
Bath •
NORTH SOMERSET
Weston-super-Mare •
SOMERSET
Taunton •
WILTSHIRE
Trowbridge •
Swindon •
SWINDON
READING
WEST BERKSHIRE
Newbury •
WOKINGHAM
WINDSOR AND MAIDENHEAD
SLOUGH
BRACKNELL FOREST
SURREY
HAMPSHIRE
Winchester •
Southampton •
SOUTHAMPTON
PORTSMOUTH
Portsmouth •
ISLE OF WIGHT
DORSET
Dorchester •
Poole •
POOLE
BOURNEMOUTH
Bournemouth •
DEVON
Exeter •
Torquay •
TORBAY
PLYMOUTH
Plymouth •
CORNWALL
Truro •

CHANNEL ISLANDS

52°N
54°N
50°N
2°W
2°W
4°W
6°W
8°W

**UNITED KINGDOM**

ISLE OF MAN
Douglas ■

ISLE OF ANGLESEY
Llangefni •
Caernarfon •
Conwy •
CONWY
DENBIGHSHIRE
Ruthin •
Mold • FLINTSHIRE
WREXHAM
Wrexham •
GWYNEDD
POWYS
Llandrindod Wells •
CEREDIGION
Aberaeron •
MERTHYR TYDFIL
BLAENAU GWENT
RHONDDA CYNON TAFF
THE VALE OF GLAMORGAN
CAERPHILLY
Cardiff ■ CARDIFF
NEATH PORT TALBOT
SWANSEA
Swansea •
CARMARTHENSHIRE
Carmarthen •
PEMBROKESHIRE
Haverfordwest •

**WALES**

**REPUBLIC OF IRELAND**

DONEGAL
Sligo •
SLIGO
LEITRIM
Carrick-on-Shannon •
FERMANAGH
Enniskillen •
OMAGH
Omagh •
STRABANE
Strabane •
DUNGANNON
Cookstown • COOKSTOWN
DUNGANNON
MONAGHAN
Monaghan •
ARMAGH
Armagh •
CRAIGAVON
BANBRIDGE
NEWRY AND MOURNE
Newry •
DOWN
CAVAN
Cavan •
LONGFORD
Longford •
ROSCOMMON
Roscommon •
MAYO
Castlebar •
GALWAY
Galway •
CLARE
Ennis •
LIMERICK
Limerick •
KERRY
Tralee •
CORK
Cork •
TIPPERARY
Clonmel •
WATERFORD
Waterford •
KILKENNY
Kilkenny •
CARLOW
Carlow •
LAOIS
Portlaoise •
OFFALY
Tullamore •
WEST MEATH
Mullingar •
MEATH
Trim •
DUBLIN
Dublin ■
Naas •
KILDARE
WICKLOW
Wicklow •
WEXFORD
Wexford •
LOUTH
Dundalk •

ANTRIM
Belfast ■ BELFAST
CARRICKFERGUS
NORTH DOWN
ARDS
CASTLEREAGH
LISBURN
Lisburn •

**South Wales** Scale 1:1 700 000

MONMOUTHSHIRE
Ebbw Vale •
Pontypool •
Cwmbran •
TORFAEN
Hengoed •
CAERPHILLY
NEWPORT
Newport •
NORTH SOMERSET
Merthyr Tydfil •
RHONDDA CYNON TAFF
Tonypandy •
Pontypridd •
BRIDGEND
Bridgend •
THE VALE OF GLAMORGAN
CARDIFF
Cardiff ■
Barry •
NEATH PORT TALBOT
Port Talbot •
SWANSEA
Swansea •

1 MERTHYR TYDFIL
2 BLAENAU GWENT

**Greater London** Scale 1:850 000

ENFIELD
BARNET
HARINGEY
WALTHAM FOREST
HARROW
HILLINGDON
BRENT
EALING
HOUNSLOW
RICHMOND UPON THAMES
KINGSTON UPON THAMES
HAMMERSMITH
CAMDEN
ISLINGTON
HACKNEY
CITY
NEWHAM
REDBRIDGE
HAVERING
BARKING
GREENWICH
BEXLEY
LEWISHAM
SOUTHWARK
LAMBETH
WANDSWORTH
MERTON
SUTTON
CROYDON
BROMLEY

1 KENSINGTON AND CHELSEA
2 CITY OF WESTMINSTER
3 HAMMERSMITH
4 TOWER HAMLETS

isles of Scilly

Transverse Mercator Projection      © Oxford University Press

Scale 1: 4 500 000

**Land height and sea depth**

metres
1000
500
300
200
100
0 — sea level
50
100
200

▴ spot height in metres

The British Isles consists of the two large islands of Great Britain and Ireland and a number of smaller islands.

Ireland

Great Britain

*Major labels:*

NORTH SEA
IRISH SEA
CELTIC SEA
ATLANTIC OCEAN
English Channel
St. George's Channel
North Channel
FRANCE

Shetland Islands — Herma Ness, Yell, Unst, Fetlar, Mainland, Whalsay, Bressay, Foula, Sumburgh Head, Fair Isle

Orkney Islands — Mull Head, North Ronaldsay, Westray, Rousay, Sanday, Stronsay, Shapinsay, Mainland, Hoy, South Ronaldsay, Duncansby Head, Pentland Firth

Cape Wrath, Butt of Lewis, Thurso, Kinnairds Head, Buchan Ness, Moray Firth, Dornoch Firth

Outer Hebrides — Lewis, Harris ▴799 Clisham, St. Kilda, North Uist, Benbecula, South Uist, Barra

Northwest Highlands, Ben Wyvis ▴1046, Loch Shin, Rona

Inner Hebrides — Skye, Cuillin Hills ▴1009, Rhum, Eigg, Coll, Tiree, Iona, Mull, Colonsay, Jura, Islay, Sound of Jura, Little Minch, The Minch

Carn Eige ▴1183, Loch Ness, Great Glen, Monadhliath Mountains, Cairngorms, Ben Macdhui ▴1310, Spey, Deveron, Don, Dee, S. Esk, N. Esk

Mallaig, Loch Linnhe, Ben Nevis ▴1344, Grampian Mountains

Loch Awe, Loch Fyne, Loch Lomond, Loch Tay, Tay, Earn, Forth, Sidlaw Hills, Ochil Hills, Firth of Tay, Fife Ness, Firth of Forth, Central Lowlands

Bute, Arran, Ayr, Clyde, Firth of Clyde, Mull of Kintyre

Southern Uplands, Merrick ▴843, Broad Law ▴840, The Cheviot ▴815, Cheviot Hills, Lammermuir Hills, St. Abb's Head, Holy Island, Tweed, Teviot, Esk, Coquet

Malin Head, Bloody Foreland, Errigal Mt. ▴752, Aran Island, Donegal Mountains, Foyle, Lough Foyle, ▴554, Sawel ▴683, Sperrin Mountains, Antrim Mtns., Rathlin Island

Donegal Bay, Lower Lough Erne, Mourne, Blackwater, Lough Neagh, Belfast Lough, Strangford Lough, Upper Lough Erne, Erne, Mourne Mtns. ▴852 Slieve Donard, Dundalk Bay

Mull of Galloway, St. Bees Head, Solway Firth, Cumbrian Mtns. ▴978 Scafell Pike, Cross Fell ▴893, Eden, Tyne, Wear, Tees, Pennines

Isle of Man ▴621 Snaefell

North York Moors ▴454, Yorkshire Dales, Swale, Nidd, Wharfe, Aire, Ouse, Derwent, Yorkshire Wolds, Holderness, Flamborough Head, Spurn Head, Humber, Morecambe Bay, Lune, Ribble

Erris Head, Rossan Point, Achill Island, Slyne Head, Aran Islands, Loop Head, Tralee Bay ▴953, Dingle Bay ▴1041 Carrauntoohill, Caha Mtns., Bantry Bay, Mizen Head, Cape Clear, Old Head of Kinsale

Lough Conn, Moy, Lough Mask, Lough Corrib, Galway Bay, Clare, Suck, Lough Ree, Shannon, Central Plain, Lough Allen, Lough Derg, Bog of Allen, Barrow, Nore, Suir, Slaney, Boyne, Dublin Bay, Wicklow Mtns. ▴926 Lugnaquillia, Wexford Bay, Carnsore Point, Galty Mtns. ▴920, Blackwater, Lee

Anglesey, Holy Island, Caernarfon Bay, Cardigan Bay, ▴1085 Snowdon, Cambrian Mtns. ▴690, Conwy, Dee, Cheshire Plain, ▴636 The Peak, Mersey, Liverpool Bay, Wirral

▴892 Cader Idris, ▴517, Teifi, Towy, Black Mtns. ▴886, Brecon Beacons, Usk, Wye, Severn, Teme, Avon, ▴330, Trent, Witham, Soar, Don

Lincoln Wolds, The Wash, ▴1, The Fens, Great Ouse, Nene, Welland, Breckland, Wensum, Bure, Norfolk Broads, Waveney, Orford Ness, Stour, The Naze

St. David's Head, St. Bride's Bay, Carmarthen Bay, Gower, Swansea Bay, Bristol Channel, ▴519 Exmoor Hills, Quantock Hills, Parrett, Mendip Hills, Salisbury Plain ▴297, Cotswold Hills, Thames, Chiltern Hills, Lea, Avon, Frome, ▴255, ▴294, Hampshire Downs, South Downs, Test, Avon, North Downs, The Weald, Medway, Romney Marsh, North Foreland

Lundy, Hartland Point, Bodmin Moor, Dartmoor ▴619, Tamar, Taw, Exe, Lyme Bay, Portland Bill, The Solent, Isle of Wight, Beachy Head, Dungeness, Strait of Dover

Land's End, Isles of Scilly, Lizard Point, Start Point, Alderney, Cap de la Hague, Guernsey, Channel Islands, Sark, Jersey, Baie de la Seine

© Oxford University Press — Transverse Mercator Projection

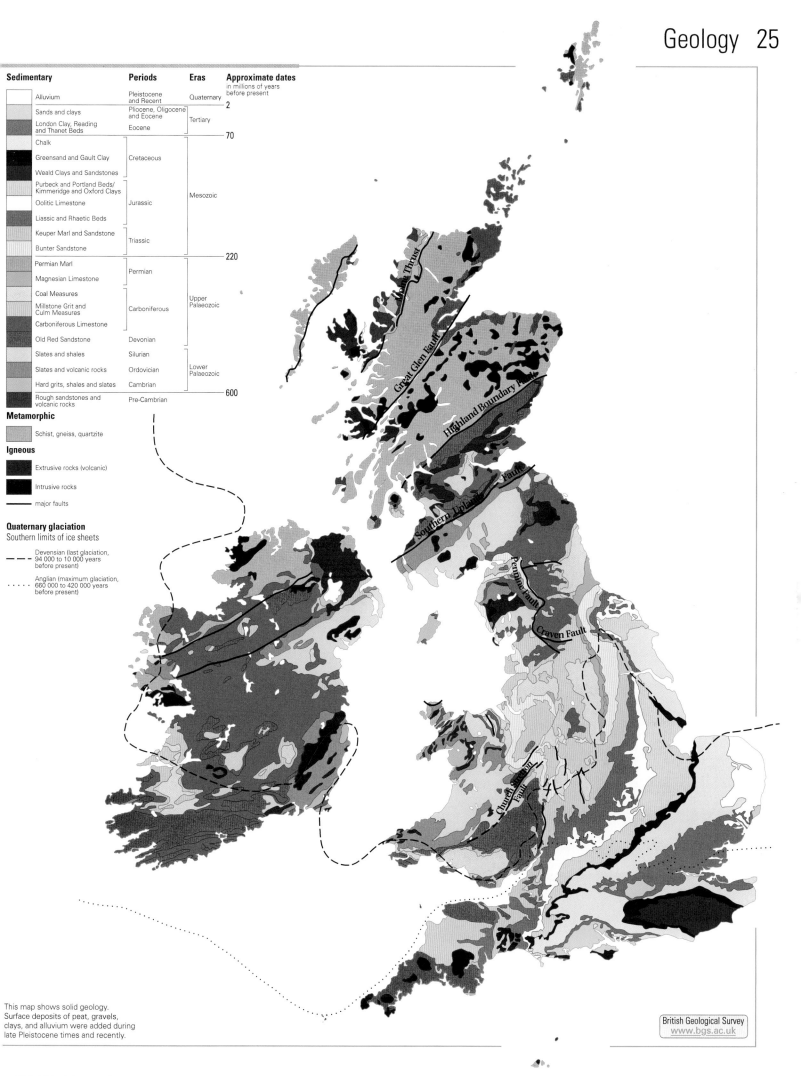

## Sedimentary

| | | Periods | Eras | **Approximate dates** in millions of years before present |
|---|---|---|---|---|
| | Alluvium | Pleistocene and Recent | Quaternary | |
| | | | | 2 |
| | Sands and clays | Pliocene, Oligocene and Eocene | Tertiary | |
| | London Clay, Reading and Thanet Beds | Eocene | | |
| | | | | 70 |
| | Chalk | | | |
| | Greensand and Gault Clay | Cretaceous | | |
| | Weald Clays and Sandstones | | | |
| | Purbeck and Portland Beds/ Kimmeridge and Oxford Clays | | Mesozoic | |
| | Oolitic Limestone | Jurassic | | |
| | Liassic and Rhaetic Beds | | | |
| | Keuper Marl and Sandstone | Triassic | | |
| | Bunter Sandstone | | | |
| | | | | 220 |
| | Permian Marl | Permian | | |
| | Magnesian Limestone | | | |
| | Coal Measures | | Upper Palaeozoic | |
| | Millstone Grit and Culm Measures | Carboniferous | | |
| | Carboniferous Limestone | | | |
| | Old Red Sandstone | Devonian | | |
| | Slates and shales | Silurian | | |
| | Slates and volcanic rocks | Ordovician | Lower Palaeozoic | |
| | Hard grits, shales and slates | Cambrian | | |
| | | | | 600 |
| | Rough sandstones and volcanic rocks | Pre-Cambrian | | |

## Metamorphic

Schist, gneiss, quartzite

## Igneous

Extrusive rocks (volcanic)

Intrusive rocks

—— major faults

## Quaternary glaciation
Southern limits of ice sheets

– – – Devensian (last glaciation, 94 000 to 10 000 years before present)

········· Anglian (maximum glaciation, 660 000 to 420 000 years before present)

This map shows solid geology. Surface deposits of peat, gravels, clays, and alluvium were added during late Pleistocene times and recently.

Moine Thrust

Great Glen Fault

Highland Boundary Fault

Southern Uplands Fault

Pennine Fault

Craven Fault

Church Stretton Fault

British Geological Survey
www.bgs.ac.uk

Scale 1: 10 000 000

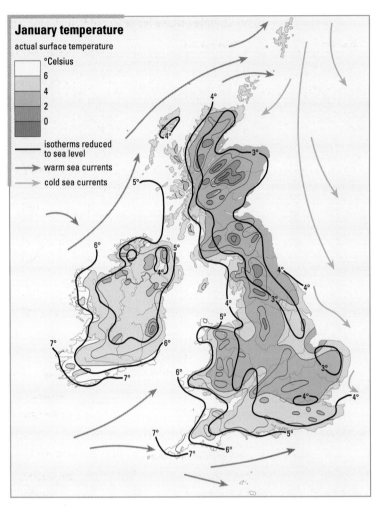

## January temperature

actual surface temperature

°Celsius
- 6
- 4
- 2
- 0

— isotherms reduced to sea level

→ warm sea currents

→ cold sea currents

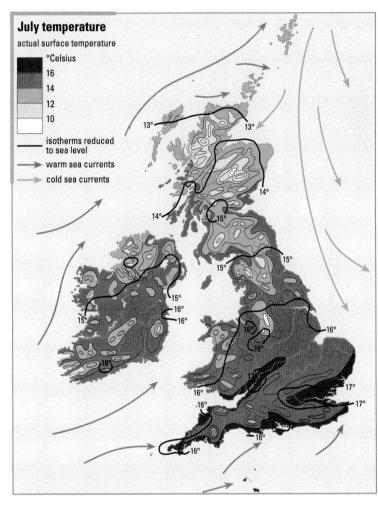

## July temperature

actual surface temperature

°Celsius
- 16
- 14
- 12
- 10

— isotherms reduced to sea level

→ warm sea currents

→ cold sea currents

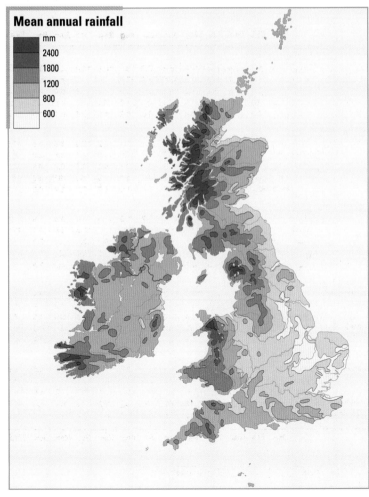

## Mean annual rainfall

mm
- 2400
- 1800
- 1200
- 800
- 600

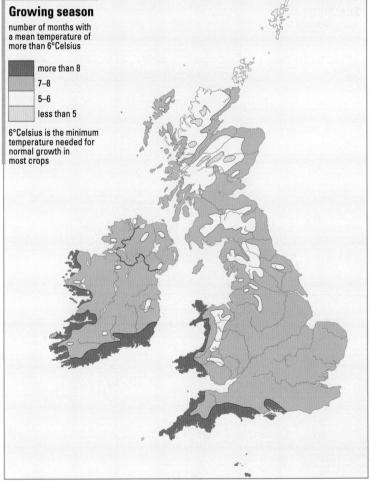

## Growing season

number of months with a mean temperature of more than 6°Celsius

- more than 8
- 7–8
- 5–6
- less than 5

6°Celsius is the minimum temperature needed for normal growth in most crops

Transverse Mercator Projection    © Oxford University Press

# Snow

average number of mornings per year with snow cover

- ■ more than 60
- ■ 40–60
- ■ 30–40
- ■ 20–30
- ■ 10–20
- □ less than 10
- □ no data

# Sunshine

average daily duration of bright sunshine, in hours

- ■ more than 5.0
- ■ 4.5–5.0
- ■ 4.0–4.5
- ■ 3.5–4.0
- □ 3.0–3.5
- □ less than 3.0

© Oxford University Press

## Climate graphs for selected British stations

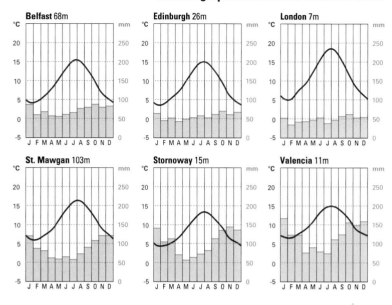

Belfast 68m · Edinburgh 26m · London 7m · St. Mawgan 103m · Stornoway 15m · Valencia 11m

## Climate stations

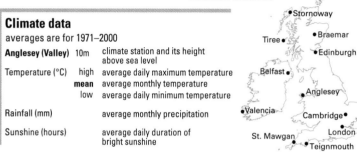

Stornoway · Braemar · Tiree · Edinburgh · Belfast · Anglesey · Valencia · Cambridge · St. Mawgan · London · Teignmouth

## Climate data

averages are for 1971–2000

**Anglesey (Valley)** 10m — climate station and its height above sea level

Temperature (°C) **high** — average daily maximum temperature
**mean** — average monthly temperature
**low** — average daily minimum temperature

Rainfall (mm) — average monthly precipitation

Sunshine (hours) — average daily duration of bright sunshine

|  |  | Jan | Feb | Mar | Apr | May | Jun | Jul | Aug | Sep | Oct | Nov | Dec | YEAR |
|---|---|---|---|---|---|---|---|---|---|---|---|---|---|---|
| **Anglesey (Valley)** | 10m |  |  |  |  |  |  |  |  |  |  |  |  |  |
| Temperature (°C) | high | 8.0 | 8.0 | 9.4 | 11.6 | 14.7 | 16.8 | 18.8 | 18.9 | 16.9 | 14.0 | 10.8 | 8.9 | 13.1 |
|  | mean | 5.8 | 5.6 | 6.9 | 8.5 | 11.3 | 13.6 | 15.7 | 15.8 | 14.0 | 11.4 | 8.4 | 6.7 | 10.3 |
|  | low | 3.5 | 3.1 | 4.3 | 5.3 | 7.8 | 10.3 | 12.5 | 12.6 | 11.1 | 8.8 | 6.0 | 4.4 | 7.5 |
| Rainfall (mm) |  | 82 | 60 | 67 | 52 | 45 | 51 | 49 | 68 | 73 | 90 | 101 | 92 | 828 |
| Sunshine (hours) |  | 1.9 | 2.9 | 3.7 | 5.9 | 7.4 | 6.8 | 6.6 | 6.2 | 4.8 | 3.5 | 2.1 | 1.5 | 4.4 |
| **Braemar** | 339m |  |  |  |  |  |  |  |  |  |  |  |  |  |
| Temperature (°C) | high | 4.1 | 4.4 | 6.4 | 9.3 | 13.1 | 15.9 | 18.1 | 17.4 | 14.2 | 10.6 | 6.8 | 4.8 | 10.5 |
|  | mean | 1.2 | 1.3 | 3.0 | 5.2 | 8.3 | 11.2 | 13.4 | 12.8 | 10.2 | 7.2 | 3.8 | 2.0 | 6.7 |
|  | low | -1.8 | -1.8 | -0.4 | 1.0 | 3.5 | 6.5 | 8.7 | 8.2 | 6.2 | 3.7 | 0.7 | -0.9 | 2.8 |
| Rainfall (mm) |  | 113 | 68 | 77 | 55 | 59 | 56 | 54 | 61 | 83 | 102 | 92 | 95 | 913 |
| Sunshine (hours) |  | 0.9 | 2.0 | 3.1 | 4.4 | 5.6 | 5.6 | 5.4 | 4.9 | 3.8 | 2.2 | 1.2 | 0.6 | 3.3 |
| **Cambridge** | 26m |  |  |  |  |  |  |  |  |  |  |  |  |  |
| Temperature (°C) | high | 7.0 | 7.4 | 10.2 | 12.6 | 16.5 | 19.4 | 22.2 | 22.3 | 18.9 | 14.6 | 9.9 | 7.8 | 14.1 |
|  | mean | 4.2 | 4.3 | 6.6 | 8.3 | 11.6 | 14.6 | 17.1 | 17.1 | 14.5 | 10.9 | 6.8 | 5.1 | 10.1 |
|  | low | 1.3 | 1.1 | 2.9 | 4.0 | 6.7 | 9.8 | 12.0 | 12.0 | 10.1 | 7.1 | 3.7 | 2.3 | 6.1 |
| Rainfall (mm) |  | 45 | 33 | 42 | 43 | 45 | 54 | 38 | 49 | 51 | 54 | 51 | 50 | 554 |
| Sunshine (hours) |  | 1.8 | 2.6 | 3.5 | 4.9 | 6.1 | 6.0 | 6.2 | 6.0 | 4.7 | 3.7 | 2.3 | 1.5 | 4.1 |
| **Teignmouth** | 3m |  |  |  |  |  |  |  |  |  |  |  |  |  |
| Temperature (°C) | high | 9.0 | 8.9 | 10.5 | 12.2 | 15.3 | 18.2 | 20.6 | 20.4 | 18.1 | 14.8 | 11.7 | 9.9 | 14.2 |
|  | mean | 6.4 | 6.2 | 7.6 | 9.0 | 12.0 | 14.7 | 17.1 | 16.9 | 14.8 | 11.9 | 8.9 | 7.4 | 11.1 |
|  | low | 3.7 | 3.5 | 4.6 | 5.7 | 8.6 | 11.2 | 13.5 | 13.4 | 11.4 | 8.9 | 6.0 | 4.8 | 8.0 |
| Rainfall (mm) |  | 102 | 83 | 68 | 55 | 52 | 51 | 36 | 57 | 67 | 83 | 84 | 113 | 850 |
| Sunshine (hours) |  | 2.0 | 2.7 | 3.8 | 6.0 | 7.0 | 7.1 | 7.4 | 6.9 | 5.3 | 3.5 | 2.8 | 1.8 | 4.7 |
| **Tiree** | 9m |  |  |  |  |  |  |  |  |  |  |  |  |  |
| Temperature (°C) | high | 7.6 | 7.4 | 8.5 | 10.1 | 12.8 | 14.5 | 16.1 | 16.3 | 14.7 | 12.4 | 9.8 | 8.3 | 11.6 |
|  | mean | 5.4 | 5.2 | 6.0 | 7.4 | 9.8 | 11.8 | 13.6 | 13.8 | 12.2 | 10.2 | 7.5 | 6.2 | 9.1 |
|  | low | 3.1 | 3.0 | 3.6 | 4.7 | 6.8 | 9.1 | 11.1 | 11.2 | 9.7 | 7.9 | 5.2 | 4.0 | 6.6 |
| Rainfall (mm) |  | 143 | 98 | 105 | 67 | 54 | 62 | 78 | 99 | 119 | 143 | 137 | 135 | 1236 |
| Sunshine (hours) |  | 1.2 | 2.3 | 3.3 | 5.5 | 7.3 | 6.6 | 5.2 | 5.2 | 4.1 | 2.7 | 1.6 | 1.0 | 3.8 |
|  |  | Jan | Feb | Mar | Apr | May | Jun | Jul | Aug | Sep | Oct | Nov | Dec | YEAR |

Met Office
www.metoffice.gov.uk

BBC Weather Centre
www.bbc.co.uk/weather

## Land use

- rough grazing
- improved pasture
- cereals
- mixed farming
- • market gardening
- forest and woodland
- built-up area

### Number of farms in the UK

|            | 1950    | 1970    | 2005    |
|------------|---------|---------|---------|
| England    | 316 485 | 192 700 | 195 900 |
| Scotland   | 74 792  | 37 576  | 51 100  |
| Wales      | 56 289  | 37 252  | 37 000  |
| N. Ireland | 86 287  | 61 124  | 27 100  |

### Average size of farms in the UK (hectares)

|            | 1950 | 1970  | 2005  |
|------------|------|-------|-------|
| England    | 33.3 | 51.4  | 47.4  |
| Scotland   | 82.9 | 165.8 | 107.9 |
| Wales      | 28.5 | 44.0  | 39.2  |
| N. Ireland | 14.0 | 17.8  | 38.0  |

### Quantity of crops harvested in the UK, 2005

million tonnes    **total 43.3 million tonnes**

- vegetables 2.7
- fruit 0.4
- other crops 12.9
- cereals 21.0
- potatoes 6.3

### Livestock in the UK, 2005

millions    **total 224.7 million**

- cattle and calves 10.4
- poultry 173.9
- sheep and lambs 35.5
- pigs 4.9

### Agricultural employment in the UK

number of workers (thousands)

**seasonal workers**
- male
- female

**regular part-time workers**
- male
- female

**regular full-time workers**
- male
- female

(bar chart, years 1984, 1992, 2005; y-axis 0–350)

Department for Environment
Food and Rural Affairs
www.defra.gov.uk

Transverse Mercator Projection

© Oxford University Press

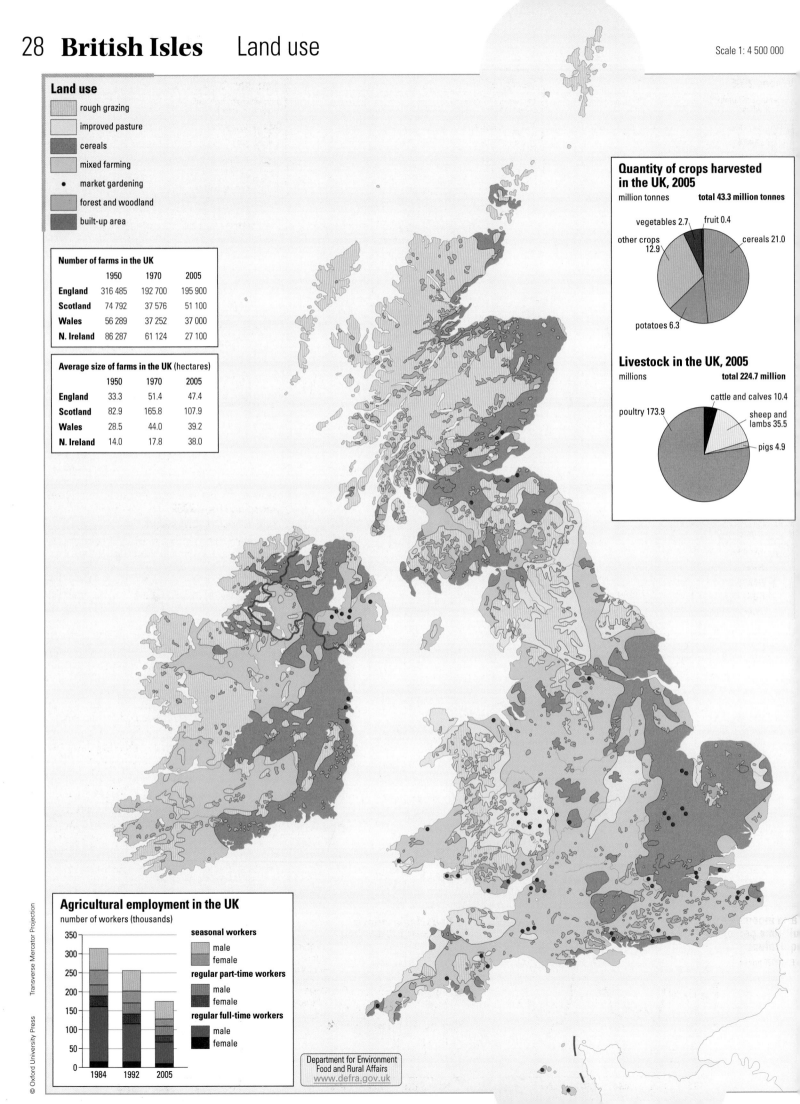

## Wheat, 2005

percentage of farmland used for wheat

- over 40%
- 30–40%
- 20–30%
- 10–20%
- 0–10%

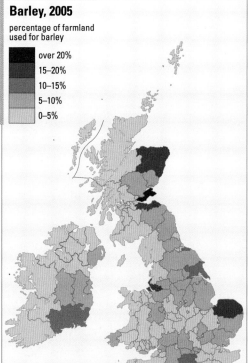

## Barley, 2005

percentage of farmland used for barley

- over 20%
- 15–20%
- 10–15%
- 5–10%
- 0–5%

## Potatoes, 2005

percentage of farmland used for potatoes

- over 3%
- 2–3%
- 1–2%
- 0.5–1%
- 0–0.5%

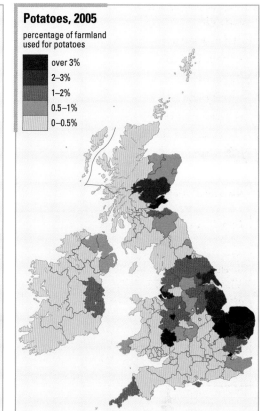

## Market gardening, 2005

percentage of farmland used for market gardening

- over 4%
- 3–4%
- 2–3%
- 1–2%
- under 1%

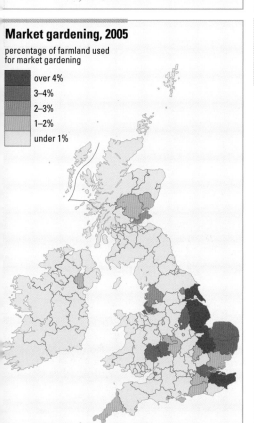

## Dairy and beef cattle, 2005

one dot represents 10 000 animals

- dairy cattle
- beef cattle

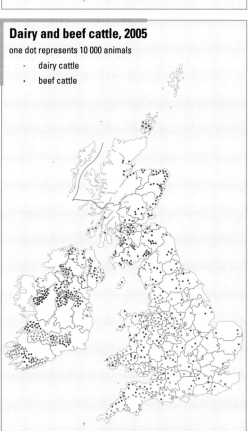

## Sheep and Pigs, 2005

one dot represents 100 000 animals

- sheep
- pigs

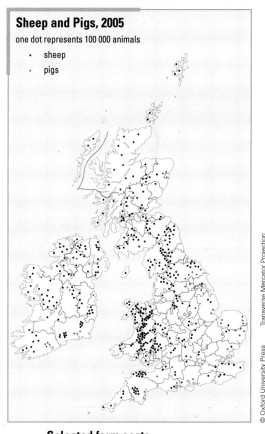

Transverse Mercator Projection

© Oxford University Press

## Farm income per full-time person equivalent

£ at 2005 prices

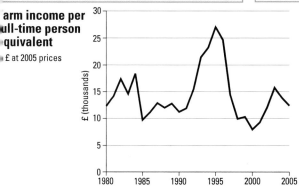

## Selected farm prices

in units where 100 = prices in 2000

- vegetables
- fruit
- animals
- potatoes
- milk
- cereals
- eggs

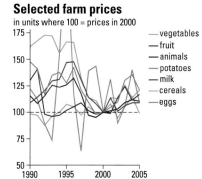

## Selected farm costs

in units where 100 = costs in 2000

- fertiliser
- energy
- machinery
- seeds
- feedstuff
- animals
- plant chemicals

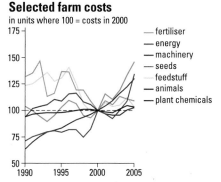

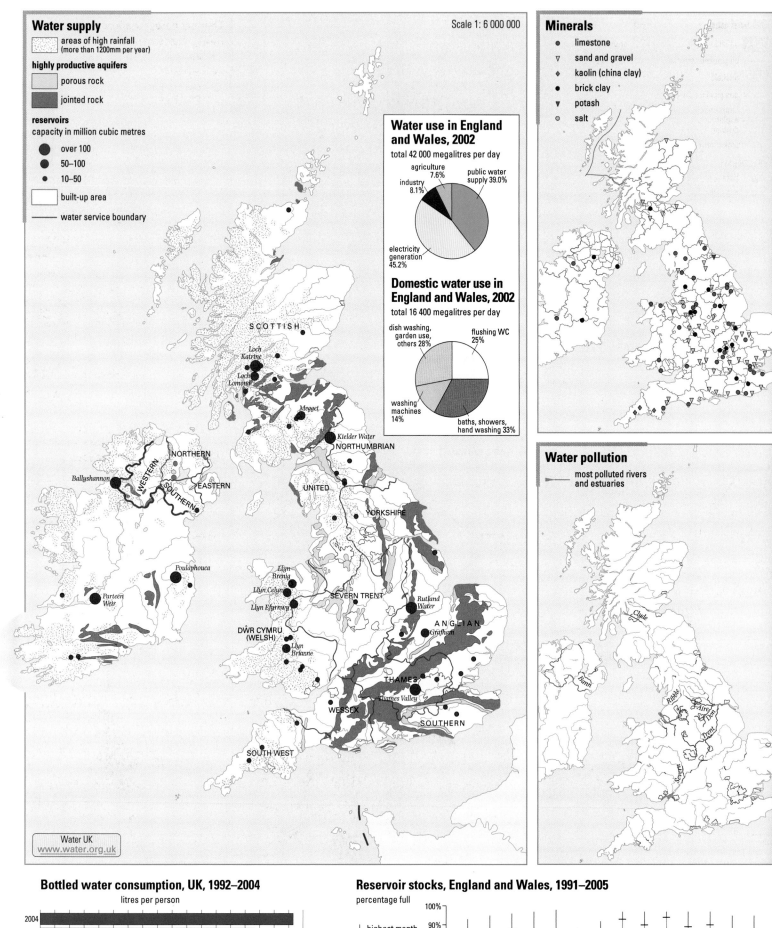

## Water supply

areas of high rainfall (more than 1200mm per year)

**highly productive aquifers**
- porous rock
- jointed rock

**reservoirs**
capacity in million cubic metres
- over 100
- 50–100
- 10–50

built-up area

water service boundary

Scale 1: 6 000 000

### Water use in England and Wales, 2002
total 42 000 megalitres per day

- agriculture 7.6%
- industry 8.1%
- public water supply 39.0%
- electricity generation 45.2%

### Domestic water use in England and Wales, 2002
total 16 400 megalitres per day

- dish washing, garden use, others 28%
- flushing WC 25%
- washing machines 14%
- baths, showers, hand washing 33%

## Minerals
- limestone
- sand and gravel
- kaolin (china clay)
- brick clay
- potash
- salt

## Water pollution
most polluted rivers and estuaries

Water UK
www.water.org.uk

*Labels on maps:* SCOTTISH, Loch Katrine, Loch Lomond, Megget, Kielder Water, NORTHUMBRIAN, NORTHERN, WESTERN, SOUTHERN, EASTERN, Ballyshannon, UNITED, YORKSHIRE, Poulaphouca, Parteen Weir, Llyn Brenig, Llyn Celyn, Llyn Efyrnwy, SEVERN TRENT, Rutland Water, ANGLIAN, Grafham, DWR CYMRU (WELSH), Llyn Brianne, THAMES, Thames Valley, WESSEX, SOUTHERN, SOUTH WEST

*Pollution map rivers:* Clyde, Bann, Ribble, Aire, Don, Trent, Severn

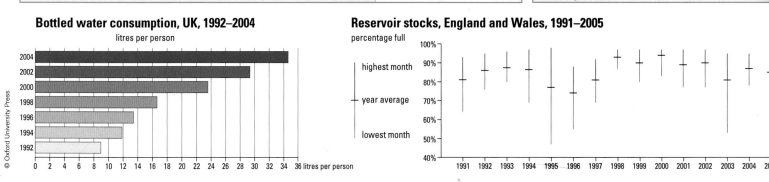

### Bottled water consumption, UK, 1992–2004
litres per person

| Year | |
|------|---|
| 2004 | ~34 |
| 2002 | ~29 |
| 2000 | ~24 |
| 1998 | ~17 |
| 1996 | ~13 |
| 1994 | ~12 |
| 1992 | ~9 |

0 2 4 6 8 10 12 14 16 18 20 22 24 26 28 30 32 34 36 litres per person

### Reservoir stocks, England and Wales, 1991–2005
percentage full

- highest month
- year average
- lowest month

1991 1992 1993 1994 1995 1996 1997 1998 1999 2000 2001 2002 2003 2004 20

© Oxford University Press

Scale 1 : 6 000 000 (main map)

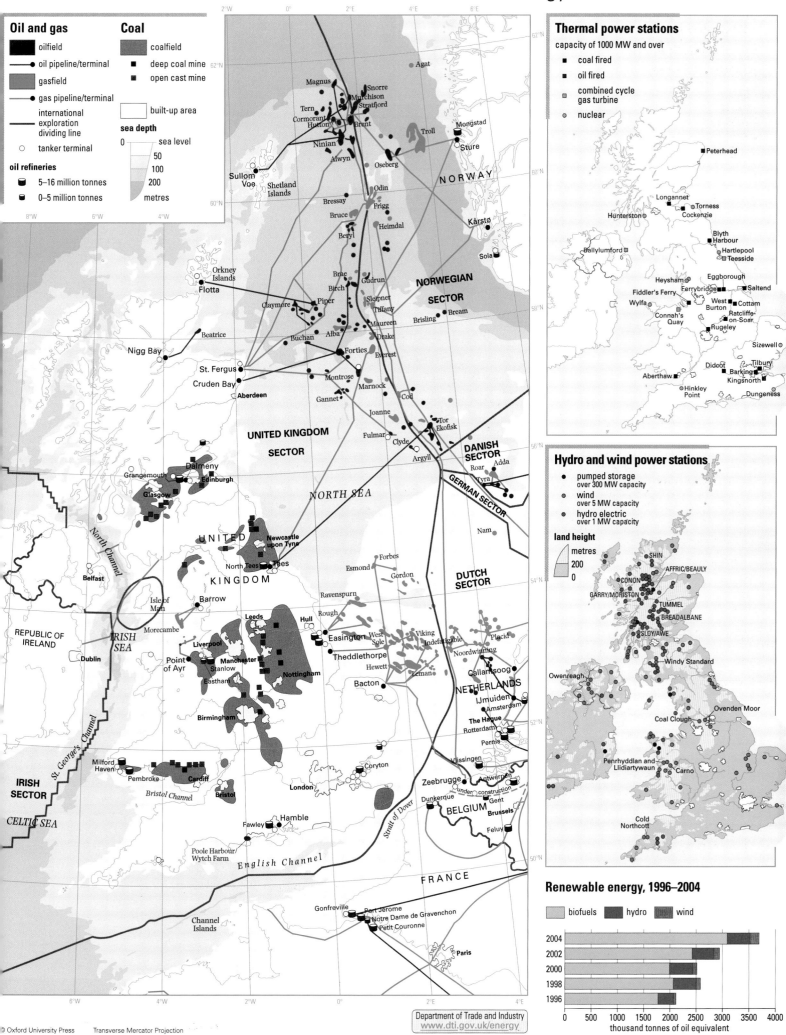

## Oil and gas

- ◼ oilfield
- ●—— oil pipeline/terminal
- ▨ gasfield
- ——— gas pipeline/terminal
- ——— international exploration dividing line
- ○ tanker terminal

**oil refineries**
- ◖ 5–16 million tonnes
- ◖ 0–5 million tonnes

## Coal

- ▨ coalfield
- ◼ deep coal mine
- ◼ open cast mine
- ☐ built-up area

**sea depth**

0 — sea level
50
100
200
metres

### Thermal power stations

capacity of 1000 MW and over

- ◼ coal fired
- ◼ oil fired
- ◼ combined cycle gas turbine
- ● nuclear

Peterhead

Longannet · Torness
Hunterston · Cockenzie
Ballylumford

Blyth Harbour
Hartlepool
Teesside

Heysham · Eggborough
Fiddler's Ferry · Ferrybridge · Saltend
Wylfa · West Burton
Connah's Quay · Cottam · Ratcliffe-on-Soar
Rugeley

Sizewell

Didcot · Tilbury
Aberthaw · Barking · Kingsnorth
Hinkley Point · Dungeness

### Hydro and wind power stations

- ● pumped storage over 300 MW capacity
- ● wind over 5 MW capacity
- ● hydro electric over 1 MW capacity

**land height**

metres
200
0

SHIN
AFFRIC/BEAULY
CONON
GARRY/MORISTON
TUMMEL
BREADALBANE
SLOY/AWE

Windy Standard

Owenreagh

Ovenden Moor

Coal Clough

Penrhyddlan and Llidiartywaun · Carno

Cold Northcott

### Renewable energy, 1996–2004

biofuels ☐  hydro ▨  wind ▨

| Year | |
|---|---|
| 2004 | |
| 2002 | |
| 2000 | |
| 1998 | |
| 1996 | |

0   500   1000   1500   2000   2500   3000   3500   4000
thousand tonnes of oil equivalent

Department of Trade and Industry
www.dti.gov.uk/energy

© Oxford University Press   Transverse Mercator Projection

### Manufacturing industry

the map shows only the main centres of selected industries

▽ chemicals
● steel
○ non-ferrous metal smelting
● metal working
◼ motor vehicles
■ railway vehicles
◻ aircraft and aerospace
■ shipbuilding and repair
△ mechanical engineering
▲ electrical engineering
△ electronics and computers
◆ clothing and footwear
◆ textiles and carpets

### Regional aid to industry

Assisted areas, eligible under European Union law for grants to increase employment opportunities

▨ tier 1 (higher level of assistance)
▨ tier 2 (lower level of assistance)

### UK employment

millions of people

agriculture, forestry, and fishing
energy and water
manufacturing
transport and communications
services

### UK manufacturing production, 2005

Total value of output £464 977 million

other 3.9%
transport equipment 14.2%
electrical; optical equipment 8.8%
machinery 7.5%
metals 9.3%
non-metallic mineral products 2.7%
rubber; plastics 4.7%
chemicals 11.0%
fuels; refining 7.0%
paper; printing; publishing 9.3%
wood products 1.6%
textiles; leather 2.4%
food; drink 17.7%

Department for Trade and Industry
www.dti.gov.uk

HIGHLANDS AND ISLANDS

Fort William

Dundee
Kinross
Markinch
Grangemouth
Kirkcaldy
Coatbridge
Leith
Broxburn
Edinburgh
Glasgow
Motherwell
Irvine
Kilmarnock
Prestwick
Mauchline
Selkirk
Cumnock
Galashiels
Hawick
Girvan

Lynemouth
Newcastle upon Tyne
Gateshead
South Shields
Prudhoe
Sunderland
Washington
Billingham
Teesside
Middlesbrough
Wilton
Whitehaven
Kendal

NORTHERN IRELAND

Donegal
Belfast
Newtownards
Craigavon
Killala
Westport
Ballieborough
Dundalk
Dunleer
Delvin
Longford
Navan
Athlone
Clane
Dublin
Galway
Ballinasloe
Tullamore
Rathcoole
Dún Laoghaire
Bray
Holyhead
Ennis
Newmarket-on-Fergus
Askeaton/Foynes
Limerick
Thurles
Arklow
Tralee
Clonmel
Killarney
Cork
Kinsale
Waterford

Nelson
Burnley
Halifax
Bradford
Blackburn
Preston
Brough
Kingston upon Hull
Leeds
Bolton
St Helens
Huddersfield
Immingham
Liverpool
Oldham
Scunthorpe
Grimsby
MERSEYSIDE
Manchester
Rotherham
Sheffield
Ince
Northwich
SOUTH YORKSHIRE
Wakefield
Sandbach
Newark
Crewe
Derby
Wrexham
Nottingham
Burnaston
Castle Donington
Stafford
Rugeley
Loughborough
Wolverhampton
Ibstock
Norwich
Walsall
Leicester
Birmingham
Solihull
Peterborough
Kidderminster
Coventry
Kettering
Redditch
Rugby
Rushden
Longbridge
Wellingborough
Cambridge
Northampton
Ipswich
Banbury
Milton Keynes
Hitchin
Cowley
Luton
Watford
Borehamwood
Chelmsford
Velindre
Ebbw Vale
Cwmbran
Swindon
Reading
Bracknell
Northfleet
Baglan Bay
Llanwern
London
Swansea
Newport
Newbury
Port Talbot
Bristol
Guildford
Bridgend
Farnborough
Godalming
Avonmouth

WEST WALES AND THE VALLEYS

Appledore
Street
Yeovil
Southampton

CORNWALL

ISLES OF SCILLY

## Employment in primary activity, 2005

percentage of the workforce employed in agriculture, forestry, fishing, mining, and quarrying, by administrative area

- over 10%
- 5–10%
- 2.5–5%
- 1–2.5%
- under 1%

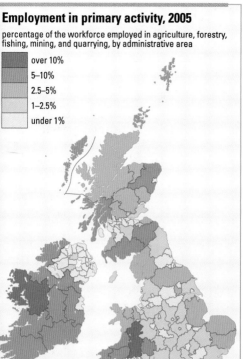

## Employment in secondary activity, 2005

percentage of the workforce employed in manufacturing, construction, and utilities, by administrative area

- over 30%
- 25–30%
- 20–25%
- 15–20%
- under 15%

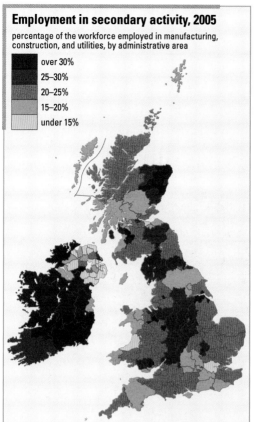

## Employment in tertiary activity, 2005

percentage of the workforce employed in services, transport, finance, and administration, by administrative area

- over 80%
- 75–80%
- 70–75%
- 65–70%
- under 65%

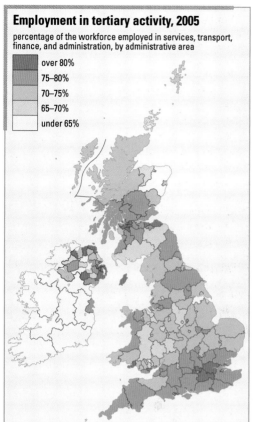

## Unemployment, 2005

percentage of the workforce unemployed, by administrative area

- over 7%
- 6–7%
- 5–6%
- 4–5%
- 3–4%
- under 3%

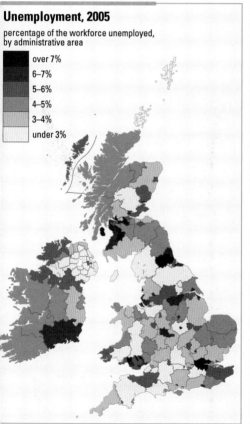

## Change in manufacturing employment, 1991–2005

percentage change in the number of people employed in manufacturing, by administrative area

**gain**
- over 20%
- 10–20%
- 0–10%

**loss**
- 0–10%
- 10–20%
- over 20%

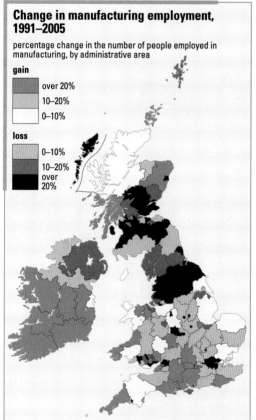

## Net jobs gains and losses, 1986–2005

thousands of jobs by former Standard Statistical Region

**gains**
300
200
100
0

**losses**
0
100
200

**activity**
- primary
- secondary
- tertiary

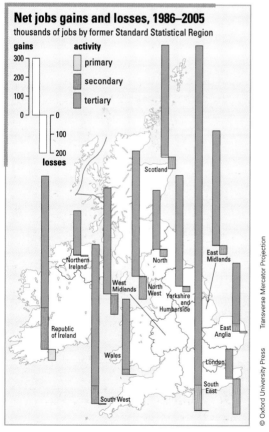

Scotland
Northern Ireland
West Midlands
North West
North
East Midlands
Yorkshire and Humberside
East Anglia
Republic of Ireland
Wales
London
South East
South West

Transverse Mercator Projection

© Oxford University Press

## UK workforce structure, 2005

Total workforce 28 117 200

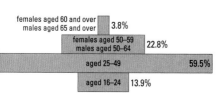

females aged 60 and over males aged 65 and over   3.8%
females aged 50–59 males aged 50–64   22.8%
aged 25–49   59.5%
aged 16–24   13.9%

## UK employment rates, 1964–2004

percentage of people of working age

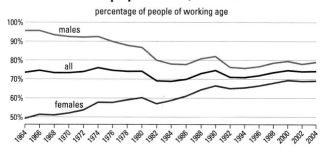

males
all
females

100%
90%
80%
70%
60%
50%

1964 1966 1968 1970 1972 1974 1976 1978 1980 1982 1984 1986 1988 1990 1992 1994 1996 1998 2000 2002 2004

## UK unemployment structure, 2005

percentage of all economically active people

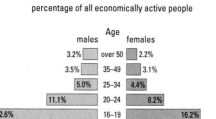

| males | Age | females |
|---|---|---|
| 3.2% | over 50 | 2.2% |
| 3.5% | 35–49 | 3.1% |
| 5.0% | 25–34 | 4.4% |
| 11.1% | 20–24 | 8.2% |
| 22.6% | 16–19 | 16.2% |

## Population density, 2004

people per square kilometre

- over 1000
- 500–1000
- 250–500
- 100–250
- 50–100
- 10–50
- under 10

## Major cities and towns

number of people

- □ over 1 000 000
- ○ 400 000–1 000 000
- ◉ 100 000–400 000
- • 25 000–100 000

Scale 1: 6 000 000

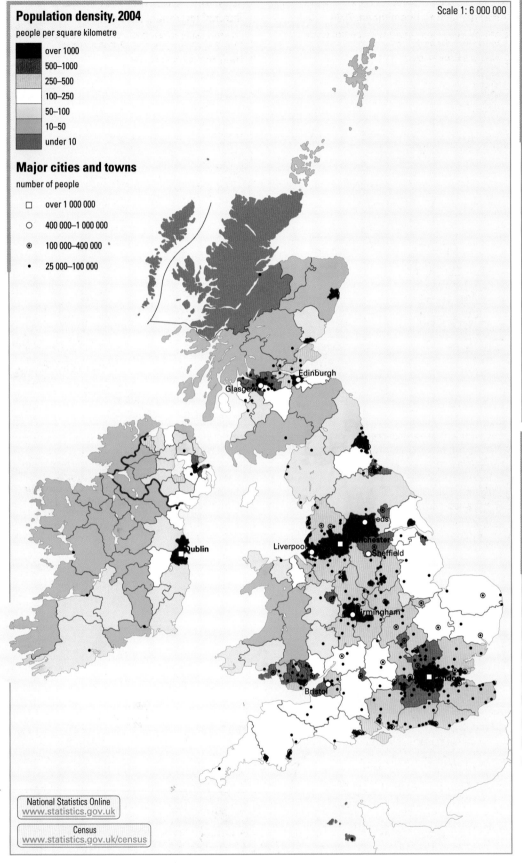

National Statistics Online
www.statistics.gov.uk

Census
www.statistics.gov.uk/census

## Young people, 2004

percentage of the population under 16 years old, by administrative area

- over 24%
- 22–24%
- 21–22%
- 20–21%
- 19–20%
- under 19%

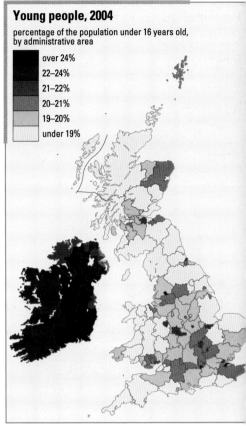

## Retired people, 2004

percentage of the population over retirement age*, by administrative area

- over 22%
- 20–22%
- 18–20%
- 16–18%
- 14–16%
- under 14%

*65 for men
60 for women

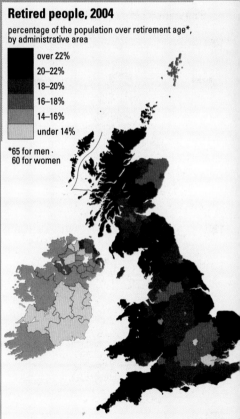

| UK population trends | 1901 | 1911 | 1921 | 1931 | 1941 | 1951 | 1961 | 1971 | 1981 | 1991 | 2001 | 2011 | 2021 |
|---|---|---|---|---|---|---|---|---|---|---|---|---|---|
| Total population (millions) | 38.24 | 42.08 | 44.03 | 46.04 | 48.22 | 50.23 | 52.81 | 55.93 | 56.35 | 57.65 | 59.62 | 60.93 | 63.64 |
| Infant mortality (deaths per 1000 live births) | 138.0 | 110.0 | 76.0 | 62.0 | 50.0 | 27.0 | 21.0 | 17.9 | 11.0 | 7.4 | 5.6 | 5.5 | 5.5 |
| Birth rate (births per 1000 people) | 28.6 | 24.5 | 22.8 | 16.3 | 14.4 | 15.9 | 17.9 | 16.1 | 13.0 | 13.8 | 12.0 | 11.5 | 11.5 |
| Death rate (deaths per 1000 people) | 16.5 | 14.3 | 11.9 | 12.5 | 13.0 | 12.6 | 12.0 | 11.5 | 11.6 | 11.3 | 10.5 | 10.0 | 10.3 |
| Life expectancy (years) | 47.0 | 52.2 | 57.3 | 60.0 | 61.0 | 68.5 | 70.9 | 71.9 | 73.8 | 76.0 | 77.5 | 79.5 | 80.5 |

*projected*

## Population change, 1981–2004

percentage change in the number of people, by administrative area

**increase**
- over 20%
- 15–20%
- 10–15%
- 5–10%
- 0–5%

**decrease**
- 0–10%
- 10–20%

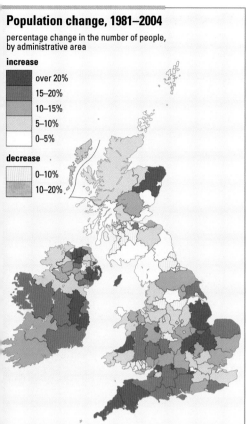

## Natural population change, 2004

difference between births and deaths per 1000 people, by administrative area

**more births than deaths**
- more than 6
- 4–6
- 2–4
- 0–2

**more deaths than births**
- 0–2
- 2–4
- 4–6
- more than 6

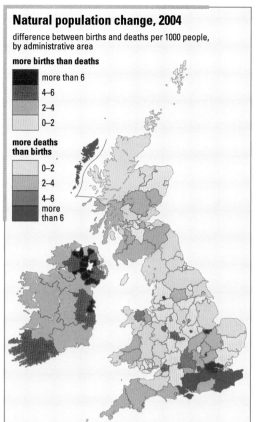

## Internal migration, 2004–2005

difference between the number moving in and the number moving out per 1000 people, by administrative area

**more people moved in than out**
- more than 6
- 3–6
- 0–3

**more people moved out than in**
- 0–3
- 3–6
- more than 6

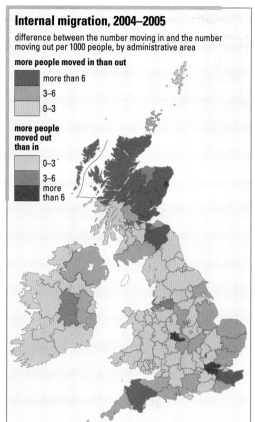

## Population structure of the UK

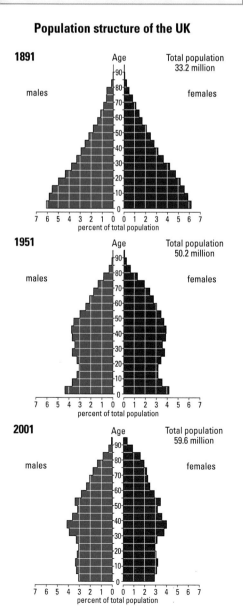

**1891**
Age
Total population 33.2 million
males   females
percent of total population

**1951**
Age
Total population 50.2 million
males   females
percent of total population

**2001**
Age
Total population 59.6 million
males   females
percent of total population

## Ethnic minority groups, 2001

members of all ethnic minority groups as a percentage of population, by administrative area

- over 16%
- 8–16%
- 4–8%
- 2–4%
- 0–2%

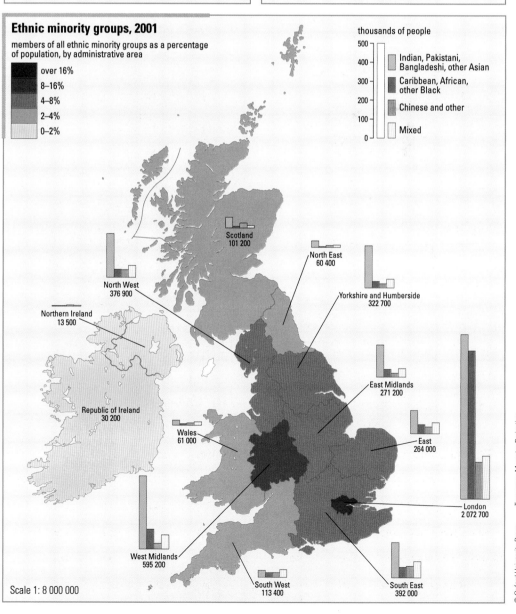

thousands of people

500
400
300
200
100
0

- Indian, Pakistani, Bangladeshi, other Asian
- Caribbean, African, other Black
- Chinese and other
- Mixed

Scotland 101 200
North East 60 400
North West 376 900
Yorkshire and Humberside 322 700
Northern Ireland 13 500
East Midlands 271 200
Republic of Ireland 30 200
East 264 000
Wales 61 000
London 2 072 700
West Midlands 595 200
South West 113 400
South East 392 000

Scale 1: 8 000 000

Transverse Mercator Projection

© Oxford University Press

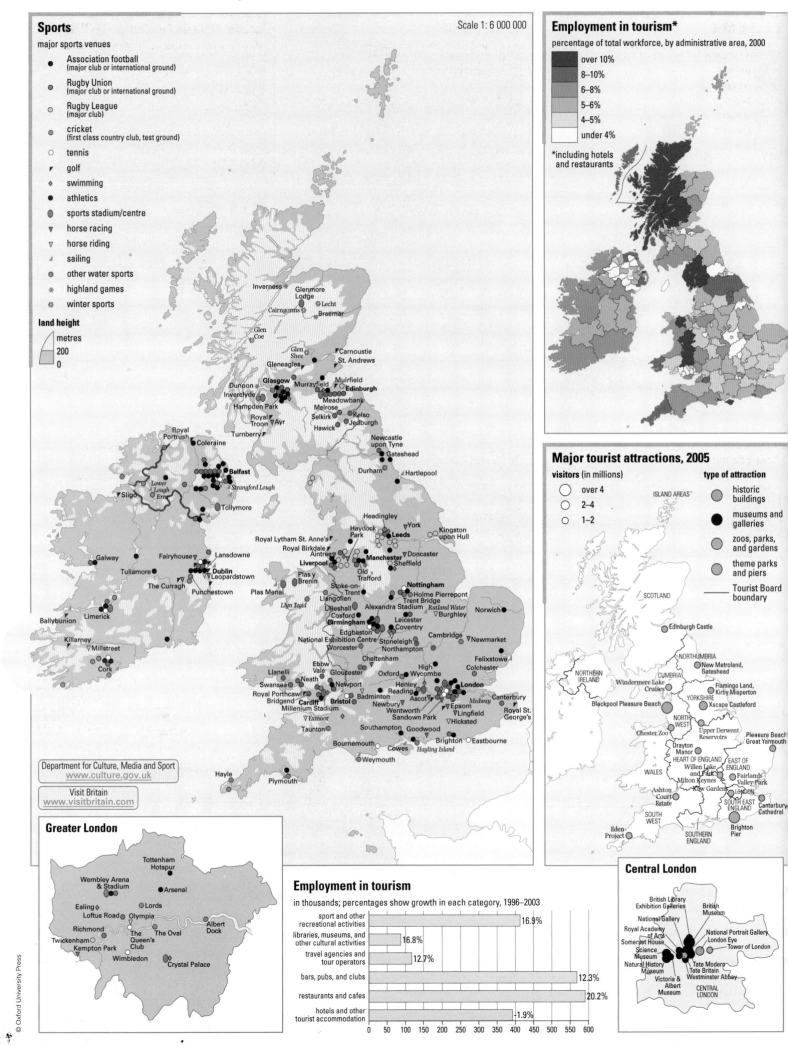

## Sports

**major sports venues**

- ● Association football (major club or international ground)
- ● Rugby Union (major club or international ground)
- ○ Rugby League (major club)
- ● cricket (first class country club, test ground)
- ○ tennis
- ⌐ golf
- ◇ swimming
- ● athletics
- ● sports stadium/centre
- ▽ horse racing
- ▽ horse riding
- ◣ sailing
- ● other water sports
- ✳ highland games
- ❀ winter sports

**land height**

metres
200
0

Scale 1: 6 000 000

Department for Culture, Media and Sport
www.culture.gov.uk

Visit Britain
www.visitbritain.com

Inverness
Glenmore Lodge
Cairngorms
Lecht
Braemar
Glen Coe
Glen Shee
Carnoustie
St. Andrews
Gleneagles
Glasgow
Murrayfield
Muirfield
Edinburgh
Dunoon
Inverclyde
Meadowbank
Hampden Park
Melrose
Royal Troon
Ayr
Selkirk
Kelso
Jedburgh
Turnberry
Hawick
Newcastle upon Tyne
Gateshead
Durham
Hartlepool
Royal Portrush
Coleraine
Belfast
Strangford Lough
Lower Lough Erne
Sligo
Tollymore
Headingley
Haydock Park
York
Kingston upon Hull
Royal Lytham St. Anne's
Leeds
Royal Birkdale
Doncaster
Galway
Fairyhouse
Lansdowne
Aintree
Manchester
Sheffield
Tullamore
Liverpool
Old Trafford
Dublin
Leopardstown
Plas y Brenin
Stoke-on-Trent
Nottingham
The Curragh
Punchestown
Plas Menai
Llangollen
Holme Pierrepont
Trent Bridge
Ballybunion
Limerick
Lilleshall
Cosford
Alexandra Stadium
Rutland Water
Burghley
Norwich
Killarney
Millstreet
Birmingham
Leicester
Coventry
Cambridge
Newmarket
Cork
Edgbaston
National Exhibition Centre
Stoneleigh
Northampton
Worcester
Cheltenham
Felixstowe
Colchester
Llanelli
Ebbw Vale
Gloucester
Oxford
High Wycombe
Swansea
Neath
Newport
Henley
Reading
London
Canterbury
Royal Porthcawl
Badminton
Ascot
Medway
Bridgend
Bristol
Newbury
Epsom
Royal St. George's
Millenium Stadium
Cardiff
Wentworth
Lingfield
Exmoor
Sandown Park
Hicksted
Taunton
Goodwood
Llyn Tegid
Southampton
Hayle
Plymouth
Bournemouth
Cowes
Hayling Island
Brighton
Eastbourne
Weymouth

## Employment in tourism*

percentage of total workforce, by administrative area, 2000

- over 10%
- 8–10%
- 6–8%
- 5–6%
- 4–5%
- under 4%

*including hotels and restaurants

## Major tourist attractions, 2005

**visitors** (in millions)
- ○ over 4
- ○ 2–4
- ○ 1–2

**type of attraction**
- ● historic buildings
- ● museums and galleries
- ● zoos, parks, and gardens
- ● theme parks and piers
- — Tourist Board boundary

ISLAND AREAS
SCOTLAND
Edinburgh Castle
NORTHUMBRIA
New Metroland, Gateshead
CUMBRIA
Windermere Lake Cruises
Flamingo Land, Kirby Misperton
YORKSHIRE
Blackpool Pleasure Beach
Xscape Castleford
NORTH WEST
Chester Zoo
Upper Derwent Reservoirs
Pleasure Beach Great Yarmouth
Drayton Manor
HEART OF ENGLAND
Willen Lake and Park
EAST OF ENGLAND
Fairlands Valley Park
WALES
Milton Keynes
Kew Gardens
LONDON
Ashton Court Estate
SOUTH EAST ENGLAND
Canterbury Cathedral
SOUTH WEST
Brighton Pier
Eden Project
SOUTHERN ENGLAND

## Greater London

Tottenham Hotspur
Wembley Arena & Stadium
Arsenal
Ealing
Lords
Loftus Road
Olympia
Richmond
The Queen's Club
Albert Dock
Twickenham
The Oval
Kempton Park
Wimbledon
Crystal Palace

## Employment in tourism

in thousands; percentages show growth in each category, 1996–2003

- sport and other recreational activities — 16.9%
- libraries, museums, and other cultural activities — 16.8%
- travel agencies and tour operators — 12.7%
- bars, pubs, and clubs — 12.3%
- restaurants and cafes — 20.2%
- hotels and other tourist accommodation — -1.9%

0  50  100  150  200  250  300  350  400  450  500  550  600

## Central London

British Library Exhibition Galleries
British Museum
National Gallery
Royal Academy of Arts
National Portrait Gallery
Somerset House
London Eye
Science Museum
Tower of London
Natural History Museum
Tate Modern
Tate Britain
Victoria & Albert Museum
Westminster Abbey
CENTRAL LONDON

## Income, 2006

average gross weekly earnings of workers in full-time employment, by administrative area

- over £475
- £425–£475
- £400–£425
- £375–£400
- £350–£375
- under £350

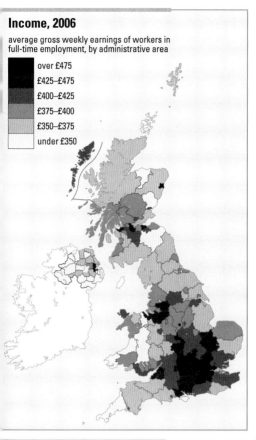

## Education, 2002

percentage of 16 year olds entering further or higher education, by administrative area

- over 90%
- 85–90%
- 80–85%
- 75–80%
- 70–75%
- under 70%

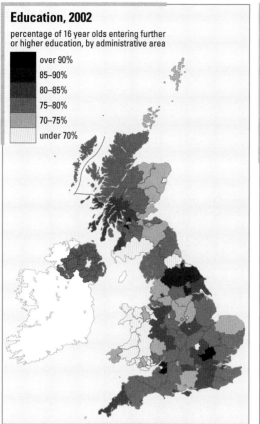

## Index of Multiple Deprivation (IMD), 2000

IMD is calculated from a number of indicators including low income, unemployment, poor health, disability, lack of education, unsatisfactory housing, and poor access to services. The map shows the 10% most deprived areas within each part of the UK.

- England
- Wales
- Scotland
- Northern Ireland

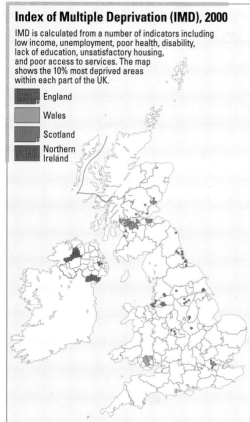

## Domestic burglaries, 2005

per 1000 households, by administrative area

- over 20
- 15–20
- 10–15
- 5–10
- under 5

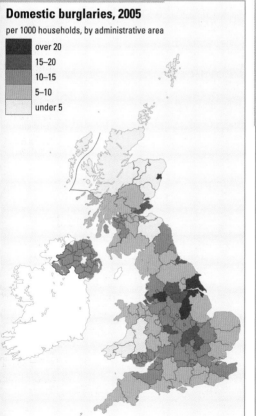

## Coronary heart disease, 2002–2004

age-standardised death rates per 100 000 people*, by administrative area

- over 50
- 40–50
- 30–40
- 20–30
- under 20

*under 65

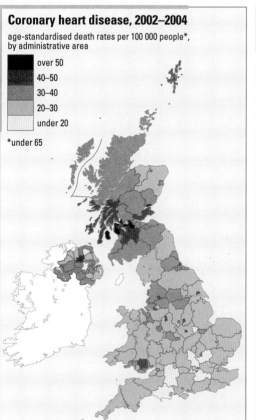

## House prices, 2006

comparative prices for similar size and style of house in similar neighbourhoods

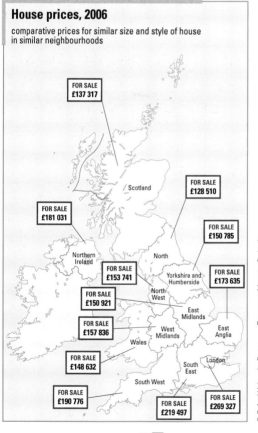

FOR SALE £137 317

FOR SALE £128 510

FOR SALE £181 031

FOR SALE £150 785

FOR SALE £153 741

FOR SALE £173 635

FOR SALE £150 921

FOR SALE £157 836

FOR SALE £148 632

FOR SALE £190 776

FOR SALE £219 497

FOR SALE £269 327

Scotland

Northern Ireland

North

Yorkshire and Humberside

North West

East Midlands

West Midlands

East Anglia

Wales

South East

London

South West

## Consumer goods, 1970–2005

percentage of UK households having use of each product

- car
- central heating
- washing machine
- dishwasher
- microwave oven
- video
- PC
- CD player
- ∞ no data

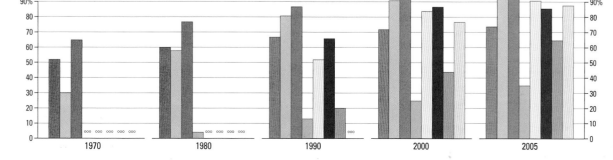

1970   1980   1990   2000   2005

Scale 1: 4 500 000

## Conservation

- National Parks*
- Areas of Outstanding Natural Beauty (England, Wales, and Northern Ireland) National Scenic Areas (Scotland)
- Heritage Coast (England and Wales) Coastal Conservation Zone (Scotland)
- internationally recognized sites (including Special Protection Areas, 'Ramsar' Sites, and Biosphere Reserves)
- Natural Heritage Sites
- Cultural Heritage Sites
- built-up area

*National parks are designated to conserve the natural beauty and cultural heritage of areas of outstanding landscape value. There are 10 national parks in England and Wales, which were designated in the 1950's following the National Parks and Access to the Countryside Act, 1949. The Broads is not officially a national park but is considered as such by the government and has had its own authority since 1989. The New Forest National Park was created in 2005. Proposals to establish the South Downs as a national park are still taking place. The National Parks (Scotland) Act was passed in July 2000, and the Cairngorms, and Loch Lomond and The Trossachs became Scotland's first national parks in 2002/3.

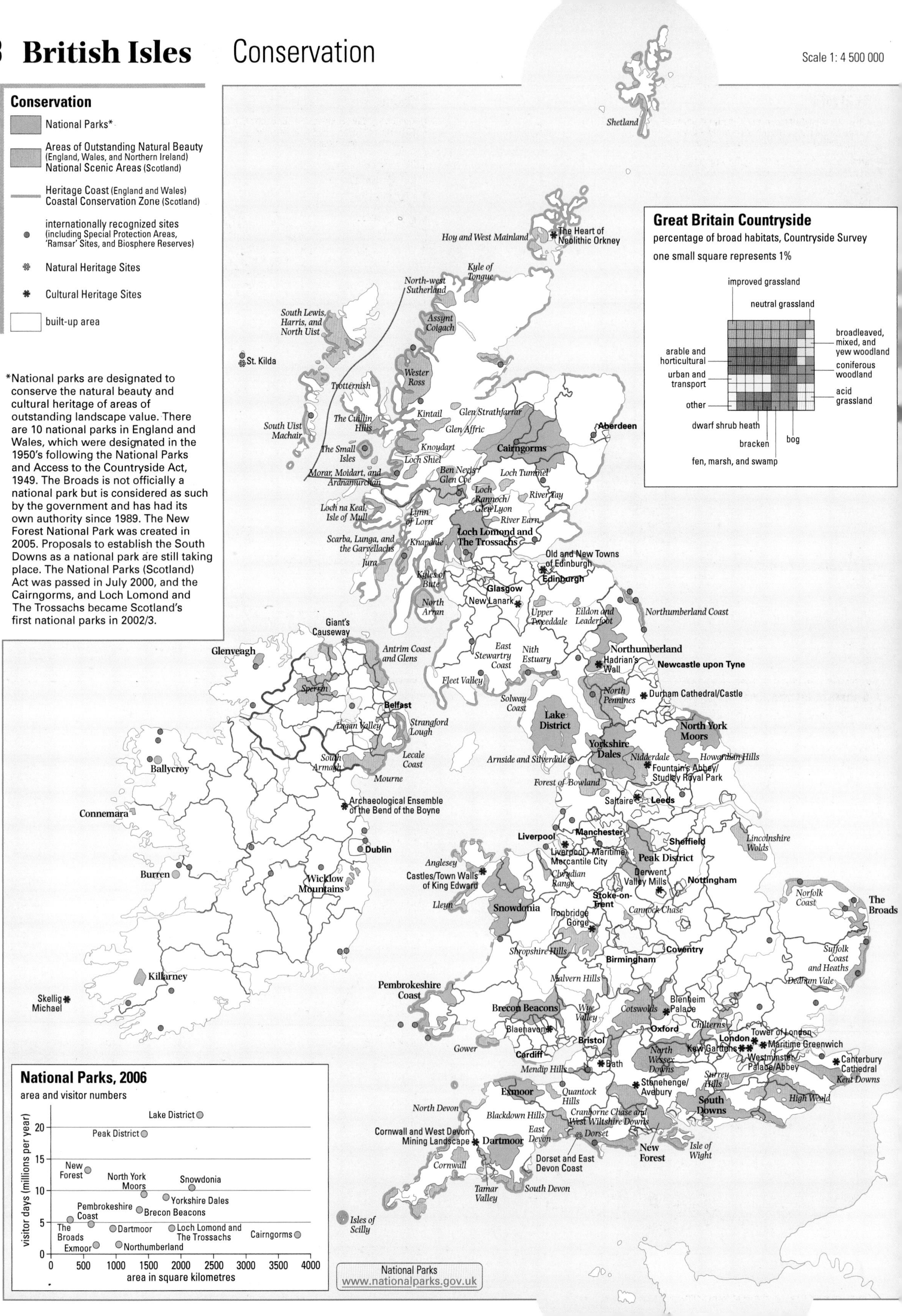
Shetland
Hoy and West Mainland
The Heart of Neolithic Orkney
Kyle of Tongue
North-west Sutherland
South Lewis, Harris, and North Uist
Assynt Coigach
St. Kilda
Wester Ross
Trotternish
South Uist Machair
The Cuillin Hills
Kintail
Glen Strathfarrar
Glen Affric
Aberdeen
The Small Isles
Knoydart
Cairngorms
Loch Shiel
Morar, Moidart, and Ardnamurchan
Ben Nevis/ Glen Coe
Loch Tummel
Loch Rannoch/ Glen Lyon
River Tay
Loch na Keal, Isle of Mull
Lynn of Lorn
River Earn
Loch Lomond and The Trossachs
Scarba, Lunga, and the Garvellachs
Knapdale
Jura
Old and New Towns of Edinburgh
Edinburgh
Kyles of Bute
Glasgow
New Lanark
North Arran
Upper Tweeddale
Eildon and Leaderfoot
Northumberland Coast
Giant's Causeway
Glenveagh
Antrim Coast and Glens
East Stewartry Coast
Nith Estuary
Northumberland
Hadrian's Wall
Newcastle upon Tyne
Fleet Valley
Sperrin
Solway Coast
North Pennines
Durham Cathedral/Castle
Belfast
Strangford Lough
Lagan Valley
Lake District
North York Moors
Yorkshire Dales
Ballycroy
South Armagh
Lecale Coast
Arnside and Silverdale
Nidderdale
Howardian Hills
Fountain's Abbey/ Studley Royal Park
Mourne
Forest of Bowland
Saltaire
Leeds
Connemara
Archaeological Ensemble of the Bend of the Boyne
Liverpool
Manchester
Sheffield
Lincolnshire Wolds
Dublin
Liverpool – Maritime Mercantile City
Peak District
Anglesey
Burren
Castles/Town Walls of King Edward
Clwydian Range
Derwent Valley Mills
Nottingham
Wicklow Mountains
Norfolk Coast
The Broads
Lleyn
Snowdonia
Stoke-on-Trent
Cannock Chase
Ironbridge Gorge
Shropshire Hills
Coventry
Birmingham
Suffolk Coast and Heaths
Killarney
Malvern Hills
Dedham Vale
Pembrokeshire Coast
Skellig Michael
Brecon Beacons
Wye Valley
Cotswolds
Blenheim Palace
Chilterns
Blaenavon
Oxford
London
Tower of London
Bristol
Maritime Greenwich
Gower
Cardiff
North Wessex Downs
Kew Gardens
Westminster Palace/Abbey
Canterbury Cathedral
Mendip Hills
Bath
Kent Downs
Surrey Hills
Stonehenge/ Avebury
Exmoor
Quantock Hills
High Weald
North Devon
South Downs
Blackdown Hills
Cranborne Chase and West Wiltshire Downs
Cornwall and West Devon Mining Landscape
Dartmoor
East Devon
Dorset
New Forest
Isle of Wight
Dorset and East Devon Coast
Cornwall
Tamar Valley
South Devon
Isles of Scilly
Great Britain Countryside
percentage of broad habitats, Countryside Survey
one small square represents 1%
improved grassland
neutral grassland
broadleaved, mixed, and yew woodland
arable and horticultural
coniferous woodland
urban and transport
acid grassland
other
dwarf shrub heath
bog
bracken
fen, marsh, and swamp
National Parks, 2006
area and visitor numbers
visitor days (millions per year)
area in square kilometres
0
5
10
15
20
500
1000
1500
2000
2500
3000
3500
4000
Lake District
Peak District
New Forest
North York Moors
Snowdonia
Yorkshire Dales
Pembrokeshire Coast
Brecon Beacons
The Broads
Dartmoor
Loch Lomond and The Trossachs
Cairngorms
Exmoor
Northumberland
National Parks
www.nationalparks.gov.uk

Transverse Mercator Projection

© Oxford University Press

## Acid rain

Environmental damage is more likely where acid deposition is high and soils (particularly those that are already acid) are more sensitive.

areas where potential damage to vegetation from nitrogen in acid rain is

- very high
- high
- moderate
- low

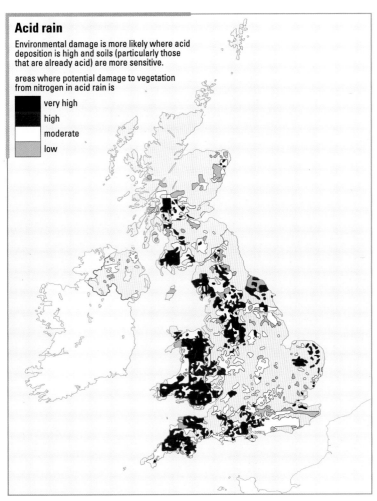

## Ozone

Number of days when ozone concentration exceeded 50 parts per billion, used to assess the potential for effects on human health.

days per year

- over 45
- 35–45
- 30–35
- 25–30
- under 25

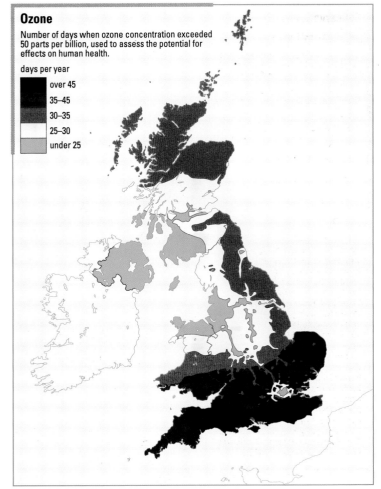

## Coastal and offshore pollution

bathing beaches heavily polluted by sewage

oil spills within UK waters
tonnes

- over 5000
- 50–5000
- 0–50

**Braer 86 248 tonnes**
5 January 1993

**Sea Empress 72 000 tonnes**
15 February 1996

*ATLANTIC OCEAN*

*NORTH SEA*

*English Channel*

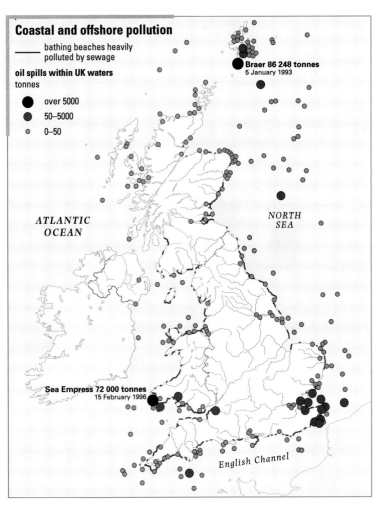

## Light pollution

Artificial light, measured by satellite. 0 means the satellite can detect no artificial light. 255 means that the detector is saturated with artificial light.

- 240–255
- 150–240
- 50–150
- 1.7–50
- 0–1.7
- no data

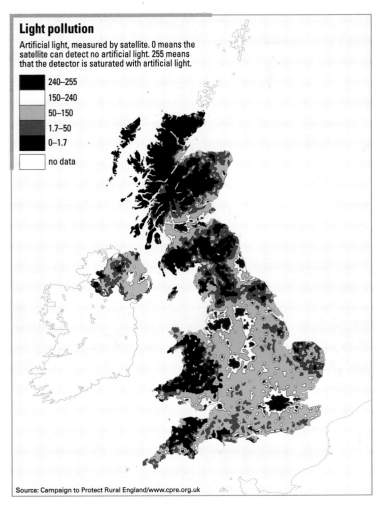

Source: Campaign to Protect Rural England/www.cpre.org.uk

Scale 1 : 7 500 000

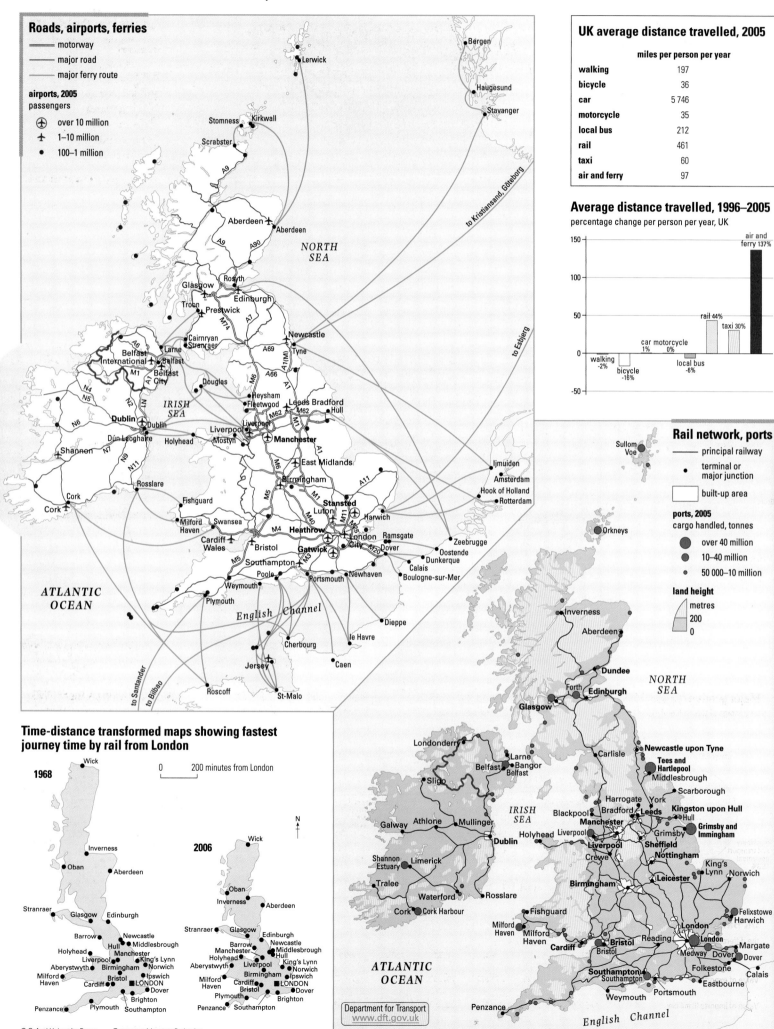

## Roads, airports, ferries

— motorway
— major road
— major ferry route

**airports, 2005**
passengers
⊕ over 10 million
✈ 1–10 million
• 100–1 million

### UK average distance travelled, 2005

| | miles per person per year |
|---|---|
| walking | 197 |
| bicycle | 36 |
| car | 5 746 |
| motorcycle | 35 |
| local bus | 212 |
| rail | 461 |
| taxi | 60 |
| air and ferry | 97 |

### Average distance travelled, 1996–2005

percentage change per person per year, UK

air and ferry 137%
rail 44%
taxi 30%
car 1%
motorcycle 0%
walking -2%
bicycle -16%
local bus -6%

### Rail network, ports

— principal railway
• terminal or major junction
☐ built-up area

**ports, 2005**
cargo handled, tonnes
● over 40 million
● 10–40 million
• 50 000–10 million

**land height**
metres
200
0

## Time-distance transformed maps showing fastest journey time by rail from London

0 — 200 minutes from London

1968

2006

Department for Transport
www.dft.gov.uk

© Oxford University Press   Transverse Mercator Projection

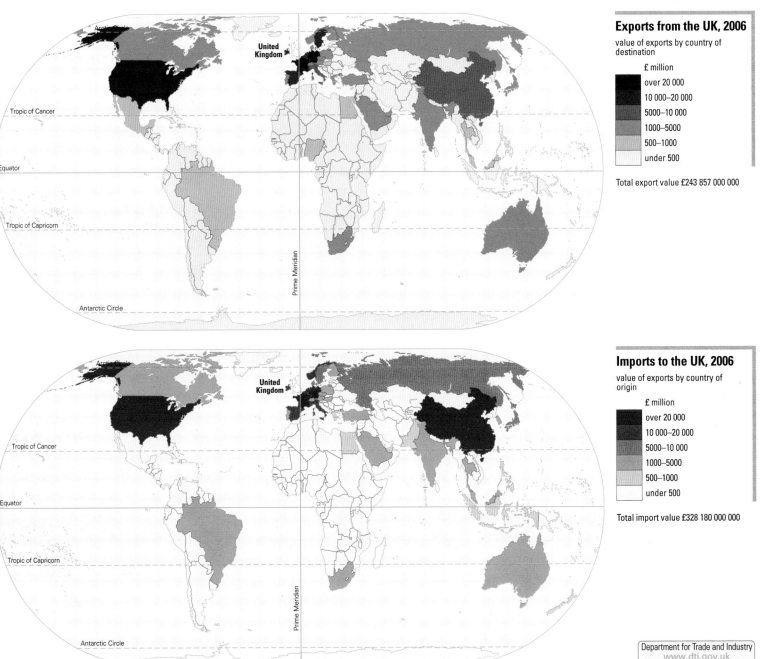

**Exports from the UK, 2006**

value of exports by country of destination

£ million

- over 20 000
- 10 000–20 000
- 5000–10 000
- 1000–5000
- 500–1000
- under 500

Total export value £243 857 000 000

**Imports to the UK, 2006**

value of exports by country of origin

£ million

- over 20 000
- 10 000–20 000
- 5000–10 000
- 1000–5000
- 500–1000
- under 500

Total import value £328 180 000 000

Department for Trade and Industry
www.dti.gov.uk

## Major goods exported, 2006

percentage of total value of exports

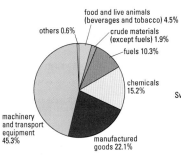

- others 0.6%
- food and live animals (beverages and tobacco) 4.5%
- crude materials (except fuels) 1.9%
- fuels 10.3%
- chemicals 15.2%
- manufactured goods 22.1%
- machinery and transport equipment 45.3%

## Major trading partners, 2006

percentage of total value of exports

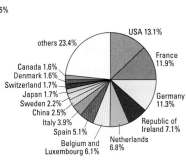

- USA 13.1%
- France 11.9%
- Germany 11.3%
- Republic of Ireland 7.1%
- Netherlands 6.8%
- Belgium and Luxembourg 6.1%
- Spain 5.1%
- Italy 3.9%
- China 2.5%
- Sweden 2.2%
- Japan 1.7%
- Switzerland 1.7%
- Denmark 1.6%
- Canada 1.6%
- others 23.4%

## Major goods imported, 2006

percentage of total value of imports

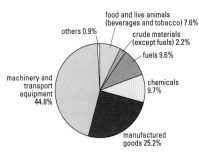

- others 0.9%
- food and live animals (beverages and tobacco) 7.6%
- crude materials (except fuels) 2.2%
- fuels 9.6%
- chemicals 9.7%
- manufactured goods 25.2%
- machinery and transport equipment 44.8%

## Major trading partners, 2006

percentage of total value of imports

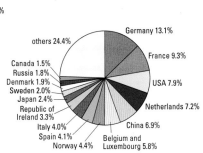

- Germany 13.1%
- France 9.3%
- USA 7.9%
- Netherlands 7.2%
- China 6.9%
- Belgium and Luxembourg 5.8%
- Norway 4.4%
- Spain 4.1%
- Italy 4.0%
- Republic of Ireland 3.3%
- Japan 2.4%
- Sweden 2.0%
- Denmark 1.9%
- Russia 1.8%
- Canada 1.5%
- others 24.4%

## UK Balance of Trade, 1994–2006

the difference in value between exports and imports

| | 1994 | 1995 | 1996 | 1997 | 1998 | 1999 | 2000 | 2001 | 2002 | 2003 | 2004 | 2005 | 2006 |
|---|---|---|---|---|---|---|---|---|---|---|---|---|---|
| Value of exports (£ million) | 135 260 | 153 577 | 167 196 | 171 923 | 164 056 | 166 198 | 188 085 | 190 055 | 186 517 | 187 846 | 190 877 | 211 616 | 243 857 |
| Value of imports (£ million) | 146 351 | 165 600 | 180 918 | 184 265 | 185 869 | 193 722 | 218 108 | 230 703 | 233 192 | 235 136 | 251 770 | 280 399 | 328 180 |

URAL MOUNTAINS
Pechora
Ural
Caspian Sea
Volga
Oka
Severnaya (N.) Dvina
Kola Peninsula
WHITE SEA
Lake Onega
Rybinsk Reservoir
Tsimlyansk Reservoir
Don
Donets
SEA OF AZOV
Crimea
BLACK SEA
Caucasus
5642 Mt. Elbrus
5123 Mt. Ararat
Lake Van
Tigris
Euphrates
Anatolian Plateau
Taurus Mountains
Kizil Irmak
Lake Tuz
Cyprus
Central Russian Uplands
Lake Ladoga
Lake Peipus
Dnepr
Bug
Bosporus
SEA OF MARMARA
Dardanelles
2917 Mt. Olympus
AEGEAN SEA
Rhodes
Crete
Cyclades
Peloponnese
Pindhos Mountains
Corfu
IONIAN SEA
5121
Inarijärvi
Kemi
Lappland
Torne
Muonio
Gulf of Finland
Saimaa
Salpausselkä
Daugava
Pripet Marshes
Pripet
Dniester
CARPATHIANS
2548
Balkan Mts.
Rodopi Planina
Danube
Tisza
Neman
Gulf of Riga
Vistula
North European Plain
Oder
Hungarian Basin
Tatry Mts.
Drava
Dinaric Alps
Sava
ADRIATIC SEA
Gulf of Taranto
APPENNINI
Vesuvius
Mt. Etna 3323
Sicily
Malta
C. Bon
G. of Gabes
MEDITERRANEAN SEA
Lofoten Islands
Indals
Dal
Klar
Lake Vänern
Lake Vättern
Öland
Lake Mälaren
Godland
Bornholm
Skane
1603
Bohemian Massif
Danube
Schwäbische Alb
Bodensee
Tauern
1277
LIGURIAN SEA
Corsica
Sardinia
Balearic Islands
Menorca
Mallorca
Ibiza
MEDITERRANEAN
TYRRHENIAN SEA
Scandinavia
Skellefte
Jostedalsbreen
Vesterålen
Hardangervidda
Skagerrak
Kattegat
Sjælland
Fyn
Weser
Elbe
Harz Mts.
Rhine
Erzgebirge
Jura
Bohemian Massif
ALPS
4807 Mt. Blanc
L. Geneva
Alpes Maritimes
Dordogne
Massif Central
GREENLAND SEA
Jan Mayen
Norwegian Basin
-3970
Prime Meridian
NORTH SEA
Frisian Islands
IJsselmeer
Waal
Meuse
Marne
Seine
Paris Basin
Loire
Rhône
Saône
Vosges
Rhine
-36
Arctic Circle
Vatnajökull
1491 Hekla
Iceland
Faroe Islands
Shetland Islands
Orkney Islands
C. Wrath
Grampians
1344 Ben Nevis
Outer Hebrides
Malin Head
Southern Uplands
British Isles
Pennines
Great Britain
Cambrian Mts.
The Wash
Thames
Str. of Dover
English Channel
Channel Islands
Brittany Pen.
Cotentin
ATLANTIC OCEAN
Rockall Bank
Ireland
Central Plain
Shannon
St. George's Channel
Scilly Is.
Bay of Biscay
C. Finisterre
Cantabrian Mts.
Central Cordilleras
Duero
Tagus
Guadiana
Sierra Morena
Guadalquivir
Betican Cordilleras
La Mancha
Ebro
Pyrénées
3404
Gulf of Lions
Garonne
West European Basin
C. de São Vicente
Str. of Gibraltar
ATLAS MOUNTAINS
Grand Erg Occidental

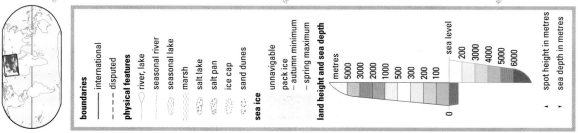

**boundaries**
— international
--- disputed
**physical features**
~~~ river, lake
seasonal river
seasonal lake
marsh
salt lake
salt pan
ice cap
sand dunes
**sea ice**
unnavigable
pack ice
— autumn minimum
— spring maximum

**land height and sea depth**

| metres | | sea level | metres |
|---|---|---|---|
| 5000 | | 200 | |
| 3000 | | 3000 | |
| 2000 | | 4000 | |
| 1000 | | 5000 | |
| 500 | | 6000 | |
| 300 | | | |
| 200 | | | |
| 100 | | | |
| 0 | | | |

• spot height in metres
▾ sea depth in metres

Scale 1: 22 000 000

0   220   440   660   880   1100 km

## July temperature

Norwegian Current

Arctic Circle

North Atlantic Drift

Westerlies

Prime Meridian

prevailing wind

cold sea current

warm sea current

-13
-18
-19
-18
-17
-20
-25
-24
-20
-15
-16
-25
25

**July temperature**

actual surface temperature

°Celsius
25
20
15
10
5

• climate station (average July temperature)

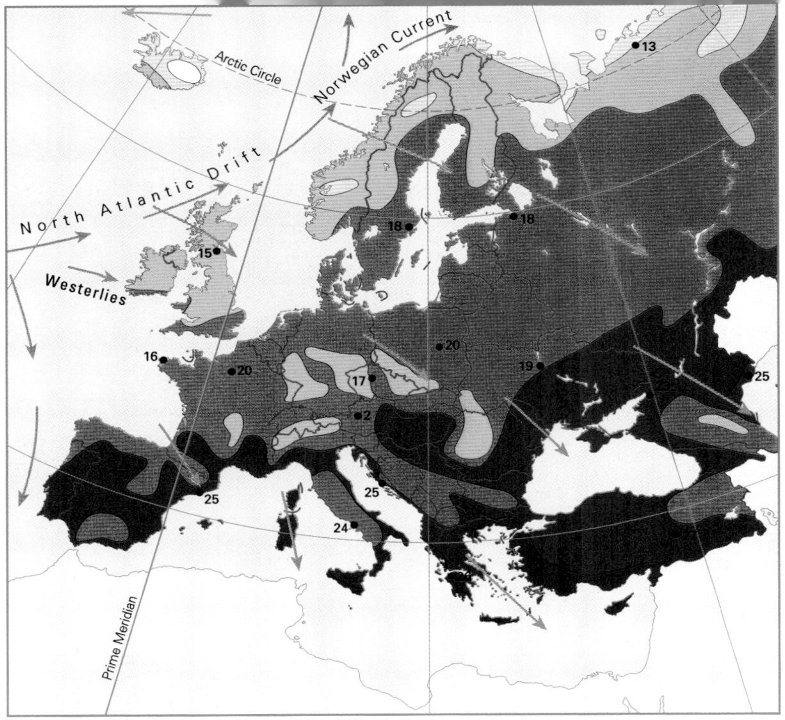

## Ecosystems

Ural Mountains

North European Plain

Scandinavia

Caucasus

ALPS

Hungarian Basin

Carpathians

ATLANTIC OCEAN

Iceland

Arctic Circle

Prime Meridian

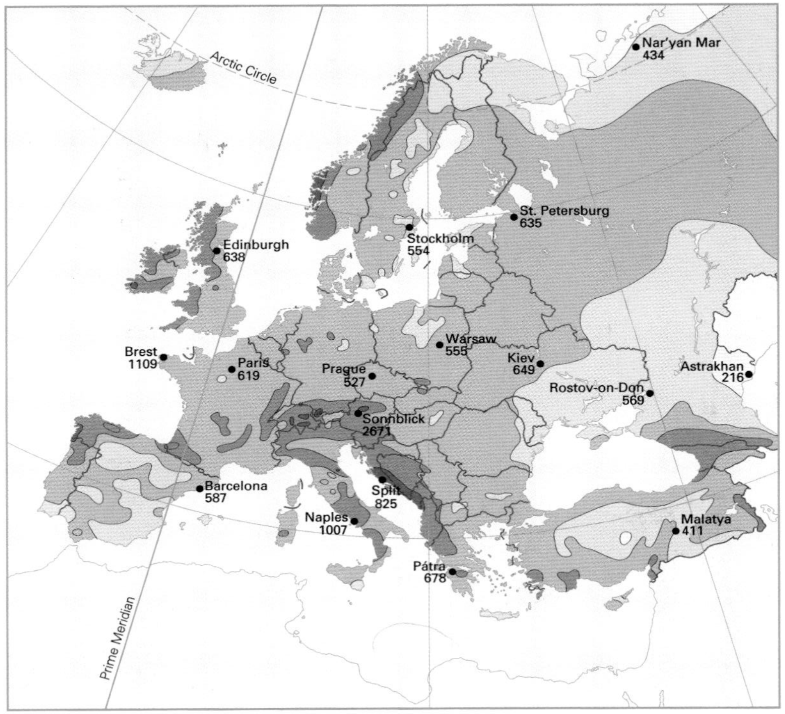

**Ecosystems**

coniferous forest
mixed forest
evergreens and shrubs
temperate grasslands
semi-desert
tundra
ice
mountains

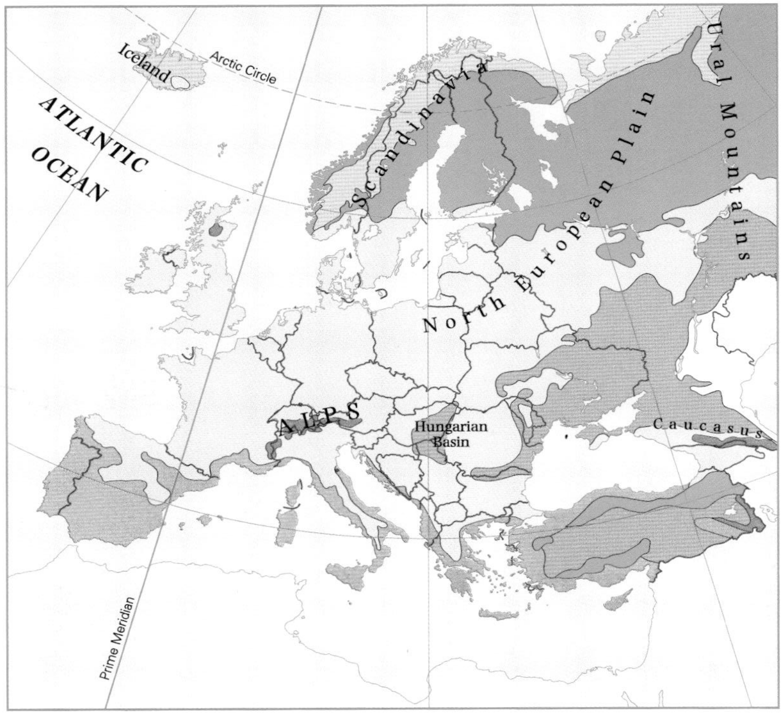

## January temperature

Norwegian Current

Arctic Circle

North Atlantic Drift

Westerlies

Prime Meridian

prevailing wind

cold sea current

warm sea current

-19
-6
-5
0
-6
-8
10
-3
-3
-2
-13
7
8
4
10
6

**January temperature**

actual surface temperature

°Celsius
10
5
0
-5
-10
-15
-20
-25

• climate station (average January temperature)

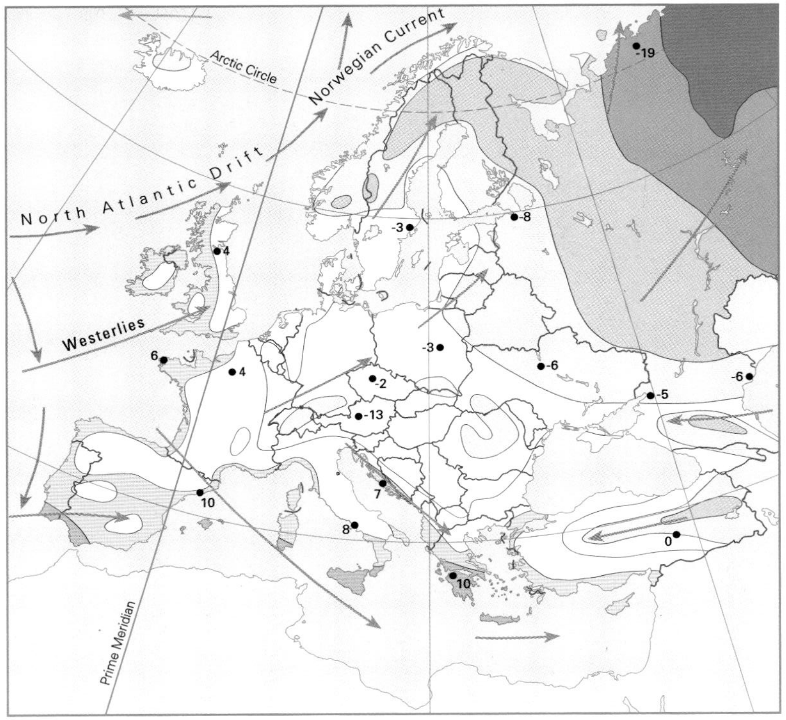

## Precipitation

Nar'yan Mar 434
Astrakhan 216
Malatya 411
St Petersburg 635
Rostov-on-Don 569
Kiev 649
Warsaw 555
Stockholm 554
Pátra 678
Sonnblick 2671
Split 825
Prague 527
Naples 1007
Edinburgh 638
Paris 619
Barcelona 587
Brest 1109

Arctic Circle

Prime Meridian

**Precipitation**

average annual precipitation

mm
2000
1000
500
250
0

• climate station (average annual precipitation)

Conical Orthomorphic Projection

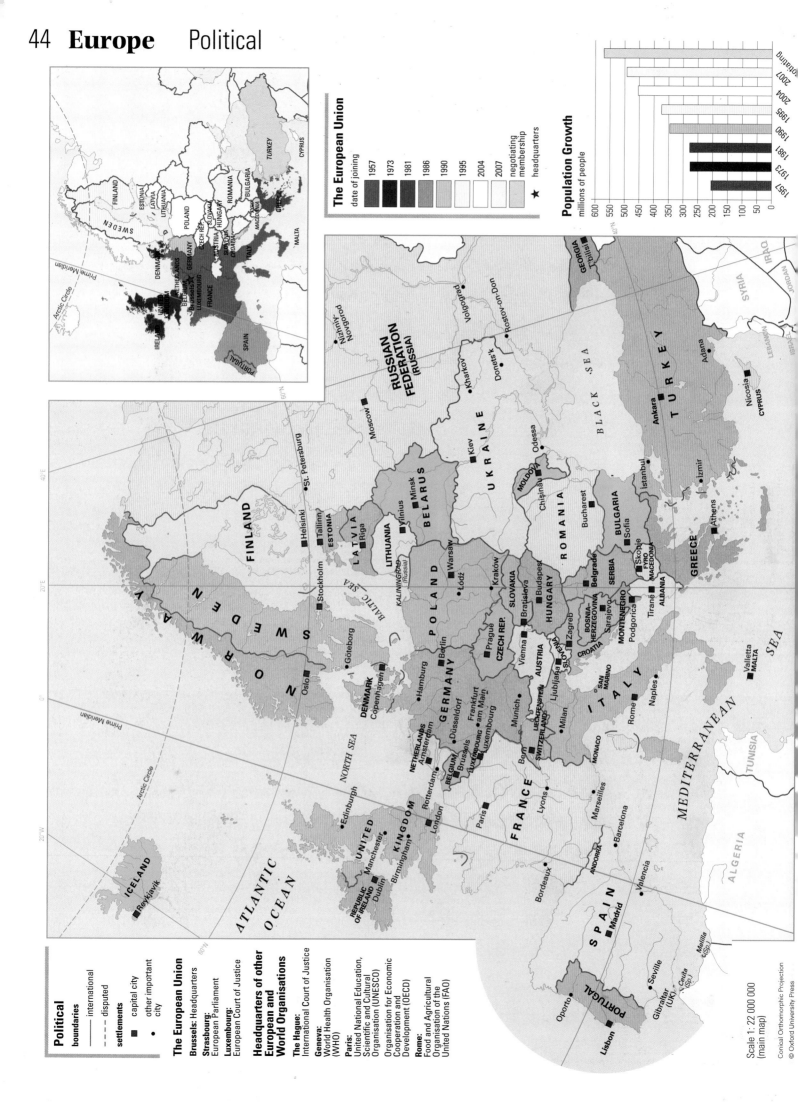

**Political**

**boundaries**
— international
--- disputed

**settlements**
■ capital city
• other important city

**The European Union**
Brussels: Headquarters
Strasbourg: European Parliament
Luxembourg: European Court of Justice

**Headquarters of other European and World Organisations**

The Hague:
International Court of Justice

Geneva:
World Health Organisation (WHO)

Paris:
United National Education, Scientific and Cultural Organisation (UNESCO)
Organisation for Economic Cooperation and Development (OECD)

Rome:
Food and Agricultural Organisation of the United Nations (FAO)

**The European Union**

date of joining
1957
1973
1981
1986
1990
1995
2004
2007
negotiating membership
★ headquarters

**Population Growth**
millions of people

1957
1973
1981
1990
1995
2004
2007

600 550 500 450 400 350 300 250 200 150 100 50 0

Scale 1: 22 000 000 (main map)

Conical Orthomorphic Projection
© Oxford University Press

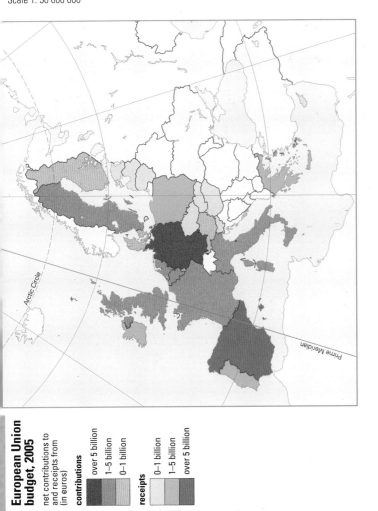

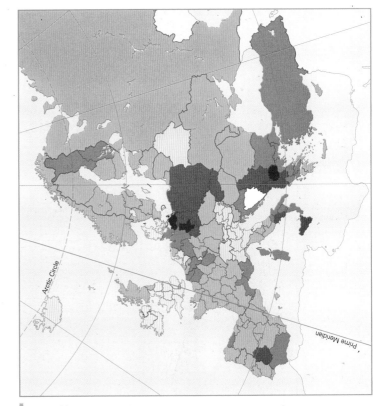

## European Union budget, 2005

net contributions to and receipts from (in euros)

**contributions**

- over 5 billion
- 1–5 billion
- 0–1 billion

**receipts**

- 0–1 billion
- 1–5 billion
- over 5 billion

## Unemployment, 2005

percentage of the work force out of work

- over 20%
- 15–20%
- 10–15%
- 5–10%
- under 5%
- no data

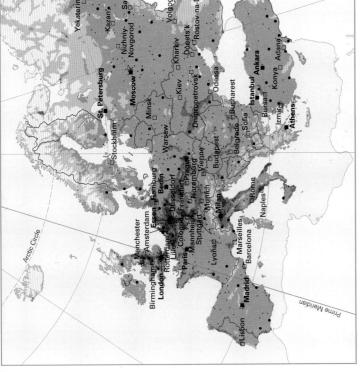

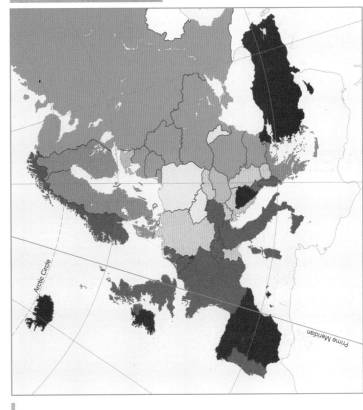

## Population density

people per square kilometre

- over 200
- 100–200
- 10–100
- 1–10
- under 1

## Major cities

population in millions

- ■ over 3
- □ 1–3
- ● 0.5–1
- • 0.1–0.5

## Population change, 2001–2006

percentage change in the number of people

**increase**

- over 4%
- 2–4%
- 1–2%
- 0–1%

**decrease**

- 0–1%
- 1–2%
- 2–4%
- over 4%

Conical Orthomorphic Projection

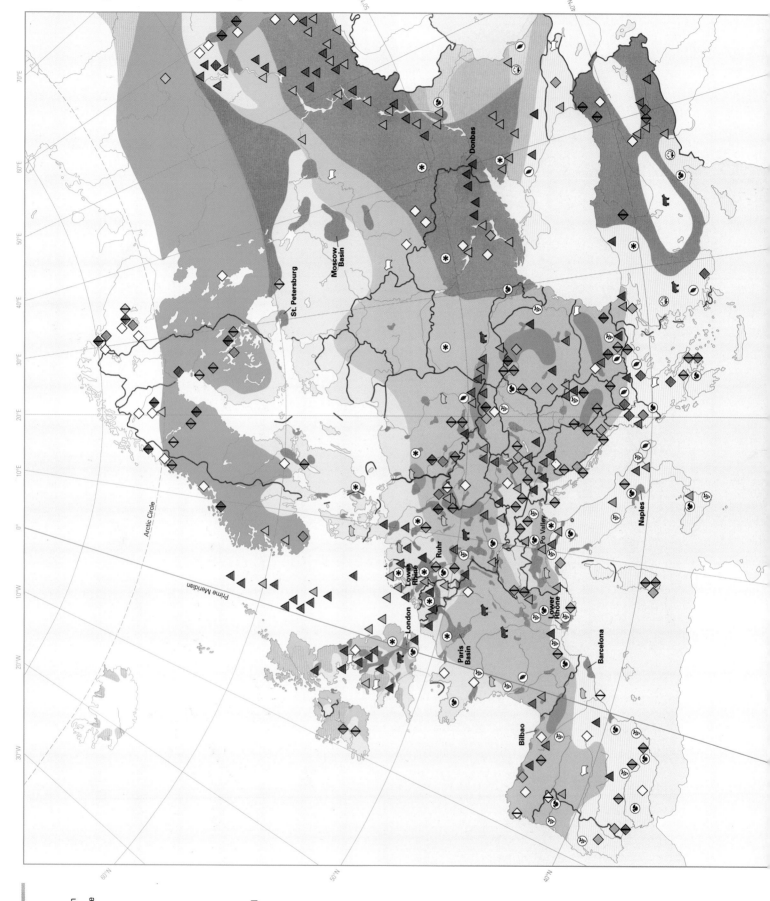

Scale 1: 22 000 000

**Land use**

- rough grazing
- shifting cultivation
- mixed subsistence
- grazing and stock rearing
- mixed farming
- grain farming
- Mediterranean farming
- dairy farming
- specialized horticulture
- forestry
- industrial areas
- unproductive land

**Livestock**
- sheep
- cattle
- pigs

**Crops**
- wine grapes
- tobacco
- fruit
- sugar
- cotton

**Minerals**
- iron ore
- manganese
- chromium
- nickel
- tin
- lead
- zinc
- copper
- bauxite

**Energy**
- coal
- oil
- gas
- hydro

Conical Orthomorphic Projection

Scale 1: 17 000 000

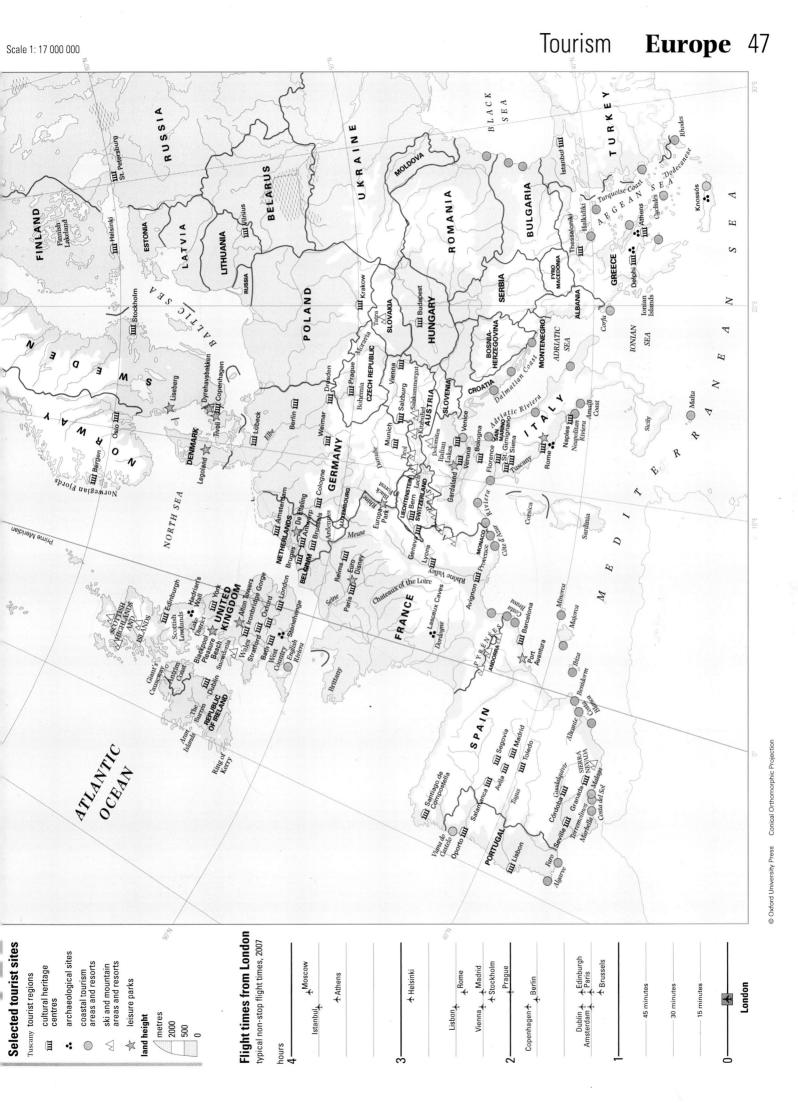

## Selected tourist sites

Tuscany tourist regions

🏛 cultural heritage centres

∴ archaeological sites

🔵 coastal tourism areas and resorts

△ ski and mountain areas and resorts

⭐ leisure parks

land height

metres
2000
500
0

**Flight times from London**

typical non-stop flight times, 2007

hours

4 — ✈ Moscow
  — ✈ Athens

  — Istanbul ✈

3 — ✈ Helsinki

  — ✈ Rome
  — ✈ Madrid
  — ✈ Stockholm
  — ✈ Prague

  — Lisbon ✈
  — Vienna ✈

2 — ✈ Berlin

  — Copenhagen ✈

  — Dublin ✈  ✈ Edinburgh
  — Amsterdam ✈  ✈ Paris
1 — ✈ Brussels

  — 45 minutes

  — 30 minutes

  — 15 minutes

0 — ✈ London

© Oxford University Press    Conical Orthomorphic Projection

NORTH SEA

Scale 1: 2 500 000

0   25   50   75   100   125 km

Conical Orthomorphic Projection
© Oxford University Press

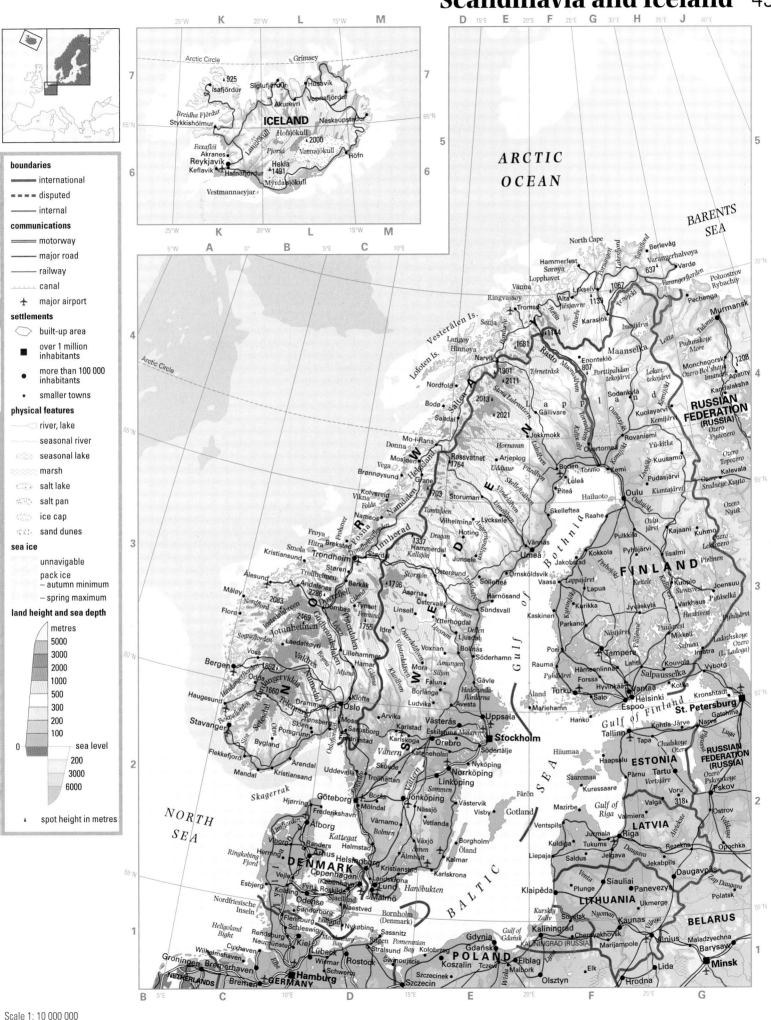

**boundaries**
─── international
---- disputed
─── internal

**communications**
═══ motorway
─── major road
─── railway
┼┼┼┼ canal
✈ major airport

**settlements**
⬡ built-up area
■ over 1 million inhabitants
● more than 100 000 inhabitants
• smaller towns

**physical features**
river, lake
seasonal river
seasonal lake
marsh
salt lake
salt pan
ice cap
sand dunes

**sea ice**
unnavigable
pack ice
– autumn minimum
– spring maximum

**land height and sea depth**
metres
5000
3000
2000
1000
500
300
200
100
0 sea level
200
3000
6000
▲ spot height in metres

Scale 1: 10 000 000

0   100   200   300   400   500 km

Conical Orthomorphic Projection
© Oxford University Press

### Iceland inset
Arctic Circle
Grímsey
925
Ísafjördur    Siglufjördur   Húsavík
             Akureyri        Vopnafjördur
Breidha Fjördur                Neskaupstadur
Stykkishólmur    **ICELAND**
Faxaflói         Hofsjökull
Akranes    Pjórsá  2000  Vatnajökull
Reykjavík   Hekla         Höfn
Keflavík  Hafnarfjördur  1491
         Mýrdalsjökull
Vestmannaeyjar
Langjökull

### Main map place names
ARCTIC OCEAN
BARENTS SEA
North Cape
Hammerfest  Berlevåg
Sørøya  Varangerhalvøya
Lakselv  637  Vardø
Vanna  Porsangen  Varangerfjorden  Poluostrov Rybachiy
Ringvassøy  Alta  Iešjavre  1139  Pechenga
Tromsø  Kautokeino  Karasjok  Murmansk
Senja  1114  Maanselka  Pudunskoye More  Monchegorsk  1208
Vesterålen Is.  Rasto  Enontekiö  807  Ozero Bol'shaya Imandra  Apatity
Langøy  1681  Torneträsk  Porttipahdan tekojärvi  Lokan tekojärvi  Kandalaksha
Hinnøya  Narvik  1901  Stora Lulevatten  Sodankylä  Kuolayarvi
Lofoten Is.  2111  Gällivare  Rovaniemi  Kuusamo  Ozero Topozero
Nordfold  2013  Jokkmokk  Övertorneå  Yli-kitka  Ozero Pyaozero
Bodø  2021  Kemijärvi  RUSSIAN FEDERATION (RUSSIA)
Saltdal  Arjeplog  Boden  Torneå  Kemi  Oulu  Ozero Srednye Kuyto
Mo-i-Rana  Uddjaur  Luleå  Tornio  Oulujärvi  Ozero Nyuk
Dønna  Røssvatnet  Piteå  Hailuoto  Kiantajärvi  Kalevala
Vega  1764  Skellefteå  Raahe  Kajaani  Kuhmo
Brønnøysund  Grane  703  Storuman  Skellefteå  Oulu  Iisalmi  Ozero Leksozero
Vikna  Namdalen  Vilhelmina  Lycksele  Pulkkila  Pyhäjärvi  Pielinen
Folda  Tünnsjøen  Hoting  Vännäs  Kokkola  FINLAND
Kolvereid  Namsos  Dragan  Umeå  Jakobstad  Iisalmi  Joensuu
Frøya  Brekstad  1337  Hammerdal  Örnsköldsvik  Lappajärvi  Kuopio  Pytäselkä
Hitra  Trondheim  Kallsjön  Östersund  Vaasa  Lapua  Jyväskylä  Varkaus  Pyhäjärvi
Smola  Stjørdal  Storsjön  Sollefteå  Kaskinen  Kurikka  Haukivesi
Kristiansund  Berkåk  1796  Åsarna  Härnösand  Parkano  Näsijärvi  Mikkeli  Imatra  Ozero Ladozhskoye (L. Ladoga)
Ålesund  Trollheimen  Åsarna  Sundsvall  Pori  Tampere  Puulavesi  Salma
Måløy  Andalsnes  2286  Yset  Linsell  Ytterhogdal  Rauma  Hämeenlinna  Lahti  Kouvola  Vyborg
Nordfjord  Dombås  Glåma  Femund  Ljusdal  Dellen  Forssa  Salpausselkä  Kotka
Flora  2083  Jotunheimen  Idre  Voxnan  Bollnäs  Åland  Hyvinkää  Vantaa  Kronshtadt
Segnefjorden  Lom  2469  Lillehammer  Österdalälven  Söderhamn  Turku  Salo  Helsinki  St. Petersburg
Voss  1755  Gudbrandsdalen  Mora  Siljan  Gävle  Åland  Espoo  Gatchina
Bergen  Valdres  Ragna  Hamar  Falun  Hedesunda-flådarna  Mariehamn  Tallinn  Kohtla-Järve  Narva
Haugesund  1862  Numedal  Mjøsa  Ludvika  Avesta  Hanko  Gulf of Finland  Luga
Odda  Hardangervidda  Drammen  Klöfta  Arvika  Hiiumaa  Haapsalu  Tapa  Chudskoye Ozero
Hardangerfjorden  1660  Telemark  Oslo  Västerås  Eskilstuna  Mälaren  Saaremaa  Pärnu  Tartu  ESTONIA  RUSSIAN FEDERATION (RUSSIA)
Stavanger  Setesdal  Tønsberg  Moss  Karlstad  Uppsala  Kuressaare  Vortsjärv  Ozero Pskovskoye
Flekkefjord  Bygland  Skien  Sarpsborg  Örebro  Stockholm  Mazirbe  Voru  Pskov
Mandal  Arendal  Fredrikstad  Karlskoga  Södertälje  Gulf of Riga  Valga  318  Ostrov
Kristiansand  Uddevalla  Vänern  Katrineholm  Ventspils  Valmiera  Opochka
Skagerrak  Skövde  Nyköping  Visby  Gotland  LATVIA  Rezekne
NORTH SEA  Trollhättan  Norrköping  Västervik  Kuldiga  Riga  Jekabpils
Hjørring  Borås  Linköping  Fårön  Tukums  Jurmala  Daugava
Frederikshavn  Mölndal  Sommen  Jelgava  Daugavpils
Ålborg  Göteborg  Jönköping  Nässjö  Borgholm  Liepaja  Saldus
Viborg  Bolmén  Vetlanda  Öland  Plunge  Venta  Jekabpils
Randers  Halmstad  Värnamo  Växjö  Borgholm  Siauliai  Panevezys  Polatsk
Herning  Helsingborg  Almhult  Kalmar  Klaipeda  LITHUANIA  Ukmerge
Århus  DENMARK  Kristianstad  Karlskrona  Kursiu  Kaunas  Vilnius  Minsk
Esbjerg  Vejle  Lund  Malmö  Hanöbukten  Marijampole  BELARUS
Kolding  Roskilde  Copenhagen (København)  Klaipeda  Kaliningrad  Maladzyechna  Barysaw
Odense  Sjaelland  Gulf of Gdansk  Sovetsk  Nyoman  Lida  Hrodna
Nordfriesische Inseln  Sønderborg  Lolland  Bornholm (Denmark)  Gdynia  KALININGRAD (RUSSIA)  Chernyakhovsk  Vilnius
Heligoland Bight  Flensburg  Naestved  Nykøbing  Sassnitz  Gdansk  Elblag  Kursky Zaliv
Groningen  Schleswig  Kiel  Mecklenburg Bay  Rügen  Pomeranian Bay  Koszalin  Malbork  Elk  Olsztyn
Bremerhaven  Rendsburg  Neumünster  Lübeck  Stralsund  Kolobrzeg  POLAND  Tczew  Wisla
Wilhelmshaven  Cuxhaven  Wismar  Rostock  Świnoujście  Szczecin
NETHERLANDS  GERMANY  Hamburg  Schwerin  Elbe

Gulf of Bothnia
Baltic Sea

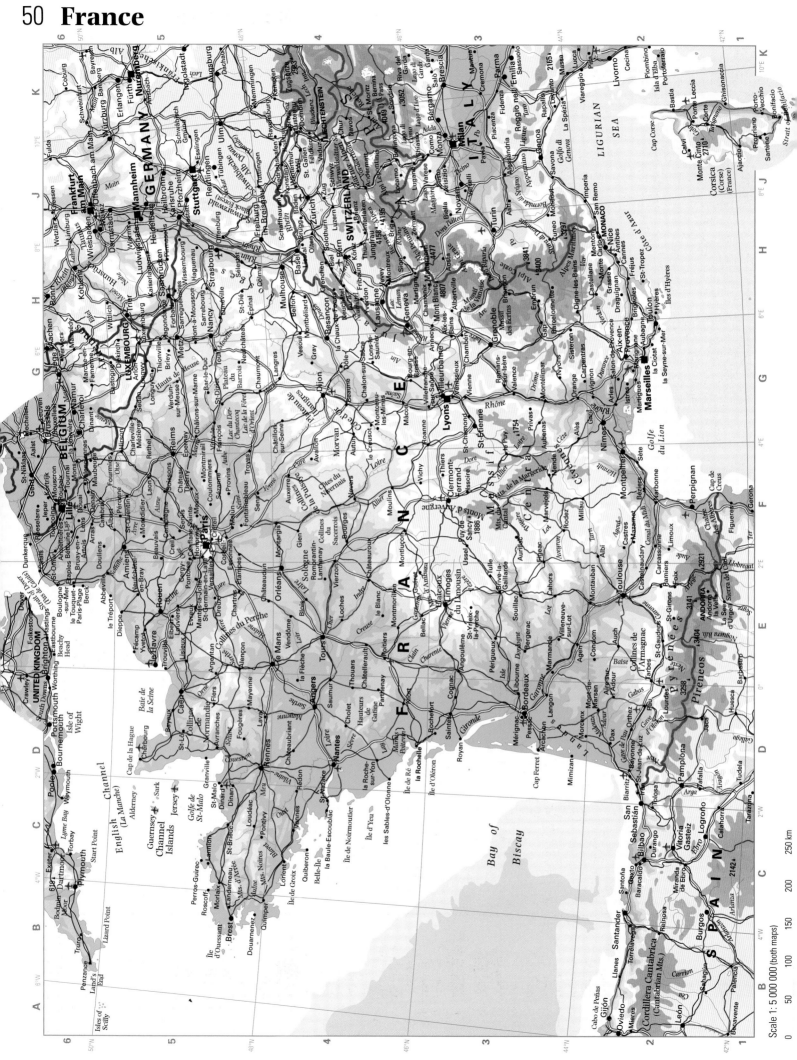

Scale 1: 5 000 000 (both maps)

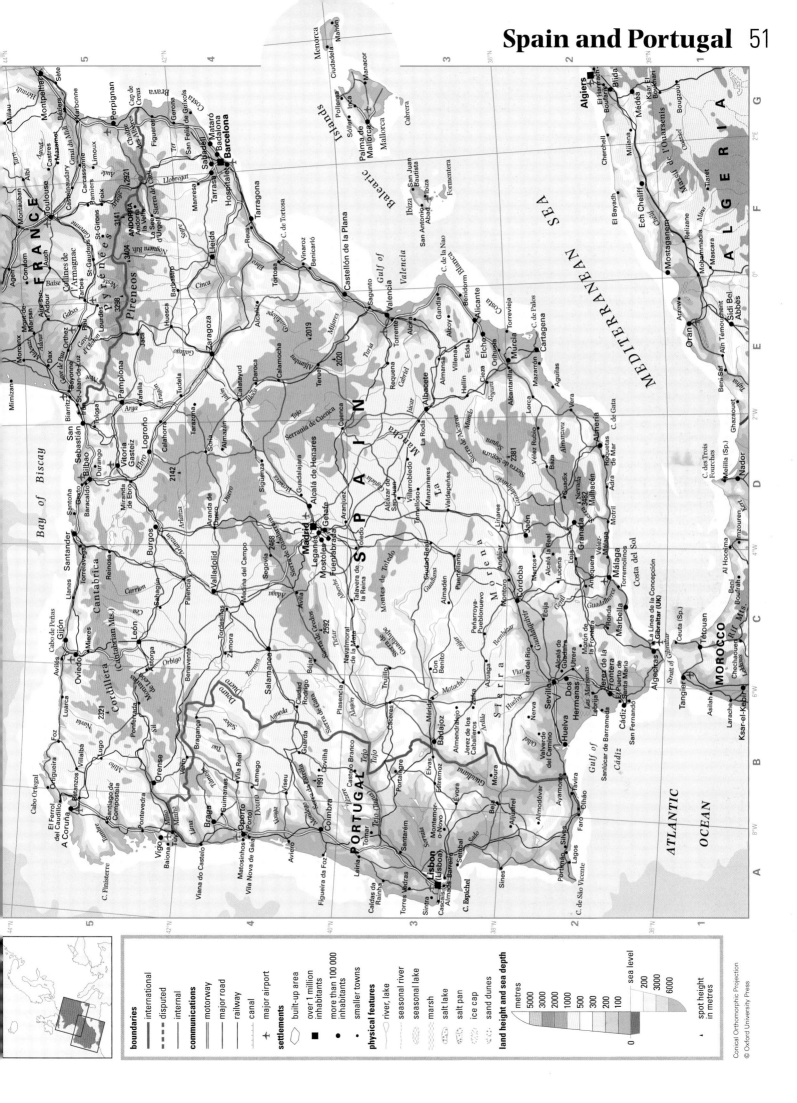

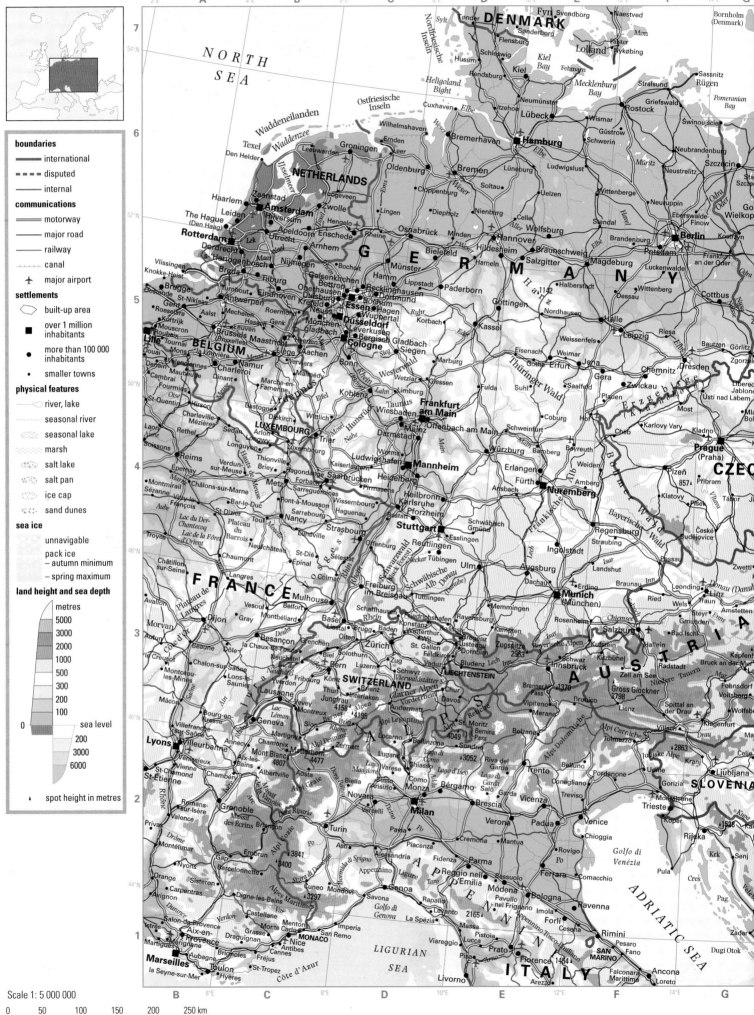

BALTIC SEA

Gulf of Gdańsk

**LITHUANIA**

Kaunas
Vilnius

Kaliningrad
KALININGRAD
(RUSSIA)
Sovetsk
Chernyakhovsk
Gusev
Marijampole
Suwałki

**BELARUS**

Orsha
Barysaw
Mahilyow
Minsk
Dzyarzhynsk
Maladzyechna
Lida
Baranavichy
Slutsk
Soligorsk
Slonim
Hrodna
Białystok
Homyel'
Rechitsa
Babruysk
Zhlobin
Mazyr
Ptsich
Pinsk
Luninyets

Wejherowo
Darłowo
Słupsk
Gdynia Sopot
Gdańsk
Koszalin
Karlino
Elbląg
Tczew
Malbork
Ostróda
Starogard Gdański
Szczecinek
Chojnice
Iława
Olsztyn
Ketrzyn
Jezioro Sniardwy
Wałcz
Jastrowie
Grudziadz
Szczytno
Ełk
Piła
Bydgoszcz
Toruń
Ciechanów
Ostrołęka
Łomża
Biebrza
Narew
Mława
Ostrów Mazowiecka
Bielsk Podlaski
Kobryn
Brest
Ratno
Pripyat
Sarny
Ptsich
Mazyr

**POLAND**

Poznań
Gniezno
Inowrocław
Włocławek
Płock
Nowy Dwor Mazowiecki
Warsaw (Warszawa)
Siedlce
Biała Podlaska
Łuków
Pruszków
Żyrardów
Sochaczew
Skierniewice
Łowicz
Kutno
Konin
Koło
Kalisz
Jarocin
Krotoszyn
Leszno
Łódź
Zgierz
Pabianice
Zduńska Wola
Piotrków Trybunalski
Radomsko
Tomaszow Mazowiecki
Radom
Puławy
Lublin
Chełm
Zamość
Vladimir Volynskiy
Luts'k
Rivne
Kovel'
Kremenets
Brody
Zolochev
Shepetovka
Novohrad Volyns'kyy
Berdychiv
Zhytomyr
Kiev
Fastov
Bila Tserkva
Kazatin

**UKRAINE**

Vinnytsya
Zhmerynka
Ternopil'
Khmel'nyts'kyy
Kopychintsy
Kam''yanets'-Podil's'kyy
Mohyliv-Podil's'kyy
Khotin
Chernivtsi
Dorohoi
Botoşani
Suceava
Rădăuţi

Zielona Góra
Nowa Sól
Głogów
Lubin
Legnica
Wrocław
Brzeg
Opole
Częstochowa
Kielce
Tarnobrzeg
Stalowa Wola
Charvonograd
L'viv
Drohobyč
Borislav
Stryy
Dolina
Ivano-Frankivs'k
Kolomyya

Wałbrzych
Kłodzko
Nysa
REPUBLIC
Olomouc
Přerov
Brno
Zlín
Opava
Ostrava
Frýdek Místek
Bielsko-Biała
Żywiec
Zakopane
Bytom
Zabrze
Gliwice
Katowice
Sosnowiec
Rybnik
Racibórz
Kraków
Tarnów
Nowy Sącz
Krosno
Jasło
Przemyśl
Sambor
Beskidy Zachodnie
CARPATHIANS
2058
1836

Znojmo
Stockerau
Klosterneuburg
Vienna Wien
Schwechat
Eisenstadt
Wiener Neustadt
Bratislava
Trnava
Nitra
Žilina
Ružomberok
Martin
Trenčín
Prievidza
Banská Bystrica
Zvolen
2663
2043
Nízke Tatry
Poprad
Prešov
1074
Košice
Rožňava
Uzhgorod
Mukachevo
Beregovo
Satu Mare

**SLOVAKIA**

Levice
Salgótarján
Miskolc
Nyíregyháza
Sighetu Marmaţiei
Borşa
Vatra Dornei
2102

Sopron
Győr
Komárno
Esztergom
Vác
Gödöllő
Gyöngyös
Eger
Balassagyarmat
1015
Tatabánya
Budapest
Székesfehérvár
Veszprém
Pápa
Cegléd
Szolnok
Karcag
Debrecen
Carei
Baia Mare
Dej
Bistriţa
Zalău
Toplita
Piatra Neamţ
Roman
Bacău
Vaslui

**HUNGARY**

Balaton
Dunaújváros
Kecskemét
Kiskunfélegyháza
Kiskunhalas
Szekszárd
Szeged
Makó
Hódmezővásárhely
Békéscsaba
Salonta
Oradea
Ciucea
Beiuş
Cluj-Napoca
Turda
Târgu Mureş
Comăneşti
Miercurea-Ciuc
Sighişoara
Medias
Baraolt
Sfântu Gheorghe
Adjud
Oneşti
Tecuci

Nagykanizsa
Kaposvár
Zalaegerszeg
Szombathely
Pécs
Baja
Subotica
Kikinda
Sombor
Zrenjanin
Arad
Lipova
Timişoara
Deva
Hunedoara
Lugoj
Caransebeş
1827
Brad
Alba Iulia
Sebeş
Sibiu
Făgăraş
Braşov
Focşani
Galaţi
Brăila
Râmnicu Sărat
Buzău

**CROATIA**

Zagreb
Sisak
Virovitica
Osijek
Vinkovci
Vukovar
Novi Sad
Vršac
Oraviţa
Reşiţa
2548
Meridionali
Petroşani
Câmpulung
Câmpina
Ploieşti
Urziceni

**ROMANIA**

Târgovişte
Titu
Slobozia
Bucharest
Călăraşi
Constanţa
Eforie
Mangalia

Prijedor
Bihać
Banja Luka
Doboj
Tuzla
Loznica
Valjevo
Šabac
Belgrade
Pančevo
Smederevo
Drobeta-Turnu-Severin
Orşova
Târgu Jiu
Petroşani
Râmnica Vâlcea
Piteşti
Slatina
Costeşti
Craiova
Roşiori de Vede
Giurgiu
Ruse
Silistra
Dobrich

**BOSNIA-HERZEGOVINA**

Zenica
2107
Sarajevo
Šibenik
Split
Čačak
1336
Kragujevac
Titovo Užice
Kraljevo
Kruševac

**SERBIA**

Vidin
Montana
Pleven
Pavlikeni
Türgovishte
Razgrad
Shumen
Varna

**BULGARIA**

**MOLDOVA**

Bălţi
Chişinău
Tighina
Tiraspol
Cimişlia
Comrat
Sarata
Bolhrad
Izmayil

**UKRAINE**

16°E  18°E  20°E  22°E  24°E  26°E  28°E  30°E

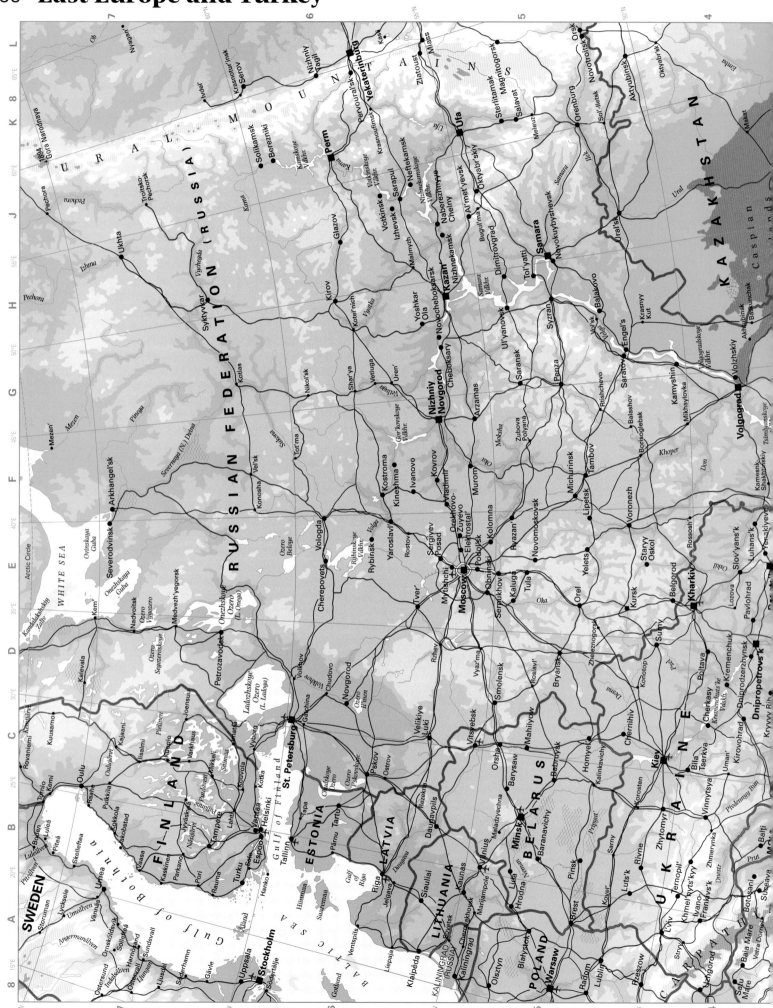

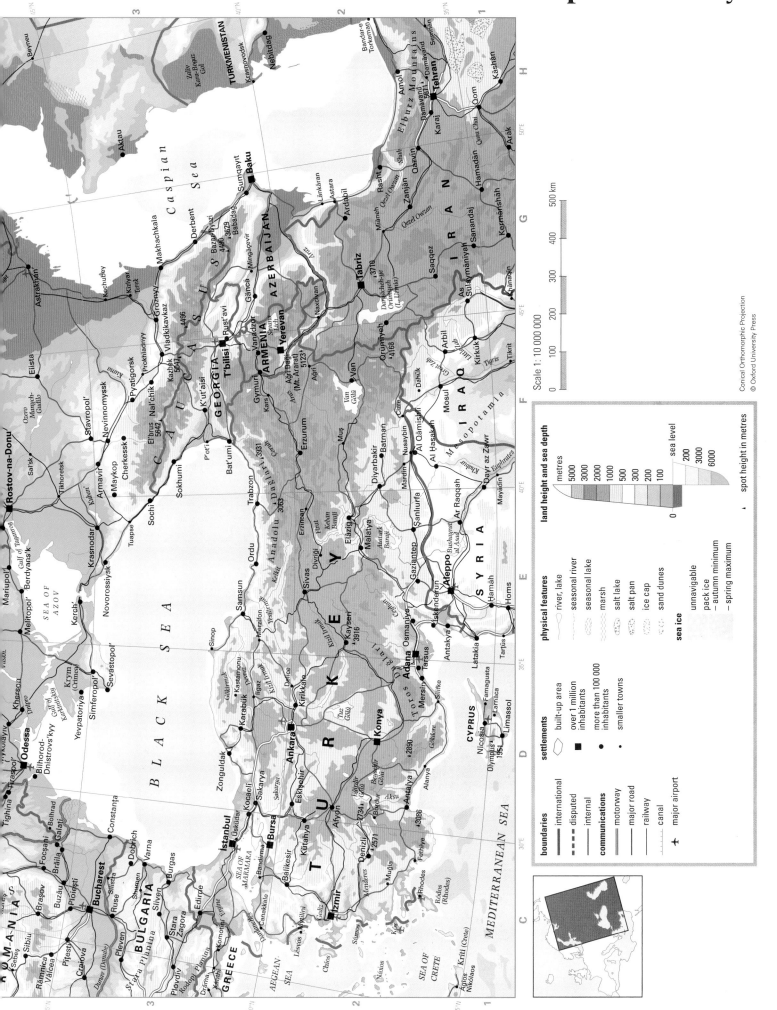

Scale 1:10 000 000

Conical Orthomorphic Projection
© Oxford University Press

**boundaries**
— international
---- disputed
— internal

**communications**
— motorway
— major road
— railway
— canal
✈ major airport

**settlements**
⬡ built-up area
■ over 1 million inhabitants
● more than 100 000 inhabitants
• smaller towns

**physical features**
river, lake
seasonal river
seasonal lake
marsh
salt lake
salt pan
ice cap
sand dunes

**sea ice**
unnavigable
pack ice
– autumn minimum
– spring maximum

**land height and sea depth**
metres
5000
3000
2000
1000
500
300
200
100
sea level
200
3000
6000
▲ spot height in metres

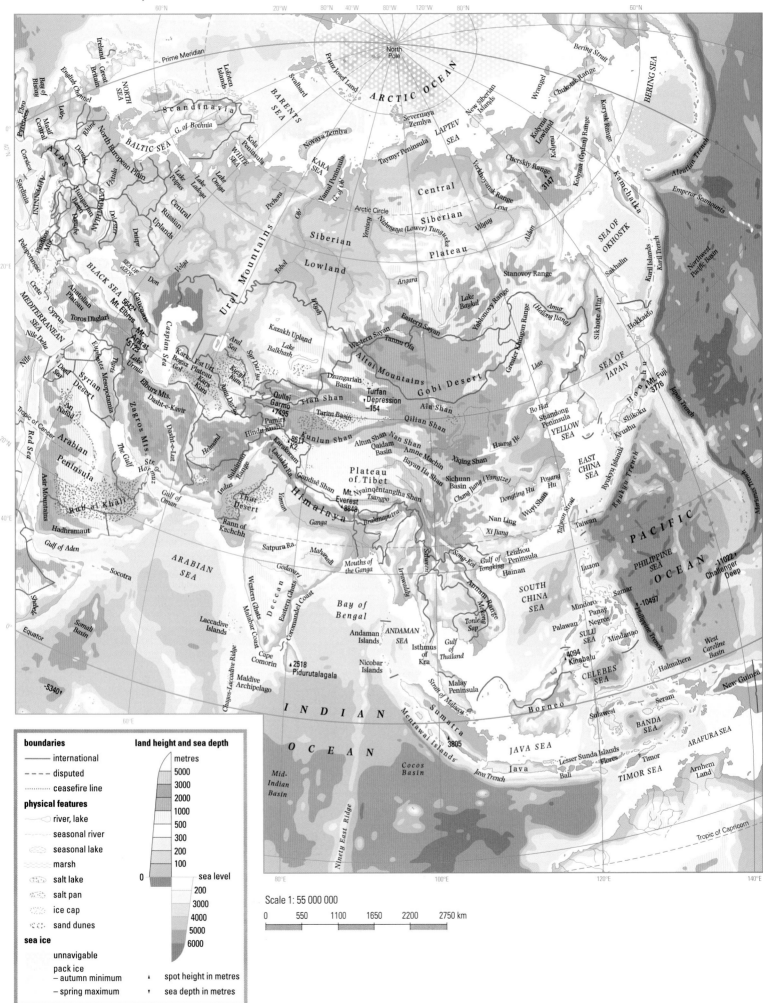

**boundaries**
— international
-- disputed
···· ceasefire line

**physical features**
— river, lake
-- seasonal river
seasonal lake
marsh
salt lake
salt pan
ice cap
sand dunes

**sea ice**
unnavigable
pack ice
– autumn minimum
– spring maximum

**land height and sea depth**

metres
5000
3000
2000
1000
500
300
200
100
0 — sea level
200
3000
4000
5000
6000

▲ spot height in metres
▼ sea depth in metres

Scale 1: 55 000 000

0   550   1100   1650   2200   2750 km

Zenithal equal Area Projection   © Oxford University Press

Scale 1: 55 000 000

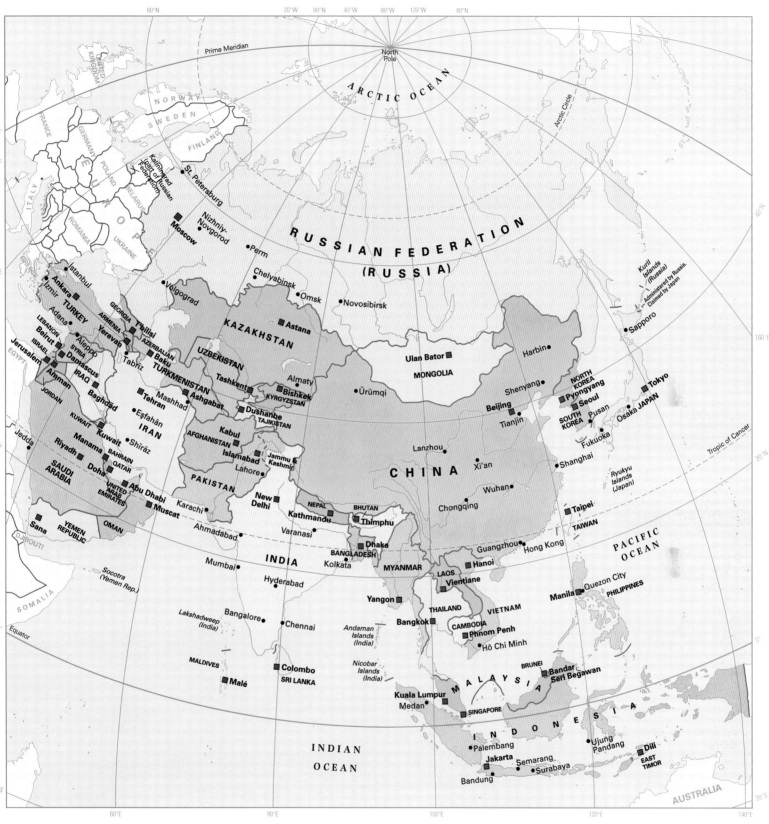

Urban and rural population, 2005

Urban and rural
population, 2005

percentage of
total population

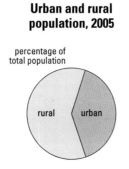

rural urban

City size as a percent
of urban population, 2005

over
10 million

5–10 million

less than
500 000

1–5 million

500 000–1 million

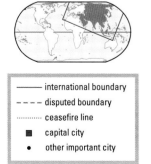

— international boundary
- - - disputed boundary
· · · · · ceasefire line
■ capital city
• other important city

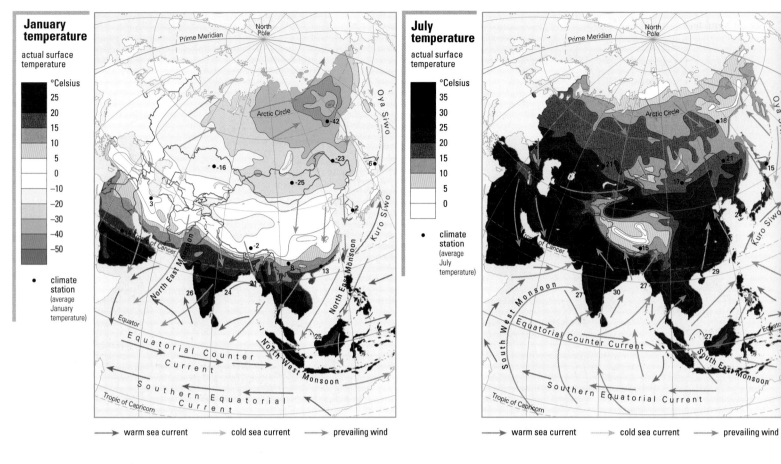

**January temperature**

actual surface temperature

°Celsius
25
20
15
10
5
0
−10
−20
−30
−40
−50

• climate station (average January temperature)

**July temperature**

actual surface temperature

°Celsius
35
30
25
20
15
10
5
0

• climate station (average July temperature)

→ warm sea current    ⇢ cold sea current    → prevailing wind

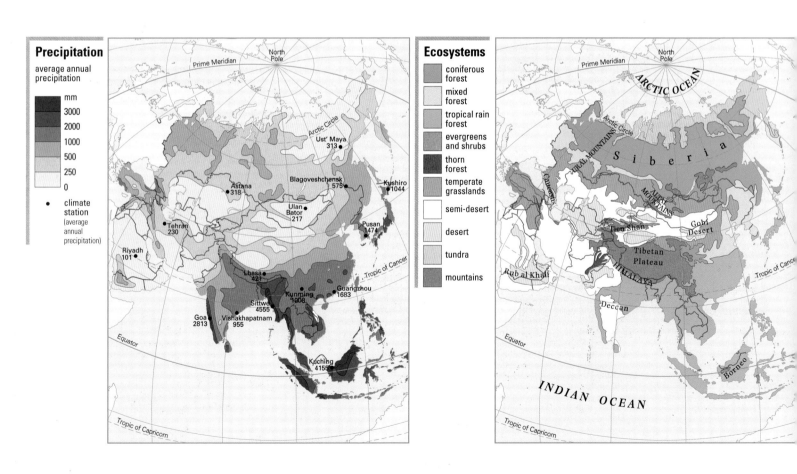

**Precipitation**

average annual precipitation

mm
3000
2000
1000
500
250
0

• climate station (average annual precipitation)

**Ecosystems**

coniferous forest
mixed forest
tropical rain forest
evergreens and shrubs
thorn forest
temperate grasslands
semi-desert
desert
tundra
mountains

Scale 1: 75 000 000

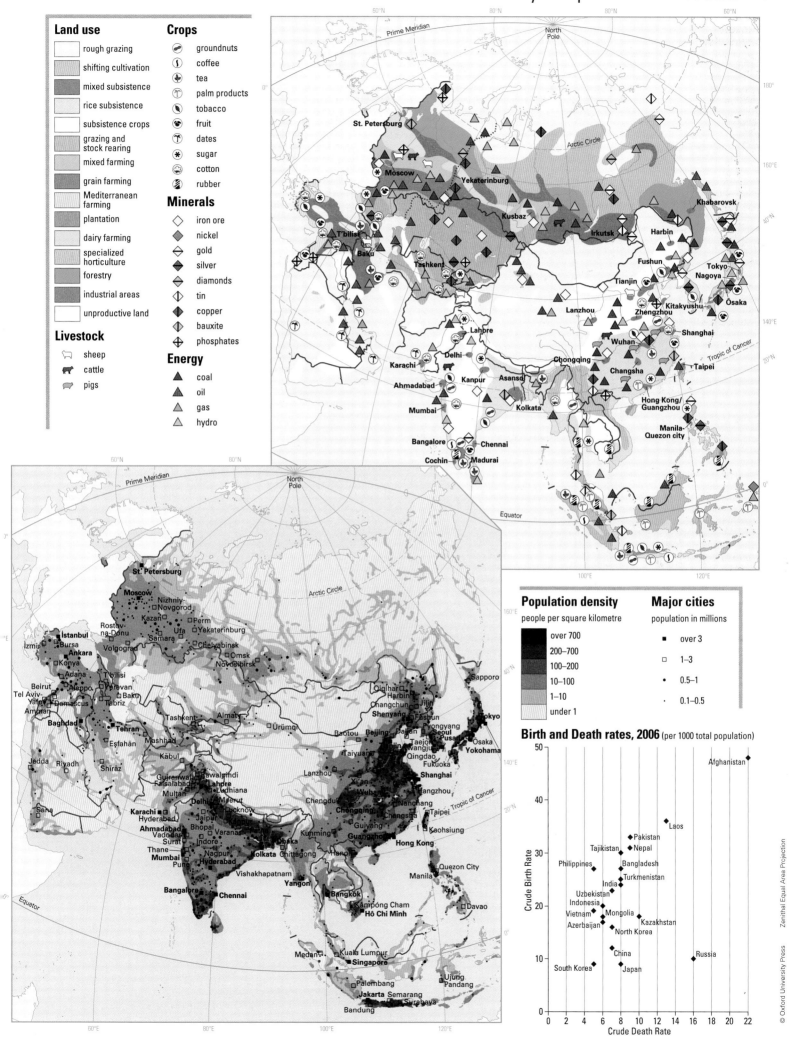

## Land use

- rough grazing
- shifting cultivation
- mixed subsistence
- rice subsistence
- subsistence crops
- grazing and stock rearing
- mixed farming
- grain farming
- Mediterranean farming
- plantation
- dairy farming
- specialized horticulture
- forestry
- industrial areas
- unproductive land

### Livestock

- sheep
- cattle
- pigs

## Crops

- groundnuts
- coffee
- tea
- palm products
- tobacco
- fruit
- dates
- sugar
- cotton
- rubber

## Minerals

- iron ore
- nickel
- gold
- silver
- diamonds
- tin
- copper
- bauxite
- phosphates

## Energy

- coal
- oil
- gas
- hydro

## Population density

people per square kilometre

- over 700
- 200–700
- 100–200
- 10–100
- 1–10
- under 1

## Major cities

population in millions

- over 3
- 1–3
- 0.5–1
- 0.1–0.5

## Birth and Death rates, 2006 (per 1000 total population)

Crude Birth Rate (vertical axis, 0–50)
Crude Death Rate (horizontal axis, 0–22)

Countries plotted: Afghanistan, Laos, Pakistan, Tajikistan, Nepal, Philippines, Bangladesh, India, Turkmenistan, Uzbekistan, Indonesia, Vietnam, Mongolia, Azerbaijan, North Korea, Kazakhstan, China, Russia, South Korea, Japan

Zenithal Equal Area Projection

© Oxford University Press

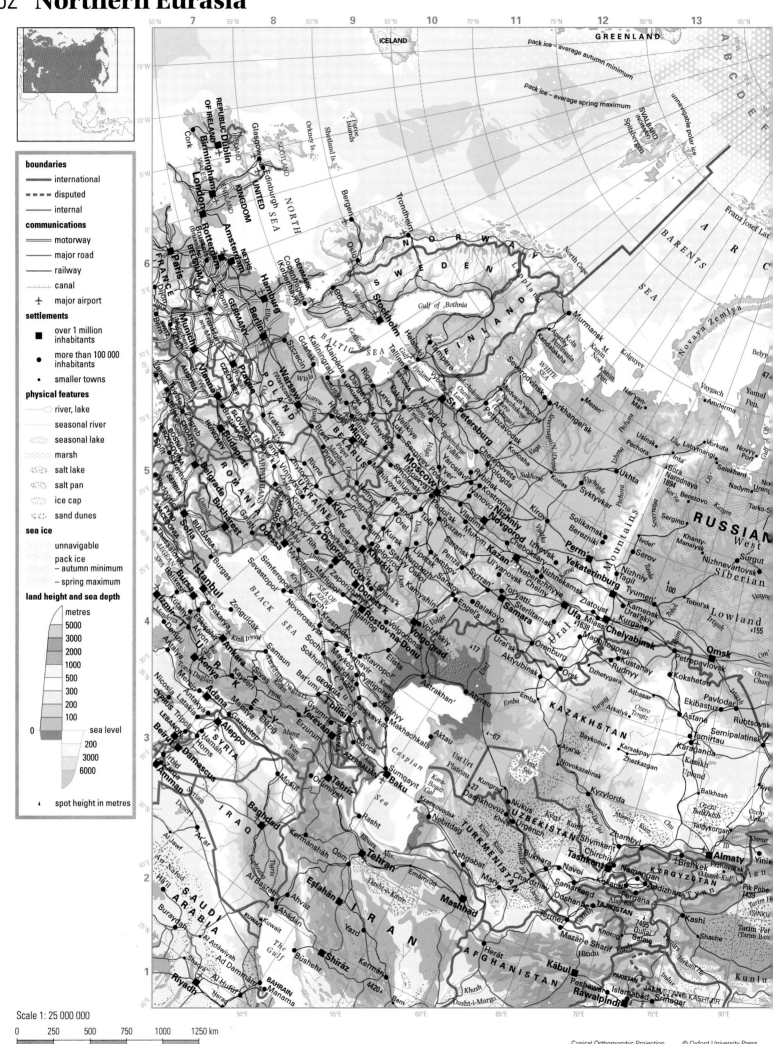

**boundaries**
— international
--- disputed
— internal
**communications**
═ motorway
— major road
— railway
+ canal
✈ major airport
**settlements**
■ over 1 million inhabitants
● more than 100 000 inhabitants
· smaller towns
**physical features**
river, lake
seasonal river
seasonal lake
marsh
salt lake
salt pan
ice cap
sand dunes
**sea ice**
unnavigable
pack ice
– autumn minimum
– spring maximum
**land height and sea depth**

metres
5000
3000
2000
1000
500
300
200
100
0 — sea level
200
3000
6000

▲ spot height in metres

Scale 1: 25 000 000

0   250   500   750   1000   1250 km

Conical Orthomorphic Projection    © Oxford University Press

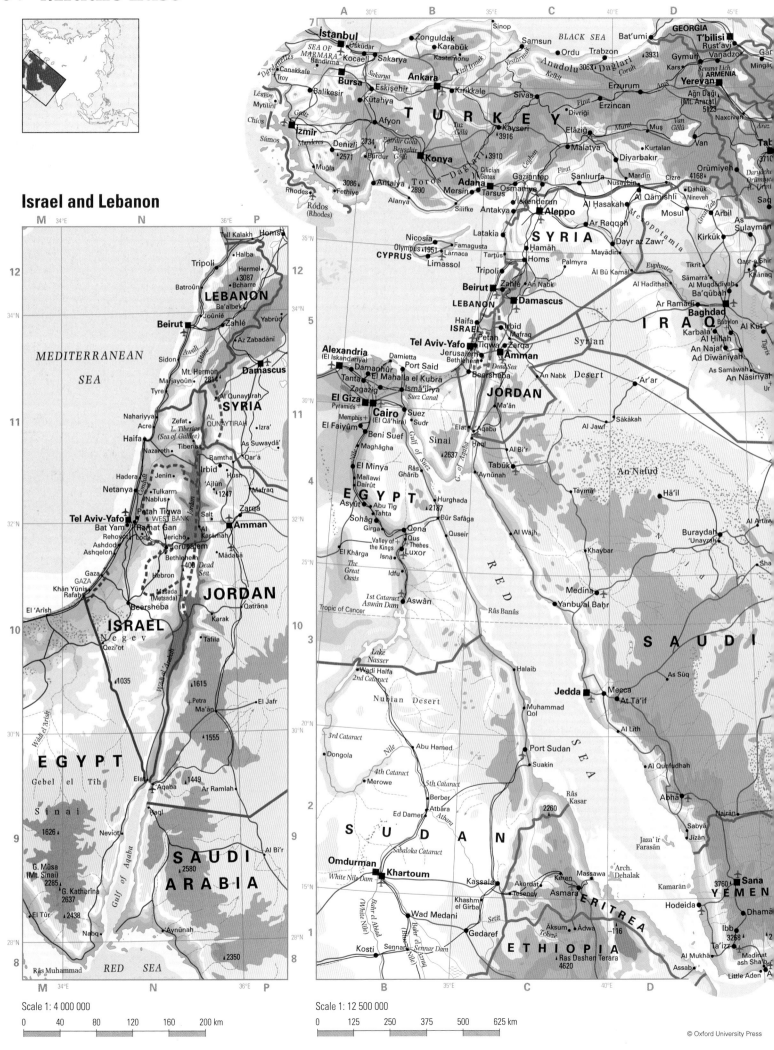

## Israel and Lebanon

Scale 1 : 4 000 000

0   40   80   120   160   200 km

Scale 1 : 12 500 000

0   125   250   375   500   625 km

© Oxford University Press

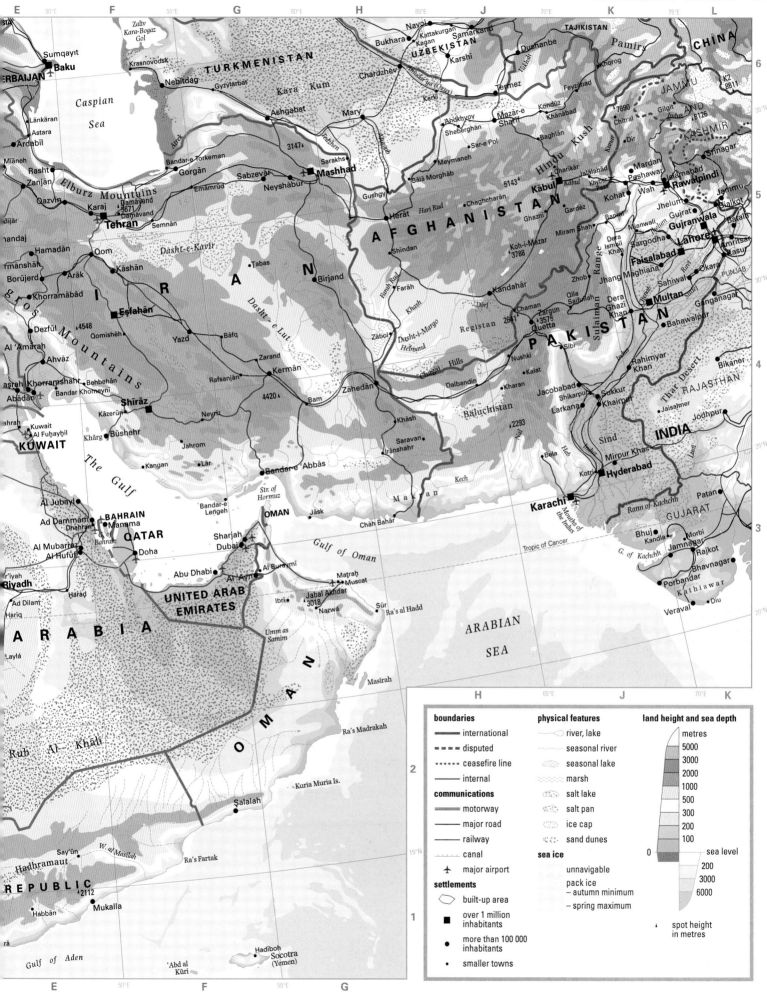

**boundaries**
- —— international
- --- disputed
- ···· ceasefire line
- —— internal

**communications**
- === motorway
- —— major road
- —— railway
- ┼┼┼ canal
- ✈ major airport

**settlements**
- ⬭ built-up area
- ■ over 1 million inhabitants
- ● more than 100 000 inhabitants
- · smaller towns

**physical features**
- river, lake
- seasonal river
- seasonal lake
- marsh
- salt lake
- salt pan
- ice cap
- sand dunes

**sea ice**
- unnavigable
- pack ice
  - autumn minimum
  - spring maximum

**land height and sea depth**

metres
- 5000
- 3000
- 2000
- 1000
- 500
- 300
- 200
- 100
- 0 — sea level
- 200
- 3000
- 6000

▲ spot height in metres

**boundaries**
— international
--- disputed
···· ceasefire line
— internal

**communications**
═══ motorway
─── major road
─── railway
┼┼┼ canal
✈ major airport

**settlements**
⬡ built-up area
■ over 1 million inhabitants
● more than 100 000 inhabitants
• smaller towns

**physical features**
~ river, lake
- - seasonal river
seasonal lake
marsh
salt lake
salt pan
ice cap
sand dunes

**sea ice**
unnavigable
pack ice
– autumn minimum
– spring maximum

**land height and sea depth**
metres
5000
3000
2000
1000
500
300
200
100
0  sea level
200
3000
6000

▲ spot height in metres

Scale 1: 12 500 000

0  125  250  375  500  625 km

**Ganges Delta, Bangladesh**
Vegetation is red, water is dark blue but paler where rich in silt.

Scale 1: 5 000 000

© Oxford University Press      Conical Orthomorphic Projection

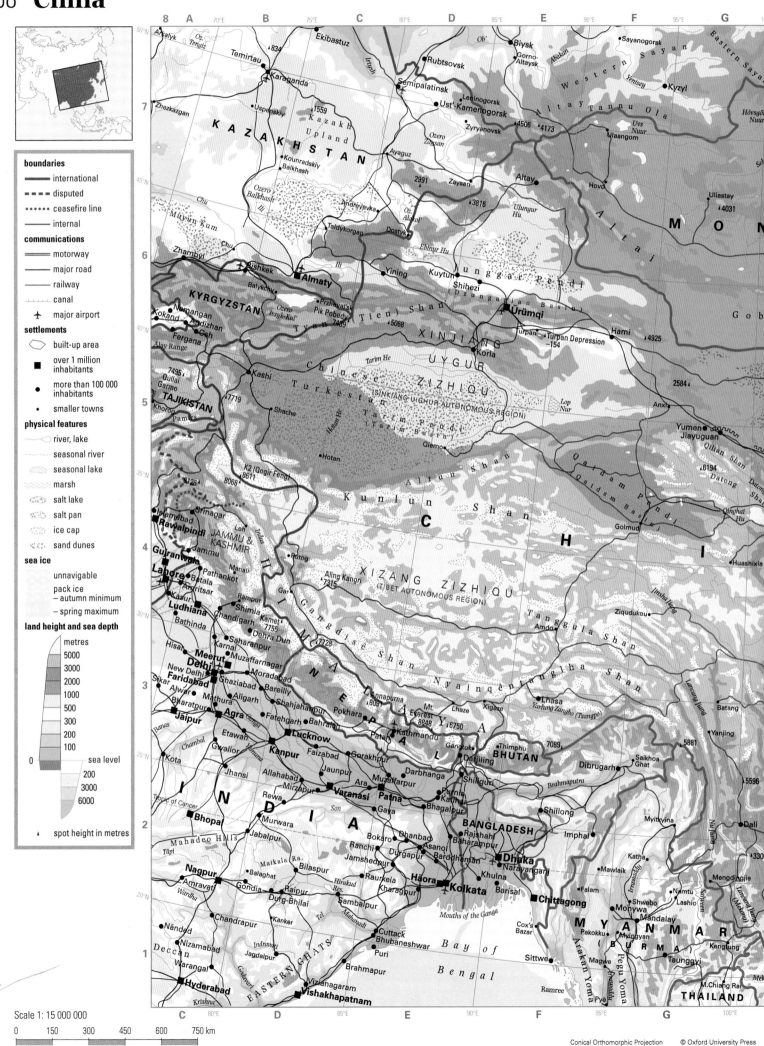

**boundaries**
- —— international
- ---- disputed
- ···· ceasefire line
- —— internal

**communications**
- ═══ motorway
- —— major road
- —— railway
- ⊥⊥⊥ canal
- ✈ major airport

**settlements**
- ⬡ built-up area
- ■ over 1 million inhabitants
- ● more than 100 000 inhabitants
- • smaller towns

**physical features**
- river, lake
- seasonal river
- seasonal lake
- marsh
- salt lake
- salt pan
- ice cap
- sand dunes

**sea ice**
- unnavigable
- pack ice
  – autumn minimum
  – spring maximum

**land height and sea depth**

metres
5000
3000
2000
1000
500
300
200
100
sea level
200
3000
6000

▲ spot height in metres

Scale 1: 15 000 000

0    150    300    450    600    750 km

Conical Orthomorphic Projection          © Oxford University Press

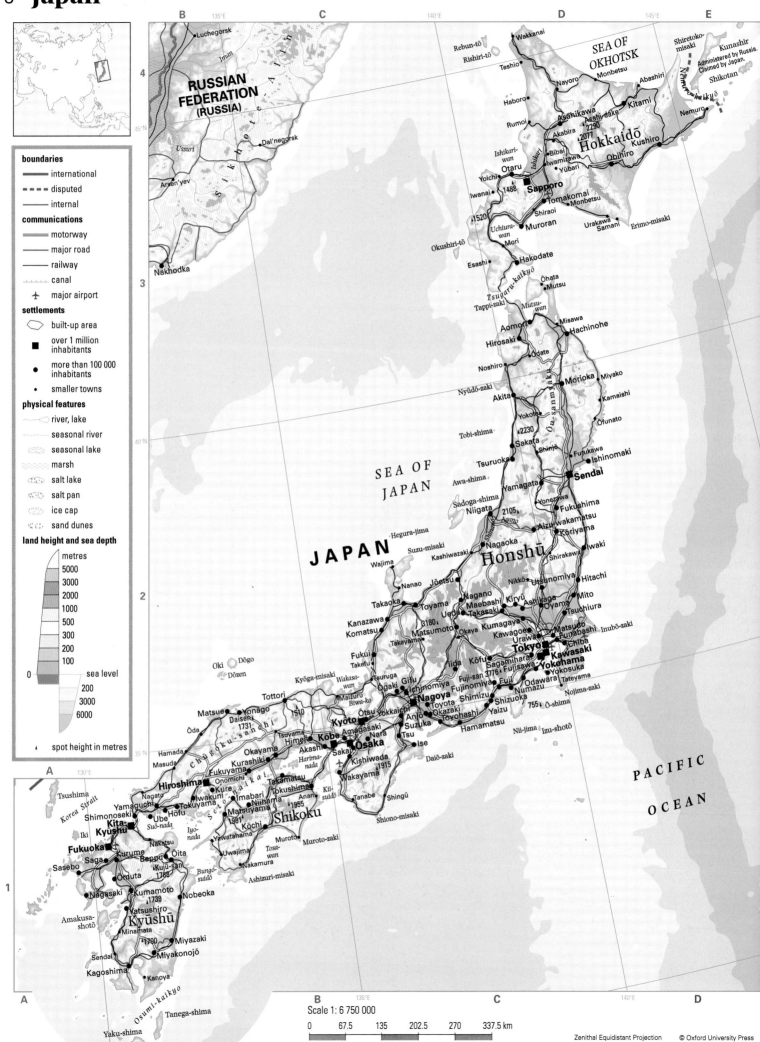

Scale 1: 6 750 000

0    67.5    135    202.5    270    337.5 km

Zenithal Equidistant Projection

© Oxford University Press

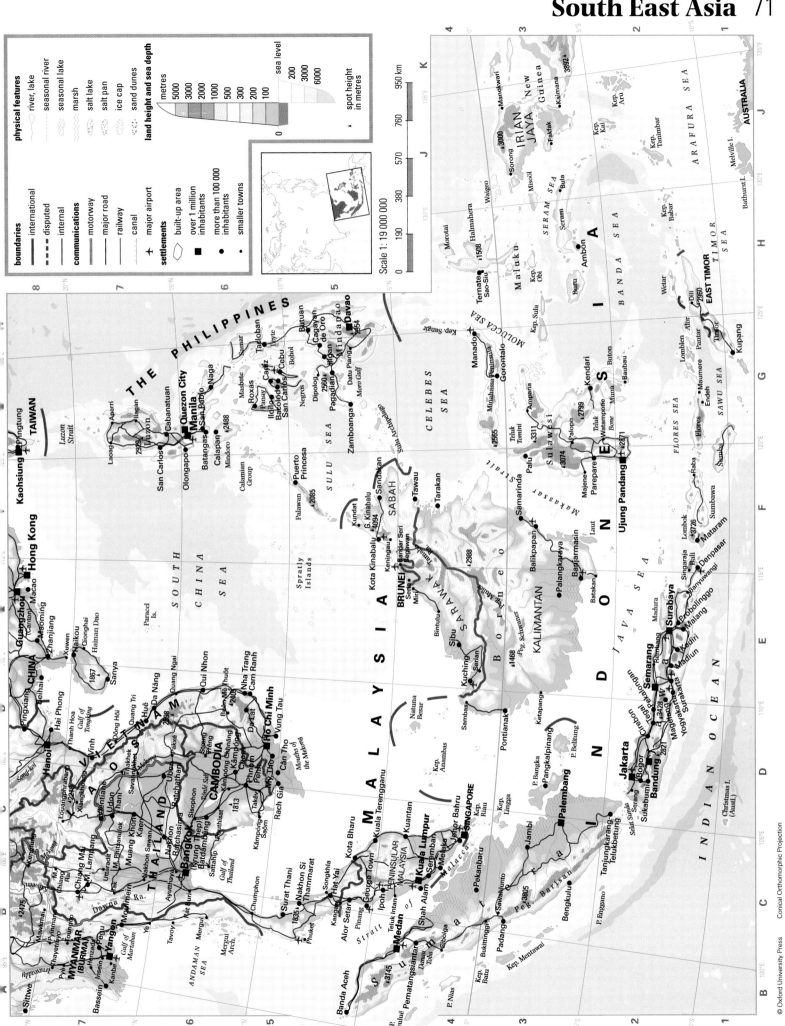

**physical features**
- river, lake
- seasonal river
- seasonal lake
- marsh
- salt lake
- salt pan
- ice cap
- sand dunes

land height and sea depth

metres
5000
3000
2000
1000
500
300
200
100
sea level
200
3000
6000

· spot height in metres

**boundaries**
- international
- disputed
- internal

**communications**
- motorway
- major road
- railway
- canal
- ✈ major airport

**settlements**
- built-up area
- ■ over 1 million inhabitants
- ● more than 100 000 inhabitants
- · smaller towns

Scale 1:19 000 000

0  190  380  570  760  950 km

Conical Orthomorphic Projection

**boundaries**
— international
-- disputed
— internal

**communications**
═ motorway
— major road
— railway
...... canal
✈ major airport

**settlements**
⬡ built-up area
◼ over 1 million inhabitants
● more than 100 000 inhabitants
• smaller towns

**physical features**
river, lake
seasonal river
seasonal lake
marsh
salt lake
salt pan
ice cap
sand dunes

**sea ice**
unnavigable
pack ice
– autumn minimum
– spring maximum

**land height and sea depth**
metres
5000
3000
2000
1000
500
300
200
100
0 sea level
200
3000
6000
▲ spot height in metres

Scale 1 : 20 000 000

0   200   400   600   800   1000 km

Zenithal Equidistant Projection     © Oxford University Press

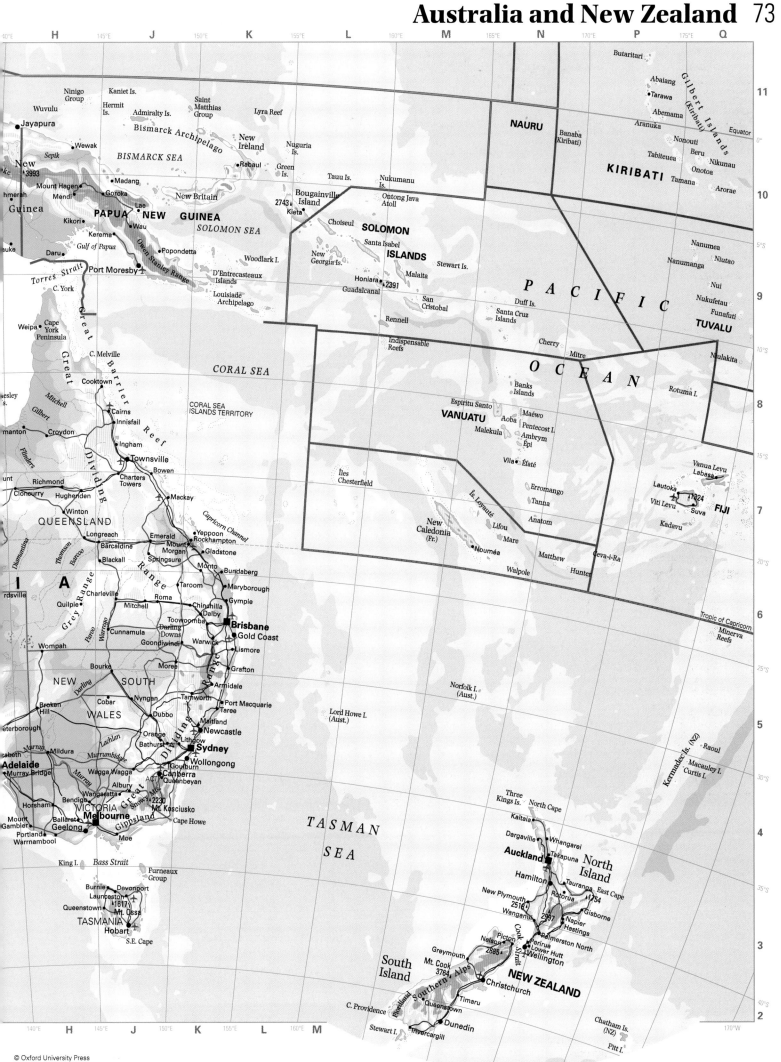

40°E H 145°E J 150°E K 155°E L 160°E M 165°E N 170°E P 175°E Q

**Butaritari**
**Abaiang**
**Tarawa**
Abemama
Aranuka
*Gilbert Islands*
*(Kiribati)*
Equator

Ninigo Group
Kaniet Is.
Hermit Is.
Admiralty Is.
Saint Matthias Group
Lyra Reef

Wuvulu
Jayapura
Wewak

**NAURU**
Banaba (Kiribati)

Nonouti
Beru
Nikunau
Onotoa

**KIRIBATI**

Tabiteuea
Tamana
Arorae

11

New
3993

*Bismarck Archipelago*

New Ireland

Nuguria Is.

**BISMARCK SEA**

0°

Mount Hagen
Mendi
Goroka
Madang

Rabaul

Green Is.

**PAPUA NEW GUINEA**

Lae
Wau

New Britain

Tauu Is.

Nukumanu Is.

Ontong Java Atoll

Nanumea
Niutao
Nanumanga

5°S

Guinea
Kikori
Kerema

*SOLOMON SEA*

Bougainville Island
2743
Kieta

Choiseul

Santa Isabel

**SOLOMON**

Stewart Is.

Nui
Nukufetau

10

Daru
Gulf of Papua
Popondetta

*Owen Stanley Range*

D'Entrecasteaux Islands

Woodlark I.

New Georgia Is.

**ISLANDS**

Malaita

Funafuti

**TUVALU**

weie
Weipa
Cape York Peninsula

Port Moresby

*Torres Strait*
C. York

Louisiade Archipelago

Honiara
2391

Guadalcanal

San Cristobal

Rennell

Duff Is.

Santa Cruz Islands

Niulakita

9

*Great*
Cooktown

C. Melville

*CORAL SEA*

Indispensable Reefs

Cherry

Mitre

10°S

kesley s.
manton
Mitchell

*Barrier*
Cairns
Innisfail

**CORAL SEA ISLANDS TERRITORY**

Banks Islands

**P A C I F I C**

Rotuma I.

8

Gilbert
Croydon

Ingham

*Reef*

Espiritu Santo
Aoba
Maéwo
Pentecost I.

**O C E A N**

nt
Flinders

Townsville
Bowen

Charters Towers

**VANUATU**

Malekula
Ambrym
Epi

Vanua Levu
Labasa

15°S

unt
Richmond
Cloncurry
Hughenden

Mackay

Vila
Éfaté

Lautoka
Viti Levu
1324

**FIJI**

Suva

7

**QUEENSLAND**

Longreach
Winton

*Dividing*

Emerald
Mount Morgan
Rockhampton

Yeppoon

*Capricorn Channel*

Îles Chesterfield

New Caledonia (Fr.)

Îs. Loyauté

Erromango

Lifou
Tanna

Anatom

Kadavu

Geva-i-Ra

20°S

I
A

*Grey Range*
*Range*

Barcaldine
Blackall

Springsure

Gladstone

Monto
Bundaberg

Noumea

Mare

Matthew
Walpole

Hunter

6

rdsville
Quilpie
Charleville

Mitchell

Roma

Taroom

Maryborough
Gympie

Chinchilla
Dalby

Tropic of Capricorn

Minerva Reefs

Bourke
Cunnamula

Goondiwindi

Toowoomba
*Darling Downs*

**Brisbane**
Gold Coast

Warwick

Lismore

Norfolk I. (Aust.)

25°S

**NEW**

Cobar
Nyngan

Moree

Tamworth

Armidale

Port Macquarie
Taree

Lord Howe I. (Aust.)

5

**SOUTH**

*Darling*
Broken Hill

Dubbo

*Dividing*

Maitland
Newcastle

**WALES**

Orange
Bathurst

Lithgow

**Sydney**

Norfolk I.

Raoul

*Kermadec Is. (NZ)*

eterborough
zabeth

Mildura

*Murrumbidgee*

*Lachlan*

Goulburn
Queanbeyan

Wollongong

Macauley I.
Curtis I.

30°S

**Adelaide**
Murray Bridge

Wagga Wagga
Albury

ACT

**Canberra**

Three Kings Is.
North Cape

Kaitaia

Horsham
Bendigo
Wangaratta

*Murray*

*Snowy Mts.*
2230

Mt. Kosciusko

North Island

Dargaville
Whangarei

35°S

Mount Gambier
Portland
Warrnambool

Ballarat
Geelong

**Melbourne**

**VICTORIA**

*Gippsland*

Moe

Cape Howe

**TASMAN**

**Auckland**
Takapuna

Hamilton

Tauranga
East Cape

King I.
*Bass Strait*

Furneaux Group

**SEA**

New Plymouth
2518

Rotorua
1754

Gisborne

Burnie
Devonport
Launceston
1617
Mt. Ossa

Wanganui
2797

Napier
Hastings

4

Queenstown

**TASMANIA**

Hobart

S.E. Cape

Picton
Nelson
Porirua
Lower Hutt

Palmerston North

*Cook Strait*
**Wellington**

3

Greymouth

Mt. Cook
3764
*Southern Alps*

**South Island**

2885

South Island

**NEW ZEALAND**

Christchurch

*Fiordland*

Mt. Cook

Timaru

C. Providence

Queenstown
Dunedin

40°S

Stewart I.

Invercargill

Chatham Is. (NZ)

Pitt I.

2

140°E H 145°E J 150°E K 155°E L 160°E M 170°W

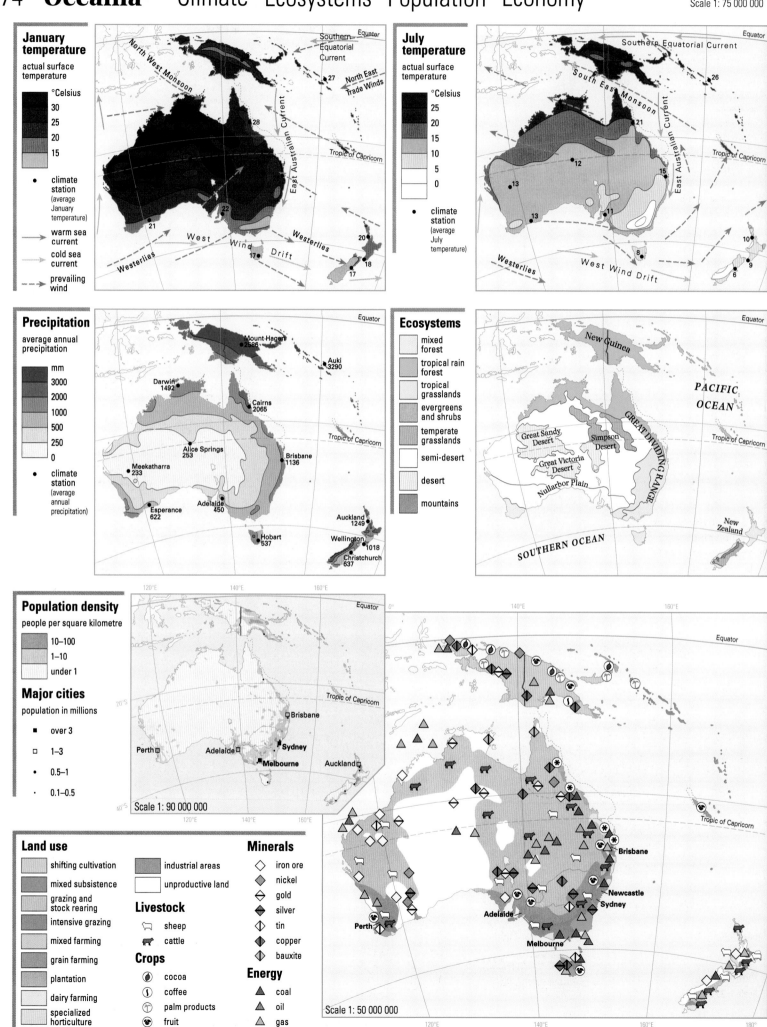

**January temperature**

actual surface temperature

°Celsius
- 30
- 25
- 20
- 15

- climate station (average January temperature)
- → warm sea current
- → cold sea current
- --→ prevailing wind

**July temperature**

actual surface temperature

°Celsius
- 25
- 20
- 15
- 10
- 5
- 0

- climate station (average July temperature)

**Precipitation**

average annual precipitation

mm
- 3000
- 2000
- 1000
- 500
- 250
- 0

- climate station (average annual precipitation)

Mount Hagen 2586
Auki 3290
Darwin 1492
Cairns 2065
Alice Springs 253
Brisbane 1136
Meekatharra 233
Esperance 622
Adelaide 450
Auckland 1249
Hobart 537
Wellington 1018
Christchurch 637

**Ecosystems**
- mixed forest
- tropical rain forest
- tropical grasslands
- evergreens and shrubs
- temperate grasslands
- semi-desert
- desert
- mountains

New Guinea
PACIFIC OCEAN
Great Sandy Desert
Simpson Desert
GREAT DIVIDING RANGE
Great Victoria Desert
Nullarbor Plain
SOUTHERN OCEAN
New Zealand

**Population density**

people per square kilometre
- 10–100
- 1–10
- under 1

**Major cities**

population in millions
- ■ over 3
- ◻ 1–3
- • 0.5–1
- · 0.1–0.5

Brisbane
Perth
Adelaide
Sydney
Melbourne
Auckland

Scale 1: 90 000 000

**Land use**
- shifting cultivation
- mixed subsistence
- grazing and stock rearing
- intensive grazing
- mixed farming
- grain farming
- plantation
- dairy farming
- specialized horticulture
- forestry
- industrial areas
- unproductive land

**Livestock**
- 🐑 sheep
- 🐂 cattle

**Crops**
- cocoa
- coffee
- palm products
- fruit
- sugar

**Minerals**
- ◇ iron ore
- ◆ nickel
- gold
- silver
- tin
- copper
- bauxite

**Energy**
- △ coal
- △ oil
- △ gas
- △ hydro

Perth
Adelaide
Melbourne
Newcastle
Sydney
Brisbane

Scale 1: 50 000 000

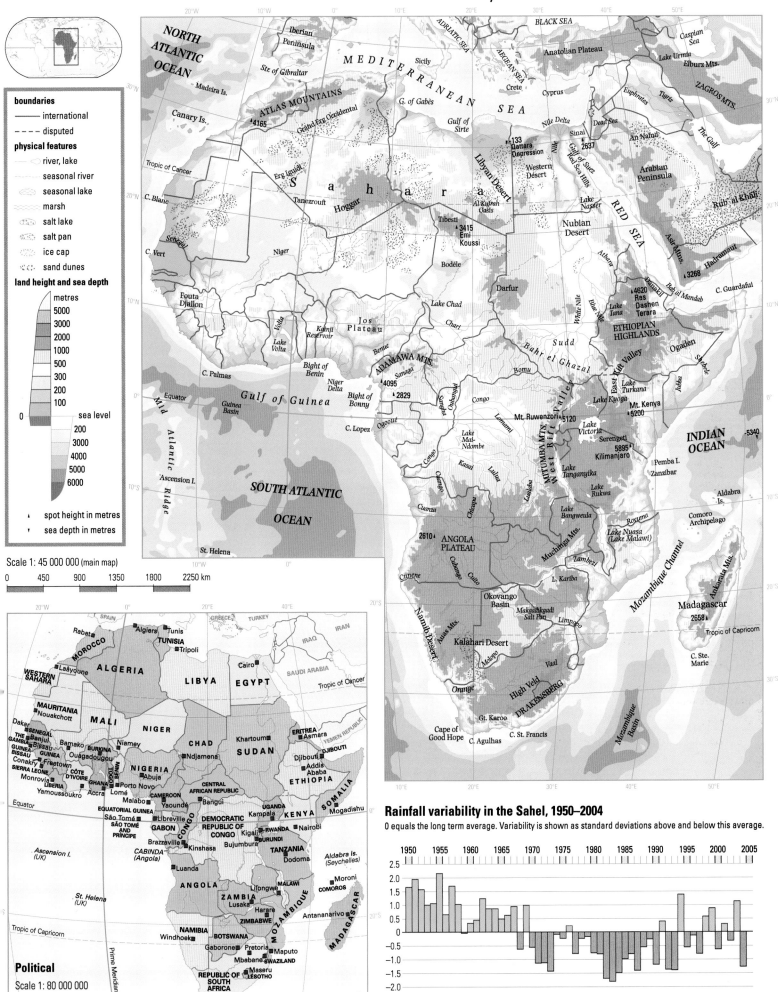

**boundaries**
— international
--- disputed

**physical features**
~ river, lake
seasonal river
seasonal lake
marsh
salt lake
salt pan
ice cap
sand dunes

**land height and sea depth**
metres
5000
3000
2000
1000
500
300
200
100
0   sea level
200
3000
4000
5000
6000

▲ spot height in metres
▼ sea depth in metres

Scale 1: 45 000 000 (main map)

0   450   900   1350   1800   2250 km

**Political**
Scale 1: 80 000 000

© Oxford University Press      Zenithal Equal Area Projection

### Rainfall variability in the Sahel, 1950–2004
0 equals the long term average. Variability is shown as standard deviations above and below this average.

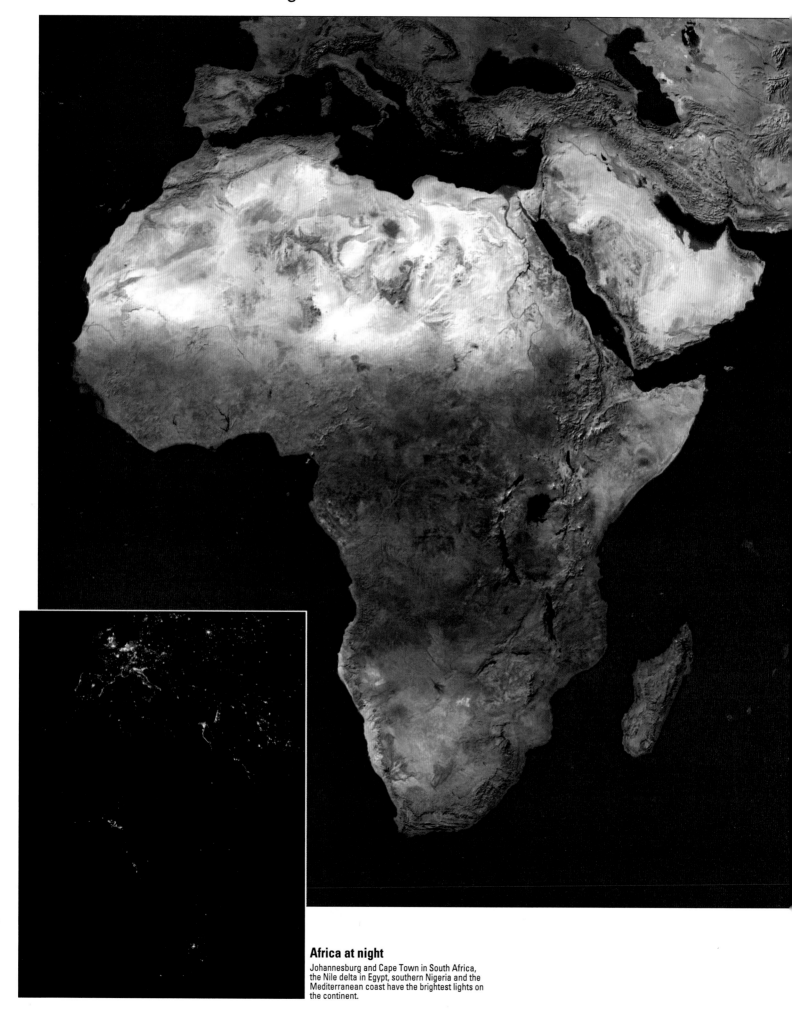

### Africa at night

Johannesburg and Cape Town in South Africa, the Nile delta in Egypt, southern Nigeria and the Mediterranean coast have the brightest lights on the continent.

Scale 1: 90 000 000

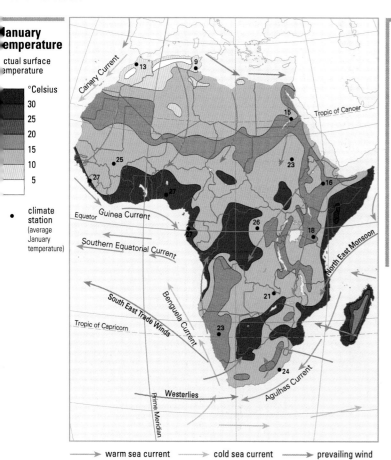

**January temperature**

actual surface temperature

°Celsius

30
25
20
15
10
5

● climate station (average January temperature)

Canary Current
Guinea Current
Equator
Southern Equatorial Current
South East Trade Winds
Benguela Current
Tropic of Cancer
Tropic of Capricorn
North East Monsoon
Westerlies
Aguilhas Current
Prime Meridian

13  9  15  25  27  27  23  16  26  27  18  21  23  24

→ warm sea current  → cold sea current  → prevailing wind

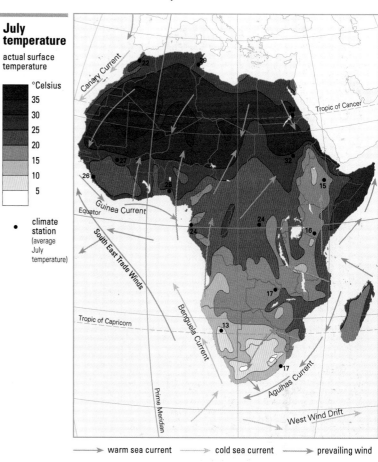

**July temperature**

actual surface temperature

°Celsius

35
30
25
20
15
10
5

● climate station (average July temperature)

Canary Current
Guinea Current
Equator
South East Trade Winds
Benguela Current
Tropic of Cancer
Tropic of Capricorn
Aguilhas Current
West Wind Drift
Prime Meridian

22  29  27  26  28  24  24  32  15  16  18  17  13  17

→ warm sea current  → cold sea current  → prevailing wind

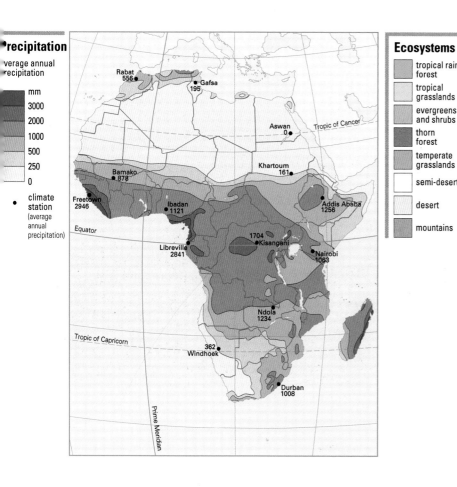

**Precipitation**

average annual precipitation

mm

3000
2000
1000
500
250
0

● climate station (average annual precipitation)

Rabat 556
Gafsa 195
Aswan 0
Khartoum 161
Bamako 878
Freetown 2946
Ibadan 1121
Addis Ababa 1256
Kisangani 1704
Libreville 2841
Nairobi 1063
Ndola 1234
Windhoek 362
Durban 1008

Tropic of Cancer
Equator
Tropic of Capricorn
Prime Meridian

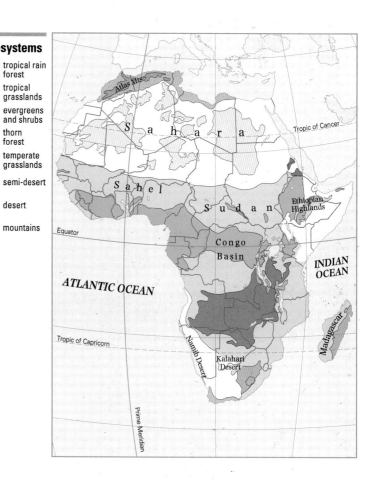

**Ecosystems**

tropical rain forest
tropical grasslands
evergreens and shrubs
thorn forest
temperate grasslands
semi-desert
desert
mountains

Atlas Mts
Sahara
Sahel
Sudan
Ethiopian Highlands
Congo Basin
Namib Desert
Kalahari Desert
ATLANTIC OCEAN
INDIAN OCEAN
Madagascar
Equator
Tropic of Cancer
Tropic of Capricorn
Prime Meridian

## Land use

| | rough grazing |
| | shifting cultivation |
| | mixed subsistence |
| | rice subsistence |
| | subsistence crops |
| | grazing and stock rearing |
| | mixed farming |
| | Mediterranean farming |
| | plantation |
| | specialized horticulture |
| | industrial areas |
| | unproductive land |

## Livestock

- sheep
- cattle
- camels

## Crops

- groundnuts
- cocoa
- coffee
- tea
- palm products
- tobacco
- fruit
- dates
- sugar
- cotton
- rubber

## Minerals

- iron ore
- gold
- silver
- diamonds
- tin
- copper
- bauxite
- phosphates

## Energy

- coal
- oil
- gas
- hydro

### Map labels (economy map)

Casablanca, Algiers, Tunis, Alexandria, Cairo, Lagos/Ibadan, Brazzaville, Kinshasa, Nairobi, Lubumbashi, Ndola, Johannesburg, Durban, Cape Town

### Map labels (population map)

Algiers, Rabat-Salé, Casablanca, Tunis, Tripoli, Alexandria, El Gîza, Cairo, Dakar, Conakry, Ibadan, Lagos, Abidjan, Accra, Douala, Omdurman, Khartoum, Addis Ababa, Mogadishu, Kampala, Nairobi, Kinshasa, Dar es Salaam, Luanda, Lusaka, Harare, Antananarivo, Pretoria, Maputo, Johannesburg, Durban, Cape Town

Tropic of Cancer
Equator
Tropic of Capricorn
Prime Meridian

Zenithal Equal Area Projection

© Oxford University Press

## Population density

people per square kilometre

| | |
| --- | --- |
| | over 700 |
| | 200–700 |
| | 100–200 |
| | 10–100 |
| | 1–10 |
| | under 1 |

## Major cities

population in millions

| | |
| --- | --- |
| ■ | over 3 |
| □ | 1–3 |
| ● | 0.5–1 |
| · | 0.1–0.5 |

## Projected population growth of selected African cities, 2005–2015

millions of people

| | 2005 | 2015 |
| --- | --- | --- |

Cities: Casablanca, Cairo, Lagos, Douala, Nairobi, Kinshasa, Dar es Salaam, Johannesburg

Scale 1 : 55 000 000 (main map)

**Selected tourist sites**
- 🏛 cultural heritage centres
- ⋰ archaeological sites
- ✳ sites of natural beauty
- ⬤ National Parks and wildlife reserves
- ⬤ coastal tourism areas and resorts

land height
metres
2000
500
0

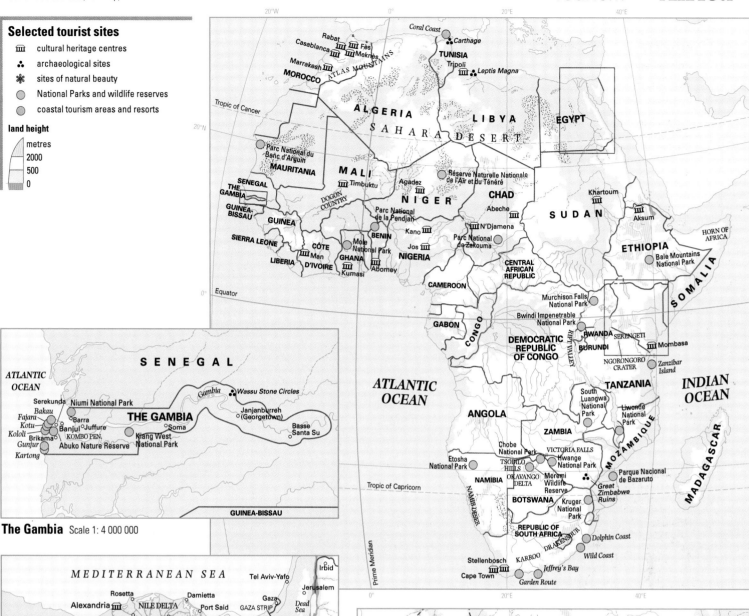

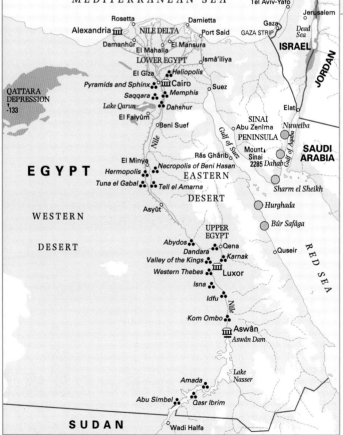

**The Gambia** Scale 1 : 4 000 000

**Nile Valley and Eastern Egypt** Scale 1 : 10 000 000

**Kenya** Scale 1 : 10 000 000

Zenithal Equal Area Projection    © Oxford University Press

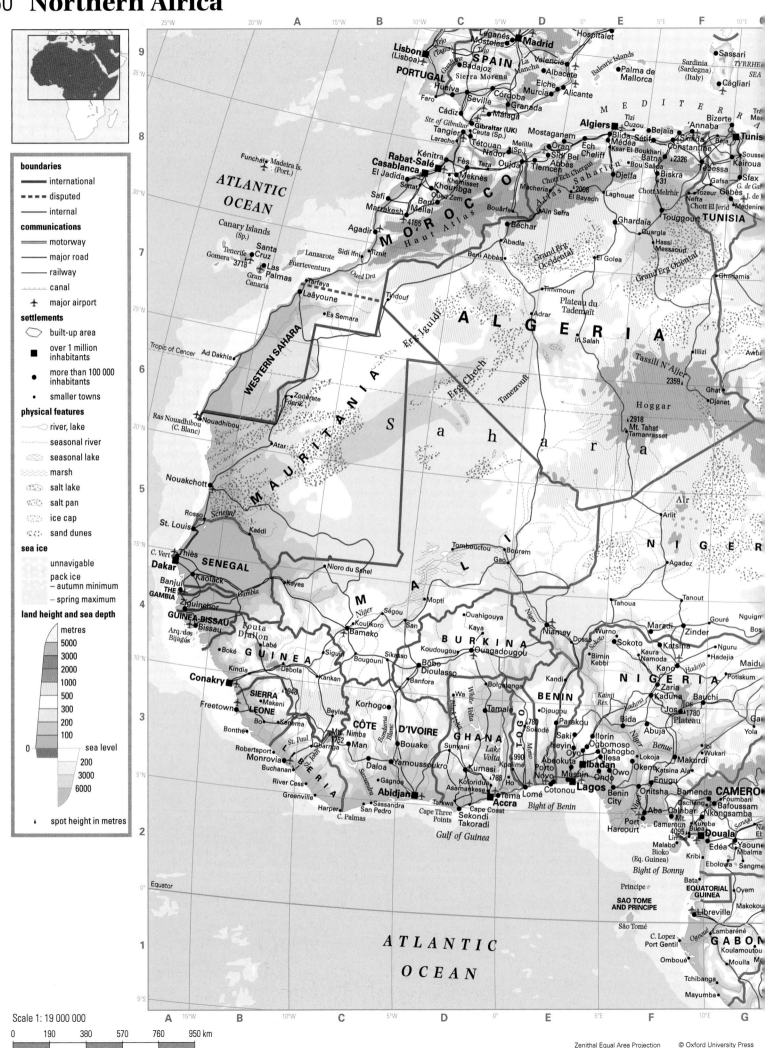

**boundaries**
—— international
- - - disputed
— internal
**communications**
=== motorway
—— major road
— railway
+++ canal
✈ major airport
**settlements**
⬡ built-up area
■ over 1 million inhabitants
● more than 100 000 inhabitants
• smaller towns
**physical features**
river, lake
seasonal river
seasonal lake
marsh
salt lake
salt pan
ice cap
sand dunes
**sea ice**
unnavigable
pack ice
– autumn minimum
– spring maximum
**land height and sea depth**
metres
5000
3000
2000
1000
500
300
200
100
0 sea level
200
3000
6000
▲ spot height in metres

Scale 1: 19 000 000

0    190    380    570    760    950 km

Zenithal Equal Area Projection    © Oxford University Press

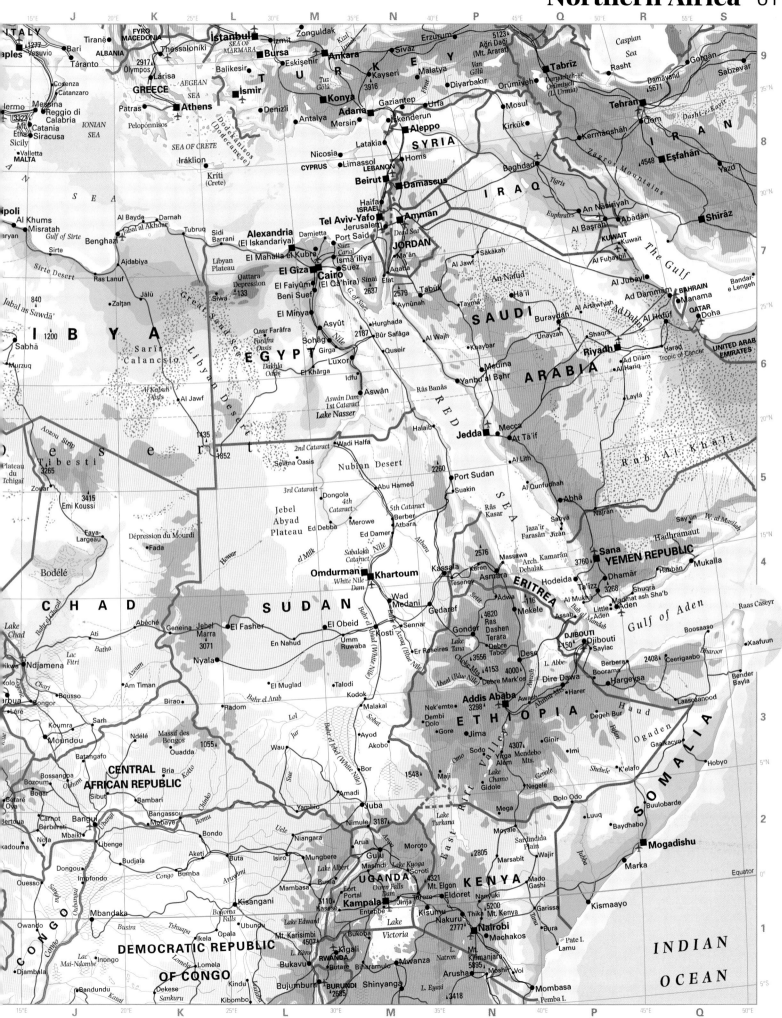

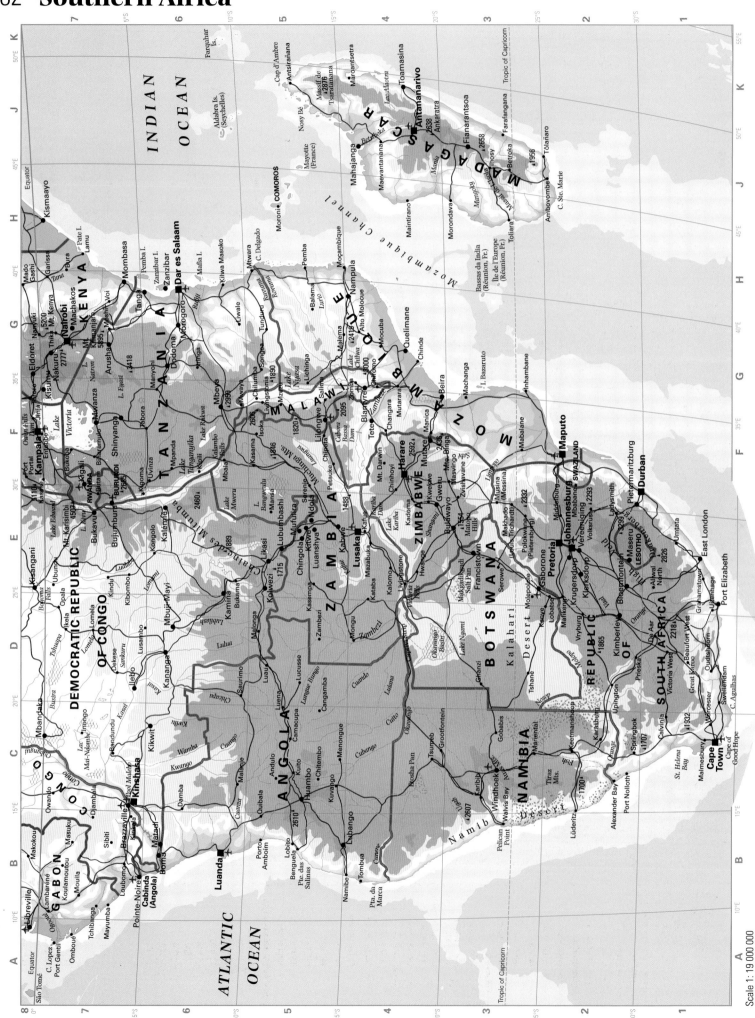

Scale 1 : 19 000 000

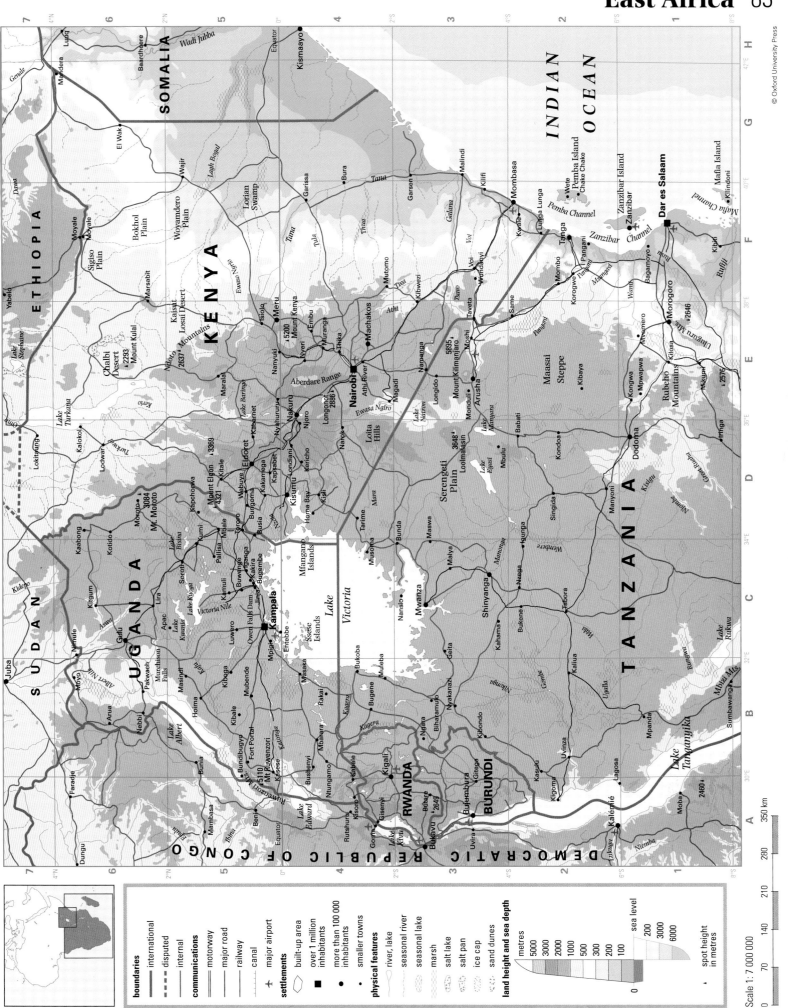

© Oxford University Press

Scale 1: 44 000 000 (main map)

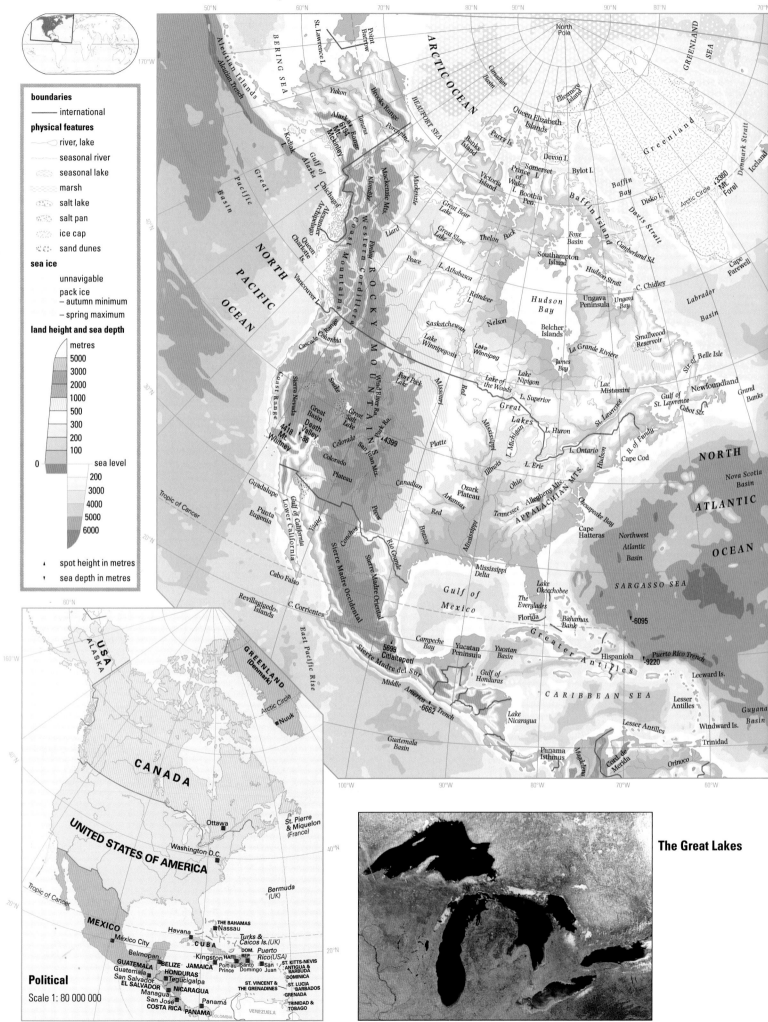

**The Great Lakes**

Political
Scale 1: 80 000 000

Oblique Mercator Projection    © Oxford University Press

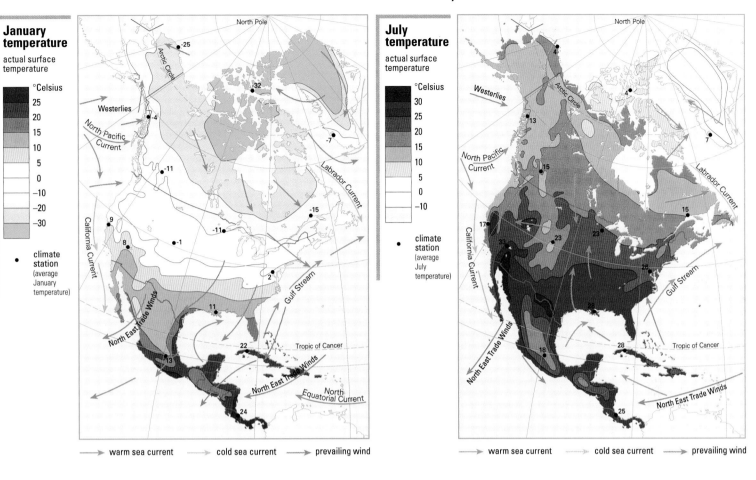

**January temperature**

actual surface temperature

°Celsius
25
20
15
10
5
0
−10
−20
−30

● climate station (average January temperature)

⟶ warm sea current ⟶ cold sea current ⟶ prevailing wind

**July temperature**

actual surface temperature

°Celsius
30
25
20
15
10
5
0
−10

● climate station (average July temperature)

⟶ warm sea current ⟶ cold sea current ⟶ prevailing wind

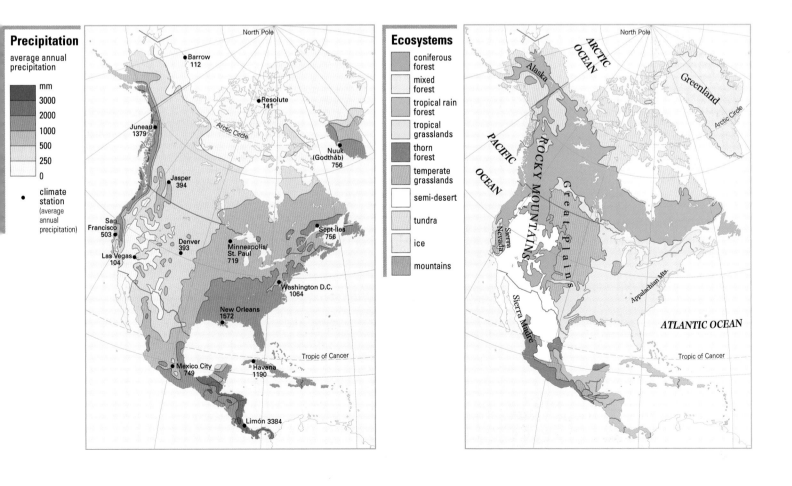

**Precipitation**

average annual precipitation

mm
3000
2000
1000
500
250
0

● climate station (average annual precipitation)

Barrow 112
Resolute 141
Juneau 1379
Nuuk (Godthåb) 756
Jasper 394
San Francisco 503
Denver 393
Minneapolis/ St. Paul 719
Sept-Îles 756
Las Vegas 104
Washington D.C. 1064
New Orleans 1572
Mexico City 749
Havana 1190
Limón 3384

**Ecosystems**

coniferous forest
mixed forest
tropical rain forest
tropical grasslands
thorn forest
temperate grasslands
semi-desert
tundra
ice
mountains

ARCTIC OCEAN
Alaska
Greenland
Arctic Circle
PACIFIC OCEAN
ROCKY MOUNTAINS
Great Plains
Sierra Nevada
Sierra Madre
Appalachian Mts.
ATLANTIC OCEAN
Tropic of Cancer
North Pole

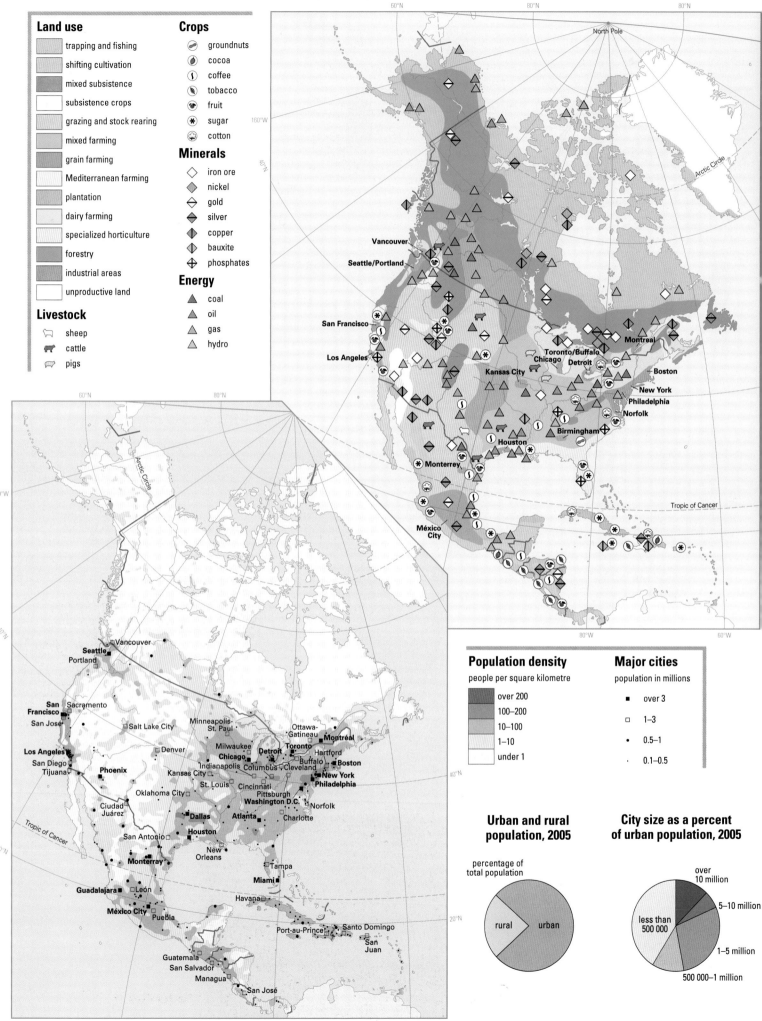

## Land use

- trapping and fishing
- shifting cultivation
- mixed subsistence
- subsistence crops
- grazing and stock rearing
- mixed farming
- grain farming
- Mediterranean farming
- plantation
- dairy farming
- specialized horticulture
- forestry
- industrial areas
- unproductive land

### Livestock

- sheep
- cattle
- pigs

## Crops

- groundnuts
- cocoa
- coffee
- tobacco
- fruit
- sugar
- cotton

## Minerals

- iron ore
- nickel
- gold
- silver
- copper
- bauxite
- phosphates

## Energy

- coal
- oil
- gas
- hydro

### Population density

people per square kilometre

- over 200
- 100–200
- 10–100
- 1–10
- under 1

### Major cities

population in millions

- over 3
- 1–3
- 0.5–1
- 0.1–0.5

### Urban and rural population, 2005

percentage of total population

rural   urban

### City size as a percent of urban population, 2005

over 10 million
5–10 million
1–5 million
less than 500 000
500 000–1 million

Scale 1: 40 000 000 (main map)

## Selected tourist sites

Great Lakes — tourist regions
🏛 cultural heritage centres
✳ sites of natural beauty
⬤ National Parks
⬤ coastal tourism areas and resorts
△ ski and mountain areas and resorts
★ leisure parks

land height

metres
2000
500
0

### Main map

120°W  100°W  80°W  60°W

**CANADA**

Vancouver  △Whistler  △Lake Louise
Seattle  △Alpental
Sun Valley  Yellowstone National Park
Squaw Valley  Salt Lake City
San Francisco 🏛  Heavenly
Sea World  Mammoth Mountain  Steamboat  Rocky Mountain National Park
Santa Cruz Beach  Yosemite National Park  Copper Mountain  Winter Park  Vail  Aspen  Snowmass
Universal Studios  Las Vegas  Grand Canyon National Park
Los Angeles 🏛  Knott's Berry Farm
Tijuana 🏛

**ROCKY MOUNTAINS**

**UNITED STATES**

Camp Snoopy
Québec 🏛
Montréal 🏛  Sunday River
Mount Snow  Killington
Niagara Falls  New England  Boston
Six Flags Great America  Chicago  Cedar Point  New York  Six Flags Hurricane Harbour
Kings Island  Washington D.C.
Memphis  Kings Dominion  Busch Gardens
Six Flags Over Georgia

**ATLANTIC OCEAN**

40°N
20°N

Walt Disney World
Universal Studios
Everglades National Park

Astro World
Houston  New Orleans
Six Flags Fiesta Texas
**Gulf of Mexico**

**MEXICO**
**BAJA CALIFORNIA**

Chihuahua 🏛
Guaymas
Tropic of Cancer
Monterrey 🏛
Mazatlan  Guadalajara 🏛
Guanajuato 🏛  Chichén Itzá  Cancún
San Blas  San Miguel de Allende  Uxmal 🏛  Isla de Cozumel
Queretaro 🏛  Yucatan Tulum
Puerto Vallarta  Tula 🏛  Teotihuacan 🏛  Yucatan Peninsula
Lago de Chapala  México City  Palenque 🏛
Lago de Patzcuaro  Morelia 🏛
Acapulco  Oaxaca 🏛
Puerto Escondido  San Cristóbal de las Casas 🏛

**PACIFIC OCEAN**

Greater Antilles
Lesser Antilles
**CARIBBEAN SEA**

---

## The Caribbean   Scale 1: 15 000 000

Havana
**CUBA**
Isla de la Juventud
Cayo Largo
Cayman Islands (UK)  Grand Cayman
Seven Mile Beach
Montego Bay
Negril Beach
**JAMAICA**  Kingston

Great Exuma  Long Island  Crooked I.
**THE BAHAMAS**
Acklins I.  Mayaguana
Caicos Passage
Great Inagua  Turks and Caicos Is. (UK)
Turks I. Passage

**West Indies**

Windward  Passage
**HAITI**  **DOMINICAN REPUBLIC**
Port-au-Prince  Santo Domingo

**Greater**  **Antilles**

Leeward Islands
Virgin Is. (UK/USA)
Cane Garden Bay  Shoal Bay
San Juan  Trunk Bay  Anguilla (UK)
**Puerto Rico (USA)**  St. Croix (USA)  St. Jean  Barbuda  **ANTIGUA AND BARBUDA**
Luquillo Beach  Antigua
**ST. KITTS AND NEVIS**
Montserrat (UK)  Grande Terre  Guadeloupe (Fr.)
Marie Galante
**DOMINICA**
Le Diamant  Martinique (Fr.)
**ST. LUCIA**
St. Vincent  **BARBADOS**
**ST. VINCENT AND THE GRENADINES**
Windward  **GRENADA**
Grand Anse Beach
Port of Spain  Tobago  **TRINIDAD AND TOBAGO**  Trinidad

**Lesser**  **Antilles**

**CARIBBEAN  SEA**

Netherland Antilles
Aruba (Neths.)  Curaçao (Neths.)  Bonaire (Neths.)
Lesser Antilles

---

## Florida   Scale 1: 8 000 000

Walt Disney World:
• The Magic Kingdom
• EPCOT Centre
• Disney-MGM Studios

Jacksonville
Marineland
Daytona Beach
John F. Kenedy Space Centre
Orlando  Cape Canaveral
Universal Studios  Walt Disney World Resort Complex
Busch Gardens
St. Petersburg  Tampa  Tampa Bay
**FLORIDA**
Sarasota  Lake Okeechobee
Charlotte Harbour  Palm Beach
Fort Myers  Fort Lauderdale
Big Cypress National Preserve  Miami Beach
Miami
Everglades National Park  Biscayne National Park
**Gulf of Mexico**
Florida Keys
Key West  Straits of Florida

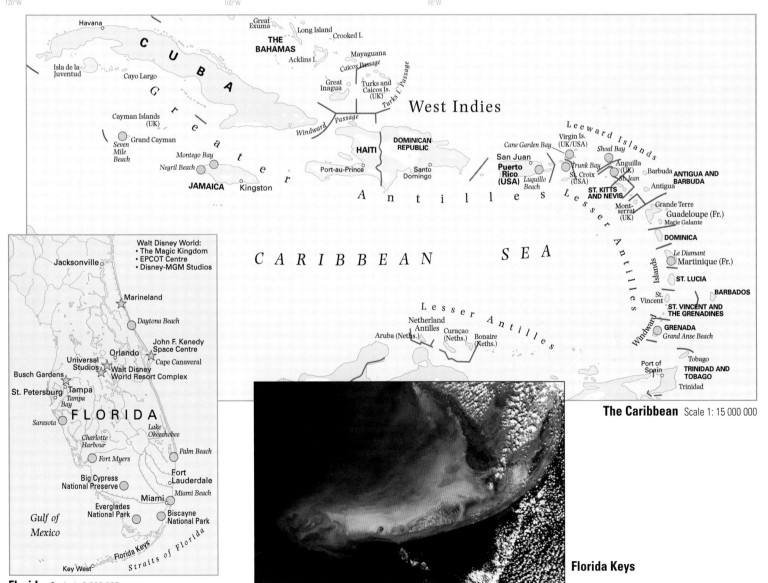

**Florida Keys**

Oblique Mercator Projection      © Oxford University Press

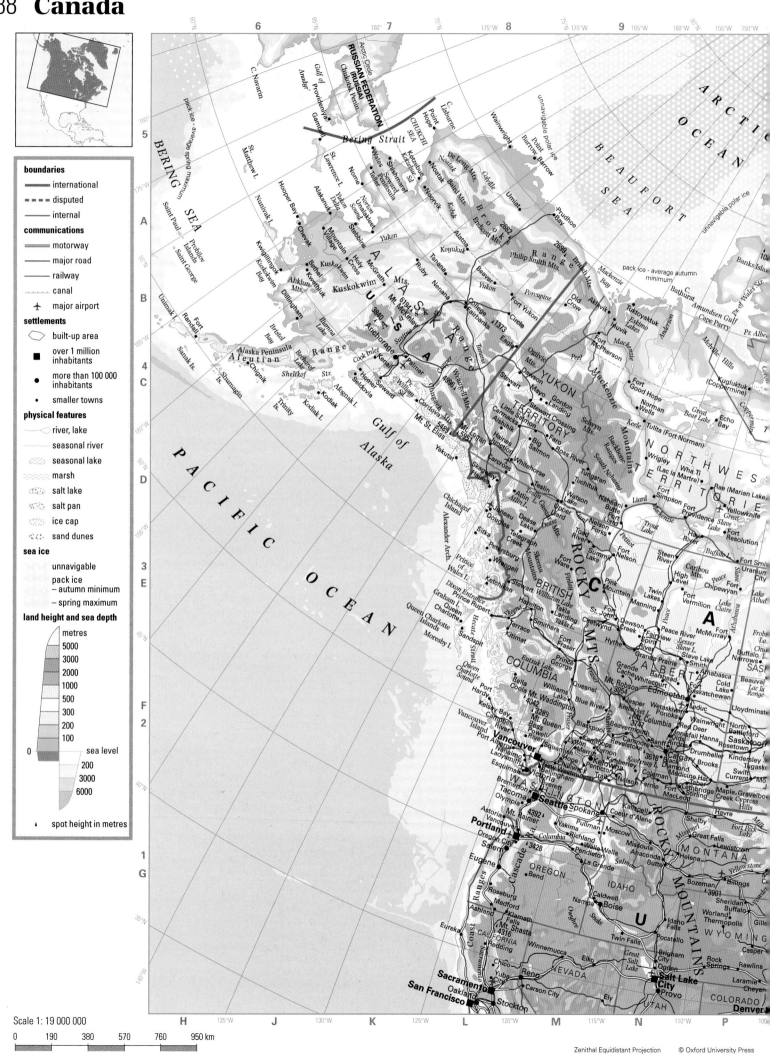

Zenithal Equidistant Projection

Scale 1 : 19 000 000

0   190   380   570   760   950 km

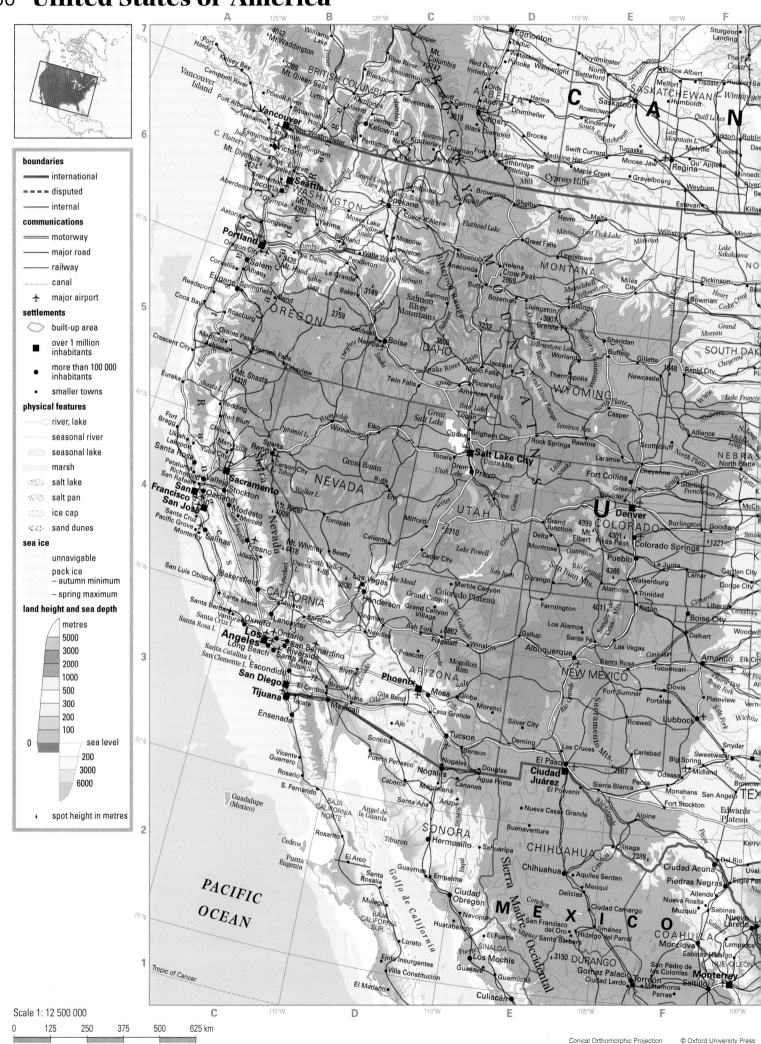

Conical Orthomorphic Projection    © Oxford University Press

Scale 1: 12 500 000

0    125    250    375    500    625 km

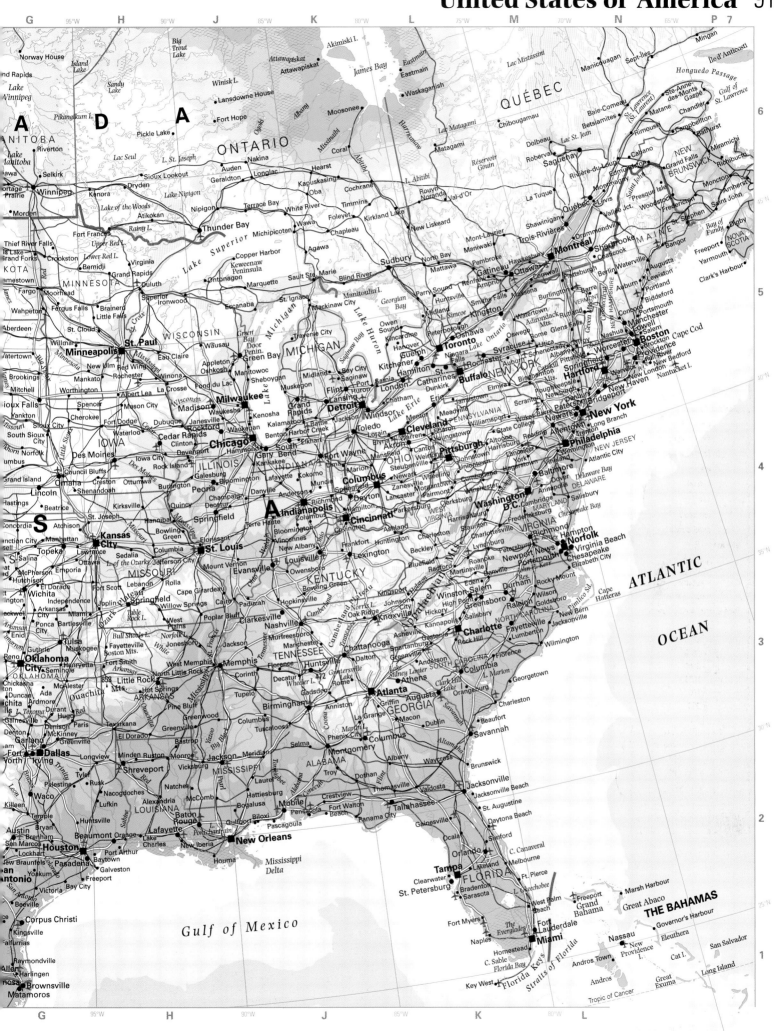

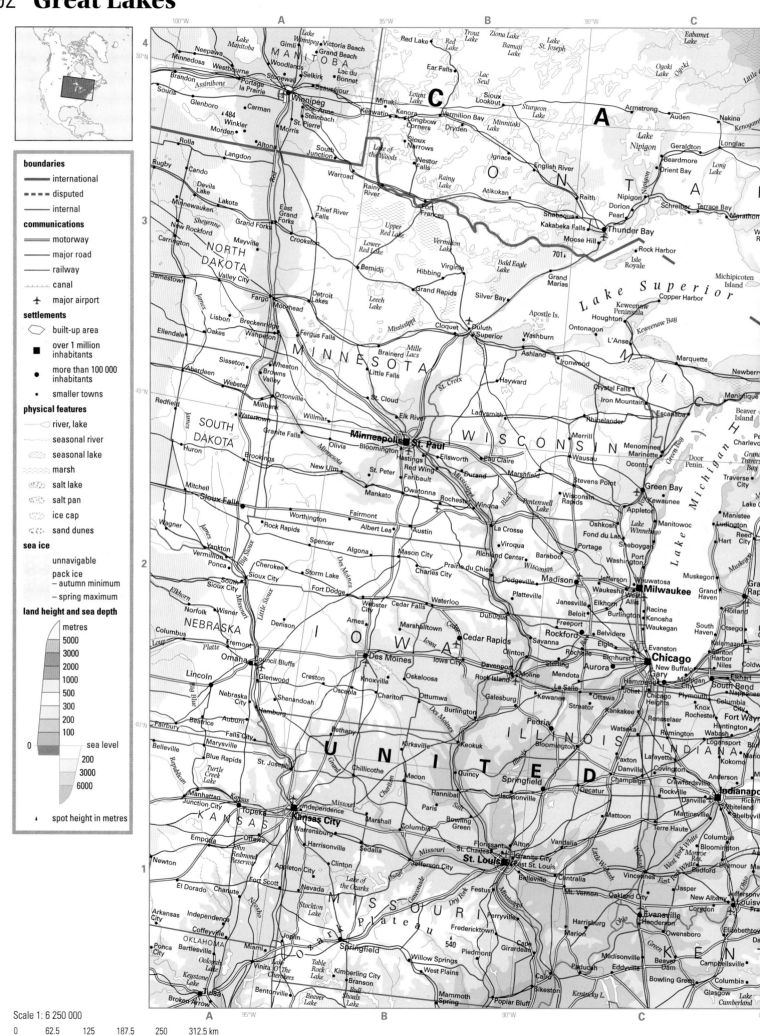

## boundaries

— international
- - - disputed
— internal

## communications
— motorway
— major road
— railway
......... canal
✈ major airport

## settlements
⬡ built-up area
■ over 1 million inhabitants
● more than 100 000 inhabitants
• smaller towns

## physical features
river, lake
seasonal river
seasonal lake
marsh
salt lake
salt pan
ice cap
sand dunes

## sea ice
unnavigable
pack ice
– autumn minimum
– spring maximum

## land height and sea depth
metres
5000
3000
2000
1000
500
300
200
100
0 sea level
200
3000
6000

▲ spot height in metres

Scale 1: 6 250 000

0    62.5    125    187.5    250    312.5 km

Conical Orthomorphic Projection      © Oxford University Press

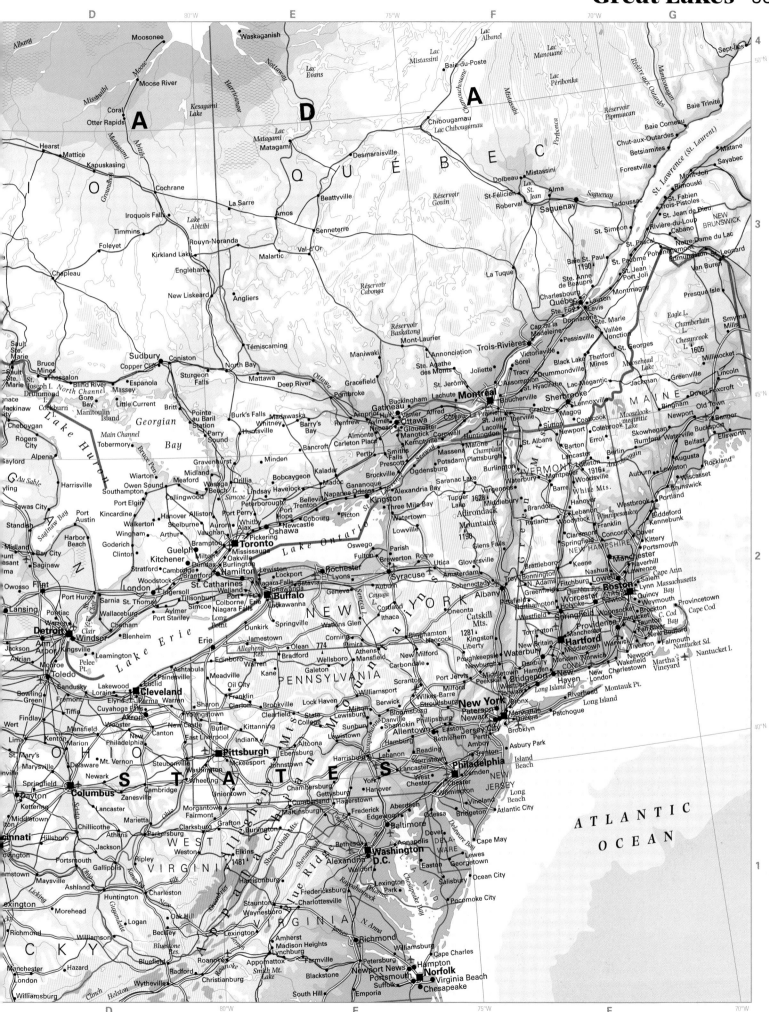

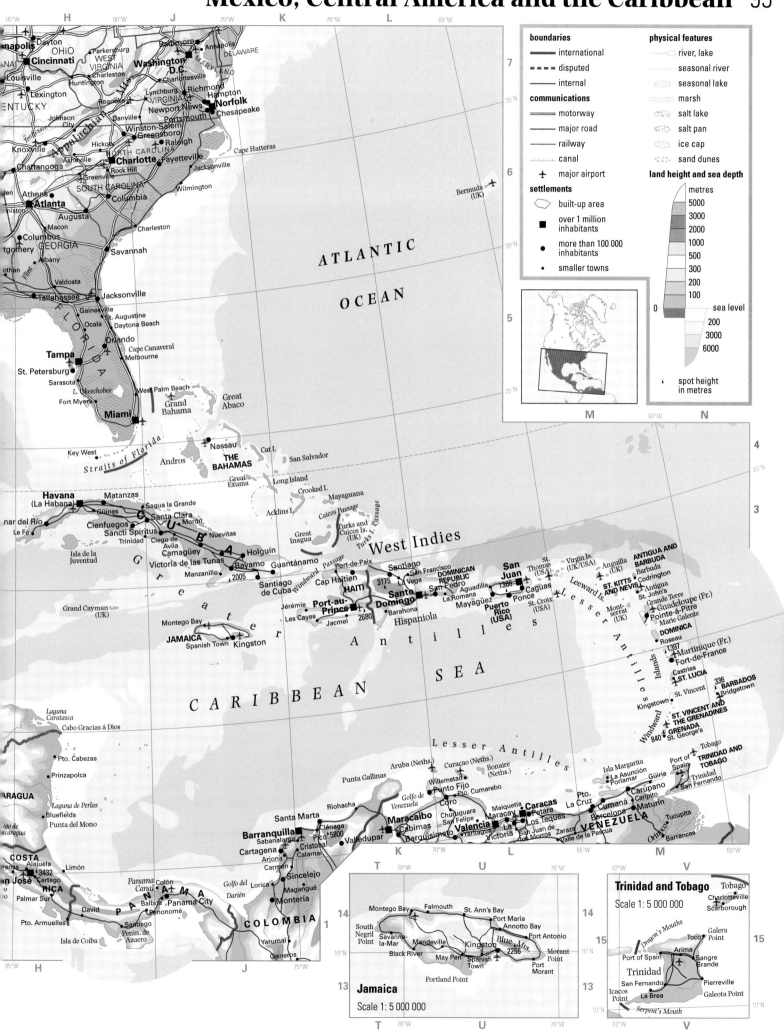

**boundaries**
— international
--- disputed
— internal

**communications**
motorway
major road
railway
canal
✈ major airport

**settlements**
built-up area
■ over 1 million inhabitants
● more than 100 000 inhabitants
• smaller towns

**physical features**
river, lake
seasonal river
seasonal lake
marsh
salt lake
salt pan
ice cap
sand dunes

**land height and sea depth**
metres
5000
3000
2000
1000
500
300
200
100
0  sea level
200
3000
6000

▲ spot height in metres

ATLANTIC OCEAN

Bermuda (UK)

CARIBBEAN SEA

West Indies

Greater Antilles

Lesser Antilles

Windward Passage

Turks Island Passage

Mona Passage

**OHIO**
Dayton
Cincinnati
Louisville
Lexington
KENTUCKY
Johnson City
Knoxville
Chattanooga
Tennessee
Parkersburg
WEST VIRGINIA
Charleston
Huntington
Roanoke
Danville
Lynchburg
VIRGINIA
Richmond
Hampton
Newport News
Norfolk
Portsmouth
Chesapeake
Winston-Salem
Greensboro
Durham
Raleigh
Hickory
NORTH CAROLINA
Charlotte
Fayetteville
Rock Hill
SOUTH CAROLINA
Greenville
Columbia
Charleston
Athens
GEORGIA
Atlanta
Augusta
Macon
Columbus
Albany
Montgomery
Tallahassee
Valdosta
Flint
FLORIDA
Gainesville
Ocala
St. Augustine
Daytona Beach
Orlando
Cape Canaveral
Melbourne
Tampa
St. Petersburg
Sarasota
L. Okeechobee
West Palm Beach
Fort Myers
Miami
Key West

Washington D.C.
MARYLAND
Baltimore
Annapolis
Annapolis
DELAWARE
Charlottesville
Cape Hatteras
Jacksonville
Wilmington
Savannah
Jacksonville

Straits of Florida
Nassau
THE BAHAMAS
Andros
Cat I.
San Salvador
Great Exuma
Long Island
Crooked I.
Acklins I.
Mayaguana
Caicos Passage
Great Inagua
Turks and Caicos Is. (UK)
Grand Bahama
Great Abaco

Havana (La Habana)
Matanzas
Sagua la Grande
Santa Clara
Morón
Güines
Cienfuegos
Sancti Spíritus
Ciego de Ávila
Camagüey
Nuevitas
Victoria de las Tunas
Bayamo
Manzanillo
2005
Holguín
Guantánamo
Santiago de Cuba
nar del Río
Le Fé
Isla de la Juventud
Trinidad
CUBA
Grand Cayman (UK)

Cap Haïtien
Port-de-Paix
HAITI
3175
Jérémie
Port-au-Prince
Les Cayes
Jacmel
2680
Santiago
San Francisco
La Vega
DOMINICAN REPUBLIC
San Pedro
Santo Domingo
La Romana
Barahona
Hispaniola
Montego Bay
JAMAICA
Spanish Town
Kingston

San Juan
Caguas
1338
Mayagüez
Ponce
Puerto Rico (USA)
St. Thomas
Virgin Is. (UK/USA)
St. Croix (USA)
Aguadilla

Anguilla (UK)
ANTIGUA AND BARBUDA
Barbuda
Codrington
St. John's
Antigua
ST. KITTS AND NEVIS
Leeward Is.
Montserrat (UK)
Grande Terre
Guadeloupe (Fr.)
Pointe-à-Pitre
Marie Galente
DOMINICA
Roseau
1397
Martinique (Fr.)
Fort-de-France
Castries
ST. LUCIA
336
BARBADOS
Bridgetown
Kingstown
St. Vincent
ST. VINCENT AND THE GRENADINES
840
GRENADA
St. George's
Lesser Antilles
Windward Is.

Tobago
Port of Spain
TRINIDAD AND TOBAGO
Trinidad
San Fernando

Laguna Caratasca
Cabo Gracias á Dios
Pto. Cabezas
Prinzapolca
NICARAGUA
Laguna de Perlas
Bluefields
Punta del Mono
icaragua

COSTA RICA
Alajuela
3432
Cartago
n José
Limón
Palmar Sur
Pto. Armuelles
Isla de Coiba
Penín. de Azuero
Santiago
David
Penonomé
PANAMA
Panama City
Balboa
Colón
Panama Canal
Golfo del Darién
COLOMBIA
Carmen
Lorica
Magangué
Montería
Sincelejo
Calamar
Arjona
Cartagena
Cristóbal
Sabanalarga
Ciénaga
Barranquilla
Santa Marta
Riohacha
Valledupar
Pico 5800
Yarumal
Cisneros

Punta Gallinas
Golfo de Venezuela
Maracaibo
Cabimas
Pico 5800
Barquisimeto
La Victoria
San Juan de los Morros
Zaraza
VENEZUELA
Aruba (Neths.)
Curaçao (Neths.)
Bonaire (Neths.)
Willemstad
Punto Fijo
Pto. Cumarebo
Coro
Churuguara
San Felipe
Maiquetía
Caracas
Petare
Los Teques
Maracay
Valencia
La Cruz
Barcelona
Cumaná
Caripito
Maturín
Güiria
Carúpano
San Fernando
Trinidad
Isla Margarita
La Asunción
Porlamar
Pto. La Cruz
Valle de la Pascua
Orinoco
Barrancas
Tucupita

**Jamaica**
Scale 1 : 5 000 000
Montego Bay
Falmouth
St. Ann's Bay
Port Maria
Annotto Bay
Port Antonio
South Negril Point
Savanna-la-Mar
Mandeville
Black River
May Pen
Spanish Town
Kingston
Blue Mts. 2256
Morant Bay
Morant Point
Portland Point

**Trinidad and Tobago**
Scale 1 : 5 000 000
Tobago
Charlotteville
Scarborough
Dragon's Mouths
Toco
Galera Point
Arima
Port of Spain
Sangre Grande
Trinidad
Pierreville
San Fernando
La Brea
Galeota Point
Icacos Point
Serpent's Mouth

© Oxford University Press

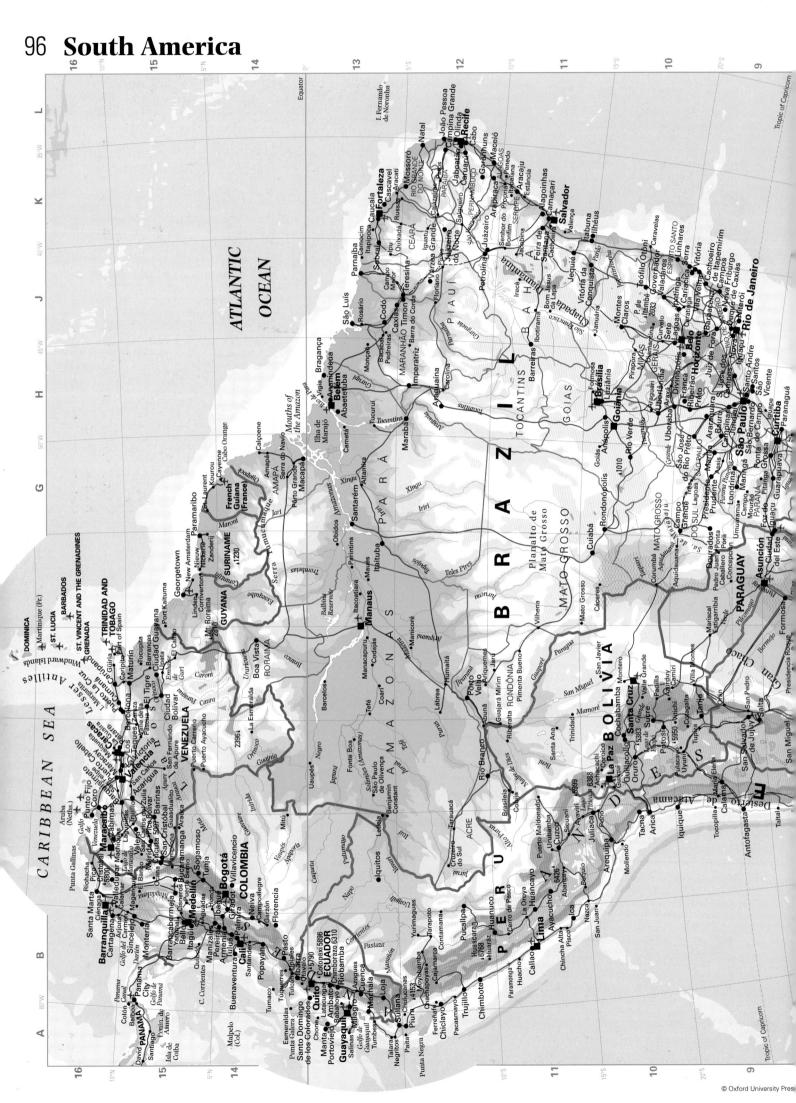

ATLANTIC
OCEAN

CARIBBEAN SEA

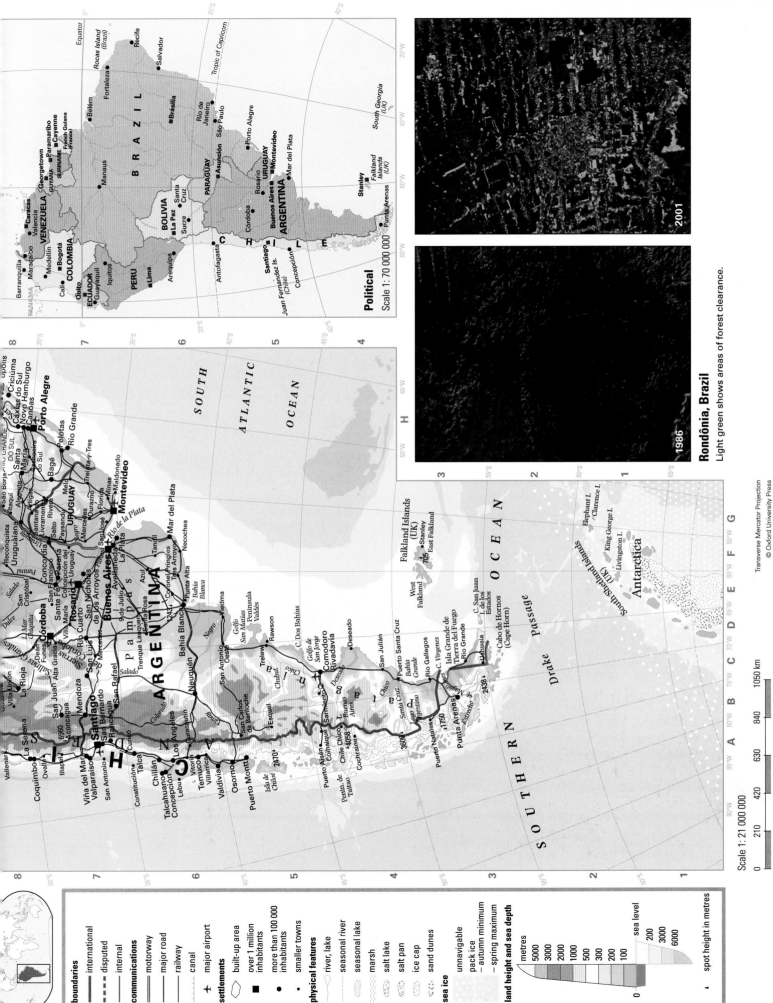

**Rondônia, Brazil**
Light green shows areas of forest clearance.

2001

1986

**Political**
Scale 1:70 000 000

Scale 1:21 000 000

Transverse Mercator Projection
© Oxford University Press

Scale 1: 70 000 000

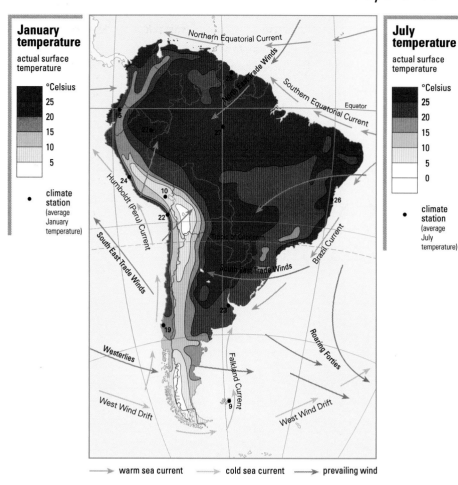

**January temperature**

actual surface temperature

°Celsius
25
20
15
10
5

● climate station (average January temperature)

Northern Equatorial Current
North East Trade Winds
Southern Equatorial Current
Equator
Humboldt (Peru) Current
South East Trade Winds
South East Trade Winds
Tropic of Capricorn
Brazil Current
Westerlies
Falkland Current
Roaring Forties
West Wind Drift
West Wind Drift

→ warm sea current    → cold sea current    → prevailing wind

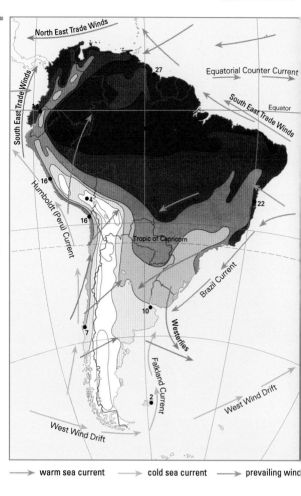

**July temperature**

actual surface temperature

°Celsius
25
20
15
10
5
0

● climate station (average July temperature)

North East Trade Winds
South East Trade Winds
Equatorial Counter Current
South East Trade Winds
Equator
Humboldt (Peru) Current
Tropic of Capricorn
Brazil Current
Westerlies
Falkland Current
West Wind Drift
West Wind Drift

→ warm sea current    → cold sea current    → prevailing wind

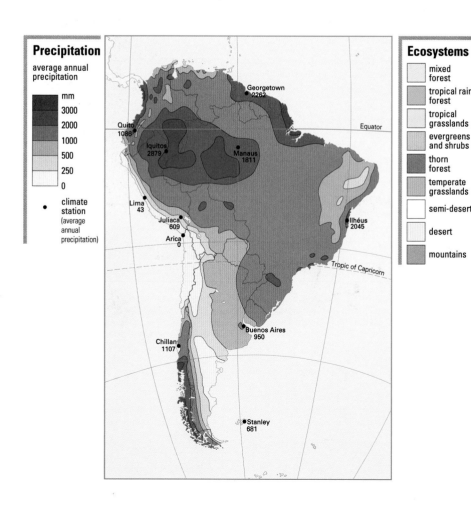

**Precipitation**

average annual precipitation

mm
3000
2000
1000
500
250
0

● climate station (average annual precipitation)

Georgetown 2262
Quito 1086
Iquitos 2879
Manaus 1811
Lima 43
Juliaca 609
Arica 0
Ilhéus 2045
Chillan 1107
Buenos Aires 950
Stanley 681
Equator
Tropic of Capricorn

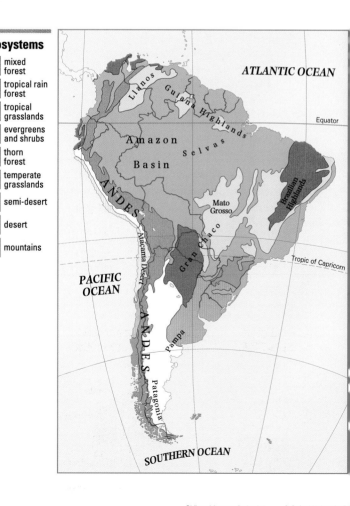

**Ecosystems**

mixed forest
tropical rain forest
tropical grasslands
evergreens and shrubs
thorn forest
temperate grasslands
semi-desert
desert
mountains

ATLANTIC OCEAN
Llanos
Guiana Highlands
Amazon Basin
Selvas
Equator
ANDES
Atacama Desert
Mato Grosso
Brazilian Highlands
PACIFIC OCEAN
Gran Chaco
Tropic of Capricorn
Pampa
ANDES
Patagonia
SOUTHERN OCEAN

Oblique Mercator Projection    © Oxford University P.

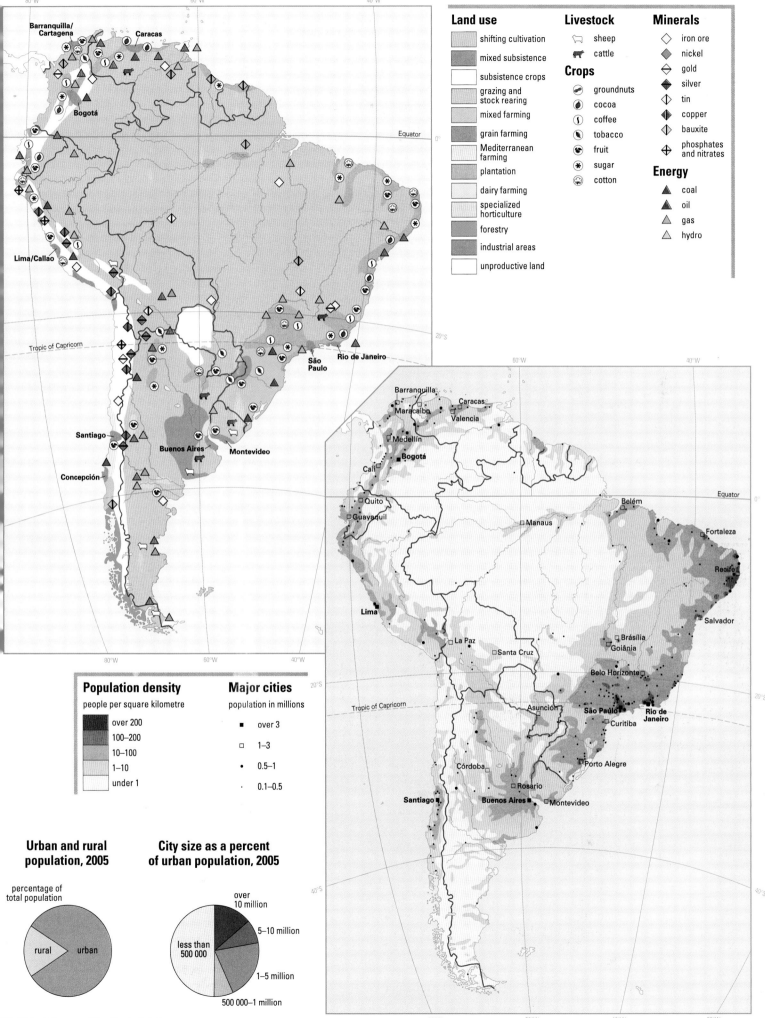

**Land use**
- shifting cultivation
- mixed subsistence
- subsistence crops
- grazing and stock rearing
- mixed farming
- grain farming
- Mediterranean farming
- plantation
- dairy farming
- specialized horticulture
- forestry
- industrial areas
- unproductive land

**Livestock**
- sheep
- cattle

**Crops**
- groundnuts
- cocoa
- coffee
- tobacco
- fruit
- sugar
- cotton

**Minerals**
- iron ore
- nickel
- gold
- silver
- tin
- copper
- bauxite
- phosphates and nitrates

**Energy**
- coal
- oil
- gas
- hydro

**Population density**
people per square kilometre
- over 200
- 100–200
- 10–100
- 1–10
- under 1

**Major cities**
population in millions
- over 3
- 1–3
- 0.5–1
- 0.1–0.5

**Urban and rural population, 2005**

percentage of total population

rural | urban

**City size as a percent of urban population, 2005**

- over 10 million
- 5–10 million
- less than 500 000
- 1–5 million
- 500 000–1 million

Scale 1 : 80 000 000

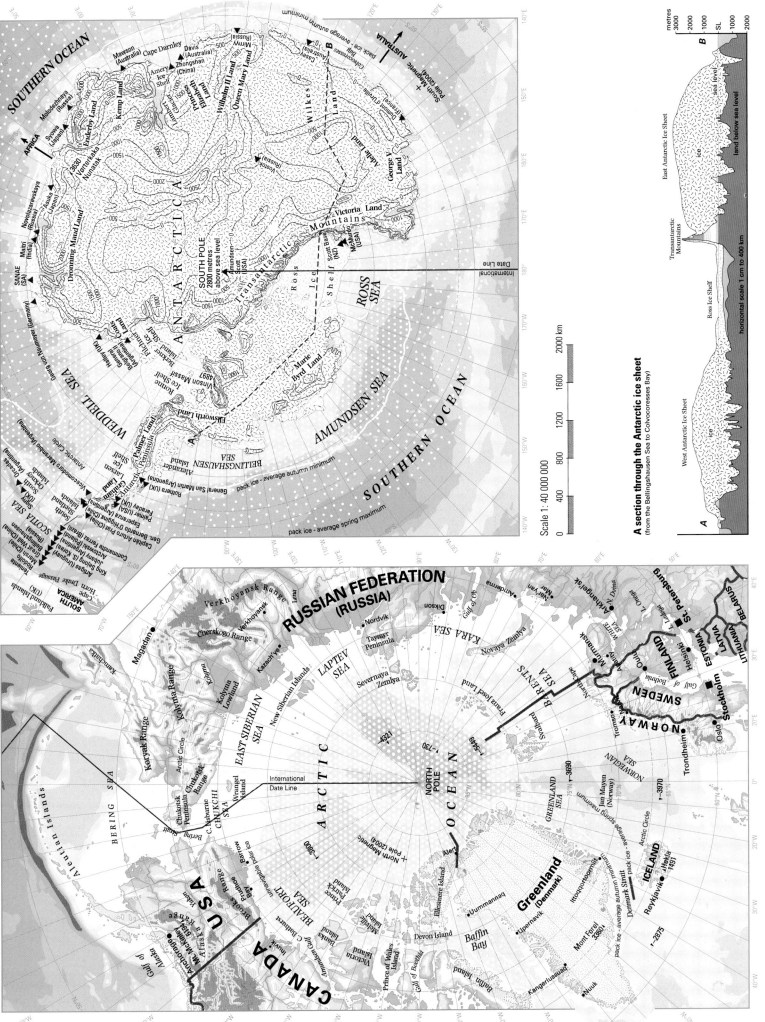

**A section through the Antarctic ice sheet**
(from the Bellingshausen Sea to Colvocoresses Bay)

Scale 1 : 40 000 000

SOUTHERN OCEAN

SOUTHERN OCEAN

WEDDELL SEA

BELLINGSHAUSEN SEA

AMUNDSEN SEA

ROSS SEA

SCOTIA SEA

A N T A R C T I C A

SOUTH POLE
2800 metres
above sea level

Dronning Maud Land

Enderby Land

Kemp Land

Princess Elizabeth Land

Wilhelm II Land

Queen Mary Land

Wilkes Land

Adélie Land

George V Land

Victoria Land

Marie Byrd Land

Ellsworth Land

Palmer Land

Coats Land

Ronne Ice Shelf

Filchner Ice Shelf

Berkner Island

Amery Ice Shelf

Ross Ice Shelf

Larsen Ice Shelf

Alexander Island

Vinson Massif 4897

Transantarctic Mountains

Antarctic Peninsula

Antarctic Circle

International Date Line

pack ice - average autumn minimum

pack ice - average spring maximum

**ARCTIC map (lower):**

RUSSIAN FEDERATION
(RUSSIA)

USA

CANADA

Greenland (Denmark)

ICELAND

NORWAY

SWEDEN

FINLAND

ESTONIA

LATVIA

LITHUANIA

BELARUS

NORTH POLE

ARCTIC OCEAN

International Date Line

Arctic Circle

BERING SEA

CHUKCHI SEA

EAST SIBERIAN SEA

LAPTEV SEA

KARA SEA

BARENTS SEA

NORWEGIAN SEA

GREENLAND SEA

BEAUFORT SEA

Baffin Bay

Denmark Strait

North Magnetic Pole (2004)

Aleutian Islands

Verkhoyansk Range

Cherskogo Range

Koryak Range

Kolyma Range

Brooks Range

Alaska Range

Reykjavik

Nuuk

St. Petersburg

Helsinki

Stockholm

Oslo

Trondheim

Tromsø

Murmansk

Arkhangel'sk

Dikson

Magadan

Norilsk

Nordvik

Verkhoyansk

Anchorage

Barrow

Alert

Hekla 1491

Mont Forel 3360

-4321

-730

-3800

-5449

-3690

-3970

-2875

Zenithal Equidistant Projection    © Oxford University Press

Equatorial scale 1: 95 000 000 (main map)

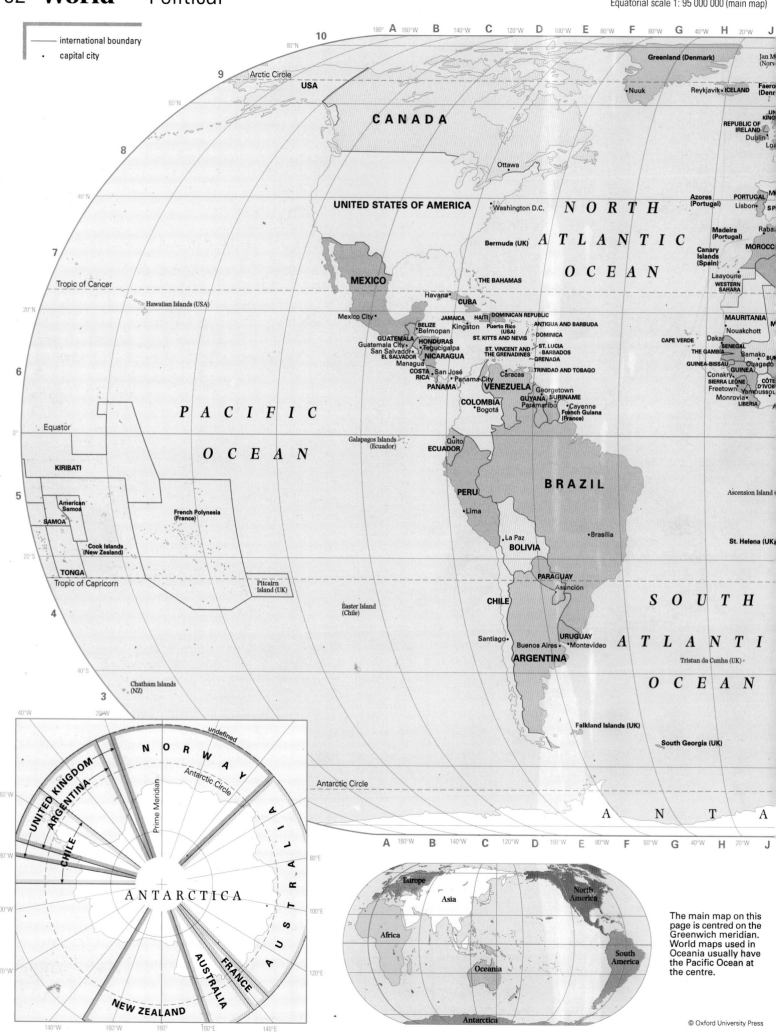

international boundary
• capital city

10  9  8  7  6  5  4  3

A 180° 160°W B 140°W C 120°W D 100°W E 80°W F 60°W G 40°W H 20°W J

80°N
Arctic Circle
60°N
40°N
Tropic of Cancer
20°N
Equator 0°
20°S
Tropic of Capricorn
40°S

**Greenland (Denmark)**
Jan M(Norv)

**USA**
Nuuk •  Reykjavik • **ICELAND**  Faeroe(Denr)

**CANADA**

UN KING
**REPUBLIC OF IRELAND**
Dublin •  Lo

Ottawa •

**UNITED STATES OF AMERICA**  • Washington D.C.

**N O R T H**

Azores (Portugal)  **PORTUGAL**
Lisbon •

**A T L A N T I C**

Madeira (Portugal)  Raba

Bermuda (UK)

**MOROCC**

**O C E A N**

Canary Islands (Spain)

**MEXICO**

Laayoune
**WESTERN SAHARA**

Hawaiian Islands (USA)

Havana •  **THE BAHAMAS**

**CUBA**

Mexico City •

**MAURITANIA**
Nouakchott •

**BELIZE**  **JAMAICA**  **HAITI**  **DOMINICAN REPUBLIC**
Belmopan  Kingston  Puerto Rico (USA)  **ANTIGUA AND BARBUDA**
**GUATEMALA**  **ST. KITTS AND NEVIS**  **DOMINICA**
Guatemala City  **HONDURAS**  **ST. LUCIA**
San Salvador • Tegucigalpa  **ST. VINCENT AND** **BARBADOS**
**EL SALVADOR**  **NICARAGUA**  **THE GRENADINES** **GRENADA**
Managua •  **TRINIDAD AND TOBAGO**
**COSTA**  • San José
**RICA**  • Panama City  Caracas •
**PANAMA**  **VENEZUELA**
Georgetown
**COLOMBIA**  **GUYANA** **SURINAME**
• Bogotá  Paramaribo •  • Cayenne
**French Guiana** (France)

**CAPE VERDE**  Dakar •
**THE GAMBIA**  **SENEGAL**
Bamako •  Ouagadou
**GUINEA-BISSAU**  **GUINEA**
Conakry •  **CÔTE** Yamoussou
**SIERRA LEONE**  **D'IVOIR**
Freetown •
Monrovia •  **LIBERIA**

**P A C I F I C**

Galapagos Islands (Ecuador)

Quito •
**ECUADOR**

**O C E A N**

**KIRIBATI**

American Samoa
French Polynesia (France)
**SAMOA**

Cook Islands (New Zealand)

**TONGA**

Easter Island (Chile)

Pitcairn Island (UK)

**PERU**
• Lima

**B R A Z I L**

Ascension Island •

La Paz •  • Brasília
**BOLIVIA**

St. Helena •

**PARAGUAY**
Asunción •

**CHILE**  **S O U T H**

Chatham Islands (NZ)

Santiago •  **URUGUAY**
Buenos Aires • • Montevideo
**ARGENTINA**

**A T L A N T I**

Tristan da Cunha (UK)

**O C E A N**

Falkland Islands (UK)

South Georgia (UK)

Antarctic Circle

A N T A T A

A 160°W B 140°W C 120°W D 100°W E 80°W F 60°W G 40°W H 20°W J

40°W  20°W

60°W
**UNITED KINGDOM**
**ARGENTINA**
80°W
**CHILE**
100°W
120°W

**N O R W A Y**
undefined

Prime Meridian

Antarctic Circle

**A N T A R C T I C A**

**A U S T R A L I A**
80°E

100°E

**FRANCE**
**AUSTRALIA**
120°E

**NEW ZEALAND**
140°W  160°W  180°  160°E  140°E

Europe
Asia
North America
Africa
Oceania
South America
Antarctica

The main map on this page is centred on the Greenwich meridian. World maps used in Oceania usually have the Pacific Ocean at the centre.

© Oxford University Press

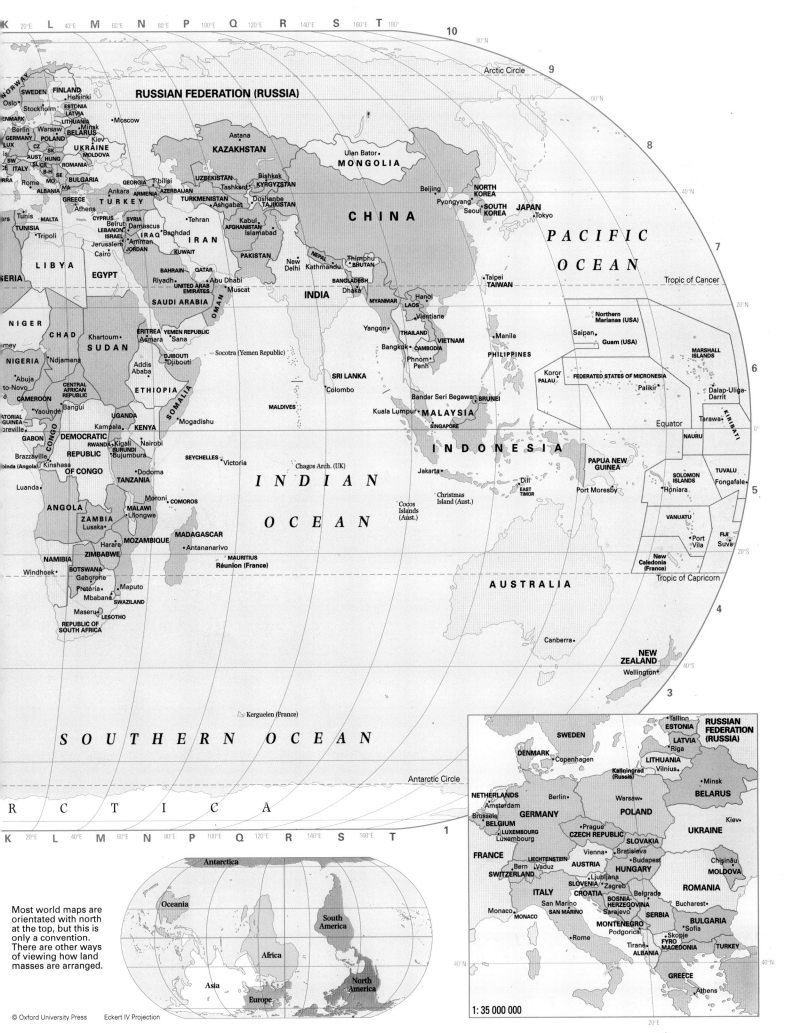

Equatorial scale 1: 95 000 000

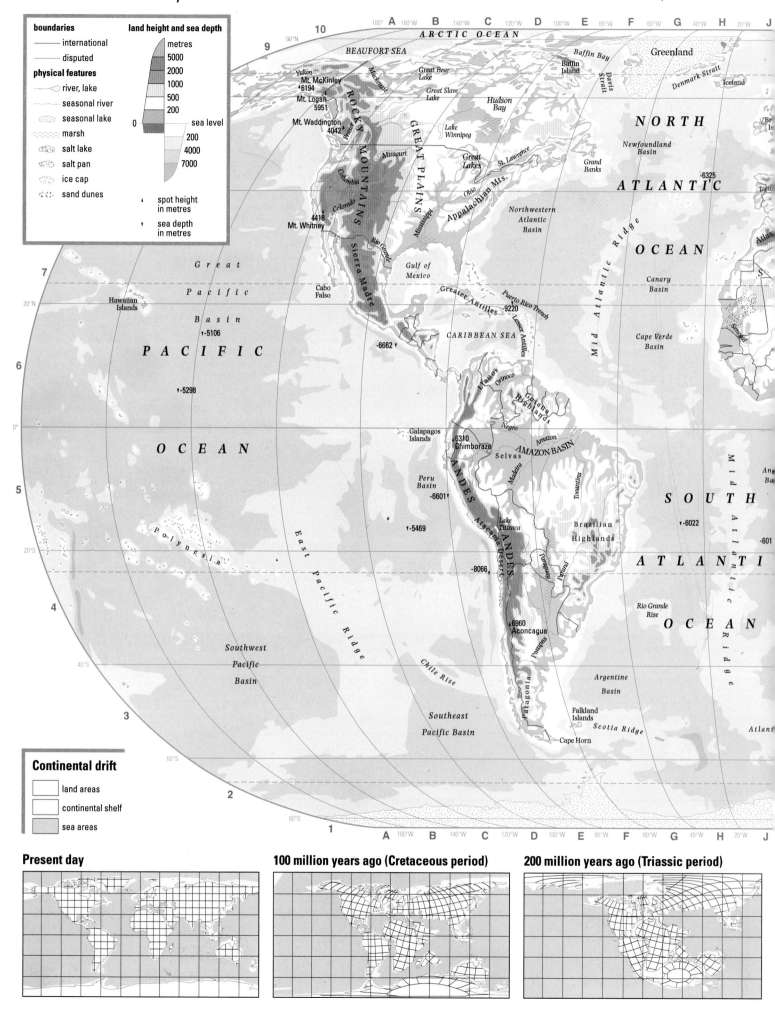

**boundaries**
—— international
········ disputed

**physical features**
~~ river, lake
--- seasonal river
seasonal lake
marsh
salt lake
salt pan
ice cap
sand dunes

**land height and sea depth**
metres
5000
2000
1000
500
200
0 ——— sea level
200
4000
7000

▲ spot height in metres
▼ sea depth in metres

**Continental drift**

land areas
continental shelf
sea areas

**Present day**

**100 million years ago (Cretaceous period)**

**200 million years ago (Triassic period)**

© Oxford University Press

The equatorial circumference of the globe is 40 075 km

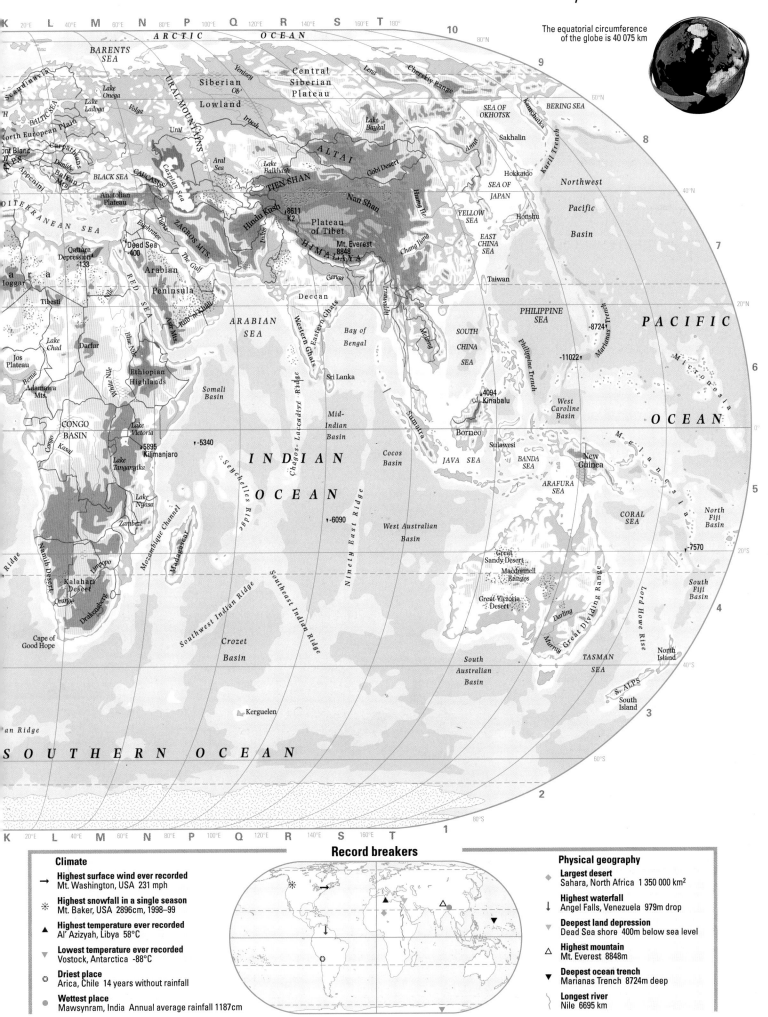

**Record breakers**

## Climate

→ **Highest surface wind ever recorded**
Mt. Washington, USA 231 mph

❊ **Highest snowfall in a single season**
Mt. Baker, USA 2896cm, 1998–99

▲ **Highest temperature ever recorded**
Al' Azizyah, Libya 58°C

▼ **Lowest temperature ever recorded**
Vostock, Antarctica -88°C

⊛ **Driest place**
Arica, Chile 14 years without rainfall

● **Wettest place**
Mawsynram, India Annual average rainfall 1187cm

## Physical geography

◆ **Largest desert**
Sahara, North Africa 1 350 000 km²

↓ **Highest waterfall**
Angel Falls, Venezuela 979m drop

▽ **Deepest land depression**
Dead Sea shore 400m below sea level

△ **Highest mountain**
Mt. Everest 8848m

▼ **Deepest ocean trench**
Marianas Trench 8724m deep

⟋ **Longest river**
Nile 6695 km

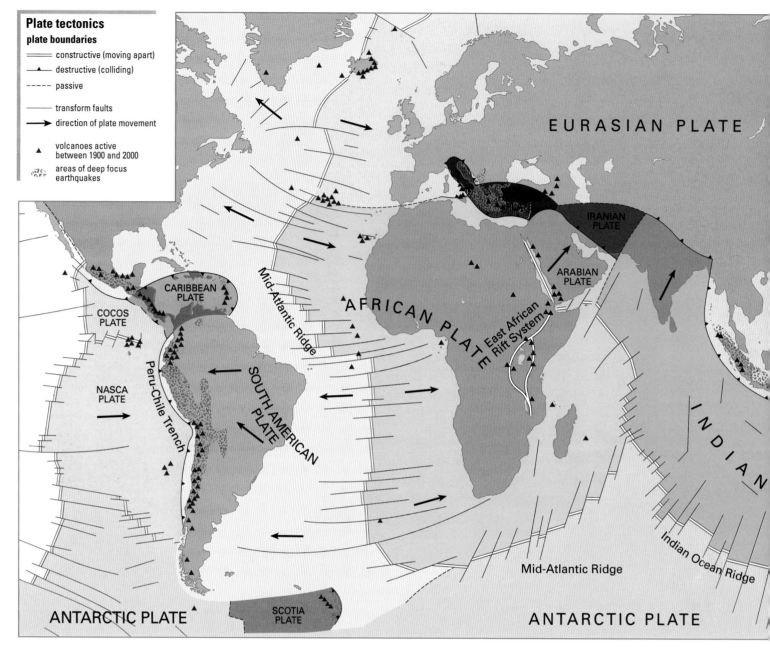

**Plate tectonics**

**plate boundaries**
- constructive (moving apart)
- destructive (colliding)
- passive
- transform faults
- direction of plate movement
- ▲ volcanoes active between 1900 and 2000
- areas of deep focus earthquakes

EURASIAN PLATE

IRANIAN PLATE

ARABIAN PLATE

CARIBBEAN PLATE

COCOS PLATE

AFRICAN PLATE

East African Rift System

Mid-Atlantic Ridge

NASCA PLATE

Peru-Chile Trench

SOUTH AMERICAN PLATE

INDIAN

Indian Ocean Ridge

Mid-Atlantic Ridge

ANTARCTIC PLATE

SCOTIA PLATE

ANTARCTIC PLATE

Mt. Etna, Italy

### Deadliest volcanic eruptions, since 1741

| Year | Place | Deaths |
|------|-------|--------|
| 1741 | Oshima, Japan | 1475 |
| 1772 | Papandayan, Indonesia | 2957 |
| 1783 | Asama, Japan | 1377 |
| 1783 | Lakagigar (Laki), Iceland | 9350 |
| 1792 | Unzen, Japan | 14 300 |
| 1815 | Tambora, Indonesia | 92 000 |
| 1882 | Galunggung, Indonesia | 4011 |
| 1883 | Krakatau, Indonesia | 36 417 |
| 1902 | Soufrière, St. Vincent | 1680 |
| 1902 | Mt. Pelée, Martinique | 29 025 |
| 1911 | Taal, Philippines | 1335 |
| 1919 | Kelut, Indonesia | 5110 |
| 1951 | Lamington, PNG | 2942 |
| 1982 | El Chichón, Mexico | 2000 |
| 1985 | Nevado del Ruiz, Colombia | 25 000 |

Latest Volcanoes
http://volcanoes.usgs.gov

Latest Earthquakes
http://earthquakes.usgs.gov

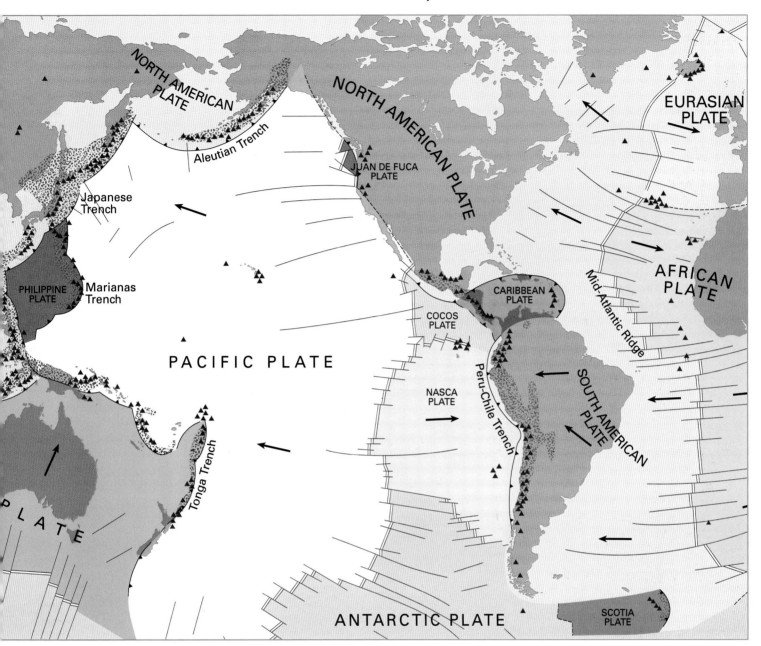

NORTH AMERICAN PLATE

Aleutian Trench

Japanese Trench

JUAN DE FUCA PLATE

NORTH AMERICAN PLATE

EURASIAN PLATE

PHILIPPINE PLATE

Marianas Trench

AFRICAN PLATE

Mid-Atlantic Ridge

CARIBBEAN PLATE

COCOS PLATE

PACIFIC PLATE

NASCA PLATE

Peru-Chile Trench

SOUTH AMERICAN PLATE

PLATE

Tonga Trench

ANTARCTIC PLATE

SCOTIA PLATE

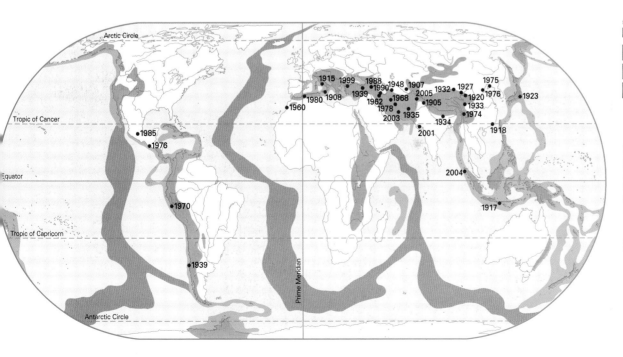

**Earthquakes**

- mobile areas (on land)
- mobile areas (under sea)
- mid-oceanic ridges
- • earthquakes causing more than 10 000 deaths, 1900–2006

**Earthquakes causing most deaths since 1900**
Indonesia (2004) 283 106
China (1976) >255 000
China (1920) 200 000
Japan (1923) 142 800
Turkmenistan (1948) 110 000
Pakistan (2005) >86 000
Italy (1908) >72 000
Peru (1970) 70 000
China (1927) 40 900
Turkey (1939) 32 700

Eckert IV Projection

Scale 1: 240 000 000

## January temperature

actual surface temperature

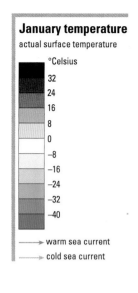

°Celsius
- 32
- 24
- 16
- 8
- 0
- −8
- −16
- −24
- −32
- −40

→ warm sea current
→ cold sea current

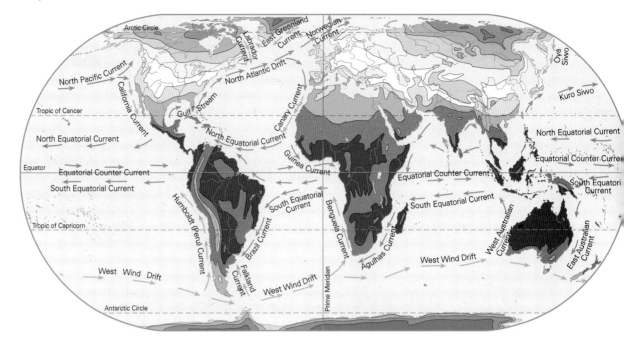

## July temperature

actual surface temperature

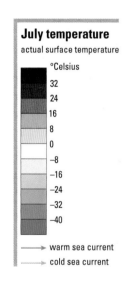

°Celsius
- 32
- 24
- 16
- 8
- 0
- −8
- −16
- −24
- −32
- −40

→ warm sea current
→ cold sea current

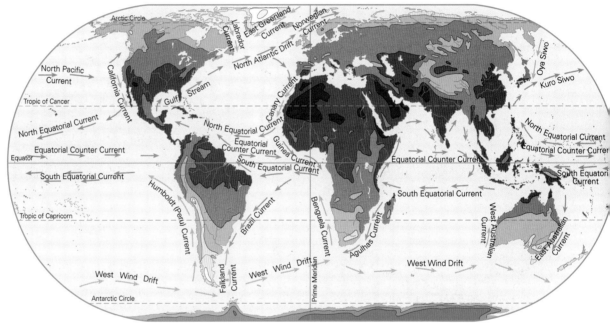

## Global warming

predicted annual mean
temperature increase
by 2050

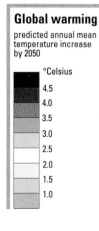

°Celsius
- 4.5
- 4.0
- 3.5
- 3.0
- 2.5
- 2.0
- 1.5
- 1.0

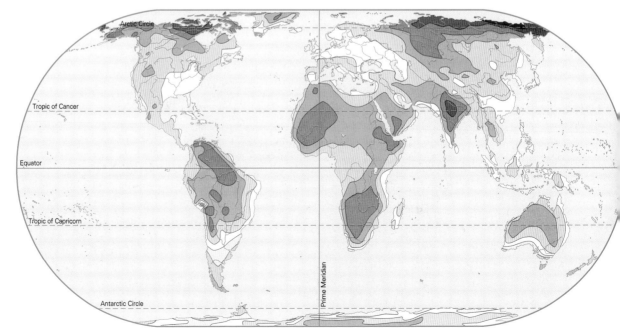

© Oxford University Press

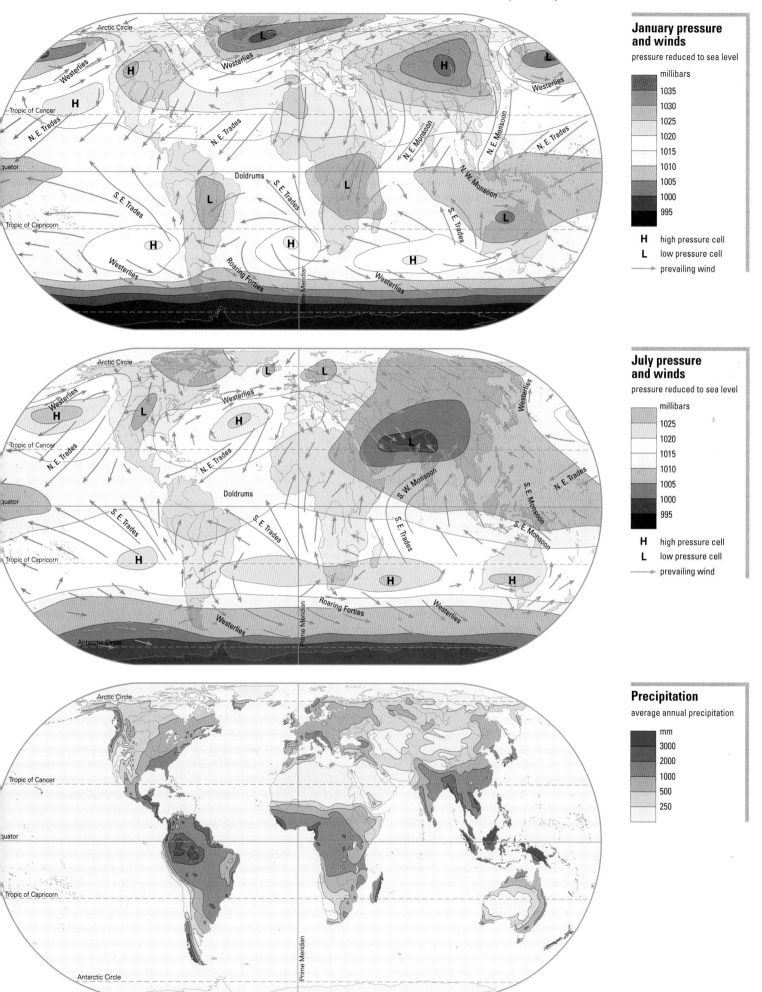

**January pressure and winds**

pressure reduced to sea level

millibars
1035
1030
1025
1020
1015
1010
1005
1000
995

H high pressure cell
L low pressure cell
→ prevailing wind

**July pressure and winds**

pressure reduced to sea level

millibars
1025
1020
1015
1010
1005
1000
995

H high pressure cell
L low pressure cell
→ prevailing wind

**Precipitation**

average annual precipitation

mm
3000
2000
1000
500
250

© Oxford University Press    Eckert IV Projection

Equatorial scale 1: 95 000 000

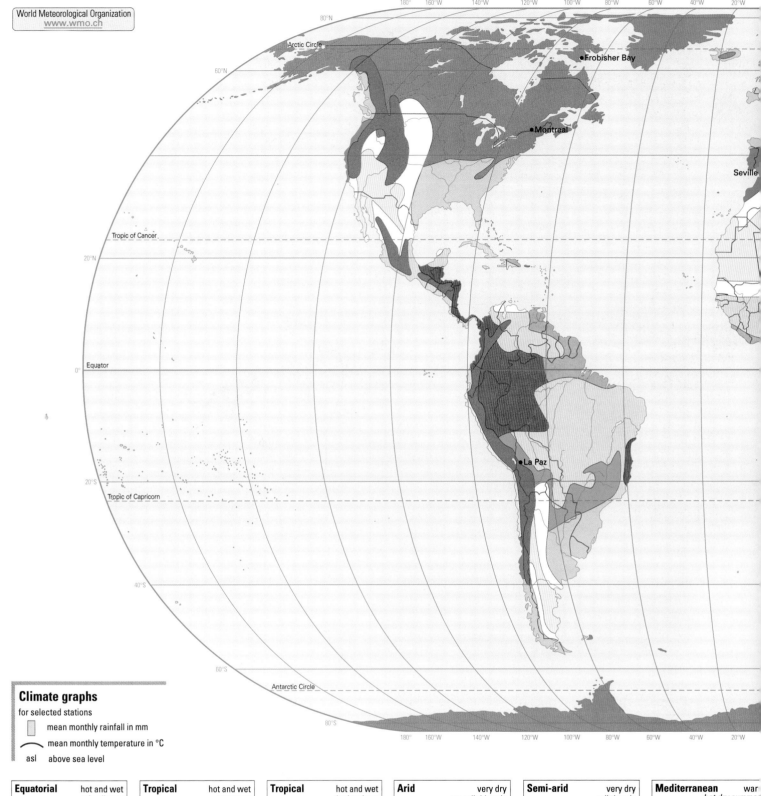

World Meteorological Organization
www.wmo.ch

**Climate graphs**

for selected stations

mean monthly rainfall in mm

mean monthly temperature in °C

asl   above sea level

| **Equatorial** | hot and wet *rain all year* |
|---|---|

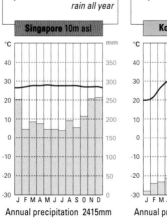

Singapore 10m asl

Annual precipitation 2415mm

| **Tropical** | hot and wet *monsoon* |
|---|---|

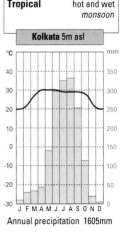

Kolkata 5m asl

Annual precipitation 1605mm

| **Tropical** | hot and wet *dry in winter* |
|---|---|

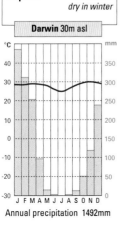

Darwin 30m asl

Annual precipitation 1492mm

| **Arid** | very dry *no reliable rain* |
|---|---|

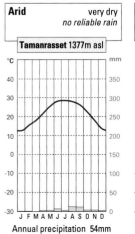

Tamanrasset 1377m asl

Annual precipitation 54mm

| **Semi-arid** | very dry *a little rain* |
|---|---|

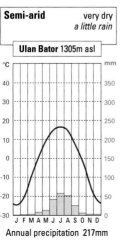

Ulan Bator 1305m asl

Annual precipitation 217mm

| **Mediterranean** | war *hot dry summer warm wet winter* |
|---|---|

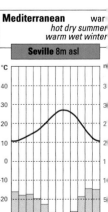

Seville 8m asl

Annual precipitation 534mm

Eckert IV Projection   © Oxford University Press

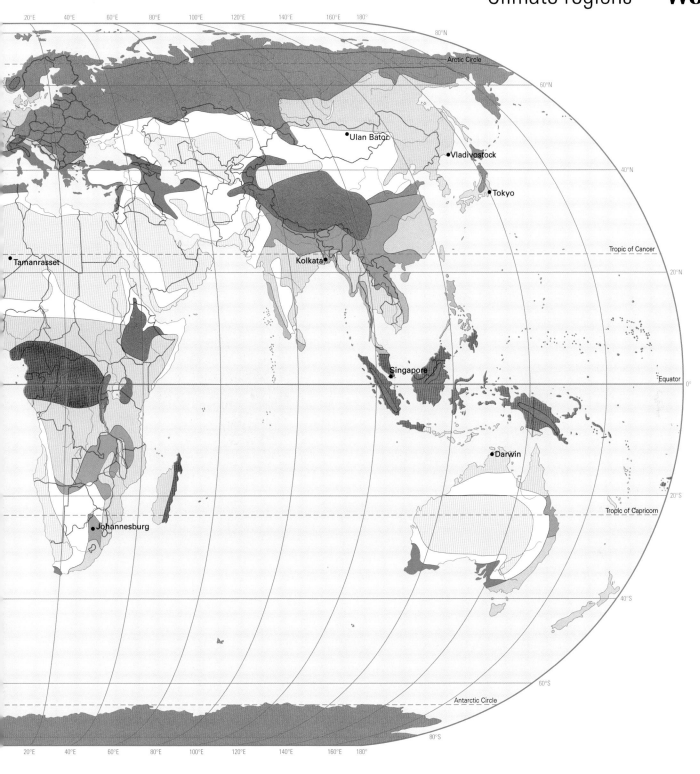

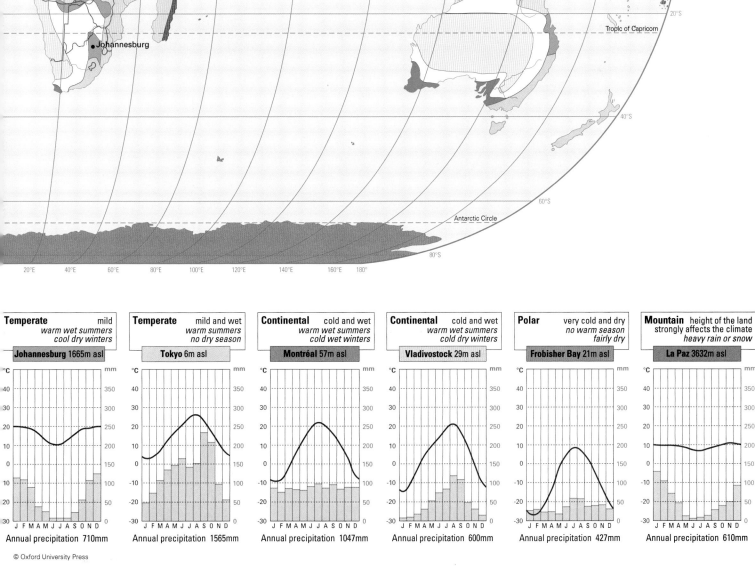

| **Temperate** mild | **Temperate** mild and wet | **Continental** cold and wet | **Continental** cold and wet | **Polar** very cold and dry | **Mountain** height of the land |
|---|---|---|---|---|---|
| *warm wet summers* *cool dry winters* | *warm summers* *no dry season* | *warm wet summers* *cold wet winters* | *warm wet summers* *cold dry winters* | *no warm season* *fairly dry* | *strongly affects the climate* *heavy rain or snow* |
| Johannesburg 1665m asl | Tokyo 6m asl | Montréal 57m asl | Vladivostock 29m asl | Frobisher Bay 21m asl | La Paz 3632m asl |

Annual precipitation 710mm | Annual precipitation 1565mm | Annual precipitation 1047mm | Annual precipitation 600mm | Annual precipitation 427mm | Annual precipitation 610mm

## Climate data

Averages are for 1961–1990

**Denver** 1626m — climate station and its height above sea level

Temperature (°C)
**high** average daily maximum temperature
**mean** average monthly temperature
**low** average daily minimum temperature

Rainfall (mm) — average monthly precipitation

BBC world weather
www.bbc.co.uk/weather/world

### Denver 1626m

| | | Jan | Feb | Mar | Apr | May | Jun | Jul | Aug | Sep | Oct | Nov | Dec | YEAR |
|---|---|---|---|---|---|---|---|---|---|---|---|---|---|---|
| Temperature (°C) | high | 6.2 | 8.1 | 11.2 | 16.6 | 21.6 | 27.4 | 31.2 | 29.9 | 24.9 | 19.1 | 11.4 | 6.9 | 17.9 |
| | mean | -1.3 | 0.8 | 3.9 | 9.0 | 14.0 | 19.4 | 23.1 | 21.9 | 16.8 | 10.8 | 3.9 | -0.6 | 10.1 |
| | low | -8.8 | -6.6 | -3.4 | 1.4 | 6.4 | 11.3 | 14.8 | 13.8 | 8.7 | 2.4 | -3.7 | -8.1 | 2.4 |
| Rainfall (mm) | | 13 | 15 | 33 | 43 | 61 | 46 | 49 | 38 | 32 | 25 | 22 | 16 | 393 |

### Georgetown 2m

| | | Jan | Feb | Mar | Apr | May | Jun | Jul | Aug | Sep | Oct | Nov | Dec | YEAR |
|---|---|---|---|---|---|---|---|---|---|---|---|---|---|---|
| Temperature (°C) | high | 28.6 | 28.9 | 29.2 | 29.5 | 29.4 | 29.2 | 29.6 | 30.2 | 30.8 | 30.8 | 30.2 | 29.1 | 29.6 |
| | mean | 26.1 | 26.4 | 26.7 | 27.0 | 26.8 | 26.5 | 26.6 | 27.0 | 27.5 | 27.6 | 27.2 | 26.4 | 26.8 |
| | low | 23.6 | 23.9 | 24.2 | 24.4 | 24.3 | 23.8 | 23.5 | 23.8 | 24.2 | 24.4 | 24.2 | 23.8 | 24.0 |
| Rainfall (mm) | | 185 | 89 | 111 | 141 | 286 | 328 | 268 | 201 | 98 | 107 | 186 | 262 | 2262 |

### Guangzhou 42m

| | | Jan | Feb | Mar | Apr | May | Jun | Jul | Aug | Sep | Oct | Nov | Dec | YEAR |
|---|---|---|---|---|---|---|---|---|---|---|---|---|---|---|
| Temperature (°C) | high | 18.3 | 18.4 | 21.6 | 25.5 | 29.4 | 31.3 | 32.7 | 32.6 | 31.4 | 28.6 | 24.4 | 20.5 | 26.2 |
| | mean | 13.3 | 14.3 | 17.7 | 21.9 | 25.6 | 27.3 | 28.5 | 28.3 | 27.1 | 24.0 | 19.4 | 15.0 | 21.9 |
| | low | 5.0 | 6.6 | 10.7 | 16.1 | 20.7 | 23.5 | 25.7 | 25.2 | 22.6 | 17.6 | 11.9 | 6.5 | 16.0 |
| Rainfall (mm) | | 43 | 65 | 85 | 182 | 284 | 258 | 228 | 221 | 172 | 79 | 42 | 24 | 1683 |

### Havana 50m

| | | Jan | Feb | Mar | Apr | May | Jun | Jul | Aug | Sep | Oct | Nov | Dec | YEAR |
|---|---|---|---|---|---|---|---|---|---|---|---|---|---|---|
| Temperature (°C) | high | 25.8 | 26.1 | 27.6 | 28.6 | 29.8 | 30.5 | 31.3 | 31.6 | 31.0 | 29.2 | 27.7 | 26.5 | 28.8 |
| | mean | 22.2 | 22.4 | 23.7 | 24.8 | 26.1 | 26.9 | 27.6 | 27.8 | 27.4 | 26.2 | 24.5 | 23.0 | 25.2 |
| | low | 18.6 | 18.6 | 19.7 | 20.9 | 22.4 | 23.4 | 23.8 | 24.1 | 23.8 | 23.0 | 21.3 | 19.5 | 21.6 |
| Rainfall (mm) | | 64 | 69 | 46 | 54 | 98 | 182 | 106 | 100 | 144 | 181 | 88 | 58 | 1190 |

### Juliaca 3827m

| | | Jan | Feb | Mar | Apr | May | Jun | Jul | Aug | Sep | Oct | Nov | Dec | YEAR |
|---|---|---|---|---|---|---|---|---|---|---|---|---|---|---|
| Temperature (°C) | high | 16.7 | 16.7 | 16.5 | 16.8 | 16.6 | 16.0 | 16.0 | 17.0 | 17.6 | 18.6 | 18.8 | 17.7 | 17.1 |
| | mean | 10.2 | 10.1 | 9.9 | 8.7 | 6.4 | 4.5 | 4.3 | 5.8 | 8.1 | 9.5 | 10.2 | 10.4 | 8.2 |
| | low | 3.6 | 3.5 | 3.2 | 0.6 | -3.8 | -7.0 | -7.5 | -5.4 | -1.4 | 0.3 | 1.5 | 3.0 | -0.8 |
| Rainfall (mm) | | 133 | 109 | 99 | 43 | 10 | 3 | 2 | 6 | 22 | 41 | 55 | 86 | 609 |

### Khartoum 380m

| | | Jan | Feb | Mar | Apr | May | Jun | Jul | Aug | Sep | Oct | Nov | Dec | YEAR |
|---|---|---|---|---|---|---|---|---|---|---|---|---|---|---|
| Temperature (°C) | high | 30.8 | 33.0 | 36.8 | 40.1 | 41.9 | 41.3 | 38.4 | 37.3 | 39.1 | 39.3 | 35.2 | 31.8 | 37.1 |
| | mean | 23.2 | 25.0 | 28.7 | 31.9 | 34.5 | 34.3 | 32.1 | 31.5 | 32.5 | 32.4 | 28.1 | 24.5 | 29.9 |
| | low | 15.6 | 17.0 | 20.5 | 23.6 | 27.1 | 27.3 | 25.9 | 25.3 | 26.0 | 25.5 | 21.0 | 17.1 | 22.7 |
| Rainfall (mm) | | 0 | 0 | 0 | 0.5 | 4 | 5 | 46 | 75 | 25 | 5 | 1 | 0 | 161 |

### Lhasa 3650m

| | | Jan | Feb | Mar | Apr | May | Jun | Jul | Aug | Sep | Oct | Nov | Dec | YEAR |
|---|---|---|---|---|---|---|---|---|---|---|---|---|---|---|
| Temperature (°C) | high | 6.9 | 9.0 | 12.1 | 15.6 | 19.3 | 22.7 | 22.1 | 21.1 | 19.7 | 16.3 | 11.2 | 7.7 | 15.3 |
| | mean | -2.1 | 1.1 | 4.6 | 8.1 | 11.9 | 15.5 | 15.3 | 14.5 | 12.8 | 8.1 | 2.2 | -1.7 | 7.5 |
| | low | -10.1 | -6.8 | -3.0 | 0.9 | 5.0 | 9.3 | 10.1 | 9.4 | 7.5 | 1.3 | -4.9 | -9.0 | 0.8 |
| Rainfall (mm) | | 1 | 1 | 2 | 5 | 27 | 72 | 119 | 123 | 58 | 10 | 2 | 1 | 421 |

### Libreville 15m

| | | Jan | Feb | Mar | Apr | May | Jun | Jul | Aug | Sep | Oct | Nov | Dec | YEAR |
|---|---|---|---|---|---|---|---|---|---|---|---|---|---|---|
| Temperature (°C) | high | 29.5 | 30.0 | 30.2 | 30.1 | 29.4 | 27.6 | 26.4 | 26.8 | 27.5 | 28.0 | 28.4 | 29.0 | 28.6 |
| | mean | 26.8 | 27.0 | 27.1 | 26.6 | 26.7 | 25.4 | 24.3 | 24.3 | 25.4 | 25.7 | 25.9 | 26.2 | 26.0 |
| | low | 24.1 | 24.0 | 23.9 | 23.1 | 24.0 | 23.2 | 22.1 | 21.8 | 23.4 | 23.4 | 23.4 | 23.4 | 23.3 |
| Rainfall (mm) | | 250 | 243 | 363 | 339 | 247 | 54 | 7 | 14 | 104 | 427 | 490 | 303 | 2841 |

### Limón 3m

| | | Jan | Feb | Mar | Apr | May | Jun | Jul | Aug | Sep | Oct | Nov | Dec | YEAR |
|---|---|---|---|---|---|---|---|---|---|---|---|---|---|---|
| Temperature (°C) | high | 27.9 | 28.6 | 29.6 | 29.6 | 28.5 | 27.5 | 27.7 | 27.7 | 27.2 | 27.0 | 27.1 | 27.7 | 28.0 |
| | mean | 24.0 | 24.3 | 25.0 | 25.8 | 26.1 | 25.9 | 25.2 | 25.6 | 25.7 | 25.4 | 25.1 | 24.3 | 25.2 |
| | low | 20.3 | 20.3 | 20.9 | 21.6 | 22.2 | 22.3 | 22.1 | 22.1 | 22.2 | 21.9 | 21.6 | 20.9 | 21.5 |
| Rainfall (mm) | | 319 | 201 | 193 | 287 | 281 | 276 | 408 | 289 | 163 | 198 | 367 | 402 | 3384 |

### Malatya 849m

| | | Jan | Feb | Mar | Apr | May | Jun | Jul | Aug | Sep | Oct | Nov | Dec | YEAR |
|---|---|---|---|---|---|---|---|---|---|---|---|---|---|---|
| Temperature (°C) | high | 2.9 | 5.3 | 11.1 | 18.2 | 23.5 | 29.2 | 33.8 | 33.4 | 28.9 | 20.9 | 11.8 | 5.7 | 18.7 |
| | mean | -0.4 | 1.5 | 6.9 | 13.0 | 17.8 | 22.9 | 27.0 | 26.5 | 22.0 | 14.8 | 7.6 | 2.4 | 13.5 |
| | low | -3.2 | -1.7 | 2.4 | 7.7 | 11.8 | 16.1 | 19.8 | 19.4 | 15.2 | 9.5 | 3.7 | -0.3 | 8.4 |
| Rainfall (mm) | | 42 | 36 | 60 | 61 | 50 | 22 | 3 | 2 | 6 | 40 | 47 | 42 | 411 |

### Manaus 84m

| | | Jan | Feb | Mar | Apr | May | Jun | Jul | Aug | Sep | Oct | Nov | Dec | YEAR |
|---|---|---|---|---|---|---|---|---|---|---|---|---|---|---|
| Temperature (°C) | high | 30.5 | 30.4 | 30.6 | 30.7 | 30.8 | 31.0 | 31.3 | 32.6 | 32.9 | 32.8 | 32.1 | 31.3 | 31.4 |
| | mean | 26.1 | 26.0 | 26.1 | 26.3 | 26.3 | 26.4 | 26.5 | 27.0 | 27.5 | 27.6 | 27.3 | 26.7 | 26.7 |
| | low | 23.1 | 23.1 | 23.2 | 23.3 | 23.3 | 23.0 | 22.7 | 23.0 | 23.5 | 23.7 | 23.7 | 23.5 | 23.3 |
| Rainfall (mm) | | 260 | 288 | 314 | 300 | 256 | 114 | 88 | 58 | 83 | 126 | 183 | 217 | 2287 |

### Meekatharra 518m

| | | Jan | Feb | Mar | Apr | May | Jun | Jul | Aug | Sep | Oct | Nov | Dec | YEAR |
|---|---|---|---|---|---|---|---|---|---|---|---|---|---|---|
| Temperature (°C) | high | 38.1 | 36.5 | 34.5 | 29.2 | 23.6 | 19.7 | 18.9 | 21.0 | 25.4 | 29.4 | 33.1 | 36.5 | 28.8 |
| | mean | 31.2 | 30.1 | 28.0 | 23.2 | 17.8 | 14.3 | 13.2 | 14.8 | 18.4 | 22.2 | 25.9 | 29.3 | 22.4 |
| | low | 24.3 | 23.7 | 21.5 | 17.1 | 11.9 | 8.9 | 7.5 | 8.5 | 11.4 | 15.0 | 18.6 | 22.1 | 15.9 |
| Rainfall (mm) | | 26 | 30 | 22 | 17 | 27 | 36 | 25 | 12 | 6 | 7 | 14 | 11 | 233 |

### Minneapolis-St. Paul 255m

| | | Jan | Feb | Mar | Apr | May | Jun | Jul | Aug | Sep | Oct | Nov | Dec | YEAR |
|---|---|---|---|---|---|---|---|---|---|---|---|---|---|---|
| Temperature (°C) | high | -6.3 | -3.0 | 4.0 | 13.6 | 20.8 | 26.0 | 28.9 | 27.1 | 21.5 | 14.9 | 5.0 | -3.6 | 12.4 |
| | mean | -11.2 | -7.8 | -0.6 | 8.0 | 14.7 | 20.1 | 23.1 | 21.4 | 15.8 | 9.3 | 0.7 | -7.8 | 7.1 |
| | low | -16.2 | -12.7 | -5.2 | 2.3 | 8.7 | 14.2 | 17.3 | 15.7 | 10.2 | 3.8 | -3.8 | -12.1 | 1.9 |
| Rainfall (mm) | | 24 | 22 | 49 | 62 | 86 | 103 | 90 | 92 | 69 | 56 | 39 | 27 | 719 |

### Ndola 1270m

| | | Jan | Feb | Mar | Apr | May | Jun | Jul | Aug | Sep | Oct | Nov | Dec | YEAR |
|---|---|---|---|---|---|---|---|---|---|---|---|---|---|---|
| Temperature (°C) | high | 26.6 | 26.9 | 27.4 | 27.5 | 26.6 | 25.1 | 25.2 | 27.5 | 30.5 | 31.5 | 29.4 | 27.0 | 27.6 |
| | mean | 20.8 | 20.8 | 21.0 | 20.5 | 18.6 | 16.5 | 16.7 | 19.2 | 22.5 | 23.7 | 22.5 | 21.0 | 20.3 |
| | low | 17.1 | 17.1 | 16.5 | 14.4 | 10.8 | 7.9 | 7.8 | 10.2 | 13.6 | 16.2 | 17.1 | 17.2 | 13.8 |
| Rainfall (mm) | | 29.3 | 249 | 170 | 46 | 4 | 1 | 0 | 0 | 3 | 32 | 130 | 306 | 1234 |

### Nuuk 70m

| | | Jan | Feb | Mar | Apr | May | Jun | Jul | Aug | Sep | Oct | Nov | Dec | YEAR |
|---|---|---|---|---|---|---|---|---|---|---|---|---|---|---|
| Temperature (°C) | high | -4.4 | -4.5 | -4.8 | -0.8 | 3.5 | 7.7 | 10.6 | 9.9 | 6.3 | 1.7 | -1.0 | -3.3 | 1.7 |
| | mean | -7.4 | -7.8 | -8.0 | -3.9 | 0.6 | 3.9 | 6.5 | 6.1 | 3.5 | -0.6 | -3.6 | -6.2 | -1.4 |
| | low | -10.1 | -10.6 | -10.6 | -6.1 | -1.5 | 1.3 | 3.8 | 3.8 | 1.6 | -2.5 | -5.8 | -8.7 | -3.8 |
| Rainfall (mm) | | 39 | 47 | 50 | 46 | 55 | 62 | 82 | 89 | 88 | 70 | 74 | 54 | 756 |

### Paris 65m

| | | Jan | Feb | Mar | Apr | May | Jun | Jul | Aug | Sep | Oct | Nov | Dec | YEAR |
|---|---|---|---|---|---|---|---|---|---|---|---|---|---|---|
| Temperature (°C) | high | 6.0 | 7.6 | 10.8 | 14.4 | 18.2 | 21.5 | 24.0 | 23.8 | 20.8 | 16.0 | 10.1 | 6.8 | 15.0 |
| | mean | 3.4 | 4.2 | 6.6 | 9.5 | 13.2 | 16.4 | 18.4 | 18.0 | 15.3 | 11.4 | 6.7 | 4.2 | 10.6 |
| | low | 0.9 | 1.3 | 2.9 | 5.0 | 8.3 | 11.2 | 12.9 | 12.7 | 10.6 | 7.7 | 3.8 | 1.7 | 6.6 |
| Rainfall (mm) | | 54 | 46 | 54 | 47 | 63 | 58 | 84 | 52 | 54 | 56 | 56 | 56 | 650 |

### Qiqihar 148m

| | | Jan | Feb | Mar | Apr | May | Jun | Jul | Aug | Sep | Oct | Nov | Dec | YEAR |
|---|---|---|---|---|---|---|---|---|---|---|---|---|---|---|
| Temperature (°C) | high | -12.7 | -7.8 | 2.3 | 12.9 | 21.0 | 26.2 | 27.8 | 26.1 | 20.1 | 11.1 | -1.3 | -10.4 | 9.6 |
| | mean | -19.2 | -14.8 | -4.5 | 6.1 | 14.4 | 20.3 | 22.8 | 20.9 | 14.0 | 4.8 | -7.1 | -16.2 | 3.5 |
| | low | -24.5 | -20.9 | -11.0 | -0.9 | 7.3 | 14.2 | 17.9 | 16.2 | 8.5 | -0.7 | -12.0 | -21.2 | -2.3 |
| Rainfall (mm) | | 1 | 2 | 5 | 15 | 31 | 64 | 138 | 94 | 45 | 19 | 4 | 3 | 421 |

### Rabat Sale 75m

| | | Jan | Feb | Mar | Apr | May | Jun | Jul | Aug | Sep | Oct | Nov | Dec | YEAR |
|---|---|---|---|---|---|---|---|---|---|---|---|---|---|---|
| Temperature (°C) | high | 17.2 | 17.7 | 19.2 | 20.0 | 22.1 | 24.1 | 26.8 | 27.1 | 26.4 | 24.0 | 20.6 | 17.7 | 21.9 |
| | mean | 12.6 | 13.1 | 14.2 | 15.2 | 17.4 | 19.8 | 22.2 | 22.4 | 21.5 | 19.0 | 15.9 | 13.2 | 17.2 |
| | low | 8.0 | 8.6 | 9.2 | 10.4 | 12.7 | 15.4 | 17.6 | 17.7 | 16.7 | 14.1 | 11.1 | 8.7 | 12.5 |
| Rainfall (mm) | | 77 | 74 | 61 | 62 | 25 | 7 | 1 | 1 | 6 | 44 | 97 | 101 | 556 |

### Sittwe 5m

| | | Jan | Feb | Mar | Apr | May | Jun | Jul | Aug | Sep | Oct | Nov | Dec | YEAR |
|---|---|---|---|---|---|---|---|---|---|---|---|---|---|---|
| Temperature (°C) | high | 28.0 | 29.4 | 31.4 | 34.1 | 31.5 | 29.5 | 28.9 | 28.9 | 30.1 | 31.1 | 30.3 | 28.5 | 30.1 |
| | mean | 21.4 | 22.7 | 24.8 | 28.9 | 28.3 | 27.1 | 26.8 | 26.7 | 27.4 | 27.6 | 25.7 | 22.6 | 25.8 |
| | low | 14.7 | 15.9 | 18.2 | 23.6 | 25.1 | 24.6 | 24.7 | 24.5 | 24.6 | 24.0 | 21.0 | 16.6 | 21.5 |
| Rainfall (mm) | | 11 | 8 | 5 | 44 | 268 | 1091 | 1155 | 1025 | 537 | 289 | 105 | 17 | 4555 |

### Stockholm 52m

| | | Jan | Feb | Mar | Apr | May | Jun | Jul | Aug | Sep | Oct | Nov | Dec | YEAR |
|---|---|---|---|---|---|---|---|---|---|---|---|---|---|---|
| Temperature (°C) | high | -0.7 | -0.6 | 3.0 | 8.6 | 15.7 | 20.7 | 21.9 | 20.4 | 15.1 | 9.9 | 4.5 | 1.1 | 10.0 |
| | mean | -2.8 | -3.0 | 0.1 | 4.6 | 10.7 | 15.6 | 17.2 | 16.2 | 11.9 | 7.5 | 2.6 | -1.0 | 6.6 |
| | low | -5.0 | -5.3 | -2.7 | 1.1 | 6.3 | 11.3 | 13.4 | 12.7 | 9.0 | 5.3 | 0.7 | -3.2 | 3.6 |
| Rainfall (mm) | | 39 | 27 | 26 | 30 | 30 | 45 | 72 | 66 | 55 | 50 | 53 | 46 | 539 |

### Tehran 1191m

| | | Jan | Feb | Mar | Apr | May | Jun | Jul | Aug | Sep | Oct | Nov | Dec | YEAR |
|---|---|---|---|---|---|---|---|---|---|---|---|---|---|---|
| Temperature (°C) | high | 7.2 | 9.9 | 15.4 | 21.9 | 28.0 | 34.1 | 36.8 | 35.4 | 31.5 | 24.0 | 16.5 | 9.8 | 22.5 |
| | mean | 3.0 | 5.3 | 10.3 | 16.4 | 22.1 | 27.5 | 30.4 | 29.2 | 25.3 | 18.5 | 11.6 | 5.6 | 17.1 |
| | low | -1.1 | 0.7 | 5.2 | 10.9 | 16.1 | 20.9 | 24.0 | 23.0 | 19.2 | 12.9 | 6.7 | 1.3 | 11.7 |
| Rainfall (mm) | | 37 | 34 | 37 | 28 | 15 | 3 | 3 | 1 | 1 | 14 | 21 | 36 | 230 |

### Wellington 8m

| | | Jan | Feb | Mar | Apr | May | Jun | Jul | Aug | Sep | Oct | Nov | Dec | YEAR |
|---|---|---|---|---|---|---|---|---|---|---|---|---|---|---|
| Temperature (°C) | high | 21.3 | 21.1 | 19.8 | 17.3 | 14.8 | 12.8 | 12.0 | 12.7 | 14.2 | 15.9 | 17.8 | 19.6 | 16.6 |
| | mean | 17.8 | 17.7 | 16.6 | 14.3 | 11.9 | 10.1 | 9.2 | 9.8 | 11.2 | 12.8 | 14.5 | 16.4 | 13.5 |
| | low | 14.4 | 14.3 | 13.5 | 11.3 | 9.1 | 7.3 | 6.4 | 6.9 | 8.3 | 9.7 | 11.3 | 13.2 | 10.5 |
| Rainfall (mm) | | 67 | 48 | 76 | 87 | 99 | 113 | 111 | 106 | 82 | 81 | 74 | 74 | 1018 |

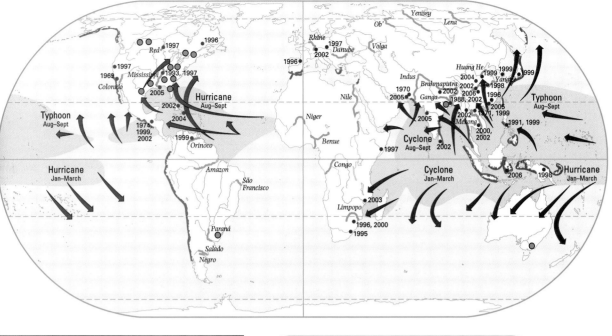

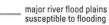

## Storms and floods

- → paths of revolving tropical storms
- areas affected by tropical storms
- coasts vulnerable to tsunamis (seismic sea waves)
- major river flood plains susceptible to flooding
- • major floods
- ● areas affected by tornadoes

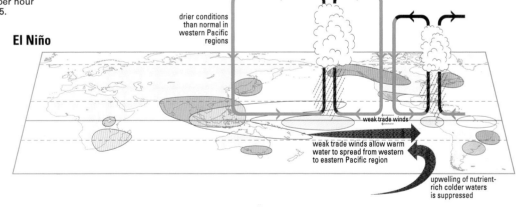

## Water

### Surplus

Enough water to support vegetation and crops without irrigation.

- large surplus
- surplus

### Deficiency

Not enough water to support vegetation and crops without irrigation. After long periods of deficiency these areas may lose their natural vegetation.

- deficiency
- chronic deficiency

## Hurricane Katrina

Winds in this hurricane reached 280km per hour and caused 1836 deaths. 29 August, 2005.

## El Niño and La Niña

Changes to normal climatic conditions as a result of El Niño and La Niña

- dryer and warmer
- dryer
- dryer and cooler
- warmer
- cooler
- wetter and warmer
- wetter
- wetter and cooler

### El Niño

drier conditions than normal in western Pacific regions

weak trade winds

weak trade winds allow warm water to spread from western to eastern Pacific region

upwelling of nutrient-rich colder waters is suppressed

### La Niña

heavier rain than normal in Western Pacific region

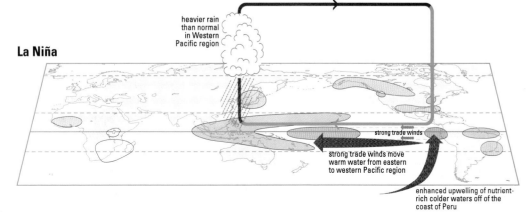

strong trade winds

strong trade winds move warm water from eastern to western Pacific region

enhanced upwelling of nutrient-rich colder waters off the coast of Peru

- air circulation
- trade winds
- sea movements

Equatorial scale 1: 105 000 000

## Ecosystems

vegetation types are those which would occur naturally without interference by people

**coniferous forest**
cone bearing trees

**deciduous and mixed forest**
leaf shedding and coniferous trees

**tropical rain forest**
many species of lush, tall trees

**tropical grasslands (savannah)**
tall grass parkland with scattered trees

**evergreen trees and shrubs**
plants and small trees with leathery leaves

**thorn forest**
low trees and shrubs with spines or thorns

**temperate grasslands**
prairies, steppes, pampas, and veld

**semi-desert**
short grasses and drought-resistant scrub

**desert**
sand and stones, very little vegetation

**tundra**
moss and lichen, with few trees

**ice**
no vegetation

**mountains**
thin soils, steep slopes,
and high altitude
affects type of
vegetation

**ice**
Aerial view of Jameson Land, towards
Liverpool Land, Greenland

**deciduous and mixed forest**
Deciduous forest with scattered white pine,
Blue Ridge Mountains, North Carolina, USA

**temperate grasslands**
Prairie, South Dakota, USA

**tropical rain forest**
Monteverde Cloud Forest Reserve,
Costa Rica

**thorn forest**
Acacia thorns, Hwange, Zimbabwe

South Dakota

Blue Ridge Mountains
North Carolina

Algarve
Portugal

Jameson Land
Greenland

Monteverde Cloud Forest Reserve
Costa Rica

Arctic Circle

Tropic of Cancer

Equator

Tropic of Capricorn

Antarctic Circle

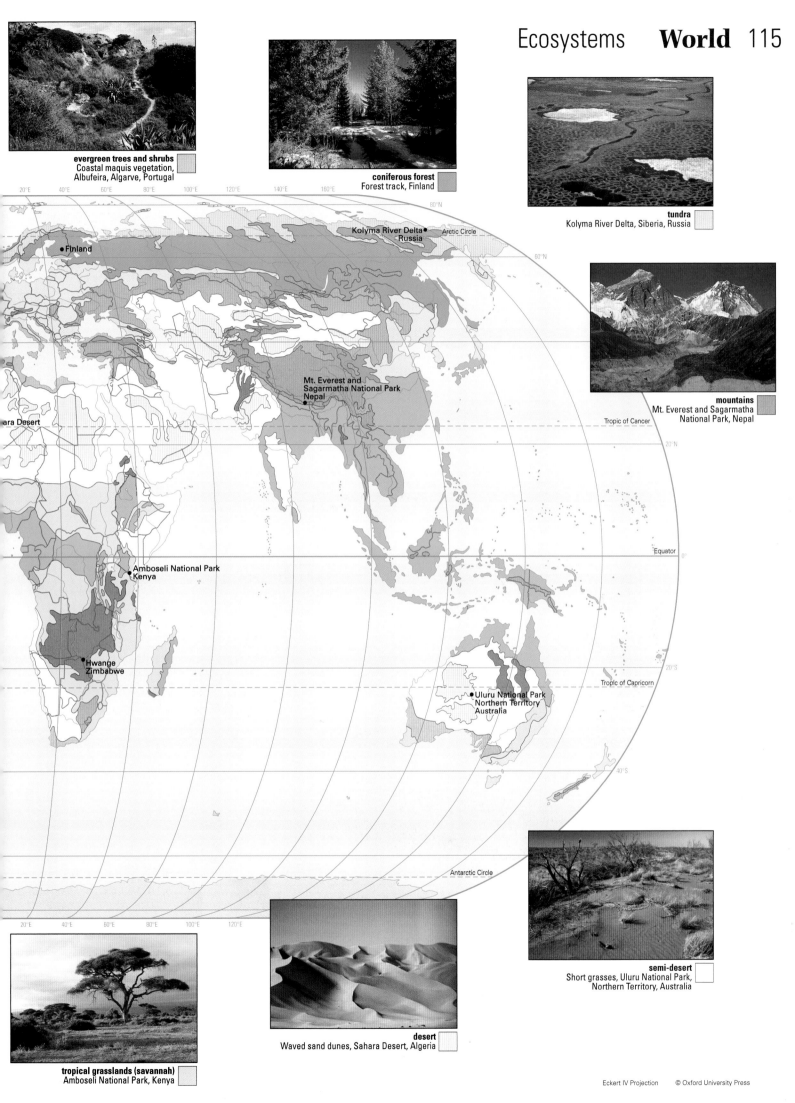

**evergreen trees and shrubs**
Coastal maquis vegetation,
Albufeira, Algarve, Portugal

**coniferous forest**
Forest track, Finland

**tundra**
Kolyma River Delta, Siberia, Russia

**mountains**
Mt. Everest and Sagarmatha
National Park, Nepal

**semi-desert**
Short grasses, Uluru National Park,
Northern Territory, Australia

**desert**
Waved sand dunes, Sahara Desert, Algeria

**tropical grasslands (savannah)**
Amboseli National Park, Kenya

Kolyma River Delta
Russia

Arctic Circle

80°N

60°N

Finland

Mt. Everest and
Sagarmatha National Park
Nepal

Tropic of Cancer

20°N

ara Desert

Equator

0°

Amboseli National Park
Kenya

Hwange
Zimbabwe

20°S

Tropic of Capricorn

Uluru National Park
Northern Territory
Australia

40°S

Antarctic Circle

20°E 40°E 60°E 80°E 100°E 120°E 140°E 160°E

20°E 40°E 60°E 80°E 100°E 120°E

Eckert IV Projection © Oxford University Press

## Population density
people per square kilometre

- over 200
- 100–200
- 50–100
- 5–50
- 1–5
- under 1

## Major cities
population in millions

- ■ over 10
- ⊡ 5–10
- ☐ 1–5

## Population structure, 2006

### World
males — Age — females

percent of total population

**Total population: 6 528 051 823**
**Land area: 148 940 000km²**

### Kenya
males — Age — females

percent of total population

**Total population: 35 890 645**
**Land area: 580 367km²**

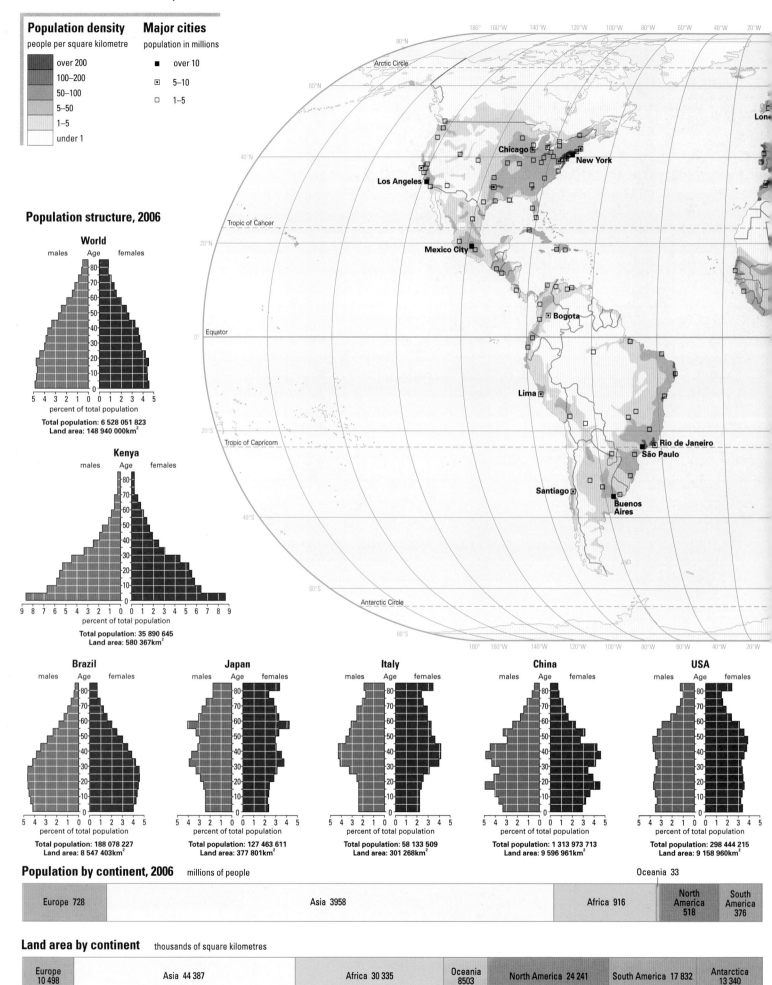

### Brazil
males — Age — females

percent of total population

**Total population: 188 078 227**
**Land area: 8 547 403km²**

### Japan
males — Age — females

percent of total population

**Total population: 127 463 611**
**Land area: 377 801km²**

### Italy
males — Age — females

percent of total population

**Total population: 58 133 509**
**Land area: 301 268km²**

### China
males — Age — females

percent of total population

**Total population: 1 313 973 713**
**Land area: 9 596 961km²**

### USA
males — Age — females

percent of total population

**Total population: 298 444 215**
**Land area: 9 158 960km²**

## Population by continent, 2006   millions of people

| Europe 728 | Asia 3958 | Africa 916 | North America 518 | South America 376 | Oceania 33 |
|---|---|---|---|---|---|

## Land area by continent   thousands of square kilometres

| Europe 10 498 | Asia 44 387 | Africa 30 335 | Oceania 8503 | North America 24 241 | South America 17 832 | Antarctica 13 340 |
|---|---|---|---|---|---|---|

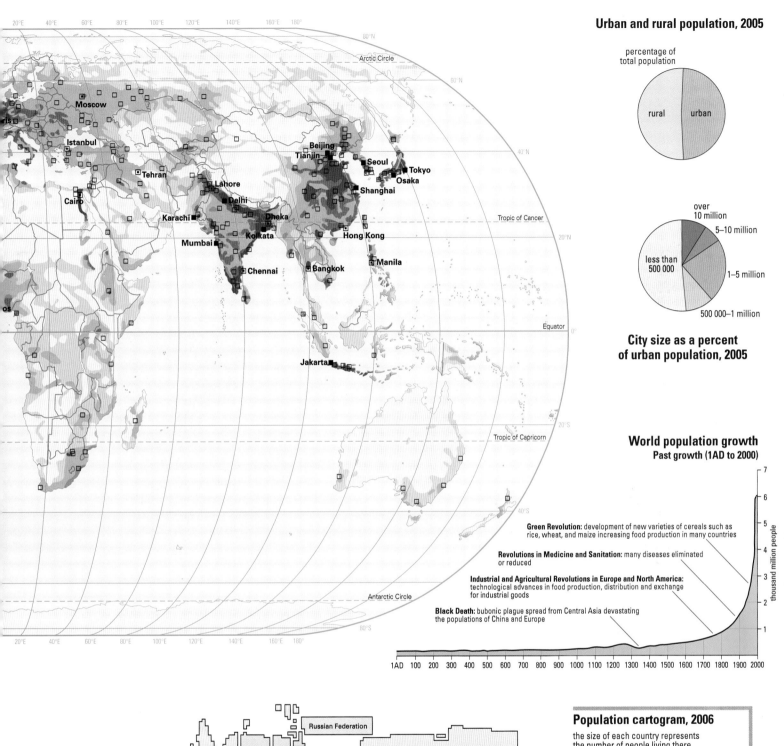

### Urban and rural population, 2005

percentage of
total population

rural | urban

over
10 million

5–10 million

less than
500 000

1–5 million

500 000–1 million

### City size as a percent
of urban population, 2005

### World population growth
**Past growth (1AD to 2000)**

**Green Revolution:** development of new varieties of cereals such as rice, wheat, and maize increasing food production in many countries

**Revolutions in Medicine and Sanitation:** many diseases eliminated or reduced

**Industrial and Agricultural Revolutions in Europe and North America:** technological advances in food production, distribution and exchange for industrial goods

**Black Death:** bubonic plague spread from Central Asia devastating the populations of China and Europe

thousand million people

1AD 100 200 300 400 500 600 700 800 900 1000 1100 1200 1300 1400 1500 1600 1700 1800 1900 2000

Map labels: Moscow, Istanbul, Tehran, Cairo, Lahore, Delhi, Karachi, Mumbai, Kolkata, Dhaka, Chennai, Beijing, Tianjin, Seoul, Tokyo, Osaka, Shanghai, Hong Kong, Bangkok, Manila, Jakarta

Arctic Circle, Tropic of Cancer, Equator, Tropic of Capricorn, Antarctic Circle

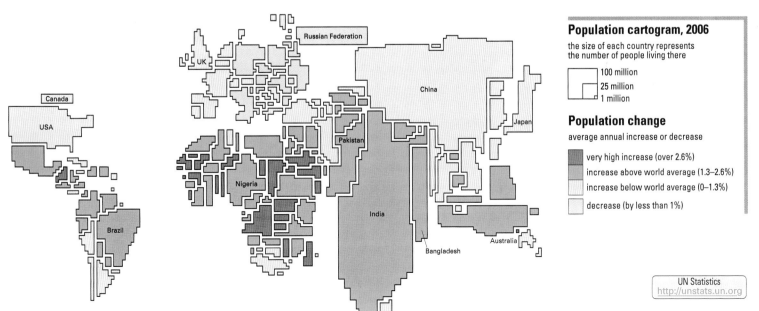

### Population cartogram, 2006

the size of each country represents
the number of people living there

100 million

25 million

1 million

### Population change

average annual increase or decrease

very high increase (over 2.6%)

increase above world average (1.3–2.6%)

increase below world average (0–1.3%)

decrease (by less than 1%)

Cartogram labels: Russian Federation, UK, Canada, USA, China, Japan, Pakistan, Nigeria, India, Brazil, Bangladesh, Australia

UN Statistics
http://unstats.un.org

## Population change, 1994–2004

percentage population gain or loss

- over 40% gain
- 30–40% gain
- 20–30% gain
- 10–20% gain
- under 10% gain
- 0–20% loss

**Highest population gain**
Marshall Islands 85.2%
United Arab Emirates 83.2%
Rwanda 65.4%
São Tomé and Príncipe 60%
Afghanistan 57.7%

United Kingdom 2.2%

**Highest population loss**
Albania -9.8%
Bosnia-Herzegovina -12.5%
Estonia -13.3%
Armenia -14.6%
Georgia -17.1%

## Fertility rate, 2006

average number of children
born to childbearing women

- over 6 children
- 5–5.9 children
- 4–4.9 children
- 3–3.9 children
- 2–2.9 children
- 1–1.9 children
- ○ countries with over 40% of the total population under the age of 15 in 2006

**Largest families**
Niger 7.9 children
Mali 7.1 children
Guinea-Bissau 7.1 children
Uganda 6.9 children
Somalia 6.9 children

United Kingdom 1.8 children

## Urban population

percentage of the population living in
urban areas

- over 80%
- 60–80%
- 40–60%
- 20–40%
- under 20%
- no data

**Most urban in 2004**
Singapore 100%
Monaco 100%
Belgium 97%
Kuwait 96%
Iceland 94%

United Kingdom 90%

**Least urban in 2004**
Papua New Guinea 13%
Lesotho 13%
Uganda 12%
Burundi 9%
East Timor 8%

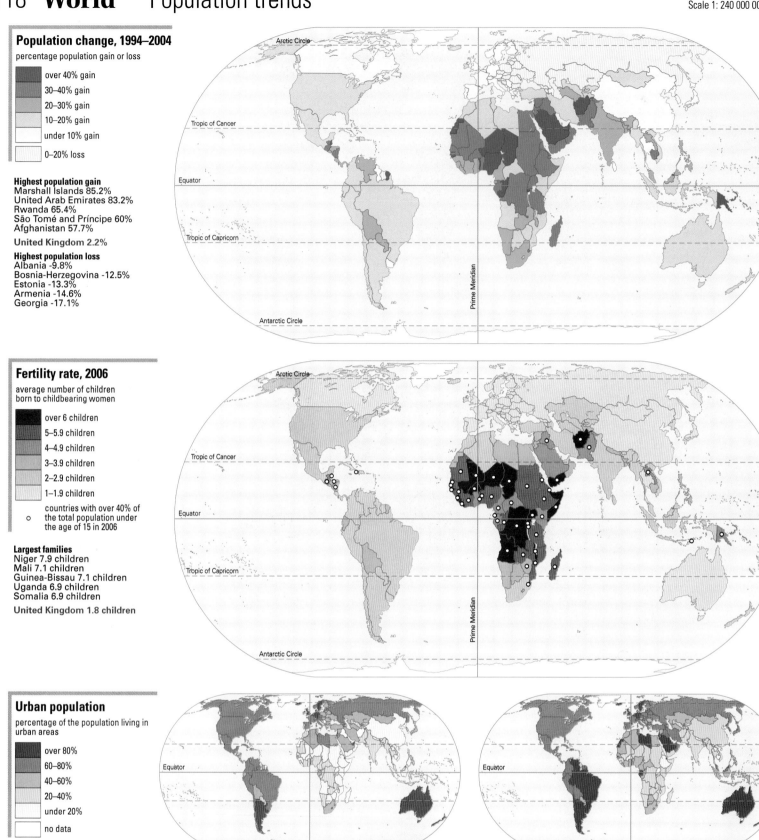

**1975**

**2004**

*projected* **2015**

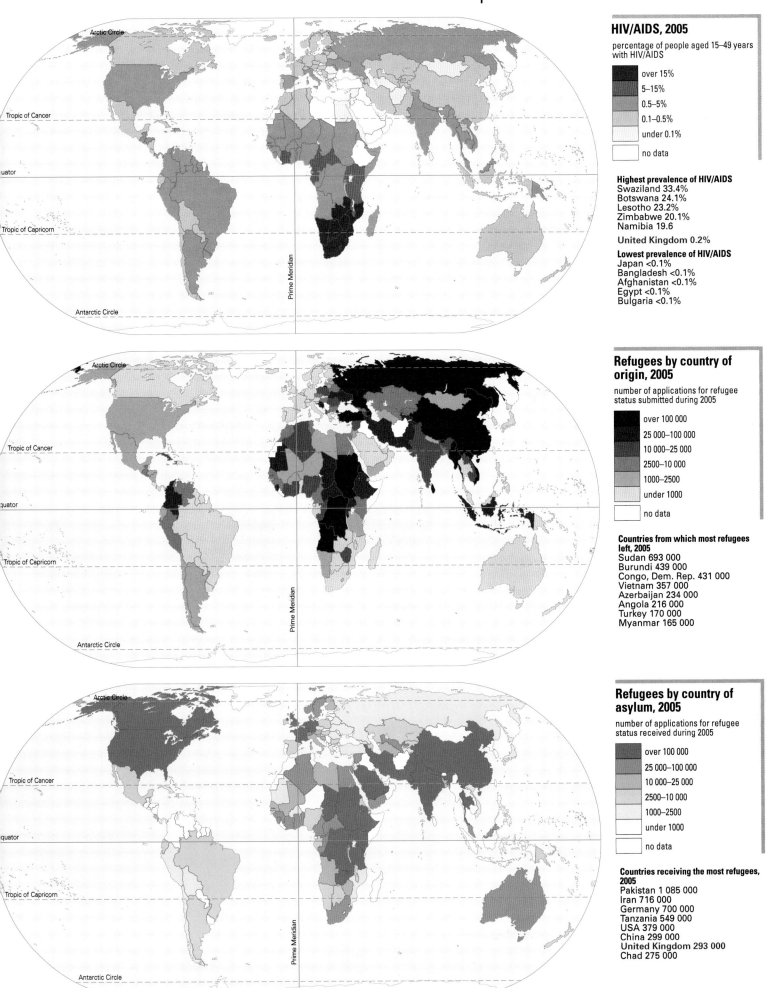

**HIV/AIDS, 2005**

percentage of people aged 15–49 years with HIV/AIDS

- over 15%
- 5–15%
- 0.5–5%
- 0.1–0.5%
- under 0.1%
- no data

**Highest prevalence of HIV/AIDS**
Swaziland 33.4%
Botswana 24.1%
Lesotho 23.2%
Zimbabwe 20.1%
Namibia 19.6

United Kingdom 0.2%

**Lowest prevalence of HIV/AIDS**
Japan <0.1%
Bangladesh <0.1%
Afghanistan <0.1%
Egypt <0.1%
Bulgaria <0.1%

**Refugees by country of origin, 2005**

number of applications for refugee status submitted during 2005

- over 100 000
- 25 000–100 000
- 10 000–25 000
- 2500–10 000
- 1000–2500
- under 1000
- no data

**Countries from which most refugees left, 2005**
Sudan 693 000
Burundi 439 000
Congo, Dem. Rep. 431 000
Vietnam 357 000
Azerbaijan 234 000
Angola 216 000
Turkey 170 000
Myanmar 165 000

**Refugees by country of asylum, 2005**

number of applications for refugee status received during 2005

- over 100 000
- 25 000–100 000
- 10 000–25 000
- 2500–10 000
- 1000–2500
- under 1000
- no data

**Countries receiving the most refugees, 2005**
Pakistan 1 085 000
Iran 716 000
Germany 700 000
Tanzania 549 000
USA 379 000
China 299 000
United Kingdom 293 000
Chad 275 000

## Purchasing power, 2004

Purchasing Power Parity (PPP) in US$
Based on Gross Domestic Product (GDP)
per person, adjusted for the local cost
of living

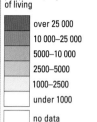

- over 25 000
- 10 000–25 000
- 5000–10 000
- 2500–5000
- 1000–2500
- under 1000
- no data

**Highest purchasing power**
Luxembourg $69 961
United States $39 676
Ireland $38 827
Norway $38 454
Iceland $33 051

United Kingdom $30 821

**Lowest purchasing power**
Congo, Democratic Republic $705
Burundi $677
Tanzania $674
Malawi $646
Sierra Leone $561

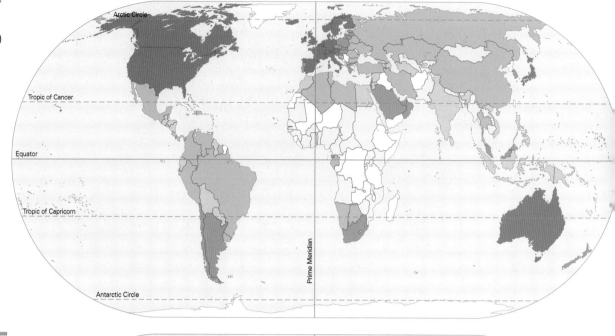

## Literacy and schooling, 2004

percentage of people aged 15 and above
who can, with understanding, both read
and write a short, simple statement on
their everyday life

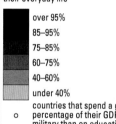

- over 95%
- 85–95%
- 75–85%
- 60–75%
- 40–60%
- under 40%
- ○ countries that spend a greater
  percentage of their GDP on the
  military than on education

**Highest literacy levels**
Georgia 100%
Slovakia 100%
Estonia 99.8%
Cuba 99.8%
Latvia 99.7%

United Kingdom 99%

**Lowest literacy levels**
Guinea 29.5%
Niger 28.7%
Chad 25.7%
Burkina 21.8%
Mali 19%

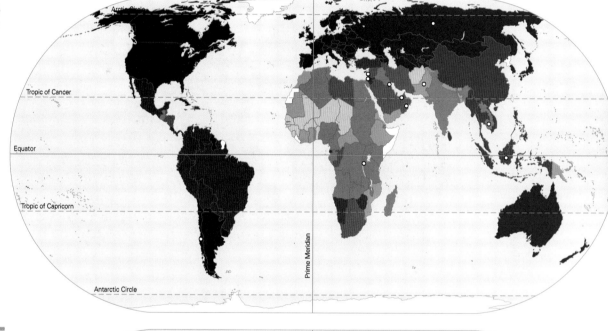

## Life expectancy, 2004

average expected lifespan of babies
born in 2004

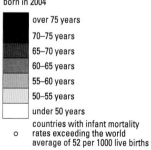

- over 75 years
- 70–75 years
- 65–70 years
- 60–65 years
- 55–60 years
- 50–55 years
- under 50 years
- ○ countries with infant mortality
  rates exceeding the world
  average of 52 per 1000 live births

**Highest life expectancy**
Japan 82 years
Iceland 81 years
Switzerland 81 years
Australia 80 years
Sweden 80 years

United Kingdom 78 years

**Lowest life expectancy**
Zambia 38 years
Zimbabwe 37 years
Lesotho 35 years
Botswana 35 years
Swaziland 31 years

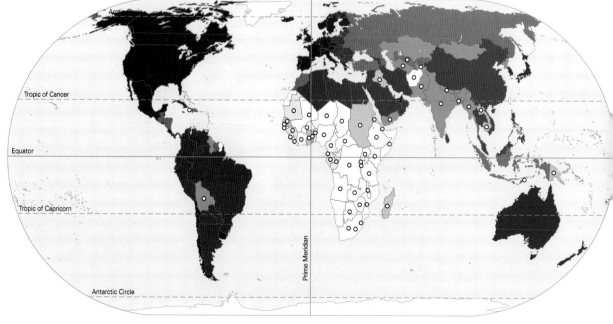

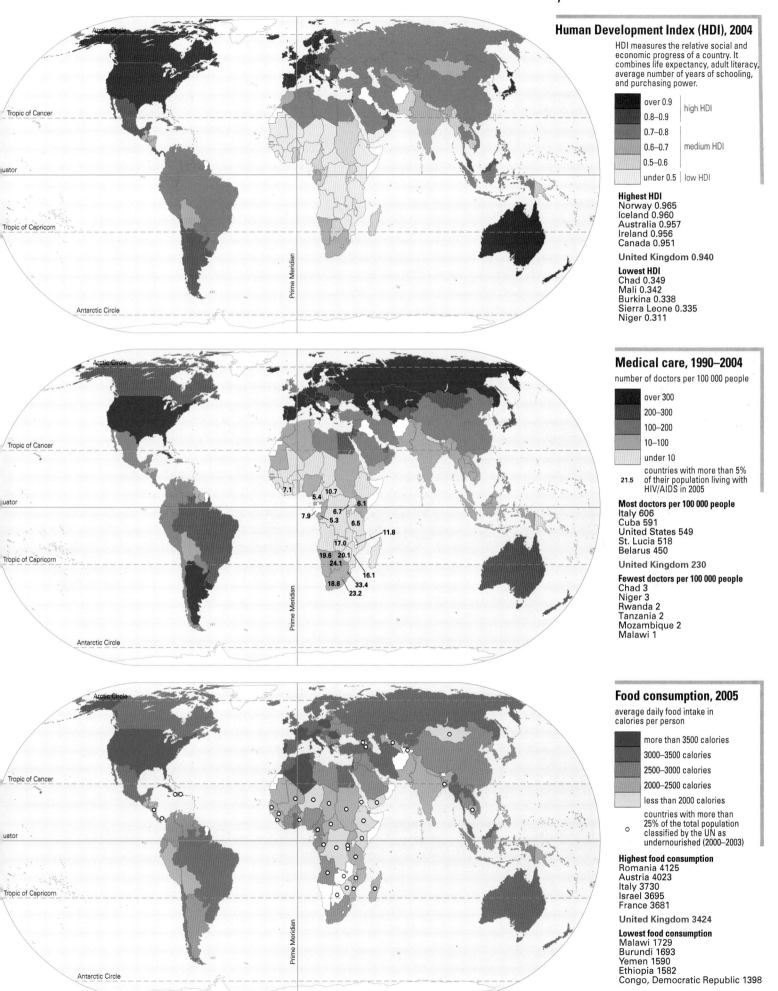

## Human Development Index (HDI), 2004

HDI measures the relative social and economic progress of a country. It combines life expectancy, adult literacy, average number of years of schooling, and purchasing power.

| | | |
|---|---|---|
| | over 0.9 | high HDI |
| | 0.8–0.9 | |
| | 0.7–0.8 | |
| | 0.6–0.7 | medium HDI |
| | 0.5–0.6 | |
| | under 0.5 | low HDI |

**Highest HDI**
Norway 0.965
Iceland 0.960
Australia 0.957
Ireland 0.956
Canada 0.951

United Kingdom 0.940

**Lowest HDI**
Chad 0.349
Mali 0.342
Burkina 0.338
Sierra Leone 0.335
Niger 0.311

## Medical care, 1990–2004

number of doctors per 100 000 people

| | |
|---|---|
| | over 300 |
| | 200–300 |
| | 100–200 |
| | 10–100 |
| | under 10 |
| 21.5 | countries with more than 5% of their population living with HIV/AIDS in 2005 |

**Most doctors per 100 000 people**
Italy 606
Cuba 591
United States 549
St. Lucia 518
Belarus 450

United Kingdom 230

**Fewest doctors per 100 000 people**
Chad 3
Niger 3
Rwanda 2
Tanzania 2
Mozambique 2
Malawi 1

## Food consumption, 2005

average daily food intake in calories per person

| | |
|---|---|
| | more than 3500 calories |
| | 3000–3500 calories |
| | 2500–3000 calories |
| | 2000–2500 calories |
| | less than 2000 calories |
| ○ | countries with more than 25% of the total population classified by the UN as undernourished (2000–2003) |

**Highest food consumption**
Romania 4125
Austria 4023
Italy 3730
Israel 3695
France 3681

United Kingdom 3424

**Lowest food consumption**
Malawi 1729
Burundi 1693
Yemen 1590
Ethiopia 1582
Congo, Democratic Republic 1398

© Oxford University Press

Scale 1: 240 000 000

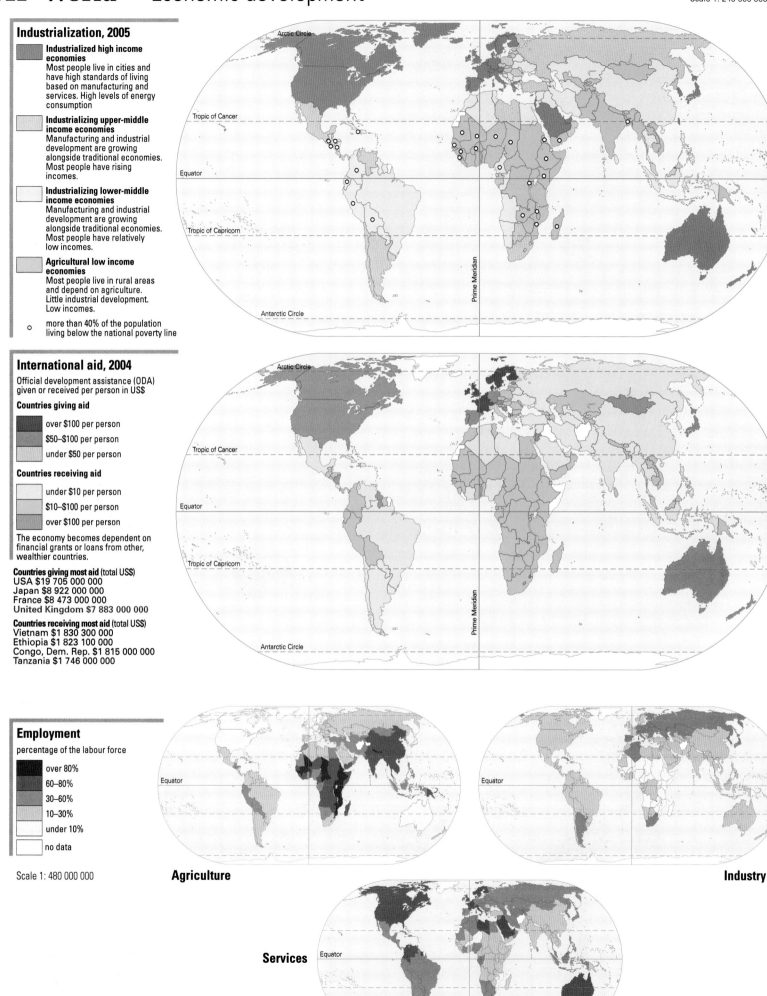

## Industrialization, 2005

**Industrialized high income economies**
Most people live in cities and have high standards of living based on manufacturing and services. High levels of energy consumption

**Industrializing upper-middle income economies**
Manufacturing and industrial development are growing alongside traditional economies. Most people have rising incomes.

**Industrializing lower-middle income economies**
Manufacturing and industrial development are growing alongside traditional economies. Most people have relatively low incomes.

**Agricultural low income economies**
Most people live in rural areas and depend on agriculture. Little industrial development. Low incomes.

○  more than 40% of the population living below the national poverty line

## International aid, 2004

Official development assistance (ODA) given or received per person in US$

**Countries giving aid**

over $100 per person

$50–$100 per person

under $50 per person

**Countries receiving aid**

under $10 per person

$10–$100 per person

over $100 per person

The economy becomes dependent on financial grants or loans from other, wealthier countries.

**Countries giving most aid** (total US$)
USA $19 705 000 000
Japan $8 922 000 000
France $8 473 000 000
United Kingdom $7 883 000 000

**Countries receiving most aid** (total US$)
Vietnam $1 830 300 000
Ethiopia $1 823 100 000
Congo, Dem. Rep. $1 815 000 000
Tanzania $1 746 000 000

## Employment

percentage of the labour force

over 80%

60–80%

30–60%

10–30%

under 10%

no data

Scale 1: 480 000 000

**Agriculture**

**Industry**

**Services**

Eckert IV Projection          © Oxford University Press

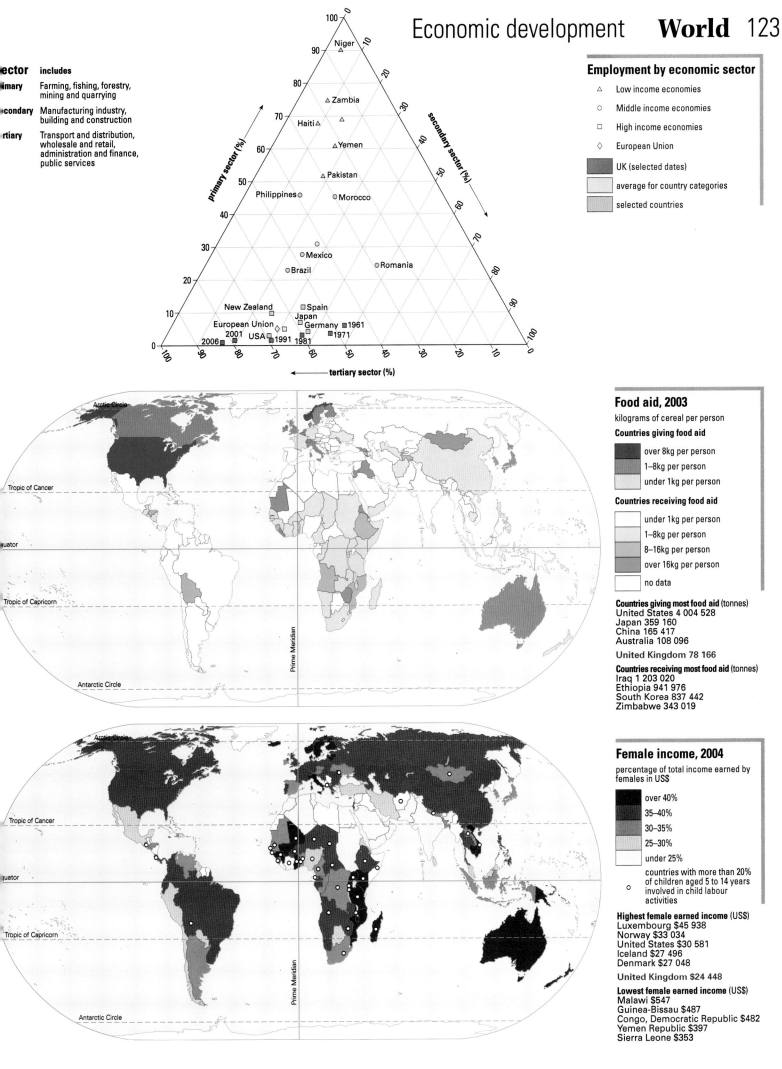

**ector** **includes**

**imary** Farming, fishing, forestry, mining and quarrying

**condary** Manufacturing industry, building and construction

**rtiary** Transport and distribution, wholesale and retail, administration and finance, public services

primary sector (%)

secondary sector (%)

← tertiary sector (%)

- Niger
- Zambia
- Haiti
- Yemen
- Pakistan
- Philippines
- Morocco
- Mexico
- Brazil
- Romania
- New Zealand
- Spain
- Japan
- European Union
- Germany 1961
- 2001
- USA 1991 1981 1971
- 2006

**Employment by economic sector**

△ Low income economies

○ Middle income economies

□ High income economies

◇ European Union

UK (selected dates)

average for country categories

selected countries

**Food aid, 2003**

kilograms of cereal per person

**Countries giving food aid**

over 8kg per person

1–8kg per person

under 1kg per person

**Countries receiving food aid**

under 1kg per person

1–8kg per person

8–16kg per person

over 16kg per person

no data

**Countries giving most food aid** (tonnes)
United States 4 004 528
Japan 359 160
China 165 417
Australia 108 096

United Kingdom 78 166

**Countries receiving most food aid** (tonnes)
Iraq 1 203 020
Ethiopia 941 976
South Korea 837 442
Zimbabwe 343 019

**Female income, 2004**

percentage of total income earned by females in US$

over 40%

35–40%

30–35%

25–30%

under 25%

○ countries with more than 20% of children aged 5 to 14 years involved in child labour activities

**Highest female earned income** (US$)
Luxembourg $45 938
Norway $33 034
United States $30 581
Iceland $27 496
Denmark $27 048

United Kingdom $24 448

**Lowest female earned income** (US$)
Malawi $547
Guinea-Bissau $487
Congo, Democratic Republic $482
Yemen Republic $397
Sierra Leone $353

## Energy production, 2004
kg oil equivalent per person

- over 25 000
- 2500–25 000
- 1000–2500
- 100–1000
- under 100
- no data

**Highest energy producers**
kg oil equivalent per person

Qatar 102 633
United Arab Emirates 73 541
Kuwait 63 191
Norway 58 937
Brunei 58 217
Equatorial Guinea 36 060
Trinidad & Tobago 31 745
Saudi Arabia 23 414
Oman 19 447
Bahrain 16 868
Libya 16 021
Canada 14 317
Turkmenistan 13 451
Australia 13 252
Gabon 9683

**United Kingdom 3945**

- North America
- Central and South America
- Europe and Eurasia
- Middle East
- Africa
- Asia Pacific

### Oil reserves
Proven recoverable reserves
World total: 156 700 000 000 tonnes

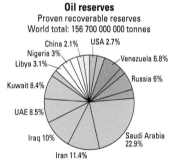

China 2.1% — USA 2.7%
Nigeria 3% — Venezuela 6.8%
Libya 3.1% — Russia 6%
Kuwait 8.4%
UAE 8.5%
Iraq 10% — Saudi Arabia 22.9%
Iran 11.4%

### Gas reserves
Proven recoverable reserves
World total: 175 780 000 000 000 m³

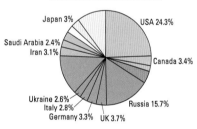

USA 3% — Venezuela 2.4%
Algeria 2.6%
Nigeria 2.8% — Russia 26.7%
UAE 3.4%
Saudi Arabia 3.8%
Qatar 14.7%
Iran 15.2%

### Coal reserves
Proven recoverable reserves
World total: 984 453 000 000 tonnes

Australia 8.3%
India 8.6% — USA 25.4%
China 11.6%
South Africa 5%
Poland 2.3% — Russia 15.9%
Kazakhstan 3.5% — Germany 6.7%
Ukraine 3.5%

### Oil consumption
World total: 3 636 600 000 tonnes

South Korea 2.9%
India 3.1% — USA 25.1%
Japan 6.8%
China 7.6%
Canada 2.6%
Mexico 2.3%
Brazil 2.3%
Germany 3.4%
Russia 3.4%
Spain 2.1% — France 2.6%
UK 2.1% — Italy 2.5%

### Gas consumption
World total: 2 331 900 000 000 m³

Japan 3% — USA 24.3%
Saudi Arabia 2.4%
Iran 3.1%
Canada 3.4%
Ukraine 2.6%
Italy 2.8% — Russia 15.7%
Germany 3.3% — UK 3.7%

### Coal consumption
World total: 2 578 400 000 tonnes oil equivalent

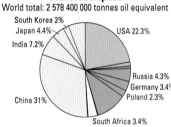

South Korea 2%
Japan 4.4% — USA 22.3%
India 7.2%
Russia 4.3%
Germany 3.4%
Poland 2.3%
China 31%
South Africa 3.4%

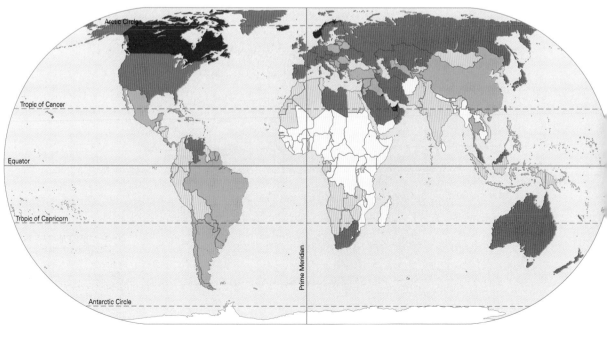

## Energy consumption, 2004
kg oil equivalent per person

- over 10 000
- 2500–10 000
- 1000–2500
- 250–1000
- under 250
- no data

**Highest energy consumers**
kg oil equivalent per person

United Arab Emirates 23 134
Bahrain 21 011
Qatar 15 286
Iceland 13 671
Trinidad and Tobago 12 563

**United Kingdom 4164**

**Lowest energy consumers**
kg oil equivalent per person

Brurundi 26
Mali 25
Cambodia 15
Afghanistan 14
Chad 8

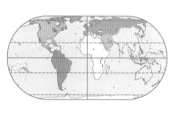

# World trade cartogram, 2005

the size of each country represents its share of total world trade

☐ 1% of world trade

▫ 0.01% of world trade

## Change in share of world trade, 1995–2005

| | | |
|---|---|---|
| ▓ over 50% | | |
| ▒ 5–50% | growth | |
| ☐ 0–5% growth or decline | little or no change | |
| ▨ 5–50 | | |
| ▨ over 50% | decline | |

Only those countries with more than 0.01% share in world trade are shown

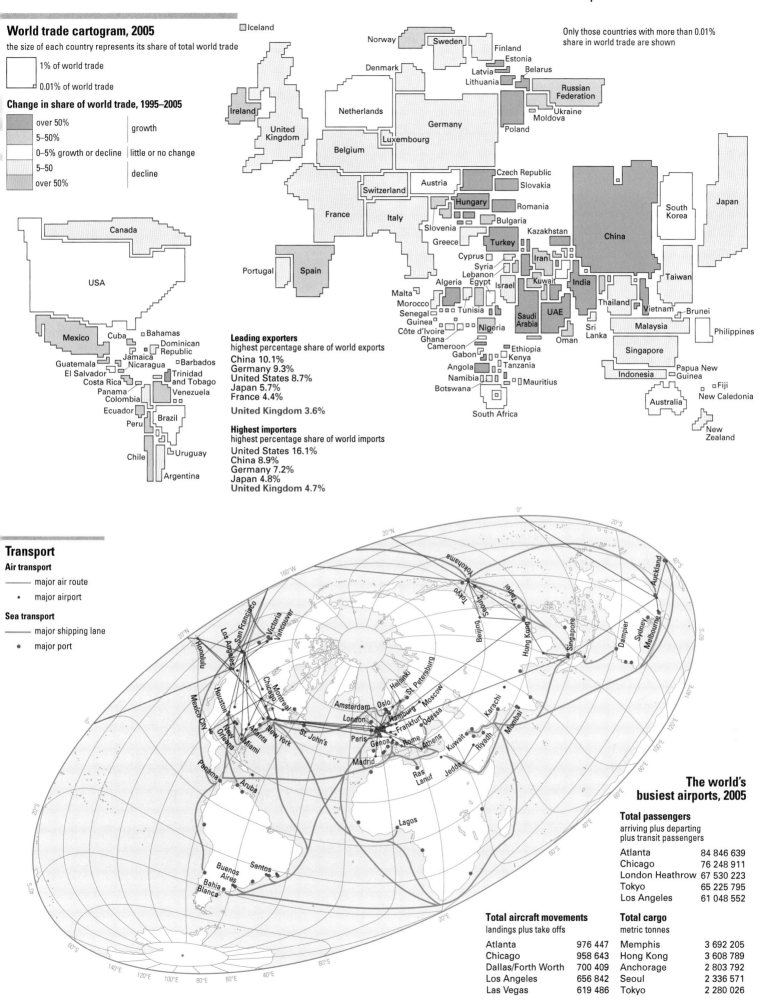

**Leading exporters**
highest percentage share of world exports
China 10.1%
Germany 9.3%
United States 8.7%
Japan 5.7%
France 4.4%

United Kingdom 3.6%

**Highest importers**
highest percentage share of world imports
United States 16.1%
China 8.9%
Germany 7.2%
Japan 4.8%
United Kingdom 4.7%

# Transport

**Air transport**

―― major air route

• major airport

**Sea transport**

―― major shipping lane

• major port

## The world's busiest airports, 2005

**Total passengers**
arriving plus departing
plus transit passengers

| | |
|---|---|
| Atlanta | 84 846 639 |
| Chicago | 76 248 911 |
| London Heathrow | 67 530 223 |
| Tokyo | 65 225 795 |
| Los Angeles | 61 048 552 |

| **Total aircraft movements** landings plus take offs | | **Total cargo** metric tonnes | |
|---|---|---|---|
| Atlanta | 976 447 | Memphis | 3 692 205 |
| Chicago | 958 643 | Hong Kong | 3 608 789 |
| Dallas/Forth Worth | 700 409 | Anchorage | 2 803 792 |
| Los Angeles | 656 842 | Seoul | 2 336 571 |
| Las Vegas | 619 486 | Tokyo | 2 280 026 |

## Desertification and tropical deforestation

- existing areas of desert
- areas with a high risk of becoming deserts
- areas with a moderate risk of becoming deserts
- existing areas of tropical rain forest
- former areas of tropical rain forest

### Countries losing greatest areas of forest ('000 hectares) 2000–2005

| | |
|---|---|
| Brazil | 3103 |
| Indonesia | 1871 |
| Sudan | 589 |
| Myanmar | 466 |
| Zambia | 445 |
| Tanzania | 412 |
| Nigeria | 410 |
| Congo, Dem. Rep. | 319 |
| Zimbabwe | 313 |
| Venezuela | 288 |

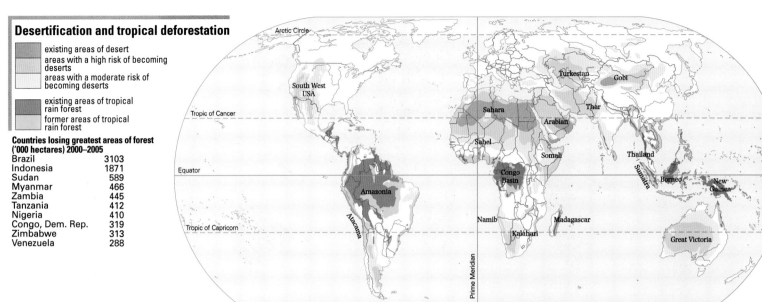

## Acid rain

### Sulphur and nitrogen emissions

Oxides of sulphur and nitrogen produced by burning fossil fuel react with rain to form dilute sulphuric and nitric acids

- areas with high levels of fossil fuel burning
- cities where sulphur dioxide emissions are recorded and exceed World Health Organization recommended levels

### Areas of acid rain deposition

Annual mean values of pH in precipitation

- pH less than 4.2 (most acidic)
- pH 4.2–4.6
- pH 4.6–5.0
- other areas where acid rain is becoming a problem

Lower pH values are more acidic. 'Clean' rain water is slightly acidic with a pH of 5.6. The pH scale is logarithmic, so that a value of 4.6 is ten times as acidic as normal rain.

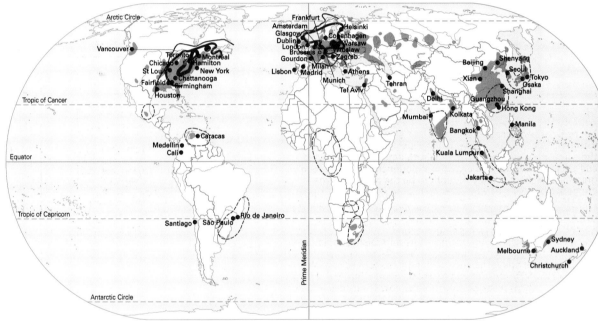

## Sea pollution

### Major oil spills

- ● over 100 000 tonnes
- • under 100 000 tonnes
- frequent oil slicks from shipping

### Other sea pollution

- severe pollution
- moderate pollution
- ▼ deep sea dump sites

### Major oil spills ('000 tonnes)

| | | |
|---|---|---|
| **1979** | *Ixtoc 1* well blow-out, Gulf of Mexico | 467 |
| **1979** | Collision of *Atlantic Empress* and *Aegean Captain*, off Tobago, Caribbean | 138 |
| **1983** | *Nowruz* well blow-out, The Gulf | 267 |
| **1989** | *Exxon Valdez* spills oil off the coast of Alaska | 37 |
| **1991** | Release of oil by Iraqi troops, *Sea Island* terminal, The Gulf | 800 |
| **2002** | *Prestige* oil tanker sinks off the coast of Spain | 63 |
| **2003** | *Tasman Spirit* tanker spills oil in Karachi Port, Pakistan | 30 |

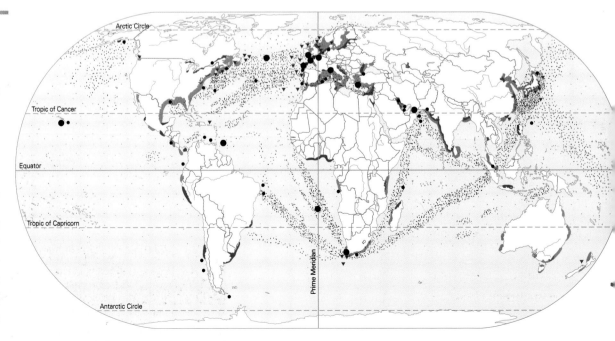

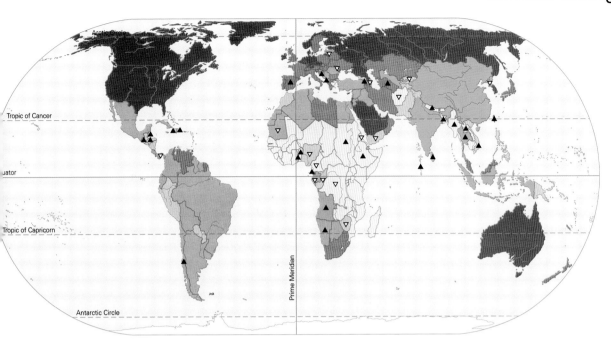

© Oxford University Press

## Carbon dioxide emissions, 2004

metric tonnes per person

| | |
|---|---|
| ▓ | over 10 |
| ▓ | 5–10 |
| ▓ | 1–5 |
| ░ | 0.5–1 |
| □ | under 0.5 |

**changes in carbon dioxide emissions per person, 1994–2004**

▲ more than a 50% increase

▽ more than a 20% decrease

**Highest carbon dioxide emissions**
metric tonnes per person
United Arab Emirates 55.92
Qatar 46.25
Bahrain 33.52
Kuwait 30.88
Trinidad and Tobago 30.03

United Kingdom 9.62

**Lowest carbon dioxide emissions**
metric tonnes per person
Mali 0.06
Cambodia 0.04
Congo, Dem. Rep. 0.03
Afghanistan 0.02
Chad 0.02

## Global warming

The Earth's climate changes naturally over long periods of time. Scientists now think that these natural cycles of change have been overtaken by a rapid rise in the temperature of the Earth's atmosphere.

Global warming is caused by the **greenhouse effect**. Greenhouses work by trapping heat from the sun. Glass panes let in sunlight but prevent heat from escaping so that plants can survive cold weather. 'Greenhouse gases' in the Earth's atmosphere work in the same way. Without them the Earth would be too cold to sustain life. However, we are now experiencing an enhanced greenhouse effect, widely thought to be the result of large quantities of heat-trapping gases escaping into the atmosphere.

These greenhouse gases include carbon dioxide, methane, nitrogen oxides and chlorofluorocarbons (CFCs) and they are caused by human activities such as burning coal and oil, increasing road and air transport, burning down forests and raising cattle. Even a small increase in temperature can have serious consequences, altering weather patterns and resulting in increased rainfall, storms or drought to different parts of the world. Rising sea levels caused by melting polar ice also threaten low-lying coastal areas.

## The natural greenhouse effect

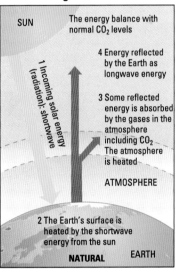

SUN — The energy balance with normal $CO_2$ levels

1 Incoming solar energy (radiation): shortwave

4 Energy reflected by the Earth as longwave energy

3 Some reflected energy is absorbed by the gases in the atmosphere including $CO_2$. The atmosphere is heated

ATMOSPHERE

2 The Earth's surface is heated by the shortwave energy from the sun

**NATURAL** EARTH

## How it alters with increased $CO_2$

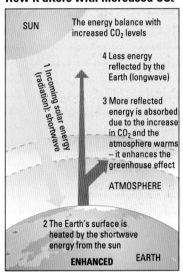

SUN — The energy balance with increased $CO_2$ levels

1 Incoming solar energy (radiation): shortwave

4 Less energy reflected by the Earth (longwave)

3 More reflected energy is absorbed due to the increase in $CO_2$ and the atmosphere warms – it enhances the greenhouse effect

ATMOSPHERE

2 The Earth's surface is heated by the shortwave energy from the sun

**ENHANCED** EARTH

## Projected change in global warming

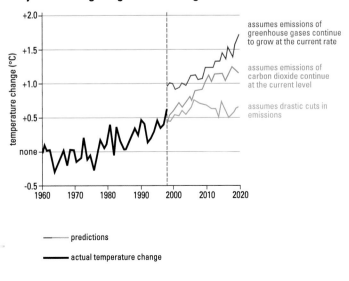

assumes emissions of greenhouse gases continue to grow at the current rate

assumes emissions of carbon dioxide continue at the current level

assumes drastic cuts in emissions

—— predictions

—— actual temperature change

## The Antarctic ozone 'hole'

Three dimensional image of ozone depletion over Antarctica in September, 1998. The lowest ozone concentration is shown in blue.

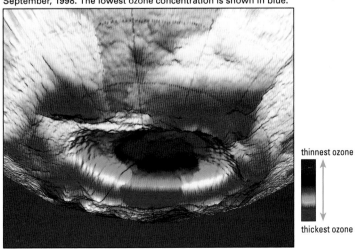

thinnest ozone

thickest ozone

Ozone in the stratosphere absorbs harmful ultra-violet rays. Pollutants in the air destroy ozone, making the ozone layer thinner. Strong winds and intense cold of the Antarctic winter concentrate the effects of pollutants so that ozone is thinnest over Antarctica in spring (September and October).

Scale 1: 125 000 000 (main map)

## Selected tourist destinations

The locations shown represent a limited selection of important tourism sites.

🏛 cultural/historical sites

✳ natural heritage sites

● resorts

● tourist cities

── main cruise routes

**land height**

metres
2000
500
0

## Top tourist destinations, 2005

| | arrivals (000's) | % change 2004–2005 |
|---|---|---|
| **France** | 76 000 | 1.2 |
| **Spain** | 55 600 | 6.0 |
| **USA** | 49 400 | 7.2 |
| **China** | 46 800 | 12.1 |
| **Italy** | 36 500 | -1.5 |
| **United Kingdom** | 30 000 | 8.0 |
| **Mexico** | 21 900 | 6.3 |
| **Germany** | 21 500 | 6.8 |
| **Turkey** | 20 300 | 20.5 |
| **Austria** | 20 000 | 3.0 |

## Market share, 2005

percent of all international tourist arrivals

| | |
|---|---|
| France | 9.4% |
| Spain | 6.9% |
| USA | 6.1% |
| China | 5.8% |
| Italy | 4.5% |
| UK | 3.7% |
| Mexico | 2.7% |
| Germany | 2.7% |
| Turkey | 2.5% |
| Austria | 2.5% |

0  2  4  6  8  10

## Earnings from tourism, 2004

tourist receipts in million $US

■ over 5000

▨ 1000–5000

▨ 250–1000

▨ 100–250

▨ under 100

☐ no data

**Highest tourist earnings (millions)**
USA $74 547
Spain $45 248
France $40 841
Italy $35 656
**United Kingdom $28 221**
Germany $27 668

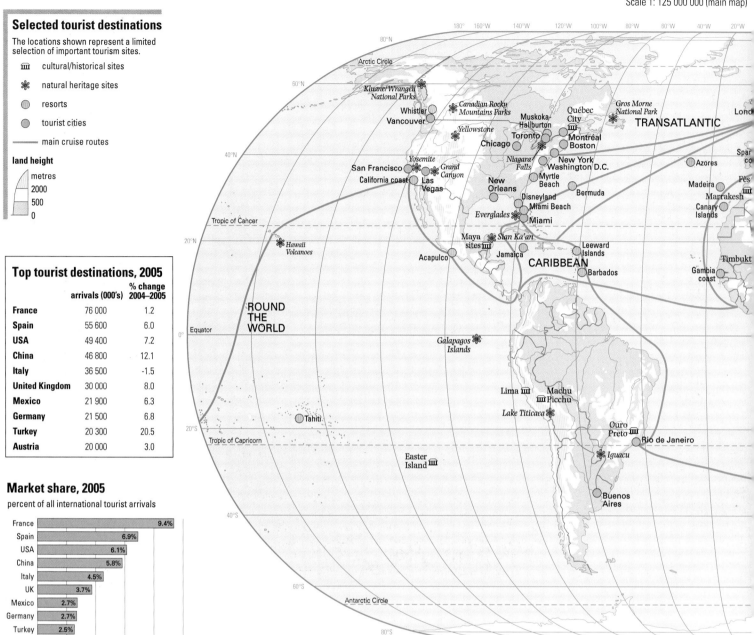

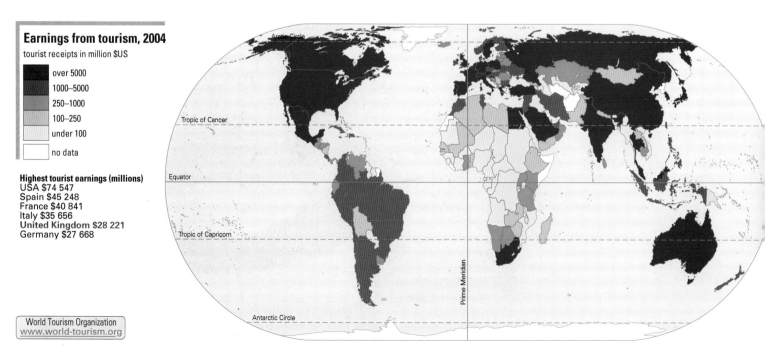

Eckert IV Projection      © Oxford University Press

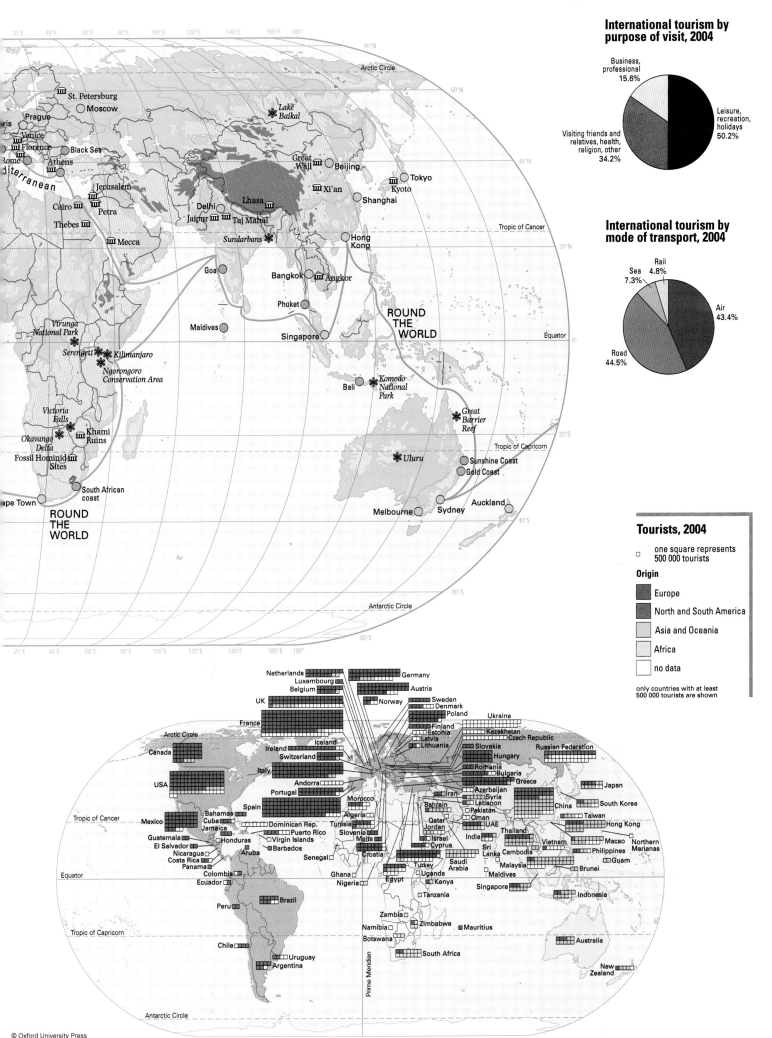

## International tourism by purpose of visit, 2004

Business, professional 15.6%

Leisure, recreation, holidays 50.2%

Visiting friends and relatives, health, religion, other 34.2%

## International tourism by mode of transport, 2004

Rail 4.8%

Sea 7.3%

Air 43.4%

Road 44.5%

## Tourists, 2004

□ one square represents 500 000 tourists

### Origin

Europe

North and South America

Asia and Oceania

Africa

no data

only countries with at least 500 000 tourists are shown

## Time zones

Minus numbers show hours behind Greenwich Mean Time (GMT). Plus numbers show hours ahead of GMT.

- even numbers of hours difference from GMT
- odd numbers of hours difference from GMT
- half an hour difference from adjacent zone
- less than half an hour difference from adjacent zone

Longitude is measured from the **prime meridian** which passes through Greenwich. There are 24 standard time zones, each of 15° of longitude. The edges of these time zones usually follow international boundaries.

The **international date line** marks the point where one calendar day ends and another begins. A traveller crossing from east to west moves forward one day. Crossing from west to east the calendar goes back one day.

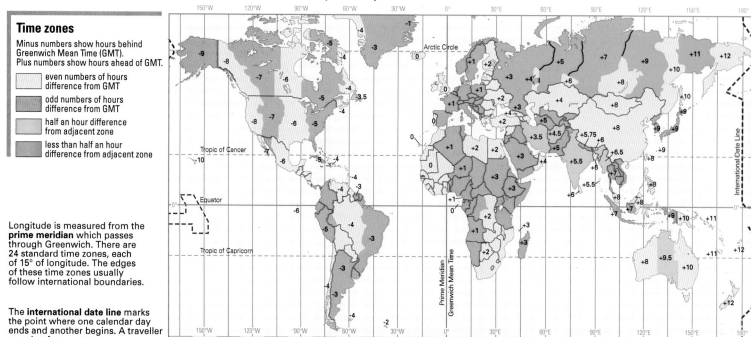

| -11 | -10 | -9 | -8 | -7 | -6 | -5 | -4 | -3 | -2 | -1 | 0 | +1 | +2 | +3 | +4 | +5 | +6 | +7 | +8 | +9 | +10 | +11 | +12 |

## Distance

Flight distance between cities in kilometres.
To convert kilometres to miles multiply by 0.62

| **Beijing** | | | | | | | | | | | | |
|---|---|---|---|---|---|---|---|---|---|---|---|---|
| 19 307 | **Buenos Aires** | | | | | | | | | | | |
| 1983 | 18 484 | **Hong Kong** | | | | | | | | | | |
| 11 710 | 8088 | 10 732 | **Johannesburg** | | | | | | | | | |
| 8145 | 11 161 | 9645 | 9071 | **London** | | | | | | | | |
| 10 081 | 9871 | 11 678 | 16 676 | 8774 | **Los Angeles** | | | | | | | |
| 12 468 | 7468 | 14 162 | 14 585 | 8936 | 2484 | **Mexico City** | | | | | | |
| 4774 | 14 952 | 4306 | 8274 | 7193 | 14 033 | 15 678 | **Mumbai** | | | | | |
| 11 000 | 8548 | 12 984 | 12 841 | 5580 | 3951 | 3371 | 12 565 | **New York** | | | | |
| 8226 | 11 097 | 9613 | 8732 | 338 | 9032 | 9210 | 7032 | 5839 | **Paris** | | | |
| 4468 | 15 904 | 2661 | 8860 | 10 871 | 14 146 | 16 630 | 3919 | 15 533 | 10 758 | **Singapore** | | |
| 8949 | 11 800 | 7374 | 11 040 | 16 992 | 12 073 | 12 969 | 9839 | 15 989 | 16 962 | 6300 | **Sydney** | |
| 2113 | 18 388 | 2903 | 13 547 | 9581 | 8823 | 11 355 | 6758 | 10 871 | 9726 | 5322 | 7823 | **Tokyo** |

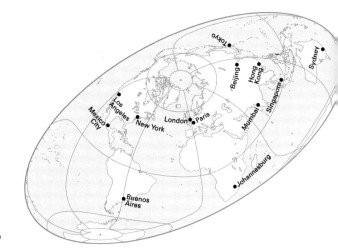

## Internet users, 2007

per 10 000 people

- over 2500
- 1000–2500
- 250–1000
- 100–250
- 25–100
- under 25

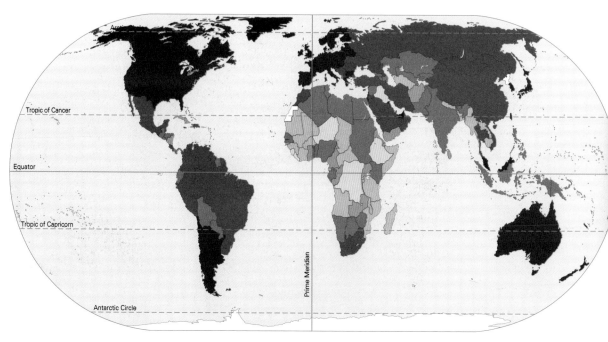

Gall Projection (Timezones)    Oblique Aitoff Projection    © Oxford University Press

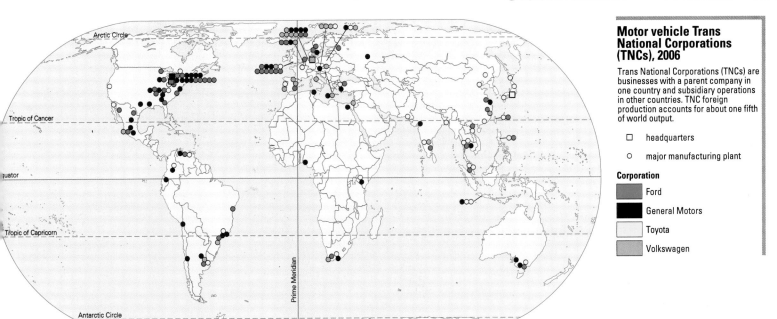

## Motor vehicle Trans National Corporations (TNCs), 2006

Trans National Corporations (TNCs) are businesses with a parent company in one country and subsidiary operations in other countries. TNC foreign production accounts for about one fifth of world output.

□    headquarters

○    major manufacturing plant

**Corporation**

     Ford

     General Motors

     Toyota

     Volkswagen

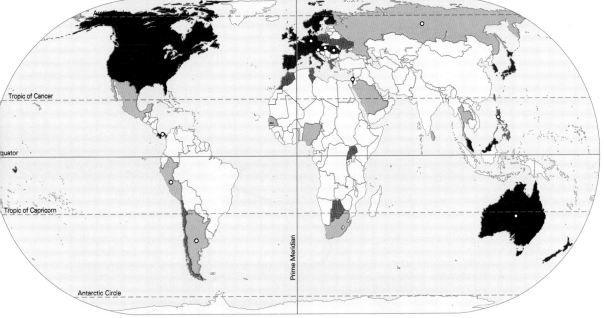

## Globalisation index, 2006

The Globalisation index measures the extent to which countries are globally connected. The index combines country data on trade, foreign investment, international travel, international telephone traffic, internet use and membership of international organisations. The map shows only the top 50 countries.

**Ranking**

     1–10 (most globalised)

     11–20

     21–30

     31–40

     41–50

○    most rapidly globalising countries

Source: A. T. Kearney/Foreign Policy magazine

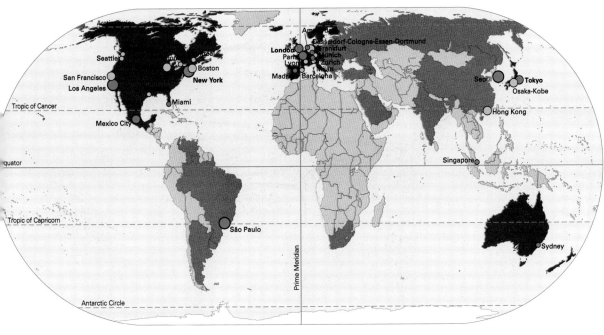

## World economy

     economic core (countries dominant in the world economy)

     semi-periphery (countries partially dependent on the core)

     periphery (countries highly dependent on the core)

## Global cities

Some geographers have identified a network of global cities arranged in a hierarchy according to the power they exert on the global economy. The map shows one view of this hierarchy. The position of each city in the hierarchy can change rapidly through time.

   cities dominating global financial markets

○   cities dominating international and national economies

○   cities dominating subnational and regional economies

**City population**

○   10–25 million

○   5–10 million

○   1–5 million

Source: Friedmann, 1995

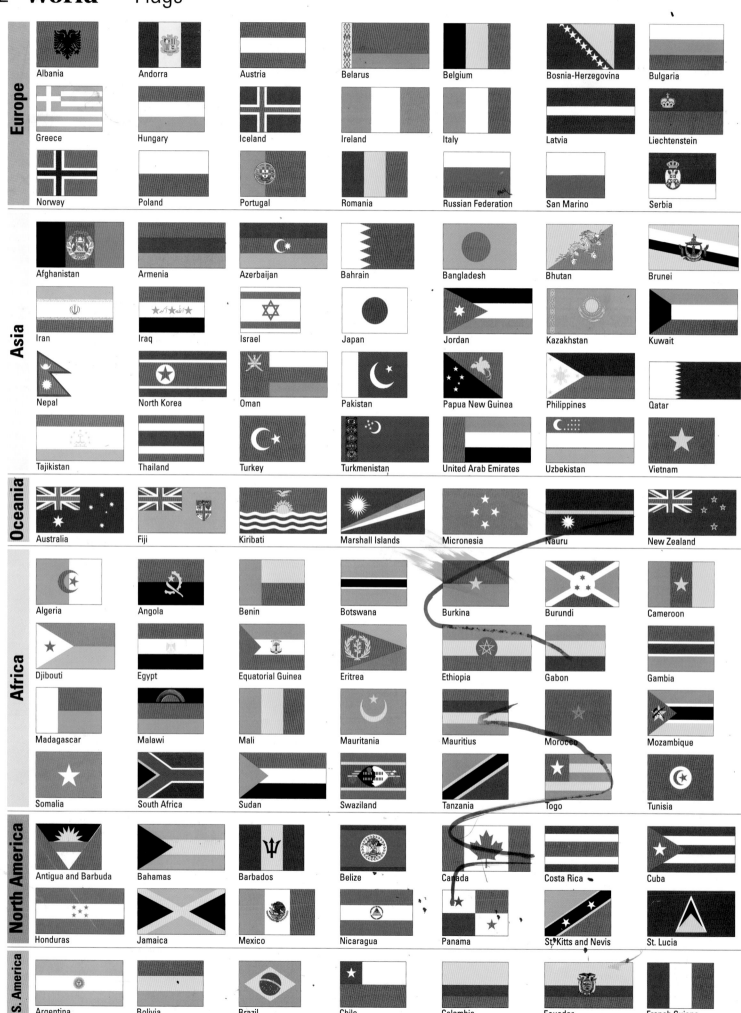

**Europe**

Albania | Andorra | Austria | Belarus | Belgium | Bosnia-Herzegovina | Bulgaria
Greece | Hungary | Iceland | Ireland | Italy | Latvia | Liechtenstein
Norway | Poland | Portugal | Romania | Russian Federation | San Marino | Serbia

**Asia**

Afghanistan | Armenia | Azerbaijan | Bahrain | Bangladesh | Bhutan | Brunei
Iran | Iraq | Israel | Japan | Jordan | Kazakhstan | Kuwait
Nepal | North Korea | Oman | Pakistan | Papua New Guinea | Philippines | Qatar
Tajikistan | Thailand | Turkey | Turkmenistan | United Arab Emirates | Uzbekistan | Vietnam

**Oceania**

Australia | Fiji | Kiribati | Marshall Islands | Micronesia | Nauru | New Zealand

**Africa**

Algeria | Angola | Benin | Botswana | Burkina | Burundi | Cameroon
Djibouti | Egypt | Equatorial Guinea | Eritrea | Ethiopia | Gabon | Gambia
Madagascar | Malawi | Mali | Mauritania | Mauritius | Morocco | Mozambique
Somalia | South Africa | Sudan | Swaziland | Tanzania | Togo | Tunisia

**North America**

Antigua and Barbuda | Bahamas | Barbados | Belize | Canada | Costa Rica | Cuba
Honduras | Jamaica | Mexico | Nicaragua | Panama | St. Kitts and Nevis | St. Lucia

**S. America**

Argentina | Bolivia | Brazil | Chile | Colombia | Ecuador | French Guiana

## Europe

 Croatia

 Czech Republic

 Denmark

 Estonia

 Finland

 France

 Germany

 Lithuania

 Luxembourg

 Macedonia, FYRO

 Malta

 Moldova

 Montenegro

 Netherlands

 Slovakia

 Slovenia

 Spain

 Sweden

 Switzerland

 Ukraine

 United Kingdom

## Asia

 Cambodia

 China

 Cyprus

 East Timor

 Georgia

 India

 Indonesia

 Kyrgyzstan

 Laos

 Lebanon

 Malaysia

 Maldives

 Mongolia

 Myanmar

 Saudi Arabia

 Seychelles

 Singapore

 South Korea

 Sri Lanka

 Syria

 Taiwan

 Yemen

## Oceania

 Northern Marianas

 Palau

 Samoa

 Solomon Islands

 Tonga

 Tuvalu

 Vanuatu

## Africa

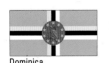 Cape Verde

 Central African Republic

 Chad

 Comoros

 Congo

 Congo, Dem. Rep.

 Côte d'Ivoire

 Ghana

 Guinea

 Guinea-Bissau

 Kenya

 Lesotho

 Liberia

 Libya

 Namibia

 Niger

 Nigeria

 Rwanda

 Sao Tomé and Pirncipe

 Senegal

Sierra Leone

Uganda

Zambia

Zimbabwe

## North America

Dominica

Dominican Republic

El Salvador

Greenland

Grenada

Guatemala

Haiti

St. Vincent & the Grenadines

Trinidad and Tobago

United States of America

## S. America

Guyana

Paraguay

Peru

Suriname

Uruguay

Venezuela

The datasets below are explained on pages 140/1

| | ooo | no data |
|---|---|---|
| | per capita | for each person |

| | Land | | Population | | | | | | | | | Employment | | |
|---|---|---|---|---|---|---|---|---|---|---|---|---|---|---|
| | Area | Arable and permanent crops | Total | Density | Change | Births | Deaths | Fertility | Infant mortality | Life expectancy | Urban | Agriculture | Industry | Service |
| | | | 2006 | 2006 | 1994–2004 | 2006 | 2006 | 2006 | 2006 | 2004 | 2004 | | | |
| | thousand km² | % of total | millions | persons per km² | % | births per 1000 | deaths per 1000 | children per mother | per 1000 live births | years | % | % | % | % |
| Afghanistan | 652 | 12.4 | 31.1 | 47.7 | 57.7 | 48 | 22 | 6.8 | 166 | 46 | ooo | ooo | ooo | ooo |
| Albania | 29 | 24.3 | 3.6 | 124.1 | -9.8 | 14 | 6 | 1.9 | 8 | 74 | 45 | 55 | 23 | 22 |
| Algeria | 2382 | 3.5 | 32.9 | 13.8 | 17.4 | 21 | 4 | 2.4 | 30 | 71 | 63 | 26 | 31 | 43 |
| Andorra | 0.5 | 2.2 | 0.07 | 140.0 | 53.8 | 11 | 4 | 1.3 | 4 | ooo | 53 | ooo | ooo | ooo |
| Angola | 1247 | 2.6 | 12.0 | 9.6 | 19.7 | 49 | 22 | 6.8 | 139 | 41 | ooo | 75 | 8 | 17 |
| Antigua and Barbuda | 0.4 | 22.7 | 0.07 | 175.0 | 51.5 | 18 | 6 | 2.3 | 21 | 74 | 39 | ooo | ooo | ooo |
| Argentina | 2780 | 12.6 | 39.9 | 14.4 | 10.4 | 18 | 8 | 2.4 | 17 | 75 | 90 | 12 | 32 | 56 |
| Armenia | 30 | 18.8 | 3.0 | 100.0 | -14.6 | 13 | 9 | 1.7 | 26 | 72 | 64 | 18 | 43 | 39 |
| Australia | 7741 | 6.3 | 20.3 | 2.6 | 12.6 | 13 | 6 | 1.8 | 5 | 81 | 88 | 6 | 26 | 68 |
| Austria | 84 | 17.4 | 8.2 | 97.6 | 0.9 | 9 | 9 | 1.4 | 4 | 79 | 66 | 8 | 38 | 54 |
| Azerbaijan | 87 | 23.2 | 8.1 | 93.1 | 9.3 | 17 | 6 | 2.0 | 9 | 67 | 52 | 31 | 29 | 40 |
| Bahamas, The | 14 | 0.9 | 0.3 | 21.4 | 9.5 | 19 | 9 | 2.3 | 13 | 70 | 90 | 5 | 16 | 79 |
| Bahrain | 0.7 | 8.5 | 0.7 | 1000.0 | 25.4 | 21 | 3 | 2.6 | 10 | 75 | 96 | 2 | 30 | 68 |
| Bangladesh | 144 | 58.5 | 147.4 | 1023.6 | 20.1 | 27 | 8 | 3.0 | 65 | 63 | 25 | 65 | 16 | 19 |
| Barbados | 0.4 | 39.5 | 0.3 | 750.0 | 13.6 | 14 | 8 | 1.7 | 14 | 75 | 52 | 14 | 30 | 56 |
| Belarus | 208 | 30.4 | 9.8 | 47.1 | -4.9 | 9 | 15 | 1.2 | 8 | 68 | 72 | 20 | 40 | 40 |
| Belgium | 33 | 25.4 | 10.4 | 315.2 | 2.9 | 11 | 10 | 1.6 | 5 | 79 | 97 | 3 | 28 | 69 |
| Belize | 23 | 4.4 | 0.3 | 13.0 | 42.2 | 27 | 5 | 3.3 | 31 | 72 | 48 | 33 | 19 | 48 |
| Benin | 113 | 25.0 | 7.9 | 69.9 | 39.3 | 41 | 12 | 5.6 | 102 | 54 | 40 | 63 | 8 | 29 |
| Bhutan | 47 | 3.5 | 2.3 | 48.9 | -44.4 | 20 | 7 | 2.9 | 40 | 63 | 11 | 94 | 2 | 4 |
| Bolivia | 1099 | 2.8 | 9.0 | 8.2 | 21.6 | 31 | 8 | 3.8 | 54 | 64 | 64 | 47 | 18 | 35 |
| Bosnia-Herzegovina | 51 | 21.3 | 4.5 | 88.2 | -12.5 | 9 | 9 | 1.2 | 7 | 74 | 45 | ooo | ooo | ooo |
| Botswana | 582 | 0.7 | 1.6 | 2.7 | 19.3 | 26 | 27 | 3.1 | 56 | 35 | 57 | 46 | 20 | 34 |
| Brazil | 8547 | 7.8 | 188.1 | 22.0 | 16.5 | 21 | 6 | 2.3 | 27 | 71 | 84 | 23 | 23 | 54 |
| Brunei | 6 | 1.2 | 0.4 | 66.7 | 40.8 | 20 | 3 | 2.4 | 9 | 77 | 73 | 2 | 24 | 74 |
| Bulgaria | 111 | 32.3 | 7.4 | 66.7 | -7.6 | 9 | 15 | 1.3 | 10 | 72 | 70 | 13 | 48 | 39 |
| Burkina | 274 | 16.1 | 13.9 | 50.7 | 37.5 | 44 | 19 | 6.2 | 81 | 48 | 18 | 92 | 2 | 6 |
| Burundi | 28 | 48.5 | 8.1 | 289.3 | 5.5 | 46 | 18 | 6.8 | 106 | 44 | 10 | 92 | 3 | 5 |
| Cambodia | 181 | 21.0 | 13.9 | 76.8 | 36.9 | 30 | 9 | 3.7 | 91 | 57 | 19 | 74 | 8 | 18 |
| Cameroon | 475 | 15.1 | 17.7 | 37.3 | 24.4 | 37 | 14 | 4.9 | 74 | 46 | 54 | 70 | 9 | 21 |
| Canada | 9971 | 4.6 | 33.1 | 3.3 | 9.9 | 11 | 7 | 1.5 | 5 | 80 | 80 | 3 | 25 | 72 |
| Cape Verde | 4 | 11.2 | 0.4 | 100.0 | 34.4 | 30 | 5 | 3.5 | 28 | 71 | 57 | 30 | 30 | 40 |
| Central African Republic | 623 | 3.2 | 4.3 | 6.9 | 13.3 | 37 | 19 | 4.9 | 94 | 39 | 38 | 80 | 3 | 17 |
| Chad | 1284 | 2.8 | 9.9 | 7.7 | 52.9 | 48 | 20 | 6.7 | 101 | 44 | 25 | 83 | 4 | 13 |
| Chile | 757 | 3.0 | 16.1 | 21.3 | 14.3 | 16 | 5 | 2.0 | 8 | 78 | 87 | 19 | 25 | 56 |
| China | 9598 | 16.0 | 1320.9 | 137.6 | 7.7 | 12 | 7 | 1.6 | 27 | 72 | 40 | 72 | 15 | 13 |
| Colombia | 1139 | 3.4 | 43.6 | 38.3 | 19.7 | 20 | 5 | 2.4 | 19 | 73 | 72 | 27 | 23 | 50 |
| Comoros | 2 | 59.2 | 0.7 | 350.0 | 18.2 | 37 | 7 | 4.9 | 59 | 64 | 36 | 78 | 9 | 13 |
| Congo | 342 | 0.7 | 3.7 | 10.8 | 50.5 | 40 | 14 | 5.3 | 75 | 52 | 60 | 49 | 15 | 36 |
| Congo, Dem. Rep. | 2345 | 3.3 | 62.7 | 26.7 | 34.3 | 45 | 14 | 6.7 | 95 | 44 | 32 | 68 | 13 | 19 |
| Costa Rica | 51 | 10.3 | 4.1 | 80.4 | 28.6 | 17 | 4 | 1.9 | 10 | 78 | 61 | 26 | 27 | 47 |
| Côte d'Ivoire | 322 | 21.4 | 17.7 | 55.0 | 23.4 | 39 | 14 | 5.1 | 104 | 46 | 45 | 60 | 10 | 30 |
| Croatia | 57 | 28.1 | 4.5 | 78.9 | -5.4 | 9 | 11 | 1.4 | 6 | 75 | 56 | 16 | 34 | 50 |
| Cuba | 111 | 34.2 | 11.4 | 102.7 | 3.2 | 11 | 7 | 1.5 | 6 | 78 | 76 | 19 | 30 | 51 |
| Cyprus | 9 | 12.2 | 0.8 | 88.9 | 24.0 | 11 | 7 | 1.5 | 5 | 79 | 69 | 14 | 30 | 56 |
| Czech Republic | 79 | 41.9 | 10.2 | 129.1 | -1.3 | 10 | 11 | 1.3 | 3 | 76 | 74 | 11 | 45 | 44 |
| Denmark | 43 | 53.0 | 5.5 | 127.9 | 3.7 | 12 | 10 | 1.8 | 4 | 77 | 86 | 6 | 28 | 66 |
| Djibouti | 23 | 0.04 | 0.5 | 21.7 | 30.6 | 31 | 12 | 4.0 | 100 | 53 | 86 | ooo | ooo | ooo |
| Dominica | 0.8 | 26.7 | 0.07 | 87.5 | 35.1 | 15 | 7 | 1.9 | 22 | 76 | 73 | ooo | ooo | ooo |
| Dominican Republic | 49 | 32.8 | 9.2 | 187.8 | 13.3 | 23 | 6 | 2.8 | 31 | 66 | 66 | 25 | 29 | 46 |
| Ecuador | 284 | 10.5 | 13.5 | 47.5 | 19.4 | 27 | 6 | 3.2 | 29 | 75 | 62 | 33 | 19 | 48 |
| Egypt | 1001 | 3.4 | 78.9 | 78.8 | 30.3 | 27 | 6 | 3.1 | 33 | 70 | 43 | 40 | 22 | 38 |
| El Salvador | 21 | 43.3 | 6.8 | 323.8 | 20.7 | 26 | 6 | 3.0 | 25 | 71 | 60 | 36 | 21 | 43 |
| Equatorial Guinea | 28 | 8.2 | 0.5 | 17.9 | 28.5 | 43 | 20 | 5.6 | 102 | 43 | 39 | 66 | 11 | 23 |
| Eritrea | 118 | 4.3 | 4.8 | 40.7 | 39.3 | 39 | 11 | 5.3 | 61 | 54 | 19 | 80 | 5 | 15 |

## Wealth | Energy and trade | Quality of life

| GNI (million US$) 2005 | Purchasing power (US$) 2004 | Growth of PP (annual %) 1990–2004 | Energy consumption (kg oil equivalent per capita) 2004 | Imports (US$ per capita) 2005 | Exports (US$ per capita) 2005 | Aid received (given) (million US$) 2004 | Human Development Index 2004 | Health care (doctors per 100 000 people) 1990–2004 | Food consumption (daily calories per capita) 2005 | Safe water (% access) 2004 | Illiteracy male (%) 2004 | Illiteracy female (%) 2004 | Higher education (students per 100 000 people) 2002 | Cars (people per car) 2000 | |
|---|---|---|---|---|---|---|---|---|---|---|---|---|---|---|---|
| ooo | ooo | ooo | 14 | ooo | ooo | ooo | ooo | ooo | ooo | ooo | ooo | ooo | ooo | 644 | Afghanistan |
| 8.0 | 4978 | 4.8 | 804 | 835 | 210 | 363 | 0.784 | 131 | 2918 | 96 | 1 | 2 | 1165 | 36 | Albania |
| 39.6 | 6603 | 0.9 | 964 | 620 | 1400 | 313 | 0.728 | 113 | 3510 | 85 | 20 | 40 | 1459 | 34 | Algeria |
| ooo | ooo | ooo | ooo | ooo | ooo | ooo | ooo | ooo | ooo | ooo | ooo | ooo | ooo | 2 | Andorra |
| 22.5 | 2180 | -1.2 | 309 | 511 | 1468 | 1144 | 0.439 | 8 | 2518 | 53 | 17 | 46 | 74 | 111 | Angola |
| ooo | 12 586 | 1.5 | 2876 | 7006 | 906 | 2 | 0.808 | 17 | 2045 | 91 | ooo | ooo | ooo | ooo | Antigua and Barbuda |
| 73.1 | 13 298 | 1.3 | 1781 | 740 | 1033 | 91 | 0.863 | 301 | 2985 | 96 | 3 | 3 | 5006 | 7 | Argentina |
| 4.4 | 4101 | 2.7 | 1508 | 586 | 315 | 254 | 0.768 | 359 | 2380 | 92 | 0 | 1 | 2504 | 1900 | Armenia |
| 73.2 | 30 331 | 2.5 | 6612 | 6163 | 5206 | (1460) | 0.957 | 247 | 3330 | 100 | ooo | ooo | 5178 | 2 | Australia |
| 06.2 | 32 276 | 2.0 | 4453 | 15 325 | 15 059 | (678) | 0.944 | 338 | 4023 | 100 | ooo | ooo | 2746 | 2 | Austria |
| 10.4 | 4153 | 5.5 | 2056 | 501 | 518 | 176 | 0.736 | 355 | 2744 | 77 | 1 | 2 | 2189 | 30 | Azerbaijan |
| ooo | 17 843 | 0.2 | 4780 | 6652 | 1619 | 5 | 0.825 | 105 | 2521 | 97 | ooo | ooo | ooo | 4 | Bahamas, The |
| ooo | 20 758 | 2.2 | 15 286 | 10 652 | 13 578 | 104 | 0.859 | 109 | ooo | ooo | 11 | 16 | 1683 | 5 | Bahrain |
| 66.7 | 1870 | 2.5 | 116 | 98 | 66 | 1404 | 0.530 | 26 | 2309 | 74 | ooo | ooo | 631 | 2808 | Bangladesh |
| ooo | ooo | ooo | 2177 | 5952 | 1333 | 29 | 0.879 | 121 | 2988 | 100 | ooo | ooo | 2730 | 7 | Barbados |
| 27.0 | 6970 | 1.6 | 2452 | 1708 | 1634 | 46 | 0.794 | 455 | 2885 | 100 | 0 | 1 | 4485 | 9 | Belarus |
| 78.7 | 31 096 | 1.7 | 6726 | 30 410 | 31 903 | (1463) | 0.945 | 449 | 3109 | ooo | ooo | ooo | 3559 | 2 | Belgium |
| 1.0 | 6747 | 2.6 | 1248 | 2032 | 737 | 7 | 0.751 | 105 | 2921 | 91 | ooo | ooo | ooo | 29 | Belize |
| 4.3 | 1091 | 1.4 | 101 | 106 | 66 | 378 | 0.428 | 4 | 2437 | 67 | 52 | 77 | 274 | 260 | Benin |
| 0.8 | 1969 | ooo | 226 | 620 | 393 | 78 | 0.538 | 5 | ooo | 62 | ooo | ooo | 90 | ooo | Bhutan |
| 9.3 | 2720 | 1.2 | 566 | 255 | 291 | 767 | 0.692 | 122 | 2128 | 85 | 7 | 19 | 3576 | 65 | Bolivia |
| 10.5 | 7032 | 12.0 | 1239 | 1816 | 615 | 671 | 0.800 | 134 | 3068 | 97 | 1 | 6 | ooo | 34 | Bosnia-Herzegovina |
| 9.9 | 9945 | 4.2 | 816 | 1854 | 2507 | 39 | 0.570 | 40 | ooo | 95 | 20 | 18 | 514 | 59 | Botswana |
| 62.0 | 8195 | 1.2 | 1233 | 416 | 635 | 285 | 0.792 | 115 | 3244 | 90 | 12 | 11 | 1737 | 11 | Brazil |
| ooo | 19 210 | ooo | 6852 | 3745 | 17 607 | 1 | 0.871 | 101 | 2610 | ooo | 5 | 10 | 1276 | 2 | Brunei |
| 26.7 | 8078 | 0.7 | 2814 | 2349 | 1515 | 622 | 0.816 | 356 | 2839 | 99 | 1 | 2 | 2981 | 5 | Bulgaria |
| 5.2 | 1169 | 1.3 | 35 | 99 | 37 | 610 | 0.342 | 6 | 2593 | 61 | 71 | 85 | 121 | 744 | Burkina |
| 0.7 | 677 | -2.5 | 26 | 35 | 15 | 351 | 0.384 | 3 | 1693 | 79 | 33 | 48 | 177 | 650 | Burundi |
| 6.1 | 2423 | 5.0 | 15 | 263 | 220 | 478 | 0.583 | 16 | 2370 | 41 | 15 | 36 | 248 | 788 | Cambodia |
| 16.4 | 2174 | 0.5 | 128 | 177 | 173 | 762 | 0.506 | 19 | 2634 | 66 | 23 | 40 | 504 | 152 | Cameroon |
| 52.6 | 31 263 | 2.1 | 10 459 | 9898 | 11 127 | (2599) | 0.950 | 214 | 3486 | 100 | ooo | ooo | 3738 | 2 | Canada |
| 1.0 | 5727 | 3.5 | 136 | 865 | 35 | 140 | 0.722 | 49 | 2875 | 80 | ooo | ooo | 415 | 133 | Cape Verde |
| 1.4 | 1094 | -0.6 | 35 | 37 | 32 | 105 | 0.353 | 8 | 2105 | 75 | 35 | 67 | 175 | 422 | Central African Republic |
| 3.9 | 2090 | 2.1 | 8 | 79 | 314 | 319 | 0.368 | 4 | 2190 | 42 | 59 | 87 | 66 | 853 | Chad |
| 95.7 | 10 874 | 3.7 | 1866 | 1997 | 2490 | 49 | 0.859 | 109 | 3079 | 95 | 4 | 4 | 3366 | 15 | Chile |
| 69.7 | 5896 | 8.9 | 1147 | 735 | 805 | 1661 | 0.768 | 106 | 2951 | 77 | 5 | 14 | 946 | 369 | China |
| 04.5 | 7256 | 0.5 | 705 | 465 | 464 | 509 | 0.790 | 135 | 2745 | 93 | 7 | 7 | 2383 | 43 | Colombia |
| 0.4 | 1943 | -0.5 | 58 | 158 | 20 | 25 | 0.556 | 15 | 1766 | 86 | ooo | ooo | 116 | 1 | Comoros |
| 3.8 | 978 | -0.2 | 122 | 354 | 1250 | 116 | 0.520 | 20 | 2026 | 58 | ooo | ooo | 418 | 119 | Congo |
| 7.0 | 705 | -6.0 | 37 | 38 | 36 | 1815 | 0.391 | 11 | 1398 | 46 | 19 | 46 | 110 | 525 | Congo, Dem. Rep. |
| 20.3 | 9481 | 2.5 | 1174 | 2264 | 1627 | 14 | 0.841 | 132 | 2618 | 97 | 5 | 5 | 2065 | 22 | Costa Rica |
| 15.7 | 1551 | -1.1 | 162 | 295 | 419 | 154 | 0.421 | 12 | 2268 | 84 | 39 | 61 | 595 | 88 | Côte d'Ivoire |
| 36.9 | 12 191 | 2.5 | 2153 | 4174 | 1983 | 121 | 0.846 | 244 | 2811 | 100 | 1 | 3 | 2511 | 5 | Croatia |
| ooo | ooo | ooo | 1037 | 632 | 238 | 91 | 0.826 | 591 | 3547 | 91 | 0 | 0 | 1704 | 57.4 | Cuba |
| ooo | 22 805 | 3.0 | 3683 | 8320 | 1926 | 60 | 0.903 | 234 | 3295 | 100 | 1 | 5 | 1815 | 4 | Cyprus |
| 14.8 | 19 408 | 2.7 | 4319 | 7495 | 7646 | 280 | 0.885 | 351 | 3303 | 100 | ooo | ooo | 2774 | 3 | Czech Republic |
| 61.8 | 31 914 | 1.7 | 3991 | 14 036 | 15 720 | (2037) | 0.943 | 293 | 3494 | 100 | ooo | ooo | 3651 | 3 | Denmark |
| 0.8 | 1993 | -1.9 | 1396 | 403 | 50 | 64 | 0.494 | 18 | 2674 | 73 | ooo | ooo | 163 | 55 | Djibouti |
| ooo | 5643 | 1.4 | 746 | 2298 | 563 | 29 | 0.793 | 50 | 3083 | 97 | ooo | ooo | ooo | 23 | Dominica |
| 21.9 | 7449 | 4.2 | 841 | 1081 | 689 | 87 | 0.751 | 188 | 2673 | 95 | 13 | 13 | ooo | 53 | Dominican Republic |
| 34.7 | 3963 | 0.2 | 724 | 779 | 764 | 161 | 0.765 | 148 | 2770 | 94 | 8 | 10 | ooo | 123 | Ecuador |
| 93.0 | 4211 | 2.5 | 829 | 268 | 144 | 1458 | 0.702 | 54 | 3274 | 98 | 17 | 41 | 3338 | 52 | Egypt |
| 16.8 | 5041 | 1.8 | 466 | 983 | 493 | 212 | 0.729 | 124 | 2680 | 84 | ooo | ooo | 1730 | 67 | El Salvador |
| ooo | 20 510 | 30.4 | 303 | 4042 | 14 254 | 30 | 0.653 | 30 | ooo | 43 | 7 | 20 | 201 | 143 | Equatorial Guinea |
| 0.8 | 977 | 0.6 | 62 | 112 | 2 | 260 | 0.454 | 5 | ooo | 60 | ooo | ooo | 128 | 760 | Eritrea |

The datasets below are explained on pages 140/

| | no data |
|---|---|
| ooo | no data |
| per capita | for each person |

| | **Land** | | **Population** | | | | | | | | | **Employment** | | |
|---|---|---|---|---|---|---|---|---|---|---|---|---|---|---|
| | Area | Arable and permanent crops | Total | Density | Change | Births | Deaths | Fertility | Infant mortality | Life expectancy | Urban | Agriculture | Industry | Service |
| | 2006 | 2006 | 2006 | 2006 | 1994–2004 | 2006 | 2006 | 2006 | 2006 | 2004 | 2004 | | | |
| | thousand km² | % of total | millions | persons per km² | % | births per 1000 | deaths per 1000 | children per mother | per 1000 live births | years | % | % | % | % |
| Estonia | 45 | 14.0 | 1.3 | 28.9 | -13.3 | 11 | 13 | 1.5 | 6 | 72 | 69 | 14 | 41 | 45 |
| Ethiopia | 1104 | 9.7 | 74.8 | 67.8 | 34.5 | 39 | 15 | 5.4 | 77 | 48 | 16 | 86 | 2 | 12 |
| Fiji | 18 | 15.6 | 0.9 | 50.0 | 2.0 | 21 | 6 | 2.5 | 16 | 68 | 50 | 46 | 15 | 39 |
| Finland | 338 | 6.5 | 5.2 | 15.4 | 2.2 | 11 | 9 | 1.8 | 3 | 79 | 61 | 8 | 31 | 61 |
| France | 552 | 35.5 | 60.9 | 110.3 | 3.6 | 13 | 9 | 1.9 | 4 | 80 | 77 | 5 | 29 | 66 |
| French Guiana | 91 | 0.1 | 0.2 | 2.2 | 49.3 | 31 | 4 | 3.9 | 10 | ooo | ooo | ooo | ooo | ooo |
| Gabon | 268 | 1.8 | 1.4 | 5.2 | 34.6 | 33 | 13 | 4.3 | 57 | 54 | 83 | 51 | 16 | 33 |
| Gambia, The | 11 | 22.6 | 1.6 | 145.5 | 39.3 | 38 | 12 | 5.1 | 75 | 56 | 53 | 82 | 8 | 10 |
| Georgia | 70 | 15.3 | 4.7 | 67.1 | -17.1 | 12 | 11 | 1.6 | 25 | 71 | 52 | 26 | 31 | 43 |
| Germany | 357 | 33.6 | 82.4 | 230.8 | 1.4 | 8 | 10 | 1.3 | 4 | 79 | 75 | 4 | 38 | 58 |
| Ghana | 239 | 26.5 | 22.5 | 94.1 | 26.8 | 33 | 10 | 4.4 | 59 | 57 | 47 | 59 | 13 | 28 |
| Greece | 132 | 29.1 | 10.7 | 81.1 | 5.5 | 10 | 10 | 1.3 | 4 | 78 | 59 | 23 | 27 | 50 |
| Greenland | 342 | ooo | 0.06 | 0.2 | 1.1 | ooo | ooo | ooo | ooo | ooo | ooo | ooo | ooo | ooo |
| Grenada | 0.3 | 35.3 | 0.09 | 300.0 | 8.7 | 19 | 7 | 2.1 | 17 | 65 | 31 | ooo | ooo | ooo |
| Guatemala | 109 | 17.5 | 12.5 | 114.7 | 30.7 | 34 | 6 | 4.4 | 35 | 68 | 47 | 52 | 17 | 31 |
| Guinea | 246 | 6.3 | 9.7 | 39.4 | 29.4 | 41 | 13 | 5.7 | 98 | 54 | 33 | 87 | 2 | 11 |
| Guinea-Bissau | 36 | 15.2 | 1.4 | 38.9 | 42.6 | 50 | 20 | 7.1 | 116 | 45 | 30 | 85 | 2 | 13 |
| Guyana | 215 | 2.4 | 0.8 | 3.7 | 8.3 | 22 | 9 | 2.3 | 46 | 64 | 28 | 22 | 25 | 53 |
| Haiti | 28 | 39.6 | 8.5 | 303.6 | 15.0 | 36 | 13 | 4.7 | 73 | 52 | 38 | 68 | 9 | 23 |
| Honduras | 112 | 12.7 | 7.3 | 65.2 | 29.1 | 31 | 6 | 3.9 | 30 | 68 | 46 | 41 | 20 | 39 |
| Hungary | 93 | 51.6 | 10.0 | 107.5 | -1.6 | 10 | 13 | 1.3 | 6 | 73 | 66 | 15 | 38 | 47 |
| Iceland | 103 | 0.07 | 0.3 | 2.9 | 12.8 | 14 | 6 | 2.1 | 2 | 81 | 93 | ooo | ooo | ooo |
| India | 3288 | 51.7 | 1111.7 | 338.1 | 20.2 | 24 | 8 | 2.9 | 58 | 64 | 29 | 64 | 16 | 20 |
| Indonesia | 1905 | 17.7 | 231.8 | 121.7 | 14.7 | 20 | 6 | 2.4 | 35 | 67 | 47 | 55 | 14 | 31 |
| Iran | 1633 | 10.4 | 65.0 | 39.8 | 13.6 | 18 | 6 | 2.0 | 32 | 71 | 66 | 39 | 23 | 38 |
| Iraq | 438 | 13.9 | 26.8 | 61.2 | 33.0 | 36 | 10 | 4.8 | 88 | 59 | ooo | 16 | 18 | 66 |
| Ireland | 70 | 16.0 | 4.1 | 58.6 | 14.3 | 15 | 7 | 1.9 | 5 | 78 | 60 | 14 | 29 | 57 |
| Israel | 21 | 19.2 | 6.4 | 304.8 | 25.9 | 21 | 5 | 2.8 | 4 | 80 | 92 | 4 | 29 | 67 |
| Italy | 301 | 36.7 | 58.1 | 193.0 | 1.0 | 10 | 10 | 1.3 | 4 | 80 | 68 | 9 | 31 | 60 |
| Jamaica | 11 | 25.8 | 2.8 | 254.5 | 5.1 | 19 | 6 | 2.3 | 24 | 71 | 53 | 25 | 23 | 52 |
| Japan | 378 | 12.6 | 127.5 | 337.3 | 1.9 | 9 | 8 | 1.3 | 3 | 82 | 66 | 7 | 34 | 59 |
| Jordan | 89 | 4.5 | 5.9 | 66.3 | 37.9 | 29 | 5 | 3.7 | 24 | 72 | 82 | 15 | 23 | 62 |
| Kazakhstan | 2717 | 8.0 | 15.2 | 5.6 | -8.0 | 18 | 10 | 2.2 | 29 | 64 | 57 | 22 | 32 | 46 |
| Kenya | 580 | 8.9 | 35.9 | 61.9 | 10.6 | 40 | 15 | 4.9 | 77 | 48 | 21 | 80 | 7 | 13 |
| Kiribati | 0.7 | 50.7 | 0.1 | 142.9 | 31.6 | 31 | 8 | 4.2 | 43 | ooo | ooo | ooo | ooo | ooo |
| Kuwait | 18 | 0.8 | 2.4 | 133.3 | 54.3 | 19 | 2 | 2.4 | 10 | 77 | 98 | 1 | 25 | 74 |
| Kyrgyzstan | 199 | 7.1 | 5.2 | 26.1 | 12.7 | 21 | 7 | 2.6 | 30 | 67 | 36 | 32 | 27 | 41 |
| Laos | 237 | 4.2 | 6.4 | 27.0 | 26.9 | 36 | 13 | 4.8 | 88 | 55 | 20 | 78 | 6 | 16 |
| Latvia | 65 | 28.8 | 2.3 | 35.4 | -9.7 | 9 | 14 | 1.3 | 7 | 72 | 68 | 16 | 40 | 44 |
| Lebanon | 10 | 30.1 | 3.9 | 390.0 | 46.3 | 19 | 5 | 2.4 | 17 | 72 | 87 | 7 | 31 | 62 |
| Lesotho | 30 | 11.0 | 2.0 | 66.7 | -1.7 | 28 | 25 | 3.5 | 91 | 35 | 19 | 40 | 28 | 32 |
| Liberia | 111 | 5.4 | 3.0 | 27.0 | 29.6 | 50 | 21 | 6.8 | 142 | 43 | ooo | ooo | ooo | ooo |
| Libya | 1760 | 1.2 | 5.9 | 3.4 | 14.3 | 27 | 4 | 3.4 | 26 | 74 | 85 | 11 | 23 | 66 |
| Liechtenstein | 0.2 | 25.0 | 0.03 | 150.0 | 0 | 11 | 6 | 1.4 | 3 | ooo | ooo | ooo | ooo | ooo |
| Lithuania | 65 | 45.8 | 3.6 | 55.4 | -8.6 | 9 | 13 | 1.3 | 7 | 73 | 67 | 18 | 41 | 41 |
| Luxembourg | 3 | ooo | 0.5 | 166.7 | 23.8 | 9 | 13 | 1.3 | 4 | 79 | 83 | ooo | ooo | ooo |
| Macedonia, FYRO* | 26 | 23.8 | 2.1 | 80.8 | 7.8 | 11 | 9 | 1.4 | 11 | 74 | 68 | 21 | 40 | 39 |
| Madagascar | 587 | 6.0 | 18.9 | 32.2 | 30.6 | 40 | 12 | 5.2 | 83 | 56 | 27 | 78 | 7 | 15 |
| Malawi | 118 | 20.6 | 13.3 | 112.7 | 25.8 | 44 | 18 | 6.0 | 76 | 40 | 17 | 87 | 5 | 8 |
| Malaysia | 330 | 23.0 | 24.4 | 73.9 | 27.3 | 20 | 4 | 2.6 | 10 | 73 | 66 | 27 | 23 | 50 |
| Maldives | 0.3 | 40.0 | 0.4 | 1333.3 | 22.0 | 18 | 3 | 2.8 | 15 | 67 | 29 | 32 | 31 | 37 |
| Mali | 1240 | 3.8 | 11.7 | 9.4 | 38.4 | 50 | 18 | 7.1 | 130 | 48 | 30 | 86 | 2 | 12 |
| Malta | 0.3 | 31.3 | 0.4 | 1333.3 | 8.7 | 9 | 7 | 1.4 | 6 | 79 | 95 | ooo | ooo | ooo |
| Marshall Islands | 0.2 | 16.7 | 0.06 | 300.0 | 85.2 | 38 | 5 | 4.9 | 29 | ooo | ooo | ooo | ooo | ooo |
| Mauritania | 1026 | 0.5 | 3.2 | 3.1 | 35.7 | 42 | 14 | 5.8 | 74 | 53 | 40 | 55 | 10 | 35 |

* Former Yugoslav Republic of Macedonia

© Oxford University Press

## Wealth | Energy and trade | Quality of life

| GNI | Purchasing power | Growth of PP | Energy consumption | Imports | Exports | Aid received (given) | Human Development Index | Health care | Food consumption | Safe water | Illiteracy male | Illiteracy female | Higher education | Cars | |
|---|---|---|---|---|---|---|---|---|---|---|---|---|---|---|---|
| 2005 | 2004 | 1990–2004 | 2004 | 2005 | 2005 | 2004 | 2004 | 1990–2004 | 2005 | 2004 | 2004 | 2004 | 2002 | 2000 | |
| million US$ | US$ | annual % | kg oil equivalent per capita | US$ per capita | US$ per capita | million US$ | | doctors per 100 000 people | daily calories per capita | % access | % | % | students per 100 000 people | people per car | |
| 12.2 | 14 555 | 4.3 | 4146 | 7453 | 5695 | 136 | 0.858 | 448 | 2744 | 100 | 0 | 0 | 4459 | 3 | Estonia |
| 11.1 | 756 | 1.5 | 29 | 58 | 12 | 1823 | 0.371 | 3 | 1582 | 22 | ooo | ooo | 150 | 1433 | Ethiopia |
| 2.7 | 6066 | 1.4 | 790 | 1899 | 828 | 64 | 0.758 | 34 | 3197 | 47 | ooo | ooo | ooo | 17 | Fiji |
| 96.9 | 29 951 | 2.2 | 6454 | 11 246 | 12 584 | (680) | 0.947 | 316 | 3387 | 100 | ooo | ooo | 5465 | 3 | Finland |
| 69.2 | 29 300 | 1.7 | 4655 | 8176 | 7559 | (8473) | 0.942 | 337 | 3681 | 100 | ooo | ooo | 3386 | 2 | France |
| ooo | ooo | ooo | 1972 | ooo | ooo | ooo | ooo | ooo | ooo | ooo | ooo | ooo | ooo | 7 | French Guiana |
| 6.9 | 6623 | -0.1 | 734 | 1007 | 3555 | 38 | 0.633 | 29 | 2705 | 88 | ooo | ooo | 580 | 7 | Gabon |
| 0.4 | 1991 | 0.2 | 66 | 155 | 5 | 63 | 0.479 | 11 | 2537 | 82 | ooo | ooo | ooo | 186 | Gambia, The |
| 5.9 | 2844 | -1.0 | 760 | 557 | 194 | 315 | 0.743 | 409 | 1797 | 82 | ooo | ooo | 3154 | 12 | Georgia |
| 75.6 | 28 303 | 1.5 | 4457 | 9383 | 11 760 | (7534) | 0.932 | 337 | 3472 | 100 | ooo | ooo | 2654 | 2 | Germany |
| 10.0 | 2240 | 1.9 | 164 | 226 | 113 | 1358 | 0.532 | 15 | 3098 | 75 | 34 | 50 | 339 | 214 | Ghana |
| 20.3 | 22 205 | 2.6 | 3395 | 4860 | 1535 | (465) | 0.921 | 438 | 3706 | ooo | 2 | 6 | 4979 | 4 | Greece |
| ooo | ooo | ooo | 3603 | ooo | ooo | ooo | ooo | ooo | ooo | ooo | ooo | ooo | ooo | ooo | Greenland |
| ooo | 8021 | 3.1 | 997 | 3099 | 376 | 15 | 0.762 | 50 | 2310 | 95 | ooo | ooo | ooo | ooo | Grenada |
| 30.3 | 4313 | 1.3 | 377 | 833 | 427 | 218 | 0.762 | 90 | 2239 | 95 | 25 | 37 | ooo | 84 | Guatemala |
| 3.9 | 2180 | 1.0 | 61 | 87 | 95 | 279 | 0.673 | 11 | 2428 | 50 | 57 | 82 | ooo | 488 | Guinea |
| 0.3 | 722 | -2.6 | 95 | 75 | 64 | 76 | 0.445 | 12 | 1949 | 59 | ooo | ooo | 35 | 267 | Guinea-Bissau |
| 0.8 | 4439 | 1.5 | 776 | 1046 | 733 | 145 | 0.349 | 48 | 2853 | 83 | ooo | ooo | ooo | 32 | Guyana |
| 3.9 | 1892 | -2.2 | 82 | 170 | 55 | 243 | 0.725 | 25 | 1945 | 54 | ooo | ooo | ooo | 252 | Haiti |
| 8.0 | 2876 | 0.2 | 361 | 622 | 235 | 642 | 0.482 | 57 | 2435 | 87 | 20 | 20 | 1388 | 165 | Honduras |
| 01.6 | 16 814 | 3.1 | 2653 | 6548 | 6157 | 303 | 0.683 | 333 | 3272 | 99 | ooo | ooo | 3515 | 4 | Hungary |
| 14.4 | 33 051 | 2.0 | 12 563 | 16 792 | 10 401 | ooo | 0.869 | 362 | 3189 | 100 | ooo | ooo | 4022 | 2 | Iceland |
| 04.1 | 3139 | 4.0 | 358 | 123 | 87 | 691 | 0.960 | 60 | 2417 | 86 | 27 | 52 | 1023 | 218 | India |
| 82.2 | 3609 | 1.8 | 518 | 315 | 391 | 84 | 0.611 | 13 | 2893 | 77 | 6 | 13 | 1373 | 86 | Indonesia |
| 77.3 | 7525 | 2.3 | 2506 | 525 | 824 | 189 | 0.711 | 45 | 3082 | 94 | 17 | 30 | 2341 | 44 | Iran |
| ooo | ooo | ooo | 1189 | ooo | ooo | ooo | 0.746 | ooo | ooo | ooo | ooo | ooo | 1325 | 35 | Iraq |
| 71.1 | 38 827 | 7.3 | 4014 | 16 351 | 26 413 | (607) | 0.956 | 279 | 3679 | ooo | ooo | ooo | 4545 | 3 | Ireland |
| 28.7 | 24 382 | 1.6 | 3519 | 6809 | 6161 | 479 | 0.927 | 382 | 3695 | 100 | 2 | 4 | 4971 | 5 | Israel |
| 72.9 | 28 180 | 1.3 | 3559 | 6480 | 6265 | (2462) | 0.940 | 420 | 3730 | ooo | 1 | 2 | 3201 | 2 | Italy |
| 9.0 | 4163 | -0.1 | 1457 | 1680 | 565 | 75 | 0.724 | 85 | 2826 | 93 | 26 | 14 | 1694 | 23 | Jamaica |
| 76.5 | 29 251 | 0.8 | 4442 | 4030 | 4656 | (8922) | 0.949 | 198 | 2679 | 100 | ooo | ooo | 3122 | 3 | Japan |
| 13.5 | 4688 | 0.5 | 1250 | 1920 | 786 | 581 | 0.760 | 203 | 2741 | 97 | 5 | 15 | 3065 | 28 | Jordan |
| 44.6 | 7440 | 1.7 | 3849 | 1146 | 1839 | 265 | 0.774 | 354 | 3200 | 86 | 0 | 1 | 3414 | ooo | Kazakhstan |
| 18.4 | 1140 | -0.6 | 129 | 179 | 96 | 635 | 0.491 | 14 | 1881 | 61 | 22 | 30 | 314 | 174 | Kenya |
| ooo | ooo | ooo | 102 | 556 | 10 | ooo | ooo | ooo | 2333 | ooo | ooo | ooo | ooo | ooo | Kiribati |
| 77.7 | 19 384 | -0.4 | 11 749 | 6419 | 17 753 | 3 | 0.871 | 153 | ooo | ooo | 6 | 9 | 1531 | 3 | Kuwait |
| 2.3 | 1935 | -1.3 | 837 | 215 | 131 | 258 | 0.705 | 251 | 3052 | 77 | 1 | 2 | 4219 | 36 | Kyrgyzstan |
| 2.6 | 1954 | 4.2 | 207 | 126 | 86 | 270 | 0.553 | 59 | 3064 | 51 | 23 | 39 | 494 | 540 | Laos |
| 15.6 | 11653 | 2.8 | 1870 | 3780 | 2243 | 165 | 0.845 | 301 | 2586 | 99 | 0 | 0 | 4722 | 5 | Latvia |
| 22.6 | 5837 | 3.7 | 1575 | 2693 | 653 | 265 | 0.774 | 325 | 3009 | 100 | ooo | ooo | 3887 | 5 | Lebanon |
| 1.7 | 2619 | 4.5 | 67 | 774 | 362 | 102 | 0.494 | 5 | ooo | 79 | 26 | 10 | 269 | 350 | Lesotho |
| 0.4 | ooo | ooo | 65 | 362 | 61 | ooo | ooo | ooo | 1943 | ooo | ooo | ooo | 1352 | 310 | Liberia |
| 32.4 | 7570 | ooo | 3326 | 1196 | 5144 | 18 | 0.798 | 129 | 2892 | ooo | ooo | ooo | 6690 | 11 | Libya |
| ooo | ooo | ooo | ooo | ooo | ooo | ooo | ooo | ooo | ooo | ooo | ooo | ooo | ooo | 2 | Liechtenstein |
| 24.6 | 13 107 | 1.4 | 2465 | 4526 | 3460 | 252 | 0.857 | 397 | 3196 | ooo | 0 | 0 | 4095 | 4 | Lithuania |
| ooo | 69 961 | 5.4 | 10 811 | 47 532 | 40 266 | (236) | 0.945 | 266 | ooo | 100 | ooo | ooo | 658 | 2 | Luxembourg |
| 5.8 | 6610 | -0.4 | 1376 | 1587 | 1003 | 248 | 0.796 | 219 | 2631 | ooo | 2 | 6 | 2202 | 7 | Macedonia, FYRO* |
| 5.4 | 857 | -1.1 | 51 | 83 | 41 | 1236 | 0.509 | 29 | 2148 | 50 | 24 | 35 | 198 | 288 | Madagascar |
| 2.1 | 646 | 0.9 | 48 | 90 | 40 | 476 | 0.400 | 2 | 1729 | 73 | 25 | 46 | 28 | 644 | Malawi |
| 25.9 | 10 276 | 3.5 | 2677 | 4521 | 5561 | 290 | 0.805 | 70 | 3013 | 99 | 8 | 15 | 2458 | 6 | Malaysia |
| 0.8 | ooo | ooo | 1116 | 2260 | 492 | 28 | 0.739 | 92 | 2791 | 83 | 4 | 4 | ooo | ooo | Maldives |
| 5.2 | 998 | 2.5 | 25 | 119 | 82 | 567 | 0.338 | 8 | 2306 | 50 | 73 | 88 | 243 | 557 | Mali |
| 5.5 | 18 879 | 3.6 | 2605 | 8915 | 5641 | 6 | 0.875 | 318 | 3451 | 100 | 14 | 11 | 1845 | 2 | Malta |
| 0.2 | ooo | ooo | ooo | ooo | ooo | ooo | ooo | ooo | ooo | ooo | ooo | ooo | ooo | ooo | Marshall Islands |
| 1.8 | 1940 | 1.2 | 422 | 244 | 184 | 180 | 0.486 | 11 | 2371 | 53 | 41 | 57 | 289 | 280 | Mauritania |

The datasets below are explained on pages 140/⬧

| | | | | | | | | | | | | | | |
|---|---|---|---|---|---|---|---|---|---|---|---|---|---|---|
| ooo no data | | | | | | | | | | | | | | |
| per capita for each person | | | | | | | | | | | | | | |

| | **Land** | | **Population** | | | | | | | | | **Employment** | | |
|---|---|---|---|---|---|---|---|---|---|---|---|---|---|---|
| | Area | Arable and permanent crops | Total | Density | Change | Births | Deaths | Fertility | Infant mortality | Life expectancy | Urban | Agriculture | Industry | Service |
| | | | 2006 | 2006 | 1994–2004 | 2006 | 2006 | 2006 | 2006 | 2004 | 2004 | | | |
| | thousand km² | % of total | millions | persons per km² | % | births per 1000 | deaths per 1000 | children per mother | per 1000 live births | years | % | % | % | % |
| Mauritius | 2 | 52.0 | 1.2 | 600.0 | 7.8 | 15 | 7 | 1.8 | 15 | 72 | 42 | 17 | 43 | 40 |
| Mexico | 1958 | 13.9 | 107.4 | 54.9 | 18.6 | 22 | 5 | 2.4 | 21 | 75 | 76 | 28 | 24 | 48 |
| Micronesia, Fed. States | 0.7 | 51.4 | 0.1 | 142.9 | -3.8 | 26 | 6 | 4.1 | 40 | ooo | ooo | ooo | ooo | ooo |
| Moldova | 34 | 64.3 | 4.3 | 126.5 | -3.4 | 11 | 12 | 1.3 | 12 | 68 | 47 | 33 | 30 | 37 |
| Mongolia | 1567 | 0.8 | 2.8 | 1.8 | 10.4 | 18 | 6 | 1.9 | 21 | 65 | 57 | 32 | 22 | 46 |
| Montenegro | 14 | ooo | 0.7 | 50.0 | ooo | 13 | 9 | 1.7 | 8 | ooo | ooo | ooo | ooo | ooo |
| Morocco | 447 | 20.8 | 33.2 | 74.3 | 15.1 | 21 | 6 | 2.5 | 40 | 70 | 58 | 45 | 25 | 30 |
| Mozambique | 802 | 5.5 | 20.5 | 25.6 | 15.6 | 41 | 20 | 5.4 | 108 | 42 | 34 | 83 | 8 | 9 |
| Myanmar | 677 | 15.7 | 47.0 | 69.4 | 14.1 | 21 | 10 | 2.5 | 75 | 61 | 30 | 73 | 10 | 17 |
| Namibia | 824 | 1.0 | 2.0 | 2.4 | 22.8 | 29 | 15 | 3.9 | 44 | 47 | 35 | 49 | 15 | 36 |
| Nauru | 0.02 | ooo | 0.01 | 500.0 | 0 | 26 | 7 | 3.4 | 42 | ooo | ooo | ooo | ooo | ooo |
| Nepal | 147 | 22.4 | 28.3 | 192.5 | 24.4 | 31 | 9 | 3.7 | 64 | 62 | 15 | 94 | 0 | 6 |
| Netherlands | 41 | 22.9 | 16.5 | 402.4 | 6.0 | 12 | 8 | 1.7 | 5 | 79 | 80 | 5 | 26 | 69 |
| New Zealand | 271 | 12.5 | 4.1 | 15.1 | 13.8 | 14 | 7 | 2.0 | 5 | 79 | 86 | 10 | 25 | 65 |
| Nicaragua | 130 | 16.6 | 5.6 | 43.1 | 30.3 | 29 | 5 | 3.3 | 36 | 70 | 59 | 28 | 26 | 46 |
| Niger | 1267 | 3.6 | 12.5 | 9.9 | 40.8 | 55 | 21 | 7.9 | 149 | 45 | 17 | 90 | 4 | 6 |
| Nigeria | 924 | 35.7 | 131.9 | 142.7 | 42.3 | 43 | 19 | 5.9 | 100 | 43 | 47 | 43 | 7 | 50 |
| Northern Marianas | 0.5 | 17.4 | 0.08 | 160.0 | 6.3 | ooo | ooo | ooo | ooo | ooo | ooo | ooo | ooo | ooo |
| North Korea | 121 | 22.4 | 23.1 | 190.9 | 7.9 | 16 | 7 | 2.0 | 21 | 63 | ooo | 38 | 32 | 30 |
| Norway | 324 | 2.7 | 4.6 | 14.2 | 6.4 | 12 | 9 | 1.8 | 3 | 80 | 77 | 6 | 25 | 69 |
| Oman | 213 | 0.3 | 3.1 | 14.6 | 31.7 | 24 | 4 | 3.4 | 10 | 74 | 72 | 44 | 24 | 32 |
| Pakistan | 796 | 27.8 | 165.8 | 208.3 | 33.3 | 33 | 9 | 4.6 | 79 | 63 | 35 | 52 | 19 | 29 |
| Palau | 0.5 | 21.7 | 0.02 | 40.0 | 17.6 | 14 | 7 | 2.1 | 18 | ooo | ooo | ooo | ooo | ooo |
| Panama | 76 | 9.2 | 3.2 | 42.1 | 23.9 | 22 | 5 | 2.7 | 19 | 75 | 70 | 26 | 16 | 58 |
| Papua New Guinea | 463 | 1.9 | 5.7 | 12.3 | 42.6 | 32 | 11 | 4.1 | 64 | 56 | 13 | 79 | 7 | 14 |
| Paraguay | 407 | 7.7 | 6.5 | 16.0 | 27.7 | 22 | 5 | 2.9 | 29 | 71 | 58 | 39 | 22 | 39 |
| Peru | 1285 | 3.4 | 28.3 | 22.0 | 18.9 | 19 | 6 | 2.4 | 33 | 70 | 72 | 36 | 18 | 46 |
| Philippines | 300 | 35.7 | 89.5 | 298.3 | 22.0 | 27 | 5 | 3.4 | 27 | 71 | 62 | 46 | 15 | 39 |
| Poland | 323 | 45.5 | 38.5 | 119.2 | -0.9 | 10 | 10 | 1.3 | 6 | 75 | 62 | 27 | 36 | 37 |
| Portugal | 92 | 29.4 | 10.6 | 115.2 | 6.0 | 10 | 10 | 1.4 | 4 | 78 | 57 | 18 | 34 | 48 |
| Qatar | 11 | 1.9 | 0.9 | 81.8 | 18.0 | 18 | 2 | 2.8 | 9 | 73 | 95 | 3 | 32 | 65 |
| Romania | 238 | 41.5 | 22.3 | 93.7 | -4.5 | 10 | 12 | 1.3 | 17 | 72 | 54 | 24 | 47 | 29 |
| Russian Federation | 17 075 | 7.4 | 142.1 | 8.3 | -2.6 | 10 | 16 | 1.3 | 11 | 65 | 73 | 14 | 42 | 44 |
| Rwanda | 26 | 52.6 | 9.6 | 369.2 | 65.4 | 43 | 3 | 6.1 | 86 | 44 | 19 | 92 | 3 | 5 |
| St. Kitts and Nevis | 0.4 | 22.2 | 0.04 | 100.0 | 16.3 | 18 | 9 | 2.4 | 15 | 70 | 32 | ooo | ooo | ooo |
| St. Lucia | 0.6 | 29.0 | 0.2 | 333.3 | 39.9 | 20 | 5 | 2.2 | 16 | 73 | 28 | ooo | ooo | ooo |
| St. Vincent & the Grenadines | 0.4 | 35.9 | 0.1 | 250.0 | -9.1 | 18 | 7 | 2.1 | 18 | 71 | 46 | ooo | ooo | ooo |
| Samoa | 3.0 | 45.4 | 0.2 | 66.7 | 22.0 | 29 | 6 | 4.4 | 20 | 70 | 22 | ooo | ooo | ooo |
| San Marino | 0.06 | 16.7 | 0.03 | 500.0 | 20.0 | 10 | 8 | 1.2 | 7 | ooo | ooo | ooo | ooo | ooo |
| Sao Tome and Principe | 1.0 | 56.3 | 0.2 | 200.0 | 60.0 | 34 | 9 | 4.1 | 80 | 63 | 57 | ooo | ooo | ooo |
| Saudi Arabia | 2150 | 1.8 | 27.0 | 12.6 | 50.4 | 30 | 3 | 4.5 | 23 | 72 | 81 | 19 | 20 | 61 |
| Senegal | 197 | 12.7 | 12.2 | 61.9 | 34.1 | 39 | 10 | 5.3 | 61 | 56 | 41 | 77 | 8 | 15 |
| Serbia | 88 | ooo | 10.1 | 114.8 | ooo | 13 | 12 | 1.8 | 10 | ooo | ooo | ooo | ooo | ooo |
| Seychelles | 0.5 | 15.6 | 0.1 | 200.0 | 35.1 | 18 | 8 | 2.1 | 16 | 73 | 53 | ooo | ooo | ooo |
| Sierra Leone | 72 | 8.4 | 6.0 | 83.3 | 27.5 | 46 | 23 | 6.5 | 163 | 41 | 40 | 68 | 15 | 17 |
| Singapore | 1 | 1.6 | 4.5 | 4500.0 | 22.8 | 10 | 4 | 1.2 | 2 | 79 | 100 | 0 | 36 | 64 |
| Slovakia | 49 | 31.8 | 5.4 | 110.2 | 1.0 | 10 | 10 | 1.3 | 7 | 74 | 56 | 12 | 32 | 56 |
| Slovenia | 20 | 9.8 | 2.0 | 100.0 | 0.6 | 9 | 9 | 1.2 | 4 | 77 | 51 | 6 | 46 | 48 |
| Solomon Islands | 29 | 2.6 | 0.6 | 20.7 | 37.4 | 34 | 8 | 4.5 | 48 | 63 | 17 | 77 | 7 | 16 |
| Somalia | 638 | 1.7 | 8.9 | 13.9 | 14.6 | 46 | 17 | 6.9 | 119 | 46 | ooo | ooo | ooo | ooo |
| South Africa | 1221 | 12.9 | 44.2 | 36.2 | 21.4 | 23 | 18 | 2.8 | 54 | 47 | 59 | 14 | 32 | 54 |
| South Korea | 99 | 18.9 | 48.8 | 492.9 | 8.0 | 9 | 5 | 1.1 | 5 | 77 | 81 | 18 | 35 | 47 |
| Spain | 506 | 37.0 | 40.4 | 79.8 | 8.5 | 11 | 9 | 1.3 | 4 | 80 | 77 | 12 | 33 | 55 |
| Sri Lanka | 66 | 29.2 | 20.7 | 313.6 | 9.6 | 19 | 6 | 2.0 | 11 | 74 | 15 | 48 | 21 | 31 |
| Sudan | 2506 | 6.6 | 41.2 | 16.4 | 35.1 | 36 | 9 | 5.0 | 64 | 57 | 40 | 70 | 8 | 22 |

## ealth     Energy and trade     Quality of life

| NI | Purchasing power | Growth of PP | Energy consumption | Imports | Exports | Aid received (given) | Human Development Index | Health care | Food consumption | Safe water | Illiteracy male | Illiteracy female | Higher education | Cars | |
|---|---|---|---|---|---|---|---|---|---|---|---|---|---|---|---|
| 05 | 2004 | 1990–2004 | 2004 | 2005 | 2005 | 2004 | 2004 | 1990–2004 | 2005 | 2004 | 2004 | 2004 | 2002 | 2000 | |
| ion S$ | US$ | annual % | kg oil equivalent per capita | US$ per capita | US$ per capita | million US$ | | doctors per 100 000 people | daily calories per capita | % access | % | % | students per 100 000 people | people per car | |
| 6.5 | 12 027 | 3.9 | 1126 | 2542 | 1724 | 38 | 0.800 | 106 | 3097 | 100 | 12 | 20 | 1050 | 26 | Mauritius |
| 3.4 | 9803 | 1.3 | 1574 | 2247 | 2073 | 121 | 0.821 | 198 | 3117 | 97 | 8 | 10 | 2095 | 11 | Mexico |
| 0.3 | ooo | ooo | ooo | ooo | ooo | ooo | ooo | ooo | ooo | ooo | ooo | ooo | ooo | ooo | Micronesia, Fed. States |
| 3.2 | 1729 | -5.3 | 729 | 550 | 259 | 118 | 0.694 | 264 | 2953 | 92 | 1 | 2 | 2429 | 25 | Moldova |
| 1.8 | 2056 | 2.4 | 843 | 450 | 413 | 262 | 0.691 | 263 | 1995 | 62 | 2 | 3 | 3376 | 104 | Mongolia |
| ooo | ooo | ooo | ooo | ooo | ooo | ooo | ooo | ooo | 2679 | ooo | ooo | ooo | ooo | ooo | Montenegro |
| 52.6 | 4309 | 1.1 | 345 | 674 | 353 | 706 | 0.640 | 51 | 3256 | 81 | 34 | 60 | 1012 | 29 | Morocco |
| 6.2 | 1237 | 4.2 | 175 | 122 | 88 | 1228 | 0.390 | 3 | 2392 | 43 | ooo | ooo | 50 | 233 | Mozambique |
| ooo | 1027 | ooo | 110 | 45 | 58 | 121 | 0.581 | 36 | 3305 | 78 | 6 | 14 | 1313 | 1274 | Myanmar |
| 6.1 | 7418 | 1.3 | 688 | 1241 | 1019 | 179 | 0.626 | 30 | ooo | 87 | 13 | 17 | 676 | 31 | Namibia |
| ooo | ooo | ooo | 4300 | ooo | ooo | ooo | ooo | ooo | ooo | ooo | ooo | ooo | ooo | ooo | Nauru |
| 7.3 | 1490 | 2.1 | 58 | 67 | 31 | 427 | 0.527 | 21 | 2341 | 90 | 37 | 65 | 463 | ooo | Nepal |
| 42.0 | 31 789 | 2.1 | 6286 | 22 001 | 24 658 | (4204) | 0.947 | 315 | 3427 | 100 | ooo | ooo | 3205 | 3 | Netherlands |
| 06.3 | 23 413 | 2.1 | 5536 | 6402 | 5301 | (212) | 0.936 | 237 | 3337 | ooo | ooo | ooo | 4729 | 2 | New Zealand |
| 4.9 | 3634 | 0.1 | 320 | 504 | 167 | 1232 | 0.698 | 37 | 2402 | 79 | 23 | 23 | ooo | 98 | Nicaragua |
| 3.3 | 779 | -0.7 | 35 | 62 | 36 | 536 | 0.311 | 3 | 1897 | 46 | 57 | 85 | 129 | 590 | Niger |
| 74.0 | 1154 | 0.8 | 201 | 131 | 321 | 573 | 0.448 | 28 | 2848 | 48 | ooo | ooo | ooo | 151 | Nigeria |
| ooo | ooo | ooo | ooo | ooo | ooo | ooo | ooo | ooo | ooo | ooo | ooo | ooo | ooo | ooo | Northern Marianas |
| ooo | ooo | ooo | 981 | ooo | ooo | ooo | ooo | ooo | 2291 | ooo | ooo | ooo | ooo | ooo | North Korea |
| 81.5 | 38 454 | 2.5 | 10 606 | 12 003 | 22 447 | (2199) | 0.965 | 313 | 3366 | 100 | ooo | ooo | 4345 | 3 | Norway |
| ooo | 15 259 | 1.9 | 3217 | 3495 | 7282 | 55 | 0.810 | 132 | ooo | ooo | 13 | 27 | 732 | 13 | Oman |
| 97.3 | 2225 | 1.6 | 312 | 163 | 102 | 1421 | 0.539 | 74 | 2446 | 91 | 37 | 64 | ooo | 161 | Pakistan |
| 0.2 | ooo | ooo | ooo | ooo | ooo | ooo | ooo | ooo | ooo | ooo | ooo | ooo | ooo | ooo | Palau |
| 15.0 | 7278 | 2.2 | 1691 | 1286 | 313 | 38 | 0.809 | 150 | 2681 | 90 | 8 | 9 | 3060 | 15 | Panama |
| ooo | 2543 | 0.5 | 344 | 294 | 542 | 266 | 0.523 | 5 | ooo | 39 | 37 | 49 | 191 | 136 | Papua New Guinea |
| 6.1 | 4813 | -0.8 | 1698 | 627 | 286 | 0 | 0.757 | 111 | 3101 | 86 | ooo | ooo | 1642 | 66 | Paraguay |
| 74.0 | 5678 | 2.1 | 523 | 447 | 615 | 487 | 0.767 | 117 | 2411 | 83 | 7 | 18 | 3078 | 48 | Peru |
| 09.7 | 4614 | 0.9 | 380 | 571 | 497 | 463 | 0.763 | 58 | 2497 | 85 | 8 | 7 | 2973 | 110 | Philippines |
| 73.1 | 12 974 | 4.0 | 2376 | 2645 | 2340 | 1525 | 0.862 | 247 | 3596 | ooo | ooo | ooo | 4935 | 5 | Poland |
| 81.3 | 19 629 | 2.1 | 2639 | 5794 | 3615 | (1031) | 0.904 | 342 | 3547 | ooo | ooo | ooo | 3801 | 3 | Portugal |
| ooo | 19 844 | ooo | 21 011 | 12 378 | 31 694 | 2 | 0.844 | 222 | ooo | 100 | 11 | 11 | 987 | 4 | Qatar |
| 34.6 | 8480 | 1.4 | 1839 | 1870 | 1282 | 916 | 0.805 | 190 | 4125 | 57 | 2 | 4 | 2599 | 10 | Romania |
| 38.1 | 9902 | -0.6 | 5237 | 876 | 1702 | 1313 | 0.797 | 425 | 3005 | 97 | 0 | 1 | 5523 | 9 | Russian Federation |
| 2.1 | 1263 | -0.1 | 34 | 45 | 14 | 468 | 0.450 | 5 | 1980 | 74 | 29 | 40 | 173 | 889 | Rwanda |
| ooo | 12 702 | 4.0 | 1060 | 4271 | 1042 | -0.1 | 0.825 | 119 | 2798 | 100 | ooo | ooo | ooo | 8 | St. Kitts and Nevis |
| ooo | 6324 | 0.4 | 858 | 3216 | 728 | -22 | 0.790 | 517 | 2159 | 98 | ooo | ooo | 138 | 21 | St. Lucia |
| 0.4 | 6398 | 1.6 | 667 | 2024 | 318 | 11 | 0.759 | 87 | ooo | ooo | ooo | ooo | ooo | 16 | St. Vincent & the Grenadines |
| 0.4 | 5613 | 4.9 | 343 | 1011 | 64 | 31 | 0.778 | 70 | 3093 | 88 | ooo | ooo | 660 | 56 | Samoa |
| ooo | ooo | ooo | ooo | ooo | ooo | ooo | ooo | ooo | ooo | ooo | 100 | 100 | ooo | 1 | San Marino |
| 0.1 | 1231 | ooo | 202 | 313 | 32 | 33 | 0.607 | 49 | ooo | 79 | ooo | ooo | 107 | 3 | Sao Tome and Principe |
| 89.2 | 13 825 | -0.1 | 5911 | 2570 | 7848 | 32 | 0.777 | 137 | 2631 | ooo | 13 | 31 | 1815 | 11 | Saudi Arabia |
| 8.2 | 1713 | 0.9 | 145 | 274 | 141 | 1052 | 0.460 | 6 | 2228 | 76 | 49 | 71 | 284 | 104 | Senegal |
| ooo | ooo | ooo | ooo | ooo | ooo | ooo | ooo | ooo | 2679 | ooo | ooo | ooo | ooo | ooo | Serbia |
| 0.7 | 16 652 | 2.1 | 3693 | 8001 | 4213 | 10 | 0.842 | 151 | 2992 | 88 | 9 | 8 | ooo | 12 | Seychelles |
| 1.2 | 561 | -5.5 | 62 | 62 | 29 | 360 | 0.335 | 3 | ooo | 57 | 53 | 76 | 162 | 131 | Sierra Leone |
| 19.8 | 28 077 | 3.8 | 11 116 | 46 075 | 52 893 | 9 | 0.916 | 140 | ooo | 100 | 3 | 11 | ooo | 10 | Singapore |
| 42.8 | 14 623 | 2.7 | 3672 | 6560 | 5932 | 235 | 0.856 | 318 | 2615 | 100 | ooo | ooo | 2813 | 4 | Slovakia |
| 34.9 | 20 939 | 3.6 | 4106 | 10 043 | 9314 | 62 | 0.910 | 225 | 3087 | ooo | ooo | ooo | 4932 | 3 | Slovenia |
| 0.3 | 1814 | -2.7 | 126 | 299 | 214 | 122 | 0.592 | 13 | 2262 | 70 | ooo | ooo | ooo | ooo | Solomon Islands |
| ooo | ooo | ooo | 31 | 74 | 36 | ooo | ooo | ooo | ooo | ooo | ooo | ooo | ooo | 876 | Somalia |
| 23.5 | 11 192 | 0.6 | 2879 | 1329 | 1106 | 617 | 0.653 | 77 | 2874 | 88 | 16 | 19 | 1482 | 11 | South Africa |
| 65.0 | 20 499 | 4.5 | 4639 | 5409 | 5889 | -68 | 0.912 | 157 | 2969 | 92 | ooo | ooo | 6712 | 6 | South Korea |
| 95.9 | 25 047 | 2.3 | 3973 | 6425 | 4313 | (2437) | 0.938 | 330 | 3285 | 100 | ooo | ooo | 4564 | 2 | Spain |
| 22.8 | 4390 | 3.8 | 242 | 450 | 323 | 519 | 0.755 | 55 | 2200 | 79 | 8 | 11 | ooo | 87 | Sri Lanka |
| 23.1 | 1949 | 3.4 | 95 | 186 | 133 | 882 | 0.516 | 22 | 2444 | 70 | 29 | 48 | 541 | 398 | Sudan |

| | | | | | | | | | | | | | | | |
|---|---|---|---|---|---|---|---|---|---|---|---|---|---|---|---|
| ∘∘∘ no data<br>per capita for each person | **Land** | | **Population** | | | | | | | | | | **Employment** | | |
| | Area | Arable and permanent crops | Total | Density | Change | Births | Deaths | Fertility | Infant mortality | Life expectancy | Urban | Agriculture | Industry | Services |
| | | | 2006 | 2006 | 1994–2004 | 2006 | 2006 | 2006 | 2006 | 2004 | 2004 | | | |
| | thousand km² | % of total | millions | persons per km² | % | births per 1000 | deaths per 1000 | children per mother | per 1000 live births | years | % | % | % | % |
| Suriname | 163 | 0.4 | 0.5 | 3.1 | -1.2 | 21 | 7 | 2.5 | 20 | 69 | 74 | 21 | 18 | 61 |
| Swaziland | 17 | 10.9 | 1.1 | 64.7 | 36.5 | 29 | 28 | 3.7 | 74 | 31 | 24 | 40 | 22 | 38 |
| Sweden | 450 | 6.0 | 9.0 | 20.0 | 2.5 | 11 | 10 | 1.8 | 2 | 80 | 84 | ∘∘∘ | ∘∘∘ | ∘∘∘ |
| Switzerland | 41 | 10.5 | 7.5 | 182.9 | 5.8 | 10 | 8 | 1.4 | 4 | 81 | 75 | 6 | 35 | 59 |
| Syria | 185 | 29.3 | 18.9 | 102.2 | 30.0 | 29 | 4 | 3.5 | 18 | 74 | 51 | 33 | 24 | 43 |
| Taiwan | 36 | ∘∘∘ | 23.0 | 638.9 | 9.4 | 9 | 6 | 1.1 | 5 | ∘∘∘ | ∘∘∘ | ∘∘∘ | ∘∘∘ | ∘∘∘ |
| Tajikistan | 143 | 7.4 | 6.9 | 48.3 | 14.9 | 30 | 8 | 3.8 | 89 | 64 | 25 | 41 | 23 | 36 |
| Tanzania | 945 | 5.4 | 37.4 | 39.6 | 31.3 | 42 | 17 | 5.7 | 68 | 46 | 24 | 84 | 5 | 11 |
| Thailand | 513 | 37.7 | 64.6 | 125.9 | 8.7 | 14 | 7 | 1.7 | 20 | 70 | 32 | 64 | 14 | 22 |
| Togo | 57 | 46.3 | 5.5 | 96.5 | 42.6 | 38 | 12 | 5.1 | 90 | 55 | 39 | 66 | 10 | 24 |
| Tonga | 0.8 | 64.0 | 0.1 | 125.0 | 3.1 | 25 | 7 | 3.1 | 19 | 72 | 24 | ∘∘∘ | ∘∘∘ | ∘∘∘ |
| Trinidad and Tobago | 5 | 23.8 | 1.1 | 220.0 | 4.0 | 14 | 8 | 1.6 | 19 | 70 | 12 | 11 | 31 | 58 |
| Tunisia | 164 | 30.0 | 10.2 | 62.2 | 13.4 | 17 | 6 | 2.0 | 21 | 74 | 65 | 28 | 33 | 39 |
| Turkey | 775 | 36.8 | 70.4 | 90.8 | 19.4 | 19 | 6 | 2.2 | 25 | 69 | 67 | 53 | 18 | 29 |
| Turkmenistan | 488 | 3.9 | 5.0 | 10.2 | 29.4 | 25 | 8 | 2.9 | 74 | 63 | 46 | 37 | 23 | 40 |
| Tuvalu | 0.02 | ∘∘∘ | 0.01 | 500.0 | 11.1 | 27 | 10 | 3.7 | 35 | ∘∘∘ | ∘∘∘ | ∘∘∘ | ∘∘∘ | ∘∘∘ |
| Uganda | 241 | 29.9 | 29.2 | 121.2 | 33.7 | 47 | 16 | 6.9 | 81 | 48 | 13 | 85 | 5 | 10 |
| Ukraine | 604 | 55.7 | 46.6 | 77.2 | -9.0 | 9 | 17 | 1.2 | 10 | 66 | 68 | 20 | 40 | 40 |
| United Arab Emirates | 84 | 3.2 | 2.6 | 31.0 | 83.2 | 15 | 1 | 2.2 | 9 | 78 | 77 | 8 | 27 | 65 |
| United Kingdom | 245 | 23.9 | 60.6 | 247.3 | 2.2 | 12 | 10 | 1.8 | 5 | 79 | 90 | 2 | 29 | 69 |
| United States of America | 9364 | 18.5 | 298.4 | 31.9 | 12.7 | 14 | 8 | 2.0 | 7 | 78 | 81 | 3 | 28 | 69 |
| Uruguay | 177 | 7.6 | 3.4 | 19.2 | 6.4 | 15 | 10 | 2.2 | 15 | 76 | 92 | 14 | 27 | 59 |
| Uzbekistan | 447 | 10.8 | 27.3 | 61.1 | 18.5 | 23 | 7 | 2.7 | 58 | 67 | 37 | 34 | 25 | 41 |
| Vanuatu | 12 | 9.8 | 0.2 | 16.7 | 19.8 | 31 | 6 | 4.0 | 27 | 69 | 23 | ∘∘∘ | ∘∘∘ | ∘∘∘ |
| Venezuela | 912 | 3.7 | 25.7 | 28.2 | 22.6 | 22 | 5 | 2.7 | 17 | 73 | 93 | 12 | 27 | 61 |
| Vietnam | 332 | 26.8 | 84.4 | 254.2 | 12.4 | 19 | 5 | 2.1 | 18 | 71 | 26 | 71 | 14 | 15 |
| Western Sahara | 252 | 0.008 | 0.4 | 1.6 | 46.3 | 28 | 8 | 3.9 | 53 | ∘∘∘ | ∘∘∘ | ∘∘∘ | ∘∘∘ | ∘∘∘ |
| Yemen | 528 | 3.2 | 21.5 | 40.7 | 34.6 | 41 | 9 | 6.2 | 75 | 61 | 27 | 61 | 17 | 22 |
| Zambia | 753 | 7.0 | 11.3 | 15.0 | 24.4 | 41 | 23 | 5.7 | 92 | 38 | 35 | 75 | 8 | 17 |
| Zimbabwe | 391 | 8.6 | 12.2 | 31.2 | 13.9 | 30 | 23 | 3.6 | 61 | 37 | 35 | 68 | 8 | 24 |

## Explanation of datasets

### Land

**Area** does not include areas of lakes and seas

**Arable and permanent crops** percentage of total land area used for arable and permanent crops

### Population

**Total** estimate for mid 2004

**Density** the total population of a country divided by its land area

**Change** percentage change in population between 1994 and 2004. Negative numbers indicate a decrease

**Births** number of births per one thousand people in one year

**Deaths** number of deaths per one thousand people in one year

**Fertility** average number of children born to child bearing women

**Infant mortality** number of deaths of children under one year per 1000 live births

**Life expectancy** number of years a baby born now can expect to live

**Urban** percentage of the population living in towns and cities

### Employment

**Agriculture** percentage of the labour force employed in agriculture

**Industry** percentage of the labour force employed in industry

**Services** percentage of the labour force employed in services

© Oxford University Press

## Wealth | Energy and trade | Quality of life

| GNI | Purchasing power | Growth of PP | Energy consumption | Imports | Exports | Aid received (given) | Human Development Index | Health care | Food consumption | Safe water | Illiteracy male | Illiteracy female | Higher education | Cars | |
|---|---|---|---|---|---|---|---|---|---|---|---|---|---|---|---|
| 2005 | 2004 | 1990–2004 | 2004 | 2005 | 2005 | 2004 | 2004 | 1990–2004 | 2005 | 2004 | 2004 | 2004 | 2002 | 2000 | |
| million US$ | US$ | annual % | kg oil equivalent per capita | US$ per capita | US$ per capita | million US$ | | doctors per 100 000 people | daily calories per capita | % access | % | % | students per 100 000 people | people per car | |
| 1.1 | 000 | 000 | 2066 | 1992 | 2115 | 24 | 0.759 | 45 | 3424 | 92 | 8 | 13 | 1196 | 8 | Suriname |
| 2.6 | 5638 | 2.1 | 454 | 1839 | 1786 | 117 | 0.500 | 16 | 000 | 62 | 19 | 22 | 452 | 38 | Swaziland |
| 59.1 | 29 541 | 1.8 | 6446 | 12 326 | 14 418 | (2722) | 0.951 | 328 | 3108 | 100 | 000 | 000 | 4276 | 2 | Sweden |
| 11.4 | 33 040 | 0.2 | 4320 | 17 013 | 17 601 | (1545) | 0.947 | 361 | 3306 | 100 | 000 | 000 | 2310 | 2 | Switzerland |
| 26.3 | 3610 | 1.5 | 1143 | 426 | 302 | 110 | 0.716 | 140 | 2906 | 93 | 14 | 26 | 549 | 107 | Syria |
| 000 | 000 | -4.8 | 44834 | 000 | 000 | 000 | 000 | 000 | 000 | 000 | 000 | 000 | 000 | 5 | Taiwan |
| 2.2 | 1202 | 1.1 | 1015 | 204 | 140 | 241 | 0.652 | 203 | 000 | 59 | 0 | 1 | 1268 | 000 | Tajikistan |
| 12.7 | 674 | 2.6 | 50 | 69 | 39 | 1746 | 0.430 | 2 | 2131 | 62 | 23 | 38 | 63 | 735 | Tanzania |
| 175.0 | 8090 | 000 | 1343 | 1840 | 1714 | -2 | 0.784 | 37 | 2657 | 99 | 5 | 10 | 3386 | 37 | Thailand |
| 2.2 | 1536 | 000 | 161 | 146 | 93 | 61 | 0.495 | 4 | 1895 | 52 | 31 | 62 | 286 | 174 | Togo |
| 000 | 7870 | 2.1 | 415 | 1222 | 98 | 19 | 0.815 | 34 | 000 | 100 | 1 | 1 | 358 | 19 | Tonga |
| 13.4 | 12 182 | 3.3 | 13 671 | 4347 | 6922 | -1 | 0.809 | 79 | 2805 | 91 | 000 | 000 | 888 | 6 | Trinidad and Tobago |
| 28.8 | 7768 | 3.2 | 834 | 1314 | 1046 | 328 | 0.760 | 134 | 3484 | 93 | 17 | 35 | 2314 | 24 | Tunisia |
| 342.0 | 7753 | 1.6 | 1282 | 1617 | 1019 | 257 | 0.757 | 135 | 3212 | 96 | 5 | 20 | 2493 | 17 | Turkey |
| 000 | 4584 | -4.4 | 4155 | 742 | 1021 | 37 | 0.724 | 418 | 3112 | 72 | 1 | 2 | 000 | 000 | Turkmenistan |
| 000 | 000 | 000 | 000 | 000 | 000 | 000 | 000 | 000 | 000 | 000 | 000 | 000 | 000 | 000 | Tuvalu |
| 8.0 | 1478 | 3.5 | 37 | 62 | 30 | 1159 | 0.502 | 8 | 2392 | 60 | 23 | 42 | 289 | 923 | Uganda |
| 71.7 | 6394 | -3.2 | 3428 | 768 | 728 | 360 | 0.774 | 295 | 2865 | 96 | 0 | 1 | 4411 | 10 | Ukraine |
| 000 | 24 056 | -0.5 | 23 134 | 17 812 | 25 469 | 6 | 0.839 | 202 | 2446 | 100 | 000 | 000 | 859 | 7 | United Arab Emirates |
| 072.7 | 30 821 | 2.2 | 4164 | 8472 | 6355 | (7883) | 0.940 | 230 | 3424 | 100 | 000 | 000 | 3740 | 2 | United Kingdom |
| 12.9 | 39 676 | 1.9 | 8567 | 5844 | 3051 | (19 705) | 0.948 | 256 | 3637 | 100 | 000 | 000 | 5537 | 2 | United States of America |
| 15.1 | 9421 | 0.8 | 1273 | 1120 | 983 | 22 | 0.851 | 365 | 3066 | 100 | 000 | 000 | 2953 | 11 | Uruguay |
| 13.6 | 1869 | 1.3 | 2108 | 140 | 181 | 246 | 0.696 | 274 | 2074 | 82 | 000 | 000 | 890 | 000 | Uzbekistan |
| 0.3 | 3051 | -0.2 | 159 | 710 | 180 | 38 | 0.670 | 11 | 2187 | 60 | 000 | 000 | 344 | 50 | Vanuatu |
| 28.1 | 6043 | -1.2 | 2882 | 912 | 2088 | 49 | 0.784 | 194 | 2509 | 83 | 7 | 7 | 2676 | 13 | Venezuela |
| 51.3 | 2745 | 5.5 | 287 | 439 | 380 | 1830 | 0.709 | 53 | 2762 | 85 | 6 | 13 | 970 | 562 | Vietnam |
| 000 | 000 | 000 | 276 | 000 | 000 | 000 | 000 | 000 | 000 | 000 | 000 | 000 | 000 | 000 | Western Sahara |
| 12.6 | 879 | 1.7 | 205 | 203 | 304 | 252 | 0.492 | 33 | 1590 | 67 | 000 | 000 | 926 | 101 | Yemen |
| 5.8 | 943 | -1.1 | 278 | 236 | 147 | 1081 | 0.407 | 12 | 000 | 58 | 24 | 40 | 232 | 107 | Zambia |
| 4.5 | 2065 | -1.9 | 423 | 179 | 140 | 187 | 0.491 | 16 | 1870 | 81 | 6 | 14 | 483 | 61 | Zimbabwe |

## Explanation of datasets

### Wealth

**GNI** Gross National Income (GNI) is the total value of goods and services produced in a country plus income from abroad.

**Purchasing power** Gross Domestic Product (GDP) is the total value of goods and services produced in a country. Purchasing power parity (PPP) is GDP per person, adjusted for the local cost of living

**Growth of PP** average annual growth (or decline, shown as a negative value in the table) in purchasing power. This figure shows whether people are becoming better or worse off

### Energy and trade

**Energy consumption** consumption of commercial energy per person shown as the equivalent in kilograms of oil

**Imports** total value of imports per person shown in US dollars

**Exports** total value of exports per person shown in US dollars

**Aid received (given)** amount of economic aid a country has received. Negative values indicate that the repayment of loans exceeds the amount of aid received. Figures in brackets show aid given

### Quality of life

**HDI** Human Development Index (HDI) measures the relative social and economic progress of a country. It combines life expectancy, adult literacy, average number of years of schooling, and purchasing power. Economically more developed countries have an HDI approaching 1.0. Economically less developed countries have an HDI approaching 0.

**Health care** number of doctors in each country per 100 000 people

**Food consumption** average number of calories consumed by each person each day

**Safe water** percentage of the population with access to safe drinking water

**Illiteracy** percentage of men and women who are unable to read and write

**Higher education** number of students in higher education per 100 000 people

**Cars** the number of people for every car

## How to use the index

To find a place on an atlas map use either the grid code or latitude and longitude.

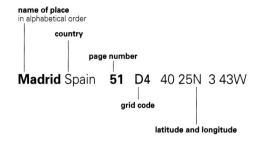

name of place
in alphabetical order

country

page number

**Madrid** Spain **51** D4 40 25N 3 43W

grid code

latitude and longitude

### Grid code

**Madrid** Spain **51** D4 40 25N 3 43W

Madrid is in grid square D4

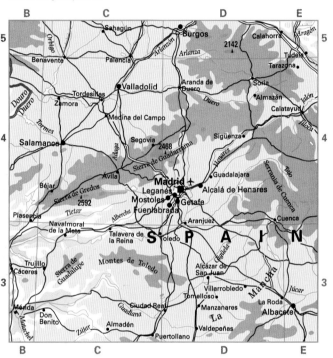

### Latitude and longitude

**Madrid** Spain **51** D4 40 25N 3 43W

Madrid is at latitude 40 degrees, 25 minutes north and 3 degrees, 43 minutes west

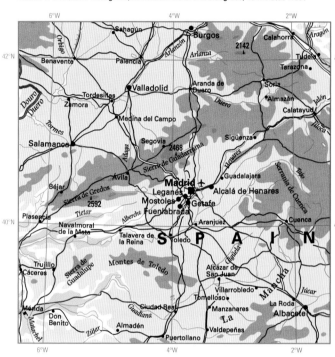

### Geographical abbreviations

| | |
|---|---|
| admin | administrative area |
| Arch. | Archipelago |
| b. | bay or harbour |
| c. | cape, point, or headland |
| can. | canal |
| co. | county |
| d. | desert |
| fj. | fjord |
| G. | Gunung; Gebel |
| g. | gulf |
| geog. reg. | geographical region |
| i. | island |
| is. | islands |
| Kep. | Kepulauan |
| l. | lake, lakes, lagoon |
| mt. | mountain, peak, or spot height |
| mts. | mountains |
| NP | National Park |
| P. | Pulau |
| p; pen | peninsula |
| Peg | Pegunungan |
| plat. | plateau |
| prov. | province |
| Pt. | Point |
| Pta. | Punta |
| Pte. | Pointe |
| Pto. | Porto; Puerto |
| r. | river |
| Ra. | Range |
| res. | reservoir |
| salt l. | salt lake |
| sd. | sound, strait, or channel |
| St. | Saint |
| Ste. | Sainte |
| Str. | Strait |
| sum. | summit |
| tn. | town or other populated place |
| v. | valley |
| vol. | volcano |

### Political abbreviations

| | |
|---|---|
| Aust. | Australia |
| Bahamas | The Bahamas |
| CAR | Central African Republic |
| Col. | Columbia |
| CDR | Congo Democratic Republic |
| Czech Rep. | Czech Republic |
| Dom. Rep. | Dominican Republic |
| Eq. Guinea | Equatorial Guinea |
| Fr. | France |
| Med. Sea | Mediterranean Sea |
| Neths | Netherlands |
| NI | Northern Ireland |
| NZ | New Zealand |
| Philippines | The Philippines |
| PNG | Papua New Guinea |
| Port. | Portugal |
| RoI | Republic of Ireland |
| RSA | Republic of South Africa |
| Sp. | Spain |
| Switz. | Switzerland |
| UAE | United Arab Emirates |
| UK | United Kingom |
| USA | United States of America |
| W. Indies | West Indies |
| Yemen | Yemen Republic |

# A

Aachen Germany 52 C5 50 46N 6 06E
Aalten Belgium 48 B4 51 56N 6 35E
Abādān Iran 65 C5 30 20N 48 15E
Abbeville France 50 E6 50 06N 1 51E
Abbey RoI 21 C3 53 06N 8 24W
Abbeyfeale RoI 21 B2 52 24N 9 18W
Abbeyleix RoI 21 D2 52 55N 7 20W
Abbeytown England 12 C3 54 51N 3 17W
Abbotsbury England 19 E2 50 40N 2 36W
Aberaeron Wales 14 B2 52 49N 44 43W
Abercarn Wales 14 C1 51 39N 3 08W
Aberchirder Scotland 9 G2 57 33N 2 38W
Aberdare Wales 14 C1 51 43N 3 27W
Aberdaron Wales 14 B2 52 49N 44 43W
Aberdeen Scotland 9 G2 57 10N 2 04W
Aberdeen USA 91 G6 45 28N 98 30W
Aberdeen City u.a. Scotland 9 G2 57 10N 2 00W
Aberdeenshire u.a. Scotland 9 G2 57 10N 2 50W
Aberdyfi Wales 14 B2 52 33N 4 02W
Aberfeldy Scotland 9 F1 56 37N 3 54W
Aberffraw Wales 14 B3 53 12N 4 28W
Aberfoyle Scotland 11 E3 56 11N 4 23W
Abergavenny Wales 14 C1 51 50N 3 00W
Abergele Wales 14 C3 53 17N 3 34W
Aberlady Scotland 11 G3 56 01N 2 51W
Aberporth Wales 14 B2 52 07N 4 34W
Abersoch Wales 14 B2 52 50N 4 31W
Abertillery Wales 14 C1 51 45N 3 09W
Aberystwyth Wales 14 B2 52 25N 4 05W
Abidjan Côte d'Ivoire 80 D3 5 19N 4 01W
Abingdon England 16 B2 51 41N 1 17W
Abington Scotland 11 F2 55 29N 3 42W
Aboyne Scotland 9 G2 57 05N 2 50W
Abu Dhabi UAE 65 F3 24 28N 54 25E
Abuja Nigeria 80 F3 9 10N 7 11E
Acapulco Mexico 94 E3 16 51N 99 56W
Accra Ghana 80 D3 5 33N 0 15W
Accrington England 12 D2 53 46N 2 21W
Achill Head RoI 20 A3 53 59N 10 13W
Achill Island RoI 20 A3 53 55N 10 05W
Achill Sound tn. RoI 20 B3 53 56N 9 54W
Achnacroish Scotland 8 D1 56 32N 5 30W
Achnasheen Scotland 9 D2 57 35N 5 06W
Ackworth Moor Top England 13 E2 53 39N 1 20W
Aclare RoI 20 C4 54 02N 8 54W
Acle England 17 E3 52 38N 1 33E
A Coruña Spain 51 A5 43 22N 8 24W
Adana Turkey 57 E2 37 00N 35 19E
Adare RoI 21 C2 52 34N 8 48W
Ad Dammām Saudi Arabia 65 F4 26 25N 50 06E
Addis Ababa Ethiopia 81 N3 9 03N 38 42E
Addlestone England 16 C2 51 22N 0 31W
Adelaide Australia 73 G4 34 56S 138 36E
Aden Yemen 64 E1 12 50N 45 03E
Aden, Gulf of Indian Ocean 65 E1 12 30N 47 30E
Adriatic Sea Med. Sea 54 F5 43 00N 15 00E
Adrigole RoI 21 B1 51 44N 9 42W
Adur r. England 16 C1 50 55N 0 20W
Adwick le Street England 13 E2 53 34N 1 11W
Aegean Sea Med. Sea 55 L3 39 00N 24 00E
AFGHANISTAN 66 A6/B6
Agen France 50 E3 44 12N 0 38E
Aghaville RoI 21 B1 51 39N 9 21W
Agra India 66 D5 27 09N 78 00E
Ağrı Dağı mt. Turkey 57 F2 39 44N 44 15E
Agropoli Italy 54 F4 40 21N 14 59E
Ahascragh RoI 20 C3 53 24N 8 20W
Ahmadabad India 66 C4 23 03N 72 40E
Ahoghill NI 10 C1 54 51N 6 22W
Ailsa Craig i. Scotland 10 D2 55 16N 5 07W
Airdrie Scotland 11 F2 55 52N 3 59W
Aire r. England 13 E2 53 40N 1 00W
Aire-sur-l'Adour France 50 D2 43 42N 0 15W
Aix-en-Provence France 50 G2 43 31N 5 27E
Aix-les-Bains France 50 G3 45 41N 5 55E
Ajaccio France 50 J1 41 55N 8 43E
Ajmer India 66 C5 26 29N 74 40E
Akron USA 91 K5 41 04N 81 31W
Alabama state USA 91 J3 32 00N 87 00W
Åland is. Finland 49 E3 60 15N 20 00E
Alaska state USA 88 D6/F6 63 10N 157 30W
Alaska, Gulf of USA 88 F5/G5 58 00N 147 00W
Alaska Range USA 88 E6/G6 62 30N 152 30W
Albacete Spain 51 E3 39 00N 1 52W
ALBANIA 55 H4/J4
Al Başrah Iraq 65 E5 30 30N 47 50E
Albert France 50 F6 50 00N 2 40E
Alberta prov. Canada 88 M4/N4 54 00N 117 30W
Albertville France 50 H3 45 40N 6 24E
Albi France 50 F2 43 56N 2 08E
Ålborg Denmark 49 C2 57 05N 9 50E
Albrighton England 15 D2 52 38N 2 16W
Albuquerque USA 90 E4 35 05N 106 38W
Alcalá de Henares Spain 51 D4 40 28N 3 22W
Alcantarilla Spain 51 E2 37 59N 1 12W

Alcázar de San Juan Spain 51 D3 39 24N 3 12W
Alcester England 15 E2 52 13N 1 52W
Alcira Spain 51 E3 39 10N 0 27W
Aldbourne England 16 B2 51 30N 1 37W
Aldbrough England 13 F2 53 50N 0 06W
Alde r. England 17 E3 52 10N 1 30E
Aldeburgh England 17 E3 52 09N 1 35E
Alderley Edge tn. England 12 D2 53 18N 2 15W
Alderney i. Channel Islands 19 E1 49 43N 2 12W
Aldershot England 16 C2 51 15N 0 47W
Aldridge England 15 E2 52 36N 1 55W
Aldsworth England 15 E1 51 48N 1 46W
Alençon France 50 E5 48 25N 0 05E
Aleppo Syria 64 C6 36 14N 37 10E
Alessándria Italy 54 C6 44 55N 8 37E
Ålesund Norway 49 C3 62 28N 6 11E
Aleutian Range USA 88 D5 56 30N 159 00W
Alexandria Egypt 81 L8 31 13N 29 55E
Alexandria Scotland 11 E2 55 59N 4 36W
Alexandroúpoli Greece 55 L4 40 51N 25 53E
Alford England 13 G2 53 17N 0 11E
Alford Scotland 9 G2 57 13N 2 42W
Alfreton England 13 E2 53 06N 1 23W
Algeciras Spain 51 C2 36 08N 5 27W
ALGERIA 80 D7/F7
Algiers Algeria 80 E9 36 50N 3 00E
Alicante Spain 51 E3 38 21N 0 29W
Alice USA 91 G2 27 45N 98 06W
Alice Springs tn. Australia 72 F6 23 42S 133 52E
Alkmaar Neths 48 C5 52 38N 4 44E
Allahabad India 66 E5 25 27N 81 50E
Allegheny Mountains USA 93 E1/2 40 00N 79 00W
Allen r. England 12 D3 54 50N 2 20W
Allendale Town England 12 D3 54 54N 2 15W
Allentown USA 91 L5 40 37N 75 30W
Alloa Scotland 11 F3 56 07N 3 49W
Alma USA 93 D2 43 23N 84 40W
Almadén Spain 51 C3 38 47N 4 50W
Almansa Spain 51 E3 38 52N 1 06W
Almaty Kazakhstan 62 K5 43 19N 76 55E
Almería Spain 51 D2 36 50N 2 26W
Älmhult Sweden 49 D2 56 32N 14 10E
Aln r. England 11 H2 55 25N 1 45W
Alness Scotland 9 E2 57 41N 4 15W
Alnwick England 11 H2 55 25N 1 42W
Alpes Maritimes mts. France/Italy 50 H2 44 15N 6 45E
Alpi Dolomitiche mts. Italy 54 D7 46 00N 12 00E
Alpi Pennine mts. Italy/Switz. 52 C3 45 55N 7 30E
Alps mts. Europe 52 D3 46 00N 7 30E
Alsager England 12 D2 53 06N 2 19W
Alston England 12 D3 54 49N 2 26W
Altai mts. Mongolia 68 F7 47 00N 92 30E
Altamira Brazil 96 G13 3 13S 52 15W
Altnaharra Scotland 9 E3 58 16N 4 27W
Alton England 16 C2 51 09N 0 59W
Altrincham England 12 D2 53 24N 2 21W
Alyth Scotland 9 F1 56 37N 3 13W
Amarillo USA 90 F4 35 14N 101 50W
Amazonas r. Brazil 96 G13 2 00S 53 00W
Amble England 11 H2 55 20N 1 34W
Ambleside England 12 D3 54 26N 2 58W
Ambon Indonesia 71 H3 3 41S 128 10E
Amersfoort Neths 48 D5 52 09N 5 23E
Amersham England 16 C2 51 40N 0 38W
Amesbury England 16 B2 51 10N 1 46W
Amfípoli Greece 55 K4 40 48N 23 52E
Amiens France 50 F5 49 54N 2 18E
Amlwch Wales 14 B3 53 25N 4 20W
Amman Jordan 64 C5 31 04N 46 17E
Ammanford Wales 14 B1 51 48N 3 58W
Ampthill England 16 C2 52 02N 0 30W
Amritsar India 66 C6 31 35N 74 56E
Amsterdam Neths 48 C5 52 22N 4 54E
Amstetten Austria 52 G4 48 08N 14 52E
Amur r. Asia 69 N8 52 30N 126 30E
Anascaul RoI 21 A2 52 09N 10 04W
Anchorage USA 88 F6 61 10N 150 00W
Ancona Italy 54 E5 43 37N 13 31E
Ancroft England 11 G2 55 42N 2 00W
Andalsnes Norway 49 C3 62 33N 7 43E
Andaman Islands India 67 G2 12 00N 94 00E
Anderlecht Belgium 48 C3 50 50N 4 20E
Andermatt Switz. 52 D3 46 38N 8 36E
Andes mts. S. America 96/97 B14/C6 10 00S 77 00W
Andorra la Vella Andorra 50 E2 42 30N 1 30E
Andover England 16 B2 51 13N 1 28W
Andreas Isle of Man 12 B3 54 22N 4 26W
Ándros i. Greece 55 L2 37 49N 24 54E
Andújar Spain 51 C3 38 02N 4 03W
Angara r. Russia 63 M8 58 00N 97 30E
Angers France 50 D4 47 29N 0 32W
Angle Wales 14 A1 51 41N 5 06W
Anglesey i. Wales 14 B3 53 18N 4 25W

Anglesey, Isle of u.a. Wales 14 B3 53 18N 4 25W
ANGOLA 82 C5
Angoulême France 50 E3 45 40N 0 10E
Anguilla i. Leeward Islands 94 P10 18 14N 63 05W
Angus u.a. Scotland 9 G1 56 45N 3 00W
Ankara Turkey 57 D2 39 56N 32 50E
'Annaba Algeria 80 F9 36 55N 7 47E
Annalong NI 10 D1 54 06N 5 55W
Annan r. Scotland 11 F2 55 05N 3 20W
Annan Scotland 11 F1 54 59N 3 16W
Annapolis USA 91 L4 38 59N 76 30W
Annapurna mt. Nepal 66 E5 28 34N 83 50E
Annbank Scotland 11 E2 55 28N 4 30W
Annecy France 50 H3 45 54N 6 07E
Annfield Plain England 13 E3 54 52N 1 45W
Ansbach Germany 52 E4 49 18N 10 36E
Anshan China 69 M6 41 05N 122 58E
Anstey England 15 E2 52 40N 1 10W
Anston England 13 E2 53 22N 1 13W
Anstruther Scotland 11 G3 56 14N 2 42W
Antalya Turkey 57 D2 36 53N 30 42E
Antananarivo Madagascar 82 J4 18 52S 47 30E
Antarctica 101
Antequera Spain 51 C2 37 01N 4 34W
Antibes France 50 H2 43 35N 7 07E
ANTIGUA & BARBUDA 94 Q9
Antofagasta Chile 96 C9 23 40S 70 23W
Antrim NI 10 C1 54 43N 6 13W
Antrim district NI 10 C1 54 40N 6 10W
Antrim Mountains NI 10 C2 55 00N 6 10W
Antwerpen Belgium 48 C4 51 13N 4 25W
Aosta Italy 54 B6 45 43N 7 19E
Apeldoorn Neths 48 D5 52 13N 5 57E
Appalachian Mountains USA 91 K4 37 00N 82 00W
Appennini mts. Italy 54 C6/F4 43 00N 12 30E
Appleby-in-Westmorland England 12 D3 53 36N 2 29W
Appledore England 18 C3 51 03N 4 12W
Appleton USA 91 J5 44 17N 88 24W
'Aqaba, Gulf of Middle East 64 D4 28 40N 34 40E
Arabian Sea Indian Ocean 65 H3 22 00N 63 00E
Araguaína Brazil 96 H12 7 16S 48 18W
Aral Sea Asia 62 H5/J6 45 00N 60 00E
Aranda de Duero Spain 51 D4 41 40N 3 41W
Aran Fawddwy mt. Wales 14 C2 52 47N 3 41W
Aran Island RoI 20 C4 55 00N 8 40W
Aran Islands RoI 21 B3 53 10N 9 50W
Aranjuez Spain 51 D4 40 02N 3 37W
Arbil Iraq 64 D6 36 12N 44 01E
Arbroath Scotland 9 G1 56 34N 2 35W
Arcachon France 50 D3 44 40N 1 11W
Arctic Ocean 101
Ardara RoI 20 C4 54 46N 8 25W
Ardbeg Scotland 10 C2 55 39N 6 05W
Ardee RoI 20 E3 53 52N 6 33W
Ardennes mts. Belgium 48 D3 50 10N 5 45E
Ardfert RoI 21 B2 52 20N 9 47W
Ardglass NI 10 D1 54 16N 5 37W
Ardle r. Scotland 9 F1 56 40N 3 30W
Ardminish Scotland 10 D2 55 42N 5 44W
Ardmore RoI 21 D1 51 57N 7 43W
Ardmore Point Scotland 10 C2 55 41N 6 01W
Ardnamurchan, Point of Scotland 8 C1 56 44N 6 14W
Ardrossan Scotland 11 E2 55 39N 4 49W
Ards district NI 10 D1 54 35N 5 35W
Ards Peninsula NI 10 D1 54 25N 5 30W
Ardvasar Scotland 8 D2 57 03N 5 55W
Arendal Norway 49 C2 58 27N 8 56E
Arequipa Peru 96 C10 16 25S 71 32W
Arezzo Italy 54 D5 43 28N 11 53E
Argentan France 50 D5 48 45N 0 01W
ARGENTINA 97 D5
Argyll and Bute u.a. Scotland 10 D3 56 10N 5 00W
Århus Denmark 49 D2 56 15N 10 10E
Arica Chile 96 C10 18 30S 70 20W
Arinagour Scotland 8 C1 56 37N 6 31W
Ariquemes Brazil 96 E12 9 55S 63 06W
Arisaig Scotland 8 D2 56 51N 5 51W
Arisaig, Sound of Scotland 8 D1 56 50N 5 50W
Arizona state USA 90 D3 34 00N 112 00W
Arkansas state USA 91 H3 34 00N 93 00W
Arkansas r. USA 90 G4 36 00N 99 00W
Arkansas City USA 91 G4 37 03N 97 02W
Arkhangel'sk Russia 62 G9 64 32N 40 40E
Arklow RoI 21 E2 52 48N 6 09W
Arles France 50 G2 43 41N 4 38E
Arlon Belgium 48 D2 49 41N 5 49E
Armadale Highland Scotland 8 D2 57 05N 5 54W
Armadale West Lothian Scotland 11 F2 55 54N 3 41W
Armagh NI 10 C1 54 21N 6 39W
Armagh district NI 10 C1 54 20N 6 40W
ARMENIA 57 F3
Armentières France 50 F6 50 41N 2 53E

Armthorpe England 13 E2 53 32N 1 03W
Arnhem Neths 48 D4 52 00N 5 53E
Arnold England 15 E2 53 00N 1 09W
Arran i. Scotland 10 D2 55 35N 5 15W
Arras France 50 F6 50 17N 2 46E
Artane RoI 20 E3 53 23N 6 12W
Arthur's Seat sum. Scotland 11 F2 55 57N 3 11W
Arthurstown RoI 21 E2 52 15N 6 57W
Aruba i. Neths 96 C16
Arun r. England 16 C1 51 00N 0 30W
Arundel England 16 C1 50 51N 0 34W
Arvika Sweden 49 D2 59 41N 12 38E
Ascoli Piceno Italy 54 E5 42 52N 13 35E
Ascot England 16 C2 51 25N 0 41W
Ash England 17 E2 51 17N 1 16E
Ashbourne England 13 E2 53 01N 1 43W
Ashbourne RoI 20 E3 53 31N 6 24W
Ashburton England 18 D2 50 31N 3 45W
Ashby-de-la-Zouch England 15 E2 52 46N 1 28W
Ashford England 17 D2 51 09N 0 53E
Ash Fork USA 90 D4 35 13N 112 29W
Ashgabat Turkmenistan 62 H4 37 58N 58 24E
Ashington England 13 E4 55 11N 1 34W
Ashkirk Scotland 11 G2 55 29N 2 50W
Ashton-in-Makerfield England 12 D2 53 29N 2 39W
Ashton-under-Lyne England 12 D2 53 29N 2 06W
Ashwell England 16 C3 52 03N 0 09W
Askeaton RoI 21 C2 52 36N 8 58W
Askern England 13 E2 53 37N 1 09W
Askrigg England 12 D3 54 19N 2 04W
Asmara Eritrea 81 N5 15 20N 38 58E
Aspatria England 12 C3 54 46N 3 20W
Assisi Italy 54 E5 43 04N 12 37E
Astana Kazakhstan 62 K7 51 10N 71 28E
Astee RoI 21 B2 52 33N 9 34W
Asti Italy 54 C6 44 54N 8 13E
Astorga Spain 51 B5 42 27N 6 04W
Astoria USA 90 B6 46 12N 123 50W
Astrakhan' Russia 62 G6 46 22N 48 04E
Asunción Paraguay 96 F7 25 15S 57 40W
Aswân Egypt 81 M6 24 05N 32 56E
Asyûṭ Egypt 81 M7 27 14N 31 07E
Athabasca Canada 88 N4 54 44N 113 15W
Athabasca, Lake Canada 88 P5 59 10N 109 30W
Athboy RoI 20 E3 53 37N 6 55W
Athenry RoI 20 C3 53 18N 8 45W
Athens Greece 55 K2 38 00N 23 44E
Atherstone England 15 E2 52 35N 1 31W
Athleague RoI 20 C3 53 34N 8 15W
Athlone RoI 20 D3 53 25N 7 56W
Áthos mt. Greece 55 L4 40 10N 24 19E
Athy RoI 21 E2 52 59N 7 00W
Atlanta USA 91 K3 33 45N 84 23W
Atlantic City USA 91 M4 39 23N 74 27W
Atlantic Ocean 104
Attleborough England 17 E3 52 31N 1 01E
Attymass RoI 20 B4 54 03N 9 04W
Aubagne France 50 G2 43 17N 5 35E
Aubenas France 50 G3 44 37N 4 24E
Auch France 50 E2 43 40N 0 36E
Auchencairn Scotland 11 F1 54 51N 3 53W
Auchterarder Scotland 11 F3 56 18N 3 43W
Auchtermuchty Scotland 11 F3 56 17N 3 15W
Auckland NZ 73 P3 36 51S 174 46E
Audley England 12 D2 53 03N 2 20W
Augher NI 10 B1 54 26N 7 08W
Aughnacloy NI 10 C1 54 25N 6 59W
Aughrim RoI 21 E2 52 52N 6 20W
Aughton England 13 E2 53 22N 1 19W
Augsburg Germany 52 E4 48 21N 10 54E
Augusta USA 91 K3 33 29N 82 00W
Auldgirth Scotland 11 F2 55 12N 3 43W
Aurillac France 50 F3 44 56N 2 26E
Austin USA 91 G3 30 18N 97 47W
AUSTRALIA 72/73
AUSTRIA 52 E3/G3
Autun France 50 G4 46 58N 4 18E
Auxerre France 50 F4 47 48N 3 35E
Avallon France 50 F4 47 30N 3 54E
Avebury England 16 B2 51 27N 1 51W
Aveiro Portugal 51 A4 40 38N 8 40W
Aveley England 17 D2 51 30N 0 15E
Avesta Sweden 49 E3 60 09N 16 10E
Avezzano Italy 54 E5 42 02N 13 26E
Aviemore Scotland 9 F2 57 12N 3 50W
Avignon France 50 G2 43 56N 4 48E
Avila Spain 51 C4 40 39N 4 42W
Avoca RoI 21 E2 52 52N 6 13W
Avon r. Warwickshire England 15 E2 52 10N 1 55W
Avon r. Hampshire England 16 B1 51 05N 1 55W
Avon r. Wiltshire England 16 A2 51 25N 2 05W
Avon r. Devon England 18 D2 50 15N 3 48W
Avon r. Scotland 9 F2 57 12N 3 50W
Avonmouth England 19 E3 51 31N 2 42W
Avranches France 50 D5 48 42N 1 21W
Axbridge England 19 E3 51 18N 2 49W

Axe r.
  Somerset England 19 E3 51 11N 2 43W
Axe r. Dorset England 19 E2 50 50N 2 50W
Axminster England 19 E2 50 47N 3 00W
Ayamonte Spain 51 B2 37 13N 7 24W
Ayers Rock mt.
  Australia 72 F5 25 18S 131 18E
Aylesbury England 16 C2 51 50N 0 50W
Aylesford England 17 D2 51 18N 0 30E
Aylesham England 17 E2 51 12N 1 11E
Aylsham England 17 E3 52 49N 1 15E
Ayr r. Scotland 11 E2 55 30N 4 10W
Ayr Scotland 11 E2 55 28N 4 38W
Ayre, Point of
  Isle of Man 12 B3 54 25N 4 22W
Aysgarth England 12 E3 54 17N 2 00W
AZERBAIJAN 57 G3
Azov, Sea of Asia 57 E4 46 00N 36 00E
Azuaga Spain 51 C3 38 16N 5 40W

# B

Babbacombe Bay
  England 18 D2 50 30N 3 30W
Bacup England 12 D2 53 42N 2 12W
Badajoz Spain 51 B3 38 53N 6 58W
Badalona Spain 51 G4 41 27N 2 15E
Baden Switz. 52 D3 47 28N 8 19E
Bad Ischl Austria 52 F3 47 43N 13 38E
Baffin Bay Canada/
  Greenland 89 X8/Z8 72 00N 65 00W
Baffin Island Canada 89 U8/W7 68 30N 70 00W
Baggy Point England 18 C3 51 09N 4 16W
Baghdad Iraq 64 D5 33 20N 44 26E
BAHAMAS, THE 95 J4
Bahía Blanca Argentina 97 E6 38 45S 62 15W
Bahia de Campeche
  Mexico 94 E4/F4 20 00N 95 00W
BAHRAIN 65 F4
Bahrain, Gulf of
  The Gulf 65 F4 25 55N 50 30E
Bahr el Abiad r. Sudan 81 M4 14 00N 32 20E
Bahr el Azraq r. Sudan 81 M4 13 30N 33 45E
Baia Mare Romania 53 L3 47 39N 23 36E
Baie de la Seine France 50 D5 49 40N 0 30W
Baildon England 13 E2 53 52N 1 46W
Bailieborough RoI 20 E3 53 54N 6 59W
Baja California p.
  Mexico 94 B5 27 30N 113 00W
Bakersfield USA 90 C4 35 25N 119 00W
Bakewell England 13 E2 53 13N 1 40W
Baku Azerbaijan 57 G3 40 22N 49 53E
Bala Wales 14 C2 52 54N 3 35W
Balaton l. Hungary 53 H3 47 00N 17 30E
Balbriggan RoI 20 E3 53 37N 6 11W
Balcombe England 16 C2 51 04N 0 08W
Baldock England 16 C2 51 59N 0 12W
Balearic Islands
  Med. Sea 51 F3/H3 40 00N 2 00E
Baleshare i. Scotland 8 B2 57 32N 7 22W
Bali i. Indonesia 71 E2/F2 8 30S 115 00E
Ballachulish Scotland 8 D1 56 40N 5 10W
Ballagan Point RoI 20 E4 54 00N 6 06W
Ballaghaderreen RoI 20 C3 53 55N 8 36W
Ballantrae Scotland 10 D2 55 06N 5 00W
Ballater Scotland 9 F2 57 03N 3 03W
Ballaugh Isle of Man 12 B3 54 18N 4 32W
Ballina RoI 20 B4 54 07N 9 09W
Ballinafad RoI 20 C4 54 02N 8 20W
Ballinagleragh RoI 20 C4 54 09N 8 01W
Ballinalack RoI 20 D3 53 38N 7 28W
Ballinalee RoI 20 D3 53 46N 7 39W
Ballinamore RoI 20 D4 54 03N 7 47W
Ballinasloe RoI 20 C3 53 20N 8 13W
Ballincollig RoI 21 C1 51 54N 8 35W
Ballindine RoI 20 C3 53 40N 8 57W
Ballingry Scotland 11 F3 56 11N 3 20W
Ballinhassig RoI 21 C1 51 49N 8 32W
Ballinrobe RoI 20 B3 53 37N 9 13W
Ballinskelligs Bay RoI 21 A1 51 46N 10 17W
Ballintra RoI 20 C4 54 35N 8 07W
Ballon RoI 21 E2 52 44N 6 46W
Ballybay RoI 20 E4 54 08N 6 54W
Ballybofey RoI 20 D4 54 48N 7 47W
Ballybunnion RoI 21 B2 52 31N 9 40W
Ballycanew RoI 21 E2 52 36N 6 18W
Ballycastle NI 10 C2 55 12N 6 15W
Ballycastle RoI 20 B4 54 17N 9 22W
Ballyclare NI 10 C1 54 45N 6 00W
Ballycolla RoI 21 D2 52 52N 7 26W
Ballyconnell RoI 20 D4 54 07N 7 35W
Ballycotton RoI 21 C1 51 50N 8 01W
Ballycotton Bay RoI 21 D1 51 51N 7 57W
Ballycroy RoI 20 B4 54 02N 9 49W
Ballydavid Head RoI 21 A2 52 14N 10 21W
Ballydehob RoI 21 B1 51 34N 9 28W
Ballydesmond RoI 21 B2 52 11N 9 14W
Ballydonegan RoI 21 A1 51 37N 10 12W
Ballydonegan Bay RoI 21 A1 51 29N 10 09W
Ballygalley Head NI 10 D1 54 54N 5 51W
Ballygowan NI 10 D1 54 30N 5 47W
Ballyhaunis RoI 20 C3 53 46N 8 46W
Ballyheige RoI 21 B2 52 24N 9 50W
Ballyheige Bay RoI 21 B2 52 24N 9 52W
Ballyhoura Mountains
  RoI 21 C2 52 17N 8 33W
Ballyjamesduff RoI 20 D3 53 52N 7 12W

Ballykinler NI 10 D1 54 17N 5 47W
Ballylanders RoI 21 C2 52 23N 8 21W
Ballylongford RoI 21 B2 52 33N 9 28W
Ballymacarbry RoI 21 D2 52 16N 7 12W
Ballymahon RoI 20 D3 53 34N 7 45W
Ballymena NI 10 C1 54 52N 6 17W
Ballymena district NI 10 C1 54 55N 6 20W
Ballymoe RoI 20 C3 53 42N 8 28W
Ballymoney NI 10 C2 55 04N 6 31W
Ballymoney district NI 10 C2 55 00N 6 20W
Ballymore
  Donegal RoI 20 D5 55 09N 7 56W
Ballymore
  Westmeath RoI 20 D3 53 29N 7 40W
Ballymote RoI 20 C4 54 06N 8 31W
Ballynahinch NI 10 D1 54 24N 5 54W
Ballynamona RoI 21 C2 52 05N 8 39W
Ballynamult RoI 21 D2 52 13N 7 40W
Ballyquintin Point NI 10 D1 54 19N 5 30W
Ballyragget RoI 21 D2 52 47N 7 20W
Ballyshannon RoI 20 C4 54 30N 8 11W
Ballyteige Bay RoI 21 E2 52 12N 6 45W
Ballyvaghan RoI 21 B3 53 07N 9 09W
Ballyvourney RoI 21 B1 51 56N 9 10W
Ballywalter NI 10 D1 54 33N 5 30W
Balmaclellan Scotland 11 E2 55 05N 4 07W
Balmoral Scotland 9 F2 57 02N 3 13W
Balrath RoI 20 E3 53 37N 6 29W
Baltic Sea Europe 49 E2/F2 55 15N 17 00E
Baltimore RoI 21 B1 51 29N 9 22W
Baltimore USA 91 L4 39 18N 76 38W
Baltinglass RoI 21 E2 52 55N 6 41W
Baltray RoI 20 E3 53 44N 6 16W
Bamako Mali 80 C4 12 40N 7 59W
Bamberg Germany 52 E4 49 54N 10 54E
Bamburgh England 11 H2 55 36N 1 42W
Bampton England 18 D2 51 00N 3 29W
Banagher RoI 21 D3 53 11N 7 59W
Banbridge NI 10 C1 54 21N 6 16W
Banbridge district NI 10 C1 54 15N 6 20W
Banbury England 16 B2 52 04N 1 20W
Banchory Scotland 9 G2 57 30N 2 30W
Bandar Seri Begawan
  Brunei 71 F4 4 53N 115 00E
Bandon RoI 21 C1 51 45N 8 45W
Bandung Indonesia 71 D2 6 57S 107 34E
Banff Canada 88 M4 51 10N 115 34W
Banff Scotland 9 G2 57 40N 2 33W
Bangalore India 66 D2 12 58N 77 35E
Bangkok Thailand 71 C6 13 44N 100 30E
BANGLADESH 67 F4/G4
Bangor NI 10 D1 54 40N 5 40W
Bangor RoI 20 B4 54 09N 9 44W
Bangor Wales 14 B3 53 13N 4 08W
Bangui CAR 81 J2 4 23N 18 37E
Banja Luka
  Bosnia-Herzegovina 55 G6 44 47N 17 11E
Banjul The Gambia 80 A4 13 28N 16 39W
Bann r. Coleraine NI 10 C2 55 05N 6 40W
Bann r. Banbridge NI 10 C1 54 20N 6 11W
Bann r. RoI 21 E2 52 39N 6 24W
Bannockburn Scotland 11 F3 56 05N 3 56W
Bannow Bay RoI 21 E2 52 13N 6 48W
Bansha RoI 21 C2 52 28N 8 04W
Banstead England 16 C2 51 19N 0 12W
Banteer RoI 21 C2 52 08N 8 54W
Bantry RoI 21 B1 51 41N 9 27W
Bantry Bay RoI 21 B1 51 35N 9 48W
Baotou China 69 J6 40 38N 109 59E
Baracaldo Spain 51 D5 43 17N 2 59W
Baranavichy Belarus 53 N6 53 09N 26 00E
BARBADOS 94 S11
Barbastro Spain 51 F5 42 02N 0 07E
Barcelona Spain 51 G4 41 25N 2 10E
Barcs Hungary 53 H2 45 58N 17 30E
Bardsey Island Wales 14 B2 52 46N 4 48W
Barents Sea
  Arctic Ocean 101 75 00N 40 00E
Bargoed Wales 14 C1 51 43N 3 15W
Bari Italy 55 G4 41 07N 16 52E
Barisal Bangladesh 67 G4 22 41N 90 20E
Barking England 17 D2 51 33N 0 06E
Barle r. England 18 D3 51 05N 3 36W
Bar-le-Duc France 50 G5 48 46N 5 10E
Barletta Italy 54 G4 41 20N 16 17E
Barmouth Wales 14 B2 52 43N 4 03W
Barnard Castle England 13 E3 54 33N 1 55W
Barnatra RoI 20 B4 54 13N 9 50W
Barnet England 16 C2 51 39N 0 12W
Barnoldswick England 12 D2 53 56N 2 16W
Barnsley England 13 E2 53 34N 1 28W
Barnstaple England 18 C3 51 05N 4 04W
Barnstaple or Bideford
  Bay England 18 C3 51 05N 4 25W
Barquisimeto
  Venezuela 96 D16 10 03N 69 18W
Barra i. Scotland 8 B1/B2 57 00N 7 25W
Barra Head Scotland 8 B1 56 47N 7 36W
Barranquilla Colombia 96 C16 11 10N 74 50W
Barra, Sound of
  Scotland 8 B2 57 06N 7 22W
Barre USA 91 M5 44 13N 72 31W
Barreiras Brazil 96 J11 12 09S 44 58W
Barreiro Portugal 51 A3 38 40N 9 05W
Barrhead Scotland 11 E2 55 48N 4 24W
Barrow r. RoI 21 E2 52 38N 6 58W
Barrow-in-Furness
  England 12 C3 54 07N 3 14W

Barry Wales 14 C1 51 24N 3 18W
Barton-upon-Humber
  England 13 F2 53 41N 0 27W
Barvas Scotland 8 C3 58 22N 6 32W
Barysaw Belarus 53 P7 54 09N 28 30E
Basel Switz. 52 C3 47 33N 7 36E
Basildon England 17 D2 51 34N 0 25W
Basingstoke England 16 B2 51 16N 1 05W
Bassenthwaite Lake
  England 12 C3 54 40N 3 13W
Bastia France 50 J2 42 14N 9 26E
Bastogne Belgium 48 D3 50 00N 5 43E
Bath England 19 E3 51 23N 2 22W
Bath and North East
  Somerset u.a. England 19 E3 51 25N 2 30W
Bathgate Scotland 11 F2 55 55N 3 39W
Bathurst Canada 89 X3 47 37N 65 40W
Batley England 13 E2 53 44N 1 37W
Baton Rouge USA 91 H3 30 30N 91 10W
Battle England 17 D1 50 55N 0 29E
Bat Yam Israel 64 N10 31 59N 34 45E
Bawdsey England 17 E3 52 01N 1 25E
Bawtry England 13 E2 53 26N 1 01W
Bayeux France 50 D5 49 16N 0 42W
Bayonne France 50 D2 43 30N 1 28W
Bayreuth Germany 52 E4 49 27N 11 35E
Bayston Hill tn.
  England 14 D2 52 40N 2 48W
Beachy Head England 17 D1 50 44N 0 16E
Beaconsfield England 16 C2 51 37N 0 39W
Beadnell Bay England 11 H2 55 32N 1 30W
Beaminster England 19 E2 50 49N 2 45W
Bear Island RoI 21 B1 51 40N 9 48W
Bearsden Scotland 11 E2 55 56N 4 20W
Bearsted England 17 D2 51 17N 0 35E
Beatrice USA 91 G5 40 17N 96 45W
Beaulieu England 16 B1 50 49N 1 27W
Beauly Scotland 9 E2 57 29N 4 29W
Beauly r. Scotland 9 E2 57 25N 4 33W
Beauly Firth Scotland 9 E2 57 30N 4 20W
Beaumaris Wales 14 B3 53 16N 4 05W
Beaune France 50 G4 47 02N 4 50E
Beauvais France 50 F5 49 26N 2 05E
Bebington England 12 D2 53 20N 2 59W
Beccles England 17 E3 52 28N 1 34E
Béchar Algeria 80 D8 31 35N 2 17W
Bedale England 13 E3 54 17N 1 35W
Bedford England 16 C3 52 08N 0 29W
Bedfordshire co.
  England 16 C2 52 08N 0 29W
Bedlington England 13 E4 55 08N 1 25W
Bedwas Wales 14 C1 51 35N 3 12W
Bedworth England 15 E2 52 29N 1 28W
Beeston England 15 E2 52 56N 1 12W
Beighton England 13 E2 53 21N 1 21W
Beijing China 69 L5 39 55N 116 26E
Beinn Dearg mt.
  Scotland 9 E2 57 47N 4 56W
Beira Mozambique 82 F4 19 49S 34 52E
Beirut Lebanon 64 C5 33 52N 35 30E
Beith Scotland 11 E2 55 45N 4 38W
Beja Portugal 51 B3 38 01N 7 52W
Bejaïa Algeria 80 F9 36 49N 5 03E
Béjar Spain 51 C4 40 24N 5 45W
BELARUS 56 B5/6
Belderg RoI 20 B4 54 18N 9 33W
Belém Brazil 96 H12 1 27S 48 29W
Belfast NI 10 D1 54 35N 5 55W
Belfast district NI 10 C1/D1 54 40N 6 05W
Belfast Lough est. NI 10 D1 54 40N 5 50W
Belford England 11 H2 55 36N 1 49W
Belfort France 50 H4 47 38N 6 52E
BELGIUM 48 B3/D3
Belgrade Serbia 55 J6 44 50N 20 30E
BELIZE 94 G3
Bellac France 50 E4 46 07N 1 04E
Bellacorick RoI 20 B4 54 07N 9 34W
Bellanagh RoI 20 D3 53 56N 7 24W
Bellavary RoI 20 B3 53 53N 9 12W
Bellingham England 12 D4 55 09N 2 16W
Bellsbank Scotland 11 E2 55 19N 4 24W
Bellshill Scotland 11 F2 55 49N 4 02W
Belmont Scotland 7 D3 60 41N 0 58W
Belmopan Belize 94 G3 17 13N 88 48W
Belmullet RoI 20 B4 54 14N 10 00W
Belo Horizonte Brazil 96 J10 19 54S 43 54W
Belper England 13 E2 53 01N 1 29W
Belton England 17 E3 52 34N 1 40E
Beltra Lough RoI 20 B3 53 55N 9 25W
Belturbet RoI 20 D4 54 06N 7 28W
Belvoir, Vale of
  England 15 F2 52 58N 0 55W
Bembridge England 16 B1 50 41N 1 05W
Ben Alder mt. Scotland 9 E1 56 49N 4 28W
Benbane Head NI 10 C2 55 14N 6 29W
Benbecula i. Scotland 8 B2 57 25N 7 20W
Ben Cleuch mt.
  Scotland 11 F3 56 11N 3 47W
Ben Cruachan mt.
  Scotland 8 D1 56 26N 5 09W
Benavente Spain 51 C4 42 00N 5 40W
Benevento Italy 54 F4 41 08N 14 46E
Bengal, Bay of
  Indian Ocean 67 F3 17 00N 88 00E
Benghazi Libya 81 K8 32 07N 20 04E
Benguela Angola 82 B5 12 34S 13 24E
Ben Hope mt. Scotland 9 E3 58 24N 4 37W

Benicarló Spain 51 F4 40 25N 0 25E
Benidorm Spain 51 E3 38 33N 0 09W
BENIN 80 E4
Benin City Nigeria 80 F3 6 19N 5 41E
Ben Klibreck mt.
  Scotland 9 E3 58 14N 4 22W
Ben Lawers mt.
  Scotland 9 E1 56 33N 4 15W
Benllech Wales 14 B3 53 19N 4 15W
Ben Lomond mt.
  Scotland 11 E3 56 12N 4 38W
Ben Loyal mt. Scotland 9 E3 58 24N 4 26W
Ben Macdui mt.
  Scotland 9 F2 57 04N 3 40W
Ben More mt.
  Highland Scotland 8 C1 56 25N 6 02W
Ben More mt.
  Stirling Scotland 9 E1 56 23N 4 31W
Ben More Assynt mt.
  Scotland 9 E3 58 07N 4 52W
Bennettsbridge RoI 21 D2 52 35N 7 10W
Ben Nevis mt. Scotland 9 E1 56 40N 5 00W
Benson USA 90 D3 31 58N 110 19W
Bentley England 13 E2 53 33N 1 09W
Benwee Head RoI 20 B4 54 21N 9 48W
Ben Wyvis mt. Scotland 9 E2 57 40N 4 35W
Beppu Japan 70 B1 33 18N 131 30E
Bérgamo Italy 54 C6 45 42N 9 40E
Bergen Norway 49 C3 60 23N 5 20E
Bergerac France 50 E3 44 50N 0 29E
Bergisch Gladbach
  Germany 52 C5 50 59N 7 10E
Bering Sea
  Pacific Ocean 100 H12/J13 60 00N 175 00W
Bering Strait
  Russia/USA 88 B7 69 00N 169 00W
Berkeley England 15 D1 51 42N 2 27W
Berkhamsted England 16 C2 51 46N 0 35W
Berkshire Downs
  England 16 B2 51 30N 1 25W
Berlin Germany 52 F6 52 32N 13 25E
Bern Switz. 52 C3 46 57N 7 26E
Bernalda Italy 55 G4 40 24N 16 44E
Berner Alpen mts.
  Switz. 52 C3/D3 46 25N 7 30E
Berneray i. Scotland 8 B2 57 45N 7 10W
Bernina Pass Switz. 52 E3 46 25N 10 02E
Berriedale Scotland 9 F3 58 11N 3 33W
Berry Head England 18 D2 50 24N 3 29W
Berwick-upon-Tweed
  England 11 G2 55 46N 2 00W
Besançon France 50 G4 47 14N 6 02E
Bessacarr England 13 E2 53 30N 1 05W
Bessbrook NI 10 C1 54 12N 6 24W
Betanzos Spain 51 A5 43 17N 8 13W
Bethersden England 17 D2 51 07N 0 45W
Bethesda Wales 14 B3 53 11N 4 03W
Bethlehem
  Middle East 64 C5 31 42N 35 12E
Béthune France 50 F6 50 32N 2 38E
Bettyhill Scotland 9 E3 58 32N 4 14W
Betws-y-Coed Wales 14 C3 53 05N 3 48W
Beverley England 13 F2 53 51N 0 26W
Bewdley England 15 D2 52 22N 2 19W
Bewl Water l. England 17 D2 51 02N 0 23E
Bexhill England 17 D1 50 50N 0 29E
Bexley England 17 D2 51 27N 0 09E
Béziers France 50 F2 43 21N 3 13E
Bharatpur India 66 D5 27 14N 77 29E
Bhopal India 66 D4 23 17N 77 28E
Bhubaneshwar India 67 F4 20 13N 85 50E
BHUTAN 67 G5
Białystok Poland 53 L6 53 09N 23 10E
Biarritz France 50 D2 43 29N 1 33W
Bicester England 16 B2 51 54N 1 09W
Biddeford USA 91 M5 43 29N 70 27W
Biddulph England 12 D2 53 08N 2 10W
Bideford England 18 C3 51 01N 4 13W
Biel Switz. 52 C3 46 27N 8 13E
Bielefeld Germany 52 D6 52 02N 8 32E
Bielsko-Biała Poland 53 J4 49 50N 19 00E
Bigbury Bay England 18 D2 50 15N 4 00W
Biggar Scotland 11 F2 55 38N 3 32W
Biggleswade England 16 C3 52 05N 0 17W
Bihać
  Bosnia-Herzegovina 54 F6 44 49N 15 53E
Bikaner India 66 C5 28 01N 73 22E
Bila Tserkva Ukraine 53 P4 49 49N 30 10E
Bilbao Spain 51 D5 43 15N 2 56W
Billericay England 17 D2 51 38N 0 25E
Billinge England 12 D2 53 30N 2 42W
Billingham England 13 E3 54 36N 1 17W
Billingshurst England 16 C2 51 01N 0 28W
Bill of Portland c.
  England 19 E2 50 31N 2 27W
Bingham England 15 F2 52 57N 0 57W
Bingley England 13 E2 53 51N 1 50W
Birchwood tn. England 13 E2 53 14N 0 33W
Birkenhead England 12 C2 53 24N 3 02W
Birmingham England 15 E2 52 30N 1 50W
Birmingham USA 91 J3 33 30N 86 55W
Birr RoI 21 D3 53 05N 7 54W
Birstall England 15 E2 52 40N 1 08W

| Place | Map | Grid | Lat | Long |
|---|---|---|---|---|
| Bishop Auckland England | 13 | E3 | 54 40N | 1 40W |
| Bishopbriggs Scotland | 11 | E2 | 55 54N | 4 14W |
| Bishop's Castle tn. England | 14 | C2 | 52 29N | 3 00W |
| Bishop's Cleeve England | 15 | D1 | 51 57N | 2 04W |
| Bishop's Lydeard England | 19 | D3 | 51 04N | 3 12W |
| Bishop's Stortford England | 17 | D2 | 51 53N | 0 09E |
| Bishopston Wales | 14 | B1 | 51 35N | 4 03W |
| Bishop's Waltham England | 16 | B1 | 50 58N | 1 12W |
| Bishopton Scotland | 11 | E2 | 55 54N | 4 31W |
| Bissau Guinea-Bissau | 80 | A4 | 11 52N | 15 39W |
| Blaby England | 15 | E2 | 52 35N | 1 09W |
| Black r. England | 20 | D3 | 53 55N | 7 42W |
| Blackburn England | 12 | D2 | 53 45N | 2 29W |
| Blackdown Hills England | 19 | D2 | 50 55N | 3 10W |
| Blackhall Colliery tn. England | 13 | E3 | 54 43N | 1 20W |
| Black Head Rol | 21 | B3 | 53 09N | 9 16W |
| Blackhope Scar mt. Scotland | 11 | F2 | 55 58N | 3 07W |
| Black Isle Scotland | 9 | E2 | 57 35N | 4 15W |
| Blackmoor Vale England | 19 | E2 | 50 56N | 2 19W |
| Black Mountains Wales | 14 | C1 | 51 55N | 3 10W |
| Black Mountain Wales | 14 | C1 | 51 50N | 3 55W |
| Blackpool England | 12 | C2 | 53 50N | 3 03W |
| Black Sea Europe | 57 | D3/E3 | 43 00N | 35 00E |
| Blacksod Bay Rol | 20 | A3/A4 | 54 05N | 10 00W |
| Blackstairs Mountains Rol | 21 | E2 | 52 33N | 6 49W |
| Blackwater r. Hampshire England | 16 | C2 | 51 22N | 0 54W |
| Blackwater r. Essex England | 17 | D2 | 51 45N | 0 50E |
| Blackwater r. Waterford Rol | 21 | D2 | 52 02N | 7 51W |
| Blackwater r. Meath Rol | 20 | E3 | 53 41N | 6 44W |
| Blackwaterfoot Scotland | 10 | D2 | 55 30N | 5 19W |
| Blackwater r. NI | 10 | C1 | 54 20N | 6 50W |
| Blackwood Wales | 14 | C1 | 51 41N | 3 13W |
| Blaenau Ffestiniog Wales | 14 | C2 | 52 59N | 3 56W |
| Blaenau Gwent u.a. Wales | 14 | C1 | 51 45N | 3 10W |
| Blaenavon Wales | 14 | C1 | 51 48N | 3 05W |
| Blagoveshchensk Russia | 63 | Q7 | 50 19N | 127 30E |
| Blaina Wales | 14 | C1 | 51 48N | 3 11W |
| Blair Atholl Scotland | 9 | F1 | 56 46N | 3 51W |
| Blairgowrie Scotland | 9 | F1 | 56 36N | 3 21W |
| Blakeney Point England | 17 | E3 | 52 58N | 1 00E |
| Blandford Forum England | 19 | E2 | 50 52N | 2 11W |
| Blantyre Malawi | 82 | F4 | 15 46S | 35 00E |
| Blantyre Scotland | 11 | E2 | 55 47N | 4 06W |
| Blarney Rol | 21 | C1 | 51 56N | 8 34W |
| Blennerville Rol | 21 | B2 | 52 15N | 9 43W |
| Blessington Rol | 21 | E3 | 53 10N | 6 32W |
| Bletchley England | 16 | C3 | 52 00N | 0 46W |
| Blidworth England | 13 | E2 | 53 09N | 1 11W |
| Blithe r. England | 15 | E2 | 52 45N | 1 50W |
| Blois France | 50 | E4 | 47 36N | 1 20E |
| Bloody Foreland Rol | 20 | C5 | 55 10N | 8 15W |
| Bludenz Austria | 52 | D3 | 47 10N | 9 50E |
| Blue Stack Mountains Rol | 20 | C4 | 54 44N | 8 03W |
| Blyth Nottinghamshire England | 13 | E2 | 53 23N | 1 03W |
| Blyth Northumberland England | 13 | E4 | 55 07N | 1 30W |
| Blyth r. England | 13 | E4 | 55 08N | 1 45W |
| Blyth r. England | 17 | E3 | 52 22N | 1 29E |
| Boa Vista Brazil | 96 | E14 | 3 23S | 55 30W |
| Bocholt Germany | 52 | C5 | 51 49N | 6 37E |
| Bochum Germany | 52 | C5 | 51 28N | 7 11E |
| Boddam Scotland | 9 | H2 | 57 28N | 1 48W |
| Boden Sweden | 49 | F4 | 65 50N | 21 44E |
| Bodensee l. Switz. | 52 | D3 | 47 40N | 9 30E |
| Bodmin England | 18 | C2 | 50 29N | 4 43W |
| Bodmin Moor England | 18 | C2 | 50 35N | 4 40W |
| Boggeragh Mountains Rol | 21 | B2/C2 | 52 00N | 8 50W |
| Bogie r. Scotland | 9 | G2 | 57 25N | 2 50W |
| Bognor Regis England | 16 | C1 | 50 47N | 0 41W |
| Bogotá Colombia | 96 | C14 | 4 38N | 74 05W |
| Böhmer Wald mts. Germany | 52 | F4 | 49 00N | 13 00E |
| Boise City USA | 90 | F4 | 36 44N | 102 31W |
| Boldon England | 13 | E3 | 54 57N | 1 27W |
| BOLIVIA | 96 | D10/E10 | | |
| Bollington England | 13 | D2 | 53 18N | 2 06W |
| Bologna Italy | 54 | E6 | 44 30N | 11 20E |
| Bolsover England | 13 | E2 | 53 15N | 1 26W |
| Bolton England | 12 | D2 | 53 35N | 2 26W |
| Bolus Head Rol | 21 | A1 | 51 45N | 10 10W |
| Bolzano Italy | 54 | D7 | 46 30N | 11 22E |
| Bonar Bridge tn. Scotland | 9 | E2 | 57 53N | 4 21W |
| Bo'ness Scotland | 11 | F3 | 56 01N | 3 37W |
| Bonifacio France | 50 | J1 | 41 23N | 9 10E |
| Bonifacio, Strait of France/Italy | 50 | J1 | 41 20N | 8 45E |
| Bonn Germany | 52 | C5 | 50 44N | 7 06E |
| Bonnybridge Scotland | 11 | F2 | 55 59N | 3 54W |
| Bonnyrigg Scotland | 11 | F2 | 55 52N | 3 08W |
| Boolakennedy Rol | 21 | C2 | 52 20N | 8 03W |
| Bootle Cumbria England | 12 | C3 | 54 17N | 3 23W |
| Bootle Merseyside England | 12 | C2 | 53 28N | 3 00W |
| Bordeaux France | 50 | D3 | 44 50N | 0 34W |
| Bordon Camp England | 16 | C2 | 51 07N | 0 53W |
| Borneo i. Indonesia/Malaysia | 71 | D3/F5 | 1 00N | 113 00E |
| Bornholm i. Denmark | 49 | D2 | 55 02N | 15 00E |
| Boroughbridge England | 13 | E3 | 54 05N | 1 24W |
| Borris in Ossory Rol | 21 | D2 | 52 57N | 7 37W |
| Borrisokane Rol | 21 | C2 | 53 00N | 8 08W |
| Borrisoleigh Rol | 21 | D2 | 52 45N | 8 00W |
| Borrowash England | 15 | E2 | 52 55N | 1 24W |
| Borth Wales | 14 | B2 | 52 29N | 4 03W |
| Boscastle England | 18 | C2 | 50 41N | 4 42W |
| BOSNIA-HERZEGOVINA | 55 | G6/H6 | | |
| Boston England | 13 | F1 | 52 29N | 0 01W |
| Boston USA | 91 | M5 | 42 20N | 71 05W |
| Boston Spa England | 13 | E2 | 53 54N | 1 21W |
| Bothnia, Gulf of Finland/Sweden | 49 | E3/F3 | 61 00N | 19 10E |
| Botoşani Romania | 53 | N3 | 47 44N | 26 41E |
| BOTSWANA | 82 | D3/E3 | | |
| Bottrop Germany | 52 | C5 | 51 31N | 6 55E |
| Boulder USA | 90 | E5 | 40 02N | 105 16W |
| Boulogne-sur-Mer France | 50 | E6 | 50 43N | 1 37E |
| Bourg-en-Bresse France | 50 | G4 | 46 12N | 5 13E |
| Bourges France | 50 | F4 | 47 05N | 2 23E |
| Bourne England | 15 | F2 | 52 46N | 0 23W |
| Bourne End England | 16 | C2 | 51 34N | 0 42W |
| Bournemouth England | 19 | F2 | 50 43N | 1 54W |
| Bournemouth u.a. England | 19 | F2 | 50 43N | 1 54W |
| Bourton-on-the-Water England | 15 | E1 | 51 53N | 1 46W |
| Bovey r. England | 18 | D2 | 50 40N | 3 50W |
| Bovey Tracey England | 18 | D2 | 50 36N | 3 40W |
| Bowes England | 12 | D3 | 54 30N | 2 01W |
| Bowland, Forest of England | 12 | D2/D3 | 54 00N | 2 40W |
| Bowmore Scotland | 10 | C2 | 55 45N | 6 17W |
| Bowness-on-Windermere England | 12 | D3 | 54 22N | 2 55W |
| Boxtel Neths | 48 | D4 | 51 36N | 5 20E |
| Boyle Rol | 20 | C3 | 53 58N | 8 18W |
| Boyne r. Rol | 20 | E3 | 53 45N | 6 25W |
| Bozeman USA | 90 | D6 | 45 40N | 111 00W |
| Brabourne Lees England | 17 | D2 | 51 08N | 1 00E |
| Brackley England | 15 | E2 | 52 02N | 1 09W |
| Bracknell England | 16 | C2 | 51 26N | 0 46W |
| Bracknell Forest u.a. England | 16 | C1 | 50 25N | 0 50W |
| Bradford England | 13 | E2 | 53 48N | 1 45W |
| Bradford-on-Avon England | 16 | A2 | 51 22N | 2 15W |
| Bradwell-on-Sea England | 17 | D2 | 51 44N | 0 54E |
| Bradworthy England | 18 | C2 | 50 54N | 4 24W |
| Braemar Scotland | 9 | F2 | 57 01N | 3 23W |
| Braga Portugal | 51 | A4 | 41 32N | 8 26W |
| Bragança Portugal | 51 | B4 | 41 47N | 6 46W |
| Brahmaputra r. India/Bangladesh | 67 | G5 | 26 40N | 93 00E |
| Brăila Romania | 53 | N2 | 45 17N | 27 58E |
| Brailsford England | 15 | E2 | 52 59N | 1 36W |
| Braintree England | 17 | D2 | 51 53N | 0 32E |
| Brampton England | 12 | D3 | 54 57N | 2 43W |
| Brandenburg Germany | 52 | F6 | 52 25N | 12 34E |
| Brandon Durham England | 13 | E3 | 54 46N | 1 38W |
| Brandon Suffolk England | 17 | D3 | 52 27N | 0 37E |
| Brandon Bay Rol | 21 | A2 | 52 15N | 10 05W |
| Brandon Mountain Rol | 21 | A2 | 52 10N | 10 10W |
| Brandon Point Rol | 21 | A2 | 52 15N | 10 05W |
| Brant r. England | 13 | F2 | 53 05N | 0 35W |
| Brasília Brazil | 96 | H10 | 15 45S | 47 57W |
| Braşov Romania | 53 | M2 | 45 39N | 25 35E |
| Bratislava Slovakia | 53 | H4 | 48 10N | 17 10E |
| Braunau Austria | 52 | F4 | 48 16N | 13 03E |
| Braunschweig Germany | 52 | E6 | 52 15N | 10 30E |
| Braunton England | 18 | C3 | 51 07N | 4 10W |
| Bray Rol | 20 | E3 | 53 12N | 6 06W |
| Bray Head Rol | 21 | A1 | 53 12N | 6 05W |
| BRAZIL | 96 | F11/H11 | | |
| Brazzaville Congo | 82 | C7 | 4 14S | 15 14E |
| Breaston England | 15 | E2 | 52 56N | 1 12W |
| Brechin Scotland | 9 | G1 | 56 44N | 2 40W |
| Brecon Wales | 14 | C1 | 51 57N | 3 24W |
| Breda Neths | 48 | C4 | 51 35N | 4 46E |
| Bregenz Austria | 52 | D3 | 47 31N | 9 46E |
| Bremen Germany | 52 | D6 | 53 05N | 8 48E |
| Bremerhaven Germany | 52 | D6 | 53 33N | 8 35E |
| Brent England | 16 | C2 | 51 34N | 0 17W |
| Brentwood England | 17 | D2 | 51 38N | 0 18E |
| Brescia Italy | 54 | D6 | 45 33N | 10 13E |
| Bressay i. Scotland | 7 | C3 | 60 08N | 1 05W |
| Brest Belarus | 56 | B5 | 52 08N | 23 40E |
| Brest France | 50 | B5 | 48 23N | 4 30W |
| Briançon France | 50 | H3 | 44 53N | 6 39E |
| Bridgend Wales | 14 | C1 | 51 31N | 3 35W |
| Bridgend u.a. Wales | 14 | C1 | 51 32N | 3 35W |
| Bridge of Dee tn. Scotland | 9 | F1 | 56 59N | 3 20W |
| Bridge of Don tn. Scotland | 9 | G2 | 57 11N | 2 05W |
| Bridge of Ericht tn. Scotland | 9 | E1 | 56 44N | 4 23W |
| Bridge of Orchy tn. Scotland | 9 | E1 | 56 30N | 4 46W |
| Bridge of Weir tn. Scotland | 11 | E2 | 55 52N | 4 35W |
| Bridgeport USA | 91 | M5 | 41 12N | 73 12W |
| Bridgetown Rol | 21 | E2 | 52 14N | 6 33W |
| Bridgnorth England | 15 | D2 | 52 33N | 2 25W |
| Bridgwater England | 19 | D3 | 51 08N | 3 00W |
| Bridgwater Bay England | 19 | D3 | 51 15N | 3 20W |
| Bridlington England | 13 | F3 | 54 05N | 0 12W |
| Bridlington Bay England | 13 | F3 | 54 03N | 0 10W |
| Bridport England | 19 | E2 | 50 44N | 2 46W |
| Brierfield England | 12 | D2 | 53 50N | 2 14W |
| Brig Switz. | 52 | C3 | 46 19N | 8 00E |
| Brigg England | 13 | F2 | 53 34N | 0 30W |
| Brighouse England | 13 | E2 | 53 42N | 1 47W |
| Brightlingsea England | 17 | E2 | 51 49N | 1 02E |
| Brighton England | 16 | C1 | 50 50N | 0 10W |
| Brighton and Hove u.a. England | 16 | C1 | 50 51N | 0 09W |
| Brignoles France | 50 | H2 | 43 25N | 6 03E |
| Bríndisi Italy | 55 | G4 | 40 37N | 17 57E |
| Brisbane Australia | 73 | K5 | 27 30S | 153 00E |
| Bristol England | 19 | E3 | 51 27N | 2 35W |
| Bristol u.a. England | 19 | E3 | 51 30N | 2 38W |
| Bristol Channel UK | 18 | C1/D1 | 51 20N | 4 00W |
| British Columbia prov. Canada | 88 | K4/K5 | 56 50N | 125 30W |
| British Isles Europe | 6 | | | |
| Briton Ferry tn. Wales | 14 | C1 | 51 38N | 3 49W |
| Brittas Rol | 20 | E3 | 53 14N | 6 27W |
| Brive-la-Gaillarde France | 50 | E3 | 45 09N | 1 32E |
| Brixham England | 18 | D2 | 50 23N | 3 30W |
| Brno Czech Rep. | 53 | H4 | 49 13N | 16 40E |
| Broad Bay Scotland | 8 | C3 | 58 15N | 6 10W |
| Broadford Rol | 21 | C2 | 52 48N | 8 38W |
| Broadford Scotland | 8 | D2 | 57 14N | 5 54W |
| Broad Haven b. Rol | 20 | B4 | 54 18N | 9 55W |
| Broadstairs England | 17 | E2 | 51 22N | 1 27E |
| Broadstone England | 19 | E2 | 50 45N | 2 00W |
| Broadway England | 15 | E2 | 52 02N | 1 50W |
| Brockenhurst England | 16 | B1 | 50 49N | 1 34W |
| Brodick Scotland | 10 | D2 | 55 35N | 5 09W |
| Bromley England | 16 | D2 | 51 31N | 0 01E |
| Bromsgrove England | 15 | D2 | 52 20N | 2 03W |
| Bromyard England | 15 | D2 | 52 11N | 2 30W |
| Brora Scotland | 9 | F3 | 58 01N | 3 51W |
| Brora r. Scotland | 9 | E3 | 58 05N | 4 00W |
| Broseley England | 15 | D2 | 52 37N | 2 29W |
| Brotton England | 13 | F3 | 54 34N | 0 56W |
| Brough East Riding of Yorkshire England | 13 | F2 | 53 44N | 0 35W |
| Brough Cumbria England | 12 | D3 | 54 32N | 2 19W |
| Brough Head Scotland | 7 | A2 | 59 09N | 3 19W |
| Broughshane NI | 10 | C1 | 54 54N | 6 12W |
| Broughton Wales | 14 | D3 | 53 10N | 3 00W |
| Broughton in Furness England | 12 | C3 | 54 17N | 3 13W |
| Broughty Ferry tn. Scotland | 9 | G1 | 56 28N | 2 53W |
| Brownhills tn. England | 15 | E2 | 52 39N | 1 55W |
| Broxburn Scotland | 11 | F2 | 55 57N | 3 29W |
| Bruay-en-Artois France | 50 | F6 | 50 29N | 2 33E |
| Brue r. England | 19 | E3 | 51 10N | 2 50W |
| Brugg Switz. | 52 | D3 | 47 29N | 8 13E |
| Brugge Belgium | 48 | B4 | 51 13N | 3 14E |
| BRUNEI | 71 | E4/F4 | | |
| Brunico Italy | 54 | D7 | 46 47N | 11 57E |
| Brunswick USA | 91 | K3 | 31 09N | 81 30W |
| Brussels Belgium | 48 | C3 | 50 50N | 4 21E |
| Bruton England | 19 | E3 | 51 07N | 2 27W |
| Bryher i. England | 18 | A1 | 49 57N | 6 21W |
| Brymbo Wales | 14 | C3 | 53 05N | 3 03W |
| Brynamman Wales | 14 | C1 | 51 49N | 3 52W |
| Brynmawr Wales | 14 | C1 | 51 49N | 3 11W |
| Bucharest Romania | 53 | N2 | 44 25N | 26 07E |
| Buchan Ness Scotland | 9 | H2 | 57 28N | 1 47W |
| Buckfastleigh England | 18 | D2 | 50 29N | 3 46W |
| Buckhaven Scotland | 11 | F3 | 56 11N | 3 03W |
| Buckie Scotland | 9 | G2 | 57 40N | 2 58W |
| Buckingham England | 16 | C2 | 52 00N | 1 00W |
| Buckinghamshire co. England | 16 | C2 | 51 50N | 0 50W |
| Buckley Wales | 14 | C3 | 53 10N | 3 05W |
| Budapest Hungary | 53 | J3 | 47 30N | 19 03E |
| Buddon Ness Scotland | 9 | G1 | 56 28N | 2 45W |
| Bude England | 18 | C2 | 50 50N | 4 33W |
| Bude Bay England | 18 | C2 | 50 50N | 4 40W |
| Budleigh Salterton England | 19 | D2 | 50 38N | 3 20W |
| Buenaventura Colombia | 96 | B14 | 3 54N | 77 02W |
| Buenos Aires Argentina | 97 | F7 | 34 40S | 58 30W |
| Buffalo USA | 91 | L5 | 42 52N | 78 55W |
| Builth Wells Wales | 14 | C2 | 52 09N | 3 24W |
| Bujumbura Burundi | 83 | A3 | 3 22S | 29 19E |
| Bukavu CDR | 81 | L1 | 2 30S | 28 50E |
| Bulawayo Zimbabwe | 82 | E3 | 20 10S | 28 43E |
| Bulford England | 16 | B2 | 51 12N | 1 46W |
| BULGARIA | 55 | K5/M5 | | |
| Bulkington England | 15 | E2 | 52 28N | 1 25W |
| Bull Point NI | 10 | C2 | 55 18N | 6 16W |
| Bunclody Rol | 21 | E2 | 52 38N | 6 40W |
| Buncrana Rol | 20 | D5 | 55 08N | 7 27W |
| Bundoran Rol | 20 | C4 | 54 28N | 8 17W |
| Bungay England | 17 | E3 | 52 28N | 1 26E |
| Bunmahon Rol | 21 | D2 | 52 08N | 7 23W |
| Bunnahown Rol | 20 | B3 | 53 24N | 9 47W |
| Bunnyconnellan Rol | 20 | B4 | 54 06N | 9 01W |
| Buraydah Saudi Arabia | 64 | D4 | 26 20N | 43 59E |
| Bure r. England | 17 | E3 | 52 47N | 1 20E |
| Burgas Bulgaria | 55 | M5 | 42 30N | 27 29E |
| Burgess Hill tn. England | 16 | C1 | 50 58N | 0 08W |
| Burghead tn. Scotland | 9 | F2 | 57 42N | 3 30W |
| Burghead Bay Scotland | 9 | F2 | 57 41N | 3 31W |
| Burgh le Marsh England | 13 | G2 | 53 10N | 0 15E |
| Burgos Spain | 51 | D5 | 42 21N | 3 41W |
| BURKINA | 80 | D4 | | |
| Burley-in-Wharfedale England | 13 | E2 | 53 55N | 1 45W |
| Burnham Market England | 17 | D3 | 52 57N | 0 44E |
| Burnham-on-Crouch England | 17 | D2 | 51 38N | 0 49E |
| Burnham-on-Sea England | 19 | D3 | 51 15N | 3 00W |
| Burnley England | 12 | D2 | 53 48N | 2 14W |
| Burnmouth Scotland | 11 | G2 | 55 50N | 2 04W |
| Burnsall England | 12 | E3 | 54 03N | 1 57W |
| Burntisland tn. Scotland | 11 | F3 | 56 03N | 3 15W |
| Burntwood England | 15 | E2 | 52 40N | 1 56W |
| Burray i. Scotland | 7 | B1 | 58 51N | 2 54W |
| Burrow Head Scotland | 11 | E1 | 54 41N | 4 24W |
| Burry Port Wales | 14 | B1 | 51 42N | 4 15W |
| Bursa Turkey | 57 | C3 | 40 12N | 29 04E |
| Burscough Bridge tn. England | 12 | D2 | 53 37N | 2 51W |
| Burton Agnes England | 13 | F3 | 54 03N | 0 19W |
| Burton Latimer England | 15 | F2 | 52 22N | 0 40W |
| Burton upon Trent England | 15 | E2 | 52 48N | 1 36W |
| BURUNDI | 83 | A3/B3 | | |
| Burwell England | 17 | D3 | 52 16N | 0 19E |
| Bury England | 12 | D2 | 53 36N | 2 17W |
| Bury St. Edmunds England | 17 | D3 | 52 15N | 0 43E |
| Bush r. NI | 10 | C2 | 55 10N | 6 30W |
| Bushey England | 16 | C2 | 51 39N | 0 22W |
| Bushmills NI | 10 | C2 | 55 12N | 6 32W |
| Bute i. Scotland | 10 | D2 | 55 50N | 5 05W |
| Bute, Sound of Scotland | 10 | D2 | 55 45N | 5 10W |
| Butler's Bridge Rol | 20 | D4 | 54 03N | 7 22W |
| Buttermere l. England | 12 | C3 | 54 32N | 3 16W |
| Buttevant Rol | 21 | C2 | 52 14N | 8 40W |
| Butt of Lewis c. Scotland | 8 | C3 | 58 30N | 6 20W |
| Buxton England | 13 | E2 | 53 15N | 1 55W |
| Bydgoszcz Poland | 53 | H6 | 53 16N | 18 00E |
| Byfield England | 15 | E2 | 52 11N | 1 14W |
| Bytom Poland | 53 | J5 | 50 21N | 18 51E |

**C**

| Place | Map | Grid | Lat | Long |
|---|---|---|---|---|
| Cabo de Hornos Chile | 97 | D2 | 56 00S | 67 15W |
| Cabo Finisterre Spain | 51 | A5 | 42 52N | 9 16W |
| Cabrera i. Spain | 51 | G3 | 39 00N | 2 59E |
| Cáceres Spain | 51 | B3 | 39 29N | 6 23W |
| Cadair Idris mt. Wales | 14 | C2 | 52 42N | 3 54W |
| Cádiz Spain | 51 | B2 | 36 32N | 6 18W |
| Cádiz, Gulf of Spain | 51 | B2 | 36 30N | 7 15W |
| Caen France | 50 | D5 | 49 11N | 0 22W |
| Caerleon Wales | 14 | D1 | 51 37N | 2 57W |
| Caernarfon Wales | 14 | B3 | 53 08N | 4 16W |
| Caernarfon Bay Wales | 14 | B3 | 53 05N | 4 30W |
| Caerphilly Wales | 14 | C1 | 51 35N | 3 14W |
| Caerphilly u.a. Wales | 14 | C1 | 51 37N | 3 5W |
| Caersws Wales | 14 | C2 | 52 31N | 3 26W |
| Cágliari Italy | 54 | C3 | 39 13N | 9 08E |
| Caha Mountains Rol | 21 | B1 | 51 40N | 9 40W |
| Caher Rol | 21 | D2 | 52 21N | 7 56W |
| Caher Island Rol | 20 | A3 | 53 43N | 10 01W |
| Cahersiveen Rol | 21 | A1 | 51 57N | 10 13W |
| Cahore Point Rol | 21 | E2 | 52 34N | 6 11W |
| Cahors France | 50 | E3 | 44 28N | 0 26E |
| Cairn Gorm mt. Scotland | 9 | F2 | 57 07N | 3 40W |
| Cairngorms mts. Scotland | 9 | F2 | 57 10N | 3 30W |
| Cairnryan Scotland | 10 | D2 | 54 58N | 5 02W |

| Place | Page | Grid | Lat | Long |
|---|---|---|---|---|
| Cairns Australia | 73 | J7 | 16 51S | 145 43E |
| Cairo Egypt | 81 | M7 | 30 00N | 31 15E |
| Caister-on-Sea England | 17 | E3 | 52 39N | 1 44E |
| Caistor England | 13 | F2 | 53 30N | 0 20W |
| Calahorra Spain | 51 | E5 | 46 19N | 1 58W |
| Calais France | 50 | E6 | 50 57N | 1 52E |
| Calamocha Spain | 51 | E4 | 40 54N | 1 18W |
| Calatayud Spain | 51 | E4 | 41 21N | 1 39W |
| Caldew r. England | 12 | C3 | 54 45N | 3 00W |
| Caldey Island Wales | 14 | B1 | 51 38N | 4 42W |
| Caldicot Wales | 14 | D1 | 51 36N | 2 45W |
| Caldwell USA | 90 | C5 | 43 39N | 116 40W |
| Calgary Canada | 88 | N4 | 51 05N | 11 05W |
| Cali Colombia | 96 | B14 | 3 24N | 76 30W |
| California state USA | 90 | C4 | 35 00N | 119 00W |
| Callan Rol | 21 | D2 | 52 33N | 7 23W |
| Callander Scotland | 11 | E3 | 56 15N | 4 13W |
| Callao Peru | 96 | B11 | 12 05S | 77 08W |
| Calligarry Scotland | 8 | D2 | 57 02N | 5 58E |
| Callington England | 18 | C2 | 50 30N | 4 18W |
| Calne England | 16 | A2 | 51 27N | 2 00W |
| Calverton England | 13 | E2 | 53 03N | 1 05W |
| Calvi France | 50 | J2 | 42 34N | 8 44E |
| Cam r. England | 17 | D3 | 52 15N | 0 11E |
| Camberley England | 16 | C2 | 51 21N | 0 45W |
| CAMBODIA | 71 | C6/D6 | | |
| Camborne England | 18 | B2 | 50 12N | 5 19W |
| Cambrai France | 50 | F6 | 50 10N | 3 14E |
| Cambrian Mountains Wales | 14 | C2 | 52 15N | 3 45W |
| Cambridge England | 17 | D3 | 52 12N | 0 07E |
| Cambridge USA | 91 | L4 | 38 34N | 76 04W |
| Cambridgeshire co. England | 16 | C3 | 52 30N | 0 00 |
| Camel r. England | 18 | C2 | 50 31N | 4 44W |
| Camelford England | 18 | C2C | 50 37N | 4 41W |
| CAMEROON | 80 | G3 | | |
| Campbeltown Scotland | 10 | D2 | 55 26N | 5 36W |
| Campina Grande Brazil | 96 | K12 | 7 15S | 35 50W |
| Campinas Brazil | 96 | H9 | 22 54S | 47 06W |
| Campobasso Italy | 54 | F4 | 41 33N | 14 39E |
| Campo Grande Brazil | 96 | G9 | 20 24S | 54 35W |
| Campos Brazil | 96 | J9 | 21 46S | 41 21W |
| Campsie Fells Scotland | 11 | E3 | 56 00N | 4 15W |
| CANADA | 88/89 | | | |
| Canadian r. USA | 90 | F4 | 35 00N | 104 00W |
| Canary Islands Spain | 80 | A7/B7 | 28 30N | 15 10W |
| Canaveral, Cape USA | 91 | K2 | 28 28N | 80 28W |
| Canberra Australia | 73 | J3 | 35 18S | 149 08E |
| Cancún Mexico | 94 | G4 | 21 09N | 86 45W |
| Canisp mt. Scotland | 9 | D3 | 58 07N | 5 03W |
| Canna i. Scotland | 8 | C2 | 57 05N | 6 35W |
| Canna, Sound of Scotland | 8 | C2 | 57 00N | 6 30W |
| Cannes France | 50 | H2 | 43 33N | 7 00E |
| Cannich Scotland | 9 | E2 | 57 12N | 4 46W |
| Cannington England | 19 | D3 | 51 09N | 3 04E |
| Cannock England | 15 | D2 | 52 42N | 2 01W |
| Cannock Chase England | 15 | D2/E2 | 52 45N | 2 04W |
| Canonbie Scotland | 11 | G2 | 55 05N | 2 57W |
| Canterbury England | 17 | E2 | 51 17N | 1 05E |
| Canvey Island England | 17 | D2 | 51 32N | 0 33E |
| Cap de la Hague France | 50 | D5 | 49 44N | 1 56W |
| Cape Clear Rol | 21 | B1 | 51 30N | 9 30W |
| Cape Cornwall England | 18 | B2 | 50 07N | 5 44W |
| Capel England | 16 | C2 | 51 10N | 0 20W |
| Cape Town RSA | 82 | C1 | 33 56S | 18 28E |
| CAPE VERDE | 102 | | | |
| Cape York Peninsula Australia | 73 | H8 | 12 30S | 142 30E |
| Cap Ferret c. France | 50 | D3 | 44 42N | 1 16W |
| Cappagh White Rol | 21 | C2 | 52 40N | 8 10W |
| Cappamore Rol | 21 | C2 | 52 37N | 8 20W |
| Cappoquin Rol | 21 | D2 | 52 08N | 7 50W |
| Capri i. Italy | 54 | F4 | 40 33N | 14 15E |
| Caprivi Strip Namibia | 82 | D4 | 17 30S | 27 50E |
| Caracas Venezuela | 96 | D16 | 10 35N | 66 56W |
| Carcassonne France | 50 | F2 | 43 13N | 2 21E |
| Cardiff Wales | 14 | C1 | 51 30N | 3 13W |
| Cardiff u.a. Wales | 14 | C1 | 51 32N | 3 14W |
| Cardigan Wales | 14 | B2 | 52 06N | 4 40W |
| Cardigan Bay Wales | 14 | B2 | 52 30N | 4 30W |
| Cargenbridge Scotland | 11 | F2 | 55 05N | 3 41W |
| Caribbean Sea Central America | 95 | J3/L3 | 15 00N | 75 00W |
| Carlingford Rol | 20 | E4 | 54 02N | 6 11W |
| Carlingford Lough NI/Rol | 10 | C1 | 54 05N | 6 10W |
| Carlisle England | 12 | D3 | 54 54N | 2 55W |
| Carlow Rol | 21 | E2 | 52 50N | 6 55W |
| Carlow co. Rol | 21 | E2 | 52 40N | 6 55W |
| Carloway Scotland | 8 | C3 | 58 17N | 6 48W |
| Carlton in Lindrick England | 13 | E2 | 53 22N | 1 06W |
| Carlton-on-Trent England | 13 | F2 | 53 10N | 0 48W |
| Carluke Scotland | 11 | F2 | 55 45N | 3 51W |
| Carmarthen Wales | 14 | B1 | 51 51N | 4 20W |
| Carmarthen Bay Wales | 14 | B1 | 51 40N | 4 30W |
| Carmarthenshire u.a. Wales | 14 | B1 | 51 55N | 4 00W |
| Carmel Head Wales | 14 | B3 | 53 24N | 4 34W |
| Carndonagh Rol | 20 | D5 | 55 15N | 7 15W |
| Carn Eige mt. Scotland | 9 | D2 | 57 22N | 5 07W |
| Carnforth England | 12 | D3 | 54 08N | 2 46W |
| Carnlough NI | 10 | D1 | 54 59N | 5 59W |
| Carnlough Bay NI | 10 | D1 | 54 59N | 5 57W |
| Carnoustie Scotland | 9 | G1 | 56 30N | 2 44W |
| Carnsore Point Rol | 21 | E2 | 52 10N | 6 22W |
| Carpathians mts. Europe | 53 | J4/M3 | 49 00N | 22 00E |
| Carpentras France | 50 | G3 | 44 03N | 5 03E |
| Carradale Scotland | 10 | D2 | 55 35N | 5 28E |
| Carrauntoohil mt. Rol | 21 | B2 | 52 00N | 9 45W |
| Carrbridge Scotland | 9 | F2 | 57 17N | 3 49W |
| Carrick Rol | 20 | C4 | 54 39N | 8 38W |
| Carrickboy Rol | 20 | D3 | 53 37N | 7 41W |
| Carrickfergus NI | 10 | D1 | 54 43N | 5 49W |
| Carrickfergus district NI | 10 | D1 | 54 45N | 5 50W |
| Carrickmacross Rol | 20 | E3 | 53 58N | 5 49W |
| Carrick-on-Shannon Rol | 20 | C3 | 53 57N | 8 05W |
| Carrick-on-Suir Rol | 21 | D2 | 52 21N | 7 25W |
| Carrigaline Rol | 21 | C1 | 51 48N | 8 24W |
| Carriganimmy Rol | 21 | B1 | 51 57N | 9 02W |
| Carrigtohill Rol | 21 | C1 | 51 55N | 8 16W |
| Carron r. Scotland | 9 | E2 | 57 53N | 4 30W |
| Carronbridge Scotland | 11 | F2 | 55 16N | 3 48W |
| Carrutherstown Scotland | 11 | F2 | 55 04N | 3 24W |
| Carryduff NI | 10 | D1 | 54 31N | 5 53W |
| Carsethorn Scotland | 11 | F1 | 54 55N | 3 35W |
| Carsphairn Scotland | 11 | E2 | 55 13N | 4 16W |
| Cartagena Colombia | 96 | B16 | 10 24N | 75 33W |
| Cartagena Spain | 51 | E2 | 37 36N | 0 59W |
| Carterton England | 16 | B2 | 51 45N | 1 35W |
| Casablanca Morocco | 80 | C8 | 33 39N | 7 35W |
| Cascade Range N. America | 90 | B5/6 | 48 00N | 121 00W |
| Caserta Italy | 54 | F4 | 41 04N | 14 20E |
| Cashel Rol | 21 | D2 | 52 31N | 7 53W |
| Casper USA | 90 | E5 | 42 50N | 106 20W |
| Caspian Sea Asia | 57 | G3/H3 | 41 00N | 50 00E |
| Cassino Italy | 54 | F4 | 41 29N | 13 50E |
| Castellane France | 50 | H2 | 43 50N | 6 30E |
| Castellón de la Plana Spain | 51 | E3 | 39 59N | 0 03W |
| Castelnaudary France | 50 | E2 | 43 18N | 1 57E |
| Castelo Branco Portugal | 51 | B3 | 39 50N | 7 30W |
| Castelvetrano Italy | 54 | E2 | 37 41N | 12 47E |
| Castlebar Rol | 20 | B3 | 53 52N | 9 17W |
| Castlebay Scotland | 8 | B1 | 56 57N | 7 28W |
| Castleblaney Rol | 20 | E4 | 54 07N | 6 44W |
| Castle Cary England | 19 | E3 | 51 06N | 2 31W |
| Castlecomer Rol | 21 | D2 | 52 48N | 7 12W |
| Castleconnell Rol | 21 | C2 | 52 43N | 8 30W |
| Castledawson NI | 10 | C1 | 54 47N | 6 33W |
| Castlederg NI | 10 | B1 | 54 42N | 7 36W |
| Castledermot Rol | 21 | E2 | 52 55N | 6 50W |
| Castle Donington England | 15 | E2 | 52 51N | 1 19W |
| Castle Douglas Scotland | 11 | F1 | 54 57N | 3 56W |
| Castlefin Rol | 20 | D4 | 54 47N | 7 35W |
| Castleford England | 13 | E2 | 43 44N | 1 21W |
| Castleisland Rol | 21 | B2 | 52 14N | 9 27W |
| Castle Kennedy Scotland | 10 | E1 | 54 54N | 4 57W |
| Castlemaine Harbour Rol | 21 | B2 | 52 08N | 9 33W |
| Castlepollard Rol | 20 | D3 | 53 41N | 7 17W |
| Castlerea Rol | 20 | C3 | 53 46N | 8 29W |
| Castlereagh district NI | 10 | D1 | 54 35N | 5 55W |
| Castletown Isle of Man | 12 | B3 | 54 04N | 4 38W |
| Castletown Scotland | 9 | F3 | 58 35N | 3 23W |
| Castletown Bearhaven Rol | 21 | B2 | 51 39N | 9 55W |
| Castletownroche Rol | 21 | C2 | 52 10N | 8 28W |
| Castlewellan NI | 10 | D1 | 54 16N | 5 57W |
| Castres France | 50 | F2 | 43 36N | 2 14E |
| Castrovillari Italy | 54 | G3 | 39 48N | 16 12E |
| Catánia Italy | 54 | F2 | 37 31N | 15 06E |
| Catanzaro Italy | 55 | G3 | 38 54N | 16 36E |
| Caterham England | 16 | C2 | 51 17N | 0 04W |
| Catlemartyr Rol | 21 | C1 | 51 55N | 8 03W |
| Catrine Scotland | 11 | E2 | 55 30N | 4 20W |
| Catshill tn. England | 15 | D2 | 52 22N | 2 03W |
| Catterick Garrison England | 13 | E3 | 54 23N | 1 40W |
| Caucasus mts. Asia | 57 | F3/G3 | 43 00N | 43 00E |
| Cavan Rol | 20 | D3 | 53 58N | 7 21W |
| Cavan co. Rol | 20 | D3/4 | 54 02N | 7 10W |
| Cawood England | 13 | E2 | 53 50N | 1 07W |
| Caxias Brazil | 96 | J13 | 4 53S | 43 20W |
| Caxias do Sul Brazil | 97 | G8 | 29 14S | 51 10W |
| Cayenne French Guiana | 96 | G14 | 4 55N | 52 18W |
| Cedar Rapids tn. USA | 91 | H5 | 41 59N | 91 39W |
| Cefalù Italy | 54 | F3 | 38 03N | 14 03E |
| Cefn-mawr Wales | 14 | C2 | 52 59N | 3 02W |
| Cellar Head Scotland | 8 | C3 | 58 25N | 6 11W |
| Celle Germany | 52 | E6 | 52 37N | 10 05E |
| Cemaes Wales | 14 | B3 | 53 24N | 4 27W |
| Cemaes Head Wales | 14 | B2 | 53 10N | 4 50W |
| CENTRAL AFRICAN REPUBLIC | 81 | J3/K3 | | |
| Ceredigion u.a. Wales | 14 | B2/C2 | 52 14N | 4 00W |
| Cergy-Pontoise France | 50 | F5 | 49 02N | 2 04E |
| Cerignola Italy | 54 | F4 | 41 16N | 15 54E |
| Cerne Abbas England | 19 | E2 | 50 49N | 2 29W |
| Cesena Italy | 54 | E6 | 44 09N | 12 15E |
| České Budějovice Czech Rep. | 52 | G4 | 48 58N | 14 29E |
| Ceuta territory Spain | 51 | C1 | 35 53N | 5 19W |
| Cévennes mts. France | 50 | F3 | 44 20N | 3 30E |
| CHAD | 81 | J4/K4 | | |
| Chadderton England | 12 | D2 | 53 33N | 2 08W |
| Chad, Lake West Africa | 81 | G4 | 13 50N | 14 00E |
| Chagford England | 18 | D2 | 50 41N | 3 50W |
| Chalfont St. Giles England | 16 | C2 | 51 39N | 0 35W |
| Chalkida Greece | 55 | K3 | 38 28N | 23 36E |
| Chalkidiki p. Greece | 55 | K4 | 40 30N | 23 00E |
| Chalmer r. England | 17 | D2 | 51 54N | 0 21E |
| Châlons-sur-Marne France | 50 | G5 | 48 58N | 4 22E |
| Chalon-sur-Saône France | 50 | G4 | 46 47N | 4 51E |
| Chambéry France | 50 | G3 | 45 34N | 5 55E |
| Chamonix France | 50 | H3 | 45 55N | 6 52E |
| Champlain, Lake USA | 93 | F2 | 45 00N | 73 00W |
| Chandigarh India | 66 | D6 | 30 44N | 76 54E |
| Changchun China | 69 | N6 | 43 53N | 125 20E |
| Chang Jiang r. China | 69 | J4 | 31 00N | 110 00E |
| Changsha China | 69 | K3 | 28 10N | 113 00E |
| Chaniá Greece | 55 | L1 | 35 31N | 24 01E |
| Channel Islands British Isles | 19 | E1 | 49 30N | 2 30W |
| Chapel-en-le-Frith England | 13 | E2 | 53 20N | 1 54W |
| Chapel St. Leonards England | 13 | G2 | 53 14N | 0 20E |
| Chapeltown England | 13 | E2 | 53 28N | 1 27W |
| Chard England | 19 | E2 | 50 52N | 2 58W |
| Charing England | 17 | D2 | 51 13N | 0 48E |
| Charlbury England | 16 | B2 | 51 53N | 1 29W |
| Charleroi Belgium | 48 | C3 | 50 25N | 4 27E |
| Charleston USA | 91 | K4 | 38 23N | 81 40W |
| Charlestown Rol | 20 | C3 | 53 58N | 8 47W |
| Charlestown of Aberlour Scotland | 9 | F2 | 57 28N | 3 14W |
| Charleville-Mézières France | 50 | G5 | 49 46N | 4 43E |
| Charlotte USA | 91 | K4 | 35 03N | 80 50W |
| Charlottesville USA | 91 | L4 | 38 02N | 78 29W |
| Charlton Kings England | 15 | D2 | 51 53N | 2 03W |
| Chartres France | 50 | E5 | 48 27N | 1 30E |
| Châteaubriant France | 50 | D4 | 47 43N | 1 22W |
| Châteaudun France | 50 | E5 | 48 04N | 1 20E |
| Châteauroux France | 50 | E4 | 46 49N | 1 41E |
| Château-Thierry France | 50 | F5 | 49 03N | 3 24E |
| Châtellerault France | 50 | E4 | 46 49N | 0 33E |
| Chatham England | 17 | D2 | 51 23N | 0 32E |
| Chatham Canada | 89 | U2 | 42 24N | 82 11W |
| Châtillon-sur-Seine France | 50 | G4 | 47 52N | 4 35E |
| Chattanooga USA | 91 | J4 | 35 02N | 85 18W |
| Chatteris England | 17 | D3 | 52 27N | 0 03E |
| Chaumont France | 50 | G3 | 48 07N | 5 08E |
| Cheadle Greater Manchester England | 12 | D2 | 53 24N | 2 13W |
| Cheadle Staffordshire England | 15 | E2 | 52 59N | 1 59W |
| Cheddar England | 19 | E3 | 51 17N | 2 46W |
| Chelmsford England | 17 | D2 | 51 44N | 0 28E |
| Cheltenham England | 15 | D2 | 51 54N | 2 04W |
| Chelyabinsk Russia | 62 | J8 | 55 12N | 61 25E |
| Chemnitz Germany | 52 | F5 | 50 50N | 12 55E |
| Chengdu China | 69 | H4 | 30 37N | 104 06E |
| Chennai India | 66 | E2 | 13 05N | 80 18E |
| Chepstow Wales | 15 | D1 | 51 39N | 2 41W |
| Cherbourg France | 50 | D5 | 49 38N | 1 37W |
| Cherkasy Ukraine | 56 | D4 | 49 27N | 32 04E |
| Chernivtsi Ukraine | 53 | M4 | 48 19N | 25 52E |
| Chertsey England | 16 | C2 | 51 23N | 0 30W |
| Cherwell r. England | 16 | B2 | 51 55N | 1 18W |
| Chesapeake USA | 91 | L4 | 36 45N | 76 15W |
| Chesham England | 16 | C2 | 51 43N | 0 38W |
| Cheshire co. England | 12 | D2 | 53 30N | 2 30W |
| Cheshire Plain England | 12 | D2 | 53 12N | 2 50W |
| Cheshunt England | 16 | C2 | 51 43N | 0 02W |
| Chesil Beach England | 19 | E2 | 50 38N | 2 50W |
| Chester England | 12 | D2 | 53 12N | 2 54W |
| Chesterfield England | 13 | E2 | 53 15N | 1 25W |
| Chester-le-Street England | 13 | E3 | 54 52N | 1 34W |
| Cheviot Hills England/Scotland | 11 | G2 | 55 25N | 2 30W |
| Cheviot, The mt. England | 11 | G2 | 55 29N | 2 20W |
| Chew r. England | 19 | E3 | 51 21N | 2 40W |
| Chiba Japan | 70 | D2 | 35 38N | 140 07E |
| Chicago USA | 91 | J5 | 41 50N | 87 45W |
| Chichester England | 16 | C1 | 50 50N | 0 48W |
| Chiclayo Peru | 96 | B12 | 6 47S | 79 47W |
| Chieti Italy | 54 | F5 | 42 21N | 14 10E |
| Chigwell England | 16 | D2 | 51 37N | 0 05E |
| CHILE | 96/97 | C5/C8 | | |
| Chillán Chile | 97 | C6 | 36 37S | 72 10W |
| Chiltern Hills England | 16 | B2/C2 | 51 40N | 1 00W |
| Chimborazo mt. Ecuador | 96 | B13 | 1 29S | 78 52W |
| Chimbote Peru | 96 | B12 | 9 04S | 78 34W |
| CHINA | 68/69 | | | |
| Chinnor England | 16 | C2 | 51 43N | 0 56W |
| Chioggia Italy | 54 | E6 | 45 13N | 12 17E |
| Chíos i. Greece | 55 | E3 | 38 00N | 26 00E |
| Chippenham England | 16 | A2 | 51 28N | 2 07W |
| Chipping Campden England | 15 | E2 | 52 03N | 1 46W |
| Chipping Norton England | 16 | B2 | 51 56N | 1 32W |
| Chipping Ongar England | 17 | D2 | 51 43N | 0 15E |
| Chipping Sodbury England | 15 | D1 | 51 33N | 2 24W |
| Chirk Wales | 14 | C2 | 52 56N | 3 03W |
| Chișinău Moldova | 53 | P3 | 47 00N | 28 50E |
| Chita Russia | 63 | P7 | 52 03N | 113 35E |
| Chittagong Bangladesh | 66 | G4 | 22 20N | 91 48E |
| Chitterne England | 16 | A2 | 51 11N | 2 02W |
| Chobham England | 16 | C2 | 51 21N | 0 37W |
| Cholet France | 50 | D4 | 47 04N | 0 53W |
| Chongqing China | 69 | J3 | 29 30N | 106 35E |
| Chorley England | 12 | D2 | 53 40N | 2 38W |
| Chorleywood England | 16 | C2 | 51 40N | 0 31W |
| Chornobyl Ukraine | 53 | Q5 | 51 17N | 30 15E |
| Christchurch England | 19 | F2 | 50 44N | 1 45W |
| Christchurch NZ | 73 | P2 | 43 32S | 172 38E |
| Chudleigh England | 18 | D2 | 50 36N | 3 45W |
| Chudskoye Ozero l. Russia/Estonia | 56 | C6 | 58 40N | 27 30E |
| Chulmleigh England | 18 | D2 | 50 55N | 3 52W |
| Chum r. England | 15 | D1 | 51 46N | 1 58W |
| Chur Switz. | 52 | D4 | 46 52N | 9 32E |
| Churchill Canada | 89 | S5 | 58 45N | 94 00W |
| Church Stoke Wales | 14 | C2 | 52 32N | 3 05W |
| Church Stretton England | 14 | D2 | 52 32N | 2 49W |
| Chute-aux-Outardes Canada | 93 | G3 | 49 17N | 67 57W |
| Cincinnati USA | 91 | K4 | 39 10N | 83 30W |
| Cinderford England | 15 | D1 | 51 50N | 2 29W |
| Cirencester England | 15 | E1 | 51 44N | 1 59W |
| Citlaltépetl mt. Mexico | 94 | E3 | 19 00N | 97 18W |
| City of Edinburgh u.a. Scotland | 11 | F2 | 55 55N | 3 15W |
| City of Kingston upon Hull u.a. England | 13 | F2 | 53 45N | 0 25W |
| Ciudad Bolívar Venezuela | 96 | E15 | 8 06N | 63 36W |
| Ciudadela Spain | 51 | G3 | 40 00N | 3 50E |
| Ciudad Guayana Venezuela | 96 | E15 | 8 22N | 62 37W |
| Ciudad Juárez Mexico | 94 | C6 | 31 42N | 106 29W |
| Ciudad Obregón Mexico | 94 | C5 | 27 28N | 109 59W |
| Ciudad Real Spain | 51 | D3 | 38 59N | 3 55W |
| Ciudad Rodrigo Spain | 51 | B4 | 40 36N | 6 33W |
| Civitavecchia Italy | 54 | D5 | 42 05N | 11 47E |
| Clachan Scotland | 10 | D2 | 55 45N | 5 34W |
| Clackmannan Scotland | 11 | F3 | 56 05N | 3 46W |
| Clackmannanshire u.a. Scotland | 11 | F3 | 56 10N | 3 40W |
| Clacton on Sea England | 17 | E2 | 51 48N | 1 09E |
| Clane Rol | 20 | E3 | 53 18N | 6 41W |
| Claonaig Scotland | 10 | D2 | 55 46N | 5 22W |
| Clara Rol | 20 | D3 | 53 20N | 7 36W |
| Clare r. Rol | 20 | C3 | 53 20N | 9 00W |
| Clare co. Rol | 21 | B2/C2 | 52 45N | 9 00W |
| Clarecastle Rol | 20 | C2 | 52 49N | 8 57W |
| Claregalway Rol | 20 | C3 | 53 21N | 8 57W |
| Clare Island Rol | 20 | A3/B3 | 53 49N | 10 00W |
| Claremorris Rol | 20 | C3 | 53 44N | 9 00W |
| Clarksville USA | 91 | J4 | 36 31N | 87 21W |
| Clashmore Rol | 21 | D2 | 52 00N | 7 49W |
| Clay Cross England | 13 | E2 | 53 10N | 1 24W |
| Claydon England | 17 | E3 | 52 06N | 1 07E |
| Clay Head Isle of Man | 12 | B3 | 54 11N | 4 25W |
| Clayton-le-Moors England | 12 | D2 | 53 47N | 2 23W |
| Clayton West England | 13 | E2 | 53 36N | 1 37W |
| Clear Island Rol | 21 | B1 | 51 26N | 9 30W |
| Clearwater USA | 91 | K2 | 27 57N | 82 48W |
| Cleator Moor England | 12 | C3 | 54 31N | 3 30W |
| Cleckheaton England | 13 | E2 | 53 44N | 1 43W |
| Cleethorpes England | 13 | F2 | 53 34N | 0 02W |
| Cleobury Mortimer England | 15 | D2 | 52 23N | 2 29W |
| Clermont-Ferrand France | 50 | F3 | 45 47N | 3 05E |
| Clevedon England | 19 | E3 | 51 27N | 2 51W |
| Cleveland USA | 91 | K5 | 43 15N | 75 50W |
| Cleveland Hills England | 13 | E3 | 54 25N | 1 15W |
| Cleveleys England | 12 | C2 | 53 53N | 3 03W |
| Clew Bay Rol | 20 | B3 | 53 50N | 9 50W |
| Clifden Rol | 20 | A3 | 53 29N | 10 01W |
| Clinton USA | 91 | H5 | 41 51N | 90 12W |
| Clisham mt. Scotland | 8 | C2 | 57 58N | 6 50W |
| Clitheroe England | 12 | D2 | 53 53N | 2 23W |
| Cloghan Rol | 20 | D3 | 53 13N | 7 53W |
| Clogheen Rol | 21 | D2 | 52 17N | 8 00W |
| Clogher NI | 10 | B1 | 54 25N | 7 10W |
| Clogherhead Rol | 20 | E3 | 53 45N | 6 13W |
| Clogher Head Rol | 20 | E3 | 53 48N | 6 13W |
| Cloghjordan Rol | 21 | C2 | 52 57N | 8 02W |
| Clonakilty Rol | 21 | C1 | 51 37N | 8 54W |
| Clonakilty Bay Rol | 21 | C1 | 51 33N | 8 50W |
| Clonaslee Rol | 20 | D3 | 53 09N | 7 31W |
| Clondalkin Rol | 20 | E3 | 53 19N | 6 24W |
| Clonee Rol | 20 | E3 | 53 25N | 6 26W |
| Clones Rol | 20 | D4 | 54 11N | 7 15W |
| Clonmany Rol | 20 | D5 | 55 16N | 7 25W |

**Clonmel** RoI 21 D2 52 21N 7 42W
**Clonroche** RoI 21 E2 52 27N 6 43W
**Clontarf** RoI 20 E3 53 22N 6 12W
**Cloondara** RoI 20 D3 53 43N 7 54W
**Cloppenburg** Germany 52 D6 52 52N 8 02E
**Cloughton** England 13 F3 54 20N 0 27W
**Clovelly** England 18 C2 51 00N 4 24W
**Clowne** England 13 E2 53 17N 1 15W
**Cluj-Napoca** Romania 53 L3 46 47N 23 37E
**Clwydian Range** Wales 14 C3 53 12N 3 20W
**Clydach** Wales 14 C1 51 42N 3 56W
**Clyde** r. Scotland 11 F2 55 40N 3 50W
**Clydebank** Scotland 11 E2 55 54N 4 24W
**Clyde River** tn. Canada 89 X8 70 30N 68 30W
**Coachford** RoI 21 C1 51 55N 8 47W
**Coalisland** NI 10 C1 54 32N 6 42W
**Coalville** England 15 E2 52 44N 1 20W
**Coast Ranges** USA 90 B4/6 41 00N 123 00W
**Coatbridge** Scotland 11 E2 55 52N 4 01W
**Cobh** RoI 21 C1 51 51N 8 17W
**Coburg** Germany 52 E5 50 15N 10 58E
**Cochin** India 66 D1 9 56N 76 15E
**Cockburnspath** Scotland 11 G2 55 56N 2 21W
**Cockenzie** Scotland 11 G2 55 58N 2 58W
**Cockermouth** England 12 C3 54 40N 3 21W
**Codó** Brazil 96 J13 4 28S 43 51W
**Codsall** England 15 D2 52 37N 2 12W
**Coggeshall** England 17 D2 51 52N 0 41E
**Cognac** France 50 D3 45 42N 0 19W
**Coimbra** Portugal 51 A4 40 12N 8 25W
**Colchester** England 17 D2 51 54N 0 54E
**Coldingham** Scotland 11 G2 55 53N 2 10W
**Coldstream** Scotland 11 G2 55 39N 2 15W
**Coleford** England 15 D1 51 48N 2 37W
**Coleraine** NI 10 C2 55 08N 6 40W
**Coleraine** district NI 10 C2 55 00N 6 40W
**Coleshill** England 15 E2 52 30N 1 42W
**Colgrave Sound** Scotland 7 D3 60 35N 0 55W
**Colintraive** Scotland 10 D2 55 56N 5 09W
**Coll** i. Scotland 8 C1 56 40N 6 35W
**Collin** Scotland 11 F2 55 04N 3 32W
**Collon** RoI 20 E3 53 47N 6 29W
**Collooney** RoI 20 C4 54 11N 8 29W
**Colmar** France 50 H5 48 05N 7 21E
**Colmonell** Scotland 10 E2 55 08N 4 55W
**Coln** r. England 15 E1 51 46N 1 50W
**Colne** England 12 D2 53 52N 2 09W
**Colne** r. England 17 D2 51 53N 0 45E
**Cologne** Germany 52 C5 50 56N 6 57E
**COLOMBIA** 96 C14
**Colombo** Sri Lanka 66 D1 6 55N 79 52E
**Colonsay** i. Scotland 10 C3 56 05N 6 15W
**Colorado** r. USA 90 D3 33 00N 114 00W
**Colorado** state USA 90 E4/F4 39 00N 106 00W
**Colorado Springs** USA 90 F4 38 50N 104 50W
**Colsterworth** England 15 F2 52 48N 0 37W
**Coltishall** England 17 E3 52 44N 1 22E
**Columbia** r. N. America 90 B6 46 00N 120 00W
**Columbus** USA 91 K5 39 59N 83 03W
**Colwyn Bay** tn. Wales 14 C3 53 18N 3 43W
**Comacchio** Italy 54 E6 44 42N 12 11E
**Combe Martin** England 18 C3 51 13N 4 02W
**Comber** NI 10 D1 54 33N 5 45W
**Comeragh Mountains** RoI 21 D2 52 19N 7 40W
**Como** Italy 54 C6 45 48N 9 05E
**Comodoro Rivadavia** Argentina 97 D4 45 56S 67 30W
**COMOROS** 82 H5
**Compiègne** France 50 F5 49 25N 2 50E
**Comrie** Scotland 9 F1 56 23N 4 00W
**Conakry** Guinea 80 B3 9 30N 13 43W
**Concepción** Chile 97 X6 36 50S 73 03W
**Concordia** USA 91 G4 39 36N 97 39W
**Condom** France 50 E2 43 58N 0 23E
**Conflans-Ste. Honorine** France 50 F5 49 01N 2 09E
**Cong** RoI 20 B3 53 33N 9 16W
**Congleton** England 12 D2 53 10N 2 13W
**CONGO** 82 C7
**Congo** r. Congo/CDR 82 J2 2 00S 17 00E
**CONGO DEMOCRATIC REPUBLIC** 82 D7/E7
**Congresbury** England 19 E2 51 23N 2 48W
**Conisbrough** England 13 E2 53 29N 1 13W
**Coniston** England 12 C3 54 22N 3 05W
**Coniston Water** England 12 C3 54 20N 3 05W
**Connah's Quay** Wales 14 C3 53 13N 3 03W
**Connecticut** state USA 91 M5 41 00N 73 00W
**Conon Bridge** Scotland 9 E2 57 33N 4 26W
**Consett** England 13 E3 54 51N 1 49W
**Constança** Romania 53 P2 44 12N 28 40E
**Constantine** Algeria 80 F9 36 22N 6 40E
**Conwy** Wales 14 C3 53 17N 3 50W
**Conwy** r. Wales 14 C3 53 10N 3 49W
**Conwy** u.a. Wales 14 C3 53 10N 3 40W
**Cookham** England 16 C2 51 33N 0 43W
**Cook, Mount** NZ 73 P2 43 36S 170 09E
**Cookstown** district NI 10 C1 54 35N 6 55W
**Coolgrange** RoI 21 D2 53 38N 7 08W
**Cootehill** RoI 20 D4 54 04N 7 05W
**Copeland Island** NI 10 D1 54 40N 5 31W
**Copenhagen** Denmark 49 C2 55 43N 12 34E
**Copiapo** Chile 97 C8 27 20S 70 23W

**Copper Harbor** USA 91 J6 47 28N 87 54W
**Coppull** England 12 D2 53 37N 2 40W
**Coquet** r. England 11 G2 55 20N 2 05W
**Coquimbo** Chile 97 C8 29 57S 71 25W
**Corbally** RoI 20 B4 54 10N 9 03W
**Corbeil-Essonnes** France 50 F5 48 36N 2 29E
**Corbridge** England 12 D3 54 58N 2 01W
**Corby** England 15 F2 52 49N 0 32W
**Cordillera Cantabrica** mts. Spain 51 B5/C5 43 00N 5 30W
**Córdoba** Argentina 97 E7 31 25S 64 11W
**Córdoba** Mexico 94 E3 18 55N 96 55W
**Córdoba** Spain 51 C2 37 53N 4 46W
**Corfe Castle** England 19 E2 50 38N 2 04W
**Corfu** Greece 55 H3 39 38N 19 55E
**Corinth** USA 91 J3 34 58N 88 30W
**Cork** RoI 21 C1 51 54N 8 28W
**Cork** co. RoI 21 C1 51 58N 8 40W
**Cork Harbour** RoI 21 C1 51 50N 8 10W
**Corraun Peninsula** RoI 20 B3 53 54N 9 51W
**Corrientes** Argentina 97 F8 27 30S 58 48W
**Corsewall Point** Scotland 10 D2 55 00N 5 10W
**Corsham** England 16 A1 51 26N 2 11W
**Corsica** i. France 50 J1/J2 42 00N 9 00E
**Corwen** Wales 14 C2 52 59N 3 22W
**Cosenza** Italy 54 G3 39 17N 16 16E
**COSTA RICA** 95 H1/2
**CÔTE D'IVOIRE** 80 C3/D3
**Cotgrave** England 15 E2 52 54N 1 03W
**Cotopaxi** mt. Ecuador 96 B13 0 40S 78 28W
**Cotswold Hills** England 15 D1/E1 51 40N 2 10W
**Cottbus** Germany 52 G5 51 43N 14 21E
**Cottenham** England 17 D3 52 18N 0 09E
**Countesthorpe** England 15 E2 52 33N 1 09W
**Coupar Angus** Scotland 9 F1 56 33N 3 17W
**Courtown** RoI 21 E2 52 38N 6 13W
**Cove Bay** tn. Scotland 9 G2 57 05N 2 05W
**Coventry** England 15 E2 52 25N 1 30W
**Coverack** England 18 B2 50 01N 5 05W
**Cowbridge** Wales 14 C1 51 28N 3 27W
**Cowdenbeath** Scotland 11 F3 56 07N 3 21W
**Cowes** England 16 B1 50 45N 1 18W
**Cox's Bazar** Bangladesh 67 G4 21 25N 91 59E
**Craigavon** NI 10 C1 54 28N 6 25W
**Craigavon** district NI 10 C1 54 30N 6 30W
**Craigellachie** Scotland 9 F2 57 29N 3 12W
**Craighouse** Scotland 10 D2 55 51N 5 57W
**Craignure** Scotland 8 D1 56 28N 5 42W
**Crail** Scotland 11 G3 56 16N 2 38W
**Craiova** Romania 53 L2 44 18N 23 47E
**Cramlington** England 13 E4 55 05N 1 35W
**Cranleigh** England 16 C2 51 09N 0 30W
**Crathie** Scotland 9 F2 57 02N 3 12W
**Craughwell** RoI 20 C3 53 14N 8 44W
**Craven Arms** England 14 D2 52 26N 2 50W
**Crawford** Scotland 11 F2 55 28N 3 40W
**Crawley** England 16 C2 51 07N 0 12W
**Credenhill** England 14 D2 52 05N 2 48W
**Crediton** England 18 D2 50 47N 3 39W
**Cree** r. Scotland 11 E2 54 50N 4 30W
**Creeslough** RoI 20 D5 55 07N 7 55W
**Creetown** Scotland 11 E1 54 54N 4 23W
**Cregganbaun** RoI 20 B3 53 42N 9 51W
**Cremona** Italy 54 D6 45 08N 10 01E
**Creswell** England 13 E2 53 16N 1 12W
**Créteil** France 50 F5 48 47N 2 28E
**Crewe** England 12 D2 53 05N 2 27W
**Crewkerne** England 19 E2 50 53N 2 48W
**Criccieth** Wales 14 B2 52 55N 4 14W
**Crickhowell** Wales 14 C1 51 53N 3 09W
**Cricklade** England 16 B2 51 39N 1 51W
**Crieff** Scotland 9 F1 56 23N 3 52W
**Crinan** Scotland 10 D3 56 06N 5 35W
**CROATIA** 55 G6
**Crofton** England 13 E2 53 39N 1 26W
**Cromarty** Scotland 9 E2 57 40N 4 02W
**Cromarty Firth** Scotland 9 E2 57 40N 4 20W
**Cromer** England 17 E3 52 56N 1 18E
**Crook** England 13 E3 54 43N 1 44W
**Crookhaven** RoI 21 B1 51 28N 9 43W
**Crookstown** RoI 21 C1 51 50N 8 50W
**Croom** RoI 21 C2 52 31N 8 43W
**Crosby** England 12 C2 53 30N 3 02W
**Cross Fell** mt. England 12 D3 54 43N 2 29W
**Crossgar** NI 10 D1 54 24N 5 45W
**Cross Hands** Wales 14 B1 51 48N 4 05W
**Crosshaven** RoI 21 C1 51 48N 8 18W
**Crossmaglen** NI 10 C1 54 05N 6 37W
**Crossmolina** RoI 20 B4 54 06N 9 20W
**Crouch** r. England 17 D2 51 38N 0 42E
**Crowborough** England 17 D2 51 03N 0 09E
**Crowland** England 15 F2 52 41N 0 11W
**Crowle** England 13 F2 53 37N 0 49W
**Crowthorne** England 16 C2 51 22N 0 49W
**Croyde** England 18 C3 51 08N 4 15W
**Croydon** England 16 C2 51 23N 0 06W
**Crumlin** NI 10 C1 54 37N 6 14W
**Crummock Water** England 12 C3 54 34N 3 18W
**Crusheen** RoI 21 C2 52 56N 8 53W
**Cruzeiro do Sul** Brazil 96 C12 7 40S 72 39W

**Crymych** Wales 14 B1 51 59N 4 40W
**CUBA** 95 J4
**Cuckfield** England 16 C2 51 00N 0 09W
**Cúcuta** Colombia 96 C15 7 55N 73 31W
**Cudworth** England 13 E2 53 35N 1 25W
**Cuenca** Ecuador 96 B13 2 54S 79 00W
**Cuenca** Spain 51 D4 40 04N 2 07W
**Cuiabá** Brazil 96 F10 15 32S 56 05W
**Cuillin Hills** Scotland 8 C2 57 15N 6 15W
**Culdaff** RoI 20 D5 55 17N 7 10W
**Cullen** Scotland 9 G2 57 41N 2 49W
**Cullompton** England 18 D2 50 52N 3 24W
**Cullybackey** NI 10 C1 54 53N 6 21W
**Culm** r. England 19 D2 50 55N 3 13W
**Culross** Scotland 11 F3 56 03N 3 35W
**Cumana** Venezuela 96 E16 10 29N 64 12W
**Cumbernauld** Scotland 11 E2 55 57N 4 00W
**Cumbria** co. England 12 C3/D3 54 35N 3 00W
**Cumbrian Mountains** England 12 C3/D3 54 30N 3 00W
**Cumnock** Scotland 11 E2 55 27N 4 16W
**Cuneo** Italy 54 B6 44 24N 7 33E
**Cupar** Scotland 9 F1 56 19N 3 01W
**Curitiba** Brazil 96 H8 25 25S 49 25W
**Cushendall** NI 10 C2 55 04N 6 04W
**Cushendun** NI 10 C2 55 07N 6 03W
**Cuxhaven** Germany 52 D6 53 52N 8 42E
**Cuzco** Peru 96 C11 13 32S 1 57W
**Cwmbran** Wales 14 C1 51 39N 3 00W
**CYPRUS** 57 D1/D2
**CZECH REPUBLIC** 52/53 G4/H4
**Częstochowa** Poland 53 J5 50 49N 19 07E

## D

**Dachau** Germany 52 E4 48 15N 11 26E
**Daingean** RoI 20 D3 53 17N 7 17W
**Dakar** Senegal 80 A4 14 38N 17 27W
**Dalbeattie** Scotland 11 F1 54 56N 3 49W
**Dalby** Isle of Man 12 B3 54 10N 4 44W
**Dalgety Bay** tn. Scotland 11 F3 56 03N 3 18W
**Dalian** China 69 M5 38 53N 121 37E
**Dalkeith** Scotland 11 F2 55 51N 3 04W
**Dallas** USA 91 G3 32 47N 96 48W
**Dalmally** Scotland 8 E1 56 24N 4 58W
**Dalmellington** Scotland 11 E2 55 19N 4 24W
**Dalry** Scotland 11 E2 55 43N 4 44W
**Dalton** USA 91 K3 34 46N 84 59W
**Dalton-in-Furness** England 12 C3 54 09N 3 11W
**Dalwhinnie** Scotland 9 E1 56 56N 4 14W
**Damascus** Syria 64 C5 33 30N 36 19E
**Danbury** England 17 D2 51 44N 0 33E
**Danville** USA 91 J5 40 09N 87 37W
**Dardanelles** sd. Turkey 57 A3 40 08N 26 10E
**Dar es Salaam** Tanzania 83 F1 6 51S 39 18E
**Darfield** England 13 E2 53 34N 1 22W
**Darjiling** India 67 F5 27 02N 88 20E
**Darling** r. Australia 73 H4 30 30S 144 00E
**Darlington** England 13 E3 54 31N 1 34W
**Darlington** u.a. England 13 E3 54 30N 1 30W
**Darmstadt** Germany 52 D4 49 52N 8 39E
**Dart** r. England 18 D2 50 30N 3 50W
**Dartford** England 17 D2 51 27N 0 13E
**Dartmouth** England 18 D2 50 21N 3 35W
**Darton** England 13 E2 53 36N 1 32W
**Darvel** Scotland 11 E2 55 37N 4 18W
**Darwen** England 12 D2 53 42N 2 28W
**Darwin** Australia 72 F8 12 23S 130 44E
**Daugava** r. Europe 49 F2 56 45N 24 30E
**Daugavpils** Latvia 49 G2 55 52N 26 31E
**Davao** Philippines 71 H5 7 05N 125 38E
**Davenport** USA 91 H5 41 32N 90 36W
**Daventry** England 15 E2 52 16N 1 09W
**Davis Strait** Canada/Greenland 89 Y7/Z6 69 00N 60 00W
**Davos** Switz. 52 D3 46 47N 9 50E
**Dawley** England 15 D2 52 40N 2 28W
**Dawlish** England 18 D2 50 35N 3 28W
**Dawros Head** RoI 20 C4 54 49N 8 34W
**Dead Sea** Israel/Jordan 64 C5 31 35N 35 30E
**Deal** England 17 E2 51 14N 1 24E
**Deel** r. RoI 21 C2 52 32N 8 57W
**Death Valley** USA 90 C4 36 00N 117 00W
**Deben** r. England 17 E3 52 02N 1 25E
**Debenham** England 17 E3 52 13N 1 11E
**Debrecen** Hungary 53 K3 47 30N 21 37E
**Decatur** USA 91 J4 39 51N 88 57W
**Deccan** plat. India 66 D3 18 00N 78 00E
**Deddington** England 16 B2 51 59N 1 19W
**Dee** r. England/Wales 14 C2 53 10N 3 11W
**Dee** r. RoI 20 E3 53 49N 6 38W
**Dee** r. Aberdeenshire Scotland 9 G2 57 05N 2 10W
**Dee** r. Dumfries and Galloway Scotland 11 E1 54 50N 4 00W
**Deel** r. RoI 20 D3 53 33N 7 07W
**Deer Sound** Scotland 7 B1 58 57N 2 47W
**Delaware** state USA 91 L4 39 00N 75 00W
**Delft** Neths 48 C5 52 00N 4 22E
**Delfzijl** Neths 48 E6 53 19N 6 56E
**Delhi** India 66 D5 28 40N 77 14E
**Delvin** RoI 20 D3 53 37N 7 05W
**Denbigh** Wales 14 C3 53 11N 3 25W

**Denbighshire** u.a. Wales 14 C3 53 05N 3 30W
**Denby Dale** tn. England 13 E2 53 35N 1 38W
**Den Helder** Neths 48 C5 52 58N 4 46E
**Denholme** England 13 E2 53 47N 1 53W
**Denison** USA 91 G3 33 47N 96 34W
**Denizli** Turkey 57 C2 37 46N 29 05E
**DENMARK** 49 C2/D2
**Denny** Scotland 11 F3 56 02N 3 55W
**Denpasar** Indonesia 71 F2 8 40S 115 14E
**Denton** England 12 D2 53 27N 2 07W
**Denver** USA 90 E4 39 45N 105 00W
**De Panne** Belgium 48 A4 51 06N 2 35E
**Derby** England 15 E2 52 55N 1 30W
**Derby City** u.a. England 15 E2 52 55N 1 30W
**Derbyshire** co. England 13 E2 53 05N 1 30W
**Derg** r. NI 10 B1 54 44N 7 30E
**Derriana Lough** RoI 21 A1/B1 51 54N 10 01W
**Derrybrien** RoI 21 C3 53 04N 8 37W
**Dersingham** England 17 D3 52 51N 0 30E
**Derwent** r. North Yorkshire England 13 F3 54 10N 0 35W
**Derwent** r. Cumbria England 12 C3 54 40N 3 30W
**Derwent** r. Derbyshire England 13 E2 53 15N 1 40W
**Derwent** r. Durham England 12 D3 54 50N 2 05W
**Derwent Reservoir** England 13 E2 53 25N 1 45W
**Derwent Water** England 12 C3 54 35N 3 09W
**Desborough** England 15 F2 52 27N 0 49W
**Desierto de Atacama** Chile 96 C9/D10 22 30S 70 00W
**Des Moines** USA 91 H5 41 35N 93 35W
**Dessau** Germany 52 F5 51 51N 12 15E
**Detroit** USA 91 K5 42 23N 83 05W
**Deveron** r. Scotland 9 G2 57 35N 2 35W
**Devil's Bridge** Wales 14 C2 52 23N 3 51W
**Devil's Lake** tn. USA 91 G6 48 03N 98 57W
**Devizes** England 16 B2 51 22N 1 59W
**Devon** co. England 18 D2 50 45N 3 50W
**Dewsbury** England 13 E2 53 42N 1 37W
**Dezful** Iran 65 E5 32 23N 48 28E
**Dhaka** Bangladesh 67 G4 23 42N 90 22E
**Didcot** England 16 B2 51 37N 1 15W
**Dieppe** France 50 E5 49 55N 1 05E
**Digby** Canada 89 X2 44 37N 65 47W
**Digne-les-Bains** France 50 H3 44 05N 6 14E
**Dijon** France 50 G4 47 20N 5 02E
**Dili** East Timor 71 H2 8 33S 125 34E
**Dinan** France 50 C5 48 27N 2 02W
**Dinara Planina** mts. Europe 55 G5 44 00N 17 00E
**Dinard** France 50 C5 48 38N 2 03W
**Dinas-Mawddwy** Wales 14 C2 52 43N 3 41W
**Dinas Powys** Wales 14 C1 51 25N 3 14W
**Dingle** RoI 21 A2 52 08N 10 15W
**Dingle Bay** RoI 21 A2 52 05N 10 15W
**Dingle Peninsula** RoI 21 A2 52 12N 10 15W
**Dingwall** Scotland 9 E2 57 35N 4 29W
**Dinnington** England 13 E2 53 22N 1 12W
**Dire Dawa** Ethiopia 81 P3 9 35N 41 50E
**Diss** England 17 E3 52 23N 1 06W
**DJIBOUTI** 81 P4
**Djibouti** Djibouti 81 P4 11 35N 43 11E
**Dnestr** r. Ukraine 56 C4 48 00N 28 00E
**Dnipro** r. Europe 57 D4 47 30N 33 00E
**Dnipropetrovs'k** Ukraine 56 D4 48 29N 35 00E
**Dobrich** Bulgaria 55 M5 43 34N 27 51E
**Dochart** r. Scotland 9 E1 56 25N 4 25W
**Docking** England 17 D3 52 55N 0 38E
**Dodekánisos** is. Greece 55 M2 37 00N 26 00E
**Dodman Point** England 18 C2 50 13N 4 48W
**Dodoma** Tanzania 83 D1 6 10S 35 40E
**Doha** Qatar 65 F4 25 15N 51 36E
**Dôle** France 50 G4 47 05N 5 30E
**Dolgellau** Wales 14 C2 52 44N 3 53W
**Dollar** Scotland 11 F3 56 09N 3 41W
**Dombas** Norway 49 C3 62 05N 9 07E
**DOMINICA** 94 Q8
**DOMINICAN REPUBLIC** 95 L3
**Don** r. England 13 E2 53 37N 1 02W
**Don** r. Russia 62 G7 50 00N 41 00E
**Don** r. Scotland 9 F2 57 15N 2 40W
**Donabate** RoI 20 E3 53 29N 6 09W
**Donaghadee** NI 10 D1 54 39N 5 33W
**Donau** r. Europe 52 D4 48 00N 16 00E
**Doncaster** England 13 E2 53 32N 1 07W
**Donegal** RoI 20 C4 54 39N 8 07W
**Donegal** co. RoI 20 C4/D4 54 55N 8 00W
**Donegal Bay** RoI 20 B4 54 30N 8 30W
**Donegal Point** RoI 21 B2 52 44N 9 39W
**Donets'k** Ukraine 56 E4 48 00N 37 50E
**Donington** England 15 F2 52 43N 2 25W
**Donoughmore** RoI 21 C1 51 57N 8 45W
**Dooagh** RoI 20 A3 53 58N 10 07W
**Doon** r. Scotland 11 E2 55 20N 4 30W
**Doonbeg** RoI 21 B2 52 44N 9 32W
**Dorchester** England 19 E2 50 43N 2 26W
**Dorchester** England 16 B2 51 39N 1 10W

Dordogne r. France 50 E3 44 55N 0 30E
Dordrecht Neths 48 C4 51 48N 4 40E
Dorking England 16 C2 51 14N 0 20W
Dornie Scotland 8 D2 57 17N 5 31W
Dornoch Scotland 9 E2 57 52N 4 02W
Dornoch Firth Scotland 9 E2/F2 57 55N 3 55W
Dorset co. England 19 E2 50 50N 2 20W
Dortmund Germany 52 C5 51 32N 7 27E
Douai France 50 F6 50 22N 3 05E
Douala Cameroon 80 F2 4 04N 9 43E
Douglas Isle of Man 12 B3 54 09N 4 29W
Douglas Scotland 11 F2 55 33N 3 51W
Douglas r. England 12 D2 53 38N 2 48W
Doulus Head RoI 21 A1 51 57N 10 19W
Doune Scotland 11 E3 56 11N 4 04W
Douro r. Portugal/Spain 51 B4 41 00N 8 30W
Dove r. England 13 E2 53 05N 1 55W
Dove Dale v. England 13 E2 53 10N 1 45W
Dover England 17 E2 51 08N 1 19E
Dover USA 91 L4 39 10N 75 32W
Dover, Strait of
 English Channel 17 E1/E2 51 00N 1 20W
Dovrefjell mts. Norway 49 C3 62 15N 9 10E
Down district NI 10 D1 54 25N 5 55W
Downham Market
 England 17 D3 52 36N 0 23E
Downpatrick NI 10 D1 54 20N 5 43W
Downpatrick Head RoI 20 B4 54 20N 9 15W
Downton England 16 B2 51 00N 1 44W
Dowra RoI 20 C4 54 11N 8 02W
Draguignan France 50 H2 43 32N 6 28E
Drakensberg mts. RSA 82 E1/2 30 00S 28 00E
Drammen Norway 49 D2 59 45N 10 15E
Draperstown NI 10 C1 54 48N 6 47W
Drava r. Europe 53 H3 46 00N 18 00E
Dreghorn Scotland 11 E2 55 37N 4 37W
Dresden Germany 52 F5 51 03N 13 45E
Drimoleague RoI 21 B1 51 40N 9 15W
Drobeta-Turnu-Severin
 Romania 53 L2 44 36N 22 39E
Drogheda RoI 20 E3 53 43N 6 21W
Droichead Nua RoI 20 E3 53 11N 6 45W
Droitwich England 15 D2 52 16N 2 09W
Dromcolliher RoI 21 C2 52 20N 8 55W
Dromore NI 10 B1 54 31N 7 28W
Dromore NI 10 C1 54 25N 6 09W
Dromore West RoI 20 C4 54 15N 8 53W
Dronfield England 13 E2 53 19N 1 27W
Drongan Scotland 11 E2 55 29N 4 30W
Drumkeeran RoI 20 C4 54 10N 8 08W
Drummore Scotland 10 E1 54 42N 4 54W
Drumnadrochit
 Scotland 9 E2 57 20N 4 30W
Drumshanbo RoI 20 C4 54 03N 8 02W
Drumsna RoI 20 D3 53 56N 8 00W
Dryden Canada 89 S3 49 48N 92 48W
Dubai UAE 65 G4 25 14N 55 17E
Dublin RoI 20 E3 53 26N 6 15W
Dublin co. RoI 20 E3 53 25N 6 10W
Dublin USA 91 K3 32 31N 82 54W
Dublin Bay RoI 20 E3 53 20N 6 05W
Dubrovnik Croatia 55 H5 42 40N 18 07E
Duddon r. England 12 C3 54 20N 3 20W
Dudley England 15 D2 52 30N 2 05W
Dudley England 13 E4 55 10N 1 20W
Duero r. Spain/Portugal 51 B4 41 25N 6 30W
Duffield England 15 E2 52 59N 1 29W
Dufftown Scotland 9 F2 57 26N 3 08W
Duisburg Germany 52 C5 51 26N 6 45E
Duleek RoI 20 E3 53 39N 6 25W
Dulnain r. Scotland 9 F2 57 20N 3 57W
Duluth USA 91 H6 46 45N 92 10W
Dulverton England 18 D3 51 03N 3 33W
Dumbarton Scotland 11 E2 55 57N 4 35W
Dumfries Scotland 11 F2 55 04N 3 37W
Dumfries and Galloway
 u.a. Scotland 11 E2/F2 55 10N 4 10W
Duna r. Hungary 53 J2/J3 46 00N 19 00E
Dunaff Head RoI 20 D5 55 17N 7 31W
Dunany Point RoI 20 E3 53 51N 6 14W
Dunav r. Europe 55 K5 44 00N 20 00E
Dunbar Scotland 11 G2 56 00N 2 31W
Dunbeath Scotland 9 F3 58 15N 3 25W
Dunblane Scotland 11 F3 56 12N 3 59W
Dunboyne RoI 20 E3 53 25N 6 29W
Duncannon RoI 21 E2 51 13N 6 55W
Duncansby Head
 Scotland 9 F3 58 39N 3 01W
Dunchurch England 15 E2 52 20N 1 16W
Dundalk RoI 20 E4 54 01N 6 25W
Dundalk Bay RoI 20 E3 53 55N 6 15W
Dundee Scotland 9 G1 56 28N 3 00W
Dundee City u.a.
 Scotland 9 F1/G1 56 30N 2 55W
Dundonald NI 10 D1 54 36N 5 48W
Dundrennan Scotland 11 F1 54 49N 3 57W
Dundrum RoI 20 E3 53 17N 6 15W
Dundrum Bay NI 10 D1 54 13N 5 45W
Dunedin NZ 73 P1 45 53S 170 30E
Dunfermline Scotland 11 F3 56 04N 3 29W
Dungannon NI 10 C1 54 31N 6 46W
Dungannon district NI 10 B1/C1 54 30N 7 05W
Dungarvan RoI 21 D2 52 05N 7 37W
Dungarvan Harbour
 RoI 21 D2 52 04N 7 35W
Dungeness c. England 17 D1 50 55N 0 58E
Dungiven NI 10 C1 54 55N 6 55W

Dunglow RoI 20 C4 54 57N 8 22W
Dungourney RoI 21 C1 51 58N 8 05W
Dunholme England 13 F2 53 18N 0 29W
Dunkeld Scotland 9 F1 56 34N 3 35W
Dunkerque France 50 F6 51 02N 2 23E
Dunkery Beacon sum.
 England 18 D3 51 11N 3 35W
Dún Laoghaire RoI 20 E3 53 17N 6 08W
Dunleer RoI 20 E3 53 50N 6 24W
Dunmanus Bay RoI 21 B1 51 30N 9 50W
Dunmanway RoI 21 B1 51 43N 9 06W
Dunmore RoI 20 C3 53 37N 8 44W
Dunmurry NI 10 C1 54 33N 6 00W
Dunnamaggan RoI 21 D2 52 29N 7 17W
Dunnet Scotland 9 F3 58 37N 3 21W
Dunnet Bay Scotland 9 F3 58 36N 3 21W
Dunnett Head Scotland 9 F3 58 40N 3 25W
Dunoon Scotland 10 E2 55 57N 4 56W
Duns Scotland 11 G2 55 47N 2 20W
Dunshaughlin RoI 20 E3 53 31N 6 33W
Dunstable England 16 C2 51 53N 0 32W
Dunvegan Scotland 8 C2 57 26N 6 35W
Dunvegan Head
 Scotland 8 C2 57 30N 6 42W
Durban RSA 82 F2 29 53S 31 00E
Durham England 13 E3 54 47N 1 34W
Durham co. England 13 E3 54 47N 1 34W
Durham USA 91 L4 36 00N 78 54W
Durlston Head England 19 E2 50 35N 1 57W
Durness Scotland 9 E3 58 33N 4 45W
Durrington England 16 B2 51 12N 1 48W
Durrow RoI 21 D2 52 51N 7 23W
Dursey Head RoI 21 A1 51 20N 10 10W
Dursey Island RoI 21 A1 51 36N 10 12W
Dursley England 15 D1 51 42N 2 21W
Dushanbe Tajikistan 62 J4 38 38N 68 51E
Düsseldorf Germany 52 C5 51 13N 6 47E
Dyce Scotland 9 G2 57 12N 2 11W
Dyfi r. Wales 14 C2 52 38N 3 50W
Dyke r. Scotland 9 F3 58 25N 4 00W
Dymchurch England 17 D2 51 02N 1 00E
Dysart Scotland 11 F3 56 08N 3 08W

**E**
Eaglescliffe England 13 E3 54 31N 1 22W
Eaglesfield Scotland 11 F2 55 04N 3 12W
Ealing England 16 C2 51 31N 0 18W
Earby England 12 D2 53 56N 2 08W
Earls Colne England 17 D2 51 56N 0 42E
Earl Shilton England 15 E2 52 35N 1 18W
Earlston Scotland 11 G2 55 39N 2 40W
Earn r. Scotland 9 F1 56 20N 3 40W
Easington England 13 E3 54 47N 1 21W
Easington England 13 G2 53 40N 0 07E
Easingwold England 13 E3 54 07N 1 11W
Easky RoI 20 C4 54 17N 8 58W
East Ayrshire u.a.
 Scotland 11 E2 55 30N 4 30W
Eastbourne England 17 D1 50 46N 0 17E
East Burra i. Scotland 7 C3 60 04N 1 19W
East Cowes England 16 B1 50 45N 1 16W
East Dean England 17 D1 50 45N 0 13E
East Dereham England 17 D3 52 41N 0 56E
East Dunbartonshire
 u.a. Scotland 11 E2 55 55N 4 15W
Eastern Ghats mts.
 India 66 D2/E3 15 00N 80 00E
Eastfield England 13 F3 54 15N 0 25W
East Grand Forks USA 92 A3 47 56N 96 59W
East Ilsley England 16 B2 51 32N 1 17W
Eastington England 15 D1 51 45N 2 20W
East Kilbride Scotland 11 E2 55 46N 4 10W
East Leake England 15 E2 52 50N 1 11W
Eastleigh England 16 B1 50 58N 1 22W
East Linton Scotland 11 G2 55 59N 2 39W
East Loch Tarbert
 Scotland 8 C2 57 53N 6 48W
East London RSA 82 E1 33 00S 27 54E
East Lothian u.a.
 Scotland 11 G2 55 56N 2 42W
Eastmain Canada 89 V4 52 10N 78 30W
East Markham England 13 F2 53 15N 0 54W
Easton England 19 E2 50 32N 2 26W
East Renfrewshire u.a.
 Scotland 11 E2 55 45N 4 25W
East Riding of Yorkshire
 u.a. England 13 F2 53 54N 0 40W
Eastriggs Scotland 11 F1 54 59N 3 10W
East Suisnish Scotland 8 C2 57 21N 6 03W
East Sussex co.
 England 17 D1 50 55N 0 10E
EAST TIMOR 71 H2
East Wittering England 16 C1 50 41N 0 53W
Eastwood England 13 E2 53 01N 1 18W
Eaton Socon England 16 C3 52 13N 0 18W
Ebbw Vale Wales 14 C1 51 47N 3 12W
Ebro r. Spain 51 D5 43 00N 4 30W
Ecclefechan Scotland 11 F2 55 03N 3 17W
Eccles England 12 D2 53 29N 2 21W
Eccleshall England 15 D2 52 52N 2 15W
Eckington England 13 E2 53 19N 1 21W
ECUADOR 96 B13
Eday i. Scotland 7 B2 59 11N 2 47W
Eday Sound Scotland 7 B2 59 10N 2 43W
Ede Neths 48 D5 52 03N 5 40E
Eden r. Cumbria England 12 D3 54 50N 2 45W
Eden r. Kent England 17 D2 51 12N 0 06E

Eden r. Scotland 11 F3 56 20N 3 15W
Eden USA 91 L4 36 30N 79 46W
Edenbridge England 16 C2 51 12N 0 04E
Edenderry RoI 20 D3 53 21N 7 35W
Eden Mouth Scotland 9 G1 56 20N 2 36W
Edessa Greece 55 K4 40 48N 22 03E
Edgeworthstown RoI 20 D3 53 42N 7 36W
Edinburgh Scotland 11 F2 55 57N 3 13W
Edmonton Canada 88 N4 53 34N 113 25W
Eeklo Belgium 48 B4 51 11N 3 34E
Eems r. Neths/Germany 48 E6 53 25N 6 55E
Efyrnwy r. Wales 14 C2 52 40N 3 15W
Egham England 16 C2 51 26N 0 34W
Egilsay i. Scotland 7 B2 59 09N 2 56W
Eglinton NI 10 B2 55 01N 7 11W
Egremont England 12 C3 54 29N 3 33W
EGYPT 81 L7/M7
Eigg i. Scotland 8 C1 56 55N 6 10W
Eindhoven Neths 48 D4 51 26N 5 30E
Elat Israel 64 B4 29 33N 34 57E
Elâzığ Turkey 57 E2 38 41N 39 14E
Elbe est. Europe 52 E6 54 00N 9 00E
Elbeuf France 50 E5 49 17N 1 01E
Elblag Poland 53 J7 54 10N 19 25E
El'brus mt. Russia 57 F3 43 21N 42 29E
Elburg Neths 48 D5 52 27N 5 50E
Elburz Mountains Iran 65 F6 36 15N 51 00E
Elche Spain 51 E3 38 16N 0 41W
El Dorado USA 91 H3 33 12N 92 40W
Elgin Scotland 9 F2 57 39N 3 20W
El Giza Egypt 81 M7 30 01N 31 12E
Elgol Scotland 8 C2 57 09N 6 06W
Elie Scotland 11 G3 56 12N 2 50W
Elland England 13 E2 53 41N 1 50W
Ellen r. England 12 C3 54 45N 3 25W
Ellesmere England 14 D2 52 54N 2 54W
Ellesmere Island
 Canada 89 U9/X10 77 30N 82 30W
Ellesmere Port England 12 D2 53 17N 2 54W
Ellon Scotland 9 G2 57 22N 2 05W
El Minya Egypt 81 M7 28 06N 30 45E
Elmira USA 91 L5 42 06N 76 50W
El Obeid Sudan 81 M4 13 11N 30 10W
El Paso USA 90 E3 31 45N 106 30W
EL SALVADOR 94 G2
Ely England 17 D3 52 24N 0 16E
Elyria USA 91 K5 41 22N 82 06W
Embleton England 11 H2 55 30N 1 37W
Emden Germany 52 C6 53 23N 7 13E
Emmeloord Neths 48 D5 52 43N 5 46E
Emmen Neths 48 E5 52 47N 6 55E
Emsworth England 16 C1 50 51N 0 56W
Emyvale RoI 20 E4 54 21N 6 58W
Enard Bay Scotland 8 D3 58 10N 5 25W
Enfield England 16 C2 51 39N 0 05W
England country UK 6 53 00N 2 00W
English Channel
 UK/France 6 50 00N 2 00W
Enid USA 91 G4 36 24N 97 54W
Ennis RoI 21 C2 52 50N 8 59W
Enniscorthy RoI 21 E2 52 30N 6 34W
Enniskean RoI 21 C1 51 44N 8 56W
Enniskerry RoI 20 E3 53 12N 6 10W
Enniskillen NI 10 B1 54 21N 7 38W
Ennistimon RoI 21 B2 52 57N 9 15W
Enschede Neths 48 E5 52 13N 6 55E
Entebbe Uganda 83 C5 0 04N 32 27E
Épernay France 50 F5 49 02N 3 58E
Épinal France 50 H5 48 10N 6 28E
Epping England 17 D2 51 42N 0 08E
Epsom England 16 C2 51 20N 0 16W
Epworth England 13 F2 53 31N 0 50W
EQUATORIAL GUINEA 80 F2/G2
Erfurt Germany 52 E5 50 58N 11 02E
Erie USA 91 K5 42 07N 80 05W
Erie, Lake Canada/USA 93 D2 42 15N 81 00W
Eriskay i. Scotland 8 B2 57 05N 7 10W
ERITREA 81 P4 14 40N 40 15E
Erlangen Germany 52 E4 49 36N 11 02E
Errigal Mountain RoI 20 C5 55 02N 8 07W
Errill RoI 21 D2 52 52N 7 40W
Erris Head RoI 20 A4 54 20N 10 00W
Erzgebirge mts. Europe 52 F5 50 00N 13 00E
Erzurum Turkey 57 F2 39 57N 41 17E
Esbjerg Denmark 49 C2 55 28N 8 28E
Escondido USA 90 C3 33 07N 117 05W
Eşfahān Iran 65 F5 32 41N 51 41E
Esha Ness c. Scotland 7 C3 60 29N 1 37W
Esher England 16 C2 51 22N 0 22W
Esk r. North Yorkshire
 England 13 F3 54 25N 0 40W
Esk r. Cumbria England 12 C3 54 25N 3 10W
Esk r. Scotland/England 11 F2 55 00N 3 00W
Eskişehir Turkey 57 D2 39 46N 30 30E
Espoo Finland 49 F3 60 10N 24 40E
Esquel Argentina 97 C5 42 55S 71 20W
Essen Germany 52 C5 51 27N 6 57E
Essex co. England 17 D2 51 46N 0 30E
Eston England 13 E3 54 34N 1 07W
ESTONIA 49 G2
Estremoz Portugal 51 B3 38 50N 7 35W
Étampes France 50 F5 48 26N 2 10E
ETHIOPIA 81 N3/P3
Etna, Mount Italy 54 F2 37 45N 15 00E
Eton England 16 C2 51 31N 0 37W
Ettrick Scotland 11 F2 55 23N 3 05W
Ettrickbridge Scotland 11 F2 55 30N 2 58W

Eugene USA 90 B5 44 03N 123 04W
Euphrates r. Asia 64 D5 34 40N 42 00E
Europoort Neths 48 C4 51 55N 4 10E
Evanton Scotland 9 E2 57 40N 4 20W
Evercreech England 19 E3 51 09N 2 30W
Everest, Mount
 China/Nepal 67 F5 27 59N 86 56E
Evesham England 15 E2 52 06N 1 56W
Evora Portugal 51 B3 38 46N 7 41W
Evreux France 50 E5 49 03N 1 11E
Evvoia i. Greece 55 L3 38 00N 24 00E
Exe r. England 18 D3 51 09N 3 36
Exeter England 18 D2 50 43N 3 31W
Exmouth England 18 D2 50 37N 3 25W
Eyam England 13 E2 53 24N 1 42W
Eye England 17 E3 52 19N 1 09E
Eyemouth Scotland 11 G2 55 25N 2 06W
Eye Peninsula Scotland 8 C3 58 10N 6 10W
Eyeries RoI 21 B1 51 41N 9 57W
Eynsham England 16 B2 51 46N 1 28W

**F**
Fairbourne Wales 14 B2 52 41N 4 03W
Fair Head NI 10 C2 55 15N 6 10W
Fair Isle Scotland 7 C2 59 32N 1 38W
Fairlight England 17 D1 50 52N 0 38E
Fairmont USA 91 K4 39 28N 80 08W
Faisalabad Pakistan 66 C6 31 25N 73 09E
Fakenham England 17 D3 52 50N 0 51E
Fal r. England 18 C2 50 16N 4 56W
Falcarragh RoI 20 C5 55 08N 8 06W
Falfurrias USA 91 G2 27 17N 98 10W
Falkirk Scotland 11 F2 55 59N 3 48W
Falkirk u.a. Scotland 11 F2 55 59N 3 45W
Falkland Scotland 11 F3 56 15N 3 13W
Falkland Islands
 S Atlantic Ocean 97 E2/F2 52 30S 60 00W
Falmouth England 18 B2 50 08N 5 04W
Fanad Head RoI 20 D5 55 17N 7 38W
Fane r. RoI 20 E3 53 58N 6 28W
Fano Italy 54 E5 43 51N 13 01E
Fareham England 16 B1 50 51N 1 10W
Faringdon England 16 B2 51 40N 1 35W
Farnborough England 16 C2 51 17N 0 46W
Farne Islands England 11 H2 55 38N 1 38W
Farnham England 16 C2 51 13N 0 49W
Farnham Royal
 England 16 C2 51 33N 0 38W
Farnworth England 12 D2 53 33N 2 24W
Faro Portugal 51 B3 37 01N 7 56W
Farranfore RoI 21 B2 52 10N 9 33W
Farrar r. Scotland 9 E2 57 15N 4 41W
Faughan r. NI 10 B1 54 54N 7 09W
Faversham England 17 D2 51 20N 0 53E
Fawley England 16 B1 50 49N 1 20W
Feale r. RoI 21 B2 52 26N 9 22W
Featherstone England 13 E2 53 41N 1 21W
Fécamp France 50 E5 49 45N 0 23E
FEDERATED STATES OF MICRONESIA
 100 F8
Feira de Santana Brazil 96 K11 12 17S 38 53W
Feldkirch Austria 52 D3 47 15N 9 38E
Felixstowe England 17 E2 51 58N 1 20E
Felling tn. England 13 E3 54 57N 1 33W
Felton England 11 H2 55 18N 1 42W
Feltwell England 17 D3 52 29N 0 33E
Fens, The England 16 C3/D3 52 45N 0 05E
Feolin Ferry tn.
 Scotland 10 C2 55 51N 6 06W
Ferbane RoI 20 D3 53 15N 7 49W
Fermanagh district NI 10 B1 54 25N 7 45W
Fermo Italy 54 E5 43 09N 13 44E
Fermoy RoI 21 C2 52 08N 8 16W
Ferndown England 19 E2 50 48N 1 55W
Ferns RoI 21 E2 52 35N 6 30W
Ferrara Italy 54 E6 44 50N 11 38E
Ferryhill tn. England 13 E3 54 41N 1 33W
Fès Morocco 80 C8 34 05N 5 00W
Fethaland, Point of
 Scotland 7 C3 60 35N 1 18W
Fethard RoI 21 D2 52 27N 7 41W
Fethard RoI 21 E2 52 11N 6 50W
Fetlar i. Scotland 7 D3 60 37N 0 52W
Fettercairn Scotland 9 G1 56 51N 2 34W
Ffestiniog Wales 14 C2 52 58N 3 55W
Fforest Fawr Wales 14 C1 51 50N 3 40W
Ffostrasol Wales 14 B2 52 06N 4 23W
Fianarantsoa
 Madagascar 82 J3 21 27S 47 05E
Fiddown RoI 21 D2 52 20N 7 19W
Fife u.a. Scotland 11 G3 56 10N 3 00W
Fife Ness c. Scotland 9 G1 56 17N 2 35W
Figeac France 50 F3 44 32N 2 01E
Figueira da Foz
 Portugal 51 A4 40 09N 8 51W
Figueres Spain 51 G5 42 16N 2 57E
FIJI 100 H6
Filey England 13 F3 54 12N 0 17W
Filton England 15 D1 51 31N 2 35W
Findhorn r. Scotland 9 F2 57 25N 3 55W
Findhorn Scotland 9 F2 57 39N 3 36W
Findhorn Bay Scotland 9 F2 57 39N 3 36W
Findochty Scotland 9 G2 57 42N 2 55W
Finglas RoI 20 E3 53 24N 6 18W
FINLAND 49 G3

Finland, Gulf of Finland 49 F2/G2 59 40N 23 30E
Finnea Rol 20 D3 53 47N 7 23W
Fintagh Bay Rol 20 C4 54 35N 8 33W
Fintona Rol 10 B1 54 30N 7 19W
Fintown Rol 20 C4 54 52N 8 07W
Fionn Loch Scotland 8 D2 57 45N 5 25W
Fionnphort Scotland 8 C1 56 19N 6 23W
Firat r. Asia 57 E2 37 30N 38 00E
Firth of Clyde Scotland 10 D2/E2 55 30N 5 00W
Firth of Forth Scotland 11 F3/G3 56 05N 3 00W
Firth of Lorn Scotland 10 D3 56 15N 6 00W
Firth of Tay Scotland 9 F1 56 25N 3 00W
Fishbourne England 16 B1 50 44N 1 12W
Fishguard Wales 14 B1 51 59N 4 59W
Flagstaff USA 90 D4 35 12N 111 38W
Flamborough England 13 F3 54 07N 0 07W
Flamborough Head
England 13 F3 54 06N 0 04W
Fleet England 16 C2 51 16N 0 50W
Fleetwood England 12 C2 53 56N 3 01W
Flekkefjord Norway 49 C2 58 17N 6 40E
Flimby England 12 C3 54 41N 3 31W
Flint Wales 14 C3 53 15N 3 07W
Flintshire u.a. Wales 14 C3 53 15N 3 10W
Flitwick England 16 C3 52 00N 0 29W
Florence Italy 54 D5 43 47N 11 15E
Florianópolis Brazil 97 H8 27 35S 48 31W
Florida state USA 91 K2 28 00N 82 00W
Florida Keys is. USA 91 K1 25 00N 80 00W
Flotta i. Scotland 7 A1 58 49N 3 07W
Fochabers Scotland 9 F2 57 37N 3 05W
Focşani Romania 53 N2 45 41N 27 12E
Fóggia Italy 55 F4 41 28N 15 33E
Folkestone England 17 E2 51 05N 1 11E
Folkingham England 15 F2 52 54N 0 24W
Fontainebleau France 50 F5 48 24N 2 42E
Fontstown Rol 21 E3 53 03N 6 53W
Fordham England 17 D3 52 19N 0 24E
Fordingbridge England 16 B1 50 56N 1 47W
Foreland p. England 16 B1 50 41N 1 04W
Foreland Point England18 D3 51 16N 3 47W
Foreness Point England17 E2 51 25N 1 27E
Forest Channel Islands 19 E1 49 25N 2 35W
Forest Row England 16 D2 51 06N 0 02E
Forfar Scotland 9 G1 56 38N 2 54W
Forlì Italy 54 E6 44 13N 12 02E
Formby England 12 C2 53 34N 3 05W
Formentera i. Spain 51 F3 38 41N 1 30E
FORMER YUGOSLAV REPUBLIC OF MACEDONIA
(FYROM) 55 J4/K4
Formosa Argentina 96 F8 26 07S 58 14W
Forres Scotland 9 F2 57 37N 3 38W
Fortaleza Brazil 96 K13 3 45S 38 35W
Fort Augustus Scotland 9 E2 57 09N 4 41W
Fort George Scotland 9 E2 57 35N 4 05W
Forth r. Scotland 11 E3 56 05N 4 05W
Fort Lauderdale USA 91 K2 26 08N 80 08W
Fort Liard Canada 88 L6 60 14N 123 28W
Fortrose Scotland 9 E2 57 34N 4 09W
Fort Saskatchewan
Canada 88 N4 53 42N 113 12W
Fortuneswell England 19 E2 50 33N 2 27W
Fort William Scotland 9 D1 56 49N 5 07W
Fort Worth USA 91 G3 32 45N 97 20W
Foula i. Scotland 7 B3 60 08N 2 05W
Foulness Island
England 17 D2 51 35N 0 57E
Foulness Point England17 D2 51 37N 0 57E
Fowey England 18 C2 50 20N 4 38W
Fowey r. England 18 C2 50 27N 4 38W
Foxford Rol 20 B3 53 58N 9 08W
Foyle r. NI/Rol 20 D4 54 55N 7 25W
Foynes Rol 21 B2 52 37N 9 06W
Foz Rol 51 B3 43 34N 7 15W
Framlingham England 17 E3 52 13N 1 21E
Frampton Cotterell
England 15 D1 51 32N 2 30W
FRANCE 50
Francistown Botswana 82 E3 21 11S 27 32E
Frankfurt am Main
Germany 52 D5 50 06N 8 41E
Frankfurt an der Oder
Germany 52 G6 52 20N 14 32E
Fraser r. Canada 88 L4 52 00N 122 00W
Fraserburgh Scotland 9 G2 57 42N 2 00W
Freckleton England 12 D2 53 46N 2 52W
Frederick USA 93 E1 39 25N 77 25W
Fredericksburg USA 91 L4 38 18N 77 30W
Frederikshavn
Denmark 49 D2 57 28N 10 33E
Fredrikstad Norway 49 D2 59 20N 10 50E
Freemount Rol 21 C2 52 17N 8 53W
Freeport Canada 89 X2 44 17N 66 19W
Freetown Sierra Leone 80 B3 8 30N 13 17W
Freiburg im Breisgau
Germany 52 C3 48 00N 7 52E
Fréjus France 50 H2 43 26N 6 44E
French Guiana territory
France 96 G14 5 00N 53 00W
Frenchpark Rol 20 C3 53 53N 8 24W
Freshwater England 16 B1 50 40N 1 30E
Fresno USA 90 C4 36 41N 119 47W
Fribourg Switz. 52 C3 46 50N 7 10E
Friedrichshafen
Germany 52 D3 47 39N 9 29E
Frinton on Sea England17 E2 51 50N 1 14E
Frodsham England 12 D2 53 18N 2 44W

Frogmore England 16 C2 51 20N 0 50W
Frome England 19 E 51 14N 2 20W
Frome r. Herefordshire
England 15 D2 52 05N 2 30W
Frome r. Somerset
England 19 E3 51 10N 2 20W
Frome r. Dorset
England 19 E2 50 42N 2 16W
Fuday i. Scotland 8 B2 57 05N 7 20W
Fuenlabrada Spain 51 D4 40 16N 3 49W
Fuerteventura i. Spain 80 B7 28 25N 14 00W
Fuji Japan 70 C2 35 10N 138 37E
Fuji-san mt. Japan 70 C2 35 23N 138 42E
Fukuoka Japan 70 B1 33 39N 130 21E
Furnace Scotland 10 D3 56 09N 5 12W
Fürth Germany 52 E4 49 28N 11 00E
Fushun China 69 M6 41 50N 123 54E
Fuzhou China 69 L3 26 09N 119 17E

**G**
GABON 82 B7
Gaborone Botswana 82 E3 24 45S 25 55E
Gadsden USA 91 J3 34 00N 86 00W
Gaeta Italy 54 E4 41 13N 13 36E
Gainsborough England 13 F2 53 24N 0 48W
Gairloch tn. Scotland 8 D2 57 42N 5 40W
Gairsay i. Scotland 7 B2 59 05N 2 58W
Galashiels Scotland 11 G2 55 37N 2 49W
Galaţi Romania 53 P2 45 27N 28 02E
Gallan Head Scotland 8 B3 58 14N 7 01W
Galley Head Rol 21 C1 51 35N 8 55W
Gallipoli Italy 55 H4 40 03N 17 59E
Gallup USA 90 E4 32 32N 108 46W
Galston Scotland 11 E2 55 36N 4 24W
Galveston USA 91 H2 29 17N 94 48W
Galway co. Rol 20 B3/C3 53 25N 8 45W
Galway Rol 20 B3 53 16N 9 03W
Galway Bay Rol 20 B3 53 15N 9 15W
Gambia r.
Senegal/The Gambia 80 B4 13 45N 13 15W
GAMBIA, THE 80 A4
Gandía Spain 51 E3 38 59N 0 11W
Ganga r. India 66 E5 25 00N 83 30E
Gangdisê Shan mts.
China 68 D4 31 00N 82 30E
Gap France 50 H3 44 33N 6 05E
Garda Italy 54 D6 45 34N 10 43E
Garden City USA 90 F4 37 57N 100 54W
Gardenstown Scotland 9 G2 57 40N 2 20W
Gare Loch Scotland 11 E3 56 03N 4 39W
Garelochhead Scotland11 E3 56 05N 4 50W
Garforth England 13 E2 53 48N 1 22W
Garlieston Scotland 11 E1 54 48N 4 22W
Garonne r. France 50 D3 44 45N 0 15E
Garrison NI 10 A1 54 25N 8 05W
Garron Point NI 10 D2 55 05N 5 57W
Garstang England 12 D2 53 55N 2 47W
Garth Wales 14 C2 52 08N 3 32W
Garthorpe England 13 F2 53 40N 0 42W
Garve Scotland 9 E2 57 37N 4 42W
Gaspé Canada 89 Y3 48 50N 64 30W
Gastonia USA 91 K4 35 14N 81 12W
Gatehouse of Fleet
Scotland 11 E1 54 53N 4 11W
Gateshead England 13 E3 54 58N 1 35W
Gatineau Canada 93 E3 45 29N 75 40W
Gatty Mountains Rol 21 C2 52 21N 8 11W
Gaydon England 15 E2 52 45N 0 34E
Gaza Middle East 64 N10 31 30N 34 28E
Gaziantep Turkey 57 E2 37 04N 37 21E
Gdańsk Poland 53 J7 54 22N 18 41E
Gdynia Poland 53 J7 54 31N 18 30E
Geleen Neths 48 D3 50 58N 5 45E
Gelligaer Wales 14 C1 51 39N 3 15W
Gelsenkirchen
Germany 52 C5 51 30N 7 05E
Geneva Switz. 52 C3 46 13N 6 09E
Genk Belgium 48 D3 50 58N 5 30E
Genoa Italy 54 C6 44 24N 8 56E
Gent Belgium 48 B4 51 02N 3 42E
Georgetown Guyana 96 F15 6 46N 58 10W
George Town Malaysia71 C5 5 25N 100 20E
GEORGIA 57 F3
Georgia state USA 91 K3 33 00N 83 00W
Gera Germany 52 F5 50 51N 12 11E
GERMANY 52
Gerona Spain 51 G4 41 59N 2 49E
Gerrards Cross
England 16 C2 51 35N 0 34W
Getafe Spain 51 D4 40 18N 3 44W
GHANA 80 D3
Giant's Causeway NI 10 C2 55 10N 6 30W
Gibraltar territory U.K. 51 C2 36 09N 5 21W
Gigha i. Scotland 10 D2 55 40N 5 45W
Gijón Spain 51 C5 43 32N 5 40W
Gila Bend USA 90 D3 32 56N 112 42W
Gilfach Goch Wales 14 C1 51 38N 3 30W
Gilford NI 10 C1 54 23N 6 22W
Gillingham Medway
England 17 D2 51 24N 0 33E
Gillingham Dorset
England 19 E3 51 02N 2 17W
Gilsland England 12 D3 55 00N 2 35W
Gironde r. France 50 D3 45 30N 0 45W
Girvan Scotland 10 E2 55 15N 4 51W
Givet Belgium 48 C3 50 08N 4 49E

Glanaman Wales 14 C1 51 47N 3 55W
Glanton England 11 H2 55 26N 1 54W
Glasgow Scotland 11 E2 55 53N 4 15W
Glasgow City u.a.
Scotland 11 E2 55 52N 4 16W
Glass r. Scotland 9 E2 57 15N 4 40W
Glassan Rol 20 D3 53 28N 7 52W
Glasson England 12 D2 54 00N 2 51W
Glastonbury England 19 E3 51 09N 2 43W
Glenaffric r. Scotland 8 D2 57 15N 5 15W
Glenbeigh Rol 21 B2 52 03N 9 56W
Glencoe Scotland 9 D1 56 40N 5 04W
Glencolumbkille Rol 20 C4 54 42N 8 44W
Glenfinnan Scotland 8 D1 56 53N 5 27W
Glengad Head Rol 20 D5 55 20N 7 11W
Glengarriff Rol 21 B1 51 45N 9 33W
Glenluce Scotland 11 E1 54 53N 4 49W
Glenamaddy Rol 20 C3 53 37N 8 35W
Glenridding England 12 D3 54 33N 2 58W
Glenrothes Scotland 11 F3 56 12N 3 10W
Glen Shee r. Scotland 9 F1 46 45N 3 25W
Glenties Rol 20 C4 54 47N 8 17W
Glin Rol 21 B2 52 34N 9 17W
Glossop England 13 E2 53 27N 1 57W
Gloucester England 15 D1 51 53N 2 14W
Gloucestershire co.
England 15 D1/E1 51 50N 2 20W
Glusburn England 12 D2 53 55N 2 01W
Glydar Fawr mt. Wales14 B3 53 05N 4 03W
Glyncorrwg Wales 14 C1 51 41N 3 38W
Glyn-neath Wales 14 C1 51 46N 3 38W
Gniezno Poland 53 H6 52 32N 17 32E
Goat Fell mt. Scotland 10 D2 55 39N 5 11W
Gobi Desert Mongolia
68/69 G6/J6 48 30N 100 00E
Godalming England 16 C2 51 11N 0 37W
Godmanchester
England 16 C3 52 19N 0 11W
Goiânia Brazil 96 H10 16 43S 49 18W
Goiás Brazil 96 G10 15 57S 50 07W
Golam Head Rol 20 B3 53 14N 9 44W
Golfo de California
Mexico 94 B5 27 00N 111 00W
Golfo di Genova Italy 54 C6 44 00N 9 00E
Golfo di Táranto Italy 55 G3/G4 40 00N 17 00E
Golfo di Venézia Italy 54 E6 45 00N 13 00E
Golspie Scotland 9 F2 57 58N 3 58W
Gomera i. Spain 80 A7 28 08N 17 14W
Good Hope, Cape of
RSA 82 C1 34 30S 19 00E
Goodland USA 90 F4 39 20N 101 43W
Goodwick Wales 14 B1 52 00N 5 00W
Goole England 13 F2 53 42N 0 52W
Gorebridge Scotland 11 F2 55 51N 3 02W
Gorey Rol 21 E2 52 40N 6 18W
Gorinchem Neths 48 C4 51 50N 4 59E
Goring England 16 B2 51 32N 1 09W
Gorizia Italy 54 E6 45 57N 13 37E
Gorseinon Wales 14 B1 51 41N 4 02W
Gort Rol 21 C3 53 04N 8 50W
Gorteen Rol 20 C3 53 22N 8 35W
Gortmore Rol 20 B3 53 36N 9 36W
Gorumna Island Rol 20 B3 53 15N 9 40W
Gosforth England 13 E4 55 01N 1 37W
Gosport England 16 B1 50 48N 1 08W
Göteborg Sweden 49 D2 57 45N 12 00E
Gotha Germany 52 E5 50 57N 10 43E
Gotland i. Sweden 49 E2 57 30N 18 40E
Göttingen Germany 52 D5 51 32N 9 57E
Gouda Neths 48 C5 52 00N 4 42E
Gourock Scotland 11 E2 55 58N 4 49W
Governador Valadares
Brazil 96 J10 18 49S 41 57W
Gower p. Wales 14 B1 51 35N 4 10W
Gowran Rol 21 D2 52 38N 7 04W
Graemsay i. Scotland 7 A1 58 56N 3 17W
Grafham Water
England 16 C3 52 18N 0 20W
Graiguenamanagh Rol 21 E2 52 32N 6 56W
Grain England 17 D2 51 28N 0 43E
Grampian Mountains
Scotland 9 E1/F1 56 45N 4 00W
Granada Spain 51 D2 37 10N 3 35W
Granard Rol 20 D3 53 47N 7 30W
Gran Canaria i. Spain 80 A7 28 00N 15 35W
Grand Canal Rol 20 D3 53 21N 6 15W
Grand Canyon USA 90 D4 36 04N 112 07W
Grand Cayman i.
Caribbean Sea 95 H3 19 20N 81 15W
Grand Rapids tn. USA 91 J5 42 57N 86 40W
Grange Rol 20 C4 54 24N 8 31W
Grangemouth
Scotland 11 F3 56 01N 3 44W
Grange-over-Sands tn.
England 12 D3 54 33N 3 09W
Grantham England 15 F2 52 55N 0 39W
Grantown-on-Spey
Scotland 9 F2 57 20N 3 58W
Granville France 50 D5 48 50N 1 35W
Grasmere England 12 D3 54 28N 3 02W
Grasse France 50 H2 43 40N 6 56E
Grassington England 13 E3 54 04N 1 59W
Gravelines France 48 A3 50 59N 2 08E
Gravesend England 17 D2 51 27N 0 24E
Gray France 50 G4 47 27N 5 35E
Grays England 17 D2 51 29N 0 20E

Greasby England 12 C2 53 23N 3 10W
Great Bardfield
England 17 D2 51 57N 0 26E
Great Bear Lake
Canada 88 L7/M7 66 00N 120 00W
Great Broughton
England 13 E3 54 27N 1 110W
Great Chesterford
England 17 D3 52 04N 0 11E
Great Coates England 13 F2 53 35N 0 08W
Great Cumbrae i.
Scotland 10 E2 55 46N 4 55W
Great Dividing Range
Australia 73 H8/J3 35 00N 148 00E
Great Driffield England 13 F3 54 01N 0 26E
Great Dunmow
England 17 D2 51 53N 0 22E
Great Eccleston
England 12 D2 53 51N 2 53W
Greater Antilles is.
West Indies 95 H4/L3 19 00N 78 00W
Greater London co.
England 16 C2 51 30N 0 10W
Greater Manchester
co. England 12 D2 53 30N 2 15W
Great Harwood
England 12 D2 53 48N 2 24W
Great Malvern England15 D2 52 07N 2 19W
Great Missenden
England 16 C2 51 43N 0 43W
Great Ormes Head
Wales 14 C3 53 21N 3 53W
Great Ouse r. England 17 D3 52 40N 0 20E
Great Salt Lake USA 90 D5 41 10N 112 40W
Great Shelford England
17 D3 52 08N 0 09E
Great Slave Lake
Canada 88 N6 62 00N 114 00W
Great Torrington
England 18 C2 51 57N 4 09W
Great Victoria Desert
Australia 72 E5/F5 28 00S 130 00E
Great Whernside sum.
England 13 E3 54 10N 1 59W
Great Wyrley England 15 D2 52 27N 2 02W
Great Yarmouth
England 17 E3 52 37N 1 44E
GREECE 55 J3/K3
Greencastle NI 10 C1 54 02N 6 06W
Greenisland tn. NI 10 D1 54 42N 5 52W
GREENLAND 89BB8/EE8
Greenlaw Scotland 11 G2 55 43N 2 28W
Greenock Scotland 11 E2 55 57N 4 45W
Greenore Rol 20 E4 54 02N 6 08W
Greenore Point Rol 21 E2 52 15N 6 18W
Greenstone Point
Scotland 8 D2 57 55N 5 37W
GRENADA 94 R11
Grenoble France 50 G3 45 11N 5 43E
Greta r. England 12 D3 54 10N 2 30W
Gretna Scotland 11 F1 54 59N 3 04W
Gretna Green Scotland11 F1 55 00N 3 04W
Greystones Rol 21 E3 53 09N 6 04W
Grimethorpe England 13 E2 53 34N 1 23W
Grimsby England 13 F2 53 35N 0 05W
Groningen Neths 48 E6 53 13N 6 35E
Grosseto Italy 54 D5 42 46N 11 07E
Grove England 16 B2 51 37N 1 25W
Groznyy Russia 62 G5 43 21N 45 42E
Gruinard Bay Scotland 8 D2 57 55N 5 30W
Guadalajara Mexico 94 D4 20 40N 103 20W
Guadalajara Spain 51 D4 40 37N 3 10W
Guadalquivir r. Spain 51 C2 37 45N 5 30W
Guadeloupe i.
Lesser Antilles 94 Q9 16 30N 61 30W
Guadiana r.
Spain/Portugal 51 B3 38 30N 7 30W
GUAM 100 E9
Guangzhou China 69 K2 23 08N 113 20E
Guantánamo Cuba 95 J4 20 09N 75 14W
Guarda Portugal 51 B4 40 32N 7 17W
GUATEMALA 94 F3
Guatemala City
Guatemala 94 F2 14 38N 90 22W
Guayaquil Ecuador 96 A13 2 13S 79 54W
Guéret France 50 E4 46 10N 1 52E
Guernsey i.
Channel Islands 19 E1 46 27N 2 35W
Guide Post England 13 E4 55 10N 1 36W
Guildford England 16 C2 51 14N 0 35W
Guimarães Portugal 51 A4 41 26N 8 19W
GUINEA 80 B4
GUINEA-BISSAU 80 A4/B4
Guisborough England 13 E3 54 32N 1 04W
Guiseley England 13 E2 53 53N 1 42W
Guiyang China 69 J3 26 35N 106 40E
Gujranwala Pakistan 66 C6 32 06N 74 11E
Gulf, The Middle East 65 F4 27 20N 51 00E
Gullane Scotland 11 G3 56 02N 2 50W
Gunnislake England 18 C2 50 31N 4 12W
Gutcher Scotland 7 D3 60 40N 1 00W
Guthrie USA 91 G4 35 53N 97 26W
GUYANA 96 F14
Gweebarra Bay Rol 20 C4 54 55N 8 30W
Gweedore Rol 20 C5 55 03N 8 14W
Gwynedd u.a. Wales 14 C2 52 45N 3 55W
Györ Hungary 53 H3 47 41N 17 40E

## H

Haarlem Neths 48 C5 52 23N 4 39E
Hacketstown RoI 21 E2 52 52N 6 33W
Haddington Scotland 11 G2 55 58N 2 47W
Hadleigh England 17 D3 52 02N 0 57E
Hadleigh England 17 D2 51 34N 0 36E
Hadley England 15 D2 52 43N 2 28W
Hagen Germany 52 C5 51 22N 7 27E
Hagley England 15 D2 52 26N 2 08W
Hagondange France 50 H5 49 16N 6 11E
Hags Head RoI 21 B2 52 56N 9 30W
Haguenau France 50 H5 48 49N 7 47E
Haifa Israel 64 B5 32 49N 34 59E
Hailsham England 17 D1 50 52N 0 16E
Hainan Dao i. China 69 J1/K1 18 50N 109 50E
Hai Phong Vietnam 69 J2 20 50N 106 41E
HAITI 95 K3
Hakodate Japan 70 D3 41 46N 140 44E
Hale England 12 D2 53 22N 2 20W
Halesowen England 15 D2 52 26N 2 05W
Halesworth England 17 E3 52 21N 1 30E
Halifax England 13 E2 53 44N 1 52W
Halifax Canada 89 Y2 44 38N 63 35W
Halkirk Scotland 9 F3 58 30N 3 30W
Halladale r. Scotland 9 F3 58 30N 3 55W
Halle Germany 52 E5 51 28N 11 58E
Hallein Austria 52 F3 47 41N 13 06E
Halmstad Sweden 49 D2 56 41N 12 55E
Halstead England 17 D2 51 57N 0 38E
Haltwhistle England 12 D3 54 58N 2 27W
Ḥamāh Syria 64 C6 35 10N 36 45E
Hamamatsu Japan 70 C1 34 42N 137 42E
Hamble-le-Rice England 16 B1 50 52N 1 19W
Hambleton Hills England 13 E3 54 15N 1 15W
Hamburg Germany 52 E6 53 33N 10 00E
Hämeenlinna Finland 49 F3 61 00N 24 25E
Hamilton Canada 89 U2 43 15N 79 50W
Hamilton NZ 73 Q3 37 47S 175 17E
Hamilton Scotland 11 E2 55 47N 4 03W
Hamm Germany 52 C5 51 40N 7 49E
Hammerfest Norway 49 F5 70 40N 23 44E
Hampshire co. England 16 B2 51 15N 1 15W
Hampshire Downs England 16 B2 51 15N 1 10W
Hamstreet England 17 D2 51 05N 0 52E
Hangzhou China 69 M4 30 18N 120 07E
Hanko Finland 49 F2 50 50N 23 00E
Hanley England 12 D2 53 01N 2 10W
Hannover Germany 52 D6 52 23N 9 44E
Hanoi Vietnam 69 J2 21 01N 105 52E
Harare Zimbabwe 82 F4 17 50S 31 03E
Harbin China 69 N7 45 45N 126 41E
Hargeysa Somalia 81 P3 9 31N 44 02E
Harlech Wales 14 B2 52 52N 4 07W
Harleston England 17 E3 52 24N 1 18E
Harlingen Neths 48 D6 53 10N 5 25E
Harlow England 17 D2 51 47N 0 08E
Haroldswick Scotland 7 D3 60 47N 0 50W
Harpenden England 16 C2 51 49N 0 22W
Harris i. Scotland 8 C2 57 50N 6 55W
Harrogate England 13 E2 54 00N 1 33W
Harrow England 16 C2 51 34N 0 20W
Hartford USA 91 M5 41 00N 72 00W
Hartington England 13 E2 53 09N 1 48W
Hartland England 18 C2 50 59N 4 29W
Hartland Point England 18 C3 51 02N 4 31W
Hartlepool England 13 E3 54 41N 1 13W
Hartlepool u.a. England 13 E3 54 41N 1 13W
Hartshill England 15 E2 52 33N 1 30W
Harwell England 16 B2 51 37N 1 18W
Harwich England 17 E2 51 57N 1 17E
Harworth England 13 E2 53 26N 1 04W
Harz mts. Europe 52 E5 52 00N 10 00E
Hascosay i. Scotland 7 D3 60 36N 1 00W
Haslemere England 16 C2 51 06N 0 43W
Haslingden England 12 D2 53 43N 2 18W
Hasselt Belgium 48 D3 50 56N 5 20E
Hastings England 17 D1 50 51N 0 36E
Hatfield South Yorkshire England 13 F2 53 36N 0 59W
Hatfield Hertfordshire England 16 C2 51 46N 0 13W
Hatherleigh England 18 C2 50 49N 4 04W
Hathersage England 13 E2 53 19N 1 38W
Hatton Scotland 9 H2 57 25N 1 55W
Haugesund Norway 49 C2 59 25N 5 16E
Haut Atlas mts. Morocco 80 C8 30 45N 6 50W
Havana Cuba 95 H4 23 07N 82 25W
Havant England 16 C1 50 51N 0 59W
Haverfordwest Wales 14 B1 51 49N 4 58W
Haverhill England 17 D3 52 05N 0 26E
Havering England 17 D2 51 34N 0 14E
Hawaiian Islands Pacific Ocean 100 J10/L9 25 00N 166 00W
Hawarden Wales 14 C3 53 11N 3 02W
Hawes England 12 D3 54 18N 2 12W
Hawick Scotland 11 G2 55 25N 2 47W
Hawkesbury Canada 89 W3 45 36N 74 38W
Hawkhurst England 17 D2 51 02N 0 30E
Haworth England 13 E2 53 50N 1 57W
Haxby England 13 E3 54 01N 1 05W

Haydon Bridge tn. England 12 D3 54 58N 2 14W
Hayle England 18 B2 50 10N 5 25W
Hay-on-Wye Wales 14 C2 52 04N 3 07W
Haywards Heath England 16 C2 51 00N 0 06W
Hazel Grove England 12 D2 53 23N 2 08W
Hazelmere England 16 C2 51 38N 0 44W
Heacham England 17 D3 52 55N 0 30E
Headford RoI 20 B3 53 28N 9 06W
Heanor England 13 E2 53 01N 1 22W
Heathfield England 17 D1 50 58N 0 15E
Hebden Bridge England 12 D2 53 45N 2 00W
Hebi China 69 K5 35 57N 114 08E
Heckington England 15 F2 52 59N 0 18W
Heckmondwike England 13 E2 53 43N 1 45W
Hedge End England 16 B1 50 55N 1 18W
Hednesford England 15 D2 52 43N 2 00W
Hedon England 13 F2 53 44N 0 12W
Heerenveen Neths 48 D5 52 57N 5 55E
Heerlen Neths 48 D3 50 53N 5 59E
Hefei China 69 L4 31 55N 117 18E
Heidelberg Germany 52 D4 49 25N 8 42E
Heighington England 13 F2 54 36N 1 37W
Heilbronn Germany 52 D4 49 08N 9 14E
Heisker is. Scotland 8 B2 57 30N 7 40W
Hekla mt. Iceland 49 L6 64 00N 19 41W
Helchteren Belgium 48 D3 51 03N 5 23E
Helena USA 90 D6 46 35N 112 00W
Helen's Bay tn. NI 10 D1 54 41N 5 50W
Helensburgh Scotland 11 E3 56 01N 4 44W
Hellifield England 12 D3 54 01N 2 12W
Helmsdale r. Scotland 9 F3 58 10N 3 50W
Helmsdale Scotland 9 F3 58 07N 3 40W
Helmsley England 13 E3 54 14N 1 04W
Helsingborg Sweden 49 D2 56 03N 12 43E
Helsinki Finland 49 F3 60 08N 25 00E
Helston England 18 B2 50 05N 5 16W
Helvellyn mt. England 12 C3 54 32N 3 02W
Hemel Hempstead England 16 C2 51 46N 0 28W
Hemsworth England 13 E2 53 38N 1 21W
Henfield England 16 C1 50 56N 0 17W
Hengelo Neths 48 E5 52 16N 6 46E
Henley-in-Arden England 15 E2 52 17N 1 46W
Henley-on-Thames England 16 C2 51 32N 0 56W
Herbertstown RoI 21 C2 52 32N 8 28W
Hereford England 14 D2 52 04N 2 43W
Herefordshire co. England 14/15
Herentals Belgium 48 C4 51 11N 4 50E
Herm i. Channel Islands 19 E1 49 28N 2 27W
Herne Germany 48 F4 51 32N 7 12E
Herne Bay tn. England 17 E2 51 23N 1 08E
Herning Denmark 49 C2 56 08N 8 59E
Hertfordshire co. England 16 C2 51 50N 0 05W
Hessle England 13 F2 53 44N 0 26W
Hetton-le-Hole England 13 E3 54 50N 1 27W
Hexham England 12 D3 54 58N 2 06W
Heysham England 12 D3 54 02N 2 54W
Heywood England 12 D2 53 36N 2 13W
Higham Ferrers England 15 F2 52 18N 0 36W
High Bentham England 12 D3 54 08N 2 30W
Higher Walton England 12 D2 53 45N 2 37W
Highland u.a. Scotland 8/9 D2/E2 57 00N 5 00W
Highworth England 16 B2 51 38N 1 43W
High Wycombe England 16 C2 51 38N 0 46W
Hildesheim Germany 52 D6 52 09N 9 58E
Hillingdon England 16 C2 51 33N 0 27W
Hillsborough NI 10 C1 54 28N 6 05W
Hilversum Neths 48 D5 52 14N 5 10E
Himalaya mts. Asia 66/67 D6/G5 28 00N 85 00E
Hinckley England 15 E2 52 33N 1 21W
Hindhead England 16 C2 51 07N 0 44W
Hindley England 12 D2 53 32N 2 35W
Hindu Kush mts. Afghanistan 66 B7/C7 35 00N 70 00E
Hiroshima Japan 70 B1 34 23N 132 27E
Hirwaun Wales 14 C1 51 45N 3 30W
Histon England 17 D3 52 15N 0 06E
Hitachi Japan 70 D2 36 35N 140 40E
Hitchin England 16 C2 51 57N 0 17W
Hobart Australia 73 J2 42 54S 147 18E
Hô Chi Minh Vietnam 71 D6 10 46N 106 43E
Hockley England 17 D2 51 35N 0 39E
Hodder r. England 12 D2 53 55N 2 30W
Hoddesdon England 16 C2 51 46N 0 01W
Hodnet England 15 D2 52 51N 2 35W
Hoek van Holland Neths 48 C5 51 59N 4 08E
Hohhot China 69 K6 40 49N 117 37E
Hokkaidō i. Japan 70 D3 43 30N 143 00E
Holbeach England 15 F2 52 48N 0 01E
Holderness p. England 13 F2 53 45N 0 05W
Hollyford RoI 21 C2 52 38N 8 06W
Hollywood RoI 21 E3 53 06N 6 35W
Holmes Chapel tn. England 12 D2 53 12N 2 22W
Holme-on-Spalding-Moor England 13 F2 53 49N 0 46W
Holmfirth England 13 E2 53 35N 1 46W
Holmhead Scotland 11 E2 55 29N 4 17W

Holsworthy England 18 C2 50 49N 4 21W
Holt England 17 E3 52 55N 1 05E
Holycross Limerick RoI 21 C2 52 38N 7 52W
Holycross Tipperary RoI 21 D2 52 38N 7 52W
Holyhead Wales 14 B3 53 19N 4 38W
Holy Island England 11 H2 55 41N 1 48W
Holy Island Wales 14 B3 53 16N 4 39W
Holywell Wales 14 C3 53 17N 3 13W
Holywood NI 10 D1 54 38N 5 50W
Homs Syria 64 C5 34 42N 36 40E
Homyel' Belarus 53 Q6 52 25N 31 00E
Honddu r. Wales 14 C1 51 50N 2 50W
HONDURAS 94 G2
Hong Kong China 69 K2 23 00N 114 00E
Honiton England 19 D2 50 48N 3 13W
Honshū i. Japan 70 C2 37 15N 139 00E
Hoo England 17 D2 51 26N 0 34E
Hoogeveen Neths 48 E5 52 43N 6 29E
Hook England 16 C2 51 17N 0 58W
Hook Head RoI 21 E2 52 10N 6 55W
Hope Wales 14 C3 53 07N 3 03W
Hopton on Sea England 17 E3 52 33N 1 43E
Horbury England 13 E2 53 41N 1 33W
Horley England 16 C2 51 11N 0 11W
Horncastle England 13 F2 53 13N 0 07W
Horn Head RoI 20 D5 55 13N 7 59W
Hornsea England 13 F2 53 55N 0 10W
Horsforth England 13 E2 53 51N 1 39W
Horsham England 16 C2 51 04N 0 21W
Horwich England 12 D2 53 37N 2 33W
Hospital RoI 21 C2 52 29N 8 25W
Hospitalet Spain 51 G4 41 21N 2 06E
Houghton-le-Spring England 13 E3 54 51N 1 28W
Hounslow England 16 C2 51 28N 0 21W
Houston USA 91 G2 29 45N 95 25W
Hove England 16 C1 50 49N 0 11W
Hovingham England 13 F3 54 10N 0 59W
Howden England 13 F2 53 45N 0 52W
Howth RoI 20 E3 53 23N 6 04W
Hoy i. Scotland 7 A1 58 48N 3 20W
Hoylake England 12 C2 53 23N 3 11W
Hoyland England 13 E2 53 30N 1 27W
Hoy Sound Scotland 7 A1 58 56N 3 20W
Hrodna Belarus 53 L6 53 40N 23 50E
Huambo Angola 82 C5 12 44S 15 47E
Huancayo Peru 96 B11 12 05S 75 12W
Huang He r. China 69 K5 38 00N 111 00E
Hucknall England 13 E2 53 02N 1 11W
Huddersfield England 13 E2 53 39N 1 47W
Hudson Bay Canada 89 T5/T6 60 00N 89 00W
Huelva Spain 51 C2 37 15N 6 56W
Huesca Spain 51 E4 42 08N 0 25W
Hugh Town England 18 A1 49 55N 6 19W
Hull r. England 13 F2 53 55N 0 20W
Hullbridge England 17 D2 51 37N 0 37E
Humaitá Brazil 96 E12 7 33S 63 01W
Humberston England 13 F2 53 32N 0 02W
HUNGARY 53 H3/K3
Hungerford England 16 B2 51 26N 1 30W
Hunmanby England 13 F3 54 11N 0 19W
Hunstanton England 17 D3 52 57N 0 30E
Huntford Scotland 11 G2 55 22N 2 28W
Huntingdon England 16 C3 52 20N 0 12W
Huntington USA 91 K4 38 24N 82 26W
Huntly Scotland 9 G2 57 27N 2 47W
Huntsville USA 91 J3 34 44N 86 35W
Huron, Lake Canada/USA 93 D2/3 45 00N 83 00W
Hurstpierpoint England 16 C1 50 56N 0 11W
Husbands Bosworth England 15 E2 52 27N 1 03W
Husum Germany 52 D7 54 29N 9 04E
Hutton Cranswick England 13 F2 53 57N 0 27W
Hyde England 12 D2 53 27N 2 04W
Hyderabad India 66 D3 17 22N 78 26E
Hyderabad Pakistan 66 B5 25 23N 68 24E
Hythe Hampshire England 16 B1 50 51N 1 24W
Hythe Kent England 17 E2 51 05N 1 05E

## I

Iaşi Romania 53 N3 47 09N 27 38E
Ibadan Nigeria 80 E3 7 23N 3 56E
Ibagué Colombia 96 B14 4 25N 75 20W
Ibiza i. Spain 51 F3 39 00N 1 20E
Ibstock England 15 E2 52 41N 1 23W
Ica Peru 96 B11 14 02S 75 48W
ICELAND 49 L7
Idaho state USA 90 D5 44 00N 115 00W
Idrigill Point Scotland 8 C2 57 21N 6 35W
Ieper Belgium 48 A3 50 51N 2 53E
Iglesias Italy 54 C3 39 19N 8 32E
Ilam England 13 E2 53 04N 1 49W
Ilchester England 19 E2 51 00N 2 41W
Ilebo CDR 82 D7 4 20S 20 35E
Îles Loyauté is. Pacific Ocean 73 N6/N7 21 00S 167 00E
Ilfracombe England 18 C3 51 13N 4 08W
Ilhéus Brazil 96 K11 14 50S 39 06W
Ilkeston England 13 E2 52 59N 1 18W
Ilkley England 13 E2 53 55N 1 50W
Illinois state USA 91 J5 40 00N 89 00W
Ilminster England 19 E2 50 56N 2 55W

Immingham England 13 F2 53 36N 0 11W
Imola Italy 54 E6 44 22N 11 43E
Imperatriz Brazil 96 H12 5 32S 47 28W
Imperia Italy 54 C5 43 53N 8 03E
Imphal India 67 G4 24 47N 93 55E
Inch Island i. RoI 20 D5 55 04N 7 30W
Inchon S. Korea 69 N5 37 30N 126 38E
Independence USA 91 G4 37 13N 95 43W
INDIA 66/67
Indiana state USA 91 J5 40 00N 86 00W
Indianapolis USA 91 J4 39 45N 86 10W
Indian Ocean 105
INDONESIA 71 C3/H3
Indore India 66 D4 22 42N 75 54E
Indus r. Pakistan 66 B5 28 00N 69 00E
Ingatestone England 17 D2 51 41N 0 22E
Ingleborough sum. England 12 D3 54 10N 2 23W
Ingleton England 12 D3 54 10N 2 27W
Ingolstadt Germany 52 E4 48 46N 11 27E
Inishannon RoI 21 C1 51 45N 8 38W
Inishbofin i. RoI 20 A3 53 38N 10 12W
Inishcrone RoI 20 B4 54 13N 9 05W
Inisheer i. RoI 21 B3 53 03N 9 30W
Inishkea North i. RoI 20 A4 54 08N 10 11W
Inishkea South i. RoI 20 A4 54 08N 10 11W
Inishmaan i. RoI 21 B3 53 05N 9 35W
Inishmore i. RoI 21 B3 53 07N 9 45W
Inishmurray i. RoI 20 C4 54 25N 8 35W
Inishowen Peninsula RoI 20 D5 55 15N 7 15W
Inishshark i. RoI 20 A3 53 37N 10 16W
Inishturk i. RoI 20 A3 53 43N 10 05W
Inn r. Europe 52 E3 48 00N 12 00E
Inner Hebrides is. Scotland 8 C1/C2 56 45N 6 45W
Innerleithen Scotland 11 F2 55 38N 3 05W
Inner Sound Scotland 8 D2 57 25N 5 55W
Innfield RoI 20 D3 53 25N 6 50W
Innsbruck Austria 52 E3 47 17N 11 25E
Inny r. RoI 21 A1 51 54N 10 06W
Interlaken Switz. 52 C3 46 42N 7 52E
Inuvik Canada 88 J7 68 16N 133 40W
Inveraray Scotland 10 D3 56 13N 5 05W
Inver Bay RoI 20 C4 54 36N 8 20W
Inverbervie Scotland 9 G1 56 51N 2 17W
Invercargill NZ 73 N1 46 25S 168 22E
Inverclyde u.a. Scotland 11 E2 55 50N 4 45W
Invergarry Scotland 9 E2 57 02N 4 47W
Invergordon Scotland 9 E2 57 42N 4 10W
Inverkeithing Scotland 11 F2 56 02N 3 25W
Invermoriston Scotland 9 E2 57 13N 4 38W
Inverness Scotland 9 E2 57 27N 4 15W
Inverquharity Scotland 9 G1 56 44N 2 59W
Inverurie Scotland 9 G2 57 17N 2 23W
Ioánnina Greece 55 J3 39 40N 20 51E
Iona i. Scotland 8 C1 56 19N 6 25W
Iónia Nisiá Greece 55 H3 39 00N 20 00E
Íos i. Greece 55 L2 36 00N 25 00E
Iowa state USA 91 H5 42 00N 94 00W
Iowa City USA 91 H5 41 39N 91 31W
Ipswich England 17 E2 52 04N 1 10E
Iquique Chile 96 C9 20 14S 70 07W
Iquitos Peru 96 C13 3 51S 73 13W
IRAN 65 F5/G5
IRAQ 64 D5
Irbid Jordan 64 C5 32 33N 35 51E
Irfon r. Wales 14 C2 52 10N 3 25W
Irish Sea British Isles 6 53 30N 5 30W
Irkutsk Russia 63 N7 52 18N 104 15E
Ironbridge England 15 D2 52 38N 2 30W
Irrawaddy r. Myanmar 71 A8 20 00N 95 00E
Irthing r. England 12 D3 55 00N 2 40W
Irthlingborough England 15 F2 52 20N 0 37W
Irtysh r. Asia 62 K8 57 30N 72 30E
Irún Spain 51 E5 43 20N 1 48W
Irvine Scotland 11 E2 55 37N 4 40W
Irvinestown NI 10 B1 54 29N 7 38W
Irving USA 91 G3 32 49N 96 57W
Ise r. England 15 F2 52 25N 00 50W
Isernia Italy 54 F4 41 35N 14 14E
Iskenderun Turkey 57 E2 36 37N 36 08E
Isla r. Scotland 9 F1 56 35N 3 10W
Isla d'Elba Italy 54 D5 42 00N 10 00E
Isla Grande de Tierra del Fuego Chile/Argentina 97 D2 54 00S 67 30W
Islamabad Pakistan 66 C6 33 40N 73 08E
Island Magee NI 10 D1 54 45N 5 40W
Islay i. Scotland 10 C2 55 48N 6 12W
Isleham England 17 D3 52 21N 0 25E
Isle of Man British Isles 12 B3 54 15N 4 30W
Isle of Portland England 19 E2 50 33N 2 27W
Isle of Purbeck England 19 E2 50 38N 2 05W
Isle of Whithorn tn. Scotland 11 E1 54 42N 4 22W
Isle of Wight u.a. England 16 B1 50 40N 1 20W
ISRAEL 64 B5/C5
Istanbul Turkey 57 C3 41 02N 28 57E
Itabuna Brazil 96 K11 14 48S 39 18W
ITALY 54 D5/E5
Itchen r. England 16 B2 51 05N 1 15W
Ithon r. Wales 14 C2 52 10N 3 25W
Itzehoe Germany 52 D6 53 56N 9 32E
Ivybridge England 18 D2 50 23N 3 56W
Ixworth England 17 D3 52 18N 0 50E

| Place | Pg | Grid | Lat. | Long. |
|---|---|---|---|---|
| Izhevsk Russia | 62 | H8 | 56 49N | 53 11E |
| Izmir Turkey | 57 | C2 | 38 25N | 27 10E |

### J

| Place | Pg | Grid | Lat. | Long. |
|---|---|---|---|---|
| Jackson USA | 91 | H3 | 32 20N | 90 11W |
| Jacksonville USA | 91 | K3 | 30 20N | 81 40W |
| Jaén Spain | 51 | D2 | 37 46N | 3 48W |
| Jaipur India | 66 | D5 | 26 53N | 75 50E |
| Jakarta Indonesia | 71 | D2 | 6 08S | 106 45E |
| Jakobstad Finland | 49 | F3 | 63 40N | 22 42E |
| JAMAICA | 95 | J3 | | |
| James Bay Canada | 89 | U4 | 53 45N | 81 00W |
| Jamestown USA | 91 | G6 | 46 54N | 98 42W |
| Jammu India | 66 | C6 | 32 43N | 74 54E |
| JAPAN | 70 | | | |
| Jarrow England | 13 | E3 | 54 59N | 1 29W |
| Jasper Canada | 88 | M4 | 52 55N | 118 05W |
| Jastrowie Poland | 53 | H6 | 53 25N | 16 50E |
| Jawa i. Indonesia | 71 | D2/E2 | 7 00S | 110 00E |
| Jedburgh Scotland | 11 | G2 | 55 29N | 2 34W |
| Jedda Saudi Arabia | 64 | C3 | 21 30N | 39 10E |
| Jefferson City USA | 91 | H4 | 38 33N | 92 10W |
| Jena Germany | 52 | E5 | 50 56N | 11 35E |
| Jerez de la Frontera Spain | 51 | C2 | 36 41N | 6 08W |
| Jericho Middle East | 64 | N10 | 31 51N | 35 27E |
| Jersey i. Channel Islands | 19 | E1 | 49 13N | 2 07W |
| Jerusalem Israel/Jordan | 64 | C5 | 31 47N | 35 13E |
| Jilin China | 69 | N6 | 43 53N | 126 35E |
| Jinan China | 69 | L5 | 36 41N | 117 00E |
| Jinja Uganda | 83 | C5 | 0 27N | 33 14E |
| João Pessoa Brazil | 96 | K12 | 7 06S | 34 53W |
| Jodhpur India | 66 | C5 | 26 18N | 73 08E |
| Joensuu Finland | 49 | G3 | 62 35N | 29 46E |
| Johannesburg RSA | 82 | E2 | 26 10S | 28 02E |
| John o'Groats Scotland | 9 | F3 | 58 38N | 3 05W |
| Johnstone Scotland | 11 | E2 | 55 50N | 4 31W |
| Joinville Brazil | 96 | H8 | 26 20S | 48 55W |
| Jönköping Sweden | 49 | D2 | 57 45N | 14 10E |
| Jonquière Canada | 89 | W3 | 48 25N | 71 16W |
| JORDAN | 64 | C5 | | |
| Jordan r. Middle East | 64 | N11 | 32 15N | 32 10E |
| Joyce Country Rol | 20 | B3 | 53 32N | 9 33W |
| Juàzeiro Brazil | 96 | J12 | 9 25S | 40 30W |
| Juba Sudan | 81 | M2 | 4 50N | 31 35E |
| Juliaca Peru | 96 | C10 | 15 29S | 70 09W |
| Juneau USA | 88 | J5 | 58 20N | 134 20W |
| Jungfrau mt. Switz. | 52 | C3 | 46 33N | 7 58E |
| Junsele Sweden | 49 | E3 | 63 40N | 16 55E |
| Jura mts. France/Switz. | 50 | G4/H4 | 46 30N | 6 00E |
| Jura i. Scotland | 10 | D2/D3 | 55 55N | 6 00W |
| Jura, Sound of Scotland | 10 | D2 | 55 45N | 5 55W |
| Jylland p. Denmark | 49 | C2 | 55 00N | 9 00E |
| Jyväskylä Finland | 49 | G3 | 62 16N | 25 50E |

### K

| Place | Pg | Grid | Lat. | Long. |
|---|---|---|---|---|
| K2 mt. China/India | 68 | C5 | 35 47N | 76 30E |
| Kābul Afghanistan | 66 | B6 | 34 30N | 69 10E |
| Kagoshima Japan | 70 | B1 | 31 37N | 130 32E |
| Kaiserslautern Germany | 52 | C4 | 49 27N | 7 47E |
| Kajaani Finland | 49 | G3 | 64 14N | 27 37E |
| Kalahari Desert Southern Africa | 82 | D3 | 23 30S | 23 00E |
| Kalamáta Greece | 55 | K2 | 37 02N | 22 07E |
| Kalémié CDR | 82 | E6 | 5 57S | 29 10E |
| Kaliavesi l. Finland | 49 | G3 | 63 00N | 27 20E |
| Kaliningrad Russia | 49 | F1 | 54 40N | 20 30E |
| Kalmar Sweden | 49 | E2 | 56 39N | 16 20E |
| Kalmthout Belgium | 48 | C4 | 51 23N | 4 29E |
| Kamchatka p. Russia | 63 | T8 | 57 30N | 160 00E |
| Kames Scotland | 10 | D2 | 55 54N | 5 15W |
| Kamina CDR | 82 | E6 | 8 46S | 25 00E |
| Kamloops Canada | 88 | L4 | 50 39N | 120 24W |
| Kampala Uganda | 83 | C5 | 0 19N | 32 35E |
| Kâmpóng Cham Cambodia | 71 | D6 | 11 59N | 105 26E |
| Kananga CDR | 82 | D6 | 5 53S | 22 26E |
| Kankakee USA | 91 | J5 | 41 08N | 87 52W |
| Kannapolis USA | 91 | K4 | 35 30N | 80 36W |
| Kano Nigeria | 80 | F4 | 12 00N | 8 31E |
| Kanpur India | 66 | E5 | 26 27N | 80 14E |
| Kansas state USA | 90/91 | G4 | 38 00N | 98 00W |
| Kansas City USA | 91 | H4 | 39 02N | 94 33W |
| Kanturk Rol | 21 | C2 | 52 10N | 8 55W |
| Kaohsiung Taiwan | 69 | M2 | 22 36N | 120 17E |
| Kapuskasing Canada | 89 | U3 | 49 25N | 82 26W |
| Karachi Pakistan | 66 | B4 | 24 51N | 67 02E |
| Kara Sea Russia | 101 | | 75 00N | 70 00E |
| Karasjok Norway | 49 | G4 | 69 27N | 25 30E |
| Karcag Hungary | 53 | K3 | 47 19N | 20 53E |
| Karlskoga Sweden | 49 | D2 | 59 19N | 14 33E |
| Karlskrona Sweden | 49 | E2 | 56 10N | 15 35E |
| Karlsruhe Germany | 52 | D4 | 49 00N | 8 24E |
| Karlstad Sweden | 49 | D2 | 59 24N | 13 32E |
| Kaskinen Finland | 49 | F3 | 62 23N | 21 10E |
| Kassala Sudan | 81 | N5 | 15 24N | 36 30E |
| Kassel Germany | 52 | D5 | 51 18N | 9 30E |
| Kathmandu Nepal | 67 | F5 | 27 42N | 85 19E |
| Katowice Poland | 53 | J5 | 50 15N | 18 59E |
| Katrineholm Sweden | 49 | E2 | 58 59N | 16 15E |
| Kattegat sd. Denmark/Sweden | 49 | D2 | 57 00N | 11 00E |
| Kaunas Lithuania | 49 | F1 | 54 52N | 23 55E |
| Kawasaki Japan | 70 | C3 | 35 30N | 139 45E |
| Kayseri Turkey | 57 | E2 | 38 42N | 35 28E |
| KAZAKHSTAN | 62 | H6/J6 | | |
| Kazan' Russia | 62 | G8 | 55 45N | 49 10E |
| Keady NI | 10 | C1 | 54 15N | 6 42W |
| Kealkill Rol | 21 | B1 | 51 45N | 9 20W |
| Kecskemét Hungary | 53 | J3 | 46 56N | 19 43E |
| Kefallonia i. Greece | 55 | J3 | 38 00N | 20 00E |
| Keighley England | 13 | E2 | 53 52N | 1 54W |
| Keith Scotland | 9 | G2 | 57 32N | 2 57W |
| Kells Rol | 20 | E3 | 53 44N | 6 53W |
| Kelowna Canada | 88 | M3 | 49 50N | 119 29W |
| Kelso Scotland | 11 | G2 | 55 36N | 2 25W |
| Kelvedon England | 17 | D2 | 51 51N | 0 42E |
| Kemnay Scotland | 9 | G2 | 57 14N | 2 27W |
| Kempston England | 16 | C3 | 52 07N | 0 30W |
| Kempten Germany | 52 | E3 | 47 44N | 10 19E |
| Kendal England | 12 | D3 | 54 20N | 2 45W |
| Kenilworth England | 15 | E2 | 52 21N | 1 34W |
| Kenmare Rol | 21 | B1 | 51 53N | 9 35W |
| Kennacraig Scotland | 10 | D2 | 55 50N | 5 27W |
| Kennet r. England | 16 | B2 | 51 30N | 1 45W |
| Kennington England | 17 | D2 | 51 09N | 0 55E |
| Kennoway Scotland | 11 | F3 | 56 12N | 3 03W |
| Kenora Canada | 89 | S3 | 49 47N | 94 26W |
| Kent co. England | 17 | D2 | 51 10N | 0 45E |
| Kentford England | 17 | D3 | 52 16N | 0 30E |
| Kentucky state USA | 91 | J4 | 37 00N | 85 00W |
| Kerkrade Neths | 48 | B3 | 50 52N | 6 04E |
| Kérkyra i. Greece | 55 | H3 | 39 00N | 19 00E |
| Kerpen Germany | 48 | B3 | 50 52N | 6 42E |
| Kerrera i. Scotland | 8 | D1 | 56 25N | 5 34W |
| Kerry co. Rol | 21 | B2 | 52 10N | 9 30W |
| Kerry Head Rol | 21 | B2 | 52 25N | 9 55W |
| Kesh NI | 10 | B1 | 54 31N | 7 43W |
| Kessingland England | 17 | E3 | 52 25N | 1 42E |
| Keswick England | 12 | C3 | 54 37N | 3 08W |
| Kettering England | 15 | F2 | 52 24N | 0 44W |
| Keynsham England | 19 | E3 | 51 26N | 2 30W |
| Key West USA | 91 | K1 | 24 34N | 81 48W |
| Keyworth England | 15 | E2 | 52 52N | 1 05W |
| Khabarovsk Russia | 63 | R6 | 48 32N | 135 08E |
| Kharkiv Ukraine | 56 | E4 | 50 00N | 36 15E |
| Khartoum Sudan | 81 | M5 | 15 33N | 32 35E |
| Kherson Ukraine | 57 | D4 | 46 39N | 32 38E |
| Khmel'nyts'kyy Ukraine | 53 | N4 | 49 25N | 26 59E |
| Khulna Bangladesh | 67 | F4 | 22 49N | 89 34E |
| Khyber Pass Afghanistan/Pakistan | 66 | C6 | 34 06N | 71 05E |
| Kidderminster England | 15 | D2 | 52 23N | 2 14W |
| Kidlington England | 16 | B2 | 51 50N | 1 17W |
| Kidsgrove England | 12 | D2 | 53 05N | 2 14W |
| Kidwelly Wales | 14 | B1 | 51 45N | 4 18W |
| Kiel Germany | 52 | E7 | 54 20N | 10 08E |
| Kielce Poland | 53 | K5 | 50 51N | 20 39E |
| Kielder Water England | 12 | D4 | 55 10N | 2 30W |
| Kiev Ukraine | 53 | Q5 | 50 25N | 30 30E |
| Kigali Rwanda | 83 | B4 | 1 56S | 30 04E |
| Kigoma Tanzania | 83 | A2 | 4 52S | 29 36E |
| Kilbaha Rol | 21 | B2 | 52 35N | 9 52W |
| Kilbeggan Rol | 20 | D3 | 53 22N | 7 30W |
| Kilberry Rol | 20 | E3 | 53 42N | 6 41W |
| Kilbirnie Scotland | 11 | E2 | 55 46N | 4 41W |
| Kilbrannan Sound Scotland | 10 | D2 | 55 30N | 5 30W |
| Kilcavan Rol | 20 | D3 | 53 11N | 7 21W |
| Kilchoan Scotland | 8 | C1 | 56 43N | 6 06W |
| Kilcock Rol | 20 | E3 | 53 24N | 6 40W |
| Kilcormac Rol | 21 | D3 | 53 10N | 7 43W |
| Kilcreggan Scotland | 11 | E2 | 56 01N | 4 48W |
| Kilcullen Rol | 21 | E3 | 53 08N | 6 45W |
| Kildare Rol | 21 | E3 | 53 10N | 6 55W |
| Kildare co. Rol | 21 | E3 | 53 10N | 6 55W |
| Kildorrery Rol | 21 | C2 | 52 15N | 8 20W |
| Kilfinnane Rol | 21 | C2 | 52 22N | 8 28W |
| Kilgetty Wales | 14 | B1 | 51 45N | 4 44W |
| Kinglass Lough Rol | 20 | C3 | 53 50N | 8 01W |
| Kilimanjaro mt. Tanzania | 83 | E3 | 3 04S | 37 22E |
| Kilkeary Rol | 21 | C2 | 52 50N | 8 07W |
| Kilkee Rol | 21 | B2 | 52 41N | 9 38W |
| Kilkeel NI | 10 | C1 | 54 04N | 6 00W |
| Kilkelly Rol | 20 | C3 | 53 53N | 8 51W |
| Kilkenny co. Rol | 21 | D2 | 52 30N | 7 10W |
| Kilkenny Rol | 21 | D2 | 52 39N | 7 15W |
| Kilkhampton England | 18 | C2 | 50 53N | 4 29W |
| Kilkieran Bay Rol | 20 | B3 | 53 18N | 9 41W |
| Kilkishen Rol | 21 | C2 | 52 48N | 8 45W |
| Kill Rol | 20 | E3 | 53 15N | 6 35W |
| Killala Rol | 20 | B4 | 54 13N | 9 13W |
| Killaloe Rol | 21 | C2 | 52 48N | 8 27W |
| Killamarsh England | 13 | E2 | 53 20N | 1 20W |
| Killarney Rol | 21 | B2 | 52 03N | 9 30W |
| Killary Harbour Rol | 20 | B3 | 53 38N | 9 55W |
| Killeigh Rol | 20 | D3 | 53 13N | 7 27W |
| Killenaule Rol | 21 | D2 | 52 34N | 7 40W |
| Killimer Rol | 21 | B2 | 52 37N | 9 24W |
| Killimor Rol | 21 | C3 | 53 10N | 8 17W |
| Killin Scotland | 9 | E1 | 56 28N | 4 19W |
| Killorglin Rol | 21 | B2 | 52 06N | 9 47W |
| Killybegs Rol | 20 | C4 | 54 38N | 8 27W |
| Killyleagh NI | 10 | D1 | 54 24N | 5 39W |
| Kilmacolm Scotland | 11 | E2 | 55 54N | 4 38W |
| Kilmacrenan Rol | 20 | D5 | 55 02N | 7 47W |
| Kilmacthomas Rol | 21 | D2 | 52 12N | 7 25W |
| Kilmallock Rol | 21 | C2 | 52 23N | 8 34W |
| Kilmaluag Scotland | 8 | C2 | 57 41N | 6 17W |
| Kilmarnock Scotland | 11 | E2 | 55 36N | 4 30W |
| Kilmona Rol | 21 | C1 | 51 58N | 8 33W |
| Kilmory Scotland | 10 | D2 | 55 55N | 5 41W |
| Kilrea NI | 10 | C1 | 54 57N | 6 33W |
| Kilrenny Scotland | 11 | G3 | 56 15N | 2 41W |
| Kilrush Rol | 21 | B2 | 52 39N | 9 30W |
| Kilsheelan Rol | 21 | D2 | 52 22N | 7 35W |
| Kilsyth Scotland | 11 | E2 | 55 59N | 4 04W |
| Kiltamagh Rol | 20 | B3 | 53 51N | 9 00W |
| Kiltealy Rol | 21 | E2 | 52 34N | 6 45W |
| Kiltullagh Rol | 21 | C3 | 53 35N | 8 35W |
| Kilwinning Scotland | 11 | E2 | 55 40N | 4 42W |
| Kimberley Canada | 88 | M3 | 49 40N | 115 58W |
| Kimberley England | 15 | E2 | 53 00N | 1 17W |
| Kimberley RSA | 82 | D2 | 28 45S | 24 46E |
| Kimbolton England | 15 | F3 | 52 18N | 0 24W |
| Kinbrace Scotland | 9 | F3 | 58 15N | 3 56W |
| Kineton England | 15 | E2 | 52 10N | 1 30W |
| Kingsbridge England | 18 | D1 | 50 17N | 3 46W |
| Kingsclere England | 16 | B2 | 51 20N | 1 14W |
| Kingscourt Rol | 20 | E3 | 53 53N | 6 48W |
| Kingskerswell England | 18 | D2 | 50 30N | 3 37W |
| Kings Langley England | 16 | C2 | 51 43N | 0 28W |
| King's Lynn England | 17 | D2 | 52 45N | 0 24E |
| Kings Muir Scotland | 11 | F2 | 55 40N | 3 12W |
| Kingsport USA | 91 | K4 | 36 33N | 82 34W |
| Kingsteignton England | 18 | D2 | 50 33N | 3 35W |
| Kingston Jamaica | 95 | U13 | 17 58N | 76 48W |
| Kingston upon Hull England | 13 | F2 | 53 45N | 0 20W |
| Kingston-upon-Thames England | 16 | C2 | 51 25N | 0 18W |
| Kingswood England | 15 | D1 | 51 28N | 2 30W |
| Kington England | 14 | C2 | 52 12N | 3 01W |
| Kingussie Scotland | 9 | E2 | 57 05N | 4 03W |
| Kinloch Scotland | 8 | C2 | 57 01N | 6 17W |
| Kinlocheil Scotland | 8 | D1 | 56 51N | 5 20W |
| Kinlochewe Scotland | 8 | D2 | 57 36N | 5 20W |
| Kinlochleven Scotland | 9 | E1 | 56 42N | 4 58W |
| Kinloch Rannoch Scotland | 9 | E1 | 56 42N | 4 11W |
| Kinloss Scotland | 9 | F2 | 57 38N | 3 33W |
| Kinlough Rol | 20 | C4 | 54 27N | 8 17W |
| Kinnaird Head Scotland | 9 | G2 | 57 40N | 2 00W |
| Kinnegad Rol | 20 | D3 | 53 27N | 7 05W |
| Kinnitty Rol | 21 | D3 | 53 06N | 7 43W |
| Kinross Scotland | 11 | F3 | 56 13N | 3 27W |
| Kinsale Rol | 21 | C1 | 51 42N | 8 32W |
| Kinsale Harbour Rol | 21 | C1 | 51 40N | 8 30W |
| Kinshasa CDR | 82 | C7 | 4 18S | 15 18E |
| Kintore Scotland | 9 | G2 | 57 13N | 2 21W |
| Kintyre p. Scotland | 10 | D2 | 55 30N | 5 35W |
| Kinvarra Rol | 21 | C3 | 53 08N | 8 56W |
| Kippax England | 13 | E2 | 53 46N | 1 22W |
| Kippford Scotland | 11 | F1 | 54 52N | 3 49W |
| Kirby Muxloe England | 15 | E2 | 52 38N | 1 14W |
| Kirkby England | 13 | D1 | 55 24N | 5 28W |
| Kirkby in Ashfield England | 13 | E2 | 53 13N | 1 15W |
| Kirkby Londsale England | 12 | D3 | 54 13N | 2 36W |
| Kirkbymoorside England | 13 | F3 | 54 16N | 0 55W |
| Kirkby Stephen England | 12 | D3 | 54 28N | 2 20W |
| Kirkcaldy Scotland | 11 | F3 | 56 07N | 3 10W |
| Kirkcolm Scotland | 10 | D1 | 54 58N | 5 04W |
| Kirkconnel Scotland | 11 | E2 | 55 23N | 4 00W |
| Kirkcowan Scotland | 11 | E1 | 54 55N | 4 36W |
| Kirkcudbright Scotland | 11 | E1 | 54 50N | 4 03W |
| Kirkgunzeon Scotland | 11 | F1 | 54 58N | 3 46W |
| Kirkham England | 12 | D2 | 53 47N | 2 53W |
| Kirkintilloch Scotland | 11 | E2 | 55 57N | 4 10W |
| Kirkmuirhill Scotland | 11 | F2 | 55 39N | 3 55W |
| Kirkpatrick Durham Scotland | 11 | F2 | 55 01N | 3 54W |
| Kirk Sandall England | 13 | E2 | 53 34N | 1 04W |
| Kirkwall Scotland | 7 | B1 | 58 59N | 2 58W |
| Kirov Russia | 62 | G8 | 58 00N | 49 38E |
| Kirovohrad Ukraine | 56 | D4 | 48 31N | 32 15E |
| Kirriemuir Scotland | 9 | F1 | 56 41N | 3 01W |
| Kirton England | 16 | C3 | 52 56N | 0 04W |
| Kisangani CDR | 81 | L2 | 0 33N | 25 14E |
| Kismaayo Somalia | 81 | P1 | 0 25S | 42 31E |
| Kisumu Kenya | 83 | D4 | 0 08S | 34 47E |
| Kita-Kyūshū Japan | 70 | B1 | 33 52N | 130 49E |
| Kitami Japan | 70 | D3 | 43 51N | 143 54E |
| Kitchener Canada | 89 | U2 | 43 27N | 80 30W |
| Kitimat Canada | 88 | K4 | 54 05N | 128 38W |
| Kitwe Zambia | 82 | E5 | 12 50S | 28 12E |
| Kitzbühel Austria | 52 | F3 | 47 27N | 12 23E |
| Klaipėda Lithuania | 49 | F1 | 55 43N | 21 07E |
| Klamath Falls tn. USA | 90 | B5 | 42 14N | 121 47W |
| Klöfta Norway | 49 | D3 | 60 04N | 11 06E |
| Knapdale Scotland | 10 | D2 | 55 52N | 5 31W |
| Knaresborough England | 13 | E3 | 54 00N | 1 27W |
| Knighton England | 14 | C2 | 52 21N | 3 03W |
| Knock Rol | 20 | C3 | 53 47N | 8 55W |
| Knockadoon Head Rol | 21 | D1 | 51 50N | 7 50W |
| Knockanevin Rol | 21 | C2 | 52 17N | 8 21W |
| Knockdrislagh Rol | 21 | C2 | 52 03N | 8 41W |
| Knocktopher Rol | 21 | D2 | 52 29N | 7 13W |
| Knokke-Heist Belgium | 48 | B4 | 51 21N | 3 19E |
| Knottingley England | 13 | E2 | 53 43N | 1 14W |
| Knowle England | 15 | E2 | 52 23N | 1 43W |
| Knoxville USA | 91 | K4 | 36 00N | 83 57W |
| Knutsford England | 12 | D2 | 53 18N | 2 23W |
| Kōbe Japan | 70 | C1 | 34 40N | 135 12E |
| Koblenz Germany | 52 | C5 | 50 21N | 7 36E |
| Kōfu Japan | 70 | C2 | 35 42N | 138 34E |
| Kokkola Finland | 49 | F3 | 62 45N | 30 06E |
| Kolhapur India | 66 | C3 | 16 40N | 74 20E |
| Kolkata India | 67 | F4 | 22 30N | 88 20E |
| Komatsu Japan | 70 | C2 | 36 25N | 136 27E |
| Komotiní Greece | 55 | L4 | 41 06N | 25 25E |
| Köniz Switz. | 52 | C3 | 46 56N | 7 25E |
| Konstanz Germany | 52 | D3 | 47 40N | 9 10E |
| Konya Turkey | 57 | D2 | 37 51N | 32 30E |
| Konz Germany | 48 | B2 | 49 42N | 6 35E |
| Koper Slovenia | 54 | E6 | 45 31N | 13 44E |
| Korbach Germany | 52 | D5 | 51 16N | 8 53E |
| Korinthiakós Kólpos g. Greece | 55 | K3 | 38 00N | 22 00E |
| Kórinthos Greece | 55 | K2 | 37 56N | 22 55E |
| Kortrijk Belgium | 48 | B3 | 50 50N | 3 17E |
| Kós i. Greece | 55 | M2 | 36 45N | 27 10E |
| Košice Slovakia | 53 | K4 | 48 44N | 21 15E |
| Koszalin Poland | 53 | H7 | 54 10N | 16 10E |
| Kotka Finland | 49 | G3 | 60 26N | 26 55E |
| Kovrov Russia | 56 | F6 | 56 23N | 41 21E |
| Kozáni Greece | 55 | J4 | 40 18N | 21 48E |
| Kragujevac Serbia | 55 | J5 | 44 01N | 20 55E |
| Kraków Poland | 53 | J5 | 50 03N | 19 55E |
| Kranj Slovenia | 54 | F7 | 46 15N | 14 20E |
| Krefeld Germany | 52 | C5 | 51 20N | 6 32E |
| Krems Austria | 52 | G4 | 48 25N | 15 36E |
| Kristiansand Norway | 49 | C2 | 58 08N | 8 01E |
| Kristianstad Sweden | 49 | D2 | 56 02N | 14 10E |
| Kriti i. Greece | 55 | L3 | 35 00N | 25 00E |
| Kryvyy Roh Ukraine | 56 | D4 | 47 55N | 33 24E |
| Kuala Lumpur Malaysia | 71 | C4 | 3 09N | 101 42E |
| Kuching Malaysia | 71 | E4 | 1 35N | 110 21E |
| Kufstein Austria | 52 | F3 | 47 36N | 12 11E |
| Kumamoto Japan | 70 | B1 | 32 50N | 130 42E |
| Kunlun Shan mts. China | 68 | D5/E5 | 36 30N | 85 00E |
| Kunming China | 69 | H3 | 25 04N | 102 41E |
| Kurashiki Japan | 70 | B1 | 34 36N | 133 43E |
| Kurgan Russia | 62 | J8 | 55 30N | 65 20E |
| Kuril Islands Russia | 63 | T6 | 50 00N | 155 00E |
| Kursk Russia | 62 | F7 | 51 45N | 36 14E |
| Kushiro Japan | 70 | D3 | 42 58N | 144 24E |
| KUWAIT | 65 | E4 | | |
| Kuwait Kuwait | 65 | E4 | 29 20N | 48 00E |
| Kuytun China | 68 | D6 | 44 30N | 85 00E |
| Kwangju S. Korea | 69 | N5 | 35 07N | 126 52E |
| Kyleakin Scotland | 8 | D2 | 57 16N | 5 44W |
| Kyle of Lochalsh Scotland | 8 | D2 | 57 17N | 5 43W |
| Kyles of Bute Scotland | 10 | D2 | 55 52N | 5 13W |
| Kylestrome Scotland | 9 | D3 | 58 16N | 5 02W |
| Kyōto Japan | 70 | C2 | 35 02N | 135 45E |
| KYRGYZSTAN | 62 | K5 | | |
| Kythira i. Greece | 55 | K2 | 36 00N | 23 00E |
| Kýthnos i. Greece | 55 | L2 | 37 25N | 24 25E |
| Kyūshū i. Japan | 70 | B1 | 32 20N | 131 00E |

### L

| Place | Pg | Grid | Lat. | Long. |
|---|---|---|---|---|
| Laâyoune Western Sahara | 80 | B7 | 27 10N | 13 11W |
| Labrador geog. reg. Canada | 89 | Y4 | 54 00N | 63 00W |
| la Chaux-de-Fonds Switz. | 52 | C3 | 47 07N | 6 51E |
| la Ciotat France | 50 | G2 | 43 10N | 5 36E |
| Lac Léman Switzerland | 52 | C3 | 46 20N | 6 20E |
| La Crosse USA | 91 | H5 | 43 48N | 91 04W |
| Lacul Razim l. Romania | 53 | P2 | 45 00N | 29 00E |
| Ladozhskoye Ozero l. Russia | 62 | F9 | 61 00N | 30 00E |
| Ladybank Scotland | 11 | F3 | 56 17N | 3 08W |
| Lagan r. NI | 10 | C1 | 54 30N | 6 05W |
| Laggan Bay b. Scotland | 10 | C2 | 55 38N | 6 17W |
| Lago di Como l. Italy | 54 | C6 | 46 00N | 9 00E |
| Lago di Garda l. Italy | 54 | D6 | 45 00N | 10 00E |
| Lago Maggiore l. Italy | 54 | C6 | 46 00N | 8 00E |
| Lagos Nigeria | 80 | E3 | 6 27N | 3 28E |
| Lagos Portugal | 51 | A2 | 37 05N | 8 40W |
| Lago Titicaca l. Peru/Bolivia | 96 | C10/D10 | 16 00S | 69 30W |
| La Grande USA | 90 | C6 | 45 21N | 118 05W |
| La Grande Rivière Canada | 89 | W4 | 54 00N | 74 00W |
| Lahore Pakistan | 66 | C6 | 31 34N | 74 22E |
| Lahti Finland | 49 | G3 | 61 00N | 25 40E |
| Lairg Scotland | 9 | E3 | 58 01N | 4 25W |
| Lakenheath England | 17 | D3 | 52 25N | 0 31E |
| La Línea de la Concepción Spain | 51 | C2 | 36 10N | 5 21W |
| La Maddalena Italy | 54 | C4 | 41 13N | 9 25E |

Lamar USA 90 F4 38 04N 102 37W
Lambay Island RoI 20 E3 53 29N 6 01W
Lambourn England 16 B2 51 31N 1 31W
Lambourn r. England 16 B2 51 27N 1 28W
Lamego Portugal 51 B4 41 05N 7 49W
Lamía Greece 55 K3 38 55N 22 26E
Lamlash 10 D2 55 32N 5 08W
Lammermuir Hills Scotland 11 G2 55 50N 2 45W
Lampeter Wales 14 B2 52 07N 4 05W
Lanark Scotland 11 F2 55 41N 3 48W
Lancashire co. England 12 D2 53 50N 2 30W
Lancaster England 12 D3 54 03N 2 48W
Lanchester England 13 E3 54 50N 1 44W
Lancing England 16 C1 50 50N 0 19W
Landerneau France 50 B5 48 27N 4 16W
Land's End c. England 18 B2 50 03N 5 44W
Landshut Germany 52 F4 48 31N 12 10E
Landskrona Sweden 49 D2 55 53N 12 50E
Langdon USA 92 A3 48 46N 98 21W
Langholm Scotland 11 F2 55 09N 3 00W
Langport England 19 E3 51 02N 2 50W
Langres France 50 G4 47 53N 5 20E
Lannion France 50 C5 48 44N 3 27W
L'Anse USA 92 C3 46 45N 88 27W
Lansing USA 91 K5 42 44N 85 34W
Lanzarote i. Spain 80 B7 29 00N 13 38W
Lanzhou China 69 H5 36 01N 103 45E
Laois co. RoI 21 D2 52 59N 7 25W
Laon France 50 F5 49 34N 3 37E
LAOS 71 C7/D7
La Paz Bolivia 96 D10 16 30S 68 10W
Lapford England 18 D2 50 52N 3 47W
La Plata Argentina 97 F6 34 52S 57 55W
Lappland geog. reg. Finland/Sweden 49 F4/G4 67 30N 20 05E
Lapua Finland 49 F3 62 57N 23 00E
L'Aquila Italy 54 E5 42 22N 13 24E
Laragh RoI 21 E3 53 00N 6 18W
Laredo USA 90 G2 27 32N 99 22W
Largs Scotland 10 E2 55 48N 4 52W
Lárisa Greece 55 K3 39 38N 22 25E
Larkhall Scotland 11 F2 55 45N 3 59W
Larne NI 10 D1 54 51N 5 49W
Larne district NI 10 D1 54 50N 6 00W
Larne Lough b. NI 10 D1 54 49N 5 49W
la Rochelle France 50 D4 46 10N 1 10W
la Roche-sur-Yon France 50 D4 46 40N 1 25W
La Roda Spain 51 D3 39 13N 2 15W
La See d'Urgel Spain 51 F5 42 22N 1 27E
la Seyne-sur-Mer France 50 G2 43 06N 5 53E
Las Palmas Spain 80 A7 28 08N 15 27W
La Spézia Italy 54 C6 44 07N 9 49E
Las Vegas USA 90 C4 36 10N 115 10W
Latakia Syria 64 C6 35 31N 35 47E
Latheron Scotland 9 F3 58 17N 3 22W
Latina Italy 54 E4 41 28N 12 53E
LATVIA 49 G2
Lauder Scotland 11 G2 55 43N 2 45W
Laugharne Wales 14 B1 51 47N 4 28W
Launceston Australia 73 J2 41 25S 147 07E
Launceston England 18 C2 50 38N 4 21W
Lauragh RoI 21 B1 51 45N 9 46W
Laurel USA 91 J3 31 41N 89 09W
Laurencekirk Scotland 9 G1 56 50N 2 29W
Laurencetown RoI 20 C3 53 14N 8 10W
Laurieston Scotland 11 E1 54 57N 4 03W
Laurieston Scotland 11 F2 55 59N 3 45W
Lausanne Switz. 52 C3 46 32N 6 39E
Laval France 50 D5 48 04N 0 45W
Lavenham England 17 D3 52 06N 0 47E
Lawrence USA 91 G4 38 58N 95 15W
Lawton USA 91 G3 34 36N 98 25W
Laxey Isle of Man 12 B3 54 14N 4 24W
Laxford Bridge tn. Scotland 9 D3 58 22N 5 01W
Lay r. France 50 D4 46 32N 1 15W
Lazonby England 12 D3 54 46N 2 41W
Lea r. England 16 C2 51 47N 0 17W
Leach r. England 15 E1 51 46N 1 44W
Leadhills Scotland 11 F2 55 25N 3 47W
Leadon r. England 15 D1 51 57N 2 21W
Leatherhead England 16 C2 51 18N 0 20W
LEBANON 64 C5
Lebanon USA 91 H4 37 40N 92 40W
le Blanc France 50 E4 46 38N 1 04E
Lebrija Spain 51 B2 36 55N 6 10W
Lecarrow RoI 20 C3 53 33N 8 00W
Lecce Italy 55 H4 40 21N 18 11E
Lechlade England 15 E1 51 43N 1 41W
le Creusot France 50 G4 46 48N 4 27E
Ledbury England 15 D2 52 02N 2 25W
Ledmore Scotland 9 E3 58 03N 4 58W
Leeds England 13 E2 53 50N 1 35W
Leek England 12 D2 53 06N 2 01W
Leenaun RoI 20 B3 53 36N 9 41W
Leeuwarden Neths 48 D6 53 12N 5 48E
Leeward Islands Lesser Antilles 95 M3 17 30N 64 00W
Lefkáda i. Greece 55 J3 38 45N 20 40E
Leganés Spain 51 D4 40 20N 3 46W
Legnica Poland 53 H5 51 12N 16 10E
le Havre France 50 E5 49 30N 0 06E
Leicester England 15 E2 52 38N 1 05W

Leicester City u.a. England 15 E2 52 38N 1 05W
Leicestershire co. England 15 E2 52 40N 1 20W
Leiden Neths 48 C5 52 10N 4 30E
Leigh England 12 D2 53 30N 2 33W
Leighton Buzzard England 16 C2 51 55N 0 41W
Leipzig Germany 52 F5 51 20N 12 25E
Leiria Portugal 51 A3 39 45N 8 49W
Leiston England 17 E3 52 13N 1 34E
Leith Hill tn. England 16 C2 51 11N 0 23W
Leitrim co. RoI 20 C4 54 05N 8 00W
Leivadiá Greece 55 K3 38 26N 22 53E
Leixlip RoI 20 E3 53 22N 6 30W
le Mans France 50 E4 48 00N 0 12E
Lemybrien RoI 21 D2 52 10N 7 31W
Lena r. Russia 63 Q10 70 00N 125 00E
Lens France 50 F6 50 26N 2 50E
Leoben Austria 52 G3 47 23N 15 06E
Leominster England 14 D2 52 14N 2 45W
León Mexico 94 D4 21 10N 101 42W
León Spain 51 C5 42 35N 5 34W
Leonding Austria 52 G4 48 19N 14 17E
le Puy France 50 F3 45 03N 3 53E
Lerwick Scotland 7 C3 60 09N 1 09W
Lesmahagow Scotland 11 F2 55 38N 3 54W
LESOTHO 82 E2
les Sables-d'Olonne France 50 D4 46 30N 1 47W
Lesser Antilles is. W. Indies 95 M2/M3 18 00N 65 00W
Lesser Slave Lake Canada 88 M5 55 25N 115 30W
Lésvos i. Greece 55 M3 39 00N 26 00E
Leswalt Scotland 10 D1 54 46N 5 05W
Letchworth England 16 C2 51 58N 0 14W
le Touquet-Paris-Plage France 50 E6 50 13N 1 36E
le Tréport France 50 E6 50 04N 1 22E
Letterfrack RoI 20 B3 53 33N 9 57W
Letterkenny RoI 20 D4 54 57N 7 44W
Leuchars Scotland 9 G1 56 23N 2 53W
Levanto Italy 54 C6 44 10N 9 37E
Leven England 13 F2 53 54N 0 19W
Leven Scotland 11 G3 56 11N 3 00W
Leverburgh Scotland 8 B2 57 45N 7 00W
Leverkusen Germany 52 C5 51 02N 6 59E
Lewes England 16 D1 50 52N 0 01E
Lewis i. Scotland 8 C3 58 15N 6 40W
Lexington USA 91 K4 38 03N 84 30W
Lexington USA 93 E1 37 47N 79 27W
Leyburn England 13 E3 54 19N 1 49W
Leyland England 12 D2 53 42N 2 42W
Leysdown on Sea England 17 D2 51 24N 0 55E
Lhasa China 68 F3 29 41N 91 10E
LIBERIA 80 B3/C3
Libourne France 50 D3 44 55N 0 14W
Libreville Gabon 80 F2 0 30N 9 25E
LIBYA 81 G7/K7
Libyan Desert North Africa 81 K7/L6 25 00N 25 00E
Lichfield England 15 E2 52 42N 1 48W
LIECHTENSTEIN 52 D3
Liège Belgium 48 D3 50 38N 5 35E
Lienz Austria 52 F3 46 51N 12 50E
Liepája Latvia 49 F2 56 30N 21 00E
Liffey r. RoI 20 E3 53 16N 6 37W
Lifford RoI 20 D4 54 50N 7 29W
Likasi CDR 82 E5 10 58S 26 47E
Lille France 50 F6 50 39N 3 05E
Lillehammer Norway 49 D3 61 06N 10 27E
Lilongwe Malawi 82 F5 13 58S 33 49E
Lima Peru 96 B11 12 06S 77 03W
Limavady NI 10 C1 54 30N 6 57W
Limavady district NI 10 B1/C1 54 50N 7 00W
Limburg Germany 52 D5 50 23N 8 04E
Limerick RoI 21 C2 52 04N 8 38W
Limerick co. RoI 21 C2 52 30N 8 40W
Limoges France 50 E3 45 50N 1 15E
Limoux France 50 F2 43 03N 2 13E
Limpopo r. Southern Africa 82 F3 22 30S 32 00E
Linares Spain 51 D3 38 05N 3 38W
Lincoln England 13 F2 53 14N 0 33W
Lincoln USA 91 G5 40 49N 96 41W
Lincolnshire co. England 13 F2 53 10N 0 20W
Lincoln Wolds England 13 F2 53 25N 0 05W
Lingen Germany 52 C6 52 32N 7 19E
Lingfield England 16 C2 51 11N 0 01W
Linköping Sweden 49 E2 58 25N 15 35E
Linlithgow Scotland 11 F2 55 59N 3 37W
Linslade England 16 C2 51 55N 0 42W
Linton England 17 D3 52 06N 0 17E
Linz Austria 52 G4 48 19N 14 18E
Liphook England 16 C2 51 05N 0 49W
Lippstadt Germany 52 D5 51 41N 8 20E
Lisballaw NI 10 B1 54 19N 7 32W
Lisbon Portugal 51 A3 38 44N 9 08W
Lisburn NI 10 C1 54 31N 6 03W
Lisburn district NI 10 C1 54 35N 6 10W
Liscannor Bay RoI 21 B2 52 55N 9 24W
Lisdoonvarna RoI 21 B3 53 02N 9 17W
Lisieux France 50 E5 49 09N 0 14E
Liskeard England 18 C2 50 28N 4 28W

Lismore RoI 21 D2 52 08N 7 55W
Lismore i. Scotland 8 D1 56 30N 5 30W
Lisnaskea NI 10 B1 54 15N 7 27W
Liss England 16 C2 51 03N 0 55W
Lisse Neths 48 C5 52 16N 4 34E
Lissycasey RoI 21 B2 52 44N 9 12W
Listowel RoI 21 B2 52 27N 9 29W
Litherland England 12 D2 53 28N 2 59W
LITHUANIA 49 F2
Littleborough England 12 D2 53 39N 2 05W
Littlehampton England 16 C1 50 48N 0 33W
Little Minch sd. Scotland 8 C2 57 45N 6 30W
Little Ouse r. England 17 D3 52 30N 0 30E
Littleport England 17 D3 52 28N 0 19E
Liverpool England 12 D2 53 25N 2 55W
Liverpool Bay England 12 D2 53 28N 3 15W
Liversedge England 13 E2 53 43N 1 41W
Livingston Scotland 11 F2 55 53N 3 32W
Livorno Italy 54 D5 43 33N 10 18E
Lizard England 18 B1 49 57N 5 13W
Lizard Point England 18 B1 49 56N 5 13W
Ljubljana Slovenia 54 F7 46 04N 14 30E
Ljusdal Sweden 49 E3 61 57N 16 05E
Llanberis Wales 14 B3 53 07N 4 06W
Llanbister Wales 14 C2 52 21N 3 19W
Llandeilo Wales 14 C1 51 53N 3 59W
Llandovery Wales 14 C1 51 59N 3 48W
Llandrindod Wells Wales 14 C2 52 15N 3 23W
Llandudno Wales 14 C3 53 19N 3 49W
Llandysul Wales 14 B2 52 02N 4 19W
Llanelli Wales 14 B1 51 42N 4 10W
Llanerchymedd Wales 14 B3 53 20N 4 22W
Llanes Spain 51 C3 43 25N 4 45W
Llanfair Caereinion Wales 14 C2 52 39N 3 20W
Llanfairfechan Wales 14 C3 53 15N 3 58W
Llanfyllin Wales 14 C2 52 46N 3 17W
Llangadfan Wales 14 C2 52 41N 3 28W
Llangadog Wales 14 C1 51 57N 3 53W
Llangefni Wales 14 B3 53 16N 4 18W
Llangollen Wales 14 C2 52 58N 3 10W
Llangurig Wales 14 C2 52 25N 3 36W
Llangynog Wales 14 C2 52 50N 3 25W
Llanharan Wales 14 C1 51 32N 3 28W
Llanidloes Wales 14 C2 52 27N 3 32W
Llanrhystud Wales 14 B2 52 18N 4 09W
Llanrwst Wales 14 C3 53 08N 3 48W
Llantrisant Wales 14 C1 51 33N 3 23W
Llantwit Major Wales 14 C1 51 25N 3 30W
Llanuwchllyn Wales 14 C2 52 52N 3 41W
Llanwrtyd Wells Wales 14 C2 52 07N 3 38W
Llanybydder Wales 14 B2 52 04N 4 09W
Lleida Spain 51 F4 41 37N 0 38E
Lleyn Peninsula Wales 14 B2 52 53N 4 30W
Llyn Brianne Resevoir Wales 14 C2 52 09N 3 43W
Llyn Celyn Wales 14 C3 53 04N 4 10W
Llyn Efyrnwy Wales 14 C2 52 50N 3 30W
Llyn Tegid Wales 14 C2 52 53N 3 38W
Loanhead Scotland 11 F2 55 53N 3 09W
Loch Affric Scotland 9 D2 57 15N 5 02W
Lochailort tn. Scotland 8 D1 56 53N 5 40W
Lochaline tn. Scotland 8 D1 56 32N 5 47W
Loch Alsh Scotland 8 D2 57 15N 5 35W
Locharbriggs Scotland 11 F2 55 06N 3 35W
Loch Assynt Scotland 9 D3/E3 58 05N 5 00W
Loch Awe Scotland 10 D3 56 15N 5 17W
Lochboisdale tn. Scotland 8 B2 57 09N 7 19W
Loch Bracadale Scotland 8 C2 57 20N 6 30W
Loch Broom Scotland 8 D2 57 52N 5 08W
Loch Caolisport Scotland 10 D2 55 53N 5 38W
Lochcarron tn. Scotland 8 D2 57 24N 5 30W
Loch Carron Scotland 8 D2 57 40N 5 45W
Loch Chroisg Scotland 8 D2 57 30N 5 10W
Loch Craignish Scotland 10 D3 56 05N 5 30W
Loch Creran Scotland 8 D1 56 30N 5 20W
Lochdon tn. Scotland 8 D2 56 35N 5 35W
Loch Duich Scotland 8 D2 57 15N 5 30W
Loch Earn Scotland 9 F1 56 23N 4 10W
Lochearnhead Scotland 9 E1 56 23N 4 18W
Loch Eil Scotland 8 D1 56 50N 5 25W
Loch Eishort Scotland 8 C2/D2 57 08N 6 00W
Loch Eriboll Scotland 9 E3 58 31N 4 41W
Loch Ericht Scotland 9 E1 56 48N 4 25W
Loch Erisort Scotland 8 C3 58 05N 6 30W
Loches France 50 E4 47 08N 1 00E
Loch Etive Scotland 8 D1 56 30N 5 10W
Loch Ewe Scotland 8 D2 57 50N 5 40W
Loch Eynort Scotland 8 B2 57 10N 7 15W
Loch Fannich Scotland 9 E2 57 40N 5 00W
Loch Fyne Scotland 10 D3 56 00N 5 20W
Loch Gairloch Scotland 8 D2 57 45N 5 45W
Lochgelly Scotland 11 F3 56 08N 3 19W
Lochgilphead Scotland 10 D3 56 03N 5 26W
Loch Glass Scotland 9 E2 57 40N 4 30W
Loch Goil Scotland 10 D3 56 10N 4 55W
Loch Gorm Scotland 10 C2 55 49N 6 24W
Loch Gruinart Scotland 10 C2 55 51N 6 21W
Loch Hope Scotland 9 E3 58 25N 4 37W
Loch Indaal Scotland 10 C2 55 45N 6 21W
Lochinver Scotland 8 D3 58 09N 5 15W
Loch Katrine Scotland 11 E3 56 16N 4 30W

Loch Ken Scotland 11 E2 55 02N 4 07W
Loch Laggan Scotland 9 E1 56 55N 4 30W
Loch Langavet Scotland 8 C3 58 05N 6 50W
Loch Leven Scotland 9 D1/E1 56 45N 5 05W
Loch Leven Scotland 9 D1 56 15N 3 23W
Loch Leven Scotland 11 F3 56 15N 3 23W
Loch Linnhe Scotland 8 D1 56 35N 5 25W
Loch Lochy Scotland 9 E1 56 58N 4 55W
Loch Lomond Scotland 11 E3 56 10N 4 35W
Loch Long Scotland 10 E3 56 05N 4 55W
Loch Lyon Scotland 9 E1 56 30N 4 35W
Lochmaben Scotland 11 F2 55 08N 3 27W
Lochmaddy Scotland 8 B2 57 36N 7 08W
Loch Maree Scotland 8 D2 57 40N 5 30W
Loch Meig Scotland 9 E2 57 05N 4 45W
Loch Melfort Scotland 10 D3 56 10N 5 30W
Loch Monar Scotland 9 D2 57 25N 5 02W
Loch Morar Scotland 9 D1 57 55N 5 45W
Loch More Scotland 9 E3 58 15N 4 55W
Loch Mullardoch Scotland 9 D2 57 27N 4 58W
Lochnagar mt. Scotland 9 F1 56 57N 3 16W
Loch Nan Clar Scotland 9 E3 58 15N 4 05W
Loch Ness Scotland 9 E2 57 02N 4 30W
Loch Nevis Scotland 8 D1/D2 57 00N 5 40W
Loch of Harray Scotland 7 A2 59 02N 3 14W
Lochranza tn. Scotland 10 D2 55 42N 5 18W
Loch Roag Scotland 8 C3 58 10N 6 50W
Loch Ryan Scotland 10 D2 55 00N 5 05W
Loch Scridain Scotland 8 C1 56 20N 6 05W
Loch Seaforth Scotland 8 C2 58 00N 6 40W
Loch Shell Scotland 8 C2 58 00N 6 25W
Loch Shiel Scotland 8 D1 56 45N 5 35W
Loch Shin Scotland 8 E3 58 05N 4 30W
Loch Snizort Scotland 8 C2 57 30N 6 30W
Loch Striven Scotland 10 D2 55 58N 5 07W
Loch Sunart Scotland 8 D1 56 40N 5 45W
Loch Sween Scotland 10 D2 55 58N 5 38W
Loch Tarbert Scotland 10 D2 55 57N 5 55W
Loch Tay Scotland 9 E1 56 31N 4 10W
Loch Torridon Scotland 8 D2 57 35N 5 46W
Lockerbie Scotland 11 F2 55 07N 3 22W
Lockhart USA 91 G2 29 54N 97 14W
Locks Heath England 16 B1 50 52N 1 17W
Loddon England 17 E3 52 32N 1 29E
Łódz Poland 53 J5 51 49N 19 28E
Lofoten Islands Norway 49 D4 68 30N 15 00E
Lofthouse Gate England 13 E2 53 44N 1 30W
Loftus England 13 F3 54 33N 0 53W
Logan, Mount Canada 88 G6 60 34N 140 25W
Logroño Spain 51 D5 42 28N 2 26W
Loire r. France 50 D4 47 20N 1 20W
Loja Spain 51 C2 37 10N 4 09W
Lolland i. Denmark 49 D1 54 45N 12 20E
Lomé Togo 80 E3 6 10N 1 21E
London Canada 89 U2 42 58N 81 15W
London England 16 C2 51 30N 0 10W
Londonderry NI 10 B1 54 59N 7 19W
Londonderry district NI 10 B1 54 50N 7 00W
Londrina Brazil 96 G9 23 18S 51 13W
Long Beach tn. USA 90 C3 33 47N 118 15W
Longbenton England 13 E4 55 02N 1 35W
Long Crendon England 16 C2 51 47N 0 59W
Long Eaton England 15 E2 52 54N 1 15W
Longford RoI 20 D3 53 44N 7 47W
Longford co. RoI 20 D3 53 40N 7 50W
Longhorsley England 13 E4 55 15N 1 46W
Longhoughton England 11 H2 56 26N 1 36W
Long Melford England 17 D3 52 05N 0 43E
Longridge England 12 D2 53 51N 2 36W
Long Sutton England 17 D2 52 47N 0 08E
Longuyon France 50 G5 49 27N 5 36E
Longwy France 50 G5 49 32N 5 46E
Lons-le-Saunier France 50 G4 46 41N 5 33E
Looe England 18 C2 51 21N 4 27W
Loop Head RoI 21 B2 52 30N 9 55W
Lora del Rio Spain 51 C2 37 39N 5 32W
Lorca Spain 51 D2 37 40N 1 41W
Loreto Italy 54 E5 43 36N 13 36E
Lorient France 50 C4 47 45N 3 21W
Los Angeles USA 90 C3 34 00N 118 15W
Lossiemouth Scotland 9 F2 57 43N 3 18W
Lostwithiel England 18 C2 50 24N 4 40W
Loudéac France 50 C5 48 11N 2 45W
Lough Allen RoI 20 C4/D4 54 15N 8 00W
Lough Arrow RoI 20 C4 54 04N 8 20W
Loughborough England 15 E2 52 47N 1 11W
Lough Carra RoI 20 B3 53 40N 9 15W
Lough Conn RoI 20 B4 54 04N 9 10W
Lough Corrib RoI 20 B3 53 10N 9 10W
Lough Cullin RoI 20 B4 53 58N 9 10W
Lough Dan RoI 21 E3 53 05N 6 17W
Lough Derg Donegal RoI 20 D4 54 35N 7 55W
Lough Derg Tipperary RoI 21 C2 52 55N 8 15W
Lough Derravaragh RoI 20 D3 53 40N 7 22W
Lough Ennell RoI 20 D3 53 28N 7 24W
Lough Eske RoI 20 C4 54 41N 8 05W
Lough Feeagh RoI 20 B3 53 57N 9 35W
Lough Finn RoI 20 C4 54 51N 8 08W
Lough Graney RoI 21 C2 52 59N 8 40W
Lough Kinale RoI 20 D3 53 46N 7 25W

Lough Leane Rol 21 B2 52 03N 9 33W
Lough Macnean Lower NI 10 B1 54 17N 7 50W
Lough Macnean Upper NI/Rol 10 B1 54 18N 7 55W
Lough Mask Rol 20 B3 53 40N 9 30W
Lough Melvin Rol/NI 20 C4 54 25N 8 05W
Lough Neagh NI 10 C1 54 35N 6 30W
Loughrea tn. Rol 20 C3 53 12N 8 34W
Lough Rea Rol 20 C3 53 11N 8 35W
Lough Ree Rol 20 D3 53 35N 8 00W
Lough Sheelin Rol 20 D3 53 48N 7 20W
Lough Swilly Rol 20 D5 55 20N 7 35W
Loughton England 16 D2 51 39N 0 03E
Louisburgh Rol 20 B3 53 46N 9 48W
Louisiana state USA 91 H3 32 00N 92 00W
Louisville USA 91 J4 38 13N 85 48W
Lourdes France 50 D2 43 06N 0 02W
Louth England 13 F2 53 22N 0 01W
Louth Rol 20 E3 53 57N 6 33W
Louth co. Rol 20 E3 53 55N 6 25W
Louviers France 50 E5 49 13N 1 11E
Lower Lough Erne NI 10 B1 54 30N 7 45W
Lowestoft England 17 E3 52 29N 1 45E
Lowick England 11 H2 55 38N 1 58W
Lowther Hills Scotland 11 F2 55 25N 3 45W
Luanda Angola 82 B6 8 50S 13 15E
Luarca Spain 51 B5 43 33N 6 31W
Lubango Angola 82 B5 14 55S 13 30E
Lubbock USA 90 F3 33 35N 101 53W
Lübeck Germany 52 E6 53 52N 10 40E
Lublin Poland 53 L5 51 18N 22 31E
Lubumbashi CDR 82 E5 11 41S 27 29E
Lucan Rol 20 E3 53 22N 6 27W
Lucca Italy 54 D5 43 50N 10 30E
Luce Bay Scotland 11 E1 54 47N 4 50W
Lucena Spain 51 C2 37 25N 4 29W
Luckenwalde Germany 52 F6 52 05N 13 11E
Lucknow India 66 E5 26 50N 80 54E
Lüderitz Namibia 82 C2 26 38S 15 10E
Ludgershall England 16 B2 51 16N 1 37W
Ludhiana India 66 D6 30 56N 75 52E
Ludlow England 14 D2 52 22N 2 43W
Ludwigshafen Germany 52 D4 49 29N 8 27E
Ludwigslust Germany 52 E6 53 20N 11 30E
Lugano Switz. 52 D2 46 01N 8 57E
Lugnaquillia mt. Rol 21 E2 52 58N 6 27W
Lugo Spain 51 B5 43 00N 7 33W
Luhans'k Ukraine 56 E4 48 35N 39 20E
Luleå Sweden 49 F4 65 35N 22 10E
Lundy i. England 18 C3 51 11N 4 40W
Lüneburg Germany 52 E6 53 15N 10 24E
Lunéville France 50 H5 48 35N 6 30E
Lurgan NI 10 C1 54 28N 6 20W
Lusaka Zambia 82 E4 15 26S 28 20E
Lusk Rol 20 E3 53 32N 6 10W
Lustenau Austria 52 D3 47 26N 9 42E
Luton England 16 C2 51 53N 0 25W
Luton u.a. England 16 C2 51 53N 0 25W
Lutterworth England 15 E2 52 28N 1 10W
**LUXEMBOURG** 48 D2/E2
Luxembourg Luxembourg 48 E2 49 37N 6 08E
Luxor Egypt 81 M7 25 41N 32 24E
Luzern Switz. 52 D3 47 03N 8 17E
Luzhou China 69 J3 28 55N 105 25E
Luzon i. Philippines 71 G7 15 00N 122 00E
L'viv Ukraine 53 M4 49 50N 24 00E
Lybster Scotland 9 F3 58 18N 3 13W
Lydd England 17 D1 50 57N 0 55E
Lydham England 14 D2 52 31N 2 59W
Lydney England 15 D1 51 43N 2 32W
Lyme Bay England 19 E2 50 40N 2 55W
Lyme Regis England 19 E2 50 44N 2 57W
Lyminge England 17 E1 51 08N 1 05E
Lymington England 16 B1 50 46N 1 33W
Lymm England 12 D2 53 23N 2 28W
Lyndhurst England 16 B1 50 52N 1 34W
Lynher r. England 18 C2 50 33N 4 25W
Lynmouth England 18 D3 51 15N 3 50W
Lynn Lake tn. Canada 89 Q5 56 51N 101 01W
Lynton England 18 D3 51 15N 3 50W
Lyons France 50 G3 45 46N 4 50E
Lytham St. Anne's England 12 C2 53 45N 3 01W

**M**

**Maam Cross** Rol 20 B3 53 27N 9 33W
Maas r. Neths 48 D4 51 50N 5 32E
Maastricht Neths 48 D3 50 51N 5 42E
Mablethorpe England 13 G2 53 21N 0 15E
Macao China 69 K2 22 10N 113 40E
Macapá Brazil 96 G14 0 04N 51 04W
Macarata Italy 54 E5 43 18N 13 27E
Macclesfield England 12 D2 53 16N 2 07W
**Macdonnell Ranges** Australia 72 F6 24 00S 132 30E
Macduff Scotland 9 G2 57 40N 2 30W
Maceió Brazil 96 K12 9 40S 35 44W
**Macgillycuddy's Reeks** mts. Rol 21 B2 52 00N 9 27W
The Machars Scotland 11 E1 54 49N 4 31W
Machrihanish Scotland 10 D2 55 26N 5 44W
Machynlleth Wales 14 C2 52 35N 3 51W

Mackenzie r. Canada 88 J7 67 00N 132 00W
**Mackenzie Mountains** Canada 88 J7/L6 66 00N 130 00W
McKinley, Mount USA 88 E6 62 02N 151 01W
McKinney USA 91 G3 33 14N 96 37W
Mâcon France 50 G4 46 18N 4 50E
Macon USA 91 K3 32 49N 83 37W
Macroom Rol 21 C1 51 54N 8 57W
**MADAGASCAR** 82 H2/J5
Madeira r. Brazil 96 E12 6 00S 61 30W
**Madeira Islands** Atlantic Ocean 80 A8 32 45N 17 00W
Madison USA 91 J5 43 04N 89 22W
Madrid Spain 51 D4 40 25N 3 43W
Maesteg Wales 14 C1 51 37N 3 40W
Magadan Russia 63 T8 59 38N 150 50E
Magdeburg Germany 52 E6 52 08N 11 37E
Maghera NI 10 C1 54 51N 6 40W
Magherafelt NI 10 C1 54 45N 6 36W
Magherafelt district NI 10 C1 54 45N 6 50W
Maghull England 12 D2 55 32N 2 57W
Mahajanga Madagascar 82 J4 15 40S 46 20E
Mahilyow Belarus 53 Q6 53 54N 30 20E
Mahón Spain 51 H3 39 54N 4 15E
Maidenhead England 16 C2 51 32N 0 44W
**Maiden Newton** England 19 E2 50 46N 2 35W
Maidstone England 17 D2 51 17N 0 32E
Maiduguri Nigeria 80 G4 11 53N 13 16E
Main r. NI 10 C1 54 50N 6 25W
Maine state USA 91 N6 45 00N 70 00W
Mainz Germany 52 D4 50 00N 8 16E
**Malabo** Equatorial Guinea 80 F2 3 45N 8 48E
Málaga Spain 51 C2 36 43N 4 25W
Malahide Rol 20 E3 53 27N 6 09W
Malange Angola 82 C6 9 32S 16 20E
Malatya Turkey 57 E2 38 22N 38 18E
**MALAWI** 82 F5
**MALAYSIA** 71 C5/E5
Mal Bay Rol 21 B2 52 40N 9 30W
**MALDIVES** 103
Maldon England 17 D2 51 45N 0 40E
Malé Maldives 59 4 10N 73 29E
**MALI** 80 C4/D5
Malin Head Rol 20 D5 55 30N 7 20W
Malin More Rol 20 C4 54 41N 8 46W
Mallaig Scotland 8 D2 57 00N 5 50W
Mallorca i. Spain 51 G3 39 50N 2 30E
Mallow Rol 21 C2 52 08N 8 39W
Malmesbury England 16 A2 51 36N 2 06W
Malmö Sweden 49 D2 55 35N 13 00E
Malpas England 12 D2 53 01N 2 46W
**MALTA** 54 F1
Maltby England 13 E2 53 26N 1 11W
Malton England 13 F3 54 08N 0 48W
**Malvern Hills** England 15 D2 52 05N 2 22W
Manacor Spain 51 G3 39 35N 3 12E
Managua Nicaragua 94 G2 12 06N 86 18W
Manama Bahrain 65 F4 26 12N 50 38E
Manaus Brazil 96 F13 3 06S 60 00W
Manchester England 12 D2 53 30N 2 15W
Manfredonia Italy 54 F4 41 37N 15 55E
Mangotsfield England 15 D1 51 29N 2 31W
Manhattan USA 93 F2 40 48N 73 58W
Manila Philippines 71 G6 14 37N 120 58E
Manitoba prov. Canada 89 R5 55 15N 100 00W
Manitoba, Lake Canada 89 R4 50 30N 98 15W
Manizales Colombia 96 B15 5 03N 75 32W
Mannheim Germany 52 D4 49 30N 8 28E
Manningtree England 17 E2 51 57N 1 04E
Manorhamilton Rol 20 C4 54 18N 8 10W
Manresa Spain 51 F4 41 43N 1 50E
Mansfield England 13 E2 53 09N 1 11W
**Mansfield Woodhouse** England 13 E2 53 10N 1 11W
Mantes-la-Jolie France 50 E5 48 59N 1 43E
Manuta Italy 54 D6 45 10N 10 47E
Manzanares Spain 51 D3 39 00N 3 23W
Maputo Mozambique 82 F2 25 58S 32 35E
Marabá Brazil 96 H12 5 23S 49 10W
Maracaibo Venezuela 96 C16 10 44N 71 37W
Marbella Spain 51 C2 36 31N 4 53W
Marburg Germany 52 D5 50 49N 8 36E
March England 17 D2 52 33N 0 06E
Mar del Plata Argentina 97 F6 38 00S 57 32W
Marden England 17 D2 51 11N 0 30E
Maresfield England 17 D2 51 00N 0 05E
Margam Wales 14 C1 51 34N 3 44W
Margate England 17 E2 51 24N 1 24E
Maribor Slovenia 54 F7 46 34N 15 38E
Marignane France 50 G2 43 25N 5 12E
**Mariscal Estigarribia** Paraguay 96 E9 22 04S 60 34W
Mariupol' Ukraine 57 E4 47 05N 37 34E
**Market Deeping** England 15 F2 52 41N 0 19W
**Market Drayton** England 15 D2 52 54N 2 29W
**Market Harborough** England 15 F2 52 29N 0 55W
Markethill NI 10 C1 54 18N 6 31W
Market Rasen England 13 F2 53 24N 0 21W
**Market Weighton** England 13 F2 53 52N 0 40W
Markinch Scotland 11 F3 56 12N 3 09W
Marlborough England 16 B2 51 26N 1 43W

**Marlborough Downs** England 16 B2 51 28N 1 50W
Marlow England 16 C2 51 35N 0 48W
Marmande France 50 E3 44 30N 0 10E
Marple England 12 D2 53 24N 2 03W
Marrakesh Morocco 80 C8 31 49N 8 00W
Marsala Italy 54 E2 37 48N 12 27E
Marsden West Yorkshire England 13 E2 53 36N 1 55W
Marsden Tyne and Wear England 13 E3 54 58N 1 21W
Marseilles France 50 G2 43 18N 5 22E
**MARSHALL ISLANDS** 100 G9/H8
**Marshfield** England 15 D1 51 28N 2 19W
**Marske-by-the-Sea** England 13 E3 54 36N 1 01W
Martigny Switz. 52 C3 46 07N 7 05E
Martigues France 50 G2 43 24N 5 03E
**Martinique** i. Lesser Antilles 94 R12 14 30N 61 00W
Martos Spain 51 C2 37 44N 3 58W
Maryland state USA 91 L4 39 00N 77 00W
Maryport England 12 C3 54 43N 3 30W
Maryport Scotland 10 E1 54 43N 3 30W
Maseru Lesotho 82 E2 29 19S 27 29E
Masham England 13 E3 54 13N 1 40W
Mashhad Iran 65 G6 36 16N 59 34E
Massa Italy 54 D5 44 02N 10 09E
**Massachusetts state** USA 91 M5 42 00N 72 00W
**Massif Central** France 50 F3 45 00N 3 30E
**Massif de la Vanoise** France 50 H3 45 20N 6 20E
Matadi CDR 82 B6 5 50S 13 32E
Mataró Spain 51 G4 41 32N 2 27E
Matera Italy 55 G4 40 40N 16 37E
Matlock England 12 E2 53 08N 1 32W
Matterhorn mt. Switz. 52 C2 45 59N 7 39E
Maubeuge France 50 F6 50 17N 3 58E
Mauchline Scotland 11 E2 55 31N 4 24W
**MAURITANIA** 80 B5/C6C
**MAURITIUS** 103
Maybole Scotland 11 E2 55 21N 4 41W
Mayenne France 50 D5 48 18N 0 37W
Maykop Russia 62 G5 44 37N 40 48E
Maynooth Rol 20 E3 53 23N 6 35W
Mayo Rol 20 B3 54 35N 9 07W
Mayo co. Rol 20 B3 53 55N 9 20W
Mazamet France 50 F2 43 29N 2 22E
Mazara del Vallo Italy 54 E2 37 40N 12 34E
Mazarrón Spain 51 E2 37 36N 1 19W
Mazatlán Mexico 94 C4 23 11N 106 25W
Mazirbe Latvia 49 E2 57 40N 22 21E
Mbabane Swaziland 82 F2 26 20S 31 08E
Mbandaka CDR 81 J2 0 03N 18 28E
Mbeya Tanzania 82 F6 8 54S 33 29E
Meath co. Rol 20 E3 35 35N 6 30W
Meaux France 50 F5 48 58N 2 54E
Mecca Saudi Arabia 64 C3 21 26N 39 49E
Medan Indonesia 71 B4 3 35N 98 39E
Medellín Colombia 96 B15 6 15N 75 36W
Mediterranean Sea 54 B2/E2 35 00N 15 00E
Medway r. England 17 D2 51 24N 0 40E
Medway u.a. England 17 D2 51 25N 0 35E
Meerut India 66 D5 29 00N 77 42E
Meig r. Scotland 9 E2 57 35N 4 50W
Mekong r. Asia 71 C8 16 00N 105 00E
Melbourn England 16 C2 52 05N 0 01E
Melbourne England 15 E2 52 49N 1 25W
Melbourne Australia 73 H3 37 45S 144 58E
Melilla territory Spain 51 D1 35 17N 2 57W
Melitopol' Ukraine 57 E4 46 51N 35 22E
Melksham England 16 A2 51 23N 2 09W
Melrose Scotland 11 G2 55 36N 2 44W
Meltham England 13 E2 53 36N 1 52W
**Melton Mowbray** England 15 F2 52 46N 0 53W
Melun France 50 F5 48 32N 2 40E
Melvich Scotland 9 F3 58 33N 3 55W
Memmingen Germany 52 E4 47 59N 10 11E
Memphis USA 91 J4 35 10N 90 00W
Menai Bridge tn. Wales 14 B3 53 14N 4 10W
Menai Strait Wales 14 B3 53 14N 4 10W
Mende France 50 F3 44 32N 3 30E
**Mendip Hills** England 19 E3 51 18N 2 45W
Mendoza Argentina 97 D7 32 48S 68 52W
Menorca i. Spain 51 G4/H3 39 45N 4 15E
Menton France 50 H2 43 47N 7 30E
Meppel Neths 48 E5 52 42N 6 12E
Merano Italy 54 D7 46 41N 11 10E
Mere England 16 A2 51 06N 2 16W
Mérida Mexico 94 G4 20 59N 89 39W
Mérida Spain 51 B3 38 55N 6 20W
Mérignac France 50 D3 44 50N 0 36W
Merrick mt. Scotland 11 E2 55 08N 4 29W
Merriott England 19 E2 50 55N 2 49W
Mersea Island England 17 D2 51 46N 0 57
Mersey r. England 12 D2 53 20N 2 53W
**Merseyside co.** England 12 D2 53 30N 3 20W
Merthyr Tydfil Wales 14 C1 51 46N 3 23W
Merthyr Tydfil u.a. Wales 14 C1 51 48N 3 23W
Merton England 16 C2 51 25N 0 12W
Metheringham England 13 F2 53 08N 0 25W
Methil Scotland 11 F3 56 12N 3 01W

Metz France 50 H5 49 07N 6 11E
**Meuse r.** Belgium/France 48 D3 50 03N 4 40E
Mevagissey England 18 C2 50 16N 4 48W
Mexborough England 13 E2 53 30N 1 17W
**MEXICO** 94 C5/E3
Mexico City Mexico 94 E3 19 25N 99 10W
Mexico, Gulf of Mexico 94 F4/G4 25 00N 90 00W
Miami USA 91 K2 25 45N 80 15W
Michigan state USA 91 J5/K5 45 00N 85 00W
**Michigan, Lake** Canada/USA 92 C2/C3 45 00N 87 00W
**Middlesbrough** England 13 E3 54 35N 1 14W
**Middlesbrough u.a.** England 13 E3 54 33N 1 04W
Middleton England 12 D2 53 33N 2 12W
**Middleton-in-Teesdale** England 12 D3 54 38N 2 04W
**Middleton-on-the-Wolds** England 13 F2 53 56N 0 33W
Middlewich England 12 D2 53 11N 2 27W
Midhurst England 16 C1 50 59N 0 45W
Midleton Rol 21 C1 51 55N 8 10W
**Midlothian u.a.** Scotland 11 F2 55 50N 3 05W
**Midsomer Norton** England 19 E3 51 17N 2 30W
Mieres Spain 51 C5 43 15N 5 46W
Mikkeli Finland 49 G3 61 44N 27 15E
Milan Italy 54 C6 45 28N 9 12E
**Milborne Port** England 19 E2 50 58N 2 29W
Mildenhall England 17 D3 52 21N 0 30E
Milestone Rol 21 C2 52 40N 8 05W
Milford Rol 20 D5 55 07N 7 43W
Milford Haven Wales 14 A1 51 44N 5 02W
Millau France 50 F3 44 06N 3 05E
Millisle NI 10 D1 54 37N 5 30W
Millom England 12 C3 54 13N 3 18W
Millport Scotland 10 E2 55 46N 4 55W
Millstreet Rol 21 B2 52 03N 9 04W
Milltown Malbay Rol 21 B2 52 52N 9 23W
Milngavie Scotland 11 E2 55 57N 4 19W
Milnthorpe England 12 D3 54 14N 2 46W
Milton Keynes England 16 C3 52 02N 0 42W
**Milton Keynes u.a.** England 16 C3 52 02N 0 42W
Milverton England 19 D3 51 02N 3 16W
Milwaukee USA 91 J5 43 03N 87 56W
Mimizan France 50 D3 44 12N 1 14W
**Minch, The sd.** Scotland 8 C3/D3 58 00N 6 00W
Mindanao i. Philippines 71 G5/H5 8 00N 125 00E
Minden Germany 52 D6 52 18N 8 54E
Mindoro i. Philippines 71 G6 13 00N 121 00E
Minehead England 18 D3 51 13N 3 29W
Mine Head Rol 21 D1 52 00N 7 35W
Mingulay i. Scotland 8 B1 56 49N 7 38W
Minneapolis USA 91 H5 45 00N 93 15W
Minnedosa Canada 89 R4 50 14N 99 50W
Minnesota state USA 91 H6 47 00N 95 00W
Minsk Belarus 56 C5 53 51N 27 30E
Minster England 17 D2 51 26N 0 49E
Minster England 17 E2 51 20N 1 19E
Minsterley England 14 D2 52 39N 2 55W
Mintlaw Scotland 9 G2 57 31N 2 00W
Mirfield England 13 E2 53 41N 1 42W
Miskolc Hungary 53 K4 48 07N 20 47E
Misratah Libya 81 G8 32 23N 15 06E
Mississippi r. USA 91 H3 35 00N 90 00W
Mississippi state USA 91 H3/J3 32 00N 90 00W
Missouri r. USA 91 H4 39 00N 93 00W
Missouri state USA 91 H4 38 00N 93 00W
Mitchelstown Rol 21 C2 52 16N 8 16W
Mito Japan 70 D2 36 22N 140 29E
Mizen Head Rol 21 B1 51 30N 9 50W
Moate Rol 20 D3 53 24N 7 58W
Mobile USA 91 J3 30 40N 88 05W
**Moçambique** Mozambique 82 H4 15 03S 40 45E
Modbury England 18 D2 50 21N 3 53W
Módena Italy 54 D6 44 39N 10 55E
Modesto USA 90 B4 37 37N 121 00W
Mödling Austria 53 H4 48 06N 16 18E
Moelfre Wales 14 B3 53 21N 4 14W
Moffat Scotland 11 F2 55 20N 3 27W
Mogadishu Somalia 81 Q2 2 02N 45 21E
Mohill Rol 20 D3 53 54N 7 52W
Mo-i-Rana Norway 49 D4 66 18N 14 00E
Mold Wales 14 C3 53 10N 3 08W
**MOLDOVA** 53 P3
Mole r. England 16 C2 51 15N 0 20W
Molfetta Italy 55 G4 41 12N 16 36E
Mölndal Sweden 49 D2 57 40N 12 00E
Mombasa Kenya 82 F2 4 04S 39 40E
**MONACO** 50 H2
**Monadhliath Mountains** Scotland 9 E2 57 10N 4 00W
Monaghan Rol 20 E4 54 15N 6 58W
Monaghan co. Rol 20 D4/E4 54 10N 7 00W
Monasterevin Rol 21 D3 53 07N 7 02W
**Mönchengladbach** Germany 52 C5 51 12N 6 25E
Moncton Canada 89 Y3 46 04N 64 50W
Mondovi Italy 54 B6 44 23N 7 49E
Moneen Rol 20 C3 53 26N 8 54W
Moneymore NI 10 C1 54 42N 6 40W
Monfalcone Italy 54 E6 45 49N 13 32E

**MONGOLIA** 68/69 G7/K7
**Moniaive** Scotland 11 F2 55 12N 3 55W
**Monifieth** Scotland 9 G1 56 29N 2 49W
**Monmouth** Wales 14 D1 51 50N 2 43W
**Monmouthshire** u.a.
Wales 14 D1 51 47N 2 55W
**Monopoli** Italy 55 G4 40 57N 17 18E
**Monrovia** Liberia 80 B3 6 20N 10 46W
**Montana** Bulgaria 55 K5 43 25N 23 11E
**Montana** state USA 90 E6 47 00N 111 00W
**Montargis** France 50 F4 48 00N 2 44E
**Montauban** France 50 E3 44 01N 1 20E
**Montbéliard** France 50 H4 47 31N 6 48E
**Mont Blanc** France/Italy 50 H3 45 50N 6 52E
**Montceau-les-Mines**
France 50 G4 46 40N 4 23E
**Mont-de-Marsan**
France 50 D2 43 54N 0 30W
**Montdidier** France 50 F5 49 39N 2 35E
**Monte Carlo** Monaco 50 H2 43 44N 7 25E
**Montélimar** France 50 G3 44 33N 4 45E
**MONTENEGRO** 55 H5
**Montepulciano** Italy 54 D5 43 0 5N 11 46E
**Monterrey** Mexico 94 D5 25 40N 100 20W
**Montes Claros** Brazil 96 J10 16 45S 43 52W
**Montevideo** Uruguay 97 F6 34 55S 56 10W
**Montgomery** USA 91 J3 32 22N 86 20W
**Montgomery** Wales 14 C2 52 34N 3 10W
**Montluçon** France 50 F4 46 20N 2 36E
**Montmirail** France 50 F5 48 52N 3 34E
**Montmorilion** France 50 E4 46 26N 0 52E
**Montoro** Spain 51 C3 38 02N 4 23W
**Montpelier** Rol 21 C2 52 45N 8 30W
**Montpellier** France 50 F2 43 36N 3 53E
**Montréal** Canada 89 W3 45 32N 73 36W
**Montreux** Switz. 52 C3 46 27N 6 55E
**Montrose** Scotland 9 G1 56 43N 2 29W
**Montserrat** i.
Lesser Antilles 94 P9 16 45N 62 14W
**Monza** Italy 54 C6 45 35N 9 16E
**Mooncoin** Rol 21 D2 52 17N 7 15W
**Moone** Rol 21 E2 52 58N 6 49W
**Moorfoot Hills** Scotland 11 F2/G2 55 50N 3 00W
**Moosonee** Canada 89 U4 51 18N 80 39W
**Mora** Sweden 49 D3 61 00N 14 30E
**Moray** u.a. Scotland 9 F2 57 20N 3 10W
**Moray Firth** Scotland 9 F2 57 45N 3 45W
**Morcenx** France 50 D3 44 02N 0 55W
**Morecambe** England 12 D3 54 04N 2 53W
**Morecambe Bay**
England 12 D3 54 10N 2 55W
**Morelia** Mexico 94 D3 19 40N 101 11W
**Moreton** England 12 C2 53 24N 3 07W
**Moretonhampstead**
England 18 D2 50 40N 3 45W
**Moreton-in-Marsh**
England 15 E1 51 59N 1 42W
**Morlaix** France 50 C5 48 35N 3 50W
**Morley** England 13 E2 53 46N 1 36W
**MOROCCO** 80 C8/D8
**Morón de la Frontera**
Spain 51 C2 37 07N 5 27W
**Moroni** Comoros 82 H5 11 40S 43 16E
**Morpeth** England 13 E4 55 10N 1 41W
**Morte Point** England 18 C3 51 10N 4 15W
**Mosborough** England 13 E2 53 19N 1 22W
**Moscow** Russia 62 F8 55 45N 37 42E
**Mosel** r.
Germany/France 52 C4 50 00N 7 00E
**Mossley** NI 10 D1 54 42N 5 57W
**Mossoró** Brazil 96 K12 5 10S 37 18W
**Mostar**
Bosnia-Herzegovina 55 G5 43 20N 17 50E
**Móstoles** Spain 51 D4 40 19N 3 53W
**Mosul** Iraq 64 D6 36 21N 43 08E
**Motherwell** Scotland 11 E2 55 48N 3 59W
**Motril** Spain 51 D2 36 45N 3 31W
**Moulins** France 50 F4 47 00N 3 48E
**Mountain Ash** Wales 14 C1 51 42N 3 24W
**Mount Bellew** Rol 20 C3 53 28N 8 30W
**Mount Leinster** Rol 21 E2 52 36N 6 42W
**Mountmellick** tn. Rol 21 D3 53 07N 7 20W
**Mountrath** Rol 21 D3 53 00N 7 27W
**Mounts Bay** England 18 B2 50 05N 5 30W
**Mountshannon** Rol 21 C2 52 56N 8 26W
**Mountsorrel** England 15 E2 52 44N 1 07W
**Moura** Portugal 51 B3 38 08N 7 27W
**Mourne Mountains** NI 10 C1 54 05N 6 05W
**Mousehole** England 18 B2 50 04N 5 34W
**Moville** Rol 20 D5 55 11N 7 03W
**Moy** NI 10 C1 54 27N 6 42W
**Moycullen** Rol 20 B3 53 20N 9 10W
**Moygashel** NI 10 C1 54 31N 6 46W
**Moyle** district NI 10 C1 55 10N 6 10W
**Moyvore** Rol 20 D3 53 22N 7 37W
**MOZAMBIQUE** 82 F3/G5
**Much Wenlock**
England 15 D2 52 36N 2 34W
**Muck** i. Scotland 8 C1 56 50N 6 15W
**Muckross** Rol 21 B2 52 01N 9 29W
**Muff** Rol 20 D5 55 04N 7 16W
**Muine Bheag** Rol 21 E2 52 41N 6 58W
**Muirkirk** Scotland 11 E2 55 31N 4 04W
**Muir of Ord** Scotland 9 E2 57 31N 4 27W
**Mulhacén** mt. Spain 51 D2 37 04N 3 19W
**Mülheim an der Ruhr**
Germany 48 E4 51 25N 6 50E

**Mulhouse** France 50 H4 47 45N 7 21E
**Mulhuddart** Rol 20 E3 53 24N 6 24W
**Mulkear** r. Rol 21 C2 52 38N 8 24W
**Mull** i. Scotland 8 D1 56 25N 6 00W
**Mullet Peninsula** Rol 20 A4 54 07N 10 05W
**Mull Head** Scotland 7 B2 59 20N 2 58W
**Mullinahone** Rol 21 D2 52 30N 7 30W
**Mullinavat** Rol 21 D2 52 22N 7 10W
**Mullingar** Rol 20 D3 53 32N 7 20W
**Mullion** England 18 B2 50 01N 5 14W
**Mull of Galloway**
Scotland 10 E1 54 38N 4 55W
**Mull of Kintyre**
Scotland 10 D2 55 17N 5 55W
**Mull of Oa** Scotland 10 C2 55 35N 6 20W
**Mull, Sound of** Scotland 8 D1 56 30N 6 00W
**Multan** Pakistan 66 C6 30 10N 71 36E
**Mumbai** India 66 C3 18 56N 72 51E
**Mundesley** England 17 E3 52 53N 1 26E
**Munich** Germany 52 E4 48 08N 11 35E
**Münster** Germany 52 C5 51 58N 7 37E
**Murcia** Spain 51 E2 37 59N 1 08W
**Murmansk** Russia 62 F10 68 59N 33 08E
**Murray** r. Australia 73 H3 35 30S 144 00E
**Murray Bridge** Australia
73 H3 35 10S 139 17E
**Murton** England 13 E3 54 49N 1 23W
**Muş** Turkey 57 F2 38 45N 41 30E
**Muscat** Oman 65 G3 23 37N 58 38E
**Mushin** Nigeria 80 B 6 30N 3 15E
**Musselburgh** Scotland 11 F2 55 57N 3 04W
**Mutare** Zimbabwe 82 F4 18 58N 32 40E
**Mutton Island** i. Rol 21 B2 52 49N 9 31W
**Mwanza** Tanzania 83 C3 2 31S 32 56E
**MYANMAR** 71 B7
**Mybster** Scotland 9 F3 58 27N 3 25W
**Mykolayiv** Ukraine 57 D4 46 57N 32 00E
**Mynydd Eppynt** Wales 14 C2 52 02N 3 35W
**Mynydd Preseli** Wales 14 B1 51 58N 4 45W
**Mytilíni** Greece 55 M3 39 06N 26 34E
**Mytishchi** Russia 56 E6 55 54N 37 47E

**N**

**Naas** Rol 20 E3 53 13N 6 39W
**Naestved** Denmark 49 D2 55 14N 11 47E
**Náfplio** Greece 55 K2 37 34N 22 48E
**Nagano** Japan 70 C2 36 39N 138 10E
**Nagasaki** Japan 70 A1 32 45N 129 52E
**Nagles Mountains** Rol 21 C2 52 10N 8 25W
**Nagoya** Japan 70 C2 35 08N 136 53E
**Nagpur** India 66 D4 21 10N 79 12E
**Nailsea** England 19 E3 51 26N 2 46W
**Nailsworth** England 15 D1 51 42N 2 14W
**Nairn** Scotland 9 F2 57 35N 3 53W
**Nairobi** Kenya 83 E4 1 17S 36 50E
**Namib Desert** Namibia 82 B3/C2 22 00S 14 00E
**NAMIBIA** 82 C3
**Nampula** Mozambique 82 G4 15 09S 39 14E
**Namur** Belgium 48 C3 50 28N 4 52E
**Nanchang** China 69 L3 28 33N 115 58E
**Nancy** France 50 H5 48 42N 6 12E
**Nanjing** China 69 L4 32 03N 118 47E
**Nantes** France 50 D4 47 14N 1 35W
**Nantwich** England 12 D2 53 04N 2 32W
**Naples** Italy 54 E4 40 50N 14 15E
**Naples** USA 91 K2 26 09N 81 48W
**Narberth** Wales 14 B1 51 48N 4 45W
**Narbonne** France 50 F2 43 11N 3 00E
**Narborough** England 15 E2 52 35N 1 11W
**Narvik** Norway 49 E4 68 26N 17 25E
**Naseby** England 15 E2 52 23N 0 59W
**Nashville** USA 91 J4 36 10N 86 50W
**Nassau** Bahamas 95 J5 25 05N 77 20W
**Nasser, Lake** Egypt 81 M6 22 35N 31 40E
**Natal** Brazil 96 K12 5 46S 35 15W
**Natchez** USA 91 H3 31 32N 91 24W
**Naul** Rol 20 E3 53 35N 6 17W
**NAURU** 100 G7
**Navan** Rol 20 E3 53 39N 6 41W
**Navenby** England 13 F2 53 06N 0 32W
**Naver** r. Scotland 9 E3 58 30N 4 10W
**Ndjamena** Chad 81 J4 12 10N 14 59E
**Néapoli** Greece 55 K2 36 31N 23 03E
**Neath** Wales 14 C1 51 40N 3 48W
**Neath Port Talbot** u.a.
Wales 14 C1 51 37N 3 43W
**Nebraska** state USA 90 F5 42 00N 102 00W
**Needham Market**
England 17 E3 52 09N 1 03E
**Needles, The** England 16 B1 50 39N 1 35W
**Nefyn** Wales 14 B2 52 56N 4 32W
**Negro** r. Brazil 96 D13 0 05S 67 00W
**Neiva** Colombia 96 B14 2 58N 75 15W
**Nelson** England 12 D2 53 51N 2 13W
**Neman** r.
Lithuania/Russia 56 C5 55 00N 22 00E
**Nenagh** Rol 21 C2 52 52N 8 12W
**Nene** r. England 15 F2 52 25N 0 30W
**Nene** r. England 17 D2 53 45N 0 10E
**NEPAL** 66/67 E5/F5
**Nephin** mt. Rol 20 B4 54 01N 9 22W
**Nephin Beg Range** Rol 20 B3/B4 54 00N 9 34W
**Nerva** Spain 51 B2 37 41N 6 33W
**Neston** England 12 C2 53 18N 3 03W
**NETHERLANDS** 48 D5/E5

**Nether Stowey**
England 19 D3 51 09N 3 10W
**Netzahualcóyotl**
Mexico 94 E3 19 24N 99 02W
**Neubrandenburg**
Germany 52 F6 53 33N 13 16E
**Neuchâtel** Switz. 52 C3 46 55N 6 56E
**Neufchâteau** France 50 G5 48 21N 5 42E
**Neufchâtel-en-Bray**
France 50 E5 49 44N 1 26E
**Neumünster** Germany 52 D7 54 05N 9 59E
**Neuruppin** Germany 52 F6 52 56N 12 49E
**Neuss** Germany 52 C5 51 12N 6 42E
**Neustrelitz** Germany 52 F6 53 22N 13 05E
**Nevada** state USA 90 C4 39 00N 118 00W
**Nevers** France 50 F4 47 00N 3 09E
**New Abbey** Scotland 11 F1 54 59N 3 38W
**New Alresford** England 16 B2 51 06N 1 10W
**Newark** USA 91 M5 40 44N 74 24W
**Newark-on-Trent**
England 13 F2 53 05N 0 49W
**New Ash Green**
England 17 D2 51 21N 0 18E
**Newbiggin-by-the-Sea**
England 13 E4 55 11N 1 30W
**Newbridge** Wales 14 C1 51 41N 3 09W
**Newbridge-on-Wye**
Wales 14 C2 52 13N 3 27W
**New Brunswick** prov.
Canada 89 X3 47 30N 66 00W
**New Buildings** NI 10 B1 54 56N 7 21W
**Newburgh** Scotland 9 F1 56 21N 3 15W
**Newburn** England 13 E3 54 59N 1 43W
**Newbury** England 16 B2 51 25N 1 20W
**New Caledonia** i.
Pacific Ocean 73 M6/N6 22 00S 165 00E
**Newcastle** NI 10 D1 54 12N 5 54W
**Newcastle Emlyn**
Wales 14 B2 52 02N 4 28W
**Newcastle-under-Lyme**
England 12 D2 53 00N 2 14W
**Newcastle upon Tyne**
England 13 E3 54 59N 1 35W
**Newcastle West** Rol 21 B2 52 27N 9 03W
**New Cumnock**
Scotland 11 E2 55 24N 4 12W
**New Deer** Scotland 9 G2 57 30N 2 12W
**New Delhi** India 66 D5 28 37N 77 14E
**Newfoundland** i.
Canada 89 Z3 48 15N 57 00W
**Newfoundland and Labrador** prov.
Canada 89 Y5/AA3 52 30N 62 30W
**New Galloway**
Scotland 11 E2 55 05N 4 10W
**New Guinea** i.
Pacific Ocean 72/73 F10/J9 5 00S 141 00E
**New Hampshire** state
USA 91 M5 43 00N 72 00W
**New Haven** USA 91 M5 41 18N 72 55W
**New Holland** England 13 F2 53 42N 0 22W
**Newick** England 16 D1 50 58N 0 01E
**Newinn** Rol 21 D2 52 26N 7 53W
**New Jersey** state USA 91 M4 40 00N 75 00W
**New Liskeard** Canada 89 V3 47 31N 79 41W
**Newlyn** England 18 B2 50 06N 5 34W
**Newmachar** Scotland 9 G2 57 16N 2 10W
**Newmains** Scotland 11 F2 55 47N 3 53W
**Newmarket** England 17 D3 52 15N 0 25E
**Newmarket** Rol 21 C2 52 13N 9 00W
**Newmarket-on-Fergus**
Rol 21 C2 52 45N 8 53W
**New Mexico** state USA 90 E3 35 00N 107 00W
**New Milton** England 16 B1 50 46N 1 40W
**New Orleans** USA 91 H2 30 00N 90 03W
**Newport** Telford and Wrekin
England 15 D2 52 47N 2 22W
**Newport** Isle of Wight
England 16 B1 50 42N 1 18W
**Newport** Essex
England 17 D2 51 58N 0 13E
**Newport** Mayo Rol 20 B3 53 53N 9 32W
**Newport** Tipperary Rol 21 C2 52 43N 8 25W
**Newport** Pembrokeshire
Wales 14 B2 52 01N 4 50W
**Newport** Newport
Wales 14 C1 51 35N 3 00W
**Newport** u.a. Wales 14 C1/D1 51 33N 3 00W
**Newport Bay** Rol 20 B3 53 51N 9 41W
**Newport News** USA 91 L4 36 59N 76 26W
**Newport-on-Tay**
Scotland 9 G1 56 27N 2 56W
**Newport Pagnell**
England 16 C3 52 05N 0 44W
**Newquay** England 18 B2 50 25N 5 05W
**New Quay** Wales 14 B2 52 13N 4 22W
**New Radnor** Wales 14 C2 52 15N 3 10W
**New Romney** England 17 D1 50 59N 0 57E
**New Ross** Rol 21 E2 52 24N 6 56W
**New Rossington**
England 13 E2 53 29N 1 04W
**Newry** NI 10 C1 54 11N 6 20W
**Newry and Mourne**
district NI 10 C1 54 10N 6 35W
**New Sauchie** Scotland 11 F3 56 08N 3 41W
**New Scone** Scotland 9 F1 56 25N 3 25W
**Newton Abbot**
England 18 D2 50 32N 3 36W

**Newton Aycliffe**
England 13 E3 54 37N 1 34W
**Newton Mearns**
Scotland 11 E2 55 45N 4 18W
**Newtonmore** Scotland 9 E2 57 04N 4 08W
**Newton Stewart**
Scotland 11 E1 54 57N 4 29W
**Newtown** Rol 21 D2 52 52N 7 07W
**Newtown** Wales 14 C2 52 32N 3 19W
**Newtownabbey** NI 10 D1 54 40N 5 54W
**Newtownabbey**
district NI 10 C1/D1 54 40N 6 05W
**Newtownards** NI 10 D1 54 36N 5 41W
**Newtown Cunningham**
Rol 20 D4 54 59N 7 31W
**Newtownhamilton** NI 10 C1 54 12N 6 35W
**Newtownmountkennedy**
Rol 21 E3 53 06N 6 07W
**Newtown St. Boswells**
Scotland 11 G2 55 34N 2 40W
**Newtownstewart** NI 10 B1 54 43N 7 24W
**New Tredegar** Wales 14 C1 51 44N 3 15W
**New York** USA 91 M5 40 40N 73 50W
**New York** state USA 91 L5 43 00N 76 00W
**NEW ZEALAND** 73
**Neyland** Wales 14 B1 51 43N 4 57W
**Niagara Falls** tn.
Canada 93 E2 43 05N 79 06W
**Niamey** Niger 80 E4 13 32N 2 05E
**NICARAGUA** 95 G2
**Nice** France 50 H2 43 42N 7 16E
**Nicobar Islands** India 67 G1 8 30N 94 00E
**Nicosia** Cyprus 57 D2 35 11N 33 23E
**Nienburg** Germany 52 D6 52 38N 9 13E
**NIGER** 80 E5/G5
**Niger** r. West Africa 80 F3 5 30N 6 15E
**NIGERIA** 80 F4/G4
**Nigg** Scotland 9 G2 57 08N 2 03W
**Nigg Bay** Highland
Scotland 9 E2 57 42N 4 01W
**Nigg Bay** Aberdeenshire
Scotland 9 G2 57 08N 2 03W
**Nijmegen** Neths 48 D4 51 50N 5 52E
**Nikopol'** Ukraine 56 D4 45 34N 34 25E
**Nile** r. Sudan/Egypt 81 M7 27 30N 31 40E
**Nîmes** France 50 G2 43 50N 4 21E
**Niort** France 50 D4 46 19N 0 28W
**Niterói** Brazil 96 J9 22 54S 43 06W
**Nith** r. Scotland 11 F2 55 20N 3 50W
**Nizhniy Novgorod**
Russia 62 G8 56 20N 44 00E
**Nordhausen** Germany 52 E5 51 31N 10 48E
**North Cape** Norway 49 F5 71 11N 25 40E
**Norfolk** co. England 17 D3 52 45N 1 00E
**Norfolk** USA 91 L4 36 54N 76 18W
**Norham** England 11 G2 55 43N 2 10W
**Normanton** England 13 E2 53 42N 1 25W
**Norrköping** Sweden 49 E2 58 35N 16 10E
**Northallerton** England 13 E3 54 20N 1 26W
**Northam** England 18 C3 51 02N 4 14W
**Northampton** England 15 F2 52 14N 0 54W
**Northamptonshire** co.
England 15 E2/F2 52 20N 1 00W
**North Ayrshire** u.a.
Scotland 11 E2 55 30N 5 05W
**North Baddesley**
England 16 B1 50 58N 1 27W
**North Ballachulish**
Scotland 8 D1 56 42N 5 11W
**North Berwick** Scotland 11 G3 56 04N 2 44W
**North Carolina** state
USA 91 L4 36 00N 80 00W
**North Channel**
British Isles 10 D1/D2 55 20N 5 50W
**North Dakota** state
USA 90/91 F6/G6 47 00N 102 00W
**North Dorset Downs**
England 19 E2 50 40N 2 30W
**North Down** co. NI 10 D1 54 40N 5 40W
**North Downs** England 16 C2 51 13N 0 30W
**North East Lincolnshire**
u.a. England 13 F2 53 30N 0 10W
**Northern Ireland** UK 10 B1/C1 54 40N 7 00W
**NORTHERN MARIANAS**
100 F9
**North Foreland** England
17 E2 51 23N 1 27E
**North Hykeham**
England 13 F2 53 12N 0 34W
**Northiam** England 17 D1 50 59N 0 36E
**North Island** NZ 73 P3/Q3 39 00N §76 00E
**North Kessock** Scotland 9 E2 57 30N 4 15W
**NORTH KOREA** 69 N5/N6
**North Lanarkshire** u.a.
Scotland 11 E2/F2 55 50N 3 55W
**Northleach** England 15 E1 51 51N 1 50W
**North Lincolnshire** u.a.
England 13 F2 53 40N 0 40W
**North Petherton**
England 19 D3 51 06N 3 01W
**North Pole**
Arctic Ocean 101 90 00N
**North Ronaldsay** i.
Scotland 7 B2 59 23N 2 26W
**North Shields** England 13 E4 55 01N 1 26W
**North Somercotes**
England 13 G2 53 28N 0 08E

North Somerset *u.a.*
England 19 E3 51 15N 2 50W
North Sound Rol 21 B3 53 11N 9 43W
North Sound, The
Scotland 7 B2 59 17N 2 45W
North Tawton England 18 D2 50 48N 3 53W
North Tidworth
England 16 B2 51 16N 1 40W
North Uist *i.* Scotland 8 B2 57 04N 7 15W
Northumberland *co.*
England 12 D4 55 10N 2 05W
North Walsham
England 17 E3 52 50N 1 24E
Northwest Highlands
Scotland 8/9 D2/E3 58 00N 5 00W
Northwest Territories
*territory* Canada 88 L6/N6 65 15N 115 00W
North Wheatley
England 13 F2 53 22N 0 52W
Northwich England 12 D2 53 16N 2 32W
North Wingfield
England 13 E2 53 09N 1 24W
North York Moors
England 13 F3 55 22N 0 45W
North Yorkshire *co.*
England 13 E3/F3 54 10N 2 10W
Norton England 13 F3 54 08N 0 48W
NORWAY 49 C2/F4
Norwich England 17 E3 52 38N 1 18E
Norwich USA 93 F2 41 32N 72 05W
Noss Head Scotland 9 F3 58 28N 3 04W
Nottingham England 15 E2 52 58N 1 10W
Nottinghamshire *co.*
England 13 E2/F2 53 20N 1 00W
Nouadhibou Mauritania 80 A6 20 54N 17 01W
Nouakchott Mauritania 80 A5 18 09N 15 58W
Novara Italy 54 C6 45 27N 8 37E
Nova Scotia *prov.*
Canada 89 Y2/Y3 44 30N 65 00W
Novgorod Russia 62 F8 58 30N 31 20E
Novi Sad Serbia 55 H6 45 15N 19 51E
Novosibirsk Russia 63 L8 55 04N 83 05E
Nubian Desert Sudan 81 M6 21 00N 33 00E
Nullarbor Plain
Australia 72 E4 32 00S 128 00E
Nuneaton England 15 E2 52 32N 1 28W
Nuoro Italy 54 C4 40 20N 9 21E
Nuremberg Germany 52 E4 49 27N 11 05E
Nuuk Greenland 89 AA6 64 10N 51 40W
Nyasa, Lake
Southern Africa 82 F5 12 00S 35 00E
Nykøbing Denmark 49 D1 54 47N 11 53E
Nyköping Sweden 49 E2 58 45N 17 03E
Nyons France 50 G3 44 22N 5 08E

## O

Oadby England 15 E2 52 36N 1 04W
Oakengates England 15 D2 52 42N 2 28W
Oakham England 16 F2 52 40N 00 43W
Oakland USA 90 B4 37 50N 122 15W
Oakley England 16 B2 51 15N 1 11W
Oakley Scotland 11 F3 56 05N 3 35W
Ob' *r.* Russia 62 J10 65 30N 66 00E
Oban Scotland 8 D1 56 25N 5 29W
Oberhausen Germany 52 D1 51 27N 6 50E
O'Briensbridge Rol 21 C2 52 45N 8 30W
Ochil Hills Scotland 11 F3 56 15N 3 30W
Odda Norway 49 C3 60 03N 6 34E
Oddsta Scotland 7 D3 60 37N 0 59W
Odense Denmark 49 D1 55 24N 10 25E
Oder *r.* Europe 52 G6 52 00N 15 30E
Odessa Ukraine 57 D4 46 30N 30 46E
Offaly *co.* Rol 20 D3 53 15N 7 35W
Offenbach am Main
Germany 52 D5 50 06N 8 46E
Offenburg Germany 52 C4 48 29N 7 57E
Ohio *state* USA 91 K5 40 00N 83 00W
Ohio *r.* USA 91 J4 38 00N 86 00W
Oilgate Rol 21 E2 52 25N 6 32W
Ōita Japan 70 B1 33 15N 131 36E
Okehampton England 18 C2 50 44N 4 00W
Oklahoma *state* USA 91 G4 36 00N 98 00W
Oklahoma City USA 91 G4 35 28N 97 33W
Öland *i.* Sweden 49 E2 56 45N 51 50E
Olbia Italy 54 C4 40 56N 9 30E
Oldbury England 15 D2 52 30N 2 00W
Oldcastle Rol 20 D3 53 46N 7 10W
Oldenburg Germany 52 D6 53 08N 8 13E
Old Fletton England 16 C3 52 34N 0 12W
Oldham England 12 D2 53 33N 2 07W
Old Head of Kinsale *c.*
Rol 21 C1 51 40N 8 30W
Oldmeldrum Scotland 9 G2 57 20N 2 20W
Olhão Portugal 51 B2 37 01N 7 50W
Ollerton England 13 E2 53 12N 1 00W
Olney England 16 C2 52 09N 0 43W
Olsztyn Poland 53 K6 53 48N 20 29E
Olten Switz. 52 C3 47 22N 7 55E
Ólympos *mt.* Greece 55 J4 40 05N 22 21E
Omagh NI 10 B1 54 36N 7 18W
Omagh *district* NI 10 B1 54 30N 7 30W
Omaha USA 91 G5 41 15N 96 00W
OMAN 65 F2/G3
Oman, Gulf of
Iran/Oman 65 G3 24 30N 58 30E

Omdurman Sudan 81 M5 15 37N 32 29E
Omeath Rol 20 E4 54 06N 6 17W
Omsk Russia 62 K8 55 00N 73 22E
Ōmuta Japan 70 B1 33 02N 130 26E
Onezhskoye Ozero *l.*
Russia 62 F9 62 00N 40 00E
Ontario *prov.* Canada 89 S4/U4 51 00N 91 00W
Ontario, Lake
Canada/USA 93 E2 43 45N 78 00W
Oola Rol 21 C2 52 33N 8 16W
Oostende Belgium 48 A4 51 13N 2 55E
Opava Czech Rep. 53 H4 49 58N 17 55E
Opole Poland 53 H5 50 40N 17 56E
Oporto Portugal 51 A4 41 09N 8 37W
Oran Algeria 80 D9 35 45N 0 38W
Orange France 50 G3 44 08N 4 48E
Oranmore Rol 20 C3 53 16N 8 54W
Orbetello Italy 54 D5 42 27N 11 07E
Örebro Sweden 49 E2 59 17N 15 13E
Oregon *state* USA 90 B5/C5 44 00N 120 00W
Oregon City USA 90 B6 45 21N 122 36W
Orel Russia 62 F7 52 58N 36 04E
Orenburg Russia 62 H7 51 50N 55 00E
Orense Spain 51 B5 42 20N 7 52W
Orford England 17 E3 52 06N 1 31E
Orihuela Spain 51 E3 38 05N 0 56W
Orinoco *r.* Venezuela 96 E15 8 00N 64 00W
Oristano Italy 54 C3 39 54N 8 36E
Orkney Islands *u.a.*
Scotland 7 A1/B2 59 00N 3 00W
Orlando USA 91 K2 28 33N 81 21W
Orléans France 50 E4 47 54N 1 54E
Ormskirk England 12 D2 53 35N 2 54W
Oronsay *i.* Scotland 10 C3 56 00N 6 15W
Orrell England 12 D2 53 33N 2 45W
Orsha Belarus 56 D5 54 30N 30 23E
Orthez France 50 D2 43 29N 0 46W
Ortigueira Spain 51 B5 43 43N 7 51W
Ortona Italy 54 F5 42 21N 14 24E
Oruro Bolivia 96 D10 17 59S 67 08W
Orvieto Italy 54 E5 42 43N 12 06E
Orwell *r.* England 17 E3 52 00N 1 15E
Ōsaka Japan 70 C1 34 40N 135 30E
Oshawa Canada 89 V2 43 53N 78 51W
Oslo Norway 49 D2 59 56N 10 45E
Osmaniye Turkey 57 E2 37 04N 36 15E
Osnabrück Germany 52 D6 52 17N 8 03E
Osorno Chile 97 C5 40 35S 73 14W
Ossett England 13 E2 53 41N 1 35W
Östersund Sweden 49 D3 63 10N 14 40E
Östervall Sweden 49 E3 62 20N 15 20E
Ostrava Czech Rep. 53 J4 49 50N 18 15E
Oswaldtwistle England 12 D2 53 44N 2 24W
Oswestry England 14 C2 52 52N 3 03W
Otford England 17 D2 51 19N 0 12E
Otley England 13 E2 53 54N 1 41W
Otranto Italy 55 H4 40 08N 18 30E
Ottawa Canada 89 V3 45 24N 75 38W
Otterburn England 12 D4 55 14N 2 10W
Ottery St. Mary
England 19 D2 50 45N 3 17W
Ouagadougou Burkina 80 D4 12 20N 1 40W
Oughterard Rol 20 B3 53 26N 9 19W
Oulart Rol 21 E2 53 30N 6 23W
Oulu Finland 49 G4 65 02N 25 27E
Oundle England 15 F2 52 29N 0 29W
Ouse *r.* North Yorkshire
England 13 E3 54 05N 1 15W
Ouse *r.* East Sussex
England 16 D1 50 55N 0 03E
Outer Hebrides *is.*
Scotland 8 B2/B3 58 00N 7 00W
Outwell England 17 D3 52 37N 0 14E
Overton England 16 B2 51 15N 1 15W
Overton Wales 14 D2 52 58N 2 56W
Oviedo Spain 51 C5 43 21N 7 18W
Owen Sound Canada 89 U2 44 3N 80 56W
Oxford England 16 B2 51 46N 1 15W
Oxfordshire *co.*
England 16 B2 51 50N 1 25W
Oxted England 16 C2 51 15N 0 01W
Oysterhaven Rol 21 C1 51 41N 8 26W
Ozero Balkhash *l.*
Kazakhstan 62 K6 46 00N 75 00E
Ozero Baykal *l.* Russia 63 N7 54 00N 109 00E
Ozieri Italy 54 C4 40 35N 9 01E

## P

Pacific Ocean 100
Padang Indonesia 71 C3 1 00S 100 21E
Paddock Wood *tn.*
England 17 D2 51 11N 0 23E
Paderborn Germany 52 D5 51 43N 8 44E
Padiham England 12 D2 53 49N 2 19W
Padstow England 18 C2 50 33N 4 56W
Padua Italy 54 D6 45 24N 11 53E
Paisley Scotland 11 E2 55 50N 4 26W
PAKISTAN 66 B5/C5
PALAU 100 D8 7 30N 134 30E
Palawan *i.* Philippines 71 F5/F6 10 00N 119 00E
Palembang Indonesia 71 C3 2 59S 104 45E
Palencia Spain 51 C5 41 01N 4 32W
Palermo Italy 54 E3 38 08N 13 23E
Palma de Mallorca
Spain 51 G3 39 35N 2 39E
Palmer USA 88 F6 61 35N 149 10W

Palmyra Syria 64 C5 34 40N 38 10E
Pamiers France 50 E2 43 07N 1 36E
Pampas *geog. reg.*
Argentina 97 E6 36 00S 63 00W
Pamplona Spain 51 E5 42 49N 1 39W
PANAMA 95 H1/J1
Panama Canal Panama 95 J1 9 00N 80 00W
Panama City Panama 95 J1 8 57N 19 30W
Pangbourne England 16 B2 51 29N 1 05W
Papa Sound Scotland 7 B2 59 20N 2 54W
Papa, Sound of Scotland 7 C3 60 19N 1 40W
Papa Stour *i.* Scotland 7 C3 60 20N 1 42W
Papa Westray *i.* Scotland 7 B2 59 22N 2 54W
PAPUA NEW GUINEA 73 H9/K9
PARAGUAY 96 F9
Paraguay *r.*
Paraguay/Argentina 96 F8 26 30S 58 00W
Paramaribo Suriname 96 F15 5 52N 55 14W
Parana Argentina 97 E7 31 45S 60 30W
Paraná *r.*
Paraguay/Argentina 96 F7 27 00S 56 00W
Paris France 50 F5 48 52N 2 20E
Parkano Finland 49 F3 62 03N 23 00E
Parma Italy 54 D6 44 48N 10 19E
Parnaíba Brazil 96 J13 2 58S 41 46W
Páros Greece 55 L2 37 04N 25 06E
Parrett *r.* England 19 E3 51 05N 2 54W
Parthenay France 50 D4 46 39N 0 14W
Partry Rol 20 B3 53 42N 9 16W
Partry Mountains Rol 20 B3 53 39N 9 27W
Paşcani Romania 53 N3 47 14N 26 46E
Passage East Rol 21 E2 52 13N 6 59W
Passage West *tn.* Rol 21 C1 51 52N 8 20W
Passau Germany 52 F4 48 35N 13 28E
Pasto Colombia 96 B14 1 12N 77 17W
Patagonia *geog. reg.*
Argentina 97 C2/D4 48 00S 70 00W
Pateley Bridge *tn.*
England 13 E3 54 05N 1 45W
Patna Scotland 11 E2 55 20N 4 30W
Patna India 67 F5 25 37N 85 12E
Patras Greece 55 J3 38 14N 21 44E
Patrickswell Rol 21 C2 52 36N 8 42W
Patrington England 13 F2 53 41N 0 02W
Pau France 50 D2 43 18N 0 22W
Pavia Italy 54 C6 45 12N 9 09E
Pavullo nel Frignano
Italy 54 D6 44 20N 10 49E
Peacehaven England 16 C1 50 47N 0 01E
Peč Serbia 55 J5 42 40N 20 19E
Pécs Hungary 53 J3 46 04N 18 15E
Peebles Scotland 11 F2 55 39N 3 12W
Peel Isle of Man 12 B3 54 14N 4 42W
Pelopónnisos *geog. reg.*
Greece 55 J2/K2 37 00N 22 00E
Pelotas Brazil 97 G7 31 45S 52 20W
Pembridge England 14 D2 52 14N 2 53W
Pembroke England 14 B1 51 41N 4 55W
Pembroke Dock Wales 14 B1 51 42N 4 56W
Pembrokeshire *u.a.*
Wales 14 A1/B1 51 50N 5 00W
Pembury England 17 D2 51 08N 0 19E
Penarth Wales 14 C1 51 27N 3 11W
Pencoed Wales 14 C1 51 31N 3 30W
Pendine Wales 14 B1 51 34N 4 35W
Penicuik Scotland 11 F2 55 50N 3 14W
Penistone England 13 E2 53 32N 1 37W
Penkridge England 15 D2 52 44N 2 07W
Penmaenmawr Wales 14 C3 53 16N 3 54W
Pennines England 12/13 D3/E2 54 30N 2 10W
Pennsylvania *state*
USA 91 L5 41 00N 78 00W
Penrhyndeudraeth
Wales 14 B2 52 56N 4 04W
Penrith England 12 D3 54 40N 2 44W
Penryn England 18 B2 50 09N 5 06W
Pensilva England 18 C2 50 30N 4 25W
Pentland Firth Scotland 7 A1 58 45N 3 10W
Pentland Hills Scotland 11 F2 55 45N 3 30W
Pen-y-ghent *sum.*
England 12 D3 54 10N 2 14W
Penygroes Wales 14 B3 53 04N 4 17W
Penzance England 18 B2 50 07N 5 33W
Pénombre Germany 52 F5 50 29N 12 08E
Périgueux France 50 E3 45 12N 0 44E
Perm' Russia 62 H8 58 01N 56 10E
Pernik Bulgaria 55 K5 42 36N 23 03E
Péronne France 50 F5 49 56N 2 57E
Perpignan France 50 F2 42 42N 2 54E
Perranporth England 18 B2 50 20N 5 09W
Perth Australia 72 C4 31 58S 115 49E
Perth Scotland 9 F1 56 24N 3 28W
Perth and Kinross *u.a.*
Scotland 9 F1 56 45N 3 50W
PERU 96 B11/C11
Perugia Italy 54 E5 43 07N 12 23E
Pesaro Italy 54 E5 43 54N 12 54E
Pescara Italy 54 F5 42 27N 14 13E
Peshawar Pakistan 66 C6 34 01N 71 40E
Pessac France 50 D3 44 49N 0 37W
Peterborough England 16 C3 52 35N 0 15W
Peterculter Scotland 9 G2 57 05N 2 16W
Peterhead Scotland 9 H2 57 30N 1 46W
Peterlee England 13 E4 54 46N 1 19W
Petersfield England 16 C1 51 00N 0 56W
Petrolina Brazil 96 J12 9 22S 40 30W
Petworth England 16 C1 50 59N 0 38W
Pevensey England 17 D1 50 49N 0 20E

Pewsey England 16 B2 51 21N 1 46W
Pforzheim Germany 52 D4 48 53N 8 41E
Phenix City USA 91 J3 32 28N 85 01W
Philadelphia USA 91 L4 40 00N 75 10W
PHILIPPINES, THE 71 G7/H5
Phnom Penh Cambodia 71 C6 11 35N 104 55E
Phoenix USA 90 D3 33 30N 112 03W
Piacenza Italy 54 C6 45 03N 9 41E
Pickering England 13 F3 54 14N 0 46W
Píndhos *mts.* Greece 55 J3 40 00N 21 00E
Pinsk Belarus 57 C5 52 08N 26 01E
Pinwherry Scotland 10 E2 55 09N 4 50W
Piombino Italy 54 D5 42 56N 10 32E
Pirineos *mts.*
Spain/France 51 E5/F5 42 50N 0 30E
Pirmasens Germany 52 C4 49 12N 7 37E
Pisa Italy 54 D5 43 43N 10 24E
Pistoia Italy 54 D5 43 56N 10 55E
Piteå Sweden 49 F4 65 19N 21 30E
Piteşti Romania 53 M2 44 51N 24 51E
Pitlochry Scotland 9 F1 56 43N 3 45W
Pitmedden Scotland 9 G2 57 19N 2 11W
Pittenweem Scotland 11 G3 56 13N 2 44W
Pittsburgh USA 91 L5 40 26N 80 00W
Piura Peru 96 A12 5 15S 80 38W
Planalto de Mato Grosso
*geog. reg.* Brazil 96F11/G11 13 00S 56 00W
Plasencia Spain 51 B4 40 02N 6 05W
Platte *r.* USA 90 F5 41 00N 100 00W
Plauen Germany 52 F5 50 29N 12 08E
Pleven Bulgaria 55 L5 43 25N 24 04E
Płock Poland 53 J6 52 32N 19 40E
Plockton Scotland 8 D2 57 20N 5 40W
Ploieşti Romania 53 M2 44 57N 26 01E
Plovdiv Bulgaria 55 L5 42 08N 24 45E
Plymouth England 18 C2 50 23N 4 10W
Plympton England 18 C2 50 23N 4 03W
Plymstock England 18 C2 50 21N 4 07W
Plynlimon *mt.* Wales 14 C2 52 28N 3 47W
Plzeň Czech Rep. 52 F4 49 45N 13 25E
Po *r.* Italy 54 D6 45 00N 10 00E
Pocklington England 13 F2 53 56N 0 46W
Podgorica
Montenegro 55 H5 42 28N 19 17E
Point-Noire *tn.* Congo 82 B7 4 46S 11 53E
Poitiers France 50 E4 46 35N 0 20E
POLAND 53 J6/K6
Polegate England 17 D1 50 50N 0 15E
Polesworth England 15 E2 52 44N 1 36W
Policoro Italy 55 G4 40 12N 16 40E
Pollensa Spain 51 G3 39 52N 3 01E
Polperro England 18 C2 50 19N 4 31W
Polýgyros Greece 55 K4 40 23N 23 25E
Pondicherry India 66 D2 11 59N 79 50E
Ponferrada Spain 51 B5 42 33N 6 35W
Pont *r.* England 12 E4 55 02N 1 55W
Ponta Grossa Brazil 96 G8 25 07S 50 09W
Pont-à-Mousson
France 50 H5 48 55N 6 03E
Pontardawe Wales 14 C1 51 44N 3 52W
Pontardulais Wales 14 B1 51 43N 4 02W
Pontefract England 13 E2 53 42N 1 18W
Ponteland England 13 E4 55 03N 1 44W
Ponte Leccia France 50 J2 42 28N 9 12E
Ponterwyd Wales 14 C2 52 25N 3 50W
Pontevedra Spain 51 A5 42 25N 8 39W
Pontivy France 50 C5 48 04N 2 58W
Pontrilas England 14 D1 51 57N 2 53W
Pontyclun Wales 14 C1 51 33N 3 23W
Pontycymer Wales 14 C1 51 36N 3 35W
Pontypool Wales 14 C1 51 43N 3 02W
Pontypridd Wales 14 C1 51 37N 3 22W
Poole England 19 F2 50 43N 1 59W
Poole *u.a.* England 19 F2 50 43N 1 59W
Poole Bay *b.* England 19 F3 50 41N 1 52W
Poolewe Scotland 8 D2 57 45N 5 37W
Pooley Bridge *tn.*
England 12 D3 54 38N 2 49W
Popacatepetl *mt.*
Mexico 94 E3 19 02N 98 38W
Pordenone Italy 54 E6 45 58N 12 39E
Pori Finland 49 F3 61 28N 21 45E
Porlock England 18 D3 51 14N 3 36W
Portadown NI 10 C1 54 26N 6 27W
Portaferry NI 10 D1 54 23N 5 33W
Portalegre Portugal 51 B3 39 17N 7 25W
Portarlington Rol 21 D3 53 10N 7 11W
Port Askaig Scotland 10 C2 55 51N 6 07W
Port-au-Prince Haiti 95 K3 18 33N 72 20W
Portavogie NI 10 D1 54 28N 5 25W
Port Elizabeth RSA 82 E1 33 58S 25 36E
Port Ellen Scotland 10 C2 55 39N 6 12W
Port Erin Isle of Man 12 B3 54 05N 4 45W
Port-Eynon Wales 14 B1 51 28N 4 12W
Port Gentil Gabon 82 A7 0 40S 8 50E
Port Glasgow Scotland 11 E2 55 56N 4 41W
Portglenone NI 10 C1 54 52N 6 29W
Port Harcourt Nigeria 80 F2 4 43N 7 05E
Porthcawl Wales 14 C1 51 29N 3 43W
Porthleven England 18 BB2 50 30N 5 21W
Porthmadog Wales 14 B2 52 55N 4 08W
Portimão Portugal 51 A2 37 08N 8 32W
Port Isaac England 18 C2 50 35N 4 49W
Portishead England 19 E3 51 30N 2 46W
Portknockie Scotland 9 G2 57 42N 2 52W
Portland USA 90 B6 45 32N 122 40W
Portlaoise Rol 21 D3 53 02N 7 17W

| Place | Page | Grid | Lat | Long |
|---|---|---|---|---|
| Portlaw RoI | 21 | D2 | 52 17N | 7 19W |
| Portlethen Scotland | 9 | G2 | 57 03N | 2 07W |
| Portmahomack Scotland | 9 | F2 | 57 49N | 3 50W |
| Port Moresby PNG | 73 | J9 | 9 30S | 147 07E |
| Portnaguran Scotland | 8 | C3 | 58 17N | 6 13W |
| Portnahaven Scotland | 10 | C2 | 55 41N | 6 31W |
| Porto Alegre Brazil | 97 | G7 | 30 03S | 51 10W |
| Port of Ness Scotland | 8 | C3 | 58 29N | 6 13W |
| Port of Spain Trinidad and Tobago | 95 | V15 | 10 38N | 61 31W |
| Porto Novo Benin | 80 | E3 | 6 30N | 2 47E |
| Porto Tórres Italy | 54 | C4 | 40 51N | 8 24E |
| Porto-Vecchio France | 50 | J1 | 41 35N | 9 16E |
| Pôrto Velho Brazil | 96 | E12 | 8 45S | 63 54W |
| Portpatrick Scotland | 10 | D2 | 54 51N | 5 07W |
| Portreath England | 18 | B2 | 50 51N | 5 17W |
| Portree Scotland | 8 | C2 | 57 24N | 6 12W |
| Portrush NI | 10 | C2 | 55 12N | 6 40W |
| Port Said Egypt | 81 | M8 | 31 17N | 6 40E |
| Portskerra Scotland | 9 | F3 | 58 33N | 3 55W |
| Portsmouth England | 16 | B1 | 50 48N | 1 05W |
| Portsmouth u.a. England | 16 | B1 | 50 48N | 1 05W |
| Portsmouth USA | 91 | L4 | 36 50N | 76 20W |
| Portsoy Scotland | 9 | G2 | 57 41N | 2 41W |
| Portstewart NI | 10 | C2 | 55 11N | 6 43W |
| Port Sudan Egypt | 81 | N5 | 19 38N | 37 07E |
| Port Talbot Wales | 14 | C1 | 51 36N | 3 47W |
| PORTUGAL | 51 | A3/B3 | | |
| Portumna RoI | 21 | C3 | 53 06N | 8 13W |
| Port Wemyss Scotland | 10 | C2 | 55 42N | 6 29W |
| Port William Scotland | 11 | E1 | 54 46N | 4 35W |
| Potenza Italy | 54 | F4 | 40 38N | 15 48E |
| Potomac r. USA | 91 | L4 | 39 10N | 77 30W |
| Potsdam Germany | 52 | F6 | 52 24N | 13 04E |
| Potter's Bar England | 16 | C2 | 51 42N | 0 11W |
| Potton England | 16 | C3 | 52 08N | 0 14W |
| Poulton-le-Fylde England | 12 | D2 | 53 51N | 3 00W |
| Powell River tn. Canada | 88 | L3 | 49 54N | 124 34W |
| Power Head RoI | 21 | C1 | 51 47N | 8 10W |
| Powfoot Scotland | 11 | F1 | 54 59N | 3 20W |
| Powys u.a. Wales | 14 | C2 | 52 10N | 3 30W |
| Poznań Poland | 53 | H6 | 52 25N | 16 53E |
| Prague Czech Rep. | 52 | G5 | 50 06N | 14 26E |
| Prato Italy | 54 | D5 | 43 53N | 11 06E |
| Prawle Point England | 18 | D2 | 50 12N | 3 44W |
| Preesall England | 12 | D2 | 53 55N | 2 57W |
| Prešov Slovakia | 53 | K4 | 49 00N | 21 10E |
| Prestatyn Wales | 14 | C3 | 53 20N | 3 24W |
| Presteigne Wales | 14 | C2 | 52 17N | 3 00W |
| Preston England | 12 | D2 | 53 46N | 2 42W |
| Prestonpans Scotland | 11 | G2 | 55 57N | 3 00W |
| Prestwich England | 12 | D2 | 53 32N | 2 17W |
| Prestwick Scotland | 11 | E2 | 55 30N | 4 37W |
| Pretoria RSA | 82 | E2 | 25 45S | 28 12E |
| Příbram Czech Rep. | 52 | G4 | 49 42N | 14 01E |
| Prince Albert Canada | 89 | P4 | 53 13N | 105 45W |
| Prince Edward Island prov. Canada | 89 | Y3 | 46 30N | 63 00W |
| Prince Rupert Canada | 88 | J4 | 54 09N | 130 20W |
| Princes Risborough England | 16 | C2 | 51 44N | 0 51W |
| Princetown England | 18 | D2 | 50 33N | 3 59W |
| Pripyats' r. Belarus | 56 | B5/C5 | 52 30N | 27 00E |
| Priština Serbia | 55 | J5 | 42 39N | 21 20E |
| Privas France | 50 | G3 | 44 44N | 4 36E |
| Prokop'yevsk Russia | 62 | L7 | 53 55N | 86 45E |
| Providence USA | 91 | M5 | 41 50N | 71 28W |
| Provins France | 50 | F5 | 48 34N | 3 18E |
| Prudhoe England | 13 | E3 | 54 58N | 1 51W |
| Prudhoe Bay tn. USA | 88 | F8 | 70 05N | 148 20W |
| Pruszków Poland | 53 | K6 | 52 10N | 20 47E |
| Prut r. Romania | 53 | P3 | 47 00N | 28 00E |
| Pskov Russia | 62 | E8 | 57 48N | 28 26E |
| Pucallpa Peru | 96 | C12 | 8 21S | 74 33W |
| Puddletown England | 19 | E2 | 50 45N | 2 21W |
| Pudsey England | 13 | E2 | 53 48N | 1 40W |
| Puebla Mexico | 94 | E3 | 19 03N | 98 10W |
| Pueblo USA | 90 | F4 | 38 17N | 104 38W |
| Puertollano Spain | 51 | C3 | 38 41N | 4 07W |
| Puerto Montt Chile | 97 | C5 | 41 28S | 73 00W |
| PUERTO RICO | 95 | L3 | | |
| Pulborough England | 16 | C1 | 50 58N | 0 30W |
| Pumsaint Wales | 14 | C2 | 52 03N | 3 58W |
| Pune India | 66 | C3 | 18 34N | 73 58E |
| Punta Arenas Chile | 97 | C3 | 53 10S | 70 56W |
| Purfleet England | 17 | D2 | 51 29N | 0 14E |
| Puri India | 67 | F3 | 19 49N | 85 54E |
| Pusan S. Korea | 69 | N5 | 35 05N | 129 02E |
| Puulavesi l. Finland | 49 | G3 | 61 50N | 26 40E |
| Pwllheli Wales | 14 | B2 | 52 53N | 4 25W |
| Pyle Wales | 14 | C1 | 51 32N | 3 42W |
| Pyongyang N. Korea | 69 | N5 | 39 00N | 125 47E |
| Pyrénées mts. France/Spain | 50 | E2 | 42 50N | 0 30E |
| Pýrgos Greece | 55 | J2 | 37 40N | 21 27E |
| Pýrgos Greece | 55 | L1 | 35 00N | 25 10E |

**Q**

| Place | Page | Grid | Lat | Long |
|---|---|---|---|---|
| QATAR | 65 | F4 | | |
| Qingdao China | 69 | M5 | 36 04N | 120 22E |
| Qiqihar China | 69 | M7 | 47 23N | 124 00E |
| Quantock Hills England | 19 | D3 | 51 10N | 3 15W |
| Québec prov. Canada | 89 | V4/X4 | 50 00N | 75 00W |
| Québec Canada | 89 | W3 | 46 50N | 71 15W |
| Queenborough England | 17 | D2 | 51 26N | 0 45E |
| Queen Charlotte Islands Canada | 88 | J4 | 53 00N | 132 30W |
| Queen Elizabeth Islands Canada | 89 | N9/S9 | 77 30N | 105 00W |
| Queensbury England | 13 | E2 | 53 46N | 1 50W |
| Queenstown Australia | 73 | J2 | 42 07S | 145 33E |
| Querétaro Mexico | 94 | D4 | 20 38N | 100 23W |
| Quetta Pakistan | 66 | B6 | 30 15N | 67 00E |
| Quezon City Philippines | 71 | G6 | 14 39N | 121 02E |
| Quiberon France | 50 | C4 | 47 29N | 3 07W |
| Quigley's Point RoI | 20 | D5 | 55 10N | 7 08W |
| Quimper France | 50 | B4 | 48 00N | 4 06W |
| Quito Ecuador | 96 | B13 | 0 14S | 78 30W |
| Quorn England | 15 | E2 | 52 45N | 1 10W |

**R**

| Place | Page | Grid | Lat | Long |
|---|---|---|---|---|
| Raahe Finland | 49 | F3 | 64 42N | 24 30E |
| Raasay i. Scotland | 8 | C2 | 57 25N | 6 05W |
| Rabat-Salé Morocco | 80 | C8 | 34 02N | 6 51W |
| Radcliffe England | 12 | D2 | 53 34N | 2 20W |
| Radcliffe on Trent England | 15 | E3 | 52 57N | 1 03W |
| Radlett England | 16 | C2 | 51 41N | 0 19W |
| Radom Poland | 53 | K5 | 51 26N | 21 10E |
| Radstadt Austria | 52 | F3 | 47 23N | 13 28E |
| Radstock England | 19 | E3 | 51 18N | 2 28W |
| Raglan Wales | 14 | D1 | 51 47N | 2 51W |
| Ragusa Italy | 54 | F3 | 36 56N | 14 44E |
| Rainford England | 12 | D2 | 53 30N | 2 48W |
| Rainier, Mount USA | 90 | B6 | 46 25N | 121 45W |
| Rainworth England | 13 | E2 | 53 08N | 1 08W |
| Raipur India | 66 | E4 | 21 16N | 81 42E |
| Rame Head England | 18 | C2 | 50 19N | 4 13W |
| Ramore Head NI | 10 | C2 | 55 13N | 6 39W |
| Ramsbottom England | 12 | D2 | 53 39N | 2 19W |
| Ramsey England | 16 | C3 | 52 27N | 0 07W |
| Ramsey Isle of Man | 12 | B3 | 54 19N | 4 23W |
| Ramsey Island Wales | 14 | A1 | 51 53N | 5 20W |
| Ramsgate England | 17 | E2 | 51 20N | 1 25E |
| Randalstown NI | 10 | C1 | 54 45N | 6 19W |
| Rangpur Bangladesh | 67 | F5 | 25 45N | 89 21E |
| Rannoch Moor Scotland | 9 | E1 | 56 35N | 4 50W |
| Rannoch Station Scotland | 9 | E1 | 5642N | 4 34W |
| Rapallo Italy | 54 | C6 | 44 21N | 9 13E |
| Raphoe RoI | 20 | D5 | 54 52N | 7 36W |
| Rastatt Germany | 52 | D4 | 48 51N | 8 13E |
| Rathangan RoI | 20 | E3 | 53 12N | 6 59W |
| Rathcoole RoI | 20 | E3 | 53 17N | 6 28W |
| Rathcormack RoI | 21 | C2 | 52 05N | 8 17W |
| Rathdowney RoI | 21 | D2 | 52 51N | 7 35W |
| Rathdrum RoI | 21 | E2 | 52 56N | 6 13W |
| Rathfriland NI | 10 | C1 | 54 14N | 6 10W |
| Rathkeale RoI | 21 | C2 | 52 32N | 8 56W |
| Rathlackan RoI | 20 | B4 | 54 18N | 9 15W |
| Rathlin Sound NI | 10 | C2 | 55 20N | 6 25W |
| Rath Luirc RoI | 21 | C2 | 52 21N | 8 41W |
| Rathmelton RoI | 20 | D5 | 55 02N | 7 38W |
| Rathmore RoI | 21 | B2 | 52 05N | 9 13W |
| Rathnew RoI | 21 | E2 | 52 58N | 6 05W |
| Rathvilly RoI | 21 | E2 | 52 53N | 6 41W |
| Ratoath RoI | 20 | E3 | 53 31N | 6 24W |
| Raton USA | 90 | F4 | 36 45N | 104 27W |
| Rattray Scotland | 9 | F1 | 56 36N | 3 20W |
| Rattray Head Scotland | 9 | H2 | 57 38N | 1 45W |
| Rauma Finland | 49 | F3 | 61 09N | 21 30E |
| Raunds England | 15 | F2 | 52 21N | 0 33W |
| Ravenglass England | 12 | C3 | 54 21N | 3 24W |
| Ravenna Italy | 54 | E6 | 44 25N | 12 12E |
| Ravensburg Germany | 52 | D3 | 47 47N | 9 37E |
| Ravenshead England | 13 | E2 | 53 40N | 1 10W |
| Rawalpindi Pakistan | 66 | C6 | 33 40N | 73 08E |
| Rawmarsh England | 13 | E2 | 53 27N | 1 21W |
| Rawtenstall England | 12 | D2 | 53 42N | 2 18W |
| Rayleigh England | 17 | D2 | 51 36N | 0 36E |
| Reading England | 16 | C2 | 51 28N | 0 59W |
| Reading u.a. England | 16 | B1/C1 | 50 25N | 1 00W |
| Reay Forest Scotland | 9 | E3 | 58 20N | 4 55W |
| Recife Brazil | 96 | L12 | 8 06S | 34 53W |
| Recklinghausen Germany | 52 | C5 | 51 37N | 7 11E |
| Red Bay NI | 10 | C2 | 55 04N | 6 01W |
| Redbourn England | 16 | C2 | 51 48N | 0 24W |
| Redbridge England | 16 | D2 | 51 34N | 0 05E |
| Redcar England | 13 | E3 | 54 37N | 1 04W |
| Redcar and Cleveland u.a. England | 13 | E3/F3 | 54 30N | 1 00W |
| Redditch England | 15 | E2 | 52 19N | 1 56W |
| Redhill tn. England | 16 | C2 | 51 14N | 0 11W |
| Redon France | 50 | C4 | 47 39N | 2 05W |
| Redruth England | 18 | B2 | 50 13N | 5 14W |
| Red Sea Middle East | 64 | C4/C2 | 27 00N | 35 00E |
| Reepham England | 17 | E3 | 52 46N | 1 07E |
| Regensburg Germany | 52 | F4 | 49 01N | 12 07E |
| Reggio di Calabria Italy | 54 | F3 | 38 06N | 15 39E |
| Regina Canada | 89 | Q4 | 50 30N | 104 38W |
| Reigate England | 16 | C2 | 51 14N | 0 13W |
| Reims France | 50 | G5 | 49 15N | 4 02E |
| Reinosa Spain | 51 | C3 | 43 01N | 4 09W |
| Rendsburg Germany | 52 | D7 | 54 19N | 9 39E |
| Renfrew Canada | 89 | V3 | 45 28N | 76 44W |
| Renfrew Scotland | 11 | E2 | 55 53N | 4 24W |
| Renfrewshire u.a. Scotland | 11 | E2 | 55 50N | 4 40W |
| Rennes France | 50 | D5 | 48 06N | 1 40W |
| Reno USA | 90 | C4 | 39 32N | 119 49W |
| REPUBLIC OF IRELAND | 20/21 | | | |
| REPUBLIC OF SOUTH AFRICA | 82 | D1/D2 | | |
| Requena Spain | 51 | E3 | 39 29N | 1 08W |
| Resistencia Argentina | 97 | F8 | 27 28S | 59 00W |
| Resolute Canada | 89 | S8 | 74 40N | 95 00W |
| Retford England | 13 | F2 | 53 19N | 0 56W |
| Rethel France | 50 | G5 | 49 31N | 4 22E |
| Reus Spain | 51 | F4 | 41 10N | 1 06E |
| Reutlingen Germany | 52 | D4 | 48 30N | 9 13E |
| Reykjavík Iceland | 49 | K6 | 64 09N | 21 58W |
| Rhayader Wales | 14 | C2 | 52 18N | 3 30W |
| Rheden Neths | 48 | E5 | 52 01N | 6 02E |
| Rheidol r. Wales | 14 | C2 | 52 23N | 3 55W |
| Rhein r. Germany | 52 | C4 | 50 30N | 8 00E |
| Rheine Germany | 52 | C6 | 52 17N | 7 26E |
| Rhode Island state USA | 91 | M5 | 41 00N | 71 00W |
| Rhondda Wales | 14 | C1 | 51 40N | 3 30W |
| Rhondda Cynon Taff u.a. Wales | 14 | C1 | 51 40N | 3 30W |
| Rhône r. Switz./France | 50 | G3 | 45 00N | 4 50E |
| Rhoose Wales | 14 | C1 | 51 26N | 3 22W |
| Rhosllanerchrugog Wales | 14 | C3 | 53 01N | 3 04W |
| Rhosneigr Wales | 14 | B3 | 53 14N | 4 31W |
| Rhossili Wales | 14 | B1 | 51 34N | 4 17W |
| Rhubodach Scotland | 10 | D2 | 55 56N | 5 09W |
| Rhum i. Scotland | 8 | C2 | 57 00N | 6 20W |
| Rhyl Wales | 14 | C3 | 53 19N | 3 29W |
| Rhymney Wales | 14 | C1 | 51 46N | 3 18W |
| Rhynie Scotland | 9 | G2 | 57 19N | 2 50W |
| Ribble r. England | 12 | D2 | 53 45N | 2 30W |
| Ribeirão Prêto Brazil | 96 | H9 | 21 09S | 47 48W |
| Riccall England | 13 | E2 | 53 51N | 1 04W |
| Richhill NI | 10 | C1 | 54 22N | 6 33W |
| Richmond England | 13 | E3 | 54 24N | 1 44W |
| Richmond upon Thames England | 16 | C2 | 51 28N | 0 19W |
| Rickmansworth England | 16 | C2 | 51 38N | 0 29W |
| Ried Austria | 52 | F4 | 48 13N | 13 29E |
| Riesa Germany | 52 | F5 | 51 18N | 13 18E |
| Rieti Italy | 54 | E5 | 42 24N | 12 51E |
| Riga Latvia | 49 | F2 | 56 53N | 24 08E |
| Rimini Italy | 54 | E6 | 44 03N | 12 34E |
| Ringabella Bay RoI | 21 | C1 | 51 46N | 8 13W |
| Ringaskiddy RoI | 21 | C1 | 51 49N | 8 18W |
| Ringwood England | 16 | B1 | 50 51N | 1 47W |
| Rio Branco tn. Brazil | 96 | D12 | 9 59S | 67 49W |
| Rio de Janeiro tn. Brazil | 96 | I8 | 22 53S | 43 17W |
| Rio de la Plata est. Uruguay/Argentina | 97 | F5 | 35 00S | 57 00W |
| Rio Grande tn. Brazil | 97 | G7 | 32 03S | 52 08W |
| Rio Grande r. Mexico/USA | 90 | E3/F3 | 30 00N | 105 00W |
| Ripley England | 13 | E2 | 53 03N | 1 24W |
| Ripon England | 13 | E3 | 54 08N | 1 31W |
| Risca Wales | 14 | C1 | 51 37N | 3 07W |
| Rishton England | 12 | D2 | 53 47N | 2 24W |
| Riva del Garda Italy | 54 | D6 | 45 53N | 10 50E |
| Riverton Canada | 89 | R4 | 51 00N | 97 00W |
| Rivne Ukraine | 53 | M5 | 50 39N | 26 10E |
| Riyadh Saudi Arabia | 65 | E3 | 24 39N | 46 46E |
| Roanne France | 50 | G4 | 46 02N | 4 05E |
| Robin Hood's Bay tn. England | 13 | F3 | 54 25N | 0 33W |
| Rochdale England | 12 | D2 | 53 38N | 2 09W |
| Rochefort France | 50 | D3 | 45 57N | 0 58W |
| Rochester Northamptonshire England | 12 | D4 | 55 16N | 2 16W |
| Rochester Medway England | 17 | D2 | 51 24N | 0 30E |
| Rochester USA | 91 | L5 | 43 12N | 77 37W |
| Rochford England | 17 | D2 | 51 36N | 0 43E |
| Rochfortbridge RoI | 20 | D3 | 53 25N | 7 18W |
| Rockhampton Australia | 73 | K6 | 23 22S | 150 32E |
| Rocky Mountains Canada/USA | 88 | K5/P2 | 55 00N | 125 00W |
| Rodel Scotland | 8 | C2 | 57 41N | 7 05W |
| Rodez France | 50 | F3 | 44 21N | 2 34E |
| Roding r. England | 17 | D2 | 51 45N | 0 15E |
| Roermond Neths | 48 | D4 | 51 12N | 6 00E |
| ROMANIA | 53 | L2/M2 | | |
| Romans-sur-Isère France | 50 | G3 | 45 03N | 5 03E |
| Rome Italy | 54 | E4 | 41 53N | 12 30E |
| Romney Marsh England | 17 | D2 | 51 03N | 0 58E |
| Romorantin-Lanthenay France | 50 | E4 | 47 22N | 1 44E |
| Romsey England | 16 | B1 | 50 59N | 1 30W |
| Rona i. Scotland | 8 | D2 | 57 32N | 5 59W |
| Ronda Spain | 51 | C2 | 36 45N | 5 10W |
| Ronse Belgium | 48 | B3 | 50 45N | 3 36E |
| Roosendaal Neths | 48 | C4 | 51 32N | 4 28E |
| Roosky RoI | 20 | D3 | 53 50N | 7 55W |
| Roquetas de Mar Spain | 51 | D2 | 36 46N | 2 35W |
| Rora Head Scotland | 7 | A1 | 58 52N | 3 26W |
| Rosario Argentina | 97 | E7 | 33 00S | 60 40W |
| Rosarno Italy | 54 | F3 | 38 29N | 15 59E |
| Roscoff France | 50 | C5 | 48 43N | 3 59W |
| Roscommon RoI | 20 | C3 | 53 38N | 8 11W |
| Roscommon co. RoI | 20 | C3 | 53 45N | 8 10W |
| Roscrea RoI | 21 | D2 | 52 57N | 7 47W |
| Rosehearty Scotland | 9 | G2 | 57 42N | 2 07W |
| Rosenheim Germany | 52 | F3 | 47 51N | 12 09E |
| Roskilde Denmark | 49 | D2 | 55 39N | 12 07E |
| Rossano Italy | 54 | G3 | 39 35N | 16 38E |
| Rossan Point RoI | 20 | C4 | 54 40N | 8 50W |
| Ross Carbery RoI | 21 | B1 | 51 35N | 9 02W |
| Rosscarbery Bay RoI | 21 | B1 | 51 32N | 9 00W |
| Rosslare RoI | 21 | E2 | 52 15N | 6 22W |
| Rosslare Harbour tn. RoI | 21 | E2 | 52 15N | 6 22W |
| Rosslare Point RoI | 21 | E2 | 52 19N | 6 21W |
| Ross-on-Wye England | 15 | D1 | 51 55N | 2 35W |
| Rostock Germany | 52 | F7 | 54 06N | 12 09E |
| Rostov-na-Donu Russia | 62 | F6 | 47 15N | 39 45E |
| Rostrevor NI | 10 | C1 | 54 06N | 6 12W |
| Rothbury England | 11 | H2 | 55 19N | 1 55W |
| Rother r. England | 16 | C1 | 51 00N | 0 50W |
| Rother r. England | 17 | D2 | 51 00N | 0 17E |
| Rotherham England | 13 | E2 | 53 26N | 1 20W |
| Rothes Scotland | 9 | F2 | 57 31N | 3 13W |
| Rothesay Scotland | 10 | D2 | 55 51N | 5 03W |
| Rothwell West Yorkshire England | 13 | E2 | 53 45N | 1 29W |
| Rothwell Northamptonshire England | 15 | F2 | 52 25N | 0 48W |
| Rotterdam Neths | 48 | C4 | 51 54N | 4 28E |
| Rottingdean England | 16 | C1 | 50 48N | 0 04W |
| Roubaix France | 50 | F6 | 50 42N | 3 10E |
| Rouen France | 50 | E5 | 49 26N | 1 05E |
| Roundwood RoI | 21 | E2 | 53 04N | 6 13W |
| Rousay i. Scotland | 7 | A2 | 59 10N | 3 00W |
| Rovigo Italy | 54 | D6 | 45 04N | 11 47E |
| Rowlands Gill England | 13 | E3 | 54 54N | 1 45W |
| Royal Leamington Spa England | 15 | E2 | 52 18N | 1 31W |
| Royal Tunbridge Wells England | 17 | D2 | 51 08N | 0 16E |
| Royan France | 50 | D3 | 45 38N | 1 02W |
| Royston South Yorkshire England | 13 | E2 | 53 37N | 1 27W |
| Royston Hertfordshire England | 16 | C3 | 52 03N | 0 01W |
| Royton England | 12 | D2 | 53 34N | 2 08W |
| Ruabon Wales | 14 | C2 | 52 59N | 3 02W |
| Ruddington England | 15 | E2 | 52 54N | 1 09W |
| Rufford England | 15 | E2 | 53 39N | 2 49W |
| Rugby England | 15 | E2 | 52 23N | 1 15W |
| Rugeley England | 15 | E2 | 52 46N | 1 55W |
| Ruhr r. Germany | 52 | D5 | 51 00N | 7 00E |
| Rumney Wales | 14 | C1 | 51 30N | 3 10W |
| Runcorn England | 12 | D2 | 53 20N | 2 44W |
| Ruse Bulgaria | 55 | M5 | 43 50N | 25 59E |
| Rush RoI | 20 | E3 | 53 32N | 6 06W |
| Rushden England | 15 | F2 | 52 17N | 0 36W |
| RUSSIAN FEDERATION | 62/63 | | | |
| Ruthin Wales | 14 | C3 | 53 07N | 3 18W |
| Rutland u.a. England | 15 | F2 | 5241N | 00 39W |
| Rutland Water England | 15 | F2 | 52 40N | 0 37W |
| RWANDA | 83 | A3/B3 | | |
| Ryazan' Russia | 62 | F7 | 54 37N | 39 43E |
| Rybinsk Russia | 62 | F8 | 58 03N | 38 50E |
| Rybnik Poland | 53 | J5 | 50 07N | 18 30E |
| Ryde England | 16 | B1 | 50 44N | 1 10W |
| Rye r. England | 13 | E3 | 54 15N | 1 10W |
| Rye England | 17 | D1 | 50 57N | 0 44E |
| Ryton England | 13 | E3 | 54 59N | 1 57W |
| Ryukyu Islands Japan | 69 | N3 | 27 30N | 127 30E |

**S**

| Place | Page | Grid | Lat | Long |
|---|---|---|---|---|
| Saalfeld Germany | 52 | E5 | 50 39N | 11 22E |
| Saarbrücken Germany | 52 | C4 | 49 15N | 6 58E |
| Sabadell Spain | 51 | G4 | 41 33N | 2 07E |
| Sacramento USA | 90 | B4 | 38 32N | 121 30W |
| Sacriston England | 13 | E3 | 54 50N | 1 38W |
| Saffron Walden England | 17 | D3 | 52 01N | 0 15E |
| Saga Japan | 70 | B1 | 33 16N | 130 18E |
| Sagunto Spain | 51 | E3 | 39 40N | 0 17W |
| Sahagún Spain | 51 | C3 | 42 23N | 5 02W |
| St. Abbs Scotland | 11 | G2 | 55 54N | 2 08W |
| St. Abb's Head Scotland | 11 | G2 | 55 55N | 2 09W |
| St. Agnes England | 18 | B2 | 50 18N | 5 13W |
| St. Albans England | 16 | C2 | 51 46N | 0 21W |
| St. Alban's or St Aldheim's Head England | 19 | E2 | 50 34N | 2 04W |
| St. Andrews Scotland | 9 | G1 | 56 20N | 2 48W |
| St. Anne Channel Islands | 19 | E1 | 49 43N | 2 12W |
| St. Asaph Wales | 14 | C3 | 53 15N | 3 26W |
| St. Austell England | 18 | C2 | 50 20N | 4 48W |
| St. Bees England | 12 | C3 | 54 29N | 3 35W |
| St. Blazey England | 18 | C2 | 50 22N | 4 43W |
| St. Bride's Bay Wales | 14 | A1 | 51 50N | 5 15W |
| St-Brieuc France | 50 | C5 | 48 31N | 2 45W |
| St. Catharines Canada | 89 | V2 | 43 10N | 79 15W |
| St-Chamond France | 50 | G3 | 45 29N | 4 32E |
| St. Clears Wales | 14 | B1 | 51 50N | 4 30W |
| St. Columb Major England | 18 | C2 | 50 26N | 4 56W |
| St. David's Wales | 14 | A1 | 51 54N | 5 16W |
| St. David's Head Wales | 14 | A1 | 51 55N | 5 19W |
| St.-Dié France | 50 | H5 | 48 17N | 6 57E |
| St.-Dizier France | 50 | G5 | 48 38N | 4 58E |
| Saintes France | 50 | D3 | 45 44N | 0 38W |
| St.-Étienne France | 50 | G3 | 45 26N | 4 23E |
| Saintfield NI | 10 | D1 | 54 28N | 5 50W |

St. Finnan's Bay RoI 21 A1 51 50N 10 23W
St. Gallen Switz. 52 D3 47 25N 9 23E
St.-Gaudens France 50 E2 43 07N 0 44E
St.-George's Grenada 94 R11 12 04N 61 44W
St. George's Channel
British Isles 21 E2 52 00N 6 00W
St.-German en-Laye
France 50 F5 48 54N 2 04E
St-Girons France 50 F2 42 59N 1 08E
St. Helens England 12 D2 53 28N 2 44W
St. Helier
Channel Islands 19 E1 49 12N 2 07W
St. Ives England 16 C3 52 20N 0 05W
St. Ives England 18 B2 50 12N 5 29W
St. Jean-de-Luz France 50 D2 43 23N 1 39W
Saint John Canada 89 X3 45 16N 66 03W
St. John's Canada 89 AA3 47 34N 52 41W
St. John's Point NI 10 D1 54 15N 5 35W
St. Johnstown RoI 20 54 56N 7 28W
St. John's Town of Dalry
Scotland 11 E2 55 07N 4 10W
St. Just England 18 B2 50 07N 5 41W
St. Keverne England 18 B2 50 03N 5 06W
St. Kilda i. Scotland 8 57 49N 8 34W
ST. KITTS AND NEVIS 94 P9
St. Lawrence r.
Canada/USA 89 X3 46 55N 55 24W
St. Leonards England 19 F2 50 50N 1 50W
St-Lô France 50 D5 49 07N 1 05W
St. Louis USA 91 H4 38 40N 90 15W
ST. LUCIA 94R11/R12
St. Malo France 50 C5 48 39N 2 00W
St. Margaret's at Cliffe
England 17 E2 51 10N 1 23E
St. Mawes England 18 B2 50 09N 5 01W
St. Monance Scotland 11 G3 56 13N 2 46W
St. Moritz Switz. 52 D3 46 30N 9 51E
St.-Nazaire France 50 C4 47 17N 2 12W
St. Neots England 16 C3 52 14N 0 17W
St.-Omer France 50 F6 50 45N 2 15E
St. Paul USA 91 H5 45 00N 93 10W
St. Peter Port
Channel Islands 19 E1 49 27N 3 32W
St. Petersburg Russia 62 F8 59 55N 30 25E
Saint-Pierre & Miquelon
is. Atlantic Ocean 89 Z3 47 00N 56 20W
St. Pölten Austria 53 G4 48 13N 15 37E
St.-Quentin France 50 F5 49 51N 3 17E
St.-Tropez France 50 H2 43 16N 6 39E
ST. VINCENT AND THE GRENADINES
94 R11
Sakhalin i. Russia 63 S7 50 00N 143 00E
Salamanca Spain 51 C4 40 58N 5 40W
Salcombe England 18 D2 50 13N 3 47W
Sale England 12 D2 53 26N 2 19W
Salen Scotland 8 D1 56 43N 5 47W
Salen Scotland 8 D1 56 31N 5 57W
Salerno Italy 54 F4 40 40N 14 46E
Salford England 12 D2 53 30N 2 16W
Salisbury England 16 B2 51 05N 1 48W
Salisbury Plain
England 16 B2 51 10N 1 55W
Salmon USA 90 D6 45 11N 113 55W
Salo Finland 49 F3 60 23N 23 10E
Salò Italy 54 D6 45 37N 10 31E
Salon-de-Provence
France 50 G2 43 38N 5 06E
Salt Jordan 64 N11 32 03N 35 44E
Salta Argentina 96 D9 24 46S 65 28W
Saltash England 18 C2 50 24N 4 12W
Saltburn-by-the-Sea
England 13 F3 54 35N 0 58W
Saltcoats Scotland 11 E2 55 38N 4 47W
Saltdal Norway 49 E4 67 06N 15 25E
Saltdean England 16 C1 50 49N 0 02W
Saltfleet England 13 G2 53 26N 0 10E
Saltillo Mexico 94 D5 25 30N 101 00W
Salt Lake City USA 90 D5 40 45N 111 55W
Salvador Brazil 96 K11 12 58S 38 29W
Salween r.
China/Myanmar 71 B8 20 00N 103 00E
Salzburg Austria 52 F3 47 48N 13 03E
Salzgitter Germany 52 E6 52 13N 10 20E
Samara Russia 62 H7 53 10N 50 10E
SAMOA 100 J6
Samsun Turkey 57 E3 41 17N 36 22E
Sana Yemen 64 D3 15 23N 44 14E
San Antonio USA 91 G2 29 25N 98 30W
San Cristóbal
Venezuela 96 C15 7 46N 72 15W
Sanda Island Scotland 10 D2 55 18N 5 35W
Sanday i. Scotland 7 B2 59 15N 2 30W
Sandbach England 12 D2 53 09N 2 22W
Sandhead Scotland 10 E1 54 48N 4 58W
Sandhurst England 16 C2 51 21N 0 48W
San Diego USA 90 C3 32 45N 117 10W
Sandown England 16 B1 50 39N 1 09W
Sandray i. Scotland 8 B1 56 53N 7 30W
Sandringham England 17 D2 52 50N 0 31E
Sandwich England 17 E2 51 17N 1 20E
Sandy England 16 C3 52 08N 0 18W
San Fernando Spain 51 B2 36 28N 6 12W
San Francisco USA 90 B4 37 45N 122 27W
San José Costa Rica 95 H1 9 59N 84 04W
San José USA 90 B4 37 20N 121 55W
San Juan Argentina 97 D7 31 33S 68 31W
San Juan Puerto Rico 95 L3 18 29N 66 08W

San Juan Bautista
Spain 51 F3 39 05N 1 31E
SAN MARINO 54 E5 44 00N 12 00E
Sanmenxia China 69 K4 34 46N 111 17E
San Miguel de Tucumán
Argentina 96 D8 26 48S 65 16W
Sanming China 69 L3 26 16N 117 35E
Sannox Scotland 10 D2 56 41N 5 08W
Sanquhar Scotland 11 F2 55 22N 3 56W
San Remo Italy 54 B5 43 48N 7 46E
San Salvador
El Salvador 94 G2 13 40N 89 10W
San Sebastián Spain 51 E5 43 19N 1 59W
San Severo Italy 54 F4 41 41N 15 23E
Santa Barbara USA 90 C3 33 29N 119 01W
Santa Cruz Bolivia 96 E10 17 50S 63 10W
Santa Cruz Spain 80 A7 28 28N 16 15W
Sante Fé Argentina 97 E7 31 35S 60 50W
Santa Fe USA 90 E4 35 41N 105 57W
Santa Maria Brazil 97 G8 29 45S 53 40W
Santa Marta Colombia 96 C16 11 18N 74 10W
Santander Spain 51 D5 43 28N 3 48W
Sant'Antioco Italy 54 C3 39 04N 8 27E
Santarém Brazil 96 G13 2 26S 54 41W
Santarém Portugal 51 A3 39 14N 8 40W
Santa Teresa Gallura
Italy 54 C4 41 14N 9 12E
Santiago Chile 97 C6 33 30S 70 40W
Santiago de Compostela
Spain 51 A5 42 52N 8 33W
Santiago del Estero
Argentina 97 E8 27 45S 64 19W
Santo Andre Brazil 96 H9 23 39S 46 29W
Santo Domingo
Dom. Rep. 95 L3 18 30N 69 57W
Santoña Spain 51 D5 43 27N 3 26W
Santos Brazil 96 H9 23 56S 46 22W
São Francisco r. Brazil 96 J11 15 00S 44 00W
São Luís Brazil 96 J13 2 34S 44 16W
Saône r. France 50 G4 46 28N 4 55E
São Paulo Brazil 96 H9 23 33S 46 39W
SÃO TOMÉ AND PRINCIPE
80 F2
Sapporo Japan 70 D3 43 05N 141 21E
Sarajevo
Bosnia-Herzegovina 55 H5 43 52N 18 26E
Saratov Russia 62 G7 51 30N 45 55E
Sardinia i. Italy 54 C3/C4 40 00N 9 00E
Sarnia Canada 89 U2 42 58N 82 23W
Sarreborough France 50 H5 48 43N 7 03E
Sarreguemines France 50 H5 49 06N 6 55E
Sartène France 50 J1 41 37N 8 58E
Saskatchewan prov.
Canada 88/89 P5/Q5 53 50N 109 00W
Saskatoon Canada 88 P4 52 10N 106 40W
Sassari Italy 54 C4 40 43N 8 34E
Sassnitz Germany 52 F7 54 32N 13 40E
Sassuolo Italy 54 D6 44 32N 10 47E
Satu Mare Romania 53 L3 47 48N 22 52E
SAUDI ARABIA 64/65 D3/F3
Sault Ste. Marie
Canada 89 U3 46 31N 84 20W
Saumur France 50 D4 47 16N 0 05W
Saundersfoot Wales 14 B1 51 43N 4 43W
Savannah USA 91 K3 32 04N 81 07W
Savona Italy 54 C6 44 18N 8 28E
Sawbridgeworth
England 17 D2 51 50N 0 09E
Sawel mt. NI 10 B1 54 49N 7 02W
Sawston England 17 D3 52 07N 0 10E
Saxilby England 13 F2 53 17N 0 40W
Saxmundham England 17 E3 52 13N 1 29E
Saxthorpe England 17 E3 52 50N 1 09E
Scafell Pike mt.
England 12 C3 54 27N 3 14W
Scalasaig Scotland 10 C3 56 04N 6 12W
Scalby England 13 F3 54 18N 0 27W
Scalloway Scotland 7 C3 60 08N 1 17W
Scalpay i. Scotland 8 C2 57 52N 6 40W
Scalpay i. Scotland 8 D2 57 15N 6 00W
Scapa Scotland 7 B1 58 58N 2 59W
Scapa Flow sd. Scotland 7 A1 58 55N 3 00W
Scarborough England 13 F3 54 17N 0 24W
Scarinish Scotland 8 C1 56 29N 6 48W
Scarp i. Scotland 8 B3 58 02N 7 08W
Scarriff RoI 21 C2 52 55N 8 37W
Scartaglin RoI 21 B2 52 10N 9 26W
Schaffhausen Switz. 52 D3 47 42N 8 38E
Schefferville Canada 89 X4 54 50N 67 00W
Schleswig Germany 52 D7 54 32N 9 34E
Schwäbisch Gmünd
Germany 52 D4 48 49N 9 48E
Schwarzwald mts.
Germany 52 D4 47 00N 8 00E
Schwaz Austria 52 E3 47 21N 11 44E
Schwechat Austria 53 H4 48 09N 16 27E
Schweinfurt Germany 52 E5 50 03N 10 16E
Schwerin Germany 52 E6 53 38N 11 25E
Schwyz Switz. 52 D3 47 02N 8 34E
Sciacca Italy 54 E2 37 31N 13 05E
Scilly, Isles of England 18 A1 49 56N 6 20W
Sconser Scotland 8 C2 57 18N 6 07V
Scotland UK 6 56 00N 4 00W
Scottish Borders u.a.
Scotland 11 F2/G2 55 30N 2 55W
Scourie Scotland 8 D3 58 20N 5 08W

Scrabster Scotland 9 F3 58 37N 3 34W
Scunthorpe England 13 F2 53 35N 0 39W
Seaford England 17 D1 50 46N 0 06E
Seaham England 13 E3 54 50N 1 20W
Seahouses England 11 H2 55 35N 1 38W
Seascale England 12 C3 54 24N 3 29W
Seaton Devon England 19 D2 50 43N 3 05W
Seaton Cumbria
England 12 C3 54 40N 3 30W
Seaton Delaval England 13 E4 55 04N 1 31W
Seattle USA 90 B6 47 35N 122 20W
Sedan France 50 G5 49 42N 4 57E
Sedbergh England 12 D3 54 20N 2 31W
Segovia Spain 51 C4 40 57N 4 07W
Seine r. France 50 E5 49 15N 1 15E
Sekondi Takoradi
Ghana 80 D2 4 59N 1 43W
Selborne England 16 C2 51 06N 0 56W
Selby England 13 E2 53 48N 1 04W
Sélestat France 50 H5 48 16N 7 28E
Selkirk Scotland 11 G2 55 33N 2 50W
Selsey England 16 C1 50 44N 0 48W
Selsey Bill p. England 16 C1 50 43N 0 48W
Semarang Indonesia 71 E2 6 58S 110 29E
Sendai Japan 70 D2 38 16N 140 52E
SENEGAL 80 A4/B4
Senlis France 50 F5 49 12N 2 35E
Sennen England 18 B2 50 03N 5 42W
Sennybridge Wales 14 C1 51 57N 3 34W
Sens France 50 F5 48 12N 3 18E
Seoul S. Korea 69 N5 37 32N 127 00E
Sept-Îles tn. Canada 89 X4 50 10N 66 00W
SERBIA 55 H6/K6
Serov Russia 62 J8 59 42N 60 32E
Serra Brazil 96 J10 20 06S 40 16W
Sérres Greece 55 K4 41 03N 23 33E
Sète France 50 F2 43 25N 3 43E
Settle England 12 D3 54 04N 2 16W
Setúbal Portugal 51 A3 38 31N 8 54W
Sevastopol' Ukraine 57 D3 44 36N 33 31E
Seven Head c. RoI 21 C1 51 34N 8 42W
Severn r.
England/Wales 14 C2 52 30N 3 15W
Severodvinsk Russia 62 F9 64 35N 39 50E
Seville Spain 51 C2 37 24N 5 59W
Seward USA 88 F6 60 05N 149 34W
SEYCHELLES 103
Sézannes France 50 F5 48 44N 3 44E
Sfântu Gheorghe
Romania 53 M2 45 51N 25 48E
Sfax Tunisia 80 G8 34 45N 10 43E
Sgurr Mór mt. Scotland 9 D2 57 42N 5 03W
Shaftesbury England 19 E3 51 01N 2 12W
Shaldon England 18 D2 51 35N 3 30W
Shanghai China 69 M4 31 06N 121 22E
Shanklin England 16 B1 50 38N 1 10W
Shannon RoI 21 C2 54 18N 8 55W
Shannon r. RoI 21 C2/B2 52 45N 8 57W
Shap England 12 D3 54 32N 2 41W
Shapinsay i. Scotland 7 B2 59 03N 2 51W
Sheerness England 17 D2 51 27N 0 45E
Sheffield England 13 E2 53 23N 1 30W
Shefford England 16 C3 52 02N 0 20W
Shelburne Canada 89 X2 43 37N 65 20W
Shenandoah USA 91 G5 40 48N 95 22W
Shenyang China 69 M6 41 50N 123 26E
Shepetovka Ukraine 55 N5 50 12N 27 01E
Shepperton England 16 C2 51 23N 0 28W
Sheppey, Isle of
England 17 D2 51 25N 0 50E
Shepshed England 15 E2 52 47N 1 18W
Shepton Mallet
England 19 E3 51 12N 2 33W
Sherborne England 19 E2 50 57N 2 31W
Sherbrooke Canada 89 W3 45 24N 71 54W
Sheringham England 17 E3 52 57N 1 12E
Sherkin Island RoI 21 B1 51 28N 9 25W
's-Hertogenbosch
Neths 48 D4 51 41N 5 19E
Shetland Islands u.a.
Scotland 7 C2/D3 60 00N 1 15W
Shieldaig Scotland 8 D2 57 31N 5 39W
Shifnal England 15 D2 52 41N 2 22W
Shijiazhuang China 69 K5 38 04N 114 28E
Shilbottle England 11 H2 55 23N 1 42W
Shildon England 13 E3 54 38N 1 39W
Shillelagh RoI 21 E2 52 45N 6 32W
Shipley England 13 E2 53 50N 1 47W
Shipston-on-Stour
England 15 E2 52 04N 1 37W
Shipton England 13 E3 54 01N 1 09W
Shiraz Iran 65 F4 29 38N 52 34E
Shirebrook England 13 E2 53 13N 1 13W
Shoeburyness England 17 D2 51 32N 0 48E
Shoreham-by-Sea
England 16 C1 50 49N 0 16W
Shotton Wales 14 C3 53 12N 3 02W
Shotts Scotland 11 F2 55 49N 3 48W
Shrewsbury England 15 D2 52 43N 2 45W
Shrewton England 16 B2 51 12N 1 55W
Shropshire co.
England 14/15 D2 52 35N 2 25W
Shumen Bulgaria 55 M5 43 17N 26 55E
Sible Hedingham
England 17 D2 51 58N 0 35E
Sicily i. Italy 54 E2/F2 37 00N 14 00E

Siderno Italy 54 G3 38 16N 16 17E
Sidi Bel Abbès Algeria 80 D9 35 15N 0 39W
Sidlaw Hills Scotland 9 F1/G1 56 30N 3 10W
Sidmouth England 19 D2 50 41N 3 15W
Siegen Germany 52 D5 50 52N 8 02E
Siena Italy 54 D5 43 19N 11 19E
SIERRA LEONE 80 B3
Sierra Madre Occidental
mts. Mexico 94 C5/D4 26 00N 107 00W
Sierra Nevada mts.
Spain 51 D2 37 00N 3 20W
Sierra Nevada mts.
USA 90 C4 37 00N 119 00W
Sighişoara Romania 53 M3 46 12N 24 48E
Sigüenza Spain 51 D4 41 04N 2 38W
Sileby England 15 E2 52 44N 1 05W
Silistra Bulgaria 55 M6 44 06N 27 17E
Silloth England 12 C3 54 52N 3 23W
Silverton England 18 D2 50 48N 3 30W
Silves Portugal 51 A2 37 11N 8 26W
Simferopol' Ukraine 57 D3 44 57N 34 05E
Simonsbath England 18 D3 51 09N 3 45W
Sinclair's Bay Scotland 9 F3 58 30N 3 07
Sines Portugal 51 A2 37 58N 8 52W
SINGAPORE 71 C4
Sintra Portugal 51 A3 38 48N 9 22W
Sion Switz. 52 C3 46 14N 7 22E
Sion Mills NI 10 B1 54 47N 7 28W
Siracusa Italy 54 F2 37 04N 15 19E
Sisak Croatia 54 G6 45 30N 16 22E
Sisteron France 50 G3 44 16N 5 56E
Sittingbourne England 17 D2 51 21N 0 44E
Sixmilebridge RoI 21 C2 52 45N 8 46W
Sjaelland i. Denmark 49 D2 55 15N 11 30E
Skagerrak sd.
Denmark/Norway 49 C2 57 30N 8 00E
Skegness England 13 G2 53 10N 0 21E
Skellefteå Sweden 49 F3 64 45N 21 00E
Skellingthorpe England 13 F2 53 14N 0 37W
Skelmanthorpe
England 13 E2 53 36N 1 40W
Skelmersdale England 12 D2 53 55N 2 48W
Skelmorlie Scotland 10 E2 55 51N 4 53W
Skelton England 13 F3 54 33N 0 59W
Skerries RoI 20 E3 53 35N 6 07W
Skibbereen RoI 21 B1 51 33N 9 15W
Skiddaw mt. England 12 C3 54 40N 3 08W
Skien Norway 49 C2 59 14N 9 37E
Skipton England 12 D2 53 58N 2 01W
Skokholm Island Wales 14 A1 51 42N 5 16W
Skomer Island Wales 14 A1 51 45N 5 18W
Skopje FYROM 55 J4 42 00N 21 28E
Skövde Sweden 49 D2 58 24N 13 52E
Skull RoI 21 B1 51 32N 9 40W
Skye i. Scotland 8 C2 57 20N 6 15W
Slaidburn England 12 D2 54 00N 2 26W
Slane RoI 20 E3 54 43N 6 33W
Slaney r. RoI 21 E2 52 24N 6 33W
Slatina Romania 53 M2 44 26N 24 22E
Slave r. Canada 88 N5 59 20N 111 10W
Slavonski Brod Croatia 55 G6 45 09N 18 02E
Sleaford England 13 F2 53 00N 0 24W
Sleat, Point of Scotland 8 C2 57 01N 6 01W
Sleat, Sound of Scotland 8 D2 57 00N 5 55W
Sledmere England 13 F3 54 04N 0 35W
Sleights England 13 F3 54 26N 0 40W
Slieve Donard mt. NI 10 D1 54 11N 5 55W
Slieve Gamph hills RoI 20 C4 54 11N 8 53W
Slieve Mish Mountains
RoI 21 B2 52 12N 10 00W
Sligo RoI 20 C4 54 17N 8 28W
Sligo co. RoI 20 C4 54 10N 8 40W
Sligo Bay b. RoI 20 C4 54 15N 8 55W
Sliven Bulgaria 55 M5 42 40N 26 19E
Slough England 16 C2 51 31N 0 36W
Slough u.a. England 16 C1 50 25N 0 40W
SLOVAKIA 53 J4/K4
SLOVENIA 54 F6
Smethwick England 15 E2 52 30N 1 58W
Smolensk Russia 62 F7 54 49N 32 04E
Smolyan Bulgaria 55 L4 41 34N 24 42E
Snaefell mt. Isle of Man 12 B3 54 16N 4 28W
Snake r. USA 90 C5 44 00N 118 00W
Sneek Neths 48 D6 53 02N 5 40E
Sneem RoI 21 B1 51 50N 9 45W
Snodland England 17 D2 51 20N 0 27E
Snowdon mt. Wales 14 B3 53 04N 4 05W
Snowy Mountains
Australia 73 J3 36 50S 147 00E
Soar r. England 15 E2 52 50N 1 15W
Soay i. Scotland 8 C2 57 08N 6 14W
Socotra i. Yemen 65 F1 12 05N 54 10E
Söderhamn Sweden 49 E3 61 19N 17 10E
Sodertälje Sweden 49 E2 59 11N 17 39E
Sofia Bulgaria 55 K5 42 40N 23 18E
Soham England 17 D3 52 20N 0 20E
Soissons France 50 F5 49 23N 3 20E
Solapur India 66 D3 17 43N 75 56E
Solent, The sd. England 16 B1 50 45N 1 25W
Soligorsk Belarus 55 N6 52 50N 27 32E
Solihull England 15 E2 52 25N 1 45W
Sollefteå Sweden 49 E3 63 09N 17 15E
Sóller Spain 51 G3 39 46N 2 42E
SOLOMON ISLANDS 73 L9/M9
Solothurn Switz. 52 C3 47 13N 7 32E
Soltau Germany 52 D6 52 59N 9 50E
Solway Firth Scotland 11 F1 54 45N 3 40W

SOMALIA 81 Q2/Q3
Somerset co. England 19 D3/E3 51 10N 3 00W
Somerton England 19 E3 51 03N 2 44W
Sompting England 16 C1 50 50N 0 21W
Sønderborg Denmark 49 C1 54 55N 9 48E
Sondrio Italy 54 C7 46 11N 9 52E
Sonning Common tn.
England 16 C2 51 31N 0 59W
Sopron Hungary 53 H3 47 40N 16 35E
Sora Italy 54 E4 41 43N 13 37E
Soria Spain 51 D4 41 46N 2 28W
Soroca Moldova 53 P4 48 08N 28 12E
Sosnowiec Poland 53 J5 50 16N 19 07E
Souillac France 50 E3 44 53N 1 29E
Southam England 15 E2 52 15N 1 23W
Southampton England 16 B1 50 55N 1 25W
Southampton u.a.
England 16 B1 50 55N 1 25W
Southampton Water sd.
England 16 B1 50 50N 1 20W
South Ayrshire u.a.
Scotland 11 E2 55 20N 4 40W
South Ballachulish
Scotland 8 D1 56 42N 5 09W
South Bank tn. England 13 E3 54 35N 1 10W
South Benfleet England 17 D2 51 33N 0 34E
Southborough England 17 D2 51 10N 0 15E
South Brent England 18 D2 50 25N 3 50W
South Carolina state
USA 91 K3 34 00N 81 00W
South Cave tn. England 13 F2 53 46N 0 35W
South Cerney England 15 E1 51 41N 1 57W
South Dakota state
USA 90 F5 45 00N 102 00W
South Dorset Downs
England 19 E2 50 40N 2 30W
South Downs England 16 C1 50 50N 0 30W
Southend u.a. England 17 D2 51 32N 0 50E
Southend Scotland 10 D2 55 20N 5 38W
Southend-on-Sea
England 17 D2 51 33N 0 43E
Southerness Point
Scotland 11 F1 54 53N 3 37W
Southern Ocean 101
South Esk r. Scotland 9 F1 56 50N 3 10W
South Foreland c.
England 17 E2 51 09N 1 23E
South Gloucestershire
u.a. England 15 D1 51 30N 2 30W
South Hayling England 16 C1 50 47N 0 59W
South Island NZ 73 N1/P2 42 30S 172 00E
South Kirkby England 13 E2 53 34N 1 20W
SOUTH KOREA 69 N5
South Lanarkshire u.a.
Scotland 11 E2/F2 55 35N 3 55W
Southminster England 17 D2 51 40N 0 50E
South Molton England 18 D3 51 01N 3 50W
South Normanton
England 13 E2 53 06N 1 20W
South Ockendon
England 17 D2 51 32N 0 18E
South Petherton
England 19 E2 50 58N 2 49W
South Pole Antarctica 101 90 00S
Southport England 12 C2 53 39N 3 01W
South Queensferry
Scotland 11 F2 55 59N 3 25W
South Shields England 13 E3 55 00N 1 25W
South Tyne r. England 12 D3 54 52N 2 30W
South Uist i. Scotland 8 B2 57 20N 7 15W
South Walls i. Scotland 7 A1 58 47N 3 11W
Southwick England 16 C1 51 01N 0 14W
Southwold England 17 E3 52 20N 1 40E
South Woodham Ferrers
England 17 D2 51 38N 0 38E
South Yorkshire co.
England 13 E2 53 30N 1 30W
Sowerby Bridge
England 13 E2 53 43N 1 54W
SPAIN 51 C3/E3
Spalding England 16 C3 52 47N 0 10W
Spárti Greece 55 K2 37 05N 22 25E
Spean Bridge tn.
Scotland 9 E1 56 53N 4 54W
Spennymoor England 13 E3 54 42N 1 35W
Sperrin Mountains NI 10 B1 54 49N 7 06W
Spey r. Scotland 9 F2 57 15N 3 45W
Spiddle Rol 20 B3 53 15N 9 18W
Spilsby England 13 G2 53 11N 0 05E
Spink Rol 21 D2 52 53N 7 12W
Spithead sd. England 16 B1 50 45N 1 10W
Spitsbergen i.
Arctic Ocean 62 D12 79 00N 15 00E
Spittal an der Drau
Austria 52 F3 46 48N 13 30E
Split Croatia 55 G5 43 31N 16 28E
Spokane USA 90 C6 47 40N 117 25W
Spoleto Italy 54 E5 42 44N 12 44E
Springfield Illinois USA 91 J4 39 49N 89 39W
Springfield Massachusetts
USA 91 M5 42 07N 72 35W
Spurn Head England 13 G2 53 36N 0 07E
SRI LANKA 66 E1
Srinagar Kashmir 66 C6 34 08N 74 50E
Stacks Mountains Rol 21 B2 52 19N 9 33W
Staffa i. Scotland 8 C1 56 30N 6 15W
Stafford England 15 D2 52 48N 2 07W

Staffordshire co.
England 15 D2/E2 52 50N 2 00W
Staines England 16 C2 51 26N 0 30W
Stainforth England 13 E2 53 36N 1 01W
Stalbridge England 19 E2 50 58N 2 23W
Stalybridge England 15 D3 53 29N 2 04W
Stamford Bridge tn.
England 13 F2 53 59N 0 55W
Standish USA 93 D2 43 59N 83 58W
Stane Scotland 11 F2 55 50N 3 47W
Stanhope England 12 D3 54 45N 2 01W
Stanley England 13 E2 53 44N 1 28W
Stanley England 13 E3 54 53N 1 42W
Stanley
Falkland Islands 97 F3 51 45S 57 56W
Stansted Mountfitchet
England 17 D2 51 54N 0 12E
Stapleford England 15 E2 52 56N 1 15W
Staplehurst England 17 D2 51 10N 0 33E
Starachowice Poland 53 K5 51 03N 21 00E
Stara Zagora Bulgaria 55 L5 42 25N 25 37E
Start Bay England 18 D2 50 16N 3 35W
Start Point England 18 D2 50 13N 3 38W
Staunton USA 91 L4 38 10N 79 05W
Stavanger Norway 49 C2 58 58N 5 45E
Staveley England 13 E2 53 16N 1 20W
Staxton England 13 F3 54 11N 0 26W
Steeping r. England 13 G2 53 10N 0 10E
Stendal Germany 52 E6 52 36N 11 52E
Stenhousemuir
Scotland 11 F3 56 02N 3 49W
Stevenage England 16 C2 51 55N 0 14W
Stevenston Scotland 11 E2 55 39N 4 45W
Stewart Canada 88 J5 55 56N 130 01W
Stewarton Scotland 11 E2 55 41N 4 31W
Stewartstown NI 10 C1 54 35N 6 41W
Steyning England 16 C1 50 53N 0 20W
Steyr Austria 52 G3 48 04N 14 25E
Stilton England 16 C3 52 29N 0 17W
Stinchar r. Scotland 11 E2 55 10N 4 50W
Stirling Canada 88 N3 49 34N 112 30W
Stirling u.a. Scotland 11 E3 56 10N 4 15W
Stirling Scotland 11 F3 56 07N 3 57W
Stockbridge England 16 B2 51 07N 1 29W
Stockerau Austria 53 H4 48 24N 16 13E
Stockholm Sweden 49 E2 59 20N 18 05E
Stockport England 12 D2 53 25N 2 10W
Stocksbridge England 13 E2 53 27N 1 34W
Stockton-on-Tees
England 13 E3 54 34N 1 19W
Stockton-on-Tees u.a.
England 13 E3 54 33N 1 24W
Stoer, Point of Scotland 8 D3 58 25N 5 25W
Stoke-on-Trent u.a.
England 12 D2 53 00N 2 10W
Stokenchurch England 16 C2 51 40N 0 55W
Stoke-on-Trent England 12 D2 53 00N 2 10W
Stoke Poges England 16 C2 51 33N 0 35W
Stokesley England 13 E3 54 28N 1 11W
Stone England 15 D2 52 54N 2 10W
Stonehaven Scotland 9 G1 56 38N 2 13W
Stonehouse Scotland 11 F2 55 43N 3 59W
Stony Stratford
England 16 C3 52 04N 0 52W
Størdal Norway 49 D3 63 18N 11 48E
Støren Norway 49 D3 63 03N 10 16E
Stornoway Scotland 8 C3 58 12N 6 23W
Storr, The mt. Scotland 8 C2 57 30N 6 11W
Storrington England 16 C1 50 55N 0 28W
Storuman Sweden 49 E4 65 05N 17 10E
Stotfold England 16 C3 52 01N 0 15W
Stour r. Warwickshire
England 15 E2 52 05N 1 45E
Stour r. Suffolk England 17 D3 52 10N 0 30E
Stour r. Kent England 17 E2 51 10N 1 10E
Stour r. Dorset England 19 E2 50 50N 2 10W
Stourbridge tn. England 15 D2 52 27N 2 09W
Stourport-on-Severn
England 15 D2 52 21N 2 16W
Stow Scotland 11 G2 55 42N 2 51W
Stowmarket England 17 E3 52 11N 1 00E
Stow-on-the-Wold
England 15 E1 51 56N 1 44W
Strabane NI 10 B1 54 49N 7 27W
Strabane district NI 10 B1 54 45N 7 30W
Strachur Scotland 10 D3 56 10N 5 04W
Stradbally Rol 21 D3 53 00N 7 08W
Stradone Rol 20 D3 53 59N 7 14W
Stralsund Germany 52 F7 54 18N 13 06E
Strangford Lough NI 10 D1 54 30N 5 35W
Stranorlar Rol 20 D4 54 48N 7 46W
Stranraer Scotland 10 D2 54 55N 5 02W
Strasbourg France 50 H5 48 35N 7 45E
Stratford-upon-Avon
England 15 E2 52 12N 1 41W
Strathaven Scotland 11 E2 55 41N 4 05W
Strathcarron Scotland 8 D2 57 26N 5 27W
Strathpeffer Scotland 8 E2 57 35N 4 33W
Strathy Scotland 9 F3 58 33N 3 59W
Strathy r. Scotland 9 E3 58 30N 4 00W
Strathy Point Scotland 9 E3 58 35N 4 02W
Stratton England 18 C2 50 50N 4 31W
Straubing Germany 52 F4 48 53N 12 35E
Street England 19 3 51 03N 2 45W
Stretford England 12 D2 53 27N 2 19W
Strímonas r. Greece 55 K4 41 00N 23 00E

Strokestown Rol 20 C3 53 47N 8 06W
Stroma i. Scotland 7 A1 58 40N 3 08W
Stromboli mt. Italy 54 F3 38 48N 15 15E
Stromeferry Scotland 8 D2 57 21N 5 34W
Stromness Scotland 7 A1 58 57N 3 18W
Stronsay i. Scotland 7 B2 59 07N 2 37W
Stronsay Firth Scotland 7 B2 59 00N 2 55W
Strontian Scotland 8 D1 56 41N 5 34W
Strood England 17 D2 51 24N 0 28E
Stroud England 15 D1 51 45N 2 12W
Strumble Head Wales 14 A2 52 02N 5 04W
Stryy Ukraine 53 L4 49 16N 23 51E
Stubbington England 16 B1 50 49N 1 13W
Studley England 15 E2 52 16N 1 52W
Sturminster Marshall
England 19 E2 50 48N 2 04W
Sturminster Newton
England 19 E2 50 55N 2 18W
Stuttgart Germany 52 D4 48 47N 9 12E
Subotica Serbia 55 H7 46 04N 19 41E
Sucre Bolivia 96 D10 19 05S 65 15W
SUDAN 81 L4/M4
Sudbury Canada 89 U3 46 30N 81 01W
Sudbury England 17 E3 52 02N 0 44E
Suffolk co. England 17 D3/E3 52 10N 1 00E
Suhl Germany 52 E5 50 37N 10 43E
Sulawesi i. Indonesia 71 F3/G3 2 00S 120 00E
Sumatera i. Indonesia 71 B4/C3 0 00 100 00E
Sumburgh Head
Scotland 7 C2 59 51N 1 16W
Summerhill Rol 20 E3 53 29N 6 44W
Sumy Ukraine 56 D5 50 55N 34 49E
Sunderland England 13 E3 54 55N 1 23W
Sundsvall Sweden 49 E3 62 22N 17 20E
Sunningdale England 16 C2 51 24N 0 37W
Superior, Lake
Canada/USA 92 C3 48 00N 88 00W
Surabaya Indonesia 71 E2 7 14S 112 45E
Surat India 66 C4 21 10N 72 54E
SURINAME 96 F14
Surrey co. England 16 C2 51 15N 0 30W
Sutton England 16 C2 51 22N 0 12W
Sutton Coldfield
England 15 E2 52 34N 1 48W
Sutton in Ashfield
England 13 E2 53 08N 1 15W
Sutton on Sea England 13 G2 53 19N 0 17E
Suwalki Poland 53 L7 54 06N 22 56E
Suzhou China 69 M4 31 21N 120 40E
Svilengrad Bulgaria 55 M4 41 45N 26 14E
Swadlincote England 15 E2 52 46N 1 33W
Swaffham England 17 D3 52 39N 0 41E
Swale r. England 12 D3 54 20N 2 00W
Swanage England 19 F2 50 37N 1 58W
Swanley England 17 D2 51 24N 0 12E
Swanlinbar Rol 20 D4 54 12N 7 42W
Swanscombe England 17 D2 51 26N 0 18E
Swansea Wales 14 C1 51 38N 3 57W
Swansea Bay Wales 14 C1 51 35N 3 55W
Swansea u.a. Wales 14 B1/C1 51 35N 4 10W
SWAZILAND 82 F2
SWEDEN 49 D2/E4
Swiebodzin Poland 53 G6 52 15N 15 31E
Swilly r. Rol 20 D4 54 55N 7 45W
Swindon England 16 B2 51 34N 1 47W
Swindon u.a. England 16 B2 51 34N 1 47W
Swinford Rol 20 C3 53 57N 8 57W
Swinoujscie Poland 52 G6 53 55N 14 18E
Swinton England 13 E2 53 30N 1 19W
SWITZERLAND 52 C3/D3
Swords Rol 20 E3 53 28N 6 13W
Sydney Australia 73 K4 33 55S 151 10E
Sylt Germany 52 D7 54 00N 8 00E
Symbister Scotland 7 C3 60 21N 1 02W
Symington Scotland 11 F2 55 37N 3 35W
Syracuse USA 91 L5 43 03N 76 10W
SYRIA 64 C6
Syzran' Russia 62 G7 53 10N 48 29E
Szczecin Poland 52 G6 53 25N 14 32E
Szeged Hungary 53 K3 46 15N 20 09E
Szombathely Hungary 53 H3 47 14N 16 38E

# T

Tábor Czech Rep. 52 G4 49 25N 14 39E
Tabriz Iran 65 E6 38 05N 46 18E
Tacoma USA 90 B6 47 16N 122 30W
Tadcaster England 13 E2 53 53N 1 16W
Tadley England 16 B2 51 21N 1 08W
Taegu S. Korea 69 N5 35 52N 128 36E
Taejon S. Korea 69 N5 36 20N 127 26E
Tafalla Spain 51 E5 42 32N 1 41W
Taff r. Wales 14 C1 51 30N 3 10W
Taghmon Rol 21 E2 52 19N 6 39W
Tain Scotland 9 E2 57 48N 4 04W
Taipei Taiwan 69 M3 25 05N 121 32E
TAIWAN 69 M2
Taiyuan China 69 K5 37 50N 112 30E
TAJIKISTAN 62 J4/K4
Tajo r. Spain/Portugal 51 B3 39 00N 7 00W
Takamatsu Japan 70 B1 34 20N 134 01E
Talca Chile 97 C6 35 28S 71 40W
Talcahuano Chile 97 C6 36 40S 73 10W
Talgarth Wales 14 C2 51 59N 3 15W
Tallaght Rol 20 E3 53 17N 6 21W
Tallahassee USA 91 K3 30 26N 84 16W
Tallinn Estonia 49 F2 59 22N 24 48E

Tallow Rol 21 C2 52 05N 8 01W
Tal-y-bont Wales 14 C2 52 29N 3 59W
Tamanrasset Algeria 80 F6 22 50N 5 28E
Tamar r. England 18 C2 50 32N 4 15W
Tambov Russia 62 G7 52 44N 41 28E
Tame r. England 15 E2 52 40N 1 45W
Tampa USA 91 K2 27 58N 82 38W
Tampere Finland 49 F3 61 32N 23 45E
Tamworth England 15 E2 52 39N 1 40W
Tandragee NI 10 C1 54 22N 6 25W
Tanganyika, Lake
East Africa 83 B1 7 00S 30 00E
Tangier Morocco 80 C9 35 48N 5 45W
Tangshan China 69 L5 39 37N 118 05E
TANZANIA 83 B1/D1
Tapachula Mexico 94 F2 14 54N 92 15W
Taransay i. Scotland 8 B2 57 55N 7 00W
Táranto Italy 55 G4 40 28N 17 15E
Tarazona Spain 51 E4 41 54N 1 44W
Tarbat Ness c. Scotland 9 F2 57 50N 3 45W
Tarbert Rol 21 B2 52 32N 9 23W
Tarbert Western Isles
Scotland 8 C2 57 54N 6 49W
Tarbert Argyle and Bute
Scotland 10 D2 55 52N 5 26W
Tarbes France 50 E2 43 14N 0 05E
Tarbet Scotland 11 E3 56 12N 4 43W
Tarbolton Scotland 11 E2 55 31N 4 29W
Târgoviște Romania 53 M2 44 56N 25 27E
Târgu Mureș Romania 53 M3 46 33N 24 34E
Tarija Bolivia 96 D9 21 33S 65 02W
Tarleton England 12 D2 53 41N 2 50W
Tarporley England 12 D2 53 10N 2 40W
Tarragona Spain 51 F4 41 07N 1 15E
Tarrasa Spain 51 G4 41 34N 2 00E
Tarsus Turkey 57 D2 26 25N 34 52E
Tartu Estonia 49 G2 58 20N 26 44E
Tashkent Uzbekistan 62 J5 41 16N 69 13E
Taunton England 19 D3 51 01N 3 06W
Taunus mts. Germany 52 D5 50 00N 8 00E
Tauranga NZ 73 Q3 37 41S 176 10E
Taverham England 17 E3 52 41N 1 10E
Tavira Portugal 51 B2 37 07N 7 39W
Tavistock England 18 C2 50 33N 4 08W
Tavy r. England 18 C2 50 36N 4 04W
Taw r. England 18 D2 50 46N 3 55W
Tay r. Scotland 9 F1 56 30N 3 25W
Taynuilt Scotland 8 D1 56 25N 5 14W
Tayport Scotland 9 G1 56 27N 2 53W
T'bilisi Georgia 57 F3 41 43N 44 48E
Tczew Poland 53 J7 54 05N 18 46E
Tebay England 12 D3 54 26N 2 35W
Tees r. England 12 D3 54 40N 1 20W
Tegucigalpa Honduras 94 G2 14 05N 87 14W
Tehran Iran 65 F6 35 40N 51 26E
Teifi r. Wales 14 B2 52 03N 4 30W
Teign r. England 18 D2 50 42N 3 48W
Teignmouth England 18 D2 50 33N 3 30W
Teith r. Scotland 11 E3 56 10N 4 08W
Tejo r. Portugal 51 B3 39 30N 8 15W
Tel Aviv-Yafo Israel 64 B5 32 05N 34 46E
Telford England 15 D2 52 42N 2 28W
Teme r. England 15 D2 52 15N 2 25W
Tempio Pausania Italy 54 C4 40 54N 9 07E
Templemore Rol 21 D2 52 48N 7 50W
Templenoe Rol 21 B1 51 51N 9 41W
Temuco Chile 97 C6 38 45S 72 40W
Tenbury Wells England 15 D2 52 19N 2 35W
Tenby Wales 14 B1 51 41N 4 43W
Tenerife i. Spain 80 A7 28 15N 16 35W
Tennessee r. USA 91 J4 35 00N 88 00W
Tennessee state USA 91 J4 35 00N 87 00W
Tenterden England 17 D2 51 05N 0 41E
Teramo Italy 54 E5 42 40N 13 43E
Teresina Brazil 96 J12 5 09S 42 46W
Termini Imerese Italy 54 E2 37 59N 13 42E
Termoli Italy 54 F4 42 00N 15 00E
Terni Italy 54 E5 42 34N 12 39E
Terracina Italy 54 E4 41 17N 13 15E
Terrasini Italy 54 E3 38 09N 13 05E
Terre Haute USA 91 J4 39 27N 87 24W
Teruel Spain 51 E4 40 21N 1 06W
Teslin Canada 88 J6 60 10N 132 42W
Test r. England 16 B2 51 05N 1 30W
Tetbury England 15 D1 51 39N 2 10W
Tetney England 13 F2 53 30N 0 01W
Tétouan Morocco 80 C9 35 34N 5 22W
Teviotdale Scotland 11 G2 55 20N 3 00W
Teviothead Scotland 11 G2 55 19N 2 56W
Tewkesbury England 15 D1 51 59N 2 09W
Texas state USA 90 G3 31 00N 100 00W
THAILAND 71 B7/C7
Thame r. England 16 B2 51 45N 1 05W
Thame England 16 C2 51 45N 0 59W
Thames r. England 16 C2 51 32N 0 50W
Thane India 66 C3 19 14N 73 02E
Thar Desert India 66 C5 27 30N 72 00E
Thatcham England 16 B2 51 25N 1 15W
Thaxted England 17 D2 51 57N 0 20E
The Downs USA 20 D3 53 30N 7 00W
The Everglades USA 91 K2 26 00N 81 00W
The Mumbles tn. Wales 14 C1 51 35N 3 59W
The Peak mt. England 15 E2 53 24N 1 51W
Thermaïkós Kólpos g.
Greece 55 K3/K4 40 00N 22 50E
The Rower tn. Rol 21 E2 52 27N 6 57W
Thessaloníki Greece 55 K4 40 38N 22 58E

Thetford England 17 D3 52 25N 0 45E
Thiers France 50 F3 45 51N 3 33E
Thimphu Bhutan 67 F5 27 32N 89 43E
Thionville France 50 H5 49 22N 6 11E
Thira i. Greece 55 L2 36 00N 25 00E
Thirsk England 13 E3 54 14N 1 20W
Thíva Greece 55 K3 38 19N 23 19E
Thomastown RoI 21 D2 52 31N 7 08W
Thompson Canada 89 R5 55 45N 97 54W
Thornaby-on-Tees England 13 E3 54 34N 1 18W
Thornbury England 15 D1 51 37N 2 32W
Thorne England 13 F2 53 37N 0 58W
Thorney England 16 C3 52 37N 0 07W
Thornhill Scotland 11 F2 55 15N 3 46W
Thornton England 12 D2 53 53N 3 00W
Thorpe-le-Soken England 17 E2 51 52N 1 10E
Thouars France 50 D4 46 59N 0 13W
Thrapston England 15 F2 52 24N 0 32W
Thuin Belgium 48 C3 50 21N 4 18E
Thun Switz. 52 C3 46 46N 7 38E
Thurcroft England 13 E2 53 24N 1 16W
Thurles RoI 21 D2 52 41N 7 49W
Thurrock u.a. England 17 D2 51 30N 0 25E
Thursby England 12 C3 54 51N 3 03W
Thurso Scotland 9 F3 58 35N 3 32W
Thurso r. Scotland 9 F3 58 20N 3 40W
Thurso Bay Scotland 9 F3 58 37N 3 34W
Tianjin China 69 L5 39 08N 117 12E
Tiberias, Lake Israel 64 N11 32 45N 35 30E
Tibesti mts. Chad 81 J6 21 00N 17 00E
Tickhill England 13 E2 53 26N 1 06W
Tighnabruaich Scotland 10 D2 55 56N 5 14W
Tigris r. Turkey/Iraq 65 E5 32 00N 46 00E
Tijuana Mexico 94 A6 32 29N 117 10W
Tilburg Neths 48 D4 51 34N 5 05E
Tilbury England 17 D2 51 28N 0 23E
Till r. England 11 G2 55 38N 2 08W
Till r. England 13 F2 53 20N 0 40W
Tillicoultry Scotland 11 F3 56 09N 2 45W
Tilt r. Scotland 9 F1 56 50N 3 45W
Timişoara Romania 53 K2 45 45N 21 15E
Timor i. Indonesia 71 G1/H2 9 00S 125 00E
Tinahely RoI 21 E2 52 48N 6 28W
Tingwall Scotland 7 A2 59 04N 3 03W
Tintagel England 18 C2 50 40N 4 45W
Tintagel Head England 18 C2 50 41N 4 46W
Tipperary RoI 21 C2 52 29N 8 10W
Tipperary co. RoI 21 D2 52 30N 8 00W
Tiptree England 17 D2 51 49N 0 45E
Tiranë Albania 55 H4 41 20N 19 49E
Tiree i. Scotland 8 C1 56 30N 6 55W
Titu Romania 53 M2 44 40N 25 32E
Tiverton England 18 D2 50 55N 3 29W
Tivoli Italy 54 E4 41 58N 12 48E
Tlemcen Algeria 80 D8 34 53N 1 21W
Toamasina Madagascar 82 J4 18 10S 49 23E
Tobercurry RoI 20 C4 54 03N 8 43W
Tobermore NI 10 C1 54 48N 6 42W
Tobermory Scotland 8 C1 56 37N 6 05W
Todmorden England 12 D2 53 43N 2 05W
Toe Head RoI 21 B1 51 30N 9 12W
Toe Head Scotland 8 B2 57 50N 7 07W
TOGO 80 E3
Tokelau Islands Pacific Ocean 100 J7 9 00S 168 00W
Tokyo Japan 70 C2 35 40N 139 45E
Toledo Spain 51 C3 39 52N 4 02W
Toledo USA 91 K5 41 40N 83 35W
Toliara Madagascar 82 H3 23 20N 43 41E
Tolmezzo Italy 54 E7 46 24N 13 01E
Tolosa Spain 51 D5 43 09N 2 04W
Tolsta Head Scotland 8 C3 58 20N 6 10W
Toluca Mexico 94 E3 19 20N 99 40W
Tomar Portugal 51 A3 39 36N 8 25W
Tomatin Scotland 9 F2 57 20N 3 59W
Tombouctou Mali 80 D5 16 49N 2 59W
Tomelloso Spain 51 D3 39 09N 3 01W
Tomintoul Scotland 9 F2 57 14N 3 22W
Tomsk Russia 63 L8 56 30N 85 05E
Tonbridge England 17 D2 51 12N 0 16E
TONGA 100 J5
Tongue Scotland 9 E3 58 28N 4 25W
Tønsberg Norway 49 D2 59 16N 10 25E
Tonyrefail Wales 14 C1 51 36N 3 25W
Toomyvara RoI 21 C2 52 51N 8 02W
Topsham England 18 D2 50 42N 3 27W
Tor Bay England 18 D2 50 27N 3 30W
Torbay England 18 D2 50 27N 3 30W
Tordesillas Spain 51 C4 41 30N 5 00W
Tore Scotland 9 E2 57 27N 4 21W
Torfaen u.a. Wales 14 C1 51 38N 3 04W
Tornio Finland 49 F4 65 50N 24 10E
Toronto Canada 89 V2 43 42N 79 46W
Torpoint England 18 C2 50 22N 4 11W
Torre del Greco Italy 54 F4 40 46N 14 22E
Torrelavega Spain 51 C3 43 21N 4 03W
Torremolinos Spain 51 C2 36 38N 4 30W
Torrente Spain 51 E3 39 27N 0 28W
Torrevieja Spain 51 E2 37 59N 0 40W
Torridge r. England 18 C2 50 56N 4 22W
Torridon Scotland 8 D2 57 33N 5 31W
Tortosa Spain 51 F4 40 49N 0 31E
Torún Poland 53 J6 53 01N 18 35E
Tory Island RoI 20 C5 55 16N 8 14W

Tory Sound RoI 20 C5 55 15N 8 05W
Totland England 16 B1 50 40N 1 32W
Totnes England 18 D2 50 25N 3 41W
Tottington England 12 D2 53 37N 2 20W
Totton England 16 B1 50 56N 1 29W
Touggourt Algeria 80 F8 33 08N 6 04E
Toul France 50 G5 48 41N 5 54E
Toulon France 50 G2 43 07N 5 55E
Toulouse France 50 E2 43 33N 1 24E
Tourcoing France 50 F6 50 44N 310E
Tours France 50 E4 47 23N 0 42E
Toward Scotland 10 E2 55 54N 4 58W
Towcester England 15 F2 52 08N 1 00W
Townsville Australia 73 J7 19 13S 146 48E
Toyama Japan 70 C2 36 42N 137 14E
Toyota Japan 70 C2 35 05N 137 09E
Tralee RoI 21 B2 52 16N 9 42W
Tralee Bay RoI 21 B2 52 20N 9 55W
Tramore RoI 21 D2 52 10N 7 10W
Tramore Bay RoI 21 D2 52 08N 7 08W
Tranent Scotland 11 G2 55 57N 2 57W
Trani Italy 55 G4 41 17N 16 25E
Trápani Italy 54 E3 38 02N 12 32E
Traun Austria 52 G4 48 14N 14 15E
Trawsfynydd Wales 14 C2 52 54N 3 55W
Tredegar Wales 14 C1 51 47N 3 16W
Tregaron Wales 14 C2 52 13N 3 55W
Tregony England 18 C2 50 16N 4 55W
Tremadog Bay Wales 14 B2 52 54N 4 15W
Trent r. England 13 F2 53 30N 0 44W
Trento Italy 54 D7 46 04N 11 08E
Tresco i. England 18 A1 49 57N 6 20W
Treviso Italy 54 E6 45 40N 12 15E
Trevose Head England 18 B2 50 33N 5 01W
Trier Germany 52 C4 49 45N 6 39E
Trieste Italy 54 E6 45 39N 13 47E
Tríkala Greece 55 J3 39 33N 21 46E
Trim RoI 20 E3 53 34N 6 47W
Tring England 16 C2 51 48N 0 40W
TRINIDAD AND TOBAGO 95 M2
Trípoli Greece 55 K2 37 31N 22 22E
Tripoli Lebanon 64 C5 34 27N 35 50E
Tripoli Libya 81 G8 32 54N 13 11E
Trois-Rivières tn. Canada 89 W3 46 21N 72 34W
Trollhättan Sweden 49 D2 58 17N 12 20E
Tromsø Norway 49 E4 69 42N 19 00E
Trondheim Norway 49 D3 63 36N 10 23E
Troon Scotland 11 E2 55 32N 4 40W
Trotternish p. Scotland 8 C2 57 00N 6 00W
Troup Head Scotland 9 G2 57 41N 2 19W
Trouville France 50 E5 49 22N 0 05E
Trowbridge England 16 A2 51 20N 2 13W
Troyes France 50 G5 48 18N 4 05E
Trujillo Peru 96 B12 8 06S 79 00W
Trujillo Spain 51 C3 39 28N 5 53W
Truro England 18 B2 50 16N 5 03W
Tuam RoI 20 C3 53 31N 8 50W
Tübingen Germany 52 D4 48 32N 9 04E
Tubruq Libya 81 K8 32 05N 23 59E
Tucson USA 90 D3 32 15N 110 57W
Tudela Spain 51 E4 42 04N 1 37W
Tudweiliog Wales 14 B2 52 55N 4 39W
Tula Russia 62 F7 54 11N 37 38E
Tulcea Romania 53 P2 45 10N 28 50E
Tulla RoI 21 C2 52 52N 8 45W
Tullamore RoI 20 D3 53 16N 7 30W
Tulle France 50 E3 45 16N 1 46E
Tullow RoI 21 E2 52 48N 6 44W
Tulsa USA 91 G4 36 07N 95 58W
Tulsk RoI 20 C3 53 47N 8 15W
Tummel r. Scotland 9 F1 56 40N 4 00W
Tummel Bridge Scotland 9 F1 56 43N 3 58W
Tunis Tunisia 80 G9 36 50N 10 13E
TUNISIA 80 F8/G8
Türgovishte Bulgaria 55 M5 43 14N 26 37E
Turgutlu Turkey 55 M3 38 30N 27 43E
Turin Italy 54 B6 45 04N 7 40E
Turkana, Lake Ethiopia/Kenya 83 D6/E6 4 00N 36 00E
TURKEY 57 C2/E2
TURKMENISTAN 62 H4/J4
Turks and Caicos Islands W. Indies 95 K4 21 30N 72 00W
Turku Finland 49 F3 60 27N 22 15E
Turnberry Scotland 10 E2 55 20N 4 50W
Turriff Scotland 9 G2 57 32N 2 28W
Tutbury England 15 E2 52 52N 1 40W
Tuttlingen Germany 52 D4 47 59N 8 49E
TUVALU 100 H7
Túy Spain 51 A5 42 03N 8 39W
Tuz Gölü l. Turkey 57 D2 38 40N 33 35E
Tuzla Bosnia-Herzegovina 55 H6 44 33N 18 41E
Tver' Russia 62 F8 56 49N 35 57E
Tweed r. Scotland/England 11 G2 55 45N 2 10W
Tweedmouth England 11 G3 55 47N 2 00W
Twin Falls tn. USA 90 D5 42 34N 114 30W
Twyford England 16 C2 51 29N 0 53W
Twyford England 16 B1 51 01N 1 19W
Tyldesley England 12 D2 53 32N 2 29W
Tylers Green England 16 C2 51 37N 0 42W
Tyndrum Scotland 9 E1 57 27N 4 44W
Tyne r. Scotland 11 G2 55 58N 2 43W

Tyne and Wear co. England 13 E3 55 00N 1 10W
Tynemouth tn. England 13 E4 55 01N 1 24W
Tynset Norway 49 D3 62 17N 10 47E
Tywi r. Wales 14 B1 51 50N 4 25W
Tywyn Wales 14 B2 52 35N 4 05W

## U

Uaupés Brazil 96 D13 0 07S 67 05W
Uberaba Brazil 96 H10 19 47S 47 57W
Uberlândia Brazil 96 H10 18 57S 48 17W
Uckfield England 17 D1 50 58N 0 05E
Uddevalla Sweden 49 D2 58 20N 11 56E
Udine Italy 54 E7 46 04N 13 14E
Uelzen Germany 52 E6 52 58N 10 34E
Ufa Russia 62 H7 54 45N 55 58E
Uffculme England 19 D2 50 54N 3 21W
UGANDA 83 B6/C6
Ugie r. 9 H2 57 31N 1 55W
Uig Scotland 8 C2 57 35N 6 22W
Uithuizen Neths 48 E6 53 24N 6 41E
Ujung Pandang Indonesia 71 F2 5 09S 119 28E
UKRAINE 56 C4/D4
Ulan Bator Mongolia 69 J7 47 54N 106 52E
Ulan-Ude Russia 63 N7 51 55N 107 40E
Ullapool Scotland 8 D2 57 54N 5 10W
Ullswater l. England 12 D3 54 35N 2 55W
Ulm Germany 52 D4 48 24N 10 00E
Ulva i. Scotland 8 C1 56 30N 6 15W
Ulverston England 12 C3 54 12N 3 06W
Umeå Sweden 49 F3 63 50N 20 15E
Unapool Scotland 8 D3 58 14N 5 01W
Ungava Bay Canada 89 X5 59 00N 67 30W
Unimak Island USA 88 C4 55 00N 164 00W
UNITED ARAB EMIRATES 65 F3
UNITED KINGDOM 6
UNITED STATES OF AMERICA 90/91
Unst i. Scotland 7 D3 60 45N 0 55W
Upavon England 16 B2 51 18N 1 49W
Upper Lough Erne NI 10 B1 54 15N 7 30W
Upper Tean England 15 E2 52 57N 2 00W
Uppingham England 15 F2 52 35N 0 43W
Uppsala Sweden 49 E2 59 55N 17 38E
Upton West Yorkshire England 13 E2 53 37N 1 17W
Upton Dorset England 19 E2 50 42N 2 02W
Ural r. Asia 62 H6 48 00N 52 00E
Ural Mountains Russia 62 H7/H9 57 00N 60 00E
Ure r. England 13 E3 54 20N 1 55W
Urlingford RoI 21 D2 52 43N 7 35W
Urmston England 12 D2 53 27N 2 21W
Urr r. Scotland 11 F2 55 05N 3 57W
URUGUAY 97 F6
Uruguay r. Uruguay/Argentina 97 F6 32 00S 57 40W
Ürümqi China 68 E6 43 43N 87 38E
Ushaw Moor tn. England 13 E3 54 47N 1 39W
Usk r. Wales 14 C1 51 55N 3 40W
Ussel France 50 F3 45 32N 2 18E
Ust'-Ilimsk Russia 63 N8 58 03N 102 39E
Utah state USA 90 D4 39 0N 112 00W
Utah Lake USA 90 D5 40 10N 111 50W
Utrecht Neths 48 D5 52 05N 5 07E
Utrera Spain 51 C2 37 10N 5 47W
Uttoxeter England 15 E2 52 54N 1 52W
UZBEKISTAN 62 J5

## V

Vác Hungary 53 J3 47 46N 19 08E
Vadodara India 66 C4 22 19N 73 14E
Valdepeñas Spain 51 D3 38 46N 3 24W
Valdivia Chile 97 C6 39 46S 73 15W
Val-d'Or Canada 89 V3 48 07N 77 47W
Valence France 50 G3 44 56N 4 54E
Valencia Spain 51 E3 39 29N 0 24W
Valencia Venezuela 96 D16 10 14N 67 59W
Valencia, Gulf of Spain 51 F3 39 30N 0 20E
Valencia Island RoI 21 A1 51 52N 10 20W
Valenciennes France 50 F6 50 22N 3 32E
Vale of Glamorgan, The u.a. Wales 14 C1 51 30N 3 30W
Valladolid Mexico 94 G4 20 40N 88 11W
Valladolid Spain 51 C4 41 39N 4 45W
Valletta Malta 54 F1 35 54N 14 32E
Valley tn. Wales 14 B3 53 17N 4 34W
Valparaíso Chile 97 C7 33 05S 71 40W
Valverde del Camino Spain 51 B2 37 35N 6 45W
Vanadzor Armenia 57 F3 40 49N 44 30E
Vancouver Canada 88 L3 49 13N 123 06W
Vancouver USA 90 B6 45 38N 122 40W
Vänern l. Sweden 49 D2 59 00N 13 30E
Van Gölü l. Turkey 57 F2 38 33N 42 46E
Vanna i. Norway 49 E5 70 05N 19 50E
Vännäs Sweden 49 E3 63 56N 19 50E
Vannes France 50 C4 47 40N 2 44W
Vantaa Finland 49 F3 60 20N 24 50E
VANUATU 73 N7
Varanasi India 66 E5 25 20N 83 00E
Vardø Norway 49 K6 70 22N 31 06E
Varese Italy 54 C6 45 49N 8 49E

Varkhaus Finland 49 G3 62 20N 27 50E
Varna Bulgaria 55 M5 43 12N 27 57E
Värnamo Sweden 49 D2 57 11N 14 03E
Vaslui Romania 53 N3 46 37N 27 46E
Västerås Sweden 49 E2 59 36N 16 32E
Västervik Sweden 49 E2 57 45N 16 38E
Vasto Italy 54 F5 42 07N 14 43E
Vatersay i. Scotland 8 B1 56 55N 7 32W
Vatra Dornei Romania 53 M3 47 20N 25 21E
Vättern l. Sweden 49 D2 58 20N 14 50E
Växjö Sweden 49 D2 56 52N 14 50E
Vejle Denmark 49 C2 55 43N 9 33E
Velebit mts. Croatia 54 F6 44 00N 15 00E
Vélez-Málaga Spain 51 C2 36 47N 4 06W
Vélez Rubio Spain 51 D2 37 39N 2 04W
Vementry i. Scotland 7 C3 60 20N 1 28W
Vendôme France 50 E4 47 48N 1 04E
VENEZUELA 96 D15
Venice Italy 54 E6 45 26N 12 20E
Venissieux France 50 G3 45 42N 4 46E
Venlo Netherland 48 E4 51 22N 6 10E
Ventnor England 16 B1 50 36N 1 11W
Ventura USA 90 C3 34 16N 119 18W
Vera Spain 51 E2 37 15N 1 51W
Veracruz Mexico 94 E3 19 11N 96 10W
Vercelli Italy 54 CC6 45 19N 8 26E
Verdun-sur-Meuse France 50 G5 49 10N 5 24E
Verín Spain 51 B4 41 55N 7 26W
Vermont state USA 91 M5 44 00N 73 00W
Verona Italy 54 D6 45 26N 11 00E
Versailles France 50 F5 48 48N 2 07E
Verviers Belgium 48 D3 50 36N 5 52E
Verwood England 19 F2 50 53N 1 52W
Vesoul France 50 H4 47 38N 6 09E
Vesuvio vol. Italy 54 F4 40 49N 14 26E
Veszprém Hungary 53 H3 47 06N 17 54E
Vetlanda Sweden 49 E2 57 26N 15 05E
Vevey Switz. 52 C3 46 28N 6 51E
Viano do Castelo Portugal 51 A4 41 41N 8 50W
Viareggio Italy 54 D5 43 52N 10 15E
Viborg Denmark 49 C2 56 28N 9 25E
Vibo Valentia Italy 54 G3 38 40N 16 06E
Vicenza Italy 54 D6 45 33N 11 32E
Vichy France 50 F4 46 07N 3 25E
Victoria Canada 88 L3 48 26N 123 20W
Victoria, Lake East Africa 83 C4 2 00S 33 00E
Vienna Austria 53 H4 48 13N 16 22E
Vienne France 50 G3 45 32N 4 54E
Vientiane Laos 71 C7 17 59N 102 38E
Vierzon France 50 F4 47 14N 2 03E
VIETNAM 71 D7
Vigo Spain 51 A5 42 15N 8 44W
Vila Nova de Gaia Portugal 51 A4 41 08N 8 37W
Vila Real Portugal 51 B4 41 17N 7 45W
Vilhelmina Sweden 49 E3 64 38N 16 40E
Villach Austria 52 F3 46 37N 13 51E
Villalba Spain 51 B5 43 17N 7 41W
Villarrobledo Spain 51 D3 39 16N 2 36W
Villefranche-sur-Saône France 50 G3 46 00N 4 43E
Villena Spain 51 E3 38 39N 0 52W
Villeneuve-sur-Lot France 50 E3 44 25N 0 43E
Villeurbanne France 50 G3 45 46N 4 54E
Viña del Mar Chile 97 C7 33 02S 71 35W
Vinaroz Spain 51 F4 40 29N 0 28E
Vipiteno Italy 54 D7 46 54N 11 27E
Virginia RoI 20 D3 53 49N 7 04W
Virginia USA 91 H6 47 30N 92 28W
Virginia state USA 91 L4 38 00N 77 00W
Virginia Water tn. England 16 C2 51 24N 0 34W
Virgin Islands W. Indies 95 M3 18 00N 64 30W
Visby Sweden 49 E2 57 32N 18 15E
Viseu Portugal 51 B4 40 40N 7 55W
Vishakhapatnam India 66 E3 17 42N 83 24E
Viterbo Italy 54 E5 42 24N 12 06E
Vitória Brazil 96 J9 20 20S 40 18W
Vitoria Gasteiz Spain 51 D5 42 51N 2 40W
Vitry-le-François France 50 G5 48 44N 4 36E
Vitsyebsk Belarus 56 D6 55 10N 30 14E
Vittoria Italy 54 F2 36 58N 14 32E
Vladimir Russia 62 G8 56 08N 40 25E
Vladivostok Russia 63 R5 43 09N 131 53E
Vlissingen Neths 48 B4 51 27N 3 35E
Voitsberg Austria 52 G3 47 04N 15 09E
Volga r. Russia 62 G6 50 00N 46 00E
Volgograd Russia 62 G6 48 45N 44 30E
Volta, Lake Ghana 80 D3 7 30N 0 30W
Vóreioi Sporádes is. Greece 55 K3/L3 39 00N 24 00E
Vosges mts. France 50 H5 48 10N 6 50E
Voss Norway 49 C3 60 38N 6 25E
Voxnan Sweden 49 E3 61 22N 15 39E
Vukovar Croatia 55 H6 45 19N 19 01E

## W

Waal r. Neths 48 D4 51 50N 5 07E
Waalwijk Neths 48 D4 51 42N 5 04E
Waddesdon England 16 C2 51 51N 0 56W

| Place | Region | Page | Grid | Lat | Long |
|---|---|---|---|---|---|
| **Waddington** England | | 13 | F2 | 53 10N | 0 32W |
| **Wadebridge** England | | 18 | C2 | 50 32N | 4 50W |
| **Wadhurst** England | | 17 | D2 | 51 04N | 0 21E |
| **Wadi Halfa** Sudan | | 81 | M6 | 21 55N | 31 20E |
| **Wainfleet All Saints** England | | 13 | G2 | 53 06N | 0 15E |
| **Wakefield** England | | 13 | E2 | 53 42N | 1 29W |
| **Wales** UK | | 14 | C2 | 52 40N | 3 30W |
| **Wallasey** England | | 12 | C2 | 53 26N | 3 03W |
| **Wallingford** England | | 16 | B2 | 51 37N | 1 08W |
| **Wallis and Futuna** is. Pacific Ocean | | 100 | J6 | 13 16S | 176 15W |
| **Walls** Scotland | | 7 | C3 | 60 14N | 1 34W |
| **Wallsend** England | | 13 | E3 | 55 00N | 1 31W |
| **Walney, Isle of** England | | 12 | C3 | 54 05N | 3 10W |
| **Walsall** England | | 15 | E2 | 52 35N | 1 58W |
| **Waltham Abbey** England | | 16 | D2 | 51 41N | 0 00 |
| **Waltham Forest** England | | 16 | C2 | 51 36N | 0 00 |
| **Waltham on the Wolds** England | | 15 | F2 | 52 49N | 0 49W |
| **Walton-le-Dale** England | | 12 | D2 | 53 45N | 2 41W |
| **Walton-on-the-Naze** England | | 17 | E2 | 51 51N | 1 16E |
| **Walvis Bay** tn. Namibia | | 82 | B3 | 22 59S | 14 31E |
| **Wanganui** NZ | | 73 | P3 | 39 56S | 175 03E |
| **Wanlockhead** Scotland | | 11 | F2 | 55 24N | 3 47W |
| **Wantage** England | | 16 | B2 | 51 36N | 1 25W |
| **Warboys** England | | 16 | C3 | 52 24N | 0 06W |
| **Ward Hill** Scotland | | 7 | A1 | 58 54N | 3 20W |
| **Ware** England | | 16 | C2 | 51 49N | 0 02W |
| **Wareham** England | | 19 | E2 | 50 41N | 2 07W |
| **Warley** England | | 15 | E2 | 52 30N | 1 59W |
| **Warlingham** England | | 16 | C2 | 51 19N | 0 04W |
| **Warminster** England | | 16 | A2 | 51 13N | 2 12W |
| **Warrenpoint** tn. NI | | 10 | C1 | 54 06N | 6 15W |
| **Warrington** England | | 12 | D2 | 53 24N | 2 37W |
| **Warsaw** Poland | | 53 | K6 | 52 15N | 21 00E |
| **Warsop** England | | 13 | E2 | 53 13N | 1 10W |
| **Warton** England | | 12 | D2 | 53 46N | 2 54W |
| **Warwick** England | | 15 | E2 | 52 17N | 1 34W |
| **Warwickshire** co. England | | 15 | E2 | 52 15N | 1 40W |
| **Washingborough** England | | 13 | F2 | 53 14N | 0 28W |
| **Washington** England | | 13 | E3 | 54 54N | 1 31W |
| **Washington** state USA | | 90 | B6/C6 | 47 00N | 120 00W |
| **Washington D.C.** USA | | 91 | L4 | 38 55N | 77 00W |
| **Wash, The** b. England | | 17 | D3 | 52 55N | 0 10E |
| **Watchet** England | | 19 | D3 | 51 12N | 3 20W |
| **Waterbeach** England | | 17 | D3 | 52 16N | 0 11E |
| **Waterford** Rol | | 21 | D2 | 52 15N | 7 06W |
| **Waterford** co. Rol | | 21 | D2 | 52 10N | 7 30W |
| **Waterford Harbour** Rol | | 21 | E2 | 52 10N | 7 00W |
| **Watergrasshill** Rol | | 21 | C2 | 52 00N | 8 20W |
| **Waterlooville** England | | 16 | B1 | 50 53N | 1 02W |
| **Waterville** Rol | | 21 | A1 | 51 50N | 10 10W |
| **Watford** England | | 16 | C2 | 51 39N | 0 24W |
| **Wath upon Dearne** England | | 13 | E2 | 53 31N | 1 21W |
| **Watlington** England | | 16 | C2 | 51 39N | 1 00W |
| **Watton** England | | 17 | D3 | 52 34N | 0 50E |
| **Waveney** r. England | | 17 | E3 | 52 30N | 1 30E |
| **Wavre** Belgium | | 48 | C3 | 50 43N | 4 37E |
| **Wear** r. England | | 12 | D3 | 54 45N | 2 05W |
| **Weaverham** England | | 12 | D2 | 53 16N | 2 35W |
| **Wedmore** England | | 19 | E3 | 51 14N | 2 49W |
| **Weedon Bec** England | | 15 | E2 | 52 14N | 1 05W |
| **Weiden** Germany | | 52 | F4 | 49 40N | 12 10E |
| **Weimar** Germany | | 52 | E5 | 50 59N | 11 20E |
| **Weissenfels** Germany | | 52 | E5 | 51 12N | 11 58E |
| **Welland** r. England | | 16 | C3 | 52 50N | 0 10 |
| **Welland** r. England | | 15 | F2 | 52 30N | 0 50W |
| **Wellingborough** England | | 15 | F2 | 52 19N | 0 42W |
| **Wellington** Telford and Wrekin England | | 15 | D2 | 52 43N | 2 31W |
| **Wellington** Somerset England | | 19 | D2 | 50 59N | 3 15W |
| **Wellington** NZ | | 73 | P2 | 41 17S | 174 46E |
| **Wells** England | | 19 | E3 | 51 13N | 2 39W |
| **Wells-next-the-Sea** England | | 17 | D3 | 52 58N | 0 51E |
| **Wels** Austria | | 52 | F4 | 48 10N | 14 02E |
| **Welshpool** Wales | | 14 | C2 | 52 40N | 3 09W |
| **Welton** England | | 13 | F2 | 54 47N | 3 00W |
| **Welwyn Garden City** England | | 16 | C2 | 51 48N | 0 13W |
| **Wem** England | | 14 | D2 | 52 51N | 2 44W |
| **Wemyss Bay** Scotland | | 10 | E2 | 55 55N | 4 53W |
| **Wendover** England | | 16 | C2 | 51 46N | 0 46W |
| **Wensum** r. England | | 17 | D3 | 52 45N | 1 10E |
| **Wenzhou** China | | 69 | M3 | 28 02N | 120 40E |
| **West Berkshire** u.a. England | | 16 | B2 | 51 28N | 1 00W |
| **West Bridgford** England | | 15 | E2 | 52 56N | 1 08W |
| **West Bromwich** England | | 15 | E2 | 52 31N | 1 59W |
| **Westbury** England | | 16 | A2 | 51 16N | 2 11W |
| **West Dunbartonshire** u.a. Scotland | | 11 | E3 | 56 02N | 4 39W |
| **Westerham** England | | 16 | D2 | 51 16N | 0 05E |
| **Western Ghats** mts. India | | 66 | C3/D2 | 15 30N | 74 00E |
| **Western Isles** u.a. Scotland | | 8 | B2/B3 | 57 45N | 7 30W |
| **WESTERN SAHARA** | | 80 | B6/B7 | | |
| **Western Sayan** mts. Russia | | 63 | M7 | 52 30N | 92 30E |
| **West Felton** England | | 14 | D2 | 52 49N | 2 58W |
| **West Haddon** England | | 15 | E2 | 52 20N | 1 04W |
| **Westhill** Scotland | | 9 | G2 | 57 11N | 2 16W |
| **West Horsley** England | | 16 | C2 | 51 16N | 0 26W |
| **West Indies** is. Caribbean Sea | | 95 | K4/L4 | 22 00N | 69 00W |
| **West Kilbride** Scotland | | 10 | E2 | 55 42N | 4 51W |
| **West Kirby** England | | 12 | C2 | 53 22N | 3 10W |
| **West Loch Tarbert** Western Isles Scotland | | 8 | B2/C2 | 57 55N | 6 52W |
| **West Loch Tarbert** Argyll and Bute Scotland | | 10 | D2 | 55 48N | 5 31W |
| **West Lothian** u.a. Scotland | | 11 | F2 | 55 50N | 3 36W |
| **Westmeath** co. Rol | | 20 | D3 | 53 30N | 7 30W |
| **West Mersea** England | | 17 | D2 | 51 47N | 0 55E |
| **West Midlands** co. England | | 15 | D2 | 52 35N | 2 00W |
| **Weston-super-Mare** England | | 19 | E3 | 51 21N | 2 59W |
| **Westport** Rol | | 20 | B3 | 53 48N | 9 32W |
| **Westport Bay** Rol | | 20 | B3 | 53 49N | 9 37W |
| **Westray** i. Scotland | | 7 | A2 | 59 18N | 3 00W |
| **West Sussex** co. England | | 16 | C1 | 51 00N | 0 25W |
| **West Thurrock** England | | 17 | D2 | 51 28N | 0 20E |
| **West Virginia** state USA | | 91 | K4 | 39 00N | 81 00W |
| **Westward Ho!** England | | 18 | C3 | 51 02N | 4 15W |
| **West Wittering** England | | 16 | C1 | 50 47N | 0 54W |
| **West Yorkshire** co. England | | 13 | E2 | 53 50N | 1 30W |
| **Wetherby** England | | 13 | E2 | 53 56N | 1 23W |
| **Wetzlar** Germany | | 52 | D5 | 50 33N | 8 30E |
| **Wexford** co. Rol | | 21 | E2 | 52 25N | 6 35W |
| **Wexford** Rol | | 21 | E2 | 52 20N | 6 27W |
| **Wexford Bay** Rol | | 21 | E2 | 52 25N | 6 10W |
| **Wexford Harbour** Rol | | 21 | E2 | 52 20N | 6 25W |
| **Wey** r. England | | 16 | C2 | 51 18N | 0 30W |
| **Weybridge** England | | 16 | C2 | 51 22N | 0 28W |
| **Weyburn** Canada | | 89 | Q3 | 49 39N | 103 51W |
| **Weymouth** England | | 19 | E2 | 50 37N | 2 25W |
| **Whaley Bridge** England | | 12 | E2 | 53 20N | 1 59W |
| **Whalley** England | | 12 | D2 | 53 50N | 2 24W |
| **Wharfe** r. England | | 12 | D3 | 54 10N | 2 05W |
| **Wharfedale** v. England | | 12 | D3 | 54 05N | 2 00W |
| **Wheatley** England | | 16 | B2 | 52 23N | 0 52W |
| **Whernside** sum. England | | 12 | D3 | 54 14N | 2 23W |
| **Whickham** England | | 13 | E3 | 54 57N | 1 40W |
| **Whitburn** England | | 13 | E3 | 54 57N | 1 21W |
| **Whitburn** Scotland | | 11 | F2 | 55 52N | 3 42W |
| **Whitby** England | | 13 | F3 | 54 29N | 0 37W |
| **Whitchurch** Shropshire England | | 15 | D2 | 52 58N | 2 41W |
| **Whitchurch** Buckinghamshire England | | 16 | C2 | 51 53N | 0 51W |
| **Whitchurch** Hampshire England | | 16 | B2 | 51 14N | 1 20W |
| **Whitefield** England | | 12 | D2 | 53 34N | 2 18W |
| **Whitegate** Rol | | 21 | C1 | 51 50N | 8 14W |
| **Whitehaven** England | | 12 | C3 | 54 33N | 3 35W |
| **Whitehead** NI | | 10 | D1 | 54 45N | 5 43W |
| **Whitehills** Scotland | | 9 | G2 | 57 40N | 2 35W |
| **White Horse, Vale of** England | | 16 | B2 | 51 35N | 1 30W |
| **Whiten Head** Scotland | | 9 | E3 | 58 34N | 4 32W |
| **Whiteparish** England | | 16 | B2 | 51 01N | 1 39W |
| **Whitfield** England | | 17 | E2 | 51 09N | 1 17E |
| **Whithorn** Scotland | | 11 | E1 | 54 44N | 4 25W |
| **Whitley Bay** tn. England | | 13 | E4 | 55 03N | 1 25W |
| **Whitney, Mount** USA | | 90 | C4 | 36 35N | 118 17W |
| **Whitsand Bay** England | | 18 | C2 | 50 20N | 4 25W |
| **Whitstable** England | | 17 | E2 | 51 22N | 1 02E |
| **Whittington** England | | 14 | C2 | 52 52N | 3 00W |
| **Whittlesey** England | | 16 | C3 | 52 34N | 0 08W |
| **Whitton** England | | 13 | F2 | 53 43N | 0 38W |
| **Whitworth** England | | 12 | D2 | 53 40N | 2 10W |
| **Wichita** USA | | 91 | G4 | 37 43N | 97 20W |
| **Wick** Scotland | | 9 | F3 | 58 26N | 3 06W |
| **Wick** r. Scotland | | 9 | F3 | 58 26N | 3 10W |
| **Wickford** England | | 17 | D2 | 51 38N | 0 31E |
| **Wickham** England | | 16 | B1 | 50 54N | 1 10W |
| **Wickham Market** England | | 17 | E3 | 52 09N | 1 22E |
| **Wicklow** Rol | | 21 | E2 | 52 59N | 6 03W |
| **Wicklow** co. Rol | | 21 | E2 | 52 55N | 6 25W |
| **Wicklow Mountains** Rol | | 21 | E2/E3 | 53 00N | 6 24W |
| **Widnes** England | | 12 | D2 | 53 22N | 2 44W |
| **Wiener Neustadt** Austria | | 53 | H3 | 47 49N | 16 15E |
| **Wierden** Neths | | 48 | E5 | 52 21N | 6 35E |
| **Wiesbaden** Germany | | 52 | D5 | 50 05N | 8 15E |
| **Wigan** England | | 12 | D2 | 53 33N | 2 38W |
| **Wigston** England | | 15 | E2 | 52 36N | 1 05W |
| **Wigton** England | | 12 | C3 | 54 49N | 3 09W |
| **Wigtown** Scotland | | 11 | E1 | 54 52N | 4 26W |
| **Wigtown Bay** Scotland | | 11 | E1 | 54 45N | 4 20W |
| **Wil** Switzerland | | 52 | D3 | 47 28N | 9 03E |
| **Wilberfoss** England | | 13 | F2 | 53 57N | 0 53W |
| **Wilhelmshaven** Germany | | 52 | D6 | 53 32N | 8 07E |
| **Willington** England | | 13 | E3 | 54 43N | 1 41W |
| **Williton** England | | 19 | D3 | 51 10N | 3 20W |
| **Wilmslow** England | | 12 | D2 | 53 20N | 2 15W |
| **Wilton** England | | 16 | B2 | 51 05N | 1 52W |
| **Wiltshire** co. England | | 16 | A2/B2 | 51 30N | 2 00W |
| **Wimborne Minster** England | | 19 | F2 | 50 48N | 1 59W |
| **Wincanton** England | | 19 | E3 | 51 04N | 2 25W |
| **Winchelsea** England | | 17 | D1 | 50 55N | 0 42E |
| **Winchester** England | | 16 | B2 | 51 04N | 1 19W |
| **Windermere** tn England | | 12 | D3 | 54 23N | 2 54W |
| **Windermere** l. England | | 12 | D3 | 54 20N | 3 10W |
| **Windhoek** Namibia | | 82 | C3 | 22 34S | 17 06E |
| **Windsor** Canada | | 89 | U2 | 42 18N | 83 00W |
| **Windsor** England | | 16 | C2 | 51 29N | 0 38W |
| **Windsor and Maidenhead** u.a. England | | 16 | C1 | 50 25N | 0 50W |
| **Windward Islands** Lesser Antilles | | 95 | M2 | 12 30N | 62 00W |
| **Wingate** England | | 13 | E3 | 54 55N | 1 23W |
| **Wingerworth** England | | 13 | E2 | 53 13N | 1 28W |
| **Winkleigh** England | | 18 | D2 | 50 51N | 3 56W |
| **Winnipeg** Canada | | 89 | R3 | 49 53N | 97 10W |
| **Winnipeg, Lake** Canada | | 89 | R4 | 52 30N | 97 30W |
| **Winnipegosis, Lake** Canada | | 89 | Q4 | 52 10N | 100 00W |
| **Winschoten** Neths | | 48 | F6 | 53 07N | 7 02E |
| **Winscombe** England | | 19 | E3 | 51 28N | 2 52W |
| **Winsford** England | | 12 | D2 | 53 11N | 2 31W |
| **Winslow** England | | 16 | C2 | 51 57N | 0 54W |
| **Winterbourne** England | | 15 | D1 | 51 30N | 2 31W |
| **Winterthur** Switz. | | 52 | D3 | 47 30N | 8 45E |
| **Winterton-on-Sea** England | | 17 | E3 | 52 43N | 1 42E |
| **Wirksworth** England | | 13 | E2 | 53 05N | 1 34W |
| **Wisbech** England | | 17 | D3 | 52 40N | 0 10E |
| **Wisconsin** state USA | | 91 | H6/J6 | 45 00N | 90 00W |
| **Wishaw** Scotland | | 11 | F2 | 55 47N | 3 56W |
| **Wisła** r. Poland | | 53 | J6 | 53 00N | 19 00E |
| **Wismar** Germany | | 52 | E6 | 53 54N | 11 28E |
| **Wissembourg** France | | 50 | H5 | 49 02N | 7 57E |
| **Witham** r. England | | 13 | F2 | 53 05N | 0 40W |
| **Witham** England | | 17 | D2 | 51 48N | 0 38E |
| **Witheridge** England | | 18 | D2 | 50 55N | 3 42W |
| **Withernsea** England | | 13 | G2 | 53 44N | 0 02E |
| **Witley** England | | 16 | C2 | 51 08N | 0 39W |
| **Witney** England | | 16 | B2 | 51 48N | 1 29W |
| **Wittenberg** Germany | | 52 | F5 | 51 53N | 12 39E |
| **Wittenberge** Germany | | 52 | E6 | 52 59N | 11 45E |
| **Wittlich** Germany | | 52 | C4 | 49 59N | 6 54E |
| **Wiveliscombe** England | | 19 | D3 | 51 03N | 3 19W |
| **Wivenhoe** England | | 17 | D2 | 51 52N | 0 58E |
| **Woburn Sands** tn. England | | 16 | C3 | 52 01N | 0 39W |
| **Woking** England | | 16 | C2 | 51 20N | 0 34W |
| **Wokingham** England | | 16 | C2 | 51 25N | 0 51W |
| **Wokingham** u.a. England | | 16 | C1 | 50 25N | 0 55W |
| **Wolfsberg** Austria | | 52 | G3 | 46 50N | 14 50E |
| **Wolfsburg** Germany | | 52 | E6 | 52 27N | 10 49E |
| **Wollaston** England | | 15 | F2 | 52 16N | 0 41W |
| **Wollongong** Australia | | 73 | K4 | 34 25S | 150 52E |
| **Wolsingham** England | | 13 | E3 | 54 44N | 1 52W |
| **Wolverhampton** England | | 15 | D2 | 52 36N | 2 08W |
| **Wolverton** England | | 16 | C3 | 52 04N | 0 50W |
| **Wombourne** England | | 15 | D2 | 52 32N | 2 11W |
| **Wombwell** England | | 13 | E2 | 53 32N | 1 24W |
| **Woodbridge** England | | 17 | E3 | 52 06N | 1 19E |
| **Woodford Halse** England | | 15 | E2 | 52 10N | 1 13W |
| **Woodhall Spa** England | | 13 | F2 | 53 09N | 0 14W |
| **Woodlands** tn. Canada | | 92 | A4 | 50 12N | 97 40W |
| **Woodstock** England | | 16 | B2 | 51 52N | 1 21W |
| **Wool** England | | 19 | E2 | 50 41N | 2 14W |
| **Woolacombe** England | | 18 | C3 | 51 10N | 4 13W |
| **Wooler** England | | 11 | G2 | 55 33N | 2 01W |
| **Wootton Bassett** England | | 16 | B2 | 51 33N | 1 54W |
| **Worcester** England | | 15 | D2 | 52 11N | 2 13W |
| **Worcester** USA | | 91 | M5 | 42 17N | 71 48W |
| **Worcestershire** co. England | | 15 | D2 | 52 15N | 2 15W |
| **Workington** England | | 12 | C3 | 54 39N | 3 33W |
| **Worksop** England | | 13 | E2 | 53 18N | 1 07W |
| **Worms** Germany | | 52 | D4 | 49 38N | 8 23E |
| **Worms Head** Wales | | 14 | B1 | 51 34N | 4 20W |
| **Worsbrough** England | | 13 | E2 | 53 33N | 1 29W |
| **Worthing** England | | 16 | C1 | 50 48N | 0 23W |
| **Wotton-under-Edge** England | | 15 | D1 | 51 39N | 2 21W |
| **Wrangle** England | | 13 | G2 | 53 02N | 0 07E |
| **Wrath, Cape** Scotland | | 9 | D3/E3 | 58 37N | 5 01W |
| **Wrexham** tn Wales | | 14 | C3 | 53 03N | 3 00W |
| **Wrexham** u.a. Wales | | 14 | C3/D3 | 53 00N | 3 00W |
| **Writtle** England | | 17 | D2 | 51 44N | 0 26E |
| **Wrocław** Poland | | 53 | H5 | 51 05N | 17 00E |
| **Wrotham** England | | 17 | D2 | 51 19N | 0 19E |
| **Wroughton** England | | 16 | B2 | 51 31N | 1 47W |
| **Wroxham** England | | 17 | E3 | 52 42N | 1 24E |
| **Wuhan** China | | 69 | K4 | 30 35N | 114 19E |
| **Wuppertal** Germany | | 52 | C5 | 51 15N | 7 10E |
| **Würzburg** Germany | | 52 | D4 | 49 48N | 9 57E |
| **Wuxi** China | | 69 | M4 | 31 35N | 120 19E |
| **Wye** England | | 17 | D2 | 51 11N | 0 56E |
| **Wye** r. England | | 16 | B2 | 51 08N | 2 01W |
| **Wylye** r. England | | 16 | A2 | 51 08N | 2 13W |
| **Wymondham** England | | 17 | E3 | 52 34N | 1 07E |
| **Wyoming** state USA | | 90 | E5 | 43 00N | 108 00W |

## X

| Place | Region | Page | Grid | Lat | Long |
|---|---|---|---|---|---|
| **Xi'an** China | | 69 | J4 | 34 16N | 108 54E |

## Y

| Place | Region | Page | Grid | Lat | Long |
|---|---|---|---|---|---|
| **Yakutsk** Russia | | 63 | Q9 | 62 10N | 129 50E |
| **Yamoussoukro** Côte d'Ivoire | | 80 | C3 | 6 50N | 5 20W |
| **Yangon** Myanmar | | 71 | B7 | 16 47N | 96 10E |
| **Yaoundé** Cameroon | | 80 | G2 | 3 51N | 11 31E |
| **Yarmouth** England | | 16 | B1 | 50 42N | 1 29W |
| **Yaroslavl'** Russia | | 62 | F8 | 57 34N | 39 52E |
| **Yate** England | | 15 | D1 | 51 32N | 2 25W |
| **Yateley** England | | 16 | C2 | 51 20N | 0 51W |
| **Yatsushiro** Japan | | 70 | B1 | 32 32N | 130 35E |
| **Yatton** England | | 19 | E3 | 51 24N | 2 49W |
| **Yaxley** England | | 16 | C3 | 52 31N | 0 16W |
| **Yeadon** England | | 13 | E2 | 53 52N | 1 41W |
| **Yealmpton** England | | 18 | D2 | 50 21N | 3 59W |
| **Yekaterinburg** Russia | | 62 | J8 | 56 52N | 60 35E |
| **Yell** i. Scotland | | 7 | C3 | 60 35N | 1 10W |
| **Yellowknife** Canada | | 88 | N6 | 62 30N | 114 29W |
| **Yelverton** England | | 18 | C2 | 50 30N | 4 05W |
| **YEMEN REPUBLIC** | | 64/65 | D2/E2 | | |
| **Yeovil** England | | 19 | E2 | 50 57N | 2 39W |
| **Yerevan** Armenia | | 57 | F3 | 40 10N | 44 31E |
| **Yokohama** Japan | | 70 | C2 | 35 27N | 139 38E |
| **York** England | | 13 | E2 | 53 58N | 1 05W |
| **York** u.a. England | | 13 | E2 | 53 58N | 1 05W |
| **York, Cape** Australia | | 73 | H8 | 10 42S | 142 32E |
| **Yorkshire Wolds** England | | 13 | F3 | 54 00N | 0 45W |
| **York, Vale of** England | | 13 | E3 | 54 10N | 1 20W |
| **Youghal** Rol | | 21 | D1 | 51 51N | 7 50W |
| **Youghal Bay** Rol | | 21 | D1 | 51 55N | 7 48W |
| **Yoxford** England | | 17 | E3 | 52 16N | 1 30E |
| **Ystalyfera** Wales | | 14 | C1 | 51 47N | 3 47W |
| **Ystrad Aeron** Wales | | 14 | B2 | 52 10N | 4 10W |
| **Ystradgynlais** Wales | | 14 | C1 | 51 47N | 3 45W |
| **Ystwyth** r. Wales | | 14 | C2 | 52 20N | 3 55W |
| **Ytterhogdal** Sweden | | 49 | D3 | 62 10N | 14 55E |
| **Yucatan** p. Mexico | | 94 | G3 | 19 00N | 89 00W |
| **Yuci** China | | 69 | K5 | 37 40N | 112 44E |
| **Yukon** r. Canada/USA | | 88 | D6 | 63 30N | 159 40W |
| **Yukon Territory** territory Canada | | 88 | H6/J6 | 64 15N | 135 00W |
| **Yumen** China | | 68 | G5 | 39 54N | 97 43E |
| **Yverdon** Switz. | | 52 | C3 | 46 47N | 6 38E |
| **Yvetot** France | | 50 | E5 | 49 37N | 0 45E |

## Z

| Place | Region | Page | Grid | Lat | Long |
|---|---|---|---|---|---|
| **Zaanstad** Neths | | 48 | C5 | 52 27N | 4 49E |
| **Zadar** Croatia | | 54 | F6 | 44 07N | 15 14E |
| **Zafra** Spain | | 51 | B3 | 38 25N | 6 25W |
| **Zagań** Poland | | 52 | G5 | 51 37N | 15 20E |
| **Zagreb** Croatia | | 54 | F6 | 45 48N | 15 58E |
| **Zagros Mountains** Iran | | 65 | E5/F5 | 32 45N | 48 50E |
| **Zakopane** Poland | | 53 | J4 | 49 17N | 19 54E |
| **Zákynthos** i. Greece | | 55 | J2 | 37 45N | 20 50E |
| **Zambezi** r. Zambia/Zimbabwe | | 82 | D4 | 16 00S | 23 00E |
| **ZAMBIA** | | 82 | D5/E5 | | |
| **Zamora** Spain | | 51 | C4 | 41 30N | 5 45W |
| **Zanzibar** Tanzania | | 83 | F1 | 6 10S | 39 12E |
| **Zaragoza** Spain | | 51 | E4 | 41 39N | 0 54W |
| **Zaria** Nigeria | | 80 | F4 | 11 01N | 7 44E |
| **Zeebrugge** Belgium | | 48 | B4 | 51 20N | 3 13E |
| **Zell-am-See** tn. Austria | | 52 | F3 | 47 19N | 12 47E |
| **Zenica** Bosnia-Herzegovina | | 55 | G6 | 44 11N | 17 53E |
| **Zermatt** Switz. | | 52 | C3 | 46 01N | 7 45E |
| **Zhengzhou** China | | 69 | K4 | 34 45N | 113 38E |
| **Zhmerynka** Ukraine | | 53 | P4 | 49 00N | 28 02E |
| **Zhytomyr** Ukraine | | 53 | P5 | 50 18N | 28 40E |
| **Zibo** China | | 69 | L5 | 36 51N | 118 01E |
| **Zielona Góra** Poland | | 53 | G5 | 51 57N | 15 30E |
| **ZIMBABWE** | | 82 | E4/F4 | | |
| **Zinder** Niger | | 80 | F4 | 13 46N | 8 58E |
| **Zlín** Czech Rep. | | 53 | H4 | 49 14N | 17 40E |
| **Zug** Switz. | | 52 | D3 | 47 10N | 8 31E |
| **Zugspitze** mt. Austria | | 52 | E3 | 47 25N | 11 00E |
| **Zürich** Switz. | | 52 | D3 | 47 23N | 8 33E |
| **Zvolen** Slovakia | | 53 | J4 | 48 34N | 19 08E |
| **Zwettl** Austria | | 52 | G4 | 48 37N | 15 11E |
| **Zwickau** Germany | | 52 | F5 | 50 43N | 12 30E |
| **Zwolle** Neths | | 48 | e5 | 52 31n | 6 06e |